T0220983

Artificial Intelligence and Machine Learning in Drug Design and Development

Scrivener Publishing
100 Cummings Center, Suite 541J
Beverly, MA 01915-6106

Publishers at Scrivener
Martin Scrivener (martin@scrivenerpublishing.com)
Phillip Carmical (pcarmical@scrivenerpublishing.com)

Artificial Intelligence and Machine Learning in Drug Design and Development

Edited by

Abhirup Khanna
School of Computer Science, University of Petroleum and Energy Studies, Dehradun, India

May El Barachi
Faculty of Engineering & Information Sciences, University of Wollongong in Dubai, Dubai Knowledge Park, United Arab Emirates

Sapna Jain
Department of Applied Sciences and Humanities (Chemistry), University of Petroleum and Energy Studies, Dehradun, India

Manoj Kumar
Faculty of Engineering & Information Sciences, University of Wollongong in Dubai, Dubai Knowledge Park, United Arab Emirates

and

Anand Nayyar
School of Computer Science, Duy Tan University, Da Nang, Viet Nam

Scrivener
Publishing

WILEY

This edition first published 2024 by John Wiley & Sons, Inc., 111 River Street, Hoboken, NJ 07030, USA and Scrivener Publishing LLC, 100 Cummings Center, Suite 541J, Beverly, MA 01915, USA
© 2024 Scrivener Publishing LLC
For more information about Scrivener publications please visit www.scrivenerpublishing.com.

All rights reserved. No part of this publication may be reproduced, stored in a retrieval system, or transmitted, in any form or by any means, electronic, mechanical, photocopying, recording, or otherwise, except as permitted by law. Advice on how to obtain permission to reuse material from this title is available at http://www.wiley.com/go/permissions.

Wiley Global Headquarters
111 River Street, Hoboken, NJ 07030, USA

For details of our global editorial offices, customer services, and more information about Wiley products visit us at www.wiley.com.

Limit of Liability/Disclaimer of Warranty
While the publisher and authors have used their best efforts in preparing this work, they make no representations or warranties with respect to the accuracy or completeness of the contents of this work and specifically disclaim all warranties, including without limitation any implied warranties of merchant-ability or fitness for a particular purpose. No warranty may be created or extended by sales representatives, written sales materials, or promotional statements for this work. The fact that an organization, website, or product is referred to in this work as a citation and/or potential source of further information does not mean that the publisher and authors endorse the information or services the organization, website, or product may provide or recommendations it may make. This work is sold with the understanding that the publisher is not engaged in rendering professional services. The advice and strategies contained herein may not be suitable for your situation. You should consult with a specialist where appropriate. Neither the publisher nor authors shall be liable for any loss of profit or any other commercial damages, including but not limited to special, incidental, consequential, or other damages. Further, readers should be aware that websites listed in this work may have changed or disappeared between when this work was written and when it is read.

Library of Congress Cataloging-in-Publication Data

ISBN 978-1-394-23416-5

Cover image: Pixabay.Com
Cover design by Russell Richardson

Set in size of 11pt and Minion Pro by Manila Typesetting Company, Makati, Philippines

Printed in the USA

10 9 8 7 6 5 4 3 2 1

Contents

11 Process and Applications of Structure-Based Drug Design   **321**
Shanmuga Sundari M., Sree Aiswarya Thotakura, Mounika Dharmana,
Priyanka Gadela and Mayukha Mandya Ammangatambu

Preface

The intersection of Artificial Intelligence (AI) and Machine Learning (ML) within the field of drug design and development represents a pivotal moment in the history of healthcare and pharmaceuticals. The remarkable synergy between cutting-edge technology and the life sciences has ushered in a new era of possibilities, offering unprecedented opportunities, formidable challenges, and a tantalizing glimpse into the future of medicine.

AI can be applied to all the key areas of the pharmaceutical industry, such as drug discovery and development, drug repurposing, and improving productivity within a short period. Contemporary methods have shown promising results in facilitating the discovery of drugs to target different diseases. Moreover, AI helps in predicting the efficacy and safety of molecules and gives researchers a much broader chemical pallet for the selection of the best molecules for drug testing and delivery. In this context, drug repurposing is another important topic where AI can have a substantial impact. With the vast amount of clinical and pharmaceutical data available to date, AI algorithms find suitable drugs that can be repurposed for alternative use in medicine. In traditional methods of drug design, searching for a drug that exhibits desired biological activities while conforming to safe pharmacological profiles can be a long, costly, and challenging task. Complex methods are employed to identify new chemical compounds that may be developed and eventually marketed as drugs. Despite all the technological progress, the process is very long, with an estimated average of 9 to 12 years, and the success rate is low, which considerably increases the total cost.

This book is a comprehensive exploration of this dynamic and rapidly evolving field. In an era where precision and efficiency are paramount in drug discovery, AI and ML have emerged as transformative tools, reshaping the way we identify, design, and develop pharmaceuticals. This book is a testament to the profound impact these technologies have had and will continue to have on the pharmaceutical industry, healthcare, and ultimately, patient well-being.

The editors of this volume have assembled a distinguished group of experts, researchers, and thought leaders from both the AI, ML, and pharmaceutical domains. Their collective knowledge and insights illuminate the multifaceted landscape of AI and ML in drug design and development, offering a roadmap for navigating its complexities and harnessing its potential. In each section, readers will find a rich tapestry of knowledge, case studies, and expert opinions, providing a 360-degree view of AI and ML's role in drug design and development. Whether you are a researcher, scientist, industry professional, policymaker, or simply curious about the future of medicine, this book offers valuable insights and a compass to navigate the exciting journey ahead.

The book comprises 19 chapters providing an overview of the state-of-the-art in the development and application of AI, ML, and DL methods in drug design and development. Chapter 1, "The Rise of Intelligent Machines: An Introduction to Artificial Intelligence," gives a foundational approach towards Artificial Intelligence and Generative AI, and comprehensively covers various ethical and societal implications of AI development. Chapter 2, "Introduction to Bioinformatics," provides a comprehensive overview of bioinformatics in terms of principles, methodologies, applications, and emerging trends while also highlighting how it serves as an interdisciplinary bridge between biology and computer science. In addition, the chapter specifies the significance of bioinformatics in various biological research domains and other application areas using real-time scenarios.

Chapter 3, "Exploring the Intersection of Biology and Computing: Road Ahead to Bioinformatics," discusses the importance of bioinformatics and also its relation to drug discovery and development. In addition, the chapter discusses the need for powerful computational resources in the field of bioinformatics, as well as data privacy and heterogeneity. Chapter 4, "Machine Learning in Drug Discovery: Methods, Applications, and Challenges," highlights the uses of Machine Learning algorithms in different phases of drug discovery and development (such as target validation); discusses the challenges and limitations inherent to ML techniques in drug discovery; and showcases various existing works on drug discovery that use ML tools and techniques and other current advancements for drug development.

Chapter 5 explores the use of AI to perform analysis on various data sources—e.g., Genomics, Proteomics, and metabolomics data—and specifies how AI-driven algorithms are employed to find associations and trends in large, complex datasets about AMR. The chapter also explains how to apply AI algorithms to optimize the design of antimicrobial compounds, facilitating the translation of AI-driven findings into clinical practice and public health policies. Chapter 6, "Artificial Intelligence Powered Molecular Docking: A Promising Tool for Rational Drug Design" presents various AI techniques in drug discovery, and highlights molecular docking along with its applications. The chapter also discusses various challenges encountered in implementing AI in docking algorithms and proposes potential solutions.

Chapter 7, "Revolutionizing Drug Discovery: The Role of AI and Machine Learning in Accelerating Medicinal Advancements," highlights the potential of AI, ML, DL, NLP, and robotics in drug design and development. Furthermore, the chapter presents a detailed analysis of ML algorithms and explores the diverse facets of AI in domains like personalized medicine, drug reallocation, safety assessments, predictive analysis, and drug formulation. Chapter 8, "Data Processing Method for AI-Driven Predictive Models for CNS Drug Discovery," presents ideas on how AI can be used to generate drugs, and highlights AI and ML advancements in CNS drug design, along with various advanced applications like drug repurposing, drug synergy prediction, de nova drug design, and drug sensitivity prediction. In addition, the chapter illustrates various pharmaceutical research directions for AI and ML in drug discovery.

Chapter 9, "Machine Learning Applications for Drug Repurposing," explores ML techniques used in drug repurposing and the challenges faced by ML in drug repurposing. It also gives research directions for the application of ML techniques in drug repurposing. Chapter 10, "Personalized Drug Treatment: Transforming Healthcare with AI," looks at the fundamentals of AI in healthcare; explores data sources and collection methods for personalized treatment; and illustrates various case studies specifying AI's impact on personalized drug treatment. In addition, the chapter discusses regulator and ethical considerations in AI-enabled personalized medicine.

Chapter 11, "Process and Applications of Structure-Based Drug Design," examines the various steps involved in structure-based drug design, and the tools and techniques used in structure-based drug design, applications. The chapter outlines the advantages and limitations of structure-based drug design, and discusses some future implications and potential impacts. Chapter 12, "AI Based Drug Development," details how AI improves drug development and the techniques required; enlists challenges and limitations of AI-based drug development; and highlights some case studies and examples to illustrate AI's importance in drug development. Chapter 13, "AI Models for Biopharmaceutical Property Prediction," describes the principles, advantages, and challenges of AI models used for biopharmaceutical property prediction; discusses ML and AL advancements in drug design and development; and enumerates the limitations and future challenges associated with the implementation of AI models for biopharmaceutical property prediction.

Chapter 14, "Deep Learning Tactics for Neuroimaging Genomics Investigations in Alzheimer's Disease," discusses deep learning tactics in the prediction, classification, and diagnosis of Alzheimer's disease, and explains deep learning-based prediction of altered genes and mRNA in Alzheimer's disease. Chapter 15, "Artificial Intelligence Techniques in the Classification and Screening of Compounds in Computer Aided Drug Design (CADD) Process," reviews the computational tools and techniques in CADD, elaborates on AI and ML methods in the molecular screening process, and illustrates the associated challenges and opportunities.

Chapter 16, "Empowering Clinical Decision Making: An In-Depth Systematic Review of AI-Driven Scoring Approaches for Liver Transplantation Problem," explores various AI-based scoring methods employed in liver transplantation to enhance clinical decision-making efficiency, and assesses the accuracy and predictive performance of these AI-based scoring methods in predicting post-transplant outcomes, encompassing graft failure, rejection, and patient survival. Furthermore, the chapter examines the impact of AI-based scoring methods on clinical decision-making efficiency pertaining to liver transplantation, while focusing on resource allocation, waiting times, workflow optimization, and overall transplant program outcomes. The chapter also analyzes the characteristics that affect how well AI-based scoring techniques are implemented and integrated into routine clinical decision-making in regards to liver transplantation.

Chapter 17, "Pushing Boundaries: The Landscape of AI-driven Drug Discovery and Development with Insights into Regulatory Aspects," highlights AI technologies used in drug design and discovery; chronicles the applications of AI in DDS and Drug DVPT; and elaborates on AI in medicine, current DVPTs, and a strategy for pharmaceutical companies. Chapter 18, "Feasibility of AI and Robotics in Indian Healthcare: A Narrative Analysis," describes various types of robotics in healthcare and thoroughly discusses the inclusion of robotics in Indian hospitals, using real-time case studies. The chapter also considers future applications of robotics and AI.

Chapter 19, "The Future of Healthcare: AIoMT- Redefining Healthcare with Advanced Artificial Intelligence and Machine Learning Techniques," explores many technologies used in drug design and development, and proposes a novel and secure AIoMT framework for smart healthcare. Additionally, the chapter discusses various case studies that demonstrate early detection of diabetic retinopathy, chatbots employed for mental health, and predictive analytics for patients' outcomes.

We are deeply grateful to everyone who helped with this book and greatly appreciate the dedicated support and valuable assistance rendered by Martin Scrivener and the Scrivener Publishing team during its publication.

Abhirup Khanna
May El Barachi
Sapna Jain
Manoj Kumar
Anand Nayyar
March 2023

The Rise of Intelligent Machines: An Introduction to Artificial Intelligence

Shamik Tiwari

School of Computer Science, UPES, Dehradun, India

Abstract

Artificial intelligence (AI) represents a field within computer science dedicated to developing intelligent machines that can execute tasks typically demanding human intelligence. AI aims to create algorithms, systems, and tools that replicate cognitive processes, including language comprehension, problem-solving, learning, and reasoning. AI is a multidisciplinary field that draws inspiration from various areas, including computer science, mathematics, neuroscience, philosophy, psychology, and linguistics. The emergence of AI has resulted in a revolutionary period in human history. Industry, society, and our perception of computer capabilities are all being influenced by the growth of intelligent machines, which are being powered by AI technology. The main concepts, purposes, latest developments, and ethical concerns of AI and intelligent machines are summarized in this chapter.

Keywords: Artificial intelligence, machine learning, neural networks, deep learning, intelligent machines, AI applications

1.1 Introduction

Artificial intelligence is the term used to describe computer systems that simulate human cognitive processes. It includes the capacity of computers to carry out operations such as problem-solving, learning, reasoning, perception, language understanding, and decision-making that ordinarily call for human intelligence. Artificial intelligence (AI) technologies attempt to build systems that duplicate and enhance human cognitive abilities, changing how we communicate with technology and our environment. The development of devices that could imitate human thought processes marked the beginning of AI. Key milestones include Alan Turing's theoretical framework for computation, the Dartmouth Workshop in 1956 that coined the term "artificial intelligence," and the development of early AI programs like the Logic Theorist and the General Problem Solver [1, 2].

Email: shamik.tiwari@ddn.upes.ac.in

Abhirup Khanna, May El Barachi, Sapna Jain, Manoj Kumar and Anand Nayyar (eds.) Artificial Intelligence and Machine Learning in Drug Design and Development, (1–22) © 2024 Scrivener Publishing LLC

The founding father of AI, Alan Turing, defines this discipline as:

"AI is the science and engineering of making intelligent machines, brilliant computer programs."

Artificial intelligence can also be defined as follows:

- The potential of a robot or other device operated by a program to carry out tasks usually performed by intelligent beings.
- A computational system with artificial intelligence displays behavior that is typically regarded to require intelligence.
- It is the replication by machines, particularly computer systems, of how human intellect works. These procedures entail self-correction, inference, and learning.
- A machine's capacity to mimic intelligent human behavior.

The critical question is "How close or how well a computer can imitate or go beyond when compared with a human being," even though the above definitions are all appropriate. Figure 1.1 provides the sub-domains of artificial intelligence.

AI can be broadly categorized into two main types [3]:

Narrow AI (weak AI): Narrow AI refers to AI systems designed and trained for specific tasks and operating within a limited domain. Examples of narrow AI applications include virtual assistants like Siri or Alexa, recommendation systems on online platforms, and image recognition algorithms.

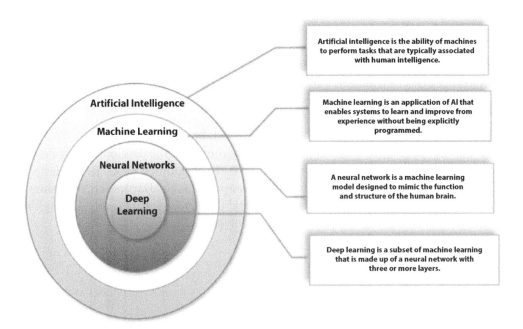

Figure 1.1 Artificial intelligence and its allied domains.

General AI (strong AI): General AI aims to replicate human-like intelligence and abilities across various tasks. It refers to AI systems that can understand, learn, and reason about various domains, just as humans do. General AI is still largely theoretical and remains a significant challenge in the field.

Organization of the Chapter

The rest of the chapter is organized as: A detailed examination of AI key components are enlightened in Section 1.2. Notable applications are explored in Section 1.3, followed by an in-depth discussion of generative AI in Section 1.4 and ethical and societal implications of AI in Section 1.5. Sections 1.6 and 1.7 focus on ethical AI development and the future of AI. And, finally, Section 1.8 concludes the chapter with future scope.

1.2   Key Components of Artificial Intelligence

Artificial intelligence is a multidisciplinary field that includes several essential elements and methods. These elements combine to allow machines to mimic human intellect and carry out activities that call for thinking, problem-solving, perception, and learning. Figure 1.2 provides the key components of artificial intelligence.

1.2.1   Machine Learning (ML)

Machine learning is a subfield of artificial intelligence that involves the development of algorithms and statistical models that enable computer systems to learn and improve their

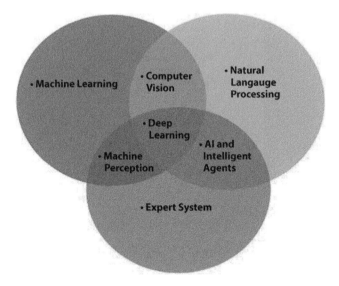

Figure 1.2 Key components of artificial intelligence.

performance on a specific task by analyzing and adapting to data without being explicitly programmed. Figure 1.3 details various machine learning algorithms [4, 5].

a. Supervised learning: In supervised learning, artificial intelligence models are developed on labeled data, where the algorithm learns to classify or predict objects based on input–output relationships. The algorithm learns to predict outcomes in labeled data by examining trends and connections between input and output variables. Examples of applications for supervised learning include fraud detection, recommendation systems, and image and speech recognition. Classification and regression are the two primary supervised learning techniques. While classification classifies data into preset groups or labels, regression forecasts continuous numeric values.

A continuous numerical output or value is predicted using regression, a supervised learning problem. The regression algorithm discovers a correlation between the input features and a continuous target variable. Regression models produce numerical values as their output, and their typical objective is to reduce the discrepancy between the projected values and the actual values in the training data. Regression algorithms commonly used include regression trees, polynomials, and linear regression. Regression tasks include assessing a patient's blood pressure based on health indicators, projecting stock prices, and predicting housing prices based on factors like square footage and location.

Classification, on the other hand, is a supervised learning activity that seeks to sort incoming data into predetermined groups or classifications. When performing classification, the algorithm learns to associate input features with specific labels or classes. A class label identifying the input's category serves as the output of a classification model. Examples of standard categorization techniques include logistic regression, decision trees, support vector machines, and neural networks. The classification of emails as spam or not, the identification of objects in photographs, and the classification of patients into different illness categories are a few examples of classification jobs.

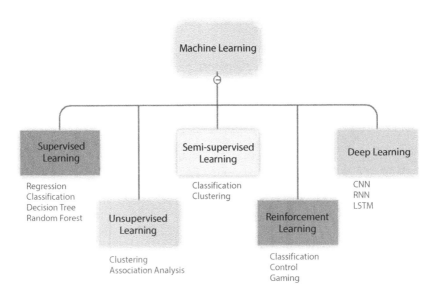

Figure 1.3 Types of machine learning algorithms.

b. Unsupervised learning: Unsupervised learning, frequently used for clustering or dimensionality reduction, entails training AI models using unlabeled data to find underlying patterns or structures within the data. Clustering, dimensionality reduction, anomaly detection, association rule learning, and generative models are just a few of the crucial methods included in unsupervised learning. Clustering algorithms like K-means group data points with similar properties, whereas dimensionality reduction techniques like PCA identify key aspects from highly dimensional data. Outliers or odd data points are found using anomaly detection, linkages in transactional data are found using association rule learning, and fresh data samples are created using generative models like GANs and VAEs. These unsupervised learning approaches play a vital role in data exploration, pattern discovery, and various applications where labeled data is scarce or unavailable, enabling valuable insights and data representations.

c. Semi-supervised learning: Semi-supervised learning uses a larger pool of unlabeled data for model training and a smaller amount of labeled data. This approach is especially helpful when obtaining labeled data is difficult or impractical. It uses the knowledge in the unlabeled data to enhance model performance using supervised and unsupervised learning techniques. Two common approaches are pseudo-labeling, in which predictions are formed on unlabeled data and utilized as pseudo-labels, and adapting conventional supervised algorithms to the semi-supervised environment. Semi-supervised learning improves model performance and makes better use of the resources available in various fields where labeled data is rare.

d. Reinforcement learning: Reinforcement learning (RL) involves an agent interacting with its surroundings and performing behaviors to maximize cumulative rewards over time. RL does not rely on labeled data like supervised learning; it learns by making mistakes instead. The agent experiments with several options and considers the effects of its choices before altering its plan to complete its objectives successfully. Applications for RL can be found in various domains, including improving recommendation systems, playing strategic games, and training autonomous robots. It addresses sequential decision-making issues, making it an essential strategy for developing intelligent, adaptable systems that can learn from experience and enhance performance in changing circumstances [6].

1.2.2   Deep Learning (DL)

Deep learning, a branch of machine learning, focuses on using multiple-layered artificial neural networks (deep neural networks) to model and complete challenging tasks. These deep neural networks are made to recognize and learn hierarchical patterns and characteristics from data automatically. Deep learning has been quite effective in applications like speech recognition, natural language processing, and image recognition. It is called "deep" because it employs numerous layers of connected artificial neurons, allowing it to handle complex and high-dimensional data representations [7] successfully.

A computer model can perform categorization tasks directly from images, text, or sound by applying deep learning techniques. Contemporary deep learning models can achieve remarkable precision, occasionally surpassing human performance. Training these models involves the utilization of a substantial dataset with labeled examples and deploying multi-layered neural network architectures. One widely used subtype of deep neural

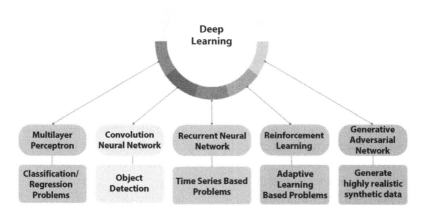

Figure 1.4 Deep learning and its types.

networks is Convolutional Neural Network (CNN or ConvNet). CNNs incorporate 2D convolutional layers and integrate learned features with input data, making them exceptionally well suited for processing 2D data, such as images. Knowing the features utilized to classify images is optional because CNNs conduct the manual feature extraction for you. Direct feature extraction from photos is how CNN operates. The pertinent features are not trained; they are discovered as the network is trained on a set of images. Thanks to this automated feature extraction, deep learning models are incredibly accurate for computer vision applications like object categorization. Figure 1.4 presents types of various deep learning approaches.

1.2.3   Expert System (ES)

An expert system, sometimes called a knowledge-based system, is a computer program or software application that simulates a human expert's judgment and problem-solving abilities in a particular subject area. Expert systems use a knowledge base of facts, laws, and heuristics that capture expertise in a particular subject area to provide intelligent advice, make recommendations, or solve issues [8]. DENDRAL, a tool for predicting molecule structure during chemical analysis, is one example of an expert system. PXDES is another illustration of an expert system that foretells the nature and severity of lung cancer.

1.2.4   Natural Language Processing (NLP)

With artificial intelligence, machines can now comprehend and interpret human language in addition to reading. It entails the development of computational models and algorithms to enable computers to comprehend, interpret, and produce human language in a meaningful and useful way. To enable computers to interact with and manage human language as if they were fluent in it, NLP comprises a wide range of tasks, including text analysis, language translation, sentiment analysis, speech recognition, and more [9].

Computational linguistics, a rule-based approach to modeling human language, is combined with other models like statistical models, machine learning, and deep learning in NLP. When combining various technological models, computers can process spoken or written words to represent human language. They can understand the complete meaning as a result, which includes the speaker's or writer's intentions and emotions. Search engine functioning is an illustration of NLP in action. Using user intent and past search history, search engines employ NLP to propose appropriate results [10].

1.2.5 Computer Vision (CV)

A subset of artificial intelligence called computer vision enables machines to interpret and understand visual information from images and videos. It encompasses diverse tasks, including image preprocessing, relevant feature extraction, object detection, image classification, and even semantic segmentation, enabling a finer understanding of image details. Computer vision finds applications across various domains, including autonomous driving, facial recognition, medical imaging, quality control in manufacturing, augmented reality, and surveillance systems [11]. This technology has fundamentally transformed our perception and interaction with the visual world surrounding us. Face recognition is one such example of computer vision. Computer vision is used in facial recognition technologies to locate specific individuals in images and movies. Law enforcement agencies can use it to track suspicious persons. However, in its most basic form, it is utilized by businesses like Meta or Google to recommend people to tag in images [12].

1.2.6 Machine Perception

Machine perception denotes the capacity of AI systems to perceive and understand their environment through sensors such as cameras, microphones, and accelerometers. By employing techniques like sensor fusion and deep learning, machines can effectively engage with their surroundings by amalgamating data from multiple modalities, identifying objects, and discerning emotions [13]. This expanded capability opens potential applications across various domains, including autonomous vehicles, healthcare diagnostics, immersive virtual experiences, and human–computer interaction. It enhances machines' ability to comprehend and respond to intricate sensory information.

1.2.7 Intelligent Agents (IAs)

Intelligent or AI agents are software entities created to interact with their surroundings and make decisions to accomplish specified goals. From straightforward rule-based systems to sophisticated decision-makers, AI agents cover many AI applications [14]. Intelligent agents, in contrast, place a more significant priority on autonomy and flexibility and are frequently used in dynamic, real-time situations, such as robots and autonomous systems. Both are essential to AI because they provide different levels of reasoning and decision-making power to handle various problems and tasks.

1.3   Applications of Artificial Intelligence

Artificial intelligence has various applications across various industries and domains, transforming our work and lives. Some notable applications of AI in various sectors are provided below [15–30].

I. Computer vision: AI has numerous applications in computer vision, where it enhances the capabilities of machines to interpret and understand visual data from the world. Figure 1.5 presents applications of artificial intelligence in the computer vision domain. The following are some critical AI applications in computer vision.

- a.   Image classification: Identifying objects or patterns within images.
- b.   Object detection: Detecting and locating specific objects within images or videos.
- c.   Facial recognition: Recognizing and verifying individuals based on facial features.
- d.   Video analytics: Analyzing video content for various purposes, such as surveillance and content recommendation.
- e.   Optical character recognition (OCR): AI-powered OCR systems can recognize and convert printed or handwritten text into machine-readable text.
- f.   Gesture recognition: AI can recognize and interpret hand gestures, enabling touchless interfaces and control in applications like gaming, virtual reality, and human–machine interaction.

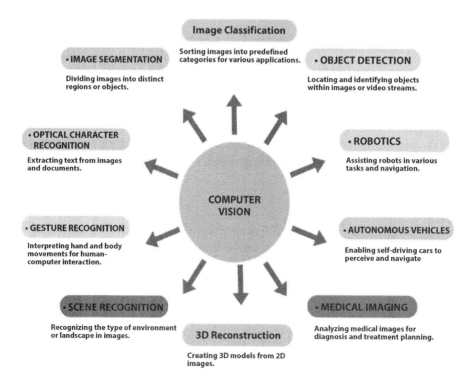

Figure 1.5 Applications of artificial intelligence in the computer vision domain.

g.   Augmented Reality (AR) and Virtual Reality (VR): AI in machine vision tracks and analyzes the user's environment, enhancing AR and VR experiences.

h.   Sports analytics: AI-enhanced cameras and vision systems analyze sports events, providing real-time data for coaching.

II. Natural language processing: AI has a wide range of applications in NLP, which is a subfield of AI focused on the interaction between computers and human language. Figure 1.6 shows common applications of natural language processing. Following are the few key applications of AI in NLP domain.

a.   Text classification: Categorizing text documents into predefined classes or categories.

b.   Sentiment analysis: The process of determining text's sentiment or emotional tone, which is commonly employed in social media monitoring and customer feedback analysis.

c.   Machine translation: NLP is used in machine translation systems such as Google Translate to translate text from one language to another automatically.

d.   Speech recognition: Speech recognition systems utilize NLP algorithms to translate spoken words into written text. This is used in voice assistants such as Siri and Google Assistant and transcription services.

e.   Question answering: NLP models can be used to create question-answering systems that can respond to user questions using a corpus of text or a knowledge base.

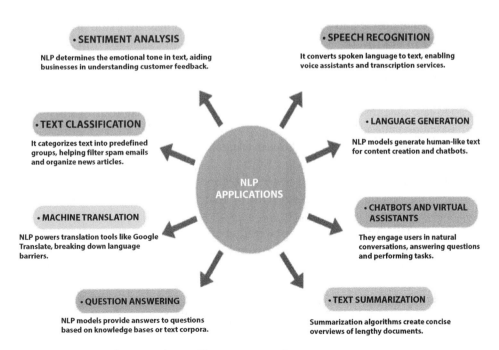

Figure 1.6 Common applications of natural language processing.

   f.   Text summarizing: Text summarizing algorithms may automatically generate succinct summaries of long text documents, making enormous amounts of information easier to comprehend.

   g.   Language generation: NLP models like GPT-3, 4 can generate human-like text, which can be used for content generation, chatbots, and creative writing assistance.

   h.   Chatbots and virtual assistants: Natural language processing is essential for developing chatbots and virtual assistants to engage in natural discussions with users, answer inquiries, and execute tasks.

   i.   Information retrieval: NLP is used in search engines to increase the search result accuracy by comprehending the user's query and web page content.

   j.   Text-to-voice (TTS) conversion: NLP technology turns written text into natural-sounding voice in TTS systems. Voiceovers, accessibility tools, and navigation systems all use this.

III. Recommendation systems: Systems that recommend goods, services, or content to customers based on their tastes and behavior are greatly aided by artificial intelligence (AI). Systems for making recommendations using AI have many uses in various sectors of the economy. The primary AI applications in recommendation systems are listed below.

   a.   Collaborative filtering: Recommending products, services, or content based on user behavior and preferences.

   b.   Content-based filtering: Recommending items based on their features and similarity to items users have shown interest in.

IV. Healthcare: AI can be used in various ways in the healthcare industry to improve administrative, diagnostic, and patient care procedures significantly. Below are a few significant uses of AI in healthcare.

   a.   Medical image analysis: Assisting in interpreting medical images, such as X-rays, MRIs, and CT scans.

   b.   Disease diagnosis: Aiding in the early detection and diagnosis of diseases based on patient data.

   c.   Drug discovery: Accelerating discovering new drugs and identifying potential drug candidates.

   d.   Drug interaction and adverse event detection: AI systems identify potential drug interactions and adverse events by analyzing patient data and medication histories.

   e.   Virtual health assistants: AI-powered chatbots and virtual assistants provide patients with medical information, answer questions, and schedule appointments.

V. Finance: In finance, AI has many uses that are revolutionizing the sector in many ways. Following are a few significant financial AI applications.

a. Credit scoring: Assessing the creditworthiness of individuals or businesses.
b. Algorithmic trading: Making financial trading decisions based on historical and real-time data.
c. Fraud detection: Identifying fraudulent transactions or activities in banking and financial systems.

VI. Autonomous Vehicles: The creation and use of autonomous vehicles (AVs) heavily relies on artificial intelligence. AVs rely on AI technologies to perceive their surroundings, make real-time decisions, and navigate safely. Following are a few significant AI uses for autonomous vehicles:

a. Self-driving cars: Enabling vehicles to navigate and make decisions autonomously using sensor data and machine learning algorithms.
b. V2X communication: AI plays a part in vehicle-to-everything (V2X) communication, which enables autonomous vehicles to communicate with other vehicles, infrastructure, and traffic control systems.

VII. Industry and manufacturing: AI applications in industries such as manufacturing are accelerating improvements in output, sustainability, and quality, resulting in more competitive and effective manufacturing processes. Below are some important AI uses in manufacturing and industry.

a. Predictive maintenance: Predicting equipment failures and optimizing maintenance schedules to reduce downtime.
b. Quality control: Identifying defects and ensuring product quality in real time on production lines.

VIII. Retail: The retail sector is changing thanks to AI, which is strengthening decision-making, enhancing operations, and improving customer experiences. The critical uses of AI in retail include the following:

a. Demand forecasting: Predicting consumer demand for products to optimize inventory management.
b. Personalized marketing: Delivering tailored marketing and product recommendations to individual customers.

IX. Marketing and advertising: By offering data-driven insights, automating tasks, and enabling more individualized and targeted campaigns, AI is having a significant impact on the marketing and advertising sector. Some prominent uses of AI in marketing and advertising are given as follows:

a. Customer segmentation: Identifying target audiences.
b. Ad click prediction: Maximizing ad campaign effectiveness.
c. Price optimization.

X. Agriculture: AI applications in agriculture promote more resilient, efficient, and sustainable farming methods. It enables farmers to meet global food demand while reducing their environmental effects. The following are some significant uses of AI in agriculture:

a. Crop monitoring: Using remote sensing and sensor data for crop health assessment and yield prediction.
b. Precision agriculture: Optimizing farming practices for efficiency and resource conservation.
c. Weed and pest control: AI-based robotic systems can autonomously identify and eliminate weeds or pests in fields.
d. Weather prediction: Models based on AI use weather data analysis to produce precise forecasts and climate predictions, which assist farmers in making plans for shifting weather patterns and modifying their farming practices accordingly.

XI. Energy management: AI is becoming increasingly important in energy management by optimizing resource allocation, increasing efficiency, and improving sustainability. The following are some of the most essential AI applications in energy management:

a. Energy consumption forecasting: Predicting energy usage to optimize energy distribution and reduce costs.
b. Smart grids: Improving the efficiency and reliability of electricity grids.

XII. Space exploration: AI advances space exploration by improving mission capabilities, data analysis, and decision-making processes. Below are some of the most important AI uses in space exploration:

a. Identifying celestial objects and anomalies in space data.
b. Autonomous rovers.
c. Exoplanet discovery.
d. Astronaut assistance.
e. Mission planning and optimization.

XIII. Gaming and entertainment: AI is transforming the gaming and entertainment industries by improving gameplay, personalizing content, and overall user experiences. Following are some of the most essential AI applications in gaming and entertainment:

a. Character behavior and strategy development in video games.
b. Create realistic character animations, making movements.
c. To enhance graphics, rendering, and physics simulations for more immersive worlds.
d. AI contributes to tracking, gesture recognition, and object recognition in VR and AR experiences, making them more interactive and immersive.

XIV. Human resources: AI is increasingly used in human resources to expedite operations and improve the overall HR experience for employees and companies. Below are some significant AI uses in human resources:

    a. Resume screening and candidate selection.
    b. Employee churn prediction.
    c. Initial screening chatbots: AI-powered chatbots can conduct preliminary screenings of candidates by asking basic questions and rating their suitability for the post.

XV. Environmental science: AI assists in data processing, modeling, monitoring, and decision-making processes in environmental research. Below are some of the most significant AI applications in environmental science:

    a. Climate modeling and prediction.
    b. Wildlife monitoring and conservation.
    c. Natural disaster prediction and response.

XVI. Sports analytics: Sports analytics involves data and statistical analysis to gain insights into various aspects of sports performance, strategy, and management. AI plays a significant role in enhancing sports analytics. Following are few AI applications in sports analytics:

    a. Performance analysis in sports.
    b. Player and team strategy optimization.

XVII. Social sciences: AI has numerous applications in social science, offering new tools and insights to researchers and policymakers. Following are some critical applications of AI in social science:

    a. Opinion mining: Analyzing public opinions and trends.
    b. Criminal behavior prediction: Identifying potential criminal activity patterns.

XVIII. Fraud detection and cybersecurity: AI is a powerful fraud detection tool. It can analyze vast data and identify patterns, anomalies, and potential threats. The following are some critical AI applications in this domain:

    a. Credit card fraud detection: Identifying suspicious transactions.
    b. Malware detection: Detecting and preventing cybersecurity threats.

XIX. Robotics: AI plays a crucial role in advancing the capabilities of robotics, enabling them to perform a wide range of tasks with greater adaptability and efficiency. Here are some critical applications of AI in the field of robotics:

    a. Industrial automation in manufacturing.
    b. Autonomous vehicles and drones.

    c.   Robotic surgery and healthcare assistance.
    d.   Search and rescue robots.

XX. Education: AI has numerous applications in the field of education, revolutionizing the way students learn and educators teach. Some critical applications are as follows:

    a.   Personalized learning platforms.
    b.   Automated grading and assessment.
    c.   Intelligent tutoring systems.
    d.   Learning analytics for educators.

XXI. Internet of Things (IoT): AI plays a significant role in enhancing the capabilities and functionality of IoT applications. The following are a few applications of AI in the field of IoT:

    a.   Smart home automation.
    b.   Industrial automation.
    c.   Healthcare monitoring.
    d.   Smart agriculture.
    e.   Supply chain management.
    f.   Smart cities.
    g.   Energy management.
    h.   Environmental monitoring.
    i.   Retail and customer engagement.
    j.   Security and surveillance.

1.4   Generative AI

Generative AI refers to a subset of artificial intelligence techniques that focus on generating content, such as text, images, music, or even video, typically in a way that appears to be created by a human. These systems are designed to learn and mimic patterns in data to produce new, creative outputs [31]. Figure 1.7 displays various generative AI-enabling technologies.

One of the most prominent generative AI models is the class of models known as generative adversarial networks (GANs). GANs consist of two neural networks: a generator and a discriminator. The generator tries to create indistinguishable data (e.g., images) from accurate data, while the discriminator tries distinguishing between real and generated data. Through a competitive training process, GANs can produce high-quality, realistic outputs, which have been used in various creative applications, including image synthesis, style transfer, and even generating artwork. Recurrent neural networks (RNNs) are a class of neural networks designed for sequential data and are commonly used in generative models like language modeling. Generative AI encompasses various enabling technologies that facilitate the generation of new content or data. Here are some key technologies that empower generative AI [32, 33]:

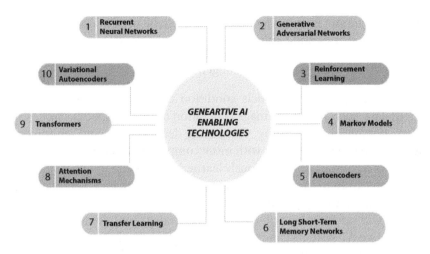

Figure 1.7 Generative AI-enabling technologies.

a. Generative adversarial networks: GANs consist of two neural networks, a generator and a discriminator, which compete to produce realistic data, often used for generating images, videos, and other content.

b. Variational autoencoders (VAEs): VAEs are probabilistic generative models that learn to encode and decode data, allowing for generating new, similar data points.

c. Transformers: Transformers, especially models like GPT (generative pre-trained transformer), have revolutionized natural language generation and other sequence-to-sequence tasks.

d. Reinforcement learning: Reinforcement learning can be used in generative AI to train agents to generate content that maximizes a specific reward, useful in-game AI and robotics.

e. Markov models: Markov models are probabilistic models used for sequence generation, often applied in speech recognition and text generation.

f. Autoencoders: Autoencoders are neural network architectures used for data compression and reconstruction, which can also be adapted for generative tasks.

g. Long short-term memory (LSTM) networks: LSTMs are a type of RNN that is particularly effective for capturing long-range dependencies in sequential data.

h. Attention mechanisms: Attention mechanisms, as used in transformers, enable models to focus on specific parts of the input data when generating output, improving performance in various generative tasks.

i. Probabilistic graphical models: These models represent complex relationships between variables and are used in generative AI for tasks like image generation and recommendation systems.

j. Monte Carlo methods: Monte Carlo methods, such as Markov chain Monte Carlo (MCMC), are used to sample from complex probability distributions, aiding in generative modeling.

k.   Neuro-evolution: Evolutionary algorithms can be used to evolve neural network architectures and parameters for generative tasks.

Figure 1.8 shows the major applications of generative AI.

l.   Conditional generative models condition content generation on specific input data, such as text-to-image generation or text-to-speech synthesis.
m.   Deep reinforcement learning: Combining deep learning and reinforcement learning to generate content with more complex interactions and behaviors.
n.   Transfer learning: Using previously learned models and optimizing them for generative tasks to increase effectiveness and performance. Generative AI is becoming increasingly well-liked as a powerful technology reshaping businesses and opening new possibilities for strategy and content production. Generative AI systems can create new content, mimic human-like reasoning, and quicken technological change by utilizing DL algorithms.

Various industries are adopting generative AI to enhance productivity, creativity, and efficiency. Figure 1.9 shows the various industries using it to expand their reach [34, 35].

a.   Entertainment and media: Creating special effects, generating realistic computer graphics, and enhancing video game experiences.

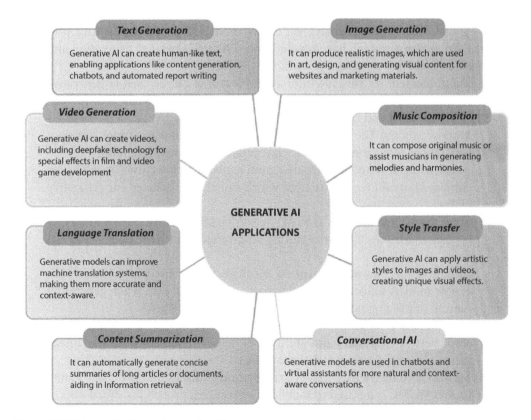

Figure 1.8 Major applications of generative AI.

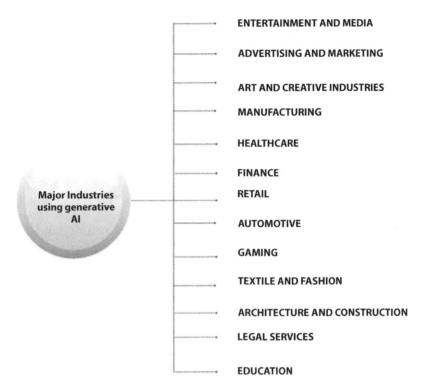

ENTERTAINMENT AND MEDIA

ADVERTISING AND MARKETING

ART AND CREATIVE INDUSTRIES

MANUFACTURING

HEALTHCARE

FINANCE

RETAIL

AUTOMOTIVE

GAMING

TEXTILE AND FASHION

ARCHITECTURE AND CONSTRUCTION

LEGAL SERVICES

EDUCATION

Major Industries using generative AI

Figure 1.9 Industries using generative AI to expand their reach, providing innovative solutions and opportunities for automation, creativity, and problem-solving.

b. Advertising and marketing: Generate personalized content, design graphics, and optimize ad campaigns.
c. Art and creative industries: Generating artwork, music, and other creative works, as well as assisting artists and musicians in the creative process.
d. Manufacturing: Design and optimize products, generate 3D models, and assist in product development.
e. Healthcare: Medical image generation, drug discovery, and predictive analytics in patient care.
f. Finance: Algorithmic trading, fraud detection, and financial data analysis.
g. Retail: Inventory management, personalized product recommendations, and visual merchandising.
h. Automotive: Designing autonomous vehicle systems and simulating driving scenarios.
i. Gaming: Creating game content, generating levels, characters, and dialogues.
j. Textile and fashion: Designing clothing and textile patterns and optimizing supply chains.
k. Aerospace: Aircraft design, simulation, and maintenance.
l. Architecture and construction: Generate designs and 3D models and simulate construction processes.

   m. Energy: Optimizing energy consumption and predicting equipment failures.
   n. Legal services: Document analysis, contract review, and legal research.
   o. Environmental sciences: Climate modeling, predicting environmental trends, and analyzing ecological data.
   p. Education: Creating educational content, generating quizzes, and personalizing learning experiences.
   q. Telecommunications: Optimize network performance, detect anomalies, and predict network failures.
   r. Hospitality: Personalized guest experiences, pricing optimization, and demand forecasting.
   s. Transportation and logistics: Route optimization, demand forecasting, and fleet management.
   t. Government and public sector: Public policy analysis, security, and disaster response planning.

1.5   Ethical and Societal Implications of AI

The ethical and societal implications of artificial intelligence (AI) are significant and multifaceted. As AI technologies continue to advance and become more integrated into various aspects of our lives, it is crucial to consider the following ethical and societal concerns [36, 37]:

   a. Bias and fairness: AI systems can perpetuate and even amplify biases present in training data. This can lead to unfair or discriminatory hiring, lending, and law enforcement outcomes. Ensuring that AI systems treat all individuals fairly and equitably, regardless of factors like race, gender, or socioeconomic status, is a major ethical challenge.
   b. Privacy: AI often relies on large datasets, raising concerns about the collection, storage, and use of personal information. Unauthorized data access and breaches can result in privacy violations. AI-powered surveillance systems, such as facial recognition, threaten individual privacy and civil liberties.
   c. Transparency and accountability: Many AI models, intense learning neural networks, are often considered "black boxes" that are difficult to interpret. Understanding how AI systems make decisions is essential for accountability and trust. Determining responsibility when AI systems make mistakes or cause harm is a legal and ethical challenge.
   d. Job displacement and economic impact: AI-driven automation can potentially displace specific jobs, particularly those involving routine and repetitive tasks. Preparing the workforce for these changes and addressing unemployment concerns is crucial. AI's impact on the economy, including shifts in labor markets, requires proactive policies and measures.
   e. Autonomy and decision-making: AI-powered autonomous systems, such as self-driving cars and drones, raise ethical questions about decision-making

in critical situations. Who is responsible for decisions made by AI in these scenarios?

f. Security: AI can be used maliciously for cyberattacks, deepfake creation, and other forms of deception. This poses threats to individuals, organizations, and governments. Developing AI-driven security measures and counter-measures is essential to address these risks.

1.6   Ethical AI Development

Ethical considerations should be an integral part of all phases of AI development, from data collection and model training to deployment and continuous monitoring. The AI research and development community is increasingly advocating for ethical principles and guidelines to be upheld [38–40].

a. Regulation and governance
Policymakers and regulators face the challenge of creating appropriate frameworks for AI technologies. Striking a balance between fostering innovation and protecting individuals and society is complex.

b. Societal acceptance and trust
Widespread trust in AI technologies is crucial for their successful adoption. Ethical practices, transparency, and accountability contribute to building and maintaining trust.

c. Bias mitigation and diversity
Efforts to reduce bias in AI must include diverse perspectives and datasets to ensure that AI systems are representative and do not favor one group over another.

d. Education and awareness
Promoting public awareness and understanding of AI's capabilities, limitations, and ethical challenges is essential for informed decision-making and responsible AI use.

1.7   Future of AI

A major revolution in both sectors and communities is anticipated because of AI and intelligent technologies. We may expect increasingly powerful and flexible systems to revolutionize our lives and work as AI technologies develop. Deep learning and neural network advancements will make AI better at deciphering complicated data patterns, advancing fields like healthcare by facilitating early diagnosis and individualized treatment regimens. Autonomous systems, from self-driving cars to AI-powered robots, will become integral to various sectors, optimizing efficiency and safety. Moreover, AI's ability to provide personalized experiences and recommendations will extend beyond virtual assistants to areas like education, revolutionizing learning experiences [41, 42].

The ethical and societal issues surrounding the use of AI are expanding along with its capabilities, however. Fairness, accountability, and openness in AI decision-making will be crucial.

By responsibly developing and regulating AI systems, we can reduce biases, safeguard personal information, and prevent job displacement. It will be crucial to strike the correct balance between innovation and ethical safeguards to shape the future of AI and intelligent machines and ultimately determine their impact on people, communities, and the global landscape [43, 44].

As technology evolves, AI is expected to:

Advance ethical AI: Efforts will continue to ensure AI systems are fair, transparent, and accountable.

Human–AI collaboration: AI will augment human capabilities, leading to new opportunities for collaboration.

Regulation and governance: Policymakers will be crucial in shaping AI's ethical and responsible development.

1.8   Conclusion

The chapter provides a fascinating summary of the state of AI. It has dug into the theoretical underpinnings and cutting-edge innovations that have elevated AI from an abstract idea to a powerful force in the contemporary world. The chapter has emphasized how AI transforms industries, offering notable improvements and efficiencies, from healthcare and banking to education and entertainment. Aside from the promise of advancement, the chapter also highlights the moral and societal conundrums that AI raises which forced us to think critically about issues of justice, responsibility, and the possible effects of automation, forcing us to take a nuanced approach to the emergence of intelligent machines. As we advance into a time where AI is developing and becoming more integrated into our daily lives, we must proceed cautiously and establish an interdependent connection between people and machines that benefits society.

References

1. Dwivedi, Y.K., Hughes, L., Ismagilova, E., Aarts, G., Coombs, C., Crick, T., Williams, M.D., Artificial Intelligence (AI): Multidisciplinary perspectives on emerging challenges, opportunities, and agenda for research, practice and policy. *Int. J. Inf. Manage.*, 57, 101994, 2021.
2. Li, H., Special section introduction: Artificial intelligence and advertising. *J. Advertising*, 48, 4, 333–337, 2019.
3. Haenlein, M. and Kaplan, A., A brief history of artificial intelligence: On the past, present, and future of artificial intelligence. *California Manage. Rev.*, 61, 4, 5–14, 2019.
4. El Naqa, I. and Murphy, M.J., *What is machine learning?* pp. 3–11, Springer International Publishing, Switzerland, 2015.
5. Janiesch, C., Zschech, P., Heinrich, K., Machine learning and deep learning. *Electron. Mark.*, 31, 3, 685–695, 2021.
6. François-Lavet, V., Henderson, P., Islam, R., Bellemare, M.G., Pineau, J., An introduction to deep reinforcement learning. *Foundations Trends® Mach. Learn.*, 11, 3–4, 219–354, 2018.
7. Zhao, Z.Q., Zheng, P., Xu, S.T., Wu, X., Object detection with deep learning: A review. *IEEE Trans. Neural Networks Learn. Syst.*, 30, 11, 3212–3232, 2019.

8. Zhou, Z.J., Hu, G.Y., Hu, C.H., Wen, C.L., Chang, L.L., A survey of belief rule-base expert system. *IEEE Trans. Systems, Man, Cybernetics: Syst.*, *51*, 8, 4944–4958, 2019.

9. Deng, L. and Liu, Y., A joint introduction to natural language processing and to deep learning. *Deep Learn. Natural Lang. Process.*, 1–22, 2018, https://doi.org/10.1007/978-981-10-5209-5_1.

10. Nadkarni, P.M., Ohno-Machado, L., Chapman, W.W., Natural language processing: An introduction. *J. Am. Med. Inf. Assoc.*, *18*, 5, 544–551, 2011.

11. Islam, A.R., Machine learning in computer vision. *Appl. Mach. Learn. Artif. Intell. Educ.*, 48–72, 2022.

12. Wu, Q., Liu, Y., Li, Q., Jin, S., Li, F., The application of deep learning in computer vision, in: *2017 Chinese Automation Congress (CAC)*, pp. 6522–6527, IEEE, 2017, October.

13. Giusti, A., Guzzi, J., Cireşan, D.C., He, F.L., Rodríguez, J.P., Fontana, F., Gambardella, L.M., A machine learning approach to visual perception of forest trails for mobile robots. *IEEE Robotics Automation Lett.*, *1*, 2, 661–667, 2015.

14. Kumaran, D., Hassabis, D., McClelland, J.L., What learning systems do intelligent agents need? Complementary learning systems theory updated. *Trends Cogn. Sci.*, *20*, 7, 512–534, 2016.

15. Tiwari, S., Kane, L., Koundal, D., Jain, A., Alhudhaif, A., Polat, K., Althubiti, S.A., SPOSDS: A smart Polycystic Ovary Syndrome diagnostic system using machine learning. *Expert Syst. Appl.*, *203*, 117592, 1–14, 2022.

16. Davenport, T.H. and Ronanki, R., Artificial intelligence for the real world. *Harvard Business Rev.*, *96*, 1, 108–116, 2018.

17. Jha, K., Doshi, A., Patel, P., Shah, M., A comprehensive review on automation in agriculture using artificial intelligence. *Artif. Intell. Agric.*, *2*, 1–12, 2019.

18. Cockburn, I.M., Henderson, R., Stern, S., The impact of artificial intelligence on innovation: An exploratory analysis, in: *The Economics of Artificial Intelligence: An Agenda*, pp. 115–146, University of Chicago Press, Chicago, USA, 2018.

19. Yu, K.H., Beam, A.L., Kohane, I.S., Artificial intelligence in healthcare. *Nat. Biomed. Eng.*, *2*, 10, 719–731, 2018.

20. Hamet, P. and Tremblay, J., Artificial intelligence in medicine. *Metabolism*, *69*, 36–S40, 2017.

21. Tiwari, S., Jain, A., Sapra, V., Koundal, D., Alenezi, F., Polat, K., Nour, M., A smart decision support system to diagnose arrhythymia using ensembled ConvNet and ConvNet-LSTM model. *Expert Syst. Appl.*, *213*, 118933, 2023.

22. Sharma, A.K., Tiwari, S., Aggarwal, G., Goenka, N., Kumar, A., Chakrabarti, P., Jasiński, M., Dermatologist-level classification of skin cancer using cascaded ensembling of convolutional neural network and handcrafted features based deep neural network. *IEEE Access*, *10*, 17920–17932, 2022.

23. Goenka, N. and Tiwari, S., Deep learning for Alzheimer prediction using brain biomarkers. *Artif. Intell. Rev.*, *54*, 7, 4827–4871, 2021.

24. Zawacki-Richter, O., Marín, V., II, Bond, M., Gouverneur, F., Systematic review of research on artificial intelligence applications in higher education–Where are the educators? *Int. J. Educ. Technol. Higher Educ.*, *16*, 1, 1–27, 2019.

25. Tiwari, S., Jain, A., Ahmed, N.M.O.S., Charu, Alkwai, L.M., Dafhalla, A.K.Y., Hamad, S.A.S., Machine learning-based model for prediction of power consumption in smart grid-smart way towards smart city. *Expert Syst.*, *39*, 5, 12832, 2022.

26. Haenlein, M. and Kaplan, A., A brief history of artificial intelligence: On the past, present, and future of artificial intelligence. *California Manage. Rev.*, *61*, 4, 5–14, 2019.

27. Xiao, S.Q. and Peng, J.C., The application of artificial intelligence technology in electrical automation control. *Appl. Mechanics Mater.*, *530*, 1049–1052, 2014.

28. Brill, T.M., Munoz, L., Miller, R.J., Siri, Alexa, and other digital assistants: A study of customer satisfaction with artificial intelligence applications. *Role Smart Technol. Decision Making*, 1st Edition, 35–70, 2022. eBook ISBN9781003307105.

29. Athey, S., The impact of machine learning on economics, in: *The economics of artificial intelligence: An agenda*, pp. 507–547, University of Chicago Press, Chicago, USA, 2018.

30. Tambe, P., Cappelli, P., Yakubovich, V., Artificial intelligence in human resources management: Challenges and a path forward. *California Manage. Rev.*, *61*, 4, 15–42, 2019.

31. Budhwar, P., Chowdhury, S., Wood, G., Aguinis, H., Bamber, G.J., Beltran, J.R., Varma, A., Human resource management in the age of generative artificial intelligence: Perspectives and research directions on ChatGPT. *Hum. Resource Manage. J.*, 33, 3, 606–659, 2023.

32. Ali, S., DiPaola, D., Breazeal, C., What are GANs?: Introducing generative adver- sarial networks to middle school students, in: *Proceedings of the AAAI Conference on Artificial Intelligence*, vol. 35, pp. 15472–15479, 2021, May.

33. Taulli, T., Introduction to generative AI: The potential for this technology is enormous, in: *Generative AI: How ChatGPT and Other AI Tools Will Revolutionize Business*, pp. 1–20, Apress, Berkeley, CA, 2023.

34. García-Peñalvo, F. and Vázquez-Ingelmo, A., What do we mean by GenAI? A systematic mapping of the evolution, trends, and techniques involved in Generative AI. *IJIMAI Magazine*, 8, 4, 1–16, 2023.

35. Fui-Hoon Nah, F., Zheng, R., Cai, J., Siau, K., Chen, L., and ChatGPT: Applications, challenges, and AI-human collaboration. *Generative AIJ. Inf. Technol. Case Appl. Res.*, 25, 3, 277–304, 2023.

36. Zohny, H., McMillan, J., King, M., Ethics of generative AI. *J. Med. Ethics*, 49, 2, 79–80, 2023.

37. Whittlestone, J., Nyrup, R., Alexandrova, A., Dihal, K., Cave, S., Ethical and societal implications of algorithms, data, and artificial intelligence: A roadmap for research. *London: Nuffield Foundation*, 2019, https://www.nuffieldfoundation.org/wp-content/uploads/2019/02/Ethical-and-Societal-Implications-of-Data-and-AI-report-Nuffield-Foundat.pdf.

38. Mittelstadt, B., Principles alone cannot guarantee ethical AI. *Nat. Mach. Intell.*, *1*, 11, 501–507, 2019.

39. Schiff, D., Biddle, J., Borenstein, J., Laas, K., What's next for ai ethics, policy, and governance? A global overview, in: *Proceedings of the AAAI/ACM Conference on AI, Ethics, and Society*, February, pp. 153–158, 2020.

40. Siau, K. and Wang, W., Artificial intelligence (AI) ethics: Ethics of AI and ethical AI. *J. Database Manage. (JDM)*, *31*, 2, 74–87, 2020.

41. Artico, F., Edge III, A.L., Langham, K., The future of artificial intelligence for the BioTech big data landscape. *Curr. Opin. Biotechnol.*, *76*, 102714, 2022.

42. Gill, S.S., Xu, M., Ottaviani, C., Patros, P., Bahsoon, R., Shaghaghi, A., Uhlig, S., AI for next generation computing: Emerging trends and future directions. *Internet Things*, *19*, 100514, 2022.

43. Ramesh, P.V., Ramesh, S.V., Aji, K., Ray, P., Tamilselvan, S., Parthasarathi, S., Rajasekaran, R., Modeling and mitigating human annotations to design processing systems with human-in-the-loop machine learning for glaucomatous defects: The future in artificial intelligence. *Indian J. Ophthalmol.*, *69*, 10, 2892, 2021.

44. Kopalle, P.K., Gangwar, M., Kaplan, A., Ramachandran, D., Reinartz, W., Rindfleisch, A., Examining artificial intelligence (AI) technologies in marketing via a global lens: Current trends and future research opportunities. *Int. J. Res. Marketing*, *39*, 2, 522–540, 2022.

Introduction to Bioinformatics

Bancha Yingngam

Department of Pharmaceutical Chemistry and Technology, Faculty of Pharmaceutical Sciences, Ubon Ratchathani University, Ubon Ratchathani, Thailand

Abstract

Bioinformatics is a crucial interdisciplinary field intersecting biology, computer science, and statistics. It acts as a pivotal catalyst in transforming life sciences and biomedical research. Despite its importance, the field grapples with issues such as overwhelming biological data volumes, inconsistent data handling standards, and a dearth of experts skilled in all intersecting disciplines. These challenges permeate academia, the pharmaceutical industry, and public health, affecting advancements in biological research, personalized medicine, and disease outbreak understanding. The chapter aims to offer an in-depth review of bioinformatics, covering its definition, significance, and inherent challenges. It intends to elevate the reader's scientific contextual understanding by detailing frequently used tools and resources, such as sequence alignment, gene and protein prediction, protein structure modeling, and complex genomic data analysis. The chapter also critically evaluates existing limitations, including data integration hurdles and the urgent need for advanced computational methods. Conclusively, it paints an optimistic picture of the future of this rapidly evolving field, highlighting the potential for breakthroughs that could profoundly enhance our understanding of life and improve health outcomes.

Keywords: Bioinformatics, biological databases, gene prediction, genomic data analysis, protein structure modeling, sequence alignment

List of Abbreviations

AI   artificial intelligence
AWS   Amazon Web Services
CML   chronic myeloid leukemia
DNA   deoxyribonucleic acid
GATK   genome analysis toolkit
ML   machine learning
MOE   molecular operating environment
PDB   Protein Data Bank
PDXs   patient-derived xenografts

Email: bancha.y@ubu.ac.th

Abhirup Khanna, May El Barachi, Sapna Jain, Manoj Kumar and Anand Nayyar (eds.) Artificial Intelligence and Machine Learning in Drug Design and Development, (23–66) © 2024 Scrivener Publishing LLC

QSAR   quantitative structure–activity relationship
RNA   ribonucleic acid

2.1   Introduction

Bioinformatics is an interdisciplinary field that analyzes and interprets complicated biological data using computing tools [1]. This bioinformatics technology arose at the intersection of biology, computer science, mathematics, and information engineering. Figure 2.1 illustrates the fundamental concept that bioinformatics is an interdisciplinary field, meaning that it combines aspects from multiple disciplines. Biology involves understanding the principles and mechanisms of life at scales ranging from the molecular (such as the structure and function of genes and proteins) to the macroscopic (such as ecosystems and evolution). Computer science is the study of algorithmic processes, computational machines, and computation itself. In the context of bioinformatics, computer science often involves the design and application of algorithms and software tools to store, analyze, and visualize biological data. Statistics involve the collection, analysis, interpretation, presentation, and organization of data. In bioinformatics, statistical methods are often used to make sense of complex biological data, such as gene expression data or genome sequences. Currently, bioinformatics has rapidly evolved as a crucial pillar of modern biological research and its related fields, including drug design and development [2]. As per a report from *Research and Markets*, the global bioinformatics market has seen a robust expansion in recent years. The market size was estimated at USD 22.85 billion in 2022 and grew to an estimated USD 27.05 billion in 2023. With a compound annual growth rate projected at 18.49%, it is anticipated that the market will burgeon to reach USD 88.84 billion by 2023 [3]. This growth can be attributed to advancements in technology and the rising importance of bioinformatics in fields such as genomics, biotechnology, and personalized medicine. The increasing market size emphasizes the commercial potential of bioinformatics, likely encouraging further investments and development in this field. The primary objective of bioinformatics is to enhance the comprehension of biological processes by investigating biological data at

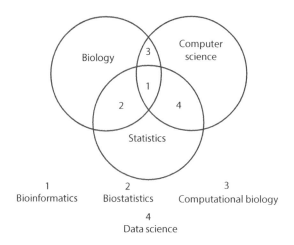

Figure 2.1 The interdisciplinary nature of bioinformatics.

diverse levels, from the molecular to the ecosystem levels. This requires making and using new algorithms, computational models, and statistical methods to obtain useful information from enormous amounts of biological data. This includes genomics, proteomics, and metabolomics [4]. Bioinformatics aims to decode the "code of life"—DNA. The Human Genome Project, which achieved the complete sequencing of the human genome around the start of the 21st century, is often viewed as the catalyst for the rapid progression of bioinformatics [5, 6]. This project produced a significant amount of data, necessitating sophisticated computational tools for its storage, retrieval, and analysis—a need that bioinformatics satisfied.

Concerning the history and evolution of bioinformatics, in the early 1960s, pioneers such as Margaret Dayhoff began developing protein and nucleic acid databases, effectively laying the foundation for what would become bioinformatics [2]. Around the same time, Paulien Hogeweg and Ben Hesper coined the term "bioinformatics" to refer to the study of information processes in biotic systems [7]. The 1970s and 1980s witnessed the development of algorithms for sequence alignment, such as the Smith-Waterman algorithm, and the establishment of important sequence databases such as GenBank [2, 8]. Several statistical approaches for phylogenetic analysis were also created during this time, reflecting the increasing processing capacity and the requirement for data interpretation tools [9]. The introduction of the human genome project in 1990, however, genuinely spurred the science of bioinformatics. This ambitious initiative attempted to sequence the complete human genome, resulting in a flood of biological data that required modern computing tools for storage, processing, and interpretation. This event marked the start of bioinformatics as scientists know it today [10]. Following the successful conclusion of the human genome project in 2003, the postgenomic period envisioned bioinformatics broadening its horizons beyond genomics. The study of several "omics" technologies, such as proteomics (the study of proteins), metabolomics (the study of metabolites), transcriptomics (the study of RNA), and many other "-omics" is now included in the areas [11–13]. Furthermore, high-throughput technologies such as next-generation sequencing (NGS) have resulted in exponential growth in biological data, reinforcing the necessity of bioinformatics in biological research [14]. Bioinformatics has been critical in accelerating developments in a variety of fields over the last two decades, including disease biomarker identification, drug discovery and development, personalized medicine, evolutionary biology, and agricultural research, among others [15, 16]. Bioinformatics tools and databases, including BLAST, FASTA, PDB, UniProt, and others, have become indispensable in current biological research. Furthermore, the combination of machine learning (ML) and artificial intelligence (AI) in bioinformatics has opened new opportunities for the interpretation of complex biological data [17, 18]. This fusion has resulted in advanced models and predictive algorithms, which have improved our understanding of biological systems at the molecular level [19]—for instance, Gupta *et al.* [20] delve into Parkinson's disease, a neurodegenerative disorder characterized by the loss of neuronal cells, which leads to cognitive impairments and synaptic dysfunction. Even with medical advancements, managing Parkinson's disease remains a formidable challenge. The keys to improving Parkinson's disease management are early prediction, diagnosis, and precise patient categorization, each of which currently faces significant obstacles. AI and ML technologies are being increasingly utilized to tackle these challenges, aiding in distinguishing Parkinson's disease patients from healthy individuals using indicators such as neuroimaging data, speech recordings, and gait abnormalities.

The authors reviewed the application of AI and ML in detecting, treating, and identifying new biomarkers related to Parkinson's disease progression and also discussed the role of these technologies in managing Parkinson's disease, focusing on altered lipidomics and the gut–brain axis. Furthermore, the authors highlighted the potential of AI and ML for the early detection of Parkinson's disease using a range of techniques, such as the analysis of speech recordings, handwriting patterns, gait irregularities, and neuroimaging data. Consequently, AI and ML can make significant contributions to the management and drug discovery processes associated with Parkinson's disease.

Bioinformatics plays a crucial role in streamlining the processes involved in the development of novel therapeutics due to its capacity to manage, analyze, and interpret vast quantities of biological data [21]. In the early phases of drug discovery, it is crucial to identify the appropriate molecular target, such as a protein or gene. Bioinformatics provides potent instruments for genomic, transcriptomic, and proteomic analyses, which can help identify potential disease biomarkers and therapeutic targets [22]. In addition, these targets can be validated *via in silico* analyses, which saves considerable time and resources. The next stage in drug discovery is to identify a chemical compound or "lead" that can interact with the identified target. Bioinformatics enables the *in silico* sifting of large compound databases, which drastically accelerates the lead identification process [23]. These leads can then be optimized using a variety of bioinformatics tools that predict the drug-like properties and possible toxicity of these compounds [24]. When experimental data are unavailable, bioinformatics plays a crucial role in predicting the three-dimensional structures of proteins [25]. This information is essential for comprehending the function of the protein and its interaction with potential pharmaceuticals. Tools such as molecular docking and dynamic simulations can shed light on how a drug bonds to its targets, thereby facilitating the design of more effective drugs [26]. Bioinformatics plays an important role in pharmacogenomics, the study of how a person's genetic makeup affects their response to medications [27]. This knowledge permits the development of individualized remedies. Modern drug design generates enormous quantities of data. Effective data management is essential for storing, retrieving, and analyzing these data. Bioinformatics provides the tools and frameworks necessary for effective data management, ensuring that valuable insights are not lost in the deluge of data [28]. Finally, the integration of ML and AI into bioinformatics has been transformative. ML algorithms can identify patterns and make predictions from complex biological data, aiding in everything from target identification to toxicity prediction [29]. AI, in combination with bioinformatics, paves the way for more efficient and successful drug discovery processes [30–32].

Objectives of the Chapter

The objectives of the chapter are:

(i)   To offer a comprehensive overview of bioinformatics, covering its core principles, methodologies, applications, and emerging trends;

(ii) To elucidate how bioinformatics serves as an interdisciplinary bridge between biology and computer science, aiding in the analysis and interpretation of complex biological data;

(iii) And, to underscore the significance of bioinformatics in various biological research domains, including but not limited to genomics, proteomics, and particularly in the area of drug discovery and development.

Organization of Chapter

The rest of the chapter is organized as follows: Section 2.2 introduces key concepts in bioinformatics, laying a foundation by discussing fundamental principles such as data structures, algorithms, and the essential aspects of molecular biology. In Section 2.3, tools and databases for bioinformatics are explored. Section 2.4 then addresses how bioinformatics can be used in different fields and the important role it plays in drug discovery and design. In Section 2.5, challenges and opportunities in bioinformatics are discussed. Section 2.6 discusses future directions of bioinformatics in drug design. This includes investigating the impact of applications using big data, ML, and AI, along with the growing field of personalized medicine, and discussing potential challenges and opportunities. And, finally, section 2.7 concludes the chapter with future scope.

2.2   Key Concepts in Bioinformatics

Before examining the intricate details of a key concept in bioinformatics, it is necessary to establish its foundation. It is crucial to provide a general overview to assist readers in comprehending the field and its fundamental components. Table 2.1 provides a glossary of key terms related to bioinformatics. A genome is the full set of genetic material in an organism, which includes all its genes. Understanding the genome is crucial in bioinformatics, as it allows one to interpret the genetic blueprint of an organism. Genome sequencing

Table 2.1 Glossary of key bioinformatics terms.

Term	Definition
Genome	The complete set of genetic material in an organism, including all of its genes.
Proteome	The entire set of proteins that is, or can be, expressed by a genome, cell, tissue, or organism at a certain time.
Transcriptome	The total amount of all the RNA molecules expressed from the genes of an organism.
Sequence alignment	A method of arranging sequences of DNA, RNA, or protein to identify regions of similarity that may be a consequence of functional, structural, or evolutionary relationships between the sequences.
Homology	It refers to the similarity in sequence of a protein or nucleic acid between species that is due to a common ancestor.

and analysis form the basis of many bioinformatic tasks, including identifying genes, predicting their function, and studying their interactions. A proteome is the complete set of proteins that can be expressed by a genome. Proteins, being the main functional units of the cell, hold vital clues about the cell's function and status. Proteomics, the study of proteomes, uses bioinformatics techniques to identify and quantify proteins, analyze their structures, and understand their functions and intersections. The transcriptome refers to the complete set of RNA molecules produced by a genome. Analyzing the transcriptome helps bioinformaticians understand what genes are active (or "expressed") at a given time, providing a snapshot of the cell's functional state. Techniques such as RNA sequencing (RNA-seq) are used to generate these data, which can then be analyzed using bioinformatics methods to glean insights into gene expression patterns. Sequence alignment is a method used to identify similarities between sequences of DNA, RNA, or proteins. This is fundamental to bioinformatics, as it allows for the comparison of genetic or protein sequences across different organisms, highlighting evolutionary relationships, predicting protein structure and function, and identifying genomic mutations. Homology, in a biological context, refers to the similarity between sequences due to the community of a gene. If a gene in one species is homologous to a gene in another species, the function of the latter will be known because it can be inferred that the former likely has a similar function. Homology also plays a crucial role in understanding evolutionary relationships between species.

As mentioned above, bioinformatics is not just about running software tools on biological data; it is a systematic process that integrates biology, computer science, and statistics to extract meaningful insight into the complexities of life. It also emphasizes that bioinformatics is an iterative process in which the results of one analysis often lead to new questions and further analysis. A common bioinformatics workflow can vary slightly depending on the specific study or type of data, but the general steps usually remain consistent. Figure 2.2 outlines a standard workflow in bioinformatics, starting with data acquisition, preprocessing, analysis (such as sequence alignment, gene prediction, and protein structure prediction), result interpretation, and hypothesis generation. The data acquisition step involves gathering the necessary biological data for analysis. These data can come from various sources, such as DNA sequencing, protein databases, gene expression databases, published literature, or online biological databases. Once the data have been acquired, it needs to be preprocessed to make it suitable for analysis which involves cleaning data to remove errors or noise, normalizing the data to ensure a fair comparison and formatting the data in a way that can be input into bioinformatics software tools—for example, in a genomic study, preprocessing involves quality control checks for DNA sequence reads and the removal of irrelevant or low-quality sequences. After preprocessing, the data were analyzed using a variety of bioinformatics tools and methods. This could involve sequence alignment (comparing sequences to each other or a reference sequence), gene prediction (identifying regions of the genome that code for proteins), or protein structure prediction (using computational techniques to predict the 3D structure of a protein from its amino acid sequence). The exact analysis steps will depend on the specific questions being asked in the study. Once the analysis is complete, the results need to be interpreted. This involves making sense of the output from the bioinformatics tools and drawing conclusions about the biological phenomena being studied. It may also involve statistical analysis to determine

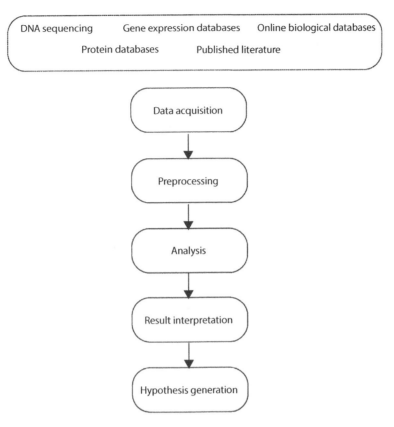

Figure 2.2 Workflow of a typical bioinformatics analysis.

the significance of the results. Finally, the interpretation of the results often leads to new hypotheses about the biological system under study. These hypotheses can then be tested in future studies, perhaps leading to new rounds of data acquisition and analysis.

Therefore, understanding the fundamental concepts is crucial to grasping the full scope of bioinformatics. These concepts are elaborated in the following sub-sections: sequence alignment, gene and protein structure prediction, computational evolutionary biology, genome assembly, biological network analysis, and the analysis of gene and protein expression and regulation.

2.2.1 Sequence Alignment

Sequence alignment stands as a cornerstone operation in the discipline of bioinformatics, playing a vital role in the analysis and comparison of DNA, RNA, and protein sequences. The insights garnered from sequence alignment can be significant, providing a window into the conservation degree among sequences, the possibility of functional correspondences, and hints toward their evolutionary origins [33]. This methodology typically bifurcates into two distinct categories: pairwise alignment and multiple sequence alignment. Table 2.2 provides a comprehensive comparison of the key differences between the methodologies used in pairwise and multiple sequence alignments [14, 34]. The criteria examined include

Table 2.2 Comparative analysis of pairwise and multiple sequence alignment methodologies.

Criteria	Pairwise alignment	Multiple sequence alignment
Definition	Involves the comparison and alignment of two sequences at a time	Involves the comparison and alignment of three or more sequences simultaneously
Use	Used to find the best matching piecewise (local) or global alignments of two query sequences	Used to identify the alignment that will produce the highest degree of similarity or conservation across all sequences
Complexity	Lower computational complexity as only two sequences are compared at a time	Higher computational complexity due to the simultaneous comparison of multiple sequences
Scoring	The alignment is scored based on the number of match/mismatch occurrences and gaps	Scoring is often a function of the sum of pairs or based on profile or probabilistic models
Algorithm examples	Smith-Waterman (local alignment), Needleman-Wunsch (global alignment)	ClustalW MUSCLE, T-COFFEE, MAFFT
Application	Ideal for comparing two very similar sequences or for finding regions of similarity within large sequences	Ideal for analyzing phylogenetic relationships, detecting conserved regions across species, and predicting protein domains and structures

the definition, use, computational complexity, scoring methods, examples of algorithms, and common applications for each alignment type. Pairwise alignment is the simpler form, involving a direct comparison between two individual sequences. Conversely, multiple sequence alignment, as its name suggests, engages with three or more sequences concurrently. The latter is more complex but can offer a broader perspective on the evolutionary relationships among multiple organisms or gene families. The computational realization of sequence alignment tasks is facilitated by various algorithms and tools, each boasting different strengths and applicable contexts. The basic local alignment search tool (BLAST) is perhaps the most recognized, offering a rapid, heuristic approach to aligning sequences [35, 36]. Meanwhile, the Smith-Waterman algorithm provides an optimal, albeit computationally more intensive, methodology for local sequence alignment [37]. For multiple sequence alignments, tools such as ClustalW have been widely adopted, demonstrating robust performance across a wide range of biological datasets [38]. The process begins with the calculation of a pairwise alignment matrix to estimate the evolutionary distance between sequences. Based on this, ClustalW was used to construct a guide phylogenetic tree using the neighbor-joining method. This tree provides an evolutionary framework that guides the subsequent progressive alignment, starting with the most closely related sequences and gradually incorporating more distantly related ones. Finally, ClustalW refines the alignment, adjusting for gaps and potentially improving alignment quality [38]. In the author's opinion, despite its effectiveness, the algorithm may not always yield the most accurate alignment, especially for more divergent sequences or extensive datasets. Thus, researchers should consider the specific demands of each analysis when selecting an alignment tool.

2.2.2   Gene and Protein Structure Prediction

The prediction of gene and protein structures represents a foundational tenet within the field of bioinformatics [39]. This discipline furnishes a portal through which one may explore and elucidate the functionality and behavioral patterns inherent to genes and proteins, thereby shedding light on the intricate processes that constitute life itself. The process of gene structure prediction is a crucial instrument for comprehending the structural organization of genetic material encapsulated within a genome. This practice involves the discernment of essential gene features such as exons, introns, and other regulatory elements [40]. A profound understanding of these components bolsters the comprehension of gene functionality, the regulatory controls it operates under, and its role within the broader context of biological phenomena. Conversely, the prediction of protein structure serves as a cornerstone for comprehending protein functionality, interactions, and molecular behavior. Given that proteins execute the majority of cellular functions, accurate prediction of their structure may yield significant insights into their functionality and potential interactions with other molecular entities [25, 39]. Such understanding contributes to advancements in drug design, facilitates disease diagnosis, and elucidates complex biological processes [41].

Several methodologies underpin the practice of gene structure prediction, as demonstrated in Table 2.3. These encompass *ab initio* prediction, which deploys statistical models to anticipate gene structure, and homology-based prediction, which relies on preexisting knowledge of gene structures in genetically analogous organisms [42]. While *ab initio* methods offer a higher degree of adaptability, they are potentially more prone to yielding false positives. In contrast, homology-based methods typically deliver superior accuracy but necessitate prior knowledge of homologous genes. Protein structure prediction primarily adheres to three methodologies: *ab initio* modeling, homology modeling, and threading [25]. *Ab initio* modeling predicts protein structure based solely on amino acid sequences but can be computationally challenging due to the enormity of potential conformations. Homology modeling, on the other hand, necessitates the availability of a similar protein's known structure. It exploits the fact that structural integrity often persists even when sequence similarity does not. Threading, otherwise known as fold recognition, aligns the target sequence with known protein folds, which proves beneficial when sequence similarity is low but fold similarity is high.

2.2.3   Computational Evolutionary Biology

Considered a cornerstone of bioinformatics, computational evolutionary biology, also known as bioinformatics in evolution, employs complex computational methodologies and algorithmic approaches to analyze and interpret biological data. These processes are primarily focused on decoding the mechanisms and patterns integral to evolution. The discipline

Table 2.3 Comparison of approaches for gene and protein structure prediction.

Prediction approach	Description	Advantages	Limitations
Gene structure prediction			
Ab initio prediction	Utilizes statistical models to predict gene structure	High adaptability	Potentially more prone to yielding false positives
Homology-based prediction	Relies on preexisting knowledge of gene structures in related organisms	Higher accuracy	Requires prior knowledge of homologous genes
Protein structure prediction			
Ab initio modeling	Predicts protein structure based solely on amino acid sequences	Can predict structure without known homologs	Computationally challenging due to the enormity of potential conformations
Homology modeling	Requires a known structure of a similar protein	Exploits structure conservation even when sequence similarity is not	Requires a known structure of a similar protein
Threading	Aligns the target sequence with known protein folds	Useful when sequence similarity is low, but fold similarity is high	Requires knowledge of known protein folds

provides a deeper understanding of the genetic and genomic complexities that characterize a vast array of organisms, ranging from simple unicellular microbes to advanced multicellular entities. For elucidating biological relationships, deciphering the dynamics of genome evolution, examining molecular evolution, and conducting an in-depth analysis of population genomics, computational evolutionary biology is indispensable. Phylogenetics is a crucial aspect of computational evolutionary biology. This subfield focuses on the examination of evolutionary interrelations among distinct biological species, with a strong foundation in the comparative study of genetic sequences across species. Phylogenetic analyses provide important insights into the sequence of speciation events, facilitate the identification of common ancestors, and assist in the prediction of functional genes or proteins.

Comparative genomics, which involves comparing the genome sequences of various species to discern evolutionary correlations, is another crucial component of computational evolutionary biology. This method helps find areas of conservation, which show that a function or structure is important, and areas of variation, which often show how a species has adapted to its environment. Comparative genomics contributes significantly to understanding genome evolution and streamlines the annotation of newly sequenced genomes by leveraging known gene sequences from phylogenetically related species. In addition, molecular evolution, a key component of computational evolutionary biology, probes the mechanisms of genetic alteration at the molecular level. This discipline involves studying alterations in the sequences of nucleotides in DNA or RNA and amino acids in proteins. Sophisticated computational methodologies enable the analysis of these alterations, thereby deciphering the drivers of evolution, including mutation, selection, genetic drift and recombination. Population genomics, on the other hand, delves into the genetic variation within and between populations, aiming to unravel how evolutionary mechanisms such as selection, migration, and genetic drift mold this variation. This field capitalizes on computational tools to analyze extensive genomic datasets, thereby offering insights into the genetic foundations of adaptation, speciation, and disease susceptibility.

2.2.4   Genome Assembly

Genomic assembly is an indispensable process central to the domain of bioinformatics. This sophisticated procedure involves the construction of a comprehensive genome sequence by assimilating shorter DNA fragments, known as reads. These reads are customarily derived from high-throughput sequencing technologies. Given the extraordinary complexity and enormity of most genomes, the assembly process is often analogized to the resolution of a monumental, complex jigsaw puzzle. The assembly of an organism's genome acts as a pivotal step toward unraveling its genetic composition and, in turn, interpreting its biological functionality. This forms the cornerstone of numerous advanced genetic studies, encompassing the identification of genetic variation, the exploration of evolutionary relationships, and the prediction of gene functions. The relevance of genomic assembly is not confined to fundamental biological research; it extends to applied disciplines such as medical genetics, microbial genomics, and agriculture.

The primary methodologies employed for genomic assembly encompass *de novo* assembly and reference-guided assembly (Table 2.4). The former, *de novo* assembly, essentially

Table 2.4 Comparison of *de novo* and reference-guided genomic assembly methods.

Methodology	Key features	Advances	Challenges
De novo assembly	Assembling genome *ab initio* without the support of a reference genome	No need for a closely related reference genome	Computationally intensive, requires advanced algorithms to assemble millions of short DNA reads
Reference-guided assembly	Assembling a genome with the aid of a preexisting sequenced genome of a closely related species	Streamlines the assembly process, less computationally intensive	Dependent on the quality and closeness of the reference genome, the potential to miss novel genomic elements unique to the target organism

involves assembling the genome *ab initio* without the support of a reference genome. This approach is computationally intensive and necessitates the employment of advanced algorithms to accurately assemble millions of short DNA reads. Conversely, reference-guided assembly capitalizes on a preexisting sequenced genome of a closely related species, using it as a reference to streamline the assembly of the new genome. Each approach exhibits unique advantages and challenges, with the selection often governed by the specific research question and the resources at hand. This underscores the vital role of judicious methodology selection in ensuring the efficacy and accuracy of the assembly process.

2.2.5   Biological Network Analysis

The biological network analysis approach enables the visualization and interpretation of the intricate web of interactions that underpins biological systems. Ranging from molecules such as genes, proteins, and metabolites to larger constructs such as cells and organisms and up to expansive structures such as entire ecosystems, the targets of biological network analysis are manifold and diverse. One prominent category of biological networks is the gene interaction network or gene regulatory network. This network elucidates the intricate interconnections among different genes, often demonstrating how the expression of a single gene can influence others. On a similar note, protein–protein interaction networks map the interactions between various proteins within an organism, thus enhancing our understanding of cellular processes and machinery. Metabolic networks constitute another essential type of biological network. They detail the complex interplay between diverse metabolic pathways within an organism, contributing significantly to our understanding of disease mechanisms and facilitating the identification of potential drug targets. Additionally, they aid in delineating the metabolic capabilities of various organisms—a facet critical to advancements in synthetic biology and biotechnology.

On a larger scale, ecological networks capture the interconnections among different species within a given ecosystem, aiding in the comprehension of ecological balance and facilitating predictions on how modifications to one species might reverberate through the ecosystem. The process of analyzing these biological networks involves sophisticated computational algorithms designed to elucidate network properties, including centrality, modularity, and robustness. Centrality measures are used to pinpoint critical nodes (be they genes, proteins, species, etc.) within the network. Modularity determines the capacity of the network to be segmented into smaller, interconnected subnetworks. Robustness denotes the network's ability to withstand and recover from perturbations. From a broader perspective, biological network analysis forms an indispensable tool in systems biology, an emerging branch of biology that strives to comprehend biological systems holistically rather than in isolation. By integrating a myriad of data types encompassing genomic, transcriptomic, proteomic, and metabolomic data, biological network analysis presents a comprehensive overview of biological systems. This approach, therefore, represents a significant stride in our ongoing endeavor to unravel the complexity of life.

2.2.6   Analysis of Gene and Protein Expression and Regulation

The analysis of gene and protein expression and regulation constitutes a central pillar within the field of bioinformatics. The ability to examine how genes and proteins are expressed and regulated is critical to understanding the cellular machinery and the processes that dictate the functionality of an organism. Gene expression analysis concerns the process by which information from a gene is used to produce a functional product, often a protein. This includes the study of transcription, the creation of RNA from a DNA template, and translation, the production of proteins from this RNA. Bioinformatics tools enable the quantification of gene expression levels using high-throughput techniques such as RNA-Seq. Understanding gene expression levels allows for insights into which genes are active or "expressed" under different conditions or stages of an organism's life cycle, which can inform studies of development, disease, and response to environmental factors.

Complementarily, the analysis of protein expression concerns the examination of the presence and quantity of proteins produced in an organism. Proteins, the workhorses of the cell, carry out many functions that are critical to life. The synthesis and degradation of each protein in a cell are tightly regulated to maintain cellular homeostasis. Through techniques such as mass spectrometry and two-dimensional gel electrophoresis, bioinformatics allows the examination of protein expression on a large scale. This aids in elucidating protein function, the effects of posttranslational modifications, and the interactions between proteins. Finally, the regulation of gene and protein expression is a complex process involving numerous regulatory elements and mechanisms, including promoters, enhancers, repressors, and small RNA molecules. Regulatory elements can be identified through comparative genomics and machine learning algorithms, which search for patterns in DNA sequences that are conserved across species and are associated with gene regulation. The study of gene regulation helps to understand how cells respond to their environment, differentiate into various cell types, and how alterations in these processes can lead to disease. These areas of focus—gene expression, protein expression, and their regulation—together form an intricate and interconnected triad that is pivotal to our understanding of biological processes.

2.3   Bioinformatics Tools and Databases

2.3.1   Publicly Available Databases

Publicly available databases represent significant repositories of diverse biological data within the realm of bioinformatics. These include, among other categories, DNA, RNA, protein sequences, protein structures, metabolic pathways, and disease-related information. Such databases not only provide data storage but also facilitate categorization, annotation, and standardization. This comprehensive management enables scientists across the world to conveniently access and utilize these data in their respective scientific pursuits. The following sub-sections detail some of the most frequently employed databases, software, and tools in this field.

2.3.1.1   GenBank

GenBank (Table 2.5) is an open-access, annotated collection of all publicly accessible nucleotide sequences and their protein translations [43]. It is part of the International Nucleotide Sequence Database Collaboration (INSDC) [44]. INSDC also includes the European Nucleotide Archive (ENA) and the DNA Data Bank of Japan (DDBJ). GenBank is routinely

Table 2.5 Overview of major biological databases.

Tool/database	URL	Description
GenBank	https://www.ncbi.nlm.nih. gov/genbank/	An open-access, annotated collection of all publicly available nucleotide sequences and their protein translations
Protein Data Bank (PDB)	http://www.rcsb.org/	A repository of 3D structural data of large biological molecules such as proteins and nucleic acids
UniProt	https://www.uniprot.org/	A comprehensive resource for protein sequence and annotation data
Ensembl	https://www.ensembl.org/	Provides genome databases for vertebrates and other eukaryotic species
KEGG	https://www.genome.jp/kegg/	A suit of databases that deal with genomes, biological pathways, diseases, drugs, and chemical substances
PubMed	https://pubmed.ncbi.nlm.nih. gov/	A freely accessible database of biomedical literature

employed by researchers worldwide because it serves as a primary repository for sequences used in molecular modeling, genomics, phylogenetics, and other fields. In particular, geneticists can use GenBank to find the DNA sequences of genes related to their research, evolutionary biologists can employ it for constructing phylogenetic trees, and bioinformaticians can use it for training and testing algorithms for gene finding or protein function prediction. GenBank is also indispensable in medical and epidemiological research—for example, researchers studying infectious diseases can use GenBank to track the spread of viruses by comparing the sequences of virus samples from different locations or times. GenBank is updated daily, and the data are distributed in several formats, including a flat-file format and as part of the NCBI Entrez system. Entrez is a search and retrieval system that integrates information from databases at NCBI, including literature (PubMed), protein sequences, and structures, genomes, genes, and more. The data in GenBank are contributed by researchers from around the world. When scientists publish a paper that includes a new DNA sequence, they usually submit that sequence to GenBank. It is important to note that while the database is curated, the accuracy of the annotation information is largely dependent on the original submitters.

2.3.1.2 RCSB Protein Data Bank (RCSB PDB)

Understanding disease pathology is critical in the search for new drugs. Biological systems are comparable to complex networks of proteins that interact and function. The SCSB PDB library contains 3D structural data for large biological molecules, such as proteins and nucleic acids [45]. These structures are derived from experimental methods such as X-ray crystallography, nuclear magnetic resonance spectroscopy, and, more recently, cryo-electron microscopy. PDB data are widely used in bioinformatics and computational biology, allowing for *in silico* drug discovery processes. Techniques such as molecular docking, virtual screening, and homology modeling rely largely on the structural data provided by the RCSB PDB. Thus, the RCSB PDB is critical in structure-based drug design, an approach in which researchers use knowledge of the 3D structure of the biological target to design new drugs. Researchers can create more efficient drugs if they have a better grasp of how chemicals attach to proteins and alter their activity. Once a target is found, the protein's 3D structure can be used to validate it, determining whether it is druggable — that is, whether it can bind with a small molecule that beneficially affects its activity.

2.3.1.3   UniProt

The Universal Protein Resource, otherwise known as UniProt, constitutes a comprehensive repository of protein sequence data coupled with relevant annotation [46]. This integrative platform is the result of a collaborative endeavor spearheaded by the European Bioinformatics Institute (EBI), the Swiss Institute of Bioinformatics (SIB), and the Protein Information Resource (PIR). UniProt enables scientific investigators to plumb the depths of the extensive protein universe, thereby facilitating the identification of potential therapeutic targets and the elucidation of underlying disease processes. Fundamentally, UniProt contributes to drug discovery through the provision of comprehensive and pertinent data concerning protein functionality. The associated annotations offer an abundance of information, spanning protein sequences, domain structures, posttranslational modifications, and variant forms. Each piece of information serves as a crucial component in comprehending disease biology and, consequently, in the pursuit of novel therapeutic compounds. Moreover, UniProt is instrumental in deciphering the functional ramifications of variations within protein sequences, offering invaluable insights into the pathophysiological mechanisms of a multitude of diseases. The incorporation of such knowledge undoubtedly enhances the capacity for targeted drug discovery and development, underscoring the indispensable role of UniProt within the scientific and medical research communities.

2.3.1.4   Ensembl

Ensembl is a comprehensive database designed to provide information on the genomes of a wide variety of species [47]. Launched in 1999, it is a project that the European Bioinformatics Institute (EBI) and the Welcome Trust Sanger Institute developed. The main purpose of Ensembl is to provide a centralized resource for genes, genomes, and related data, which include DNA sequences, protein sequences, gene locations, chromosome mapping, variant data, and comparative genomics. Ensembl is unique in how it generates annotation data. Instead of curating data from other databases, Ensembl creates its gene annotations by integrating several types of data, including direct evidence (such as cDNA and protein sequences) and indirect evidence (such as comparative genomics). In terms of its application, Ensembl is a valuable resource for those working in genomics research and related fields. It is commonly used for bioinformatics studies and provides a basis for developing more specific databases and tools. Researchers can use Ensembl to explore gene functions, variations, and their possible implications for diseases. The Ensembl project also includes several tools for visualizing, exploring, and manipulating genomic data. These include the Ensembl genome browser, which is a web-based tool for visualizing genomic data, and BioMart, a data mining tool. The Ensembl project is continually updated, with releases occurring approximately every two to three months. Each release includes updates to data, software, and tools, ensuring that Ensembl remains a state-of-the-art resource for genomics research. Finally, Ensembl promotes an ethos of open data, meaning that all of its resources are freely available to anyone without any restrictions, fostering collaboration and transparency in the scientific community.

2.3.1.5   KEGG

Kyoto Encyclopedia of Genes and Genomes (KEGG) is a suite of databases that integrate genomic, chemical, and systemic functional information [48]. Originating from Japan, it has been providing a significant contribution to the scientific community since its development in 1995 by the bioinformatics center at Kyoto University. KEGG contains several databases that cover different types of data. The databases include KEGG GENES, which provides information on gene sequences and functions; KEGG PATHWAY, which presents information about biochemical pathways; KEGG DISEASE, which offers data on diseases and their associated genes and pathways; KEGG DRUG, which compiles information about drugs and their targets; and KEGG COMPOUND, which encompasses data about small molecules.

KEGG has wide-ranging applications in both the academic and industrial sectors. Its databases are used for understanding the high-level functions and utilities of biological systems, including cells, organisms, and ecosystems, from genomic and molecular information [49]. The primary use of KEGG is to facilitate the interpretation of large-scale datasets generated by genome sequencing and other high-throughput experimental technologies in genomics, transcriptomics, proteomics, and metabolomics [50]. One of KEGG's unique features is its pathway maps, which represent knowledge of the molecular interactions and reaction networks for metabolism, genetic information processing, environmental information processing, cellular processes, organismal systems, human diseases, and drug development [51]. These maps help scientists visualize complex biological interactions more simply and understandably. In addition, KEGG provides an application programming interface that allows programmers to integrate KEGG data into their software or tools. It also has built-in tools for browsing and searching databases. This interface to KEGG is designed to support a wide range of bioinformatics software and data analysis pipelines. While KEGG, provides an array of useful information, it does have significant limits—for example, it may take some time for newly discovered genes, pathways, or chemicals to be included in the database. Furthermore, route maps are mostly based on the knowledge of model organisms and may not fully represent the particular conditions of nonmodel organisms. Future efforts could include broadening and deepening the databases, increasing update frequency, and improving the representation of biological complexity.

2.3.1.6   PubMed

PubMed, a freely accessible search engine for biomedical literature, has become an indispensable tool in bioinformatics [52]. This database comprises more than 30 million citations for biomedical literature, spanning fields such as life science, medical topics, chemical entities, and bioinformatics. As a prominent and widely used platform, PubMed plays an important role in various aspects of bioinformatics, leveraging computational methods to analyze biological data. PubMed provides an immense amount of biomedical text data that can be used for mining biological and medical information. Bioinformatics uses data mining algorithms to extract valuable insights from massive datasets, including but not limited to information about gene–disease associations, protein interactions, drug–target relationships, and disease–therapy correlations. In addition, the massive dataset available in PubMed is an excellent resource for training ML models. These models can be used for tasks such as text mining, semantic analysis, and automatic summarization in the bioinformatics domain.

2.3.2   Software and Tools for Data Analysis

An avalanche of biological data of astounding complexity and volume has accompanied bioinformatics as it has exploded onto the scientific scene thanks to rapid advancements in sequencing technologies and high-throughput methodologies. These data, while promising unprecedented insights into the workings of life's mechanisms, also present a significant challenge. It requires accurate and efficient interpretation. To address this need, a variety of specialized software and tools have been designed and developed. Table 2.6 summarizes the comparison of bioinformatics software tools. These computational tools act as crucial linchpins in the bioinformatics workflow, enabling the ability to dissect, analyze, and visualize data, conduct rigorous statistical tests, build predictive models, and perform a myriad of other functions crucial to bioinformatic analysis. The sub-section highlights some of the

Table 2.6 Comparison of bioinformatics software tools.

Software name	Functionality	Ease of use	Platform compatibility	Open-source or proprietary
BLAST	Sequence alignment	Intermediate	Windows, macOS, Linux	Open source
Clustal Omega	Multiple sequence alignment	Intermediate	Web-based	Open source
BioEdit	Sequence alignment, sequence manipulation	Intermediate	Windows	Freeware
PyMOL	Molecular visualization	Advanced	Windows, macOS, Linux	Open source and proprietary versions
Cytoscape	Network data integration, visualization, and analysis	Advanced	Windows, macOS, Linux	Open source

Note: Ease of use can vary among different users based on their familiarity with such tools and overall computer proficiency.

most widely used and impactful software and tools, which have proven indispensable in transforming raw bioinformatics data into meaningful, actionable biological knowledge.

2.3.2.1   BLAST (Basic Local Alignment Search Tool)

The Basic Local Alignment Search Tool or BLAST is a fundamental software application in bioinformatics. BLAST, which was developed by the National Center for Biotechnology Information (NCBI), enables the comparison of query nucleotide or protein sequences against a database of sequences. This facilitates the identification of regions of local similarity between them. The principal elements of the BLAST software include sequence query, database selection, algorithm selection, alignment, and scoring. BLAST, for instance, permits users to input a query sequence, which can be either a nucleotide or protein sequence. The user can select the database against which the query sequence will be compared during database selection. Depending on the user's research interests, this database could be a broad, general database such as GenBank or a more specialized database. Table 2.7 provides a detailed comparison of the BLAST algorithm and other commonly used bioinformatics algorithms by providing a comprehensive overview, highlighting the key differences and applications of each method, with a particular focus on the BLAST algorithm.

Regarding algorithm selection, BLAST includes a suite of algorithms to accommodate various types of sequence comparisons, including BLASTN (for nucleotide–nucleotide comparison), BLASTP (for protein-protein comparison), BLASTX (which compares a nucleotide query sequence translated in all reading frames to a protein sequence database), TBLASTN (which compares a protein query sequence against a nucleotide sequence database dynamically translated in all reading frames), and TBLASTX (which compares the six-frame translations of a nucleotide query sequence database). In addition, BLAST creates

Table 2.7 Common bioinformatics algorithms and their applications.

Algorithm name	Description of applications
BLAST (Basic Local Alignment Search Tool)	An algorithm used for comparing primary biological sequence information. It is widely used for finding regions of local similarity between sequences, allowing for differences such as gaps and mismatches.
Smith-Waterman	A dynamic programming algorithm is used for local sequence alignment. It is useful for finding all possible alignments and similarities within a large sequence.
Needleman-Wunsch	Another dynamic programming algorithm but used for global sequence alignment. It is used to align two sequences in their entirety, making it suitable for comparing sequences of a roughly equal size.
FASTA	This is an algorithm for comparing protein or nucleotide sequences against sequence databases and calculates significant similarities. It is faster than BLAST but can miss some of the more nuanced alignments.

alignments of the query sequence with sequences in the database, scores these alignments based on a scoring matrix, and then provides results containing details about the most similar sequences, their alignments, and their statistical significance [53]. BLAST is effective and can rapidly search enormous databases due to its use of heuristic algorithms. It has been extensively used in numerous bioinformatics fields, including gene discovery, protein function prediction, and phylogenetic analysis [54]. Notably, its functionality extends to mapping the field of homology among genes and proteins, leading to a greater understanding of evolutionary relationships. Furthermore, the BLAST algorithm forms the basis for other more specialized tools and databases. This makes it an indispensable component of the bioinformatics toolkit.

2.3.2.2 CLUSTAL Omega and CLUSTALW

CLUSTAL Omega and CLUSTALW are two widely used algorithms for multiple sequence alignment. Both were developed by the CLUSTAL team, but both algorithms differ in various aspects, including speed, accuracy, and methods of operation. The understanding and usage of these tools are fundamental in bioinformatics, particularly when aligning nucleotide or protein sequences. CLUSTALW, which stands for CLUSTAL W (weight), is a more traditional algorithm that has been widely used in the field since the 1990s. It operates on a progressive alignment approach. The process involves creating a dendrogram by performing pairwise sequence alignments, which are then used to guide the multiple-sequence alignment. The strength of CLUSTALW lies in its flexibility, which allows users to manipulate gap penalties and weight matrices, and its ability to handle smaller datasets effectively [38]. However, due to its progressive nature, the algorithm is not ideal for large datasets, as inaccuracies in the early stages of alignment can propagate through the dataset.

CLUSTAL Omega is a newer algorithm and an improvement over CLUSTALW in several ways [55]. It is designed to align large numbers of sequences more efficiently and accurately than CLUSTALW. CLUSTAL Omega uses seeded guide trees and hidden Markov model profiles for sequence alignment, which improves both the speed and quality of the alignments.

The algorithm follows three main steps, namely:

1) It constructs pairwise alignments to create a guide tree.
2) It uses this guide tree to produce a hidden Markov model profile for each subgroup of sequences.
3) Finally, it merges these hidden Markov models to create the final alignment.

While CLUSTAL Omega has improved speed and accuracy over CLUSTALW, particularly for larger datasets, it has less user control over parameters such as gap penalties and substitution matrices. The choice between CLUSTAL Omega and CLUSTALW depends largely on the specific needs of the task at hand. For smaller datasets and tasks where manual control over alignment parameters is crucial, CLUSTALW may be the preferred choice. However, for larger datasets where speed and alignment accuracy are prioritized, CLUSTAL Omega offers a more efficient solution.

2.3.2.3   *BioPython, BioPerl, Bioconductor, and BioJava*

These four software tools—BioPython, BioPerl, Bioconductor, and BioJava—represent essential resources in the field of bioinformatics. They are open-source packages dedicated to providing tools for computational biology and bioinformatics. Each is built on a different programming language (Python, Perl, R, and Java), catering to diverse user preferences and requirements. The choice between these tools depends largely on the user's preferred programming language, the specific needs of the project, and the kind of biological data being dealt with.

1) BioPython

BioPython is a set of tools written in Python, an easy-to-learn, versatile programming language widely used in data analysis. This tool provides resources for bioinformatics, such as sequence analysis, protein structure, population genetics, and phylogenetics. It simplifies the process of reading, writing, and manipulating biological data and can interact with online services such as NCBI and Exasy. It is an ideal tool for Python-loving biologists who need to incorporate computational methods into their work [56].

2) BioPerl

BioPerl offers a comprehensive collection of Perl modules that facilitate the development of Perl scripts for bioinformatics applications. Perl was one of the first languages to be widely used in bioinformatics and is known for its text manipulation capabilities, which are often required when dealing with biological data. BioPerl excels at sequence alignment, accessing bioinformatics databases, and performing rapid tasks on ".fasta" and ".fastg" files [57].

3) Bioconductor

Bioconductor is an open-source and open-development software project for the analysis and comprehension of genomic data, primarily based on the R programming language. It is rich in statistical analysis functions and graphical representation methods, offering over 1,700 bioinformatics packages. It is especially well regarded for its tools for the analysis of high-throughput genomic data, such as microarrays and next-generation sequencing data. Bioconductor's key strengths are its advanced statistical techniques and its extensive visualization capabilities, which are highly appreciated in analyzing complex genomic datasets [58].

4) BioJava

BioJava is an open-source project that provides a Java framework for processing biological data. It includes objects for manipulating sequences, file parsers, biological databases, tools for making sequence analysis graphical user interfaces (GUIs), and powerful analysis and statistical routines. It is a good choice for bioinformaticians who are looking to incorporate object-oriented programming into their work. Although Java requires more upfront learning than Python or Perl, its "write once, run anywhere" concept is a significant advantage for creating portable software solutions [59].

2.3.2.4   *GATK (Genome Analysis Toolkit)*

GATK is an advanced, open-source bioinformatics software suite developed at the Broad Institute. It is widely used to analyze high-throughput sequencing data, particularly in the field of genomics. The primary goal of GATK is to offer a comprehensive set of tools to assist researchers in processing and interpreting genomic data, such as whole-genome sequencing (WGS), whole exome sequencing (WES), and targeted sequencing projects. The GATK toolkit is especially renowned for its best-practice pipelines that guide users through the complex steps of data analysis. This includes processes such as data preprocessing (base quality score recalibration and indel realignment), variant discovery (SNP and indel calling), and postprocessing of variant calls (variant filtering and annotation). It provides robust, reliable, and efficient solutions for both germline and somatic variant detection and genotyping [60].

HaplotypeCaller is one of the most popular tools in the GATK suite. It can call both SNPs and indels at the same time by using a local *de novo* assembly of haplotypes in an active region [61]. By doing so, it provides a more accurate model for representing the inherent uncertainty in the data, leading to higher accuracy in variant calling. GATK is built on a flexible and expandable framework that allows it to handle various types of data and genomic analyses. Moreover, it is continuously updated and refined, incorporating the latest scientific findings and methods in genomics research. However, while GATK is powerful, it can also be computationally intensive and might require significant resources for large datasets. It also has a somewhat steep learning curve, particularly for researchers new to bioinformatics. Despite these challenges, the toolkit's accuracy, robustness, and comprehensive nature make it a go-to resource for genomics researchers worldwide.

2.3.2.5   PyMOL

PyMOL (https://pymol.org/2/) is a widely used, user-friendly molecular visualization system developed by Warren DeLano and commercially maintained by Schrödinger, Inc. It is a powerful tool for visualizing the structures of large molecules, such as proteins, nucleic acids (DNA and RNA), and chemical compounds. It is open-source and available for use on various operating systems, including Windows, macOS, and Linux.

The key features and uses of PyMOL include the following:

1) Molecular rendering: PyMOL can display molecules in several types (cartoon, stick, surface, spheres, dots, etc.). This makes it useful for a variety of applications.
2) 3D visualization: PyMOL provides tools for rotation, zooming, and translation of the 3D molecular structure. This allows users to examine molecular structures from various angles and perspectives.
3) Analysis tools: PyMOL can measure distances, angles, and dihedral angles in molecules. It can also display hydrogen bonds, hydrophobic interactions, and other types of molecular interactions.
4) Molecular editing: PyMOL allows users to modify molecular structures, which helps study the effects of mutations on protein structure and function.
5) Movie making: PyMOL can create animations of molecular motions, which can be exported as movie files. This is particularly useful for presentations and teaching.

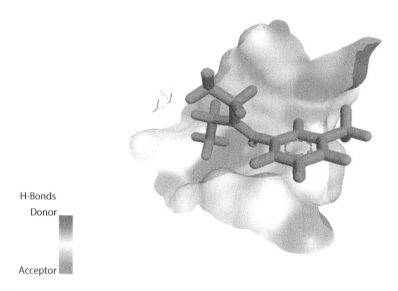

H-Bonds
Donor

Acceptor

Figure 2.3 Illustration of the interaction between the binding pocket of 3K1E and citronellal, visualized using PyMOL software.

6) Scripting: PyMOL has a built-in Python interpreter that allows for complex scripting and automation. This provides the potential for customization and the development of new tools within the software.

In the field of bioinformatics, PyMOL is commonly used for tasks such as visualizing protein structures, analyzing protein-ligand interactions, and preparing figures for scientific publications. Researchers also use it to understand the structural implications of genetic mutations, which can be helpful in areas such as drug discovery and development—for instance, during the exploration of potential mosquito-repellent molecules, the author conducted an extensive screening of various volatile substances. This process involved examining interactions with 3K1E, which refers to the crystal structure of the odorant binding protein 1 (AaegOBP1) derived from *Aedes aegypti*, a species of mosquito. This analysis enabled the identification of potential repellent substances. The study, detailed at the provided link (https://doi.org/10.2210/pdb3K1E/pdb), led to the discovery of citronellal as a promising candidate. Citronellal, a common component of citronella oil, was found to effectively interact with the 3K1E binding pocket, indicating its potential as a mosquito repellent. These interactions and their implications are visually represented in Figure 2.3. This research underscores the vital role of bioinformatics in public health by aiding in the development of more effective mosquito repellents, which could contribute significantly to the prevention of mosquito-borne diseases.

2.3.2.6   Cytoscape

Cytoscape is a highly regarded open-source bioinformatics software platform used for visualizing complex networks. While it is primarily used in the fields of molecular biology and genomics, it is versatile and can handle any type of network data [62]. Cytoscape's strength lies in its ability to integrate biomolecular interaction networks with annotations, gene expression profiles, and other state data. The basic premise of Cytoscape is that it allows the user to import a network of interactions (for example, protein–protein interactions, gene-regulatory networks, or metabolic pathways) and then layer on additional data such as gene expression levels, cellular processes, or disease states. This facilitates the generation of intricate and insightful visualizations that can aid in understanding complex biological processes and patterns. Beyond basic network visualization, Cytoscape provides an excess of features that further support bioinformatic analysis. It can integrate a multitude of data types and sources, including local and remote databases. Cytoscape can be extended to incorporate new functionalities using plugins, of which there are many available covering various biological analyses and features. It provides sophisticated methods for network layout, filtering, and the manipulation of node and edge attributes. Cytoscape plugins such as BiNGO and ClueGO facilitate functional enrichment analysis, providing insights into the biological themes prevalent in large gene sets. It can generate high-quality images suitable for use in scientific publications. One notable aspect of Cytoscape is its extensive community support. A vast array of plugins, regular updates, and an active user forum make it adaptable and suitable for many types of analyses [63].

2.3.2.7 MOE (Molecular Operating Environment)

The MOE is a fully integrated, user-friendly software suite for computational chemistry, molecular modeling, and bioinformatics. The chemical computing group developed it, and it offers a wide range of tools for small molecule and biologics-based discovery research and development. MOE's broad applicability encompasses areas such as cheminformatics, structure-based design, bioinformatics, molecular modeling, and simulations, making it an essential tool for both academia and industry [64]. It offers the capacity to handle both small molecules and large biological systems, allowing users to model and simulate biochemical interactions, making it invaluable for drug discovery and design. The key functionalities of MOE include molecular modeling and simulations, structure-based design, ligand-based design, bioinformatics and cheminformatics, and data analysis. MOE provides a comprehensive suite of modeling tools, including protein and nucleic acid builders, homology modeling, conformational search methods, and molecular dynamics simulations. For structure-based design, MOE is equipped with tools for protein–ligand docking, *de novo* design, pharmacophore modeling, and free energy calculations, enabling researchers to model and predict the interactions between potential drugs and their biological targets. MOE can generate 2D and 3D QSAR models, offering virtual screening and compound library design capabilities. MOE includes sequence alignment tools, secondary structure prediction tools, tools for clustering, data visualization, and cheminformatics capabilities, including structure–activity relationships (SAR) and chemical library design. In addition, MOE's robust data analysis capabilities, such as statistical analysis and ML tools, can be used to understand and interpret complex datasets.

2.3.3 Cloud-Based Platform for Bioinformatics

Cloud-based platforms for bioinformatics are increasingly being adopted due to their capacity to handle vast amounts of data and provide high computational power, often at a lower cost than traditional, locally hosted servers. These platforms provide scalable resources, enabling researchers to process large datasets flexibly and efficiently. Table 2.8 highlights the comparison of different cloud-based platforms for bioinformatics. The following subsections highlights some of the most commonly used cloud-based platforms.

2.3.3.1   Google Genomics

Google Genomics, part of the Google Cloud Platform (GCP), is a cloud-based service designed to store, process, explore, and share large, complex genomic datasets [65]. It offers a suite of services that facilitate a broad array of bioinformatics analyses, leveraging the robust and scalable infrastructure of GCP. The Google Genomics service is built on Google's core data storage and computing technologies, inheriting their efficiency, reliability, and scalability. It allows researchers to move large volumes of genomic data to the cloud seamlessly, overcoming the storage challenges that often accompany such large datasets.

Table 2.8 Comparison of different cloud-based platforms for bioinformatics.

Platform	Provider	Key features	Notable use cases
Google Cloud Genomics	Google	Integration with Google's AI tools, highly scalable, data sharing, and collaboration capabilities	Genomic data processing, population genomics
Amazon Web Services (AWS) Bioinformatics	Amazon	High-performance computing, large data storage, robust security, easy integration with AWS	Genomic sequencing, protein structure prediction
Azure for Genomics	Microsoft	Seamless integration with Azure services, highly scalable, supports various bioinformatics tools	Precision medicine, genome-wide association studies
IBM Genomics	IBM	Integration with IBM's AI capabilities, data security, scalability	Genomic research, personalized medicine
Galaxy	Independent	Open source, widely used for genomics research, active community, supports many bioinformatics tools	Data analysis in genomics, variant detection
Seven Bridges Genomics	Independent	Designed for genomics, strong collaboration feature, regulatory compliance	Large-scale genomic sequencing, collaborative research projects

At the heart of Google Genomics is the BigQuery platform, a highly scalable, serverless, and highly available multicloud data warehouse. BigQuery allows for rapid exploration of genomic datasets using SQL-like queries, enabling researchers to mine genomic data quickly and efficiently. This is particularly useful when dealing with vast datasets, such as those generated by next-generation sequencing techniques. Furthermore, Google Genomics also integrates popular bioinformatics tools and supports standard genomic formats (such as FASTQ, BAM, and VCF files). Its compatibility with the Genome Analysis Toolkit (GATK) and other tools facilitates a wide range of genomic analyses, from variant calling to genome-wide association studies (GWAS). In terms of collaboration, Google Genomics promotes data sharing and cooperative work. Researchers can control who has access to their data, enabling secure collaboration. Moreover, public genomic datasets can be imported and analyzed alongside private data, making them a useful tool for comparative genomics. Google Genomics, therefore, provides an efficient and scalable solution for storing, analyzing, and sharing genomic data. By harnessing the power of cloud computing, it allows researchers to focus on their research questions without worrying about computational resources, making it an invaluable tool in modern bioinformatics.

2.3.3.2   Amazon Web Services (AWS) for Genomics

AWS for genomics is a highly scalable cloud computing platform specifically designed to support genomics research [66]. It offers a suite of services that cater to the extensive computational needs of genomic data storage, processing, analysis, and collaboration. A key feature of AWS for genomics is its vast storage capability, capable of handling the significant volumes of data typically associated with genomic research. AWS offers several storage options, including Amazon S3 (Simple Storage Service), which is optimized for data archiving and backup, and Amazon Glacier, which provides low-cost storage for data archiving and long-term backup. AWS for genomics also excels at providing high computational power. It supports distributed computing, which allows for the efficient processing of large datasets. It is scalable, meaning that computational resources can be adjusted according to the demands of the project. This includes high-performance computing (HPC) options, GPU instances for machine learning applications, and FPGA instances for hardware acceleration. The platform offers seamless integration with popular bioinformatics tools and supports commonly used genomic data formats. AWS has partnered with various genomics software providers to ensure that their tools work smoothly on the AWS infrastructure. This includes tools for read alignment, variant calling, and functional annotation, among others. AWS for genomics also supports collaborative research. It provides advanced security features, including encryption and access controls, that allow secure sharing of data and results. Furthermore, it supports the use of Jupyter notebooks, facilitating reproducible research and collaboration. Lastly, AWS provides a pay-as-you-go model, meaning that researchers only pay for the resources that they actually use. This model, combined with the scalability of AWS, makes it a cost-effective solution for genomics research, particularly for projects with variable computational demands.

2.3.3.3   Microsoft Azure for Research

Microsoft Azure for Research is a powerful cloud computing platform designed to support research across a wide variety of disciplines, including bioinformatics and genomics [67].

By leveraging the robust infrastructure and advanced computing capabilities of Azure, researchers can handle extensive datasets and conduct sophisticated computational analyses with ease and efficiency. A critical aspect of Microsoft Azure for Research is its vast storage capabilities. It can comfortably accommodate the large volumes of data typically generated in bioinformatics research, such as high-throughput sequencing data. Azure provides several storage solutions, such as Azure Blob storage for unstructured data and Azure file storage for shared storage scenarios. In terms of computational resources, Azure for Research offers a scalable and versatile environment. It supports high-performance computing (HPC), GPUs for ML tasks, and a variety of virtual machines that can be tailored to the specific needs of a research project. This scalability allows researchers to dynamically adjust their computational resources according to their project requirements, improving efficiency and cost-effectiveness.

Microsoft Azure for research also provides seamless integration with popular bioinformatics tools and pipelines, supporting a wide array of analyses from sequence alignment to variant calling and genome assembly. Furthermore, Azure's support for container technology, such as Docker and Kubernetes, allows for the creation of reproducible and portable computational environments, which are particularly useful in bioinformatics research. Collaboration is another area where Azure excels. Azure provides comprehensive security features, including encryption and strict access controls, enabling secure data sharing among researchers. Furthermore, Azure Notebooks support Jupyter Notebooks, promoting reproducible research and collaborative analysis. Azure's pricing model is also geared toward supporting research, with a pay-as-you-go system that ensures researchers only pay for the resources they use. There are also grants available for researchers through the Azure for Research program, further enhancing its accessibility.

2.3.3.4   IBM Watson for Genomics

IBM Watson for Genomics is a cloud-based, AI-driven platform designed to support genomic research [68]. By leveraging IBM Watson's AI capabilities, this platform allows researchers to annotate, interpret, and understand the functional implications of genetic variants derived from next-generation sequencing data, thereby accelerating genomics research and its clinical applications. One of the unique selling points of IBM Watson for genomics is its ability to integrate and analyze structured and unstructured biomedical data. The platform uses AI to extract relevant information from vast amounts of genomic data, medical literature, guidelines, and study databases, helping researchers decipher the functional implications of genetic variations. Watson's AI algorithms continuously learn and update their knowledge base with new findings, ensuring the provision of up-to-date insights. Furthermore, Watson for Genomics offers a highly scalable cloud-based environment capable of handling the extensive storage and computational demands of genomics research. Watson's deep learning algorithms are also highly efficient, significantly reducing the time taken to analyze genomic datasets compared to traditional methods. In terms of collaboration, Watson for Genomics promotes data sharing and cooperative work. It offers advanced security measures that ensure safe and secure data sharing among researchers. Additionally, it allows for the generation of detailed yet comprehensible genomic reports that can be shared with collaborators or even patients, supporting personalized medicine efforts. A noteworthy application of IBM Watson for Genomics is in the field of cancer research, where it is used to identify potential therapeutic targets based on the unique genetic profile of a patient's tumor. However, its applications are not limited to oncology; it can be employed in any research where genomic data interpretation is needed.

2.3.3.5 Galaxy

Galaxy is an open-source, web-based platform for accessible, reproducible, and transparent computational biomedical research [69]. Designed to make computational biology accessible to researchers who do not have computer programming experience, Galaxy offers a user-friendly interface for conducting complex bioinformatics analyses. Galaxy provides an environment where users can perform, reproduce, and share complete analyses. This is achieved through its web-based user interface, which enables users to create, run, and share workflows without having to write code. The platform includes a broad range of popular bioinformatics tools, and new tools can be added by the user community, which contributes to the versatility of the platform. The platform is not confined to a specific set of tools or disciplines. It supports large-scale research in various fields of genomics, transcriptomics, proteomics, metagenomics, and more. Tools for quality control, data cleaning, visualization, statistical analysis, and many other tasks can be found in Galaxy.

One of the key features of Galaxy is its focus on reproducibility. Every analysis performed on Galaxy is automatically tracked and stored in a format that allows researchers to repeat and understand the computational methods used. This also facilitates the sharing of workflows and results with collaborators, promoting collaborative research. Galaxy can run on personal computers, local servers, or cloud computing platforms, offering flexibility to suit various computational needs and resources. Cloud-based instances of Galaxy, such as Galaxy on Amazon Web Services (AWS) or Galaxy on the Google Cloud Platform (GCP), can provide increased computational resources and facilitate large-scale analyses. Moreover, the Galaxy Project fosters an active and supportive community, which helps in the continuous development and improvement of the platform. This community also provides substantial resources for learning how to best use the Galaxy platform.

2.3.3.6 Seven Bridges Genomics

Seven Bridges Genomics is a cloud-based platform designed to facilitate bioinformatic and genomic research by providing a unified environment for data analysis, management, and collaboration [70]. The platform's intuitive interface and robust computational infrastructure cater to both experienced bioinformaticians and researchers without extensive coding experience, making it a versatile tool in the field of genomics. The platform offers extensive storage and computing resources capable of managing the large volumes of data typical in genomics. With its efficient data compression and transfer capabilities, Seven Bridges Genomics optimizes data storage and reduces the time required for data transfer.

One of the defining features of Seven Bridges Genomics is its comprehensive toolset for genomic data analysis. The platform provides access to over 800 bioinformatics tools and workflows, including widely used tools for sequence alignment, variant calling, and RNA-seq analysis. The platform also supports the Common Workflow Language (CWL), enabling the creation of reproducible and portable workflows. Additionally, Seven Bridges Genomics places a strong emphasis on collaboration. The platform provides sophisticated data-sharing capabilities, enabling researchers to share both raw data and analysis results securely. It also allows for the sharing of workflows, promotes reproducible research, and fosters collaboration within the scientific community. Seven Bridges Genomics also integrates seamlessly with public databases such as The Cancer Genome Atlas (TCGA) and the 1000 Genomes Project. This feature allows researchers to incorporate publicly available data into their analyses or compare their results with existing datasets, broadening the scope of potential research questions. Seven Bridges Genomics operates on a pay-as-you-go pricing model, meaning that researchers only pay for the computational resources that they use. This model, in combination with the scalability of the platform, ensures a cost-effective analysis for projects of any size.

2.4   Applications in Bioinformatics

The importance of bioinformatics is profound in various areas of life sciences. It spans genomic and proteomic sequence analysis to structural biology, drug discovery, and systems biology. Its applications have radically accelerated the pace of discovery, offering new insights into the complex world of biology and playing a pivotal role in personalized medicine. The following sub-sections will delve into the numerous applications of bioinformatics. Figure 2.4 illustrates how bioinformatics aids in predicting protein structures, mapping biomolecular sequences, tracing evolutionary gene trees, designing primers, and more, thereby significantly contributing to our understanding of biological systems and disease mechanisms.

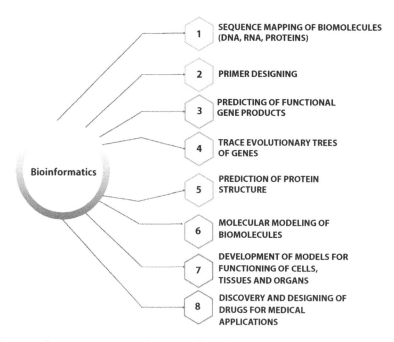

Figure 2.4 Diagram illustrating various applications of bioinformatics.

2.4.1   Sequence Mapping of Biomolecules (DNA, RNA, and Proteins)

Bioinformatics is fundamental to the sequence mapping of biomolecules such as DNA, RNA, and proteins, forming the backbone of genomic and proteomic research. With the advent of high-throughput sequencing technologies, large volumes of sequence data are generated, necessitating efficient bioinformatics tools for analysis. For DNA, bioinformatics allows researchers to map raw sequence reads to reference genomes, detect genetic variations, and understand their potential functional implications. Similarly, in RNA-Seq analysis, bioinformatics aids in mapping transcript sequences, quantifying gene and transcript expression levels, and detecting alternative splicing events. For proteins, bioinformatics tools are used to predict the amino acid sequence based on the DNA sequence, identify functional domains, and explore posttranslational modifications. These sequence mapping processes provide essential insights into the function of these biomolecules, their interactions, and their role in health and disease. Therefore, bioinformatics serves as a key enabling technology in the study and understanding of the molecular blueprints of life.

2.4.2   Primer Design

Bioinformatics plays an integral role in the design of primers, which are sequences of nucleic acids that serve as starting points for DNA synthesis in procedures such as polymerase chain reaction (PCR), DNA sequencing, and genetic testing. The selection of an appropriate primer sequence is crucial to ensuring the specificity and efficiency of these procedures. Bioinformatics tools, such as primer design software, can analyze a given DNA sequence to identify suitable primer binding sites, considering factors such as primer length, melting temperature, GC content, and the potential for secondary structure or primer–dimer formation. These tools can also verify the specificity of the designed primers against whole-genome sequences to avoid nonspecific amplification. Additionally, in multiplex PCR, bioinformatics can help design multiple primer sets that can operate concurrently without interfering with each other. Therefore, bioinformatics not only enhances the accuracy and efficiency of primer design but also expedites the overall process, making it an essential tool in molecular biology and genetic research.

2.4.3   Prediction of Functional Gene Products

Bioinformatics is fundamental in predicting functional gene products, a crucial step in deciphering the complexity of biological systems and understanding the basis of diseases. From a given DNA sequence, bioinformatics tools can identify potential genes and their structures, which include coding regions (exons), noncoding regions (introns), and regulatory elements. Once the genes are identified, sequence analysis can predict the resultant RNA and protein sequences. The functional annotation of these predicted gene products is performed using various bioinformatics databases and tools, which compare the predicted sequences with those of known function. This process can identify potential homologs, conserved domains, and motifs, providing insights into the probable function of the gene product. Additionally, bioinformatics can predict posttranslational modifications and interaction partners of the protein, offering further clues about its function. In the context of diseases, predicting functional gene products can reveal pathogenic mutations and potential therapeutic targets. Therefore, bioinformatics plays an indispensable role in predicting and functionally analyzing gene products, which has significant implications for both biology and medicine.

2.4.4   Trace Evolutionary Trees of Genes

Bioinformatics plays a pivotal role in tracing evolutionary trees, or phylogenies, of genes, a process that provides significant insights into the history of life and the molecular mechanisms underlying evolution. This process, known as phylogenetic analysis, involves the use of computational tools and algorithms to align sequences, calculate genetic distances, and construct phylogenetic trees. By comparing the sequences of a particular gene across different species, scientists can infer the evolutionary relationships among those species, understand the timing of evolutionary events, and identify the functional changes brought about by genetic variations over time. These evolutionary trees also allow us to understand how genes have evolved, duplicated, or been lost over millions of years. Moreover, phylogenetic analyses aid in identifying conserved sequences that play crucial roles in maintaining an organism's function and survival. Consequently, by enabling the tracing of evolutionary gene trees, bioinformatics enhances our understanding of evolution, biodiversity, and the complex relationship between genotype and phenotype.

2.4.5   Prediction of Protein Structure

Bioinformatics is indispensable in the field of protein structure prediction, which is fundamental to understanding the relationship between a protein's structure and its function. Given that the experimental determination of protein structures is often resource intensive and time consuming, computational methods offer a valuable alternative. Starting from the primary amino acid sequence of a protein, bioinformatics tools are used to predict secondary structural features such as alpha helices, beta sheets, and turns. Following this, advanced algorithms such as homology modeling, threading, and *ab initio* methods are employed to predict the three-dimensional structure of the protein. These models are crucial for gaining insights into protein functions, interactions, and enzymatic activities. Additionally, predicted protein structures are immensely valuable in drug discovery processes, where they facilitate the identification of potential drug targets and the design of drug molecules. Thus, bioinformatics plays an essential role in protein structure prediction, significantly advancing our understanding of protein biology and its applications in therapeutics.

2.4.6   Molecular Modeling of Biomolecules

Bioinformatics plays a pivotal role in the molecular modeling of biomolecules, a key process in understanding biological functions and interactions at the atomic level. This process encompasses the creation of three-dimensional structures of DNA, RNA, and proteins based on their sequence data, providing significant insights into their functions. Molecular dynamics simulations, a tool within bioinformatics, are utilized to study the physical movements and conformational changes of these biomolecules, revealing how they interact with each other and their environment. The modeling of complex biomolecular interactions, such as protein–protein, protein–DNA, or protein–ligand interactions, is critical to understanding cellular processes and the molecular basis of diseases. Furthermore, these models are essential in the field of rational drug design, where potential drugs are screened and optimized based on their predicted interactions with target molecules. Hence, the application of bioinformatics to molecular modeling forms the foundation for understanding biological systems and developing therapeutic interventions.

2.4.7   Development of Models for the Functioning of Cells, Tissues, and Organs

In the field of systems biology, bioinformatics plays a critical role in developing comprehensive models that elucidate the functioning of cells, tissues, and organs. Due to the immense complexity of biological systems, sophisticated computational models are essential to understanding and predicting their behaviors. Bioinformatics tools assist in decoding vast amounts of genomic, transcriptomic, proteomic, and metabolomic data to uncover intricate interactions and regulatory networks within cells. These networks can then be modeled to provide insights into cellular functions and to predict how changes in these networks can lead to diseases. On a larger scale, bioinformatics aids in tissue- and organ-level modeling by utilizing data about cell-cell interactions and communication as well as spatial and temporal patterns of gene expression. These models can help predict tissue or organ responses to various stimuli or pathological conditions and can be used to simulate the impact of potential therapeutic interventions. By integrating and interpreting multiscale data, bioinformatics significantly contributes to our understanding of complex biological systems, ultimately assisting in the development of more effective and targeted treatment strategies.

2.4.8   Drug Design and Development

Bioinformatics analysis serves as a powerful accelerant in the stages of drug discovery, notably in the identification of drug targets, screening, and refinement of drug candidates, as well as in the characterization of side effects and prediction of drug resistance [71]. This process typically involves the comparative analysis of high-throughput molecular data derived from patients, animal disease models, human cell lines, and normal controls. The principal objectives of bioinformatics in drug discovery include (1) establishing a link between disease symptoms and genetic mutations, epigenetic modifications, and other modulations of gene expression mediated by environmental factors; (2) identifying drug targets capable of restoring cellular function or eliminating dysfunctional cells; (3) predicting and refining drug candidates to achieve the intended therapeutic outcomes while minimizing side effects; and (4) assessing the environmental health impact and potential for drug resistance. These objectives underscore the pivotal role that bioinformatics plays in navigating the complex landscape of drug discovery.

Omics data have a broad range of applications in drug discovery, as summarized in Table 2.9. This includes data from genomics (the study of genes), transcriptomics (the study of mRNA transcripts), proteomics (the study of proteins), metabolomics (the study of metabolites), and many other "-omics" fields. In the context of target identification and validation, omics data can identify and validate new drug targets by studying the genes, proteins, and metabolites involved in disease processes—for instance, genomics data can reveal genes mutated in certain diseases, while proteomics data can identify proteins that are over- or under-expressed. In terms of drug repurposing, omics data can reveal new uses for existing drugs—for example, by comparing the transcriptomic profiles of cells treated with different drugs, researchers may identify drugs that induce similar responses and thus could potentially be used to treat the same disease. In precision medicine, omics data can help stratify patients into different groups on the basis of their genetic or molecular profiles, allowing for more personalized treatment strategies—for instance, genomic

Table 2.9 Summary of omics data and their applications in drug discovery.

Omics data type	Description	Use in drug discovery	Databases
Genomics	Genomics involves the study of the entire genome of an organism, including the structure, function, evolution, and mapping of genomes	Identification of disease-related genes and genetic variants as potential drug targets; predicting drug response based on an individual's genetic makeup for personalized medicine	dbGaP GWAS Catalog GWAS central PharmGKB
Transcriptomics	Transcriptomics is the study of the complete set of RNA transcripts produced by the genome under specific circumstances or in a specific cell	Understanding changes in gene expression profiles in response to disease or drug treatment can inform the development of new therapeutic strategies; identification of novel drug targets and biomarkers	ArrayExpress DrugMatrix Expression Atlas GEO repository LINCS 1000 TG-GATE
Proteomics	Proteomics involves the large-scale study of proteins, including their structures, functions, and interactions	Understanding the function and interaction of proteins in biological systems to identify potential drug targets; discovering biomarkers for disease diagnosis and prognosis; analyzing changes in protein expression or modification in response to drug treatment	PRIDE Archive Peptide Atlas ProteomicsDB Human Proteome Map Human Proteome Atlas

(Continued)

Table 2.9 Summary of omics data and their applications in drug discovery. (*Continued*)

Omics data type	Description	Use in drug discovery	Databases
Metabolomics	Metabolomics is the study of the complete set of metabolites within a biological sample, which can provide insights into the functional state of cells	Identifying changes in metabolite levels in response to disease or drug treatment, which can inform drug development; discovering biomarkers for disease diagnosis, prognosis, and prediction of drug response	Human Metabolome Madison Metabolomics Golm Metabolome Database MassBank MetaboLights MetabolomeExpress

Note: Each omics data type provides a different layer of information about biological systems and can be used individually or in combination for drug discovery.

data can be used to identify patients likely to respond to a specific drug on the basis of their genetic makeup. Importantly, omics data, particularly genomic data, play a crucial role in pharmacogenomics, the study of how an individual's genetic makeup influences their response to drugs. This can lead to personalized drug prescriptions that maximize efficacy and minimize side effects. Omics data can also help elucidate the mechanisms of action of drugs—for example, proteomics data can reveal the proteins that a drug interacts with, while metabolomics data can show how a drug affects cellular metabolism. Furthermore, omics data can aid in the discovery of biomarkers and measurable indicators of the biological state or response to drug treatment. These biomarkers can be used in clinical trials to assess the efficacy and safety of new drugs.

Furthermore, the application of bioinformatics to drug design can be broadly categorized into several approaches, including ligand-based, target-based, *de novo*, and structure-based drug design. Each method holds a unique role and application within the overall process of drug discovery and development, as summarized in Table 2.10. For ligand-based approaches, these methods rely on the knowledge of previously identified bioactive molecules (ligands) that interact with the target of interest. One of the main techniques within ligand-based approaches is quantitative structure–activity relationship (QSAR) modeling. QSAR models correlate the chemical structure of compounds to their biological activity, which allows for the prediction of the activity of new compounds. Similarly, pharmacophore modeling is another ligand-based method in which the spatial arrangement of key features in a drug necessary for its activity is identified. These models can be used to search databases of compounds for those with similar properties, potentially also interacting with the target.

Concerning target-based approaches, these techniques begin with a well-defined drug target, typically a protein whose activity can be modulated to achieve a therapeutic effect. The most common technique in this category is molecular docking, which predicts the binding affinity and orientation of a potential drug within the target's active site. The 3D structure of the protein is often determined using X-ray crystallography or NMR spectroscopy or, if the experimental structure is not available, it may be predicted using computational

Table 2.10 Summary of the different bioinformatics and drug design approaches along with their roles.

Drug design approach	Description	Role
Ligand-based approaches	Ligand-based approaches involve the use of known active compounds (ligands) to design new drug candidates. The techniques used include 3D quantitative structure–activity relationship (3D QSAR) modeling and pharmacophore modeling.	Used when the structure of the target is not known. These approaches aim to find or design new compounds with similar properties to known active compounds.
Target-based approaches	Target-based approaches involve the use of knowledge about the biological target of the drug. This approach often involves techniques such as docking, where the interactions between a potential drug and its target are predicted.	Used when the structure of the target is known. The aim is to design drugs that interact effectively with the target, often by fitting into an active site on the target.
De novo approaches	*De novo* drug design involves the use of computational methods to design new drug molecules from scratch, based on the characteristics of the target site.	Used when the structure of the target is known. These approaches aim to design new drugs that fit well with the target site, often when known ligands are not available or not effective.
Structure-based drug design (SBDD)	Structure-based drug design involves the use of the 3D structure of the biological target to design drugs. This often involves X-ray crystallography or NMR spectroscopy to determine the structure of the target and computational methods to design drugs.	Used when the 3D structure of the target is known. The aim is to design drugs that interact effectively with the 3D structure of the target, often by fitting into an active site on the target.

Note: Each approach has its own strengths and weaknesses, and the choice of approach often depends on the specific circumstances of the drug design project.

methods. The *de novo* drug design approach aims to design novel drug-like molecules from scratch, given a defined set of chemical building blocks and a target active site. To assemble the components into new molecules that fit well within the active site and have good, predicted activity, *de novo* drug design can use the rules of medicinal chemistry, information about the active site from experimental or computational methods, and optimization algorithms as guides. In addition, structure-based drug design relies on knowledge of the three-dimensional structure of the biological target, which is mainly obtained by

X-ray crystallography, NMR spectroscopy, or cryo-electron microscopy. Detailed structural information enables the design of drugs that can bind to the functional sites of the target. The techniques used in SBDD include molecular docking, where potential drugs are computationally fitted into the active site of the target, and molecular dynamics simulations, which can provide a dynamic view of drug–target interactions. All these approaches have unique strengths and can be used individually or in combination to guide the drug discovery process.

Table 2.11 presents several case studies to provide a clearer understanding of the applications of bioinformatics in drug design and development. Each study showcases the unique ways in which bioinformatics can significantly contribute to advancements in modern therapeutics—for instance, Ghaffari *et al.* [72] conducted a phase I/II trial to explore an alternative approach for patients with chronic myeloid leukemia (CML) who showed persistent molecular residual disease despite at least 15 months of treatment with imatinib, a drug that significantly improved CML treatment but did not lead to complete remission in

Table 2.11 Case studies of bioinformatics in drug discovery and development.

Case study	Research question	Bioinformatics methods used	Key finding	Reference
1. PR1/ BCR-ABL multipeptide vaccination development for chronic myeloid leukemia	How to target the BCR-ABL oncogene, the cause of chronic myeloid leukemia?	BCR-ABL transcription	A combination of immunotherapy with imatinib target therapy was identified as a potent inhibitor of the PR1/BCR-ABL oncogene, leading to its successful use in chronic myeloid leukemia treatment.	Ghaffari *et al.* [72]
2. HIV protease inhibitors	How to stop HIV replication in patients?	Computational chemistry and antiviral activity against the darunavir-resistant HIV-1 variant	Successful development of drugs like darunavir that inhibit the HIV protease, thus preventing the maturation of the virus	Ma *et al.* [73]
3. Personalized medicine for brain metastases from breast cancer	Can we predict the response of individual breast cancer patients to specific therapies?	Genomic data analysis, specifically gene expression profiling	Identified specific genetic signatures associated with responsiveness to certain breast cancer treatments, enabling more personalized treatment strategies	Morikawa *et al.* [74]

all patients. These patients were administered PR1/BCR-ABL multipeptide vaccinations. At 1 month after vaccination, four of the patients experienced a substantial decrease in their BCR-ABL transcript levels, with four achieving a major molecular response (MMR). Upon a follow-up of 7 years, the vaccinations were found to have led to MMR in five patients and a complete molecular response (CMR) in one patient. However, upon discontinuing imatinib in two patients who had achieved MMR following vaccination, there was a resurgence and relapse of leukemia. This indicates that a combined approach of immunotherapy and imatinib treatment could potentially improve the long-term clinical and molecular responses in CML patients.

The escalating occurrence of drug-resistant HIV-1 variants necessitates the immediate development of robust protease inhibitors capable of combating these multidrug-resistant strains. In a study by Ma *et al.* [73], a new series of HIV-1 protease inhibitors were synthesized, incorporating phenols or polyphenols as the P2 ligands and various sulfonamide analogs as the P2 ligands. Many of these novel inhibitors displayed impressive antiviral activity and enzymatic inhibition. Specifically, inhibitors 15d and 15f exhibited potent inhibitory activity in the low picomolar range, with 15f proving particularly effective against the darunavir-resistant HIV-1 variant. Molecular modeling studies further clarified the interactions between these inhibitors and the enzyme cavity, providing valuable insights that could aid in the future refinement of these potent inhibitors.

In 2023, Morikawa *et al.* [74] unveiled potential therapeutic strategies for brain metastases. Brain metastases often harbor unique molecular characteristics, presenting potential targets for therapeutic interventions. The researchers studied the molecular profiles of 12 brain metastases derived from breast cancer, juxtaposing them with the primary breast tumors. Authors crafted six patient-derived xenografts (PDXs) from these brain metastases, employing these PDXs as a platform for potential molecular target investigation. Remarkably, numerous alterations identified in the primary tumors were also found in the brain metastases, particularly in the immune-related and metabolic pathways. When exposed to over 350 drugs, these PDXs exhibited a high sensitivity to histone deacetylase and proteasome inhibitors. This investigation underscored significant molecular disparities between paired primary breast tumors and brain metastases. Concurrent with existing clinical trials that use genomic profiling of tumors, their functional precision medicine strategy proposes a valuable augmentation by expanding potential therapeutic avenues for brain metastases originating from breast cancer.

2.5 Challenges and Opportunities in Bioinformatics

Bioinformatics presents several unique challenges that must be navigated for successful drug development. One of the primary challenges in bioinformatics is dealing with the sheer volume and complexity of biological data. This issue stems from advancements in high-throughput screening and next-generation sequencing, which have dramatically increased the rate of data generation. Consequently, managing, analyzing, and interpreting this deluge of data are daunting tasks that require sophisticated computational algorithms and significant storage capabilities. Additionally, issues related to data quality and standardization pose considerable challenges in bioinformatics. Biological experiments, influenced by a multitude of variables, often yield inconsistent and noisy data. Additionally, the lack of standard formats for representing and exchanging data makes it harder to combine and compare data from different sources. This could make it harder for bioinformatics tools to predict how safe and effective a drug will be. Nonetheless, it is vital to recognize that these challenges also present opportunities. These problems can be solved by making data management systems smarter, improving artificial intelligence and machine learning, and working to standardize data [75–77]. This will help bioinformatics in drug discovery and development reach its full potential [78, 79].

2.6 Future Directions of Bioinformatics in Drug Design

The future of bioinformatics in drug design holds immense potential, particularly as technologies evolve and computational power continues to increase. As the intricacies of biological systems deepens, the role of bioinformatics in drug discovery is set to advance even further. Table 2.12 outlines some of the future directions of bioinformatics in drug design and development. One key area of growth lies in the development and refinement of algorithms for more accurate protein structure prediction and drug–target interaction simulations. Enhanced prediction capabilities can streamline the process of identifying viable drug

Table 2.12 Future directions of bioinformatics in drug design and development.

Future direction	Description
Enhanced algorithms for protein structure prediction and drug–target interaction simulations	The development and refinement of algorithms for accurate protein structure prediction and drug–target interaction simulations can streamline drug target identification and expedite the early stages of drug discovery.
Integration of ML and AI	The incorporation of machine learning and AI techniques into bioinformatics will enable more efficient processing of large and complex biological datasets, leading to more precise and reliable predictions.
Multiomics data integration	Combining data from genomics, transcriptomics, proteomics, and metabolomics can provide a holistic understanding of disease processes and drug interactions at different levels of biological function, unveiling new drug targets and therapeutic strategies.
Bioinformatics in personalized medicine	With the growing accessibility of personalized genomic data, bioinformatics will play a vital role in analyzing these datasets, linking genetic variations to disease risks, predicting individual responses to drugs, and assisting in the design of personalized therapeutic strategies.
Biomarker identification	Bioinformatics can help in the identification of biomarkers for early disease detection, patient stratification, and monitoring drug responses, thereby aiding in the realization of the full potential of personalized medicine.

targets and accelerate the early stages of drug discovery. Moreover, integrating machine learning and artificial intelligence will allow for a more efficient processing of large, complex biological datasets, resulting in more precise and reliable outputs.

The increasing focus on multiomics data integration is another exciting future direction in bioinformatics with the potential to revolutionize drug design. Currently, genomics, transcriptomics, proteomics, and metabolomics data are often analyzed independently. However, integrating these multiomics data can provide a more comprehensive understanding of disease processes and drug interactions across various levels of biological function. Such integrative analyses can reveal new drug targets and therapeutic strategies that might be missed when analyzing each type of data separately. Bioinformatics tools and strategies will be pivotal in facilitating this integration, managing the complexity and volume of multiomics data and extracting meaningful, actionable insights.

Personalized medicine is another field where bioinformatics is poised to make a significant impact. With advancements in sequencing technologies and the decreasing costs of genome sequencing, personalized genomic data are becoming increasingly accessible. Bioinformatics will play a vital role in analyzing these vast datasets, linking genetic variations to disease risks, predicting individual responses to drugs, and aiding in the design of personalized therapeutic strategies. Moreover, bioinformatics can assist in identifying biomarkers for early disease detection, patient stratification, and monitoring drug responses, thereby helping to realize the full potential of personalized medicine. As we move into the future, the role of bioinformatics in drug design and discovery is set to become even more central and impactful.

2.7   Conclusion and Future Scope

Bioinformatics, the application of computational technology to manage and analyze biological data, has dramatically transformed the landscape of drug discovery. The chapter explains the rich and multifaceted landscape of bioinformatics, exploring its many applications and profound implications for the field of drug design and development. As a combination of biology, computer science, and information technology, bioinformatics has proven to be an indispensable tool in the handling and analysis of complex biological datasets. The capabilities of bioinformatics to manage, analyze, and interpret large-scale biological data have revolutionized the approach to drug discovery and development. It has facilitated the decoding of genomic sequences, the understanding of genetic variations, the prediction of protein structures and functions, and the identification of novel therapeutic targets, thereby accelerating the transition from fundamental research to clinical applications. Particularly noteworthy is the capacity of bioinformatics to enable *in silico* modeling of drug–target interactions. This powerful tool allows scientists to simulate and study molecular interactions at an unprecedented scale and speed, significantly reducing the time and cost associated with traditional laboratory and clinical trials. Moreover, bioinformatics provides a robust platform for the application of AI and ML algorithms, which have shown remarkable potential in identifying patterns and making predictions from vast genomic, proteomic, and metabolomic data. Such applications further enhance the efficiency and precision of drug design processes, opening up new avenues for personalized medicine and drug repurposing. However, the integration of bioinformatics into the drug design and development process is not without challenges. Issues related to data quality, computational resource needs, model interpretability, and data privacy and security need to be addressed. Furthermore, ethical considerations surrounding data usage and the potential biases in algorithmic predictions necessitate the establishment of stringent regulations and standards. Despite these difficulties, bioinformatics holds enormous promise for the development and design of drugs in the future. The advancements it has fostered are transforming our understanding of biological systems and their interactions with therapeutic agents. It has catalyzed the evolution of drug discovery and development from a primarily experimental field into a data-intensive and computation-driven discipline. As knowledge moves forward, it is exciting to envision how further advancements in bioinformatics, coupled with AI and ML technologies, will reshape the landscape of pharmaceutical research. These technologies hold the potential to make drug discovery and development more efficient, economical, and personalized, marking a new era in healthcare. In conclusion, bioinformatics stands at the forefront of the ongoing revolution in drug design and development. It is evident that its role, buoyed by the power of AI and ML, will continue to be integral to the future of pharmaceutical research and healthcare.

References

1. Hasija, Y., Chapter 6 - Structural bioinformatics, in: *All About Bioinformatics: From Beginner to Expert,* Y. Hasija (Ed.), pp. 135–152, Academic Press, London, United Kingdom, 2023, https://doi.org/10.1016/B978-0-443-15250-4.00005-8.
2. Hasija, Y., Chapter 1 - What is bioinformatics?, in: *All About Bioinformatics: From Beginner to Expert,* Y. Hasija (Ed.), pp. 1–17, Academic Press, London, United Kingdom, 2023, https://doi.org/10.1016/B978-0-443-15250-4.00012-5.
3. Research and Markets, 2023, July 23. https://www.researchandmarkets.com/ reports/4829802/global-bioinformatics-market-by-product#src-pos-2.
4. Banimfreg, B.H., A comprehensive review and conceptual framework for cloud com puting adoption in bioinformatics. *Healthcare Analytics, 3,* 100190, 2023, https://doi.org/10.1016/j.health.2023.100190.
5. Nakamae, K. and Bono, H., Genome editing and bioinformatics. *Gene Genome Editing, 3-4,* 100018, 2022, https://doi.org/10.1016/j.ggedit.2022.100018.
6. Romdhane, L., Bouhamed, H., Ghedira, K., Ben Hamda, C., Louhichi, A., Jmel, H., . . . Rebai, A., The morbid cutaneous anatomy of the human genome revealed by a bioinformatic approach. *Genomics, 112,* 6, 4232–4241, 2020, https://doi.org/10.1016/j.ygeno.2020.07.009.
7. Iqbal, N. and Kumar, P., From data science to bioscience: Emerging era of bioinformatics applications, tools and challenges. *Proc. Comput. Sci., 218,* 1516–1528, 2023, https://doi.org/10.1016/j.procs.2023.01.130.
8. Qazi, S. and Raza, K., Chapter 1 - Translational bioinformatics in healthcare: Past, present, and future, in: *Translational Bioinformatics in Healthcare and Medicine,* K. Raza and N. Dey (Eds.), vol. 13, pp. 1–12, Academic Press, London, United Kingdom, 2021, https://doi.org/10.1016/B978-0-323-89824-9.00001-X.
9. Yu, J., Blom, J., Glaeser, S.P., Jaenicke, S., Juhre, T., Rupp, O., Goesmann, A., A review of bioinformatics platforms for comparative genomics. Recent developments of the EDGAR 2.0 platform and its utility for taxonomic and phylogenetic studies. *J. Biotechnol., 261,* 2–9, 2017, https://doi.org/10.1016/j.jbiotec.2017.07.010.

10. Shoaib, M., Singh, A., Gulati, S., Kukreti, S., Chapter 8 - Mapping genomes by using bioinformatics data and tools, in: *Chemoinformatics and Bioinformatics in the Pharmaceutical Sciences*, N. Sharma, H. Ojha, P.K. Raghav, R.K. Goyal (Eds.), pp. 245–278, Academic Press, London, United Kingdom, 2021, https://doi.org/10.1016/B978-0-12-821748-1.00002-6.

11. Nisar, N., Mir, S.A., Kareem, O., Pottoo, F.H., Chapter 4 - Proteomics approaches in the identification of cancer biomarkers and drug discovery, in: *Proteomics*, S. Ali, S. Majid, M.U. Rehman (Eds.), pp. 77–120, Academic Press, London, United Kingdom, 2023, https://doi.org/10.1016/B978-0-323-95072-5.00001-8.

12. Palermo, A., Metabolomics- and systems-biology-guided discovery of metabolite lead compounds and druggable targets. *Drug Discovery Today*, 28, 2, 103460, 2023, https://doi.org/10.1016/j.drudis.2022.103460.

13. Xing, J., Shankar, R., Ko, M., Zhang, K., Zhang, S., Drelich, A., Chen, B., Deciphering COVID-19 host transcriptomic complexity and variations for therapeutic discovery against new variants. *iScience*, 25, 10, 105068, 2022, https://doi.org/10.1016/j.isci.2022.105068.

14. Larson, N.B., Oberg, A.L., Adjei, A.A., Wang, L., A clinician's guide to bioinformatics for next-generation sequencing. *J. Thoracic Oncol.*, 18, 2, 143–157, 2023, https://doi. org/10.1016/j.jtho.2022.11.006.

15. Ayo, F.E., Awotunde, J.B., Ogundokun, R.O., Folorunso, S.O., Adekunle, A.O., A decision support system for multi-target disease diagnosis: A bioinformatics approach. *Heliyon*, 6, 3, 03657, 2020, https://doi.org/10.1016/j.heliyon.2020.e03657.

16. Roy, S., Principles and validation of bioinformatics pipeline for cancer next-generation sequencing. *Clinics Lab. Med.*, 42, 3, 409–421, 2022, https://doi.org/10.1016/j. cll.2022.05.006.

17. Mitra, D., Mitra, D., Sabri Bensaad, M., Sinha, S., Pant, K., Pant, M., Das Mohapatra, P.K., Evolution of bioinformatics and its impact on modern bio-science in the twenty-first century: Special attention to pharmacology, plant science and drug discovery. *Comput. Toxicol.*, 24, 100248, 2022, https://doi.org/10.1016/j.comtox.2022.100248.

18. Levy, J., Lu, Y., Montivero, M., Ramwala, O., McFadden, J., Miles, C., Vaickus, L., Artificial Intelligence, Bioinformatics, and pathology: Emerging trends part I—An introduction to machine learning technologies. *Adv. Mol. Pathol.*, 5, 1, 24, 2022, https://doi.org/10.1016/j. yamp.2023.01.001.

19. Theodosiou, A.A. and Read, R.C., Artificial intelligence, machine learning and deep learning: Potential resources for the infection clinician. *J. Infection*, 87, 4, 287–294, 2023, https://doi.org/10.1016/j.jinf.2023.07.006.

20. Gupta, R., Kumari, S., Senapati, A., Ambasta, R.K., Kumar, P., New era of artificial intelligence and machine learning-based detection, diagnosis, and therapeutics in Parkinson's disease. *Ageing Res. Rev.*, 90, 102013, 2023, https://doi.org/10.1016/j.arr.2023.102013.

21. Wang, C., Wang, L., Li, Q., Wu, W., Yuan, J., Wang, H., Lu, X., Computational drug discovery in ankylosing spondylitis–induced osteoporosis based on data mining and bioinformatics analysis. *World Neurosurgery*, 174, 8–, 16, 2023, https://doi.org/10.1016/j.wneu.2023.01.092.

22. O'Connor, L.M., O'Connor, B.A., Lim, S.B., Zeng, J., Lo, C.H., Integrative multiomics and systems bioinformatics in translational neuroscience: A data mining perspective. *J. Pharm. Anal.*, 13, 8, 836–850, 2023, https://doi.org/10.1016/j.jpha.2023.06.011.

23. Browne, R.B., Vishwakarma, J.N., Borah, V.V., Pegu, R.K., Roy, J.D., Chapter 7 - *In silico* application of data science, genomics, and bioinformatics in screening drug candidates against COVID-19, in: *Data Science for Genomics*, A.K. Tyagi and A. Abraham (Eds.), pp. 107–128, Academic Press, London, United Kingdom, 2023, https://doi.org/10.1016/B978-0-323-98352-5.00016-1.

24. Sarigiannis, D.A., Stratidakis, A.K., Karakitsios, S.P., *In silico* methods and *in silico* toxicology, in: *Encyclopedia of Toxicology (Fourth Edition)*, P. Wexler (Ed.), pp. 503– 507, Academic Press, United Kingdom, 2023, https://doi.org/10.1016/ B978-0-12-824315-2.01173-8.

25. Paiva, V. d. A., Gomes, I. d. S., Monteiro, C.R., Mendonça, M.V., Martins, P.M., Santana, C.A., . . . Silveira, S. d. A., Protein structural bioinformatics: An overview. *Comput. Biol. Med.*, *147*, 105695, 2022, https://doi.org/10.1016/j.compbiomed.2022.105695.

26. Ajala, A., Uzairu, A., Shallangwa, G.A., Abechi, S.E., Ramu, R., Al-Ghorbani, M., Natural product inhibitors as potential drug candidates against Alzheimer's disease: Structural-based drug design, molecular docking, molecular dynamic simulation experiments, and ADMET predictions. *J. Indian Chem. Soc.*, *100*, 5, 100977, 2023, https://doi. org/10.1016/j.jics.2023.100977.

27. Shah, I.M., Ali, A., Wani, R.F.C., Malla, B.A., Dar, M.A., Wali, A., Ahmad, M., Chapter 14 - Computational and pharmacogenomic resources, in: *Pharmacogenomics*, S.A. Ganie, A. Ali, M.U. Rehman, A. Arafah (Eds.), pp. 345–362, Academic Press, London, United Kingdom, 2023, https://doi. org/10.1016/B978-0-443-15336-5.00005-1.

28. Silva, P.J. and Ramos, K.S., 7.03 - Trends and implementation of preemptive pharmacogenomic testing, in: *Comprehensive Precision Medicine*, K.S. Ramos (Ed.), vol. 2, pp. 363–381, Elsevier, Netherlands, 2024, https://doi.org/10.1016/ B978-0-12-824010-6.00053-8.

29. Chen, Z., Wang, W., Zhang, Y., Xue, X., Hua, Y., Identification of four-gene signature to diagnose osteoarthritis through bioinformatics and machine learning methods. *Cytokine*, *169*, 156300, 2023, https://doi.org/10.1016/j.cyto.2023.156300.

30. Hasija, Y., Chapter 9 - A machine learning approach to bioinformatics, in: *All About Bioinformatics: From Beniner to Expert*, Y. Hasija (Ed.), pp. 203–224, Academic Press, London, United Kingdom, 2023, https://doi.org/10.1016/ B978-0-443-15250-4.00010-1.

31. Alzubi, J., Nayyar, A., Kumar, A., Machine learning from theory to algorithms: An overview. *J. Physics: Conf. Ser.*, *1142*, 012012, 2018, https://doi.org/10.1088/1742-6596/1142/1/012012.

32. Kumar, A., Krishnamurthi, R., Nayyar, A., Sharma, K., Grover, V., Hossain, E., A novel smart healthcare design, simulation, and implementation using healthcare 4.0 processes. *IEEE Access*, *8*, 118433–118471, 2020, https://doi.org/10.1109/ACCESS.2020.3004790.

33. Sofi, M.Y., Shafi, A., Masoodi, K.Z., Chapter 5 - Pairwise sequence alignment, in: *Bioinformatics for Everyone*, M.Y. Sofi, A. Shafi, K.Z. Masoodi (Eds.), pp. 37–45, Academic Press, London, United Kingdom, 2022, https://doi.org/10.1016/B978-0-323-91128-3.00013-6.

34. Amorim, A.R., Zafalon, G.F.D., Contessoto, A., d., G., Valêncio, C.R., Sato, L.M., Metaheuristics for multiple sequence alignment: A systematic review. *Comput. Biol. Chem.*, *94*, 107563, 2021, https://doi.org/10.1016/j.compbiolchem.2021.107563.

35. Talamantes-Becerra, B., Carling, J., Georges, A., omicR: A tool to facilitate BLASTn alignments for sequence data. *SoftwareX*, *14*, 100702, 2021, https://doi.org/10.1016/j. softx.2021.100702.

36. Naorem, L.D., Sharma, N., Raghava, G.P.S., A web server for predicting and scanning of IL-5 inducing peptides using alignment-free and alignment-based method. *Comput. Biol. Med.*, *158*, 106864, 2023, https://doi.org/10.1016/j.compbiomed.2023.106864.

37. Väth, P., Münch, M., Raab, C., Schleif, F.M., PROVAL: A framework for comparison of protein sequence embeddings. *J. Comput. Mathematics Data Sci.*, *3*, 100044, 2022, https://doi. org/10.1016/j.jcmds.2022.100044.

38. Sofi, M.Y., Shafi, A., Masoodi, K.Z., Chapter 8 - CLUSTALW software, in: *Bioinformatics for Everyone*, M.Y. Sofi, A. Shafi, K.Z. Masoodi (Eds.), pp. 75–84, Academic Press, London, United Kingdom, 2022, https://doi.org/10.1016/B978-0-323-91128-3.00003-3.

39. Ayub, F., Ahmed, H., Sohail, T., Shahzad, K., Celik, F., Wang, X., Simsek, S., Cao, J., Bioinformatics-based prediction and screening of immunogenic epitopes of Toxoplasma gondii rhoptry proteins 7, 21 and 22 as candidate vaccine target. *Heliyon*, *9*, 7, 18176, 2023, https://doi. org/10.1016/j.heliyon.2023.e18176.

40. Singh, N., Nath, R., Singh, D.B., Splice-site identification for exon prediction using bidirectional LSTM-RNN approach. *Biochem. Biophysics Rep.*, *30*, 101285, 2022, https:// doi.org/10.1016/j. bbrep.2022.101285.

41. Cao, D., Wang, C., Zhou, L., Identification and comprehensive analysis of ferroptosis-related genes as potential biomarkers for the diagnosis and treatment of proliferative diabetic retinopathy by bioinformatics methods. *Exp. Eye Res.*, 232, 109513, 2023, https://doi.org/10.1016/j.exer.2023.109513.

42. Lu, J., An, S., Ma, J., Yang, Y., Zhang, L., Yu, P., Zhang, H., Topoisomerase II α gene as a marker for prognostic prediction of hepatocellular carcinoma: A bioinformatics analysis. *Chin. Med. Sci. J.*, 37, 4, 331–339, 2022, https://doi.org/10.24920/004006.

43. The National Library of Medicine, 2023, July 23, https://pubmed.ncbi.nlm.nih.gov/.

44. International Nucleotide Sequence Database Collaboration, 2023, July 23, https://www.insdc.org/.

45. RCSB Protein Data Bank (RCSB PDB), 2023, July 23, https://www.rcsb.org/.

46. Uniprot, 2023, July 23, https://www.uniprot.org/.

47. Ensembl, 2023, July 23, https://ensemblgenomes.org/.

48. KEGG, 2023, July 23, https://www.genome.jp/kegg/.

49. Palù, M., Basile, A., Zampieri, G., Treu, L., Rossi, A., Morlino, M.S., Campanaro, S., KEMET – A python tool for KEGG Module evaluation and microbial genome annotation expansion. *Comput. Struct. Biotechnol. J.*, 20, 1481–1486, 2022, https://doi.org/10.1016/j.csbj.2022.03.015.

50. Chen, H., Zhang, Y., Awasthi, S.K., Liu, T., Zhang, Z., Awasthi, M.K., Effect of red kaolin on the diversity of functional genes based on Kyoto Encyclopedia of Genes and Genomes pathways during chicken manure composting. *Bioresource Technol.*, 311, 123584, 2020, https://doi.org/10.1016/j.biortech.2020.123584.

51. Yu, R., Wang, Y., Liang, Q., Xu, Y., Yusf, A.E., Sun, L., Identification of potential biomarkers and pathways for sepsis using RNA sequencing technology and bioinformatic analysis. *Heliyon*, 9, 4, 15034, 2023, https://doi.org/10.1016/j.heliyon.2023.e15034.

52. PubMed. (2023, July 23), https://www.ncbi.nlm.nih.gov/

53. Xu, M., Xu, C., Chen, M., Xiao, Z., Wang, Y., Xu, Y., Xu, D., Comparative analysis of commonly used bioinformatics software based on omics. *Gene Rep.*, 32, 101800, 2023, https://doi.org/10.1016/j.genrep.2023.101800.

54. Sofi, M.Y., Shafi, A., Masoodi, K.Z., Chapter 10 - NCBI BLAST, in: *Bioinformatics for Everyone*, M.Y. Sofi, A. Shafi, K.Z. Masoodi (Eds.), pp. 95–102, Academic Press, London, United Kingdom, 2022c, https://doi.org/10.1016/B978-0-323-91128-3.00021-5.

55. Mustafa, S., Akhtar, Z., Asif, M., Amjad, M., Ijaz, M., Latif, M., Iqbal, F., Novel missense variants in FGFR1 and FGFR3 causes short stature in enrolled families from Pakistan. *Meta Gene*, 26, 100778, 2020, https://doi.org/10.1016/j.mgene.2020.100778.

56. Cornish, T.C., Kricka, L.J., Park, J.Y., A Biopython-based method for comprehensively searching for eponyms in Pubmed. *MethodsX*, 8, 101264, 2021, https://doi.org/10.1016/j.mex.2021.101264.

57. Agapito, G., Computing Languages for Bioinformatics: BioPerl, in: *Encyclopedia of Bioinformatics and Computational Biology*, S. Ranganathan, M. Gribskov, K. Nakai, C. Schönbach (Eds.), pp. 187–194, Academic Press, London, United Kingdom, 2019, https://doi.org/10.1016/B978-0-12-809633-8.20365-8.

58. Sepulveda, J.L., Using R and bioconductor in clinical genomics and transcriptomics. *J. Mol. Diagnostics*, 22, 1, 3–20, 2020, https://doi.org/10.1016/j.jmoldx.2019.08.006.

59. Guzzi, P.H., Computing languages for bioinformatics: Java, in: *Encyclopedia of Bioinformatics and Computational Biology*, S. Ranganathan, M. Gribskov, K. Nakai, C. Schönbach (Eds.), pp. 206–208, Academic Press, London, United Kingdom, 2019, https://doi.org/10.1016/B978-0-12-809633-8.20368-3.

60. Naj, A.C., Lin, H., Vardarajan, B.N., White, S., Lancour, D., Ma, Y., DeStefano, A.L., Quality control and integration of genotypes from two calling pipelines for whole genome sequence

data in the Alzheimer's disease sequencing project. *Genomics*, *111*, 4, 808–818, 2019, https://doi.org/10.1016/j.ygeno.2018.05.004.

61. Park, J., Bakhtiari, M., Popp, B., Wiesener, M., Bafna, V., Detecting tandem repeat variants in coding regions using code-adVNTR. *iScience*, *25*, 8, 104785, 2022 https://doi.org/10.1016/j.isci.2022.104785.

62. Rian, K., Hidalgo, M.R., Çubuk, C., Falco, M.M., Loucera, C., Esteban-Medina, M., Dopazo, J., Genome-scale mechanistic modeling of signaling pathways made easy: A bioconductor/cytoscape/web server framework for the analysis of omic data. *Comput. Struct. Biotechnol. J.*, *19*, 2968–2978, 2021, https://doi.org/10.1016/j.csbj.2021.05.022.

63. Tran, T.-D. and Nguyen, M.-T., C-Biomarker.net: A Cytoscape app for the identification of cancer biomarker genes from cores of large biomolecular networks. *Biosystems*, *226*, 104887, 2023, https://doi.org/10.1016/j.biosystems.2023.104887.

64. Rauf, A., Al-Awthan, Y.S., Bahattab, O., Shah, Z.A., Rashid, U., Bawazeer, S., Rengasamy, K.R.R., Potent urease inhibition and *in Silico* docking study of four secondary metabolites isolated from Heterophragma adenophyllum Seem. *South Afr. J. Bot.*, *142*, 201–205, 2021. https://doi.org/10.1016/j.sajb.2021.06.031.

65. Google Genomics, 2023, July 23, https://cloud.google.com/life-sciences-solutions.

66. Amazon Web Services (AWS) for Genomes, 2023, July 23. https://aws.amazon.com/health/genomics/.

67. Microsoft Azure for Research, 2023, July 23, https://www.microsoft.com/en-us/azure-academic-research/.

68. IBM Watson for Genomes, 2023, July 23, https://researcher.watson.ibm.com/.

69. Galaxyproject, 2023, July 23, https://galaxyproject.org/.

70. Seven Bridges Genomes, 2023, July 23. https://www.sevenbridges.com/.

71. Yingngam, B., New drug discovery, in: *Multidisciplinary Applications of Natural Science for Drug Discovery and Integrative Medicine*, M. Aslam and M. Ahmad (Eds.), pp. 134–184, IGI Global, Pennsylvania, United States, 2023, https://doi.org/10.4018/978-1-6684-9463-9.ch005.

72. Ghaffari, S.H., Osfouri, E., Ahmadvand, M., Bashash, D., Ghaffari, P., Niavarani, A., Ghavamzadeh, A., The long-term outcome and efficacy of PR1/BCR-ABL multipeptides vaccination in chronic myeloid leukemia: Results of a 7-year longitudinal investigation. *IJBC*, *14*, 4, 84–94, 2022, https://doi.org/10.58209/ijbc.14.4.84.

73. Ma, L., Wen, J., Dong, B., Zhou, J., Hu, S., Wang, J., Cen, S., Design and evaluation of novel hiv-1 protease inhibitors containing phenols or polyphenols as p2 ligands with high activity against DRV-resistant hiv-1 variants. *Int. J. Mol. Sci.*, *23*, 22, 14178, 2022, https://doi.org/10.3390/ijms232214178.

74. Morikawa, A., Li, J., Ulintz, P., Cheng, X., Apfel, A., Robinson, D., Merrill, N., Optimizing precision medicine for breast cancer brain metastases with functional drug response assessment. *Cancer Res. Commun.*, *3*, 6, 1093–1103, 2023, https://doi.org/10.1158/2767-9764.Crc-22-0492.

75. Kumar, S., Nayyar, A., Paul, A., *Swarm intelligence and evolutionary algorithms in healthcare and drug development*, CRC Press, New York, United States, 2019, http://dx.doi.org/10.1201/9780429289675.

76. Zivkovic, M., Bacanin, N., Venkatachalam, K., Nayyar, A., Djordjevic, A., Strumberger, I., Al-Turjman, F., COVID-19 cases prediction by using hybrid machine learning and beetle antennae search approach. *Sustain. Cities Soc.*, *66*, 102669, 2021, https://doi.org/10.1016/j.scs.2020.102669.

77. Nayyar, A., Gadhavi, L., Zaman, N., Machine learning in healthcare: Review, opportunities and challenges, in: *Machine Learning and the Internet of Medical Things in Healthcare*, K.K.

Singh, M. Elhoseny, A. Singh and A.A. Elngar (Eds.), pp. 23-45, Academic Press, London, 2021, https://doi.org/10.1016/B978-0-12-821229-5.00011-2.

78. Durgam, R., Devarakonda, N., Nayyar, A., Eluri, R., Improved genetic algorithm using machine learning approaches to feature modelled for microarray gene data, in: *Soft Computing for Security Applications: Proceedings of ICSCS 2021*, Springer, Singapore, pp. 859–872, 2022, https:// doi.org/10.1007/978-981-16-5301-8_60.

79. Solanki, A., Kumar, S., Nayyar, A., *Handbook of Research on Emerging Trends and Applications of Machine Learning*, IGI Global, Pennsylvania, United States, 2020, https://doi. org/10.4018/978-1-5225-9643-1.

Exploring the Intersection of Biology and Computing: Road Ahead to Bioinformatics

Ahmed Mateen Buttar[1]*, Muhammad Nouman Arshad[1] and Anand Nayyar[2]

[1]Department of Computer Science, University of Agriculture Faisalabad, Faisalabad, Punjab, Pakistan
[2]Graduate School, Faculty of Information Technology, Duy Tan University, Da Nang, Vietnam

Abstract

The fields of biology, computer science, statistics, and mathematics are all brought together in the field of bioinformatics. Utilizing computer tools to decode, analyze, and manage huge amounts of biological data, particularly genomic sequences, which are beyond the capabilities of normal scientific methodologies, is the core objective of the future bioinformatics. The chapter provides an introduction to bioinformatics and discusses the importance of the field in comprehending complex biological systems. The fields of precision medicine, drug development, and evolutionary biology are all driven by bioinformatics. In addition to that, it discusses sequence alignment, the analysis of gene and protein expression, databases, tools, and machine learning related to bioinformatics. Concerns in the field of bioinformatics include the quality and integration of data, concerns pertaining to data privacy and security, and the requirement for efficient algorithms to manage the complexity and variety of biological data. The chapter presents an overview of bioinformatics, including its applications and the potential impact it will have on research in the biological sciences. In this era of big data, the field of bioinformatics has had a profound impact on biological research, paving the way for new avenues of scientific exploration and medical advancement. This chapter also emphasizes the importance of continuously improving data quality, integration, privacy, and security, as well as the development of algorithmic solutions, in order to effectively apply bioinformatics to the management of vast amounts of diverse biological information.

Keywords: Genomics, precision medicine, health informatics, HPC, E-science, tools and algorithms

3.1 Introduction

Several subfields of science can benefit from the application of bioinformatics since it integrates biological data with information storage, distribution, and analysis. Bioinformatics gives a holistic perspective that permits the identification of unifying biological principles and makes it possible to make innovative discoveries in the biological sciences. In a typical bioinformatics study, scientists use software to generate and analyze data, design new

---

Corresponding author: ahmedmatin@hotmail.com

Abhirup Khanna, May El Barachi, Sapna Jain, Manoj Kumar and Anand Nayyar (eds.) *Artificial Intelligence and Machine Learning in Drug Design and Development*, (67–92) © 2024 Scrivener Publishing LLC

algorithms and databases, or apply statistical methods to examine relationships among vast data sets. These activities are all part of the field's overarching goal to better understand biological systems. In the field of bioinformatics, genetic sequences, protein samples, cell populations, and even photographs of biomedical conditions can all be analyzed.

The objective of bioinformatics is to analyze and make sense of the information structures underlying biological processes. The fields of genomics and genetics make substantial use of bioinformatics. Using the information obtained through sequencing, bioinformatics allows for the assembly, alignment, and annotation of genomes as well as the discovery of genes and regulatory elements and the construction of phylogenies. The fields of functional genomics, structural genomics, proteomics, biotechnology, and medicines all benefit greatly from the application of bioinformatics. It is helpful in the formulation of pharmaceuticals, the production of vaccines, the investigation of metabolic pathways, the interpretation of genetic variations, and the forecasting of protein structures.

Therefore, the field of bioinformatics is an expanding one that plays an essential role in biological research. Both basic biological research and medical treatment are increasingly dependent on the data and computations provided by bioinformatics. The field of bioinformatics may lead to the discovery of new living systems, which would aid in the treatment of sickness and contribute to an overall improvement in the quality of life in the future.

This chapter provides an introduction to bioinformatics, which is the intersection of biology and computation. The exponential growth of biological data that has been created over the past few decades by technology and our increased understanding of biological systems has necessitated the development of novel methods for its storage, management, and analysis. Because of this desire, the field of bioinformatics developed. The chapter discusses the storing, distributing, and analyzing of data in the field of bioinformatics. For the purpose of producing more accurate analyses of biological data, bioinformatics brings together biology, computer science, mathematics, and statistics. This chapter demonstrates that data management is only one aspect of bioinformatics. The field of bioinformatics assists researchers in making sense of massive amounts of complicated biological data. Researchers have the potential to get fresh insights into biological processes as well as an improved understanding of these phenomena.

The ability to test hypotheses, make discoveries, and make predictions based on data has been made possible by the development of bioinformatics. Genomes, proteomics, and analysis of metabolic pathways, as well as the discovery and creation of new drugs, have all been made possible by bioinformatics. The difficulty and the transformational potential of bioinformatics are both acknowledged in this chapter. The field deals with the heterogeneity of data, concerns relating to privacy and ethics, and the requirements for computing resources. This chapter presents a comprehensive summary of bioinformatics, offering readers the opportunity to investigate the field's intricacies as well as its potential. Students, scientists, and anyone else interested in the revolutionary potential of biology and computing for contemporary science are encouraged to participate.

This chapter, "Exploring the Intersection of Biology and Computing: Road Ahead to Bioinformatics," is written with the expectation that readers will come from a wide variety of educational and professional experiences. It explains what bioinformatics is, its history, and the core concepts behind it. The comprehension of novices to the field is improved by having this foundational information. After this introduction, the principles of bioinformatics and its applications will be discussed. For the purpose of better organizing and understanding biological data, computational methods are utilized. In bioinformatics, genomic, proteomic, and metabolomics data are handled, all of which are topics covered in this chapter.

This chapter discusses some of the most significant uses of bioinformatics. In it, topics such as genomic sequencing, predicting the functions of genes and proteins, analyzing biological networks and pathways, drug discovery and design, predicting diseases, and personalized medicine are covered. The fundamental approaches and techniques used in bioinformatics are also discussed. Among these are machine learning, sequence alignment, search, phylogenetic analysis, molecular modeling and simulation, and phylogenetic tree reconstruction.

In addition to this, the chapter discusses the necessity for powerful computational resources in the field of bioinformatics as well as data privacy and heterogeneity. It provides a glimpse of the field's potential. In the final part of the chapter, the primary software, databases, and tools of bioinformatics are discussed, demonstrating how theory is used in practice. This chapter provides an overview of bioinformatics, including its significance, uses, and challenges. It lays the groundwork for a more in-depth investigation of this topic in subsequent chapters.

3.1.1   Medical Data

Bioinformatics organizes and retrieves biological databases. These databases contain DNA, protein, gene annotations, protein structures, pathways, and more.

GenBank has DNA sequences from numerous animals. Genomics involves gene, genome, and EST annotations. GenBank stores all published nucleotide sequences and protein translations. NCBI and the International Nucleotide Sequence Database Collaboration (INSDC) maintain this database. GenBank and its colleagues receive sequences from over 100,000 organisms from labs worldwide. Scientists can explore the database for genomic sequences of thousands of animals and species for their research.

GenBank: It contains genetic sequencing, EST, STS, and other data. Researchers in academia and industry utilize GenBank for phylogenetics, protein sequence/function prediction after gene expression, and protein structure modeling. In conjunction with ENA and DDBJ, GenBank provides sequence data. To create a global database, the three groups collect a percentage of the sequence data published worldwide and share it. Automated annotation systems, sequence submitters, and database curators collaborate to annotate sequences and maintain database quality. GenBank strives to assure data accuracy; however, it does not verify annotations.

UniProt (protein sequences): Several sources list protein names, functions, domains, and post-translational modifications. Data about protein sequences and annotations can be found in the Universal Protein Resource, also known as UniProt. It is a project that is worked on jointly by the EBI, SIB, and PIR. The UniProt database is a resource for scientists that is free, comprehensive, and of a high quality. It focuses on the sequence and function of proteins. The database contains proteins that have been described as well as those that are anticipated. The information that can be found on this central hub for protein function is precise, consistent, and extensive. It is divided into two sections: one that has been manually reviewed and is called UniProtKB/Swiss-Prot and the other is called TrEMBL.

Sequences from UniProtKB and UniParc are grouped together in this database, which allows for coverage of the sequence space at many resolutions while hiding repetitive sequences. The protein sequences obtained from a variety of sources, including those stored in other databases, are reliable and comprehensive. Updated databases are made available by the UniProt project every 4 weeks in order to refine and enrich the data. Researchers studying a single protein as well as those studying complex biological systems make use of UniProt.

PDB: It stores experimental protein, nucleic acid, and complex-assembly three-dimensional structures. Structural biology examines protein structures, interactions, and drug design. Proteins and nucleic acids (DNA and RNA) have three-dimensional structural data in the Protein Data Bank (PDB). Experimental methods like X-ray crystallography, NMR spectroscopy, and cryo-electron microscopy reveal these molecules' shape and organization, revealing their cell functions and interactions. The Worldwide Protein Data Bank (wwPDB) manages the PDB, which was founded in 1971 by the Research Collaborator for Structural Bioinformatics (RCSB) in the US, the Protein Data Bank Europe (PDBe), the Protein Data Bank Japan (PDBj), and BioMagResBank (BMRB).

The PDB helps bioinformaticians, structural biologists, computational chemists, and other scientists develop new drugs and therapies, design novel proteins with tailored functions, and teach structural biology. Academics and students can freely obtain structural data from the PDB database. Users can study the three-dimensional structure of molecules using molecular graphics software.

Ensembl: This genome browser and annotation database annotates multiple genomes. It shows genes, regulatory elements, genetic variants, and comparative genomics. Ensembl is a big, high-quality genetic database. EBI and Welcome Trust Sanger Institute maintain it. Ensembl intends to centralize genome-wide data from vertebrates and model animals for researchers. It aids researchers in gene function analysis. Ensembl includes genome structure, gene variants (such SNPs), gene expression, comparative genomics, and more. It funds research on disease, pharmaceuticals, evolution, and biodiversity.

The Ensembl browser lets people visualize data in the genome and view a genomic area, gene structures, variations, and species genomes. Ensembl also offers sequence alignment and variation effect prediction bioinformatics tools and APIs. As of September 2021, Ensembl supports data from over 100 species, including humans, mice, zebrafish, and others, and its resources are free and updated monthly.

KEGG: It contains genetic, chemical, and systemic functioning data. Pathways, illnesses, therapeutics, and molecular interactions are studied. Kyoto Encyclopedia of Genes and Genomes (KEGG) incorporates genomic, chemical, and systemic functional data. It is maintained by Japan's Kyoto University Bioinformatics Centre. KEGG's databases and tools let researchers understand the cell, organism, and ecosystem's high-level functions and utility from molecular data. Pathways, genetic information, and higher-level systemic processes can be examined in these biological systems.

The KEGG PATHWAY database depicts biological processes like metabolism, genetic information processing, environmental information processing, organismal systems, and human diseases. These pathways encapsulate current molecular interaction knowledge and can be utilized for data visualization, high-throughput data interpretation, and teaching. As of September 2021, researchers worldwide use KEGG for genomes, transcriptomic, proteomics, and metabolomics.

Reactome (selected biological pathways): It covers metabolism, signaling, and gene regulation. Reactome is a free, open-source, curated, and peer-reviewed biological pathway database. It provides intuitive pathway visualization, interpretation, and analysis bioinformatics tools. Reactome is an organized network of chemical changes that describes signal transmission, transport, DNA replication, metabolism, and other biological functions. Reactome emphasizes human biology and model organisms. The database lets researchers compare the high-level operations of the human biological system to other species. The Ontario Institute for Cancer Research in Canada, the European Bioinformatics Institute in UK, and New York University Langone Medical Centre in US collaborated on Reactome project.

Reactome, like other pathway databases, lets academics analyze their data inside recognized pathways. This can reveal a dataset's biological functionalities. Reactome data, including scientific literature, are manually selected for accuracy and relevance. The database is updated with biological research findings. Reactome, used in genomics, proteomics, and systems biology, contains information on thousands of events involving tens of thousands of proteins and tiny chemicals as of September 2021.

EMBL databases: EMBL-Bank has nucleotide sequences, while EMBL-EBI contains protein sequences, gene expression data, and functional genomics data.

Bioinformatics provides computational methods for biological data analysis. These methods include data storage, retrieval, analysis, modeling and simulation, and visualization. Bioinformatics' first problem is managing massive biological data from genome sequencing, proteomic analysis, and other high-throughput methods. Bioinformaticians create GenBank for DNA sequences and Protein Data Bank for protein structures to manage this data. These databases store, retrieve, and share biological data efficiently as well as analyze data after storing it. This may entail matching novel sequences with existing ones to detect similarities and differences.

Bioinformatics simulates biological systems, from modeling the ecology to modeling a protein's 3D structure. Molecular dynamics simulations can predict atom movement and interaction. Bioinformatics requires visualization. It helps interpret complex biological data and can uncover patterns and insights not immediately obvious from raw data. PyMOL is used for molecular structures and Cytoscape for biological networks. Bioinformatics turns biological data into useful information. It turns huge, complex, and seemingly incoherent data into useful insights for biological and medical research using computer methods.

3.1.2 Sequence Alignment and Searching

Bioinformatics aligns DNA, RNA, and protein sequences to find commonalities, trends, and functions. These processes are needed for sequence conservation, evolutionary links, protein structure prediction, and gene or protein recognition. These algorithms align using match scores, mismatch penalties, and gap penalties. Sequences are aligned pairwise. MSA residue conservation aligns three or more sequences. MSA algorithms include ClustalW, MUSCLE, and T-Coffee. MSA determines evolutionary links, conserved areas, and protein structures. BLAST compares query sequences to sequence databases, quickly finds local sequence similarities, and delivers matched significance E-values [1].

HMMs capture the probabilistic patterns of amino acids or nucleotides in sequences and can be trained to represent specific protein families or domains. HMM-based algorithms like HMMER are used for protein domain identification and functional annotation.

Profile Hidden Markov Models (HMMs) are extensions of HMMs that incorporate multiple sequence alignments as "profiles" to represent conserved sequence patterns. They are effective for searching sequence databases, detecting remote homologs, and identifying protein families. Tools such as HMMER and HHpred use profile HMMs for sequence searching.

3.1.3   Genomics and Functional Genomics

Genome sequencing, assembly, annotation, and analysis show gene, regulatory element, and non-coding region architecture. Genome Assembly Bioinformatics programs assemble the genome from contigs. Genome annotation locates functional, regulatory, non-coding, and genetic elements and predicts genes, biological roles, regulatory patterns, and locations. Comparative genomics investigates genome evolution. It explains genome evolution, gene function, and phenotypes. Functional genomics studies genome functions and connections, expression, protein–protein interactions, regulatory networks, and gene functions. RNA-seq tracks gene expression through time and tissues. Bioinformatics finds differentially expressed genes and regulatory networks using transcriptome data. Functional genomics involves promoters, enhancers, and transcription factor binding sites. GO databases employ experimental or computational gene functional terms. Functional genomics uses genetics, transcriptomic, proteomics, and metabolomics. Functional and bioinformatics genomics describe genome structure, function, and control and advance personalized medicine, gene therapy, crop improvement, and more in medicine, agriculture, and biotechnology [2]. Bioinformatics has evolved significantly since its inception and has become increasingly important in various aspects of biological research and applications as enlisted follows:

DNA sequencing: The development of automated DNA sequencing techniques in the 1970s and 1980s led to a massive increase in the amount of DNA sequence data generated. Bioinformatics played a crucial role in managing, analyzing, and interpreting this data, leading to advancements in genomics and molecular biology.

Genomic databases: The establishment of genomic databases, such as GenBank, provided a centralized repository for DNA sequence data. Bioinformatics tools were developed to store, retrieve, and analyze this vast amount of information, facilitating comparative genomics, gene discovery, and genome-wide studies.

Sequence alignment and homology: Bioinformatics introduced algorithms for sequence alignment, allowing researchers to compare DNA, RNA, and protein sequences. Sequence alignment helps identify conserved regions, functional motifs, and evolutionary relationships, aiding in the understanding of gene function and evolutionary history.

Gene annotation and prediction: Bioinformatics methods have been instrumental in annotating genes and predicting their functions based on sequence analysis. This information is crucial for understanding gene regulation, protein structure, and function as well as identifying potential drug targets.

Structural biology: Bioinformatics tools and algorithms have contributed significantly to the field of structural biology. They aid in the prediction of protein structures, analysis

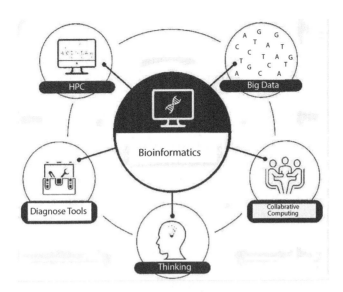

Figure 3.1 Workflow of bioinformatics problem solving process.

of protein folding patterns, and identification of protein–ligand interactions, enabling drug discovery and design.

Systems biology: Bioinformatics plays a vital role in systems biology, which focuses on understanding biological systems as a whole. It integrates data from various sources, such as genomics, transcriptomics, proteomics, and metabolomics, to build comprehensive models of biological processes and networks.

Personalized medicine: Bioinformatics is crucial in the era of personalized medicine, where genetic information is used to tailor medical treatments to individual patients. It enables the identification of disease-associated genetic variations, prediction of drug responses, and identification of biomarkers for diagnosis and prognosis.

Next-generation sequencing (NGS): The advent of NGS technologies has revolutionized genomics by enabling the high-throughput and cost-effective sequencing of entire genomes, transcriptomes, and epigenomes. Bioinformatics is essential for managing and analyzing the massive amounts of data generated by NGS platforms as shown in Figure 3.1 [3].

3.1.4   Proteomics and Protein Structure Prediction

Proteomics, structure prediction, and bioinformatics examine protein structure, function, and interactions as well as examine protein sequences, post-translational modifications, protein–protein interactions, and structure prediction. Proteomics is the large-scale study of proteins, their abundance, changes, relationships, and biological roles. Protein identification, measurement, and characterization explain biological processes. Bioinformatics tools find proteins by matching MS data to database protein sequences. Label-free and stable isotope labeling evaluate protein expression. Bioinformatics analyzes proteomics, statistics, and differentially expressed proteins [4]. Bioinformatics predicts, identifies, and characterizes PTMs such phosphorylation, acetylation, glycosylation, and ubiquitination. These findings explain protein function, signaling networks, and sickness.

Protein–protein interactions: Proteomics investigates biological systems' complex protein–protein networks. Protein interaction databases, network analysis, and computational modeling predict and analyzes PPIs, construct interaction networks, and discover functional modules. Amino acid sequences predict protein three-dimensional structures. It influences protein function, drug development, and interactions. Comparative or homology modeling predicts protein structures based on sequence similarity to empirically established structures (templates). Template-based bioinformatics methods model target protein structure. *Ab initio* approaches predict protein structures without templates. Physics, energy minimization, and statistical potentials predict protein folding [5].

Fold recognition: Protein sequences are matched to fold databases. Threading, sequence profiles, and machine learning predict protein folds in bioinformatics and validate protein structures. Ramachandran plot analysis, energy evaluation, and structural comparison uncover anticipated structure faults using bioinformatics. Bioinformatics proteomics and protein structure prediction highlight protein function, connection, and structure–function linkages.

3.1.5 Metabolomics

Bioinformatics metabolomics analyzes small molecules. To understand cellular function, metabolism, and illness, metabolites are quantified and analyzed. Systems biology uses metabolomics. Bioinformatics finds and annotates metabolites. Bioinformatics finds chemicals in experimental mass or NMR spectra using spectral similarity and functional, metabolic, and biological metabolites. KEGG, MetaboLights, HMDB, and PubChem list metabolite properties, biological roles, and pathways [6].

Bioinformatics offers many tools for handling biological data. These technologies help analyze, interpret, and predict genomic, proteomic, and metabolomic data. An organism's genome is genomic data. Genomes are sequenced, annotated, and visualized using bioinformatics tools like BLAST, FASTA, genome assemblers, and genome browsers. PLINK and GATK also study the genetic variation between species. Large-scale protein study is proteomic data. Mascot and SEQUEST identify proteins from mass spectrometry data. SWISS-MODEL and Phyre2 predict protein structures, whereas STRING and Cytoscape investigate protein–protein interactions and pathways.

Metabolomic data includes all small-molecule metabolites in a biological system. XCMS and MZmine pre-process and analyze mass spectrometry metabolomic data. MetaboAnalyst and Cytoscape visualize and understand metabolomic data. HMDB (Human Metabolome Database) helps identify and comprehend these compounds. These tools and methods evolve to address the biological data's complexity and volume. Many bioinformatics tools are user-friendly and do not need programming, making them accessible to a wide spectrum of researchers. Python and R are useful for more complicated studies.

Bioinformatics has many biological and medical research applications. High-throughput sequencing generates huge genomic data. Bioinformatics tools like Velvet, BWA, Bowtie, and MAKER predict gene locations and functions, whereas *de novo* assemblers and aligners assemble raw data into whole genomes. Bioinformatics techniques predict gene and protein function by comparing sequences or structures to known functions. BLAST and

Swiss-Prot (manually annotated and reviewed protein sequences) are utilized for this. Bioinformatics reveals complicated molecular relationships. Cytoscape visualizes these relationships, whereas KEGG provides metabolic and signaling pathway information.

Bioinformatics speeds drug research by predicting protein 3D structures (SWISS-MODEL, Phyre2), simulating protein–drug interactions (molecular docking, AutoDock), and assessing drug effects on biological pathways (GSEA, Gene Set Enrichment Analysis). Genomic data helps bioinformatics forecast illness risk. PLINK finds disease-associated variations in genetic data, and patient data-trained algorithms can predict disease progression or outcomes. In customized medicine, genetics determine treatment. Bioinformatics helps interpret genomic data, identify disease-associated genetic variations (GATK), and predict treatment responses (pharmacogenomics). Bioinformatics has transformed biological science and medicine, allowing discoveries and cures unimaginable just a few decades ago. Bioinformatics technologies and methods will continue to improve our understanding of life and illness treatment.

The following key points explain how bioinformatics normalize and analyze platform-specific metabolomics data:

Data prep: Baseline correction, noise reduction, peak alignment, and normalization decrease metabolomics data technical variations and artefacts. XCMS, MZmine, and MetaboAnalyst are extracted. Bioinformatics statistically analyzes metabolomics using t-tests, ANOVA, PCA, PLS-DA, and clustering. These approaches discover differentially expressed metabolites, sample groups, and metabolic signatures linked with specific conditions or phenotypes.

Integrative metabolic pathway analysis: Genomes, transcriptomic, proteomics, and metabolomics explain biological systems. Metabolomics data are mapped into metabolic pathways to find enriched pathways, functional modules, and metabolic pathway perturbations. PathVisio, MetScape, and MetaboAnalyst map routes. Metabolomics and other omics data can build biological networks and uncover molecular and regulatory linkages. Cytoscape and Network Analyst uncover metabolic network hubs, modules, and key metabolites. Metabolomics data show biological system activities, illness causes, and biomarkers. System biology metabolomics models biology and clarifies cell–organism interactions and regulatory networks [7].

Biomarker discovery: Metabolomics detects disease, phenotypic, and pharmacological biomarkers. Machine learning, feature selection, and route enrichment verify diagnostic, prognostic, and therapeutic biomarkers. Bioinformatics metabolomics shows metabolic pathways, biological activity, and disease. It aids personalized medicine, pharmaceutical development, and complex biological systems.

Objectives of the Chapter

The objectives of the chapter are:

- To examine how a computer approaches, handles, and evaluates biological data;
- To grasp how bioinformatics tools and methodologies manage genomic, proteomic, metabolomics, etc., data;

- To explain bioinformatics applications such as genomic sequencing, gene and protein function prediction, biological network and pathway analysis, drug discovery and design, disease prediction, and personalized medicine;
- To explore bioinformatics' ethical issues, including data privacy, heterogeneity, and computing resource requirements;
- To explore bioinformatics' potential benefits to science and medicine;
- And, to introduce bioinformatics' main software, databases, and tools, offering readers a practical perspective on bioinformatics theory.

Organization of the Chapter

The rest of the chapter is organized as follows: Section 3.2 explores bioinformatics in systems biology. Section 3.3 highlights tools and techniques in bioinformatics. Section 3.4 enlightens bioinformatics in precision medicine. Section 3.5 illustrates challenges in bioinformatics, followed by research directions in Section 3.6. Finally, Section 3.7 concludes the chapter with future scope.

3.2 Bioinformatics in Systems Biology

3.2.1 Introduction to Systems Biology

Bioinformatics uses genomes, transcriptomic, proteomics, and metabolomics in systems biology. Genes, proteins, and metabolites are modeled by computers. Systems biology examines complex biological systems. Omics integration systems biology investigates genomes, transcriptomic, proteomics, and metabolomics. Researchers can see biological systems and molecular–biological process links by merging data sets. Network analysis models complicated biological interactions in systems biology. Networks indicate metabolic, regulatory, or molecular interactions. Network-based analysis shows system hubs, modules, and key functions. Math and computers simulate systems biology, model regulatory, feedback, and dynamic processes. Simulations and computer analysis assist systems biologists in predicting system behaviors. Data-driven methods machine learning, statistical modeling, and data integration help systems biology make sense of huge, complicated biological datasets. These methods illustrate patterns, biomarkers, phenotypes, and biological system principles. Systems biology hypothesizes and evaluates biological system regulation. Experimental validation confirms computational model predictions. Modeling, experimentation, and refining assist in comprehending systems as shown Figure 3.2 [8].

Systems-level understanding: Systems biology studies biological system emergent features. Emergent features change system functionality. Systems biologists examine complicated biology. Systems biology uses computational models and biological data to describe biological complexity and behavior.

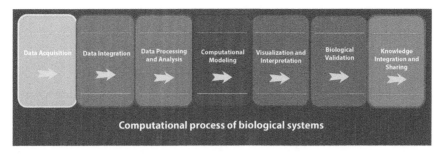

Figure 3.2 System flow diagram of biological systems in bioinformatics.

3.2.2   Data Integration in Systems Biology

Systems biology uses bioinformatics. Biology requires multi-omics data analysis. Data integration helps researchers find new relationships, routes, and emerging features in complex biological systems. Systems biology uses genomes, transcriptomic, proteomics, and metabolomics. These databases improve biological system and gene–protein–metabolite research. Omics data demonstrates system-wide molecular actors, functional modules, and regulatory linkages. Omics molecular interaction networks are integrated. Genes, proteins, and metabolites form complicated networks. Integrating networks helps researchers find functional connections, predict protein–protein interactions, and understand biological processes [9].

Gene expression, protein–protein interaction, and metabolic pathway data reveal co-regulated genes, novel gene functions, and regulatory mechanisms. Statistical modeling, machine learning, and computers fuse data from multiple sources. Systems biology studies phenotypes and molecules. Molecular data, patient characteristics, illness progression, and therapeutic outcomes can reveal biomarkers, assess disease prognosis, and modify medicines. Math models systems biology. Mathematical biological models predict and hypothesize. Gene expression, protein–protein interaction networks, and metabolic pathway data help characterize system behavior.

Visualizing related datasets aids data integration. Visualizations help researchers understand biology, trends, and system activity. Network diagrams, heat maps, pathway maps, and multidimensional plots let researchers evaluate cross-data type interactions. Systems biology requires data integration to understand complexity and dynamics, traits, biological processes, and regulatory mechanisms. Integrating heterogeneous data helps researchers see biological systems holistically, facilitating tailored treatment, pharmaceutical development, and biotechnological applications [10].

3.2.3   Network Analysis in Systems Biology

Network analysis in system biology and bioinformatics examines complex biological relationships between genes, proteins, metabolites, and other substances—modeling, studying, and understanding biological networks. Systems biology network analysis exposes system behavior, functional modules, regulatory mechanisms, and emergent properties.

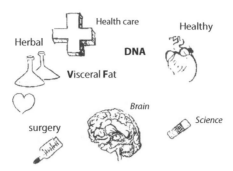

Figure 3.3 An interdisciplinary field that develops methods for understanding biological data.

- Gene regulatory networks track transcription factors and enhancers. Gene expression, chromatin immunoprecipitation, and computers determine GRNs.
- Metabolic networks show biological processes and metabolite transport—metabolomics, fluxomics, and metabolic pathway databases.
- Node degree connections, genes, proteins, and metabolites form biological networks. Degree analysis finds strongly connected information hubs.
- Network hubs between, closeness, and eigenvector centralities measure network nodes' influence. These indicators highlight key nodes that affect information flow, bottlenecks, or metabolic processes.
- Visualizing biological networks aids analysis. Heat maps, node-link diagrams, force-directed, and circular layouts visualize—visualizing networks, functional units, and links.

Functional enrichment pathway study: This determines if a network or gene/protein group over-represents biological pathways or gene sets. Pathways or activities significantly associated to genes/proteins are revealed using enrichment analysis. Functional enrichment finds Gene Ontology and protein domains in networks. It identifies network component functional themes, molecular functions, and biological processes [11].

Network simulation biological networks simulate time and perturbation. ODEs and Boolean models simulate network dynamics, predict system behavior, and investigate genetic or environmental perturbations on network output. Systems biology network analysis shows how complex biological systems work. It has biological process regulatory mechanisms, functional modules, and emergent properties as shown in Figure 3.3 [12].

3.3   Tools and Techniques in Bioinformatics

3.3.1   Commonly Used Bioinformatics Software

The following are the most commonly used Bioinformatics software's by researchers:

- Emboss: Sequence, protein structure, genome annotation, and other bioinformatics operations.
- Gromacs: Protein structure and interaction simulations.
- Qiagen clc: Bio, DNA, RNA, and protein sequence alignment, primer design, gene expression analysis, variant calling.
- Bioconductor: Statistical and computational gene expression, routing, and visualization techniques.
- Galaxy: Online data analysis and bioinformatics tools.
- Cytoscape: Bionetwork visualization and analysis tool. Several plugins visualize complicated molecular interaction networks.
- PhyloSuite: Reconstructing, retrieving, aligning, and visualizing trees improve evolutionary biology (bioinformatics programs) [13].

Bioinformatics principles include machine learning, sequence alignment and search methods, phylogenetic analysis, molecular modeling, and simulation. Bioinformatics increasingly predicts from vast, complicated datasets using machine learning. Machine learning predicts protein structures, gene functions, illness outcomes, and medication responses. Bioinformatics uses decision trees, neural networks, support vector machines, and deep learning. Bioinformatics relies on these to compare fresh sequences to database entries. BLAST and FASTA can search databases for query sequences. Alignment algorithms construct genomes, find homologous genes and proteins, and predict function.

This determines species or gene evolutionary relationships. Bioinformaticians can generate phylogenetic trees by comparing organism sequences. MEGA and PHYLIP are phylogenetic analysis tools. These anticipate and simulate protein and biomolecule three-dimensional structures. Predicting structure can reveal function and medication targets. GROMACS, AMBER, SWISS-MODEL, and Phyre2 are molecular dynamics and structural prediction tools. Bioinformatics relies on these methods, which are upgraded to manage growing biological data. They help us understand biological data and predict biological systems for research and treatment.

3.3.2 Machine Learning in Bioinformatics

Bioinformatics machine learning finds patterns, correlations, and predictions in vast biological data. Machine learning matches genes, patterns, and protein structure and function. These tasks often use HMMs, SVMs, and RNNs. ML examines microarray or RNA sequencing data. Hierarchical and K-means group similar-expressing genes. Machine learning detects, measures, and predicts mass spectrometry post-translational alterations. Classification, regression, and neural networks determine protein abundance. AI predicts protein structure, protein folding, structure, and interaction predictions. AI predicts drug–target interactions, prospects, and toxicity. Machine learning evaluates enormous chemical libraries for biological activity. Chemical structure-based QSAR models predict pharmacological action [14].

Genomes, transcriptomic, proteomics, and metabolomics comprise machine learning. Multi-view and data fusion reveal biological component relationships. Genomic, clinical, and imaging data predict and diagnose disease. These models diagnose, risk-assess, and treat cardiovascular and neurological diseases and cancer. Bioinformatics uses decision trees, random forests, support vector machines, neural networks, deep learning, and ensemble approaches. Indeed bioinformatics in systems biology is being used in cardiovascular, neurological, and cancer research to produce diagnostic tools, risk assessment models, and treatment strategies. These models evaluate complicated biological data including genomes, transcriptomics, proteomics, and metabolomics to understand disease mechanisms and patient features. Decision trees, random forests, SVM, neural networks, deep learning, and ensemble techniques are increasingly used to forecast disease outcomes, analyze disease causes, and build individualized treatments. Biological factors are utilized to classify patients into risk categories [15]. Genetic markers, lifestyle factors, and other clinical data can indicate a patient's cardiovascular disease risk. SVMs can classify diseased patients based on biological data. Gene expression data can be used by SVMs to categorize tumor samples as malignant or benign. Neural networks and deep learning are excellent for processing complicated and high-dimensional biological data. Convolutional neural networks (CNNs) are used to analyze MRI scans for neurological diseases and histopathological images for cancer diagnosis. RNNs and LSTMs can assess time-series data like heart rate or brain waves to identify cardiovascular or neurological problems. Ensembl approaches use many machine learning models to forecast, improving model accuracy and robustness. In difficult decision boundaries when no model performs well, they are useful. These algorithms predict or classify new data using tagged data patterns. Machine learning in bioinformatics investigates biological processes, disease mechanisms, and treatments on huge biological databases. Figure 3.4 shows how researchers might use massive data sets for personalized health, drug discovery, and precision agriculture [16].

Figure 3.4 Purposed genome bioinformatics competencies.

3.3.3   Cloud Computing in Bioinformatics

Cloud computing handles huge bioinformatics datasets. Cloud platforms handle massive biological data sets. Cloud storage protects genomics, proteomics, and other high-throughput sequencing data. Bioinformatics requires fast computing. Cloud computing offers powerful HPC clusters and virtual machines. HPC clouds enable genome assembly, variant calling, and molecular dynamics simulations [17].

On-demand, scalable cloud bioinformatics tools and pipelines: Pre-configured bioinformatics software lets researchers analyze and interpret massive biological datasets. Cloud computing enables researchers to collaborate. Researchers discuss data, analysis, and difficult problems. Cloud computing scales biological processes. Cloud resources let researchers handle peak demands and scale down during low activity, maximizing resource consumption and cost. Cloud computing reproduces bioinformatics workflows. Docker, Next flow, and Snake make or can replicate analysis pipelines. Git and cloud platforms manage analysis and modification workflows [18].

Cloud computing supports AI/ML. Cloud-based AI provides prediction models, image analysis, and biological data insights. Bioinformatics AI uses pre-trained and custom cloud-based machine learning models. Cloud computing saves money because researchers pay for what they use. Projects without infrastructure investments can use computational resources cost-effectively. Cloud computing in bioinformatics helps researchers overcome computational and storage constraints, accelerate data processing, improve cooperation, and try new methodologies. Cloud technologies can handle expanding biological data [19].

3.4   Bioinformatics in Precision Medicine

3.4.1   Definition and Importance of Precision Medicine

Bioinformatics powers precision medicine as it studies DNA, gene expression, and epigenetics. Mutations impact disease and treatment, genetic abnormalities, and patient-specific treatment. Reference databases and functional prediction assess gene variants, diagnose, and prognosticate.

Biomarker discovery: Bioinformatics finds genomic, transcriptomic, proteomic, or metabolomics signals that predict disease susceptibility, prognosis, or therapy response. Bioinformatics finds tailored therapeutic molecular signatures using multi-omics data, statistics, and machine learning. Genomic and proteomic data help bioinformatics algorithms uncover and repurpose pharmaceutical targets. Bioinformatics finds druggable targets using disease-associated genes, pathways, and protein structures. Bioinformatics aids doctors in drug selection. Patient-specific genetic, clinical, and molecular data informs diagnosis, prognosis, and treatment [20].

Pharmacogenomics: Bioinformatics discovers drug-responsive genes. Pharmacogenomics detects drug–drug interactions, dosage, and adverse effects, enhancing medicine safety and efficacy. Bioinformatics integrates genomic, clinical, and imaging data. Bioinformatics helps researchers uncover disease causes, progression, and treatment trends in vast data sets [21].

Bioinformatics models complicated biological, pharmacological, and pathological pathways—optimizing therapy, genetic impacts, and drug–target interactions.

Bioinformatics and precision medicine assist clinicians in diagnosing, treating, and enhancing patient outcomes. Personalizing care promotes health and reduces hazards [22].

3.4.2   Role of Bioinformatics in Precision Medicine

Bioinformatics analyzes genomic, clinical, and molecular data for precision medicine. Bioinformatics studies DNA, gene expression, and epigenetics. Mutations impact disease and treatment—genetic abnormalities and patient-specific treatment. Bioinformatics finds genetic variations. Reference databases and functional prediction assess gene variants—diagnose and prognosticate [23].

Biomarker discovery: Bioinformatics finds genomic, transcriptomic, proteomic, or metabolomics signals that predict disease susceptibility, prognosis, or therapy response. Bioinformatics finds tailored therapeutic molecular signatures using multi-omics data, statistics, and machine learning. Genomic and proteomic data help bioinformatics algorithms uncover and repurpose pharmaceutical targets. Bioinformatics finds druggable targets using disease-associated genes, pathways, and protein structures. Bioinformatics reuses drugs. Bioinformatics helps doctors customize treatment. Patient-specific genetic, clinical, and molecular data informs diagnosis, prognosis, and treatment [24].

Medical biomarker development is essential to personalized medicine. Biomarkers, measurable substances, structures, or processes in the body, can signify normal or pathological biological states. Proteins, genes, or other substances, biological activities, or physical features can change. Biomarkers can be used for illness diagnosis, prognosis, treatment prediction, and patient monitoring. Researchers use genomes, proteomics, and metabolomics to find biomarkers in healthy and sick samples. An assay must be designed to assess a possible biomarker in biological material. Validation ensures that this test measures the biomarker reliably and consistently.

To demonstrate clinical value, the biomarker is examined in broader patient populations. This step uses robust statistical analysis to confirm that the biomarker can reliably distinguish between states or predict clinical outcomes. If verified, the biomarker can be used clinically. Performance is monitored after implementation. Biomarker discovery is difficult and multidisciplinary. Biomarkers can help diagnose, forecast disease course, guide treatment, and track illness progression or response to treatment. They could boost patient outcomes and personalized therapy.

Pharmacogenomics: Bioinformatics discovers drug-responsive genes. Pharmacogenomics detects drug–drug interactions, dosage, and adverse effects, enhancing medicine safety and efficacy. Bioinformatics integrates genomic, clinical, and imaging data. Bioinformatics helps researchers uncover disease causes, progression, and treatment trends in vast data sets. Bioinformatics models complicated biological, pharmacological, and pathological pathways—optimizing therapy, genetic impacts, and drug–target interactions. Bioinformatics and precision medicine assist clinicians to diagnose, treat, and enhance patient outcomes. Customization improves health and reduces hazards [25].

Pharmacogenomics studies how genetics affect pharmacological responsiveness. It is crucial to "personalize medicine," which uses genetic and genomic data to adapt drugs, therapies, and interventions to individual patients. Pharmacogenomics holds that genetic diversity, such as SNPs, gene duplications, and epigenetic alterations, can affect pharmaceutical responsiveness. It affects medication absorption, distribution, metabolism, target function, and immune response. Drug-transporting proteins can be affected by gene variations. This affects drug distribution and target site concentration.

Genes affect drug-metabolizing enzymes: Some genetic variations cause enzymes to work faster, metabolizing a medication too quickly and limiting its efficacy. Some variations cause lower enzyme activity or non-functioning enzymes, slowing medication metabolization and increasing adverse effects. Drugs usually work by interacting with proteins, usually receptors or enzymes. Genetic differences can change pharmacological targets, affecting efficacy. Genetic differences may increase the likelihood of hypersensitivity or bad responses for particular medicines.

Pharmacogenomics testing can detect genetic polymorphisms that may predict a drug's efficacy or side effects, allowing doctors to tailor treatment to each patient. It also promises to reduce medicine and dose trial-and-error. As of September 2021, pharmacogenomics testing is increasingly employed in oncology to adapt medicines, but it is not yet routine in all areas of medicine. Cost, access to testing, comprehending test results, and ethical, legal, and societal issues may affect its wider acceptance.

3.4.3   Pharmacogenomics and Personalized Medicine

Bioinformatics and genetics study pharmacogenomics. CPIC guidelines interpret pharmaceutical response-related genetic variations. Bioinformatics and pharmacogenomics correlations improve efficacy and safety in these guidelines. These cases show bioinformatics' versatility in biology and medicine. Bioinformatics analyzes enormous genomic, transcriptomic, and clinical data to improve diagnostics, therapies, and the understanding of complex biological systems [26].

Pharmacogenomics studies pharmacological responsiveness and genes. Pharmacology and genetics are used in this new field to create safe, efficacious, and genetically customized pharmaceuticals. Current medications are "one size fits all," yet they do not work for everyone. It is hard to tell who will benefit from a drug, who will not, and who will have bad drug reactions. Drug reactions cause many US hospitalizations and deaths. Researchers are discovering how genes affect medicine response through the Human Genome Project.

Pharmacogenomics testing determines how genetic differences affect drug responses. These tests may help your doctor identify the optimal drugs and dosages and forecast drug reactions. Drug makers can use gene-derived protein structures to make medicines. Targeting a gene or protein makes these medications more effective. Doctors can analyze a patient's genetic profile and prescribe the optimum pharmacological therapy from the start, including dosage modifications to avoid side effects. Patients will be screened for genetic illness predisposition. This allows early detection and effective prevention.

Lower healthcare costs: Reduced trial-and-error patient treatment, adverse drug responses, and therapeutic efficacy will save healthcare costs. Pharmacogenomics promises personalized medications based on genetics. Understanding a person's genetic makeup is regarded to be essential to personalized medicine. Environment, nutrition, age, lifestyle, and health all affect a person's response to drugs.

3.4.4 Case Study

TCGA cancer research uses bioinformatics. Cancer genomic profiling gave TCGA huge genomic, transcriptomic, and clinical data. TCGA bioinformatics revealed cancer subtypes, driver mutations, and therapy targets.

Epidemic analysis: Bioinformatics tracked and understood the 2014 West African Ebola outbreak. The Ebola genome sequencing showed its genesis, transmission, and evolution. Bioinformatics found viral genome therapeutic targets. Bioinformatics controlled viruses. Bioinformatics improves agricultural breeding. Bioinformatics analyzes wheat breeding population genomic data for genomic selection. This identifies disease resistance, yield, and nutritional quality genes. Bioinformatics speeds crop breeding. Bioinformatics was used to study the human microbiome (HMP). The research examined metagenomics data from many body sites to understand the human microbiome and health and disease. Bioinformatics described microbial diversity, species, and microbiota function [27].

Bioinformatics could transform science and medicine. It revolutionizes life and illness treatment in basic biological research, clinical medicine, and healthcare. Genomic, proteomic, and metabolomics data can be processed and analyzed using bioinformatics tools. This helps find new genes, proteins, and biological molecules, comprehend their roles, and decipher complex biological processes and networks. Bioinformatics analyzes genomic or other omics data to find disease-associated genetic variations. This can help with early diagnosis, disease prediction, and therapy efficacy. Bioinformatics helps develop customized medicine, which tailor's therapies to patients' genetics or other traits. Pharmacogenomics examines how genes affect drug responsiveness.

Bioinformatics techniques detect therapeutic targets, predict target molecule structures, and create new medications. This accelerates medication discovery and lowers expenses. Bioinformatics can track and model illness spread, identify population health hazards, and improve disease preventive and control methods. Bioinformatics can help produce crop varieties with higher yields, disease resistance, or other desirable qualities by studying agricultural species' genomes. Bioinformatics helps research microbial communities in different habitats, assess biodiversity, and forecast ecosystem changes. In the future, bioinformatics will accelerate biological research, improve healthcare, and improve our understanding of the planet [28].

3.5 Challenges in Bioinformatics

3.5.1 Data Volume and Complexity

Bioinformatics deals with vast amounts of data that are generated from various biological sources and experimental techniques. The volume and complexity of bioinformatics data continue to increase rapidly due to advancements in high-throughput technologies and the availability of large-scale sequencing and omics datasets [29].

Genomics and transcriptomic: Genomic sequencing and transcriptomic profiling generate massive amounts of data. Whole-genome sequencing projects, such as the Human Genome Project, have produced billions of base pairs of DNA sequence data. Transcriptomic studies using RNA sequencing (RNA-seq) generate transcript abundance data for thousands of genes across multiple samples, resulting in large expression matrices [30].

Proteomics: Mass spectrometry-based proteomics generates large-scale protein identification and quantification data. The identification of proteins from complex samples, post-translational modifications, and protein–protein interactions contribute to the complexity of proteomics data. Metagenomics studies microbes. Microorganism metagenomics sequencing requires bioinformatics. Bioinformatics uses medical, spatial transcriptomic, and microscopy images. Complex algorithms examine big photos [31].

Bioinformatics links genomes, transcriptomics, proteomics, and clinical data. Modern computers analyze enormous multidimensional datasets for integrative research. Multiple-sample bioinformatics assesses genes and proteins. Multi-hypothesis testing, dimensionality reduction, and high-dimensional datasets require statistical and machine learning methodologies. Bioinformatics examines longitudinal data. Analyzing temporal dynamics, patterns, and changes requires specific methods [32].

Bioinformatics stores genomic and health data. Bioinformatics faces privacy, security, sharing, and analysis. Complex bioinformatics data requires scalable computational tools, efficient storage and retrieval, and advanced analytical methods. Cloud, parallel, and distributed computing handle massive datasets and expensive analysis. Data integration, visualization, and machine learning examine huge bioinformatics datasets.

3.5.2   Data Integration and Standardization

Bioinformatics organizes biological data. Public databases, assays, healthcare records, and publications provide bioinformatics data. Integrating data reveals biology. Ontologies and controlled vocabularies standardize biological entity and concept annotation and classification. GO and MeSH standardize gene, protein, illness, and other biological item categorization, simplifying data integration. Linking gene identifiers across databases unifies gene expression, functional annotation, and genetic variation [33].

Standardizing metadata includes experimental settings, sample properties, and data processing. Simplified exchange, repeatability, and interpretation. Bioinformatics uses FASTA, FASTQ, BED, and BAM. Community-driven data exchange standards like CDISC clinical data standards enable data integration across platforms and applications. Bioinformatics standardizes data quality. MIAME and FGE share functional genomics and microarray data. Standards and submission requirements ensure quality and interoperability in public data repositories and databases. Standardizing data and metadata in these repositories improve data integration. Bioinformatics standardization and integration enable data exchange, cross-study comparisons, and strong analytical methods. Bioinformatics research is repeatable, reliable, and useful, enabling collaboration to understand biological systems and improve patient care [34].

3.5.3   Reproducibility of Bioinformatics Analysis

Bioinformatics needs reproducibility copying a study's data, techniques, and computational environment. Science needs reproducibility. Sharing data, code, and analysis methods makes researchers accountable.

Methodological progress: Replicable assessments show process shortcomings. Replicating and critiquing analyses improves bioinformatics. Docker or singularity containers hold analytic techniques, environment, program dependencies, and configurations (easy multi-system analysis). Sharing analytic code and scripts with instructions lets others replicate the study and get consistent findings.

Open science: Open-access repositories and publications promote transparency, reproducibility, and cooperation. Continuous integration and automated testing reproduce code and script changes. Automated testing ensures analytical pipeline functionality and consistency. These repeatable strategies help boost bioinformatics research [35].

3.5.4   Privacy and Security Concerns

Bioinformatics deals with sensitive and personal data, including genomic information, medical records, and other identifiable information. Consequently, privacy and security concerns are of paramount importance in bioinformatics.

Data privacy: Bioinformatics data often contains personally identifiable information (PII) or protected health information (PHI). Protecting the privacy of individuals is crucial, and researchers must adhere to ethical and legal guidelines when collecting, storing, and sharing such data. Anonymization and de-identification techniques can be applied to remove or encrypt identifiable information while maintaining data utility. Only authorized people should access sensitive bioinformatics data. User authentication, RBAC, and other security approaches limit data access by role and responsibility.

Backup: Secure data storage systems prevent breaches. Secure data storage, backups, and disaster recovery avoid data loss, unauthorized changes, and availability.

Data sharing and consent: Bioinformatics researchers collaborate with other groups. Informed consent, data use agreements, and data sharing guidelines are necessary for privacy and compliance.

Data anonymization and utility: Balancing data anonymization with data utility is a challenge in bioinformatics. While anonymization techniques aim to protect privacy, they should not compromise the usefulness of the data for research purposes. Striking a balance between privacy and data utility is crucial to enable meaningful analysis while protecting individual identities.

Security audits and compliance: Regular security audits and compliance assessments help identify vulnerabilities in bioinformatics systems and ensure adherence to relevant data protection regulations, such as the General Data Protection Regulation (GDPR) or the Health Insurance Portability and Accountability Act (HIPAA).

Bioinformatics researchers must follow ethics to protect the study participants' privacy and confidentiality (consent, data security, and ethical research). Bioinformatics researchers need privacy and security training. Researchers should study data privacy, security, and dangers to reduce risks. Bioinformatics privacy and security require technical, organizational, and legal measures. Bioinformatics, data privacy experts, and security professionals must collaborate to protect privacy and advance bioinformatics research [36].

Bioinformatics allows breakthroughs in biology and medicine, but it also raises ethical issues that must be addressed. In genetics and customized medicine, bioinformatics uses sensitive personal data. For privacy and rights, this data must be maintained and utilized securely. Genetic information misuse could lead to employment or insurance discrimination.

The Health Insurance Portability and Accountability Act (HIPAA) in the USA and the General Data Protection Regulation (GDPR) in Europe guarantee data privacy, although bioinformatics can make this difficult. Genomic, protein, and phenotypic data make up biological data. Data storage, metadata, and analysis may vary by type. This heterogeneity makes bioinformatics data integration and comparison difficult. Data standardization and interoperability must be maintained across databases and technologies.

Bioinformatics tasks, especially those involving huge datasets, demand significant computational resources. Research capacities differ between well-resourced and low-resourced institutions because such resources are pricey. This creates a "digital divide" where certain researchers cannot use bioinformatics. Other ethical considerations may occur. To use bioinformatics ethically, these challenges must be addressed. Researchers, ethicists, and regulators must address these issues as technology and data grow.

3.6   Research Directions

Bioinformatics is a fascinating science that uses computing to solve complex biological problems. Bioinformatics is growing more crucial as big data and precision medicine take over. This field offers significant research opportunities, namely:

- Now that whole-genome sequencing is cheap, we have access to massive genetic data. These data can help identify illness genes and generate individualized treatments. Developing algorithms and tools to evaluate massive data volumes to gain meaningful and actionable insights is difficult.
- Genomics, transcriptomics, proteomics, metabolomics, and other "omics" technologies are revealing biological systems. Integrating these various data types into a coherent system image is difficult. Data integration strategies can help us understand complicated biological processes.
- High-throughput technologies have drastically increased biological data size and complexity. Data analysis is increasingly using machine learning and AI. These methods must be modified to accommodate biological data's noise, missing data, and high dimensionality.
- Genes, proteins, and interactions are nodes in biological networks. Understanding these networks and developing methods to study them can reveal biological system and disease processes.
- Protein and RNA structures are essential for understanding their function and designing drugs. Computational tools can predict and analyze these structures.
- Bioinformatics improves medication design and pharmacogenomics. Bioinformatics can anticipate medication targets, design pharmaceuticals using computer models, and research how genetic variations affect drug reactions.
- Our bodies' microbiomes are vital to our health. Microbiome data analysis requires bioinformatics tools.
- Privacy, permission, and usage of personal genomic data are growing problems. Bioinformatics researchers must examine these ethical issues.

3.7 Conclusion and Future Scope

Technology, data, and computers promote bioinformatics. Single-cell genomics and scRNA-seq show lineage, heterogeneity, and linkages. High-dimensional single-cell omics data demands excellent bioinformatics. Integrating genomic, transcriptomic, proteomic, and metabolomics expands. Multi-omics displays disease etiology, complicated biological processes, and biomarkers. Understanding omics layer interactions requires integrative bioinformatics and computational frameworks. Bioinformatics predicts, patterns, and links events. Image analysis, protein structure prediction, drug discovery, and disease diagnosis use deep learning algorithms, neural networks, and other ML methods. Complex bioinformatics data requires visualization and interactive analysis. Interactive heat maps, network visualizations, and 3D modeling help researchers understand complex biological data.

Bioinformatics supports genetic and molecular therapies. Genomic, clinical, and bioinformatics data reveal disease groups, predictive biomarkers, and tailored treatments. Microbiome analysis microorganisms' genomes are popular. Bioinformatics is needed for microbiome species, pathways, and disease linkages. Next-generation sequencing technologies, such as long-read sequencing platforms, are increasingly being used to generate long and contiguous DNA or RNA sequences. Analyzing long-read sequencing data presents unique computational challenges, including *de novo* genome assembly, structural variant detection, and isoform identification. The increasing volume and complexity of bioinformatics data necessitate scalable and efficient computational infrastructure. Cloud computing platforms provide on-demand access to high-performance computing resources, facilitating large-scale data processing, storage, and analysis. Big data analytics frameworks, such as Apache Hadoop and Spark, enable the distributed processing of bioinformatics data and accelerate analysis pipelines.

Data privacy and ethics: With the growing emphasis on data privacy and ethical considerations, emerging trends focus on ensuring the secure storage, sharing, and analysis of sensitive biological and clinical data. Privacy-preserving methods, ethical guidelines, and data governance frameworks are being developed to address the challenges associated with data privacy and protection. These emerging trends in bioinformatics highlight the ongoing advancements and the potential for transformative impact in understanding biological systems, improving healthcare outcomes, and driving innovation in the life sciences. Adapting to these trends requires interdisciplinary collaboration, continual development of computational tools, and staying abreast of technological advancements.

Future Scope and Potential Opportunities

Bioinformatics offers numerous opportunities for researchers, professionals, and industries Bioinformatics assists target identification, virtual screening, molecular modeling, and medication repurposing. Computational methods can identify drug targets and predict efficacy from large genomic and proteomic data. Bioinformatics-guided healthcare uses genomic, clinical, and lifestyle data. Genetic profiles help bioinformatics predict drug reactions, risks, and treatment. Genetic counseling bioinformatics analyzes medical genetic sequencing data. Bioinformatics develops variant calling, interpretation, and genetic disease diagnosis and also assist in genetic counselors. Farmer-friendly bioinformatics finds genes, breed markers, and enhances crop productivity. Bioinformatics aids plant disease research, genetic diversity management, and sustainable farming.

Microbiome research interests: Bioinformatics examines complex microbiome data to understand how microbes affect health, disease, and ecosystem dynamics. It promotes eco-conservation, probiotics, and personalized diet. Bioinformatics studies complicated biological systems utilizing enormous data, computer modeling, and simulation. Biology requires computational systems. Biology studies gene regulation, metabolic, and signaling networks.

Bioinformatics and big data are connected. Bioinformatics and data analysis experts analyze biological datasets, construct prediction models, and execute data-driven solutions. There is a continuous demand for the development of bioinformatics software, algorithms, and tools. Opportunities exist for professionals with expertise in programming, data analysis, and algorithm development to create innovative solutions for data processing, analysis, visualization, and interpretation. Bioinformatics expertise is highly sought after in biotechnology and pharmaceutical companies. Bioinformatics contribute to research and development activities, target identification, clinical trials, data analysis, and regulatory compliance. The growing importance of bioinformatics has created a demand for educators and trainers who can impart knowledge and skills in the field. Opportunities exist in academia, training institutions, and online platforms to teach bioinformatics, develop courses, and mentor the next generation of bioinformatics. These are just a few examples of the potential opportunities in bioinformatics. As the field continues to evolve, new avenues and applications are likely to emerge, offering diverse career prospects and avenues for impactful research and innovation.

References

1. Alam, M.S., Sultana, A., Reza, M.S., Amanullah, M., Kabir, S.R., Mollah, M.N.H., Integrated bioinformatics and statistical approaches to explore molecular biomarkers for breast cancer diagnosis, prognosis and therapies. *PloS One*, 17, 5, 0268967, 2022.
2. Giorgi, F.M., Ceraolo, C., Mercatelli, D., The R language: An engine for bioinformatics and data science. *Life*, 12, 5, 648, 2022.
3. Engevik, K.A., Engevik, M.A., Engevik, A.C., Bioinformatics reveal elevated levels of Myosin Vb in uterine corpus endometrial carcinoma patients which correlates to increased cell metabolism and poor prognosis. *PloS One*, 18, 1, 0280428, 2023.
4. Troeltzsch, M., Gogl, M., Berndt, R., Troeltzsch, M., Oral lichen planus following the administration of vector-based COVID-19 vaccine (Ad26. COV2. S). *Oral. Dis.*, 2021.
5. Saha, S., Di Cataldo, S., Giannessi, F., Cucciari, A., Von Der Linden, W., Boeri, L., Mapping superconductivity in high-pressure hydrides: The superhydra project. *Phys. Rev. Mater.*, 7, 5, 054806, 2023.
6. Debnath, S., Kant, A., Bhowmick, P., Malakar, A., Purkaystha, S., Jena, B.K., Azam, F., The enhanced affinity of WRKY reinforces drought tolerance in solanum lycopersicum L.: An innovative bioinformatics study. *Plants*, 12, 4, 762, 2023.
7. Pur, D.R., Krance, S., Pucchio, A., Bassi, A., Miranda, R.N., Felfeli, T., Emerging applications of bioinformatics and artificial intelligence in the analysis of biofluid markers involved in retinal

occlusive diseases: A systematic review. *Graefe's Arch. Clin. Exp. Ophthalmol.*, *261*, 2, 317–336, 2023.

8. Baeza, J.A., An introduction to the Special Section on Crustacean Mitochondrial Genomics: Improving the assembly, annotation, and characterization of mitochondrial genomes using user-friendly and open-access bioinformatics tools, with decapod crustaceans as an example. *J. Crustacean Biol.*, *42*, 1, 12, 2022.

9. Chen, H., Xu, J., Wei, S., Jia, Z., Sun, C., Kang, J., Zhang, M., RABC: Rheumatoid arthritis bioinformatics center. *Nucleic Acids Res.*, *51*, D1, 1381–1387, 2023.

10. Cantelli, G., Bateman, A., Brooksbank, C., Petrov, A., II, Malik-Sheriff, R.S., Ide-Smith, M., McEntyre, J., The european bioinformatics institute (EMBL-EBI) in 2021. *Nucleic Acids Res.*, 50, D1, D11–D19, 2022.

11. Olson, R.D., Assaf, R., Brettin, T., Conrad, N., Cucinell, C., Davis, J.J., Stevens, R.L., Introducing the bacterial and viral bioinformatics resource center (BV-BRC): A resource combining PATRIC, IRD and ViPR. *Nucleic Acids Res.*, 51, D1, 678–689, 2023.

12. Marcroft, T.A., Rasmussen, C., Kelley, S.T., Computing in bioinformatics and engaged student learning: Student perspectives on anticipatory activities and innovative apps. *J. Coll. Sci. Teach.*, *52*, 2, 3–5, 2022.

13. Shen, W., Song, Z., Zhong, X., Huang, M., Shen, D., Gao, P., Song, X., Sangerbox: A comprehensive, interaction-friendly clinical bioinformatics analysis platform. *Imeta*, *1*, 3, 36, 2022.

15. Banu, J.F., Rajeshwari, S.B., Kallimani, J.S., Vasanthi, S., Buttar, A.M., Sangeetha, M., Bhargava, S., Modeling of hyperparameter tuned hybrid CNN and LSTM for prediction model. *Intell. Autom. Soft Comput.*, *33*, 3, 1393–1405, 2022.

16. Bain, S.A. *et al.*, Bringing bioinformatics to schools with the 4273pi project. *PloS Comput. Biol.*, 18, 1, 1–12, 2022, doi: 10.1371/journal.pcbi.1009705.

17. Hossain, M.A., Sohel, M., Rahman, M.H., Hasan, M., II, Khan, M.S., Amin, M.A.,... Peng, S., Bioinformatics and *In silico* approaches to identify novel biomarkers and key pathways for cancers that are linked to the progression of female infertility: A comprehensive approach for drug discovery. *PloS One*, 18, 1, 0265746, 2023.

18. Li, Z., Zhang, Z., Feng, S., Wang, J., Guo, X., Sun, H., Design of model-free speed regulation system for permanent magnet synchronous linear motor based on adaptive observer. *IEEE Access*, *10*, 68545–68556, 2022.

19. Shah, S.U., Hameed, A., Ali Almazroi, A., Alqarni, M.A., Agent-based data extraction in bioinformatics. *Secur. Commun. Netw.*, 2022, Mar 26, 2022.

20. Hasan, M., II, Rahman, M.H., Islam, M.B., Islam, M.Z., Hossain, M.A., Moni, M.A., Systems biology and bioinformatics approach to identify blood based signatures molecules and drug targets of patient with COVID-19. *Inf. Med. Unlocked*, *28*, 100840, 2022.

21. Yurina, V. and Adianingsih, O.R., Predicting epitopes for vaccine development using bioinformatics tools. *Ther. Adv. Vaccines Immunother.*, 10, 25151355221100218, 2022.

22. Ricke, S.C., Dittoe, D.K., Tarcin, A.A., Rothrock Jr., M.J., Communicating the utility of the microbiome and bioinformatics to small flock poultry producers. *Poultry Sci.*, *101*, 5, 101788, 2022.

23. Upadhyay, A., Kovalev, A.A., Zhuravleva, E.A., Kovalev, D.A., Litti, Y.V., Masakapalli, S.K., Vivekanand, V., A review of basic bioinformatic techniques for microbialcommunity analysis in an anaerobic digester. *Fermentation*, *9*, 1, 62, 2023.

24. Bharadwaj, K.K., Ahmad, I., Pati, S., Ghosh, A., Sarkar, T., Rabha, B., Wan Rosli, W., II, Potent bioactive compounds from seaweed waste to combat cancer through bioinformatics investigation. *Front. Nutr.*, *9*, 889276, 2022.

25. Hassan, M.U. and Williamson, M.P., Bioinformatic analysis of WxL domain proteins. *Saudi J. Biol. Sci.*, *30*, 2, 103526, 2023.

26. Miura, N. and Okuda, S., Current progress and critical challenges to overcome in the bioinformatics of mass spectrometry-based metaproteomics. *Comput. Struct. Biotechnol. J.*, 21, 1140–1150, 2023.

27. Su, Y., Tian, X., Gao, R., Guo, W., Chen, C., Chen, C.,... Lv, X., Colon cancer diagnosis and staging classification based on machine learning and bioinformatics analysis. *Comput. Biol. Med.*, 145, 105409, 2022.

28. Buttar, A.M., Bano, M., Akbar, M.A., Alabrah, A., Gumaei, A.H., Toward trustworthy human suspicious activity detection from surveillance videos using deep learning. *Soft Comput.*, 1–13, 2023.

29. Krotova, A., Byadovskaya, O., Shumilova, I., van Schalkwyk, A., Sprygin, A., An indepth bioinformatic analysis of the novel recombinant lumpy skin disease virus strains: From unique patterns to established lineage. *BMC Genom.*, 23, 1, 396, 2022.

30. Sultana, A., Alam, M.S., Liu, X., Sharma, R., Singla, R.K., Gundamaraju, R., Shen, B., Single-cell RNA-seq analysis to identify potential biomarkers for diagnosis, and prognosis of non-small cell lung cancer by using comprehensive bioinformatics approaches. *Trans. Oncol.*, 27, 101571, 2023.

31. Vijh, D., Imam, M. A., Haque, M. M. U., Das, S., Islam, A., Malik, M. Z., Network pharmacology and bioinformatics approach reveals the therapeutic mechanism of action of curcumin in Alzheimer disease. *Metab. Brain Dis.*, 38, 4, 1205–1220, 2023.

32. Vickers, N.J., Animal communication: When I'm calling you, will you answer too? *Curr. Biol.*, 27, 14, 713–715, 2017.

33. Kazybay, B., Ahmad, A., Mu, C., Mengdesh, D., Xie, Y., Omicron N501Y mutation among SARS-CoV-2 lineages: *In silico* analysis of potent binding to tyrosine kinase and hypothetical repurposed medicine. *Travel Med. Infect. Dis.*, 45, 102242, 2022.

34. Yang, Y. and Lawson, D.J., HTRX: An R package for learning non-contiguous haplotypes associated with a phenotype. *Bioinf. Adv.*, 3, 1, 38, 2023.

35. Cho, S., Sohn, Y.D., Kim, S., Rajakumar, A., Badell, M.L., Sidell, N., Yoon, Y.S., Reduced angiovasculogenic and increased inflammatory profiles of cord blood cells in severe but not mild preeclampsia. *Sci. Rep.*, 11, 1, 3630, 2021.

36. Yoon, H.S., Cho, C.H., Yun, M.S., Jang, S.J., You, H.J., Kim, J.H., Ko, G., Akkermansia muciniphila secretes a glucagon-like peptide-1-inducing protein that improves glucose homeostasis and ameliorates metabolic disease in mice. *Nat. Microbiol.*, 6, 5, 563–573, 2021.

4

Machine Learning in Drug Discovery: Methods, Applications, and Challenges

Geetha Mani[1]* and Gokulakrishnan Jayakumar[2]

[1]Department of Control and Automation, School of Electrical Engineering, Vellore Institute of Technology, Vellore Campus, Vellore, Tamil Nadu, India
[2]School for Environment and Sustainability, University of Michigan – Ann Arbor, Ann Arbor, MI, United States

Abstract

In recent times, the pharmaceutical industry has leveraged cutting-edge technologies to gather insights from intricate biological systems. Advances in technology have spurred a growing interest in applying machine learning (ML) and deep learning (DL) approaches to generate potential therapeutic hypotheses for drug discovery and development (DD&D). These approaches offer a suite of frameworks and accompanying toolkits that enhance the discovery and decision-making processes for well-defined problems using diverse, large-scale data. In this domain, ML algorithms can be integrated across all phases of DD&D. Among their many potential applications are target validation, the identification of prognostic biomarkers, the predictive analytics of drug–protein interactions and drug toxicity, and the data analysis of digital pathology in clinical trials. This chapter delivers a comprehensive overview of both unsupervised and supervised ML algorithms that drug discovery scientists and researchers have employed, along with their advantageous applications. Utilizing ML algorithms in drug discovery and development holds the promise of significantly trimming the time, costs, and resources associated with traditional methodologies and experimentation. However, the adoption of ML in drug discovery encounters numerous challenges. In order to navigate obstacles in validating ML methods, enhancing decision-making, raising awareness of ML approaches, and pinpointing risk failures in drug discovery, it is imperative to generate accurate and methodical data during clinical trials. This chapter also offers a brief introduction to the literature on DD&D through ML methods that have been implemented at various stages of drug development.

Keywords: Pharmaceutical industry, drug discovery and development, unsupervised learning, supervised machine learning, deep learning, decision making, predictive analytics

4.1 Introduction

Artificial intelligence (AI) is the approximation or emulation of the intellectual capacity of humans in machines. The objectives of AI encompass the enhancement of computer-based

---

Corresponding author: geethamr@gmail.com

Abhirup Khanna, May El Barachi, Sapna Jain, Manoj Kumar and Anand Nayyar (eds.) Artificial Intelligence and Machine Learning in Drug Design and Development, (93–116) © 2024 Scrivener Publishing LLC

learning, reasoning, and perception. Currently, AI is applied in various sectors, ranging from finance to healthcare [40]. AI encompasses a broad spectrum of applications and employs various algorithms to interpret and extract knowledge from data. It is closely related to disciplines such as linear algebra, probability theory and statistics, machine learning (ML), and computational intelligence methods, including neural networks and fuzzy logic models [50].

ML, a subset of AI, is a field that involves machines imitating human actions or behaviors. Artificial intelligence systems are employed to perform intricate tasks in a manner comparable to human problem solving approaches [56]. Both AI and ML techniques involve complex applications such as classification, regression, prediction, and optimization [48]. ML plays a paramount role in utilizing different types of real-world data, where a specific model must be defined with its parameters. Through training in the available data, the machines learn and acquire proficiency in the model, allowing them to make future predictions and extract information from new data [40, 50, 56].

In recent times, there has been a marked increase in the use of machine learning approaches in the pharmaceutical industry [16]. As technological advancements continue to shape various industries, the potential of machine learning to revolutionize drug discovery, clinical trials, personalized medicine, and healthcare outcomes has attracted the interest of researchers, pharmaceutical companies, and healthcare professionals alike. ML algorithms have the potential to analyze large datasets, recognize patterns, and generate insights that can improve the efficiency and effectiveness of drug development, patient care, and decision making. The pharmaceutical sector hopes to accelerate innovation, refine therapies, and ultimately improve the lives of people around the world by embracing machine learning [13]. In 2020, MIT scientists employed a machine learning algorithm to uncover a powerful new antibiotic compound. Laboratory tests revealed the drug's effectiveness in eliminating a variety of difficult bacteria that cause diseases, including strains that are resistant to all existing antibiotics. The researchers used a computer model that was able to quickly analyze more than 100 million chemical compounds in a few days, with the aim of finding antibiotics that work differently than existing drugs [71]. This model was successful in treating infections in two different mouse models.

The use of machine learning and AI is advantageous in providing assistance in the delivery of drugs for the treatment of infectious diseases. This is due to a number of factors. First, it has the ability to identify essential components in intricate datasets, enabling accurate predictions without the requirement of repeating biological experiments. This makes it beneficial for drug creation, drug combination selection, and drug dose optimization. Second, machine learning can reveal hidden patterns and establish new rules, allowing the prediction of antimicrobial resistance and optimization of the medication delivery system even in the absence of prior genomic knowledge. Third, its fast data processing and analysis capabilities allow the early prediction of adverse treatment outcomes, facilitating timely interventions against infections associated with AMR. Fourth, by incorporating computational software into clinical gadgets and/or mobile devices, machine learning can be used as a viable tool for making clinical decisions regarding anti-infective drug delivery systems. Finally, it can adjust and gain knowledge from new factors in real time, enhance its execution, and create adaptable drug delivery systems to suit the ongoing development of pathogens, patients, and antimicrobial agents.

Integration of machine learning in the pharmaceutical industry attempts to address significant business concerns such as decreasing attrition rates and total expenses.

Pharmaceutical companies can increase their ability to find viable drug candidates and optimize the drug development process by employing machine learning algorithms [16, 73]. Machine learning allows for the efficient study of large amounts of data, resulting in enhanced decision making through pattern identification. This not only reduces attrition rates but also streamlines processes, improves efficiency, and increases the likelihood of successful outcomes. Integration of machine learning in the pharmaceutical business corresponds to the strategic goals of lowering attrition rates and costs, ultimately encouraging a more sustainable and effective approach to drug discovery [34].

This chapter examines the utilization of unsupervised and supervised machine learning algorithms in drug discovery. It is suggested that the use of these algorithms could significantly reduce the time, cost, and resources required for traditional methods and experiments. However, to ensure the accuracy of ML techniques, improve decision-making, increase awareness of ML approaches, and identify potential risks, it is necessary to collect precise and methodical data during clinical trials. The chapter also provides a brief summary of the literature on machine learning tools and approaches utilized in various phases of drug development. In this chapter, the following questions are studied in different sections:

- What are the uses of machine learning algorithms in different phases of drug discovery and development, such as target validation?
- What challenges and limitations exist in using ML techniques in drug discovery and how can these challenges be overcome to improve decision making, validate ML approaches, increase awareness, and identify potential risk failures?
- What is the existing work on drug discovery using ML tools and techniques and what advancements have been made in the utilization of these approaches during the various phases of drug development?

Organization of Chapter

The rest of the chapter is organized as: Section 4.2 focuses on the practical applications of AI and ML, which include target validation, drug toxicity prediction, drug-target interaction prediction, and drug bioactivity prediction. Section 4.3 delves into the specific AI and ML methods utilized in drug discovery, including support vector machines (SVMs), logistic regression, naive Bayes, k-nearest neighbors (kNN), decision trees, ensemble learning, and neural networks. Section 4.4 addresses the challenges associated with the implementation of AI and ML in drug discovery, encompassing aspects such as data quality and quantity, integration and interoperability, lack of domain expertise, validation and regulation approval, ethical considerations, cost and infrastructure requirements, limited generalization capability, and collaboration and data sharing. And, finally, section 4.5 concludes the chapter with future scope.

4.2 Applications of AI and ML in Drug Discovery

The applications of machine learning approaches have been demonstrated in a variety of areas of drug discovery and development.

4.2.1   Target Validation

Drug discovery relies on the regulation of molecular target activity, as it enables the development of drugs that are effective in combating diseases [29]. A crucial phase in the drug development process is target identification. It involves developing a therapeutic hypothesis to control how these targets are regulated, which ultimately affects how the infection turns out. Both *in vivo* and *ex vivo* models are used for target validation, with a focus on ensuring that the identified targets are relevant to the condition being addressed [79]. Numerous clinical resources, including metabolomic, transcriptomic, and proteomic profiles, as well as publicly accessible databases, are used to help identify and validate these targets. The application of ML in target identification is becoming increasingly popular as more data-driven experiments become available. Based on known features, connections to causality, and previously identified targets, ML methods can predict potential targets from a variety of aspects.

4.2.2   Drug Toxicity Prediction

The term "toxicity" describes the unfavorable consequences that chemicals can have on humans. To recognize substances that could be detrimental to human health, the assessment of toxicity is a critical component of the drug discovery process [74]. However, conventional *in vivo* studies frequently require animal research, which increases the cost of drug development. In contrast, computational approaches have the benefit of predicting the toxicity of substances more accurately and efficiently. In order to predict chemical toxicity, a variety of AI-based approaches have been developed [74, 78].

A DeepTox predictive model utilizes a three-layer deep neural network (DNN) to assess the toxicity of chemicals [43]. The model first cleanses and verifies the data before encoding the remaining compounds with molecular descriptors. For the DNN, these descriptions act as input. The DeepTox pipeline is improved by improving the number of hidden units, the

learning rate, and the dropout rate, among other hyperparameters. DeepTox beats other algorithms in accurately predicting toxicity, according to a comparison study utilizing the Tox21 dataset.

4.2.3   Drug–Target Interaction Prediction

Investigating the connections between chemical compounds and protein targets within living organisms is a key part of drug–target interaction (DTI) prediction. This is a fundamental step in the discovery of new drugs [35]. DTI has historically been calculated using experimental methods such as co-immunoprecipitation, phage display technology, and yeast two-hybrid. When used for DTI prediction, these techniques take time. *In silico* prediction of DTI is now feasible due to the vast amount of biological data accessible. As a result, machine learning methods are increasingly being used for DTI prediction [9].

Deep learning-based approaches usually outperform other approaches in DTI prediction [35, 77]. First, the corresponding characteristics of chemicals and proteins are used to encode them. The utilization of deep learning techniques is enabled by the embedding of features of chemicals and proteins. This has enabled the creation of models based on convolutional neural networks, deep belief neural networks, and multiple layer perceptrons for the prediction of drug–protein interactions, which has significantly expedited the drug discovery process [77].

4.2.4   Drug Bioactivity Prediction

The lack of bioactivity of several drugs produced from natural sources is a prevalent issue in drug discovery. As a result, determining drug bioactivity has become a significant area of focus [3]. Although *in vitro* and *in vivo* tests can simulate how molecules function in the human body, they are costly and time consuming [21]. In contrast, artificial intelligence methods provide a time- and money-efficient method for predicting drug bioactivities, such as anticancer, antiviral, and antibacterial effects. The difficulty of determining drug bioactivities has been successfully addressed by these AI techniques [3, 21].

4.3   AI and ML Methods to Drug Discovery

Artificial intelligence is essential in the progression of drug design, utilizing machine learning techniques and taking advantage of pharmacological information. Unlike speculative improvements, AI has the potential to convert medical information into reusable methods, thus improving the field [57, 73]. The remarkable computational power of ML algorithms lies in their ability to acquire knowledge without explicit programming. The concept of computational "learning" has immense potential to revolutionize various fields and applications [19, 40, 47]. By embracing a diverse range of techniques, ML algorithms are driven by the classical trio of supervised learning, unsupervised learning, and reinforcement learning, which are further enhanced by disruptive methodologies such as deep learning, adversarial learning, transfer learning, and metalearning. This dynamic interplay continually gives rise to novel models like long short-term memory and generative adversarial networks as well as applications spanning natural language processing, object recognition, forecasting, and more [17, 31].

The illustration in Figure 4.1 displays the three primary approaches to ML: supervised, unsupervised, and reinforcement learning. These are the core paradigms of machine learning. Each approach has its unique characteristics and applications. Supervised learning is a type of machine learning in which a model is trained using labeled data. This data consists of input features (independent variables) and the corresponding output labels (dependent variables). The model is then taught to map the input features to the output labels. The objective is to acquire knowledge of a connection between the input characteristics and the output labels so that the model can accurately predict or classify future, unseen data. Supervised learning algorithms involve predicting continuous values (regression) or assigning discrete labels or categories (classification) to input data. Examples of such algorithms are linear regression, logistic regression, support vector machines (SVMs), decision trees, and neural networks.

Unsupervised learning is a machine learning technique where a model learns from unlabeled data. Unlike supervised learning, there are no explicit output labels provided. The objective is to uncover concealed patterns, structures, or associations within the data without any prior understanding. Unsupervised learning algorithms focus on finding meaningful representations of the data. This can include clustering, dimensionality reduction, and

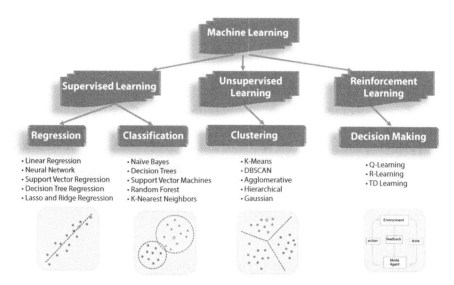

Figure 4.1 Machine learning paradigms.

anomaly detection. Popular algorithms in unsupervised learning are k-means clustering, hierarchical clustering, principal component analysis (PCA), and generative adversarial networks (GANs).

Reinforcement learning is a form of machine learning in which an agent is trained to take actions in a given environment to maximize a reward. An agent is interacting with its environment, taking actions and receiving rewards or penalties in response. The goal of the agent is to learn the best policy that will result in the highest cumulative reward over time. Reinforcement learning models learn through trial and error. They receive feedback from the environment after each action, allowing them to update their strategy and improve their decision-making over time.

Various ML approaches, including random forest, naive Bayesian classifier, logistic regression, linear discriminant analysis, neural networks, support vector machine (SVM), and more, are commonly employed in the literature. These approaches enable AI to excel in feature extraction and generalization, empowering deep learning techniques in drug design [1, 13]. Supervised learning approaches employ classifiers and regression algorithms to meet specific objectives, such as predicting continuous or categorical data elements. On the other hand, unsupervised methods are utilized to construct models for data clustering, aiming to uncover patterns or relationships within the data without predefined labels.

The feature design in traditional machine learning approaches frequently necessitates human intervention. Deep learning systems, on the other hand, automate this process by employing multi-layer feature extraction algorithms that may turn simple features into advanced ones. The availability of larger datasets allows for this acceleration [8, 56]. Deep learning methods produce more exact results by lowering generalization errors, giving them an advantage over traditional approaches. Convolutional neural networks (CNNs), recurrent neural networks (RNNs), autoencoders, and deep neural networks (DNNs) are among the deep learning approaches used in this area.

AI algorithms are used extensively in drug research and development, enhancing data analysis and prediction. Support vector machines (SVMs), random forests (RF), and multi-layer perceptrons (MLPs) are well-established models that have proved their usefulness in drug development, as evidenced by their widespread appearance in the scientific literature [13].

4.3.1 Support Vector Machines

Support vector machines (SVMs) are powerful supervised learning methods widely used for classification and regression tasks [66]. SVMs have several benefits, such as their ability to work in high-dimensional spaces and situations where the number of dimensions (i.e., shape) is greater than the total samples (i.e., number of data points). They use a subset of training points, known as support vectors, which makes them memory efficient. Additionally, SVMs are versatile, as they can be used for both linear and non-linear classification. SVMs also demonstrate versatility by allowing the use of various kernel functions, including the option to define custom kernels. However, SVMs have certain limitations. When working with a large number of features relative to the number of samples, it is essential to be judicious in the selection of kernel functions and regularization terms to prevent overfitting. Also, SVMs do not directly provide probability estimates, and calculating these probabilities typically requires computationally expensive techniques like five-fold cross-validation [60]. The mathematical decision of SVM can be expressed as follows:

$$y(x) = w_1 \phi(x_1) + w_2 \phi(x_2) + w_3 \phi(x_3) + \cdots + w_n \phi(x_n) + b$$

The weights $W = [w_1, w_2, w_3, \cdots, w_n]$ and bias b of a support vector machine (SVM) are derived from the training dataset. The kernel function ϕ can take several forms, including linear, Gaussian, or radical basis function. The support vectors, which are the samples near the decision boundary, dictate the weight W and bias b. Training an SVM aims to find the weight W and bias b that can linearly separate the training data samples and enlarge the margin of the high-dimensional latent space defined by the kernel function ϕ. The objective of the classification problem is to identify a function capable of effectively distinguishing between two classes based on the provided examples. Additionally, the classifier should exhibit strong generalization capabilities when exposed to new, unseen examples [20]. Achieving this does not require compromising generality.

In Figure 4.2, there exist numerous linear classifiers capable of separating the data, yet only a single classifier that optimizes the margin exists, which is the maximum distance between it and the nearest data point of each class. This linear classifier is referred to as the optimal separating hyperplane: $(w, x^i) + b = 0$, where x^i is the data, and w and b are the hyperplane parameters.

4.3.2 Logistic Regression

Logistic regression is well recognized as a highly effective machine learning technique for assessing clinical data in medical applications. This technique is highly beneficial when attempting to determine the probability of a sample belonging to a certain class. As a

Figure 4.2 Linear classifiers for binary classification (two classes).

discriminative model, logistic regression computes the posterior probability by plotting the feature vector against the output class, without taking into account the joint distribution of the features and target variables [33]. It can be defined mathematically as follows:

$$P(Y = y) = \frac{1}{1 + e^{(w_1x_1 + w_2x_2 + w_3x_3 + \cdots + w_nx_n + b)}}$$

The weights W and the bias b are the parameters that are learned from the training dataset. W is a vector of length n containing elements w_1, w_2, w_3, $\cdots$, w_n.

Figure 4.3 shows the schematic diagram of logistic regression. It provides interpretability by estimating the coefficients for each input feature, which allows for a more in-depth comprehension of feature significance. This method is computationally efficient and can manage large datasets. It generates probabilistic output, allowing for the inclusion of uncertainty in decision-making [30]. In comparison to advanced methods, the model is resistant to outliers and requires less data preprocessing. Logistic regression, on the other hand,

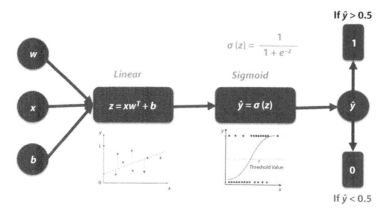

Figure 4.3 Schematic diagram of logistic regression.

presupposes a linear decision boundary and feature independence, limiting its performance in non-linear instances and correlated feature relationships. It is intended primarily for binary classification, but it can be expanded to multiclass situations. Furthermore, extreme outliers and non-numerical data can have an impact on its performance. Understanding these advantages and disadvantages is critical when deciding whether logistic regression is appropriate for given tasks and datasets [67].

4.3.3   Naive Bayes

The naive Bayes (NB) algorithm is grounded in the Bayes theorem, which computes the posterior probability of each class based on the feature vectors and their prior probabilities. In this model, the joint distribution of feature vectors and class labels is considered. The model uses the posterior probability to make a decision, assuming that the features are mutually independent [76]. The NB approach calculates the posterior probability as follows:

$$\arg\max_y P(Y = y | X_1 = x_1, \cdots\cdots X_n = x_n)$$

$$\propto \text{argmax}_y P(Y = y) \prod_{i=1}^{n} P(F_i = x_i \,|\, Y = y)$$

The predicted class, denoted by Y, is determined by the maximum posterior probability, and P is the probability. Further mathematical information on naive Bayes can be found in the work [15, 76].

The NB machine learning algorithm is well known for its superior performance in multiclass prediction tasks. It is simple to use and very effective. It continues to be extensively used and has been utilized in biological informatics since 1961. Naive Bayes' interpretability, which enables us to understand how each feature contributed to the final prediction, is one of its significant benefits. It is essential to be aware, however, that Naive Bayes is based on the assumption that all input features are independent, which may not be the reality in actual datasets. When working with complex data, this assumption may limit its usefulness [15].

4.3.4   k-Nearest Neighbors

The k-nearest neighbors (k-NN) algorithm, introduced by Cover and Hart in 1967, belongs to the category of instance-based machine learning methods that retain all training samples [75]. When predicting for a test sample, k-NN directly examines the associations between the test data and instances in the training dataset to determine the result [65]. For a specific test dataset sample $\vec{x}_{test}$, its k-nearest neighbors are identified by the data samples $\vec{x}_1, \vec{x}_2, \cdots, \vec{x}_k$ that have the k smallest distances (computed using a distance metric). The final outcome is obtained by:

$$y(\vec{x}_{test}) = D\left(\left[\, y(\vec{x}_1), y(\vec{x}_2), \cdots, y(\vec{x}_k)\,\right]\right)$$

Figure 4.4 Schematic diagram of k-nearest neighbors.

The label of the k-th sample closest to $\vec{x}_{test}$ is represented as y $(\vec{x}_k)$. If y is a categorical label for classification, then D acts as a voting function. If y is a continuous label for regression, then D functions as an averaging operation [75]. The graphical depiction of k-NN can be seen in Figure 4.4.

The performance of the k-nearest neighbors algorithm is influenced by the parameter k. To find the best k, cross-validation (CV) or optimization methods are typically employed. This algorithm has multiple benefits, including its simplicity, non-parametric properties, localized learning, the absence of a training phase, and versatility for both classification and regression tasks. It can deliver adequate results in small datasets with an even distribution of positive and negative samples. However, it has drawbacks such as computational complexity, susceptibility to feature scaling and high-dimensional data, lack of interpretability, and sensitivity to imbalanced datasets [65, 75]. These considerations should be weighed when deciding whether to employ k-NN for a particular application.

4.3.5   Decision Trees and Random Forest

Decision trees are machine learning algorithms which rely on their predictions on a set of rules. They are organized as tree-like representations. The root node of the tree symbolizes the entire training dataset, while branch nodes signify decision points and leaf nodes represent the outcomes of the cumulative decisions [69]. The data is separated using established splitting criteria into more compact, homogeneous subsets at each branch node. Until a set of requirements is satisfied, this procedure iteratively divides the data into ever-narrower subsets. These circumstances could be exceeding a maximum depth limit or having all samples inside a subset have the same label [6]. There are several well-liked decision tree algorithms, and they all use various splitting criteria. ID3 and Classification And Regression Tree (CART) methods are notable examples. These algorithms are essential for building decision trees and choosing the best data-splitting criteria [6, 69]. Figure 4.5 depicts the schematic diagram of decision trees.

Decision trees have several advantages, including interpretability, non-parametric nature, feature importance identification, ability to handle non-linear relationships, and handling

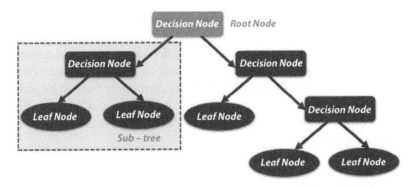

Figure 4.5 Schematic diagram of decision tree.

missing values. However, they easily overfit and react quickly to even minute variations in the data, struggle with linear modeling, exhibit bias towards dominant features, and lack global optimization. Ensemble methods like random forests or gradient boosting can help mitigate some of these limitations [61].

A random forest typically denotes a machine learning model that combines multiple decision trees through the "bagging" method [22]. This ensemble technique is specifically tailored for random forests, where the predictions of individual tree models, characterized by low bias, high variability, and overfitting to the training dataset, are aggregated. By amalgamating the predictions from diverse decision trees, random forests enhance the overall effectiveness of the ML model [22, 63]. Figure 4.6 illustrates the schematic representation of a random forest.

Random forests have several advantages, including their robustness against overfitting, high prediction accuracy, feature importance analysis, flexibility for various data types, and ability to handle missing values. However, they have limitations in terms of interpretability,

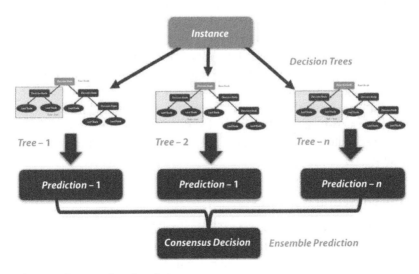

Figure 4.6 Schematic diagram of random forest.

computational cost, model size, black box nature, and sensitivity to noisy data. It is crucial to consider these factors when deciding to use random forests in a specific scenario [37].

Decision trees and random forests emulate human decision-making processes by answering a series of questions (the splitting rules at the branch nodes) that can be easily traced through a tree's branch nodes [6]. These methods are commonly favored by end users. The outcomes of the tree can be verified through empirical experimentation, potentially leading to novel insights. Moreover, the tree is adept at addressing challenges posed by incomplete or missing data in the dataset.

4.3.6   Ensemble Learning

Boosting is a powerful ensemble learning approach that uses many models with the same structure to improve prediction accuracy and reliability. This method seeks to improve predictions by integrating the strengths of various models. Ensemble learning involves creating multiple models with randomly generated parameters, which then come together to form a set. When the results/predictions of these models are combined, the resultant prediction is more reliable, as it reduces noise, bias, and variation. Compared to using a single model, the boost method offers improved accuracy and reliability. Several boosting algorithms have been developed to cater to different scenarios. These include adaptive boosting (AdaBoost) [59], gradient tree boosting (GTB) [45], extreme gradient boosting (XGBoost) [11], and categorical boosting (CatBoost) [55]. Each of these algorithms brings its own unique benefits and techniques to enhance the ensemble learning process.

AdaBoost is a machine learning technique that combines multiple weak models into a single robust model through iterative processes, thereby improving performance. It assigns learnable weights to each sample, controlling their importance during training of weak models. At each step, the weights of incorrectly classified data samples are increased, while the weights of correctly classified data samples are decreased. This ensures that subsequent iterations focus more on the samples that are harder to classify, with greater weights. On the other hand, gradient tree boosting (GTB) uses a collection of decision trees trained by optimizing the gradient direction of individual samples and their associated residuals. Extreme gradient boosting (XGBoost) adheres to similar principles, optimizing the objective function, tree size, and weight magnitudes to prevent overfitting.

CatBoost is an improved version of the standard gradient boosting approach that addresses two critical issues: dealing with categorical information and preventing target leakage. The boosting approach is extensively used in various research because of its several advantages. It uses ensemble learning to improve prediction accuracy over individual classifiers. It handles correlated data effectively and naturally supports sparse, non-linear, and/or imbalanced dataset. It can highlight key aspects, providing useful insights for decision-making.

4.3.7   Artificial Neural Networks

Artificial neural networks (ANN) consists of linked artificial neurons that serve as the fundamental information processing units [26]. As shown in Figure 4.7, ANNs are also known as neural networks because they mimic the neurons found in the human brain. Neurons constitute the essential elements of an ANN, with each neuron characterized by:

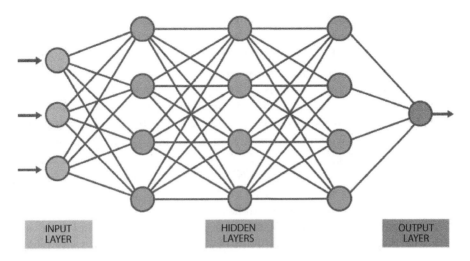

INPUT
LAYER

HIDDEN
LAYERS

OUTPUT
LAYER

Figure 4.7 Schematic diagram of ANN [26].

$$z(x) = f\,(w_1x_1 + w_2x_2 + \cdots w_nx_n + b)$$

where f denotes the activation function, which could be the Sigmoid function or rectified linear unit (ReLU), and z(x) represents the neuron's output for a given input x. The neuron's weights $W = [w_1, w_2, \cdots, w_n]$ and bias b are determined through the training data *via* backpropagation. Inspired by the human brain, the neuron is a nonlinear mathematical construct designed to approximate nonlinear relationships between inputs and outputs.

An artificial neural network (ANN) usually has at least three layers: 1) an input layer that directly receives data, with each neuron representing a specific feature value, 2) a hidden layer that transmits information from the input layer to the output layer by applying weighted linear combinations and non-linear activation functions, and 3) an output layer that produces the final results. Each layer contains multiple neurons, and every neuron is connected to all neurons in the following layer, allowing for the information flow from input to output. An ANN with more than two layers functioning in a feedforward manner is referred to as a multi-layer perceptron (MLP) [68].

The architecture of an ANN is determined by the number of hidden layers and the neurons within those layers. ANNs can vary in the number of layers and neurons within each layer. During training, the neural network learns through backpropagation of errors, calculated based on the difference between the network's output and the target values. The network's weights and biases are then modified to minimize errors on the training samples [52].

Deep learning has gained significant attention recently and has proven useful across diverse fields. Essentially, deep learning is a type of artificial neural network (ANN) characterized by a high number of hidden layers. The deep convolutional neural network (DCNN) is frequently employed when handling high-dimensional input data, such as images, utilizing shared kernels to decrease the number of parameters. Unlike traditional ANNs, DCNNs often feature more hidden layers, varying from 3 to 10 or even up to 100 layers [24]. This depth allows deep neural networks to successfully learn from extensive datasets by extracting pertinent features from the training data samples. The term "ANNs" encompasses all forms of neural networks discussed in this chapter, including standard artificial neural networks, multi-layer perceptrons, and convolutional neural networks.

In summary, every model has its own set of strengths and weaknesses when applied to real-world data. Generally speaking, models with fewer parameters tend to be more interpretable but are less capable than models with a higher parameter count.

Multiple linear regression is often utilized in drug–target interactions, whereas decision trees are used to analyze adverse drug effects [5, 10, 23, 39, 70]. To investigate drug–drug interactions, logistic regression (LR) is used. Support vector machines are useful for compound classification, whereas convolutional neural networks (CNN) excel at predicting bioactivity. Recurrent neural networks (RNN) are important in drug design from scratch, and generative adversarial networks (GAN) aid in molecule discovery. Clustering techniques like k-means assists in drug candidate selection, and hierarchical clustering is applied for molecular scaffold analysis. Dimension reduction techniques such as principal component analysis (PCA) find utility in quantitative structure–activity relationship (QSAR), and t-distributed stochastic neighbor embedding (t-SNE) is employed for chemical space mapping.

These methods serve as valuable tools in various aspects of pharmaceutical research and analysis.

4.4 Challenges

While AI and ML have shown great promise in drug discovery, there are several challenges that need to be addressed, as shown in Figure 4.8.

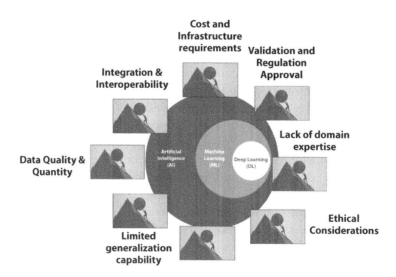

Figure 4.8 Challenges of AI and ML in drug discovery.

Table 4.1 Databases for drug discovery.

Database and URL	Description
ChEMBL (https://www.ebiac.uk/chembl)	A collection of bioactive molecules with drug-like characteristics, which includes chemical, bioactivity, and genomic information, has been created to facilitate drug development.
ChemDB (http://cdb.ics.uci.edu)	This database contains 5 million commercially available small molecules and their associated physicochemical properties, which can be either predicted or experimentally determined. It is a comprehensive chemical database.
DGIdb (http://www.dgidb.org)	A database containing DTI (Drug-Target Interaction) and druggable genomic data from more than 30 reliable sources is available.
DrugBank (http://www.drugbank.ca)	A repository of pharmaceuticals containing objectives, three-dimensional models, and other pertinent data.
DTC (http://drugtargetcommons.fimm.fi)	A platform for obtaining drug-target bioactivity information and classifying targets is being crowd-sourced.
INPUT (http://cbcb.cdutcm.edu.cn/INPUT)	This platform provides a network pharmacology approach to traditional Chinese medicine, with 29,812 identified compounds from 4,716 Chinese plants.
PubChem (https://pubchem.ncbi.nlm.nih.gov/)	A chemistry database that is open to the public and contains information data about molecules and their characteristics is an invaluable asset for chemists.
SIDER (http://sideeffects.embl.de)	A database that stores data on controlled drugs and any adverse reactions that have been documented.

4.4.1 Data Quality and Quantity

The availability of large and high-quality datasets for training and validation is critical to the development of AI and ML models. These models excel in detecting patterns, making predictions, and extracting insights from data, but they require a large amount of diverse and representative data to generalize [51, 54]. Obtaining such information, however, offers substantial hurdles, particularly in the context of uncommon diseases or unique patient populations. One significant difficulty is the scarcity of data on rare diseases or specific patient populations. Because these disorders impact a small number of people, there are frequently no centralized archives or detailed data sources [44]. As a result, researchers and organizations may find it difficult to collect enough data to accurately capture the characteristics of these situations. Furthermore, access to patient information may be restricted due to privacy concerns and data protection requirements, thus complicating the search for appropriate datasets [36, 44].

To address these issues, research institutes, hospitals, and technology businesses can collaborate to combine their resources, knowledge, and data. By establishing collaborations and sharing information, these entities can jointly contribute to the creation of larger and more representative databases. Collaborations also allow for the exchange of domain knowledge and the study of diverse views, which improves the overall quality and diversity of the data obtained. There are various public databases accessible, such as BindingDB, Drug-bank, ZINC, PUBCHEM, and REAL chemical databases. Table 4.1 shows these various databases and their URLs. Additionally, utilizing sophisticated technologies and novel ways can assist in overcoming data shortage in uncommon diseases or specific patient populations [13, 44]. From the application standpoint, using artificial intelligence can help in data augmentation, which is the generation of synthetic data or variations on current data. These enhanced datasets can complement the limited available data while also improving the diversity and representation of the training datasets [62].

4.4.2   Integration and Interoperability

The integration and analysis of pharmaceutical data pose significant challenges due to the scattered nature of the information across diverse sources and formats. To properly exploit the capabilities of AI and ML methods, it is important to emphasize data format compatibility and standardization within the pharmaceutical domain [80].

Interoperability refers to the abilities of various systems and datasets to communicate, exchange, and use information in an efficient way. In the broader setting of pharmaceutical data, achieving interoperability requires constructing common standards and protocols that enable the integration and harmonization of data from multiple sources [12]. This ensures that data can be easily shared, integrated, and analyzed across many platforms, apps, and organizations. Interoperability promotes rapid data aggregation, improves data quality and integrity, and allows academics and healthcare practitioners to gain valuable insights from integrated data.

Data format standardization is strongly related to interoperability and essential for efficient data integration and analysis. The pharmaceutical business can ensure consistency and uniformity in how data is gathered, maintained, and communicated by adopting standardized data formats, such as industry-wide data models or ontologies [12, 80]. Standardization improves data comprehension, minimizes ambiguity and errors, and allows for smooth data integration and analysis across systems and organizations. It also makes AI and ML model creation and deployment easier by providing a uniform framework for data representation and processing.

Collaboration among diverse stakeholders is essential to establish interoperability and standardization in the pharmaceutical industry. Pharmaceutical businesses, regulatory agencies, research institutes, technology suppliers, and other relevant entities must work together to establish industry-wide data standards, promote data sharing efforts, and develop inter-operability frameworks. Regulatory organizations can play an important role in encouraging the use of standardized data formats and interoperable systems by developing recommendations and regulations.

4.4.3 Lack of Domain Expertise

Some AI and ML models, such as deep learning neural networks, can be black boxes, making interpreting their decision-making process difficult. This can be an issue for regulatory authorities and healthcare practitioners who must comprehend how a model works in order to rely on its predictions [25].

There are several approaches that can be used to solve this issue. One method is to employ interpretability approaches, which can aid in explaining how a model makes decisions [41, 44]. Another method is to employ more transparent models, such as decision trees or linear models. It should be noted that interpretability is not always required. In some circumstances, the accuracy of a model may be more significant than its interpretability. In other circumstances, though, it may be critical for a model to be both accurate and interpretable [13].

The pharmaceutical industry is still in the early phases of incorporating AI and machine learning into drug research. As these technologies advance, it is critical to address the issues of interpretability and transparency. This will aid in ensuring that these technologies are used responsibly and effectively [2, 28, 32, 38, 46, 53, 64].

4.4.4 Validation and Regulation Approval

Obtaining regulatory approval for AI and ML algorithms in drug discovery is a difficult process due to the requirement to demonstrate its dependability, accuracy, and safety in accordance with regulatory standards [14]. This is critical because these algorithms have the ability to influence human health, necessitating thorough review to verify accuracy, reliability, and the absence of safety problems [27].

Validating AI and ML-based algorithms in drug discovery can be challenging by noisy and inadequate patient data, which can result in biased or inaccurate models. Researchers are addressing issues by using strategies such as data augmentation and hyperparameter tuning to improve model accuracy as well as developing ways for understanding model complexities to better evaluate safety risks [18, 62]. Despite the limitations, the potential benefits of AI and ML-based drug development algorithms are huge. These algorithms can be used to find new drug targets, create new medications, and predict drug efficacy and safety. As these technologies advance, they are anticipated to play an increasing role in the drug discovery process [13].

AI and ML in drug discovery involve collaboration between domain experts such as biologists, chemists, and pharmacologists as well as data scientists. Bridging the gap between these disciplines and establishing efficient communication is imperative for successful AI and ML integration.

4.4.5 Ethical Considerations

The integration of AI and ML in drug discovery raises ethical concerns related to privacy, data security, and biases. To maintain transparency, fairness, and accountability, it is crucial to address these implications. While AI and ML offer valuable enhancements to efficiency and accuracy in drug discovery, it is essential to carefully navigate the ethical considerations associated with their usage [7].

Bias in AI and ML algorithms is a major concern, arising from inadequate representation in training data that can lead to inaccurate predictions for certain populations [4, 49]. Privacy breaches are another worry as these algorithms often rely on vast datasets, including sensitive information, which, if not adequately protected, can be exploited for discrimination or targeted marketing purposes. Addressing these concerns is crucial for ensuring fair and unbiased outcomes while safeguarding the individuals' privacy.

In drug discovery, ethical considerations include transparency, fairness, and accountability to avoid discrimination and ensure responsible use. Developing guidelines that prioritize these principles can help researchers and policymakers ensure the responsible and beneficial application of AI and ML technologies for the benefit of society.

4.4.6   Cost and Infrastructure Requirements

Implementing AI and ML technologies necessitates significant computational resources and infrastructure, which may be difficult for smaller enterprises or research institutions with low resources [42, 58]. AI and machine learning are important technologies for increasing the efficiency and accuracy of drug discovery. However, these technologies can be costly to adopt and necessitate specialized knowledge. Smaller enterprises and academic institutions may find it challenging to implement AI and ML as a result of this [4].

There are several approaches to this problem. One solution is to employ cloud computing platforms, which can provide pay-as-you-go access to strong processing resources and infrastructure. It is paramount to highlight that the cost of integrating AI and ML technologies is not the sole consideration. These technologies may also take years to develop and execute. Before deciding whether to use AI or machine learning, it is critical to assess the costs and benefits of these technologies. Despite the challenges, AI and ML are becoming increasingly important in the drug discovery process. As these technologies continue to develop, they are likely to become more affordable and accessible to smaller organizations and research institutions [7].

4.4.7   Limited Generalization Capability

AI and machine learning models that have been trained on certain datasets and conditions may struggle to generalize to other datasets or scenarios. It is important to ensure that models are resilient and generalizable across populations, diseases, and experimental situations [8, 72]. AI and machine learning are important technologies for increasing the efficiency and accuracy of drug discovery. However, because these models are frequently trained on specific datasets and situations, their capacity to generalize to other datasets or scenarios is limited. Overfitting, in which the model learns the noise in the training data rather than the underlying patterns, might result from this [72].

There are several approaches that can be used to solve this issue. Data augmentation is one way, which involves artificially increasing the training dataset by adding additional data that is comparable to the original data [62]. Transfer learning is another strategy that involves training a model on a broad dataset of comparable tasks before fine-tuning it on the single job of interest. It is also critical to make sure that the models are resistant to noise and outliers. This can be accomplished through the use of techniques such as regularization and dropout.

Hence, it is possible to improve the robustness and generalizability of AI and ML models for drug discovery by following these steps. This will help to ensure that these models can make accurate predictions in a range of contexts [13].

4.4.8 Collaboration and Data Sharing

The pharmaceutical industry's need to protect data for competitive reasons prevented collaboration and data sharing, limiting the application of AI and ML in drug discovery. To realize the full potential of these technologies, it is indispensable to encourage collaboration and data sharing across researchers and organizations. This can be achieved through interdisciplinary collaboration, regulations, data standardization, and ongoing research and development efforts, ensuring the appropriate and successful use of AI and ML in drug discovery.

Interdisciplinary collaboration brings academics from several disciplines together to address common difficulties, establishing a collaborative and open environment for data sharing. Regulatory frameworks promote responsible data sharing by defining quality, security, and research use guidelines. Data standardization includes the development of uniform formats and protocols to allow seamless data exchange between companies. Ongoing R&D activities are focused on improving the accuracy and efficacy of AI and ML systems through the development of new algorithms, training datasets, and performance evaluation.

By addressing these issues, the pharmaceutical sector can realize the full promise of artificial intelligence and machine learning in drug discovery. This can result in the discovery of novel drugs and treatments that can help patients live better.

4.5 Conclusion and Future Directions

The pharmaceutical sector has adopted the utilization of artificial intelligence (AI) technology, incorporating machine learning (ML) algorithms and deep learning approaches into their everyday activities. ML techniques have found application in various areas of drug development and healthcare, although not without challenges. ML models in medical science have demonstrated their ability to predict and analyze compound structures, enabling the identification of alternative tools and molecules with desirable properties. Deep learning models have shown promise in many applications, contributing to improved success rates in clinical trials. As AI technology continues to advance in the field of computer-aided drug development, it brings powerful data mining capabilities. However, certain issues persist, such as the performance and interpretation of deep learning methods, the need for explainability in "black-box" models, and the optimization of neural networks' training parameters. Addressing these challenges will be crucial to harnessing the full potential of AI in drug discovery and development.

Medical science and web innovation have been combined to improve deep learning algorithms and increase the ability to make well-informed decisions on the adverse effects of treatments. The entire drug research and development process is anticipated to undergo a radical transformation in the upcoming years thanks to AI technology. Automated AI systems must successfully integrate a variety of data sources to enable this change.

References

1. Adekoya, O.C. *et al.*, A mini-review on the application of machine learning in polymer nanogels for drug delivery. *Mater. Today: Proc.*, 62, S141–S144, 2022.
2. Ali, S. *et al.*, Towards pattern-based change verification framework for cloud-enabled healthcare component-based. *IEEE Access*, 8, 148007–148020, 2020.
3. Andi, H.K., AI-powered drug detection system utilizing bioactivity prediction and drug release tracking. *J. Artif. Intell.*, 4, 4, 263–273, 2022.
4. Arabi, A.A., Artificial intelligence in drug design: Algorithms, applications, challenges and ethics. *Future Drug Discovery*, 3, 2, 59, 2021.
5. El-Attar, N.E. *et al.*, Deep learning model for classification and bioactivity prediction of essential oil-producing plants from Egypt. *Sci. Rep.*, 10, 1, 21349, 2020.
6. Bansal, M., Goyal, A., Choudhary, A., A comparative analysis of K- nearest neighbour, genetic, support vector machine, decision tree, and long short term memory algorithms in machine learning. *Decis. Anal. J.*, 3, 100071, 2022.
7. Blanco-Gonzalez, A. *et al.*, The role of ai in drug discovery: Challenges, opportunities, and strategies. *Pharmaceuticals*, 16, 6, 891, 2023.
8. Cerchia, C. and Lavecchia, A., New avenues in artificial-intelligence-assisted drug discovery. *Drug Discov. Today*, 28, 103516, 2023.
9. Chen, R. *et al.*, Machine learning for drug-target interaction prediction. *Molecules*, 23, 90, 2208, 2018.
10. Chen, W. *et al.*, Artificial intelligence for drug discovery: Resources, methods, and applications. *Mol. Therapy-Nucleic Acids*, 31, 691–702, 2023.
11. Chen, X. *et al.*, EGBMMDA: Extreme gradient boosting machine for MiRNA-disease association prediction. *Cell Death Dis.*, 9, 1, 3, 2018.
12. Chin, L. and Khozin, S., A digital highway for data fluidity and data equity in precision medicine. *Biochim. Biophys. Acta (BBA)-Reviews Cancer*, 1876, 1, 188575, 2021.
13. Dara, S. *et al.*, Machine learning in drug discovery: A review. *Artif. Intell. Rev.*, 55, 3, 1947–1999, 2022.
14. Ebrahimian, S. *et al.*, FDA-regulated AI algorithms: Trends, strengths, and gaps of validation studies. *Acad. Radiol.*, 29, 4, 559–566, 2022.
15. Frank, E. *et al.*, Naive Bayes for regression. *Mach. Learn.*, 41, 5–25, 2000.
16. Gaudelet, T. *et al.*, Utilizing graph machine learning within drug discovery and development, in: *Briefings in Bioinformatics*, vol. 22, p. 159, 2021.
17. Geetha, M., Manikandan, P., Jerome, J., Soft computing techniques based optimal tuning of virtual feedback PID controller for chemical tank reactor, in: *2014 IEEE Congress on Evolutionary Computation (CEC)*, pp. 1922–1928, IEEE, 2014.
18. Geetha, M. *et al.*, Real-time implementation and performance analysis of two dimension PID fuzzy controller for continuous stirred tank reactor, in: *2013 Fourth International Conference on Computing, Communications and Networking Technologies (ICCCNT)*, pp. 1–5, IEEE, 2013.
19. Ghildiyal, S., Mani, G., Nersisson, R., Electromyography pattern- recognition based prosthetic limb control using various machine learning techniques. *J. Med. Eng. Technol.*, 46, 5, 370–377, 2022.
20. Gunn, S.R. *et al.*, Support vector machines for classification and regression. *ISIS Tech. Rep.*, 14, 1, 5–16, 1998.

21. Gupta, R. *et al.*, Artificial intelligence to deep learning: Machine intelligence approach for drug discovery. *Mol. Divers.*, 25, 1315–1360, 2021.

22. Haddouchi, M. and Berrado, A., A survey of methods and tools used for interpreting random forest, in: *2019 1st International Conference on Smart Systems and Data Science (ICSSD)*, pp. 1–6, IEEE, 2019.

23. Hammann, F. *et al.*, Prediction of adverse drug reactions using decision tree modeling. *Clin. Pharmacol. Ther.*, 88, 52–59, 2010.

24. Harrison, P.J. *et al.*, Deep-learning models for lipid nanoparticle-based drug delivery. *Nanomedicine*, 16, 1097–1110, 2021.

25. He, J. *et al.*, The practical implementation of artificial intelligence technologies in medicine. *Nat. Med.*, 25, 30–36, 2019.

26. What is a Neural Network?, 2023. https://www.tibco.com/https://www.tibco.comreference-center/what-is-a-neural-network (accessed June 10, 2023).

27. Hwang, T.J., Kesselheim, A.S., Vokinger, K.N., Lifecycle regulation of artificial intelligence– and machine learning–based software devices in medicine. *JAMA*, 322, 2285–2286, 2019.

28. Ilmudeen, A. and Nayyar, A., Novel designs of smart healthcare systems: Technologies, architecture, and applications, in: *Machine Learning for Critical Internet of Medical Things: Applications and Use Cases*, pp. 125–151, Springer, Springer Cham, Germany, 2022.

29. Keiser, M.J. *et al.*, Predicting new molecular targets for known drugs. *Nature*, 462, 175–181, 2009.

30. Kleinbaum, D.G. *et al.*, *Logistic Regression*, Germany, 2002.

31. Koshiyama, A., Firoozye, N., Treleaven, P., Algorithms in future capital markets, *ICAIF '20: Proceedings of the First ACM International Conference on AI in Finance*, 1–8, 2020. Available at SSRN 3527511.

32. Kumar, A. *et al.*, A novel smart healthcare design, simulation, and implementation using healthcare 4.0 processes. *IEEE Access*, 8, 118433–118471, 2020.

33. LaValley, M.P., Logistic regression. *Circulation*, 117, 18, 2395–2399, 2008.

34. Lavecchia, A., Machine-learning approaches in drug discovery: Methods and applications. *Drug Discov. Today*, 20, 3, 318–331, 2015.

35. Lee, I. and Nam, H., DeepConv-DTI: Prediction of drug-target interactions via deep learning with convolution on protein sequences. *PLoS Comput. Biol.*, 15, 6, 1007129, 2019.

36. Leelananda, S.P. and Lindert, S., Computational methods in drug discovery. *Beilstein J. Organic Chem.*, 12, 1, 2694–2718, 2016.

37. Lenhof, K. *et al.*, Simultaneous regression and classification for drug sensitivity prediction using an advanced random forest method. *Sci. Rep.*, 12, 1, 13458, 2022.

38. Mahapatra, B., Krishnamurthi, R., Nayyar, A., Healthcare models and algorithms for privacy and security in healthcare records, in: *Security and Privacy of Electronic Healthcare Records: Concepts, Paradigms and Solutions*, p. 183, 2019.

39. Maltarollo, V.G. *et al.*, Advances with support vector machines for novel drug discovery. *Expert Opin. Drug Discov.*, 14, 1, 23–33, 2019.

40. Mani, G., Viswanadhapalli, J.K., Sriramalakshmi, P., AI powered IoT based real-time air pollution monitoring and forecasting. *J. Physics: Conf. Ser.*, 2115, 1, 012016, 2021.

41. Manikandan, P., Geetha, M., Jerome, J., Weighted fuzzy fault tolerant model predictive control, in: *2014 IEEE International Conference on Fuzzy Systems (FUZZ- IEEE)*, pp. 83–90, IEEE, 2014.

42. Manikandan, P. *et al.*, Real-time implementation and performance analysis of an intelligent fuzzy logic controller for level process, in: *2013 Fourth International Conference on Computing, Communications and Networking Technologies (ICCCNT)*, pp. 1–6, IEEE, 2013.

43. Mayr, A. *et al.*, DeepTox: Toxicity prediction using deep learning. *Front. Environ. Sci.*, 3, 80, 2016.

44. Miller, M.A., Chemical database techniques in drug discovery. *Nat. Rev. Drug Discov.*, 1, 3, 220–227, 2002.

45. Natekin, A. and Knoll, A., Gradient boosting machines, a tutorial. *Front. Neurorobotics*, 7, 21, 2013.

46. Nayyar, A., Gadhavi, L., Zaman, N., Machine learning in healthcare: Review, opportunities and challenges. *Mach. Learn. Internet Med. Things Healthcare*, 7, 23–45, 2021.

47. Pandiyan, M., Jayakumar, S., Sivaraman, N., Indian Patent, India, 2020, IN201841047826.

48. Pandiyan, M., Jayakumar, S., Sivaraman, N., Indian Patent, India, 2020, IN 201841024297.

49. Pandiyan, M. and Mani, G., Embedded low power analog CMOS fuzzy logic controller chip for industrial applications, in: *2015 IFIP/IEEE International Conference on Very Large Scale Integration (VLSI-SoC)*, pp. 43–48, IEEE, 2015.

50. Pandiyan, M. and Mani, G., Takagi Sugeno fuzzy expert model based soft fault diagnosis for two tank interacting system. *Arch. Control Sci.*, 24, 3, 271–287, 2014.

51. Pandiyan, M. and Mani, G., Wearable ECG SoC for wireless body area networks: implementation with fuzzy decision making chip, in: *VLSI-SoC: Design for Reliability, Security, and Low Power: 23rd IFIP WG 10.5/IEEE International Conference on Very Large Scale Integration, VLSI-SoC 2015*, Daejeon, Korea, October 5-7, 2015, pp. 67–86, Springer, 2016, Revised Selected Papers.

52. Patel, J. and Patel, A., Artificial neural networking in controlled drug delivery, in: *Artificial Neural Network for Drug Design, Delivery and Disposition*, pp. 195–218, 2016.

53. Pramanik, P.K.D., Pareek, G., Nayyar, A., Security and privacy in remote healthcare: Issues, solutions, and standards, in: *Telemedicine Technologies: Big Data, Deep Learning, Robotics, Mobile and Remote Applications for Global Healthcare*, pp. 201–225, 2019.

54. Priestley, M., O'Donnell, F., Simperl, E., A survey of data quality requirements that matter in ML development pipelines. *ACM J. Data Inf. Qual.*, 15, 2, 1–39, 2023.

55. Prokhorenkova, L. *et al.*, CatBoost: Unbiased boosting with categorical features. *Adv. Neural Inf. Process. Syst.*, 31, 2018, 2017.

56. Murphy, K.P., *Machine learning, a probabilistic perspective*, Taylor & Francis, MIT Press, United States, 2014.

57. Sahu, M. *et al.*, Artificial intelligence and machine learning in precision medicine: A paradigm shift in big data analysis. *Prog. Mol. Biol. Trans. Sci.*, 190, 1, 57–100, 2022.

58. Santa Maria Jr., J.P., Wang, Y., Camargo, L.M., Perspective on the challenges and opportunities of accelerating drug discovery with artificial intelligence. *Front. Bioinf.*, 3, 1121591, 2023.

59. Schapire, R.E., Explaining adaboost, in: *Empirical Inference: Festschrift in Honor of Vladimir N. Vapnik*, pp. 37–52, 2013.

60. Schölkopf, B. *et al.*, New support vector algorithms. *Neural Comput.*, 12, 5, 1207–1245, 2000.

61. Schöning, V. and Hammann, F., How far have decision tree models come for data mining in drug discovery? *Expert Opin. Drug Discov.*, 13, 12, 1067–1069, 2018.

62. Serov, N. and Vinogradov, V., Artificial intelligence to bring nanomedicine to life. *Adv. Drug Deliv. Rev.*, 184, 114194, 2022.

63. Shaikhina, T. *et al.*, Decision tree and random forest models for outcome prediction in antibody incompatible kidney transplantation. *Biomed. Signal Process. Control*, 52, 456–462, 2019.

64. Sharma, K., Singh, H., Sharma, D.K., Kumar, A., Nayyar, A., Krishnamurthi, R., Dynamic models and control techniques for drone delivery of medications and other healthcare items in COVID-19 hotspots, in: *Emerging Technologies for Battling Covid-19: Applications and Innovations*, pp. 1–34, 2021.

65. Shen, M. *et al.*, Development and validation of k-nearest-neighbor QSPR models of metabolic stability of drug candidates. *J. Med. Chem.*, 46, 14, 3013–3020, 2003.

66. Smola, A.J. and Schölkopf, B., A tutorial on support vector regression. *Stat Comput.*, 14, 199–222, 2004.

67. Sperandei, S., Understanding logistic regression analysis. *Biochemia Med.*, 24, 1, 12–18, 2014.

68. Sutariya, V. *et al.*, Artificial neural network in drug delivery and pharmaceutical research. *Open Bioinf. J.*, 7, 1, 49–62, 2013.

69. Swain, P.H. and Hauska, H., The decision tree classifier: Design and potential. *IEEE Trans. Geosci. Electron.*, 15, 3, 142–147, 1977.

70. Talevi, A. *et al.*, Machine learning in drug discovery and development part 1: A primer. *CPT: Pharmacometrics & Syst. Pharmacol.*, 9, 3, 129–142, 2020.

71. Trafton, A., Artificial intelligence yields new antibiotic, https://news.mit.edu/2020/artificial -intelligence-identifies-new-antibiotic-0220.2020 (accessed June 10, 2023).

72. Tripathi, N. *et al.*, Applications of artificial intelligence to drug design and discovery in the big data era: A comprehensive review. *Mol. Divers.*, 25, 3, 1643–1664, 2021.

73. Vamathevan, J. *et al.*, Applications of machine learning in drug discovery and development. *Nat. Rev. Drug Discovery*, 18, 6, 463–477, 2019.

74. Vo, A.H., Van Vleet, T. R., Gupta, R. R., Liguori, M. J., Rao, M. S. An overview of machine learning and big data for drug toxicity evaluation. *Chem. Res. Toxicol.*, 33, 1, 20–37, 2019.

75. Wang, A.X., Chukova, S.S., Nguyen, B.P., Ensemble k-nearest neighbors based on centroid displacement. *Inf. Sci.*, 629, 313–323, 2023.

76. Webb, G., II, Keogh, E., Miikkulainen, R., Naïve Bayes, in: *Encyclopedia of machine learning*, vol. 15, pp. 713–714, 2010.

77. Yang, Z. *et al.*, ML-DTI: mutual learning mechanism for interpretable drug–target interaction prediction. *J. Phys. Chem. Lett.*, 12, 17, 4247–4261, 2021.

78. Zhang, L. *et al.*, Applications of machine learning methods in drug toxicity prediction. *Curr. Topics Med. Chem.*, 18, 12, 987–997, 2018.

79. Zhang, L. *et al.*, From machine learning to deep learning: Progress in machine intelligence for rational drug discovery. *Drug Discovery Today*, 22, 11, 1680–1685, 2017.

80. Zohuri, B. and Behgounia, F., Application of artificial intelligence driving nanobased drug delivery system, in: *A Handbook of Artificial Intelligence in Drug Delivery*, pp. 145–212, Elsevier, Netherlands, 2023.

5

Artificial Intelligence for Understanding Mechanisms of Antimicrobial Resistance and Antimicrobial Discovery: A New Age Model for Translational Research

Yashaswi Dutta Gupta and Suman Bhandary*

Department of Biological Sciences, School of Life Science and Biotechnology, Adamas University, Kolkata, West Bengal, India

Abstract

Antimicrobial resistance (AMR) presents an escalating global health crisis, characterized by bacteria's growing resistance to conventional antibiotics. Understanding AMR mechanisms and developing innovative antimicrobials demand harnessing powerful tools such as artificial intelligence (AI) as potent solutions for this crisis. The chapter's primary objective is to underscore AI's battle against AMR *via* a twofold analysis—by highlighting AI's predictive potential in deciphering factors that foster AMR proliferation and outlining emerging prospects like AI-empowered diagnostic tools and AI-optimized personalized treatment strategies. We aim to critically assess diverse AI methodologies in demonstrating their efficacy in deciphering extensive bacterial genetic datasets. Along with AI's predictive powers for estimating the likelihood of drug resistance, it enables the identification of previously unidentified targets for antimicrobial action. This chapter meticulously merges an exploration of AI techniques with their practical deployment, furnishing a panoramic view of the field's present landscape and underlining AI's burgeoning role in combating AMR. In addition to assessing the current state, we also aim to review and identify the future areas of potential research in this field. Ultimately, this chapter accentuates AI's capacity as a cornerstone in ongoing efforts to mitigate AMR's impact, transcending boundaries and catalyzing a transformative shift in healthcare approaches.

Keywords: Artificial intelligence, antimicrobial resistance, machine learning, diagnostic tool, antibiotic discovery, biofilm

5.1 Introduction

Antimicrobial resistance (AMR) refers to the phenomenon where microorganisms such as bacteria, viruses, fungi, and parasites develop the ability to withstand the effects of drugs that were previously able to effectively treat infections caused by these organisms [1].

Corresponding author: suman_bhandary@yahoo.co.in

Abhirup Khanna, May El Barachi, Sapna Jain, Manoj Kumar and Anand Nayyar (eds.) Artificial Intelligence and Machine Learning in Drug Design and Development, (117–156) © 2024 Scrivener Publishing LLC

This happens when the microorganisms undergo evolutionary changes that enable them to defend themselves against antimicrobial agents, making the drugs less effective or even completely ineffective [2]. With bacteria exhibiting mounting resistance to conventional antibiotics, antimicrobial resistance (AMR) poses an escalating global health challenge [3]. Apart from rendering previously effective treatments unproductive, AMR can significantly increase morbidity, mortality, and healthcare costs [4].

AMR is caused by several factors, including misuse of antimicrobial agents, inadequate infection prevention and control measures, and the natural ability of microorganisms to adapt and evolve [2]. The discovery of new antimicrobial agents is critical to fighting AMR and providing effective treatment options [5]. However, traditional trial-and-error approaches in antimicrobial discovery is beleaguered by mounting challenges such as the rising rates of AMR, escalating costs of antimicrobial discovery with diminishing rates of success, and extremely prolonged timelines of drug discovery [6]. As the urgency to combat AMR rises rapidly, the demand for developing innovative strategies to combat AMR becomes evident [7].

The scope of this problem is vast, with AMR threatening to undermine many of the advances made in modern medicine. It is estimated that by 2050, AMR could result in 10 million deaths per year and cost the global economy up to $100 trillion [8]. In addition to its impact on human health, AMR also has significant implications for animal health and food security [9]. To address this challenge, there is a need for coordinated action at the global level. This includes efforts to reduce the overuse and misuse of antibiotics, promote the development of new antimicrobial agents, and improve the surveillance and monitoring of AMR [10]. There is also a need for increased investment in research and development to better understand the mechanisms underlying AMR and develop new strategies for combating drug-resistant bacteria.

The problem at hand is twofold: First, there is a need to enhance our understanding of AMR mechanisms in order to develop more effective strategies for combating drug-resistant bacteria [11]. Second, there is a pressing need for the discovery of new antimicrobial agents to replenish the dwindling arsenal of effective antibiotics [12]. Amid this landscape, artificial intelligence (AI) has emerged as a potent tool, offering solutions to these pressing challenges. AI has the potential to address both of these challenges by providing new insights into AMR mechanisms and accelerating the discovery of novel antimicrobial compounds. However, realizing this potential will require the development and application of advanced AI methodologies. In addition to these challenges, there are also broader issues related to AMR that need to be addressed. These include the need for improved stewardship of existing antibiotics to ensure their continued effectiveness as well as efforts to reduce the spread of drug-resistant infections through improved infection control practices [13, 14].

The application of machine learning technology in the healthcare domain can assist medical practitioners by providing faster and more accurate solutions [15]. In this chapter we aim to assess how AI algorithms such as machine learning, deep learning, etc., play a pivotal role in understanding the mechanisms of AMR to enable the analysis of vast genomic datasets to provide insights to the elusive mechanisms of AMR emergence [16]. This chapter also attempts to shed light on the applications of AI in offering a treasure trove of strategies to overcome antibiotic resistance. We shall delve into the vast arsenal of AI-powered solutions from predicting AMR patterns to optimizing treatment regimens [17]. By integrating genetic and clinical data, AI models can predict the regulation of AMR and guide clinicians towards more precise and informed treatment decisions. Optimizing antibiotics and potential drug combinations also substantiate the ability of AI and the promise it holds in tackling multi-drug-resistant pathogens [18]. Since the incorporation of AI has unprecedented potential for improving patient care, we shall aim to highlight the importance of AI in augmenting the antibiotic stewardship programs to minimize the risks of the emergence of AMR [19, 20]. In essence, this chapter puts into the spotlight the use of AI in understanding the mechanisms of antimicrobial resistance and antimicrobial discovery to revolutionize translational research by providing valuable insights, accelerating the development of new therapies, and enabling precision medicine approaches to combat the growing threat of AMR.

Objectives of the Chapter

Utilizing cutting-edge computational techniques to address the complex challenges posed by AMR and speed up the process of discovering new antimicrobial agents are the goals of using AI to understand the mechanisms of AMR and antimicrobial discovery.

The specific objectives of this chapter are to:

(a) Utilize artificial intelligence in the analysis of various data sources, such as genomics, proteomics, and metabolomics data, to elucidate the molecular mechanisms behind antibiotic resistance;

(b) Create AI-driven algorithms to find associations and trends in large, complex datasets pertaining to AMR;

(c) Create AI-driven prediction models to forecast the establishment and spread of antibiotic resistance;

(d) Use artificial intelligence (AI) techniques to examine microbial genomes and proteomes to find new therapeutic targets;

(e) Apply AI algorithms to optimize the design of antimicrobial compounds, including changing chemical structures to increase the efficacy and reduce the likelihood of resistance development;

(f) Use AI algorithms to optimize the virtual screening of large chemical libraries for potential antimicrobial compounds;

(g) And, to facilitate the translation of AI-driven findings into clinical practice and public health policies.

Organization of the Chapter

The rest of the chapter is organized as follows: Section 5.2 elaborates on the commonly used artificial intelligence algorithms for AMR. Section 5.3 illustrates AI for understanding the mechanisms of AMR and antimicrobial discovery. Section 5.4 highlights the strategies to overcome antibiotic resistance. Section 5.5 focuses on the applications of artificial intelligence for antimicrobial resistance, followed by Section 5.6 which covers the challenges towards practical implementation, and finally, Section 5.7 concludes the chapter with future scope.

5.2 Commonly Used Artificial Intelligence Algorithms for AMR

To combat AMR, AI is implemented in developing algorithms that can be used to analyze large datasets of genomic data and biochemical datasets and perform an efficient analysis of data conferred from clinical studies and trials, all of which can be used to identify discrete or emerging patterns of AMR. There are many different AI algorithms that are used to understand the underlying principles of AMR such as machine learning (ML) algorithms like naïve Bayes (NB), decision trees (DT), random forests (RF), and support vector machines (SVM) and deep learning (DL) algorithms such as artificial neural networks (ANN) [21].

AI algorithms based on predictive modeling are crucial in identifying and anticipating AMR patterns. These algorithms employ ML algorithms such as SVMs and RFs to discern hidden relationships between genetic variations, virulence factors, and drug resistance [22]. This method of predictive modeling enables researchers to forecast the emergence of AMR strains and take proactive measures. Genomic data is also a crucial factor in unraveling the genetic basis of AMR. AI algorithms can be designed to facilitate whole-genome analysis to identify resistance-conferring mutations and specific genes associated with AMR [23]. This would enable researches to tailor therapeutic interventions based on genetic susceptibility in order to achieve maximum treatment efficacy. AI algorithms can speed up the slow and costly traditional drug discovery methods by simulating how potential drug candidates interact with bacterial targets. Techniques such as virtual screening, molecular docking simulations, and deep learning-based approaches can identify compounds that bind strongly to drug-resistant targets [24]. This can lead to the faster discovery of new antibiotics, providing a stronger defense against evolving resistant strains [25]. A few examples of the implementation of AI algorithms to combat AMR are as follows:

    i.   Naïve Bayes (NB): It is a probabilistic ML algorithm that can be used to predict the likelihood of the occurrence of an event [26]. NB is based on Bayes' theorem, which describes the relationship between the probability of an event occurring given some evidence and the probability of the evidence given the event [27]. In the context of AMR, NB can be used to calculate the probability of a bacterial strain developing resistance to an antibiotic given its genetic makeup and other relevant factors [28]. NB algorithms can also predict the probability of bacterial infection and the likelihood of occurrence of AMR. This prediction can be used to tailor a more empirical method of prescribing antibiotic therapy, which, in a clinical setting, holds potential to reduce incidences of AMR in patients [29].

   ii.   Decision trees (DT): These are powerful machine learning algorithms that can be used for classification and regression tasks, including identifying patterns and relationships between variables [30]. DT is a supervised ML algorithm for regression and classification analysis. DT follows a set of if–else conditions to predict an output based on the condition parameters. DTs work by recursively partitioning the data into subsets based on the values of the input features, with the goal of maximizing the separation between the different classes [31]. DTs can be used to combat AMR by providing a framework for evaluating treatment strategies and making informed decisions about antibiotic usage. In a study by Voermans *et al.*, [32] the use of a decision-analytics framework to evaluate the use of a procalcitonin (PCT)-guided algorithm for antibiotic stewardship was employed. The study focused on the clinical and economic outcomes of treatment strategies while considering the costs of hospital charges and antibiotic therapies and the outcome of potential benefits if antibiotic usage was reduced. Such a model can be implemented in clinical settings to calculate the costs of effective treatments and probabilities of each outcome, providing a cost-effective analysis for hospitals to make informed decision regarding allocating resources and funds for treatments with maximum efficiency while mitigating the risks of the emergence of AMR.

iii. Random forests (RF): RFs are an extension of DTs that build multiple trees and combine their predictions to improve accuracy and reduce overfitting. In an RF model, the algorithm constructs a forest based on a set of DTs [33]. RF algorithms are robust ML algorithms as they provide more accurate features for data selection and handling high-dimension datasets [34]. By training RFs on large datasets of bacterial genomes and their corresponding antibiotic resistance profiles, researchers can identify genetic markers associated with resistance and use this information to guide the antibiotic treatment regime for reducing the chances of AMR relapse [35]. RF algorithms can also be used to identify potential antibiotic combination therapies against different strains of bacteria. The RF models, by combining genomic and chemical information, can predict the efficiency of proposed antibiotic combinations [36]. This approach can help minimize the risks of AMR by identifying effective combination therapies that target multiple mechanisms of resistance, reducing the likelihood of bacteria developing resistance to any single antibiotic. By using RF algorithms to guide the development of new combination therapies, researchers can potentially improve treatment outcomes and reduce the spread of antibiotic-resistant infections.

iv. Support vector machines (SVM): It is another popular algorithm for classification and regression tasks. SVMs work by finding the hyperplane that maximally separates the different classes in the data. This hyperplane is defined by a subset of the training examples called support vectors, which lie closest to the decision boundary [37]. By training SVMs on large datasets of bacterial genomes and their corresponding antibiotic resistance profiles, researchers can identify genetic markers associated with AMR. SVM models have been used in AMR studies by scanning the whole genomic sequences of microbes to predict the phenotypes responsible for AMR [23] and predict the emergence of AMR based on genomic data [38].

v. Deep learning (DL): Deep learning is a branch of machine learning that focuses on creating models and solutions for challenging issues using artificial neural networks (ANN). It draws ideas from the way that neurons work together in the human brain to process and send information. These ANNs used in DL are made up of numerous layers of connected nodes (neurons) that gradually retrieve higher-level attributes from the input data [39].

Huge volumes of biological and chemical data can be analyzed by DL algorithms to find potential new drug candidates. It helps speed up the drug discovery process by discovering compounds with antibacterial characteristics and predicting the interactions between molecules. DL algorithms can be developed for the possibility that a certain bacteria will become resistant to a particular drug. This can aid healthcare professionals in making better-informed decisions regarding the administration of antibiotics and therapeutic approaches. By training ANNs on large datasets of bacterial genomes and their corresponding antibiotic resistance profiles, researchers can identify complex patterns and relationships between genetic markers and antibiotic resistance. This information can then be used to guide the development of new antibiotics that target these specific resistance mechanisms [25]. DL models can quickly detect the existence of drug-resistant microbes by examining data from diagnostic tests, such as DNA sequencing or gene expression analyses [16]. This may result in more personalized as well as effective plans for therapy.

5.3   AI for Understanding Mechanisms of AMR and Antimicrobial Discovery

Traditional approaches to uncover the underlying mechanism of AMR and antimicrobial discovery have been inadequate due to several limitations. To overcome these limitations, AI has emerged as a promising contender as it can analyze large datasets with great efficiency and identify patterns and relationships in data which may not be apparent to the human eye.

5.3.1   Understanding the Mechanisms of AMR

The important intrinsic factors that influence the development of AMR include antimicrobial ineffectiveness, microbial physiology impeding drug–target interactions, mutations in microbes, genotypic and phenotypic alterations in microorganisms, etc. [22]. It may be apparent that many of these changes may go unnoticed by the human eye; this is where AI steps in. AI and ML techniques pose an optimism stance in bridging the gap that may help us understand the mechanistic principles and discrepancies that confer the occurrence of AMR.

Few ML methods have been developed where researchers have studied how microbial cells react to antimicrobial drugs and then used ML algorithms based on this data to create models and algorithm frameworks to train antimicrobial classifiers—for instance, an ML model named MorphEUS was developed; it used high-throughput fluorescence microscopy to study the morphological profiling based on the action of antimicrobial agents [40]. MorphEUS rapidly characterized the mechanistic cellular pathways of drug action based on the morphological changes of the microbial cell. The algorithm was based on k-nearest neighbor analysis of the drug profiles. Algorithms like MorphEUS can be developed for mutant microbial strains with known drug resistance to study the mechanisms of drug activity on different cellular pathways of the strain. This could be potentially helpful in identifying novel pathways with potential to bypass the AMR. Deep and sophisticated scanning of the microbial sequences can be performed using AI and ML approaches to find genotypic and phenotypic changes that may result in the development of AMR. Genome sequencing is a cost-effective method of extracting genome data from drug-resistant strains of microbes [41]. To design models for these evaluations, WGS data is first collected based on clinical data available in WGS databases. The WGS data consists of genetic information of normal, resistant as well as susceptible isolates of microbes. Important features regarding genetic variations, feature alleles, etc., are then extracted, which act as reference features in training ML models [42, 43]. After training these models on ML frameworks, the data is then tested against test data or unknown data to validate the performance efficiency of the ML model. Various evaluation metrics can also be used to investigate the efficiency of the test output [44]. ML algorithms like logistic regression (LR), support vector machine (SVM), random forest (RF), and convolutional neural network (CNN) were investigated to predict AMR in *Escherichia coli* for four different antibiotics [42]. By leveraging the genetically encoded data evaluated by whole-genome sequencing (WGS), the authors reported that their models could effectively predict AMR without the prior required knowledge of AMR genes in the microbial strain. This study demonstrated the ability of models based on WGS methods to efficiently predict AMR genes. Another classifier named metabolic allele classifier (MAC), which implemented the use of WGS to determine AMR based on the analysis of genetic factors, was also evaluated [45]. Based on the genotypic and phenotypic data of *Mycobacterium tuberculosis*, the authors trained a machine learning model to accurately predict AMR phenotypes and interpretable biochemical aspects such as involvement of metabolic pathways to provide an insight of the underlying mechanistic principles of AMR. Implementation of a ML model in genome-wide studies such as this can be successful in providing accurate and precise insights into the phenotypic variations that lead to AMR as well as an understanding of the biochemical principles such as the metabolic pathways involved in regulating the mechanistic principles of AMR.

5.3.2 AI for Antimicrobial Discovery

AI and applied ML models can play crucial roles in accelerating pharmaceutical research by aiding in antimicrobial discovery. ML models can be applied to investigate new drug targets, design novel drug molecules, repurpose drug, optimize existing formulations, etc. [46].

5.3.2.1 Targeting and Validation of Potential Targets

It is the first and a significantly important step in identifying potential molecules or cellular components in microbes that are associated in regulating crucial pathways in disease progression and can be targeted by potential drug candidates [47]. Potential targets can be identified with the help of a plethora of genomic, proteomic, and clinical data from databases available online. Genomic data analysis can provide ample information of potential genes or proteins that are associated with a particular disease or its role in regulating the critical metabolic pathways of a disease [48]. ML algorithms can subsequently be employed to find patterns in genomic data that may be relevant in the discovery of antimicrobial agents to control the progression of a particular disease. Gene expression is a highly reliable approach to creating a ML model that screens genomic data. This analysis investigates the regulation of genes in normal and diseased states to provide a comparative analysis of both. Network-based ML models can be based on the genetic data provided by the screening to identify key protein or metabolic pathway data that are critical in disease progression [49]. ML models must be developed in a way that may further validate the target data obtained after prospective targets have been identified. To determine if a target is likely to have a specific ailment, AI models must effectively cross-validate the target data. A group of researchers designed an ML model that predicted disease-associated genes which could be potential drug targets based on genomic data and system analysis [50]. The ML-based approach included a range of data, including gene expression profiles, protein–protein interaction profiles, and others to predict the likelihood of druggable vs. non-druggable targets and morbid vs. normal genes. The authors also cross-validated the ML model to substantiate its robustness by training and testing multiple subsets of the data. This paper demonstrates the efficiency of ML-based frameworks in target identification and validation. Table 5.1 presents a few examples of AI models that have been incorporated to predict AMR genes based on the analysis of microbial genomic data.

Table 5.1 AI models employed for predicting AMR genes.

ML-based model	Purpose and application	Reference
DeepARG	Scans metagenomic data to predict AMR genes using deep learning	[43]
AntiSMASH	Predicts biosynthetic gene clusters of secondary metabolites in bacterial and fungal genomes using SVM, HMM, pHMM	[51]
Resistance Gene Identifier (RGI)	Predicts antibiotic resistomes from protein or nucleotide data based on homology and SNP models using HMM	[52]
ResFinder	Identification of acquired antimicrobial resistance genes in whole-genome using BLAST sequence analysis	[53]
ArgANNOT	Predicts existing and novel AMR genes in bacterial genomes using BLAST sequence analysis	[54]
PRGPred	Predicts domains of resistance gene analogues using SVMs	[55]
Meta-MARC	Predicts of diverse antimicrobial resistance sequences using hierarchical, DNA-based hidden Markov models	[56]
MEGAResand AMR++	Classifies resistome sequences directly from FASTA using k-mer-based metagenomic classifier	[57]
ARGMiner	Analyzes all of the information available from several AMR gene databases and provides information on potential AMR genes carried by pathogens using RF algorithm	[58]

5.3.2.2   Drug Repurposing

Drug repurposing is a cost-effective method to re-use pre-approved drugs for new interventions in disease control. Making a new pharmaceutical drug or antimicrobial agent would take years of research and a large, long-term investment. AI can be of potential aid in accelerating antimicrobial discovery by effectively finding means to repurpose drugs [59]. Prasad and Kumar [60] highlighted the potential of AI and ML-based approaches in repurposing drugs for SARS-CoV-2. The authors initially highlighted the importance of available databases such as genomic data, clinical data, protein, and structural data, all of which can be screened by AI algorithms to find potential targets involved in regulating SARS-CoV-2. ML algorithms can be used to analyze these large datasets, and based on known drug–target interactions or protein data, the algorithms can be used to identify subtle patterns to predict novel targets or drug–target interactions. Authors also discussed the importance of AI programs in virtual screening such as being able to perform molecular docking and molecular dynamic simulations [60]. As new targets are identified, these virtual screening approaches can be used to evaluate binding affinity or simulate the drug–target interactions virtually to evaluate the efficiency of the predicted datasets. AI approaches such as homology modeling, molecular dynamics, and protein structure prediction can be used to aid in drug-repurposing studies to identify potential drugs or drug–targets that may be helpful in regulating the disease progression.

In retrospect, the research paper [60] also provides a practical insight into a critical and concerning topic that anomalies like a global pandemic may occur at any point of time in the future. It is apparent that, during an emergency to tackle a global pandemic like SARS-CoV-2, creating a novel drug having negligible side effects in a very short span of time is next to impossible. AI here can play an important role as a first line of defense in repurposing existing drugs to combat a new disease.

5.3.2.3   Novel Antimicrobial Peptide (AMP) Discovery

AI plays a critical role in *de novo* drug and peptide discovery as ML models can be made to generate novel compounds to accelerate antimicrobial discovery. AI algorithms can predict chemical structures that may exhibit antimicrobial activity similar to known structures of antimicrobial agents. This approach may aid in exploring a vast and potentially untapped chemical avenue to create novel antimicrobial compounds to overcome existing antimicrobial resistance mechanisms [61]. AMPs are highly valuable therapeutic candidates to combat antimicrobial resistant microbes [62]—for instance, a novel deep-learning model, DEEP-AmPEP30, was developed to enhance the prediction accuracy of short-length AMPs [63]. The DEEP-AmPEP30 model was trained on a comprehensive dataset of known AMPs. Based on the data, the AI model assessed the discriminative patterns present in the AMPs using data from amino acid compositions, peptides, physicochemical data, and evolutionary data. Appropriate training and cross-validation algorithms were employed to substantiate the robustness of the AI model. Yan *et al.* [63] reported that DEEP-AmPEP30 was 77% more accurate than existing models in predicting AMPs with potential antimicrobial activity. The algorithm predicted a novel short AMP sequence with potency similar to that of ampicillin and strong antimicrobial activity against *Bacillus subtilis* and *Vibrio parahaemolyticus*. In another study by Porto *et al.* [64], ML models were incorporated to

Table 5.2 AI models employed for the discovery of antimicrobial peptides.

ML-based model	Purpose and application	Reference
Deep-AmPEP30	Predicts short length AMPs using data trained on reduced amino acids composition and convolutional neural network	[63]
AmPEP	Implements sequence-based analysis based on distribution patterns of amino acid properties and random forest algorithm to predict AMPs	[65]
Co-AMPpred	Incorporates composition-based sequence and physicochemical features to train feature selection model for predicting AMPs	[66]
AMPpred-EL	An ensemble learning model combined with LightGBM and logistic regression algorithms to efficiently predict AMPs	[67]
AMP-BERT	A deep learning model with an optimized di-directional encoder representations from transformers (BERT) to identify candidate AMPs for clinical research	[68]
Peptide Ranker	Uses algorithms like SVMs and RFs to predict the potency of AMPs	[69]
iAMPPred	Uses SVM algorithm to predict and identify AMPs	[70]

predict novel AMPs from guava. The AI model was trained to rapidly screen a vast variety of peptide sequences and predict the ones with potent antimicrobial activity. Using the AI model, authors were able to predict a novel AMP, Guavanin-2, which demonstrated potent antimicrobial activity against Gram-negative bacteria.

The potential of AI-based models in predicting novel AMPs can significantly confer potential in accelerating research in antimicrobial discovery in novel drug discovery. Table 5.2 provides examples of AI models for discovery of AMPs.

5.3.2.4   Optimizing Drug Formulations

AI models can be incorporated to optimize drug formulations in order to achieve maximum effectiveness from them. Based on data available on online databases regarding physicochemical properties of chemical compounds, structure, and stability of chemicals, etc., ML algorithms can predict the most suitable formulation for potent antimicrobial activity. Landin and Rowe [71] emphasized the use of ML algorithms such as artificial neural networks (ANN), genetic algorithms, and fuzzy logic to assist in optimizing drug formulations. Optimizing drug formulations can help researchers enhance the antimicrobial activity by targeting specific sites, increasing the bioavailability, and having a prolonged release, all of which can assist in improving the therapeutic efficacy of the antimicrobial drug.

5.4   Strategies to Overcome Antibiotic Resistance

The rampant over-use of antibiotics had led to a global rise in antibiotic resistance at an alarming level. Lack of advancing pharmaceutical research to combat this threat poses a major challenge in the pipeline for the discovery of new antibiotics [72]. AI has been a revolutionary approach in accelerating the drug discovery process to overcome antibiotic resistance by predicting novel antibiotic molecules, *de novo* drug design, antimicrobial susceptibility testing, and improved diagnosis [73].

5.4.1   Discovering Novel Antibiotic Compounds

ML holds great potential in assisting the global fight against antibiotic resistance by predicting novel compounds with potent antimicrobial activity. AI and ML approaches can assist efficiently in all stages of drug discovery such as target identification and validation, feature selection of biomarkers, and clinical trials [74]. A ground-breaking testament to the feasibility of this concept was presented with the discovery of a novel antimicrobial compound using a ML-based approach by Stokes *et al.* [25]. Authors used a ML model based on neural molecular representations to predict antimicrobial compounds from a library of more than 107 million compounds. The model predicted a novel molecule, later named *halicin*, as a potent antimicrobial with a chemical structure different from that of existing antimicrobials. The molecule was also predicted to have low toxicity to humans. Authors tested halicin against multi-drug-resistant species like *Clostridium difficile*, *Acinetobacter baumannii*, and *Mycobacterium tuberculosis*. The novel molecule halicin showed potent antimicrobial activity against the three. To test its clinical efficacy, *in vivo* tests on mouse wound models of *Acinetobacter baumannii* were also performed as they have known AMR to all known antibiotics. The researchers found that a halicin-containing ointment was successfully able to clear out the *A. baumannii* infection within 24 h of topical application. A study for the development of AMR to halicin was also investigated. The authors found that *E. coli* did not develop resistance towards halicin after a 30-day treatment regime, but in contrast, *E. coli* developed resistance to a commonly used antibiotic ciprofloxacin within 1–3 days of treatment and developed a 200% increase in antibiotic resistance after 30 days. In a very recent publication from the Stokes Lab, authors discovered yet another new antibiotic capable of killing a deadly, drug-resistant superbug—*Acinetobacter baumannii*. The authors incorporated the use of ML models to scan and analyze a vast chemical space of 7,500 molecules to screen for those that inhibited the activity of *A. baumannii*. The dataset obtained from the growth inhibition results was used to train a neural network, leading to the discovery of *Abaucin*—a narrow-spectrum antibiotic compound with a potent antibacterial activity against A. *baumannii*. Further tests and research revealed that the antibiotic activity of *Abaucin* was attributed to the perturbation of lipoprotein trafficking through a mechanism involving LoIE. *In vivo* tests also validated the potency of *Abaucin* in controlling A. *baumannii* infection in a mouse wound model [75]. Both of these studies emphasize and highlight the imperative role AI plays in contributing to the urgent and pressing need of discovering novel antibiotics that humans on their own may not be able to achieve. As we have discussed in previous sections, the discovery of AMPs also holds great potential in combating antibiotic resistance. DL algorithms can be trained on a database of anti-microbial peptides with known antibiotic activity to predict novel peptide sequences [76]. Wu *et al.* [77] developed an AI model based on amino acid prediction titled "novel AMP" to perform quicker predictions for AMPs. The AI model was successfully able to predict a novel AMP molecule DP7 which showed a significantly potent antibiotic activity towards microbial as well as antibiotic-resistant strains. The DP7 AMP was also found to be less cytotoxic to human cells.

These studies highlight the importance of AI algorithms in the discovery of antibiotic molecules. This approach holds a promising optimism towards identifying novel antibiotic compounds to overcome antibiotic resistance to address the urgent need for new therapeutic options in the global combat against AMR.

5.4.2   Antibiotic Repurposing and Optimization

As discussed in the previous sections, apart from predicting new antibiotic compounds, AI algorithms can be used to screen existing antibiotics having potential as repurposed drugs for a different disease [59]. This can enable researchers to investigate alternate mechanisms of action which can be used to effectively treat antibiotic resistant bacteria. Based on the physicochemical properties of antibiotic drugs available in online databases, AI models can be trained to find patterns to optimize the drug formulation while minimizing the risks of antibiotic resistance [71]. By optimizing the pharmacokinetic properties of the drug, researchers will be able to improve the targeting to resistant bacteria and reduce the risks of emergence of new antibiotic resistance.

5.4.3   Optimization of Combinatorial Therapy

Combination therapy refers to the use of two or more combinations of different drugs to work synergistically to increase the therapeutic efficacy by targeting different disease pathways. Over the last few decades, combination therapy has been used widely to combat the growing antimicrobial resistance. Combination therapy in combating AMR has three variations: (a) different drug molecules inhibit different microbial pathways, (b) drug molecules inhibit different targets belonging to the same metabolic pathway, and (c) synergistic drug molecules inhibit the same metabolic pathway in different ways [78]. However, complications like drug–drug interactions and dose calculation need to be addressed alongside to ensure effective therapeutic outcomes and minimize AMR emergence [79]. Using different drug combinations may lead to harmful side effects and systemic toxicity. However, to efficiently screen potential drug combinations by conventional clinical techniques, it would take tedious hours of manual screening and data processing from results which are both difficult and expensive. The application of AI and ML algorithms can be incorporated to improve the therapeutic efficacy by comprehensive screening of potential drug combinations while reducing the risks of AMR [80].

ML-based approaches hold great potential combination therapy by addressing three problems: (a) predicting the sensitivity of the drug combination, (b) predicting the synergy of the drug combination, and (c) classifying the predicted drug synergy [81]. The ML-based prediction of the sensitivity of drug combinations allows researchers to predict the treatment response to different drug combinations. ML algorithms can predict the effectiveness of drug combinations based on clinical data available online. This can help develop novel combinations that can have various effective outcomes in treating different diseases. comboFM is an example of a ML model that predicts drug combination response cellular genome features and chemical descriptors of drug molecules from experimental data [82]. Predicting the synergy of drug combinations is a key in identifying the degree of the combined effect of the two drugs. ML algorithms can predict the drug combination synergy by comprehensively analyzing features from the chemical database of drugs and gene expression data. Deep neural network algorithms like DeepSynergy were among the first ML models to be developed for predicting drug combination synergy based on a model trained on a chemical and genomic database [83]. DECREASE is also a robust ML model that can predict both synergistic and antagonistic drug combinations by prediction of synergies from response values of drug dose. DECREASE is efficient in the prediction of antibacterial, antiviral, and antifungal drug combinations as well [84]. Predicting drug synergy classification uses ML-based methods which involve the comprehensive analysis of the chemical features of the drugs in combination to predict the potency of the combination. An amalgamation of genomic data of target proteins along with the data from the chemical space can potentially assist significantly in creating the best combination of drugs to treat a disease. SyDRa is a suitable example for this ML-based approach as SyDRa model is a RF algorithm trained to analyze the chemical structures of therapeutic compounds, target molecules, and pharmacogenomic data to predict an efficient drug combination [18]. These ML-based algorithms highlight how AI can be integrated with chemical and genomic data to predict effective and synergistic drug combinations.

In a research communication, a deep learning ML model, ComboNET, to predict synergistic drug combinations for Covid-19 was proposed [85]. The model was trained on graph convolutional network, drug–target interaction, to predict drug binding to target and the antiviral activity of single therapeutic agents to predict synergistic drug combinations to effectively treat SARS-Cov-2. The ComboNET model predicted two potent drug combinations—remdesivir + reserpine and remdesivir + IQ-1S—with both combinations having high *in vitro* activity with reduced risks of systemic toxicity for treating Covid-19. Another ML model, INDIGO, was developed to predict antibiotic drug combinations [36]. The model incorporated a framework based only on chemogenomic interactions to predict synergistic and antagonistic antibiotic combinations. The authors strongly believe that ML-based approaches such as INDIGO can drastically reduce the time it will take to discover clinically significant antibiotic combinations; being equipped with the genomic data can assist as well in targeting essential pathways to circumvent or suppress the development of AMR.

5.4.4 Strengthening the Antibiotic Stewardship Program

The term "stewardship" refers to the practices that safeguard valuable resources of a community. Most antibiotics that are given to patients who are not in the ICU are reported to be unnecessary and can also result in adverse side effects [86]. Antibiotic stewardship is a strategy to quantify and improve antibiotic prescription by clinicians and their usage by patients [87]. The optimum dosage and duration of using antibiotics is crucial not only to maximize effective infection treatment but also to protect patients from developing an antibiotic resistance [88]. The central aim of ASP is providing improved patient care which, in turn, results in a decrease in usage, quantity, and length of treatment with antibiotics [86]. A short-course antibiotic therapy approach for the patients suspected of ventilator-associated pneumonia was proposed, followed by reassessment of the patients to determine if sustained therapy is essential. This method reduced the usage of unnecessary antibiotic exposure to patients [89]. In another study, it was reported that randomized patients at a hospital received either physician-recommended standard care or an antibiotic treatment based on ASP. The patients in the ASP were reported as three times more likely to receive suitable antibiotic therapy as opposed to the other patients and that the patients under the ASP were two times more likely to recover from infection and were 80% less likely to have a treatment failure. In order to have successful antibiotic stewardship programs, there are seven key principles involved, which include the following: leadership commitment, a single leader responsible for outcomes, a single pharmacy leader, tracking of antibiotic use, regular reporting of antibiotic use and resistance, educating providers on use and resistance, and specific improvement interventions [86].

The empiric antibiotic prescribing which is the initial drug prescribed by clinicians is mostly an educated guesswork based on the pathogen and its susceptibility to different antibiotics. However, the testing and data accumulation may take several days, which delays the appropriate treatment period and could have adverse effects on the patient, which is why doctors often suggest antibiotics that have the ability to treat all possible pathogens. This decision by a physician might not be ideal as they end up suggesting broad spectrum antibiotics in cases where a narrow spectrum antibiotic would have been more effective. Therefore, AI and ML can help in antibiotic prescribing. Predictive analysis is based on individualized predictions and suggestions and by applying this strategy in the healthcare sector; predictive models can be trained using the electronic medical records to augment the accuracy and dependability of empiric antibiotic prescribing. AI models can be trained using statistical data to predict patient-specific information. Input of correct variables and appropriate training will help AI models to estimate real-time probabilities of infection quantitatively for individual patients also taking AMR into consideration—for example, at Stanford, an ML model was able to compare an initial empiric antibiotic prescribed at the beginning of infection with the final resistance profiles obtained. Using this ML model strategy will not only provide information on the scalpel narrow spectrum antibiotic to be given to the patient but will also improve stewardship and security [90]. In another study, a learning module was able to recognize patterns in the data linked with incorrect prescriptions. This learning module was also able to recognize patterns for inappropriate prescriptions that the baseline system was unable to predict [91]. The use of AI to predict AMR based on clinical datasets requires the model to be able to justify suitable reasons behind its predictions. An interpretable AI method that analyzes patterns in individual patient data to recognize features that contribute to AMR was also employed and evaluated. This strategy helps assess the credibility of the predictions [92]. Cai *et al.* [93] trained an ANN using microbiological and clinical statistics of women suffering from recurrent urinary tract infections (rUTIs) to predict the efficacy of empiric antimicrobial prescription. The ANN was able to predict clinical efficacy with a sensitivity and specificity of 87.8% and 97.3%, respectively. The neural network was able to recognize diverse variables that influenced the decision output of the ANN for different therapies, which proposes that ANN can be trained and used as a guide in antimicrobial stewardship [93]. Sethi *et al.* [19] developed a Bayesian network (BN) using AI models for antibiotic stewardship in a pediatric intensive care unit (PICU) which recognized antibiotic usage and resistance patterns and detected areas where the usage of antibiotics could be further improved.

5.5 Applications of Artificial Intelligence for Antimicrobial Resistance

So far, we have discussed some of the critical practices of incorporating AI for AMR such as discovery of novel antibacterial compounds, predicting novel AMPs with potent activity against bacteria, drug repurposing and optimization, personalized medicine, etc. Apart from predicting antibacterial compounds, AI also has foundations in combating antiviral, antifungal, and antiparasitic resistance. AI algorithms can also be trained for the surveillance of genomic data to predict AMR before it occurs, use existing clinical data for rapid diagnostics for AMR, and for vaccine development against AMR.

5.5.1 AI in Combating Antifungal Resistance

AI has the ability to effectively contest antifungal resistance by efficient detection and management of predicted resistance markers and fungal targets for resistance genes. As discussed in the previous sections, AI models can be modeled to perform deep scans of genomic or phenotypic data to predict antimicrobial resistance genes [42]. A similar model for pan-genomic analysis of fungal genes can be used to predict antifungal resistance. In a research study, an ML algorithm was developed to predict the resistance genes of an emerging, multi-drug-resistant fungus, *Candida auris* [94]. Li *et al.* [94] evaluated the ability of ML models trained on WGS data 358 strains of *Candida auris*. The ML classifiers then predicted the drug resistance models for *C. auris* against different antifungal drugs, evaluated on area under curve (AUC) values. A recursive feature elimination with cross-validation (RFECV) incorporated with a ML classifier was used to rank drug-resistant mutations in *C. auris*. In their overall findings, the authors reported that the ML model could accurately predict and rank drug-resistant mutation genes in *C. auris*. Apart from this, the model was also able to predict a few novel resistance mutations in the fungal genes associated with resistance to antifungal drugs like fluconazole, micafungin, and amphotericin B. This study highlighted the significance of incorporation of ML classifiers in predicting existing and novel antifungal resistance genes which is of critical importance in advancing research in antifungal resistance.

The functional knowledge of genes involved in antifungal resistance and their metabolic pathways involved provide key insights to advancing pharmaceutical research in this context as well. Information regarding significant mutation genes responsible for antifungal resistance can be utilized as targets for antifungal molecules. Exemplifying this concept through a research study, an ML model was conjugated with chemogenomic interactions of a lethal fungal pathogen *Candida albicans* to develop novel antifungal targets [95]. Using their AI model, Fu *et al.* [95] were able to identify three previously uncharacterized, essential genes of *C. albicans*—Krp1, Emf1, and Tif33. Experimental validation of these genes determined their roles in kinetochore regulation, directing mitochondrial integrity and translation initiation, respectively. The authors also performed a comprehensive screening of 9,600 chemical compounds to investigate compounds with antifungal activity against essential genes of *C. albicans*. At post-screening evaluation, the authors identified a compound *N-pyrimidinyl-beta-thiophenylacrylamide* (NP-BTA) which was found to have a compelling antifungal activity against *C. albicans* and had antifungal activity against drug-resistant *C. auris* and *C. glabrata*. A chemogenomic analysis suggested that NP-BTA

Table 5.3 ML models employed for combating antifungal resistance.

ML algorithm(s) used	Purpose and application	Reference
Logistic regression (LR), support vector classifier (SVC, including SVC RBF and SVC linear), K-nearest neighbors (KNN), decision tree (DT), ensemble learning (including random forest, AdaBoost, and gradient boosting), and naive Bayes (including BernoulliNB and GaussianNB)	Cost-effective and efficient ML-based method to identify fungal drug resistance genes involved in the regulation of resistance mechanisms in *C. auris*	[94]
Random forest, logistic regression, and LDA	Incorporation of ML models to MALDI-TOF MS data to identify fluconazole resistance in *C. albicans* to develop a time-efficient diagnostic tool with same-day results	[96]
Random forest	Using ML and chemogenomic interactions to identify essential fungal genes with previously uncharacterized functions with potential as novel targets for anti-fungal agents	[95]
Artificial neural network	Demonstrated the ability of ANN in predicting the antifungal activity of imidazole derivatives against *C. albicans* to identify potent anti-fungal agents	[97]
Regression analysis	Incorporated ML model, homology modeling, and molecular dynamics to inspect the molecular mechanisms of anti-fungal drug trimethoprim (TMP) in *Pneumocystis jirovecii*	[98]
Deep learning	Developed *Deep-AFPpred* to predict anti-fungal peptides from protein sequences using 1DCNN-BiLSTM deep learning algorithm	[99]
Random forest, logistic regression, and support vector machine	ML model to screen for prognostic factors of candidemia	[100]

was efficiently able to target an essential gene in *C. albicans* known as *glutaminyl-tRNA synthetase* (GLN4). This study highlights how ML algorithms can be used to identify novel gene targets for antifungal compounds which can assist in developing new therapeutic research in regulating antifungal resistance. Table 5.3 provides some examples of ML algorithms for combating antifungal resistance.

5.5.2 AI in Combating Antiviral Resistance

AI holds significant potential in abetting the accelerating research in fighting antiviral resistance. Antiviral drug resistance occurs due to prolonged antiviral drug therapy or antiviral replication occurring during therapeutic regimes [101]. ML models can be applied to

Table 5.4 ML models employed for combating antiviral resistance.

ML algorithm(s) used	Purpose and application	Reference
Multilayer perceptron (MLP), bidirectional recurrent neural network (BRNN), and convolutional neural network (CNN)	ML model for predicting drug resistance mutations in HIV-1 sequences	[109]
Multivariable logistic regression (MLR), elastic net (EN), random forest (RF), gradient boosting machine (GBM), and feedforward neural network (FNN) machine learning algorithms	ML algorithms to predict direct-acting antiviral (DAA) treatment failure among patients infected with hepatitis-C virus (HCV)	[110]
Support vector machine, random forest, naïve Bayes-based classifiers, deep neural network	Incorporation of ML models to virtually screen and discover new antiviral compounds against yellow fever virus (YFV)	[111]
Support vector machine (SVM), naive Bayes (NB), hierarchy of multi-label classifiers (HOMER), multi-label k-nearest neighbors (MLkNN), predictive clustering trees (PCT), random k-label sets (RAkEL)	Predicting drug resistance in HIV from patient and medical records without genotype resistance testing	[112]
Support vector machine (SVM), random forest, deep learning using multiple neural network architectures, and hyper parameters	Using feature-informed ML model to predict potential antiviral peptides	[113]
Receiver operating characteristic (ROC) and the respective area under the curve (ROC-AUC) analysis	Sequence-to-structure-based approach to predict drug resistance in HIV-1 by analyzing molecular interactions of HIV-1 protease binding sites	[114]

(Continued)

Table 5.4 ML models employed for combating antiviral resistance. (*Continued*)

ML algorithm(s) used	Purpose and application	Reference
Neural network	To predict virus mutations for the early detection of drug resistance in Newcastle disease virus (NDV)	[115]
Neural Network and Decision Trees	ML models to detect influenza A resistance to antiviral drugs oseltamivir and adamantane	[116]
2 CML (random forest [RF] and extreme gradient boosting [XGBoost]) and 4 DL (deep neural networks [DNN], graph convolutional network [GCN], graph attention network [GAT], and fingerprint and graph neural network [FP-GNN]) algorithms	Developed VDBB, an ML-based predictive framework for target and cell infection assays to support various antiviral drug discovery-related tasks, such as biological activity prediction, virtual screening, compound repositioning, and target fishing	[117]
Restricted Boltzmann machines (RBMs)	Efficient and robust ML model to predict and classify drug resistance in HIV protease	[118]

large-scale genomic and clinical data to predict the pattern of antiviral resistance genes and discover novel resistant genes for antiviral resistance mutations as well. One such study incorporated the use of ML algorithms trained to classify reverse transcriptase (RT) sequences of HIV to predict antiviral drug-resistant mutations [102]. Based on the results obtained by the ML model, Blassel *et al.* [102] discovere six new drug-resistant mutations of HIV—L228R, L228H, E203K, D218E, I135L, and H208Y. This study highlighted how the discovery of novel mutations in the viral genome can be useful in identifying novel antiviral therapeutic strategies. From a pharmaceutical point of view, ML models can also be applied for predicting the viral response to antiviral therapies. Another study by Zazzi *et al.* [103] evaluated a ML model, EuResist, to predict outcomes for antiviral therapy [103]. The EuResist model was used to collect clinical data from HIV genomic data and HIV patient records of 49,000 cases from different countries. Based on the patient's clinical data and the HIV sequence found in that patient, the ML model could predict a suitable antiviral drug therapy regime for the patient. The model was reported to provide reliable therapy combinations with an accuracy of 76%. AI models like EuResist are examples of how ML models can be incorporated for personalized medicine in reducing the risks of antiviral resistance. ML techniques can also be utilized for developing new antiviral compounds and optimizing the potency of existing antivirals to suppress the progress of antiviral resistance [104]. A vast amount of chemical, genomic, and clinical data is available for rising viral threats like HIV, Ebola, and coronavirus, etc. This data can be integrated into ML models to predict viral resistance patterns and novel drug resistance genes which can assist in the discovery of novel antivirals to combat antiviral resistance. In the last decade, many studies involving

ML approaches have been incorporated in discovering antiviral drug candidates for viral threats like Sars-Cov2 [105], Ebola [106], and HIV [107]. The development of new antivirals using ML approaches can enable researchers to bypass existing resistance mechanisms of viral pathogens to provide an efficient and potent therapeutic approach while negating the risk of emergence of AMR [108]. Table 5.4 provides some examples of ML algorithms for combating antiviral resistance.

5.5.3   AI in Combating Antiparasitic Resistance

By harnessing the capabilities of AI in exploring antiparasitic resistance, researchers can offer new methods for discovering new patterns for antiparasitic resistance in parasitic

Table 5.5 ML models employed for combating antiparasitic resistance.

ML-algorithm(s) used	Purpose and application	Reference
Decision tree, elastic net, extreme random tree, gradient boosting, Lasso Lars, LightGBM, random forest, and stochastic gradient decent algorithms	Using ML to accurately predict artemisinin drug resistance in *Plasmodium falciparum* isolates and predict the parasite clearance rate of malaria parasite isolates based on *in vitro* transcriptional profiles	[119]
Deep learning	Using ML-based approach to predict drug resistance loci for both *Plasmodium falciparum* and *Plasmodium vivax*	[121]
Deep learning to build QSAR models	Deep learning approach to predict the antiplasmodial activity and cytotoxicity of previously untested chemical agents against sensitive and drug-resistant strains of *Plasmodium falciparum*	[122]
Deep neural network	Incorporation of neural network algorithms with heterogeneous cellular assays to predict underlying mechanism of drug action in malaria-parasite *Plasmodium falciparum*	[123]
Naïve Bayes, random forest, J48, and SMO	Computational modeling to identify and predict the biological activity of novel anti-leishmanial compounds targeting the pyruvate kinase enzyme of *Leishmania mexicana* (LmPK)	[124]
Random forest	ML model for predicting bioactive anti-malarial molecules that inhibit the activity of aspartyl amino peptidase (M18AAP) in *Plasmodium falciparum*	[125]
LightGBM (tree-based gradient boosting method)	Robust ML model to predict conserved-expression transcription biomarkers related to artemisinin treatment resistance	[120]

pan genomes, predicting new therapeutic options, and optimizing treatment methods to bypass antiparasitic resistance. In an Ensemble ML approach evaluated by Ford *et al.* [119], the authors discussed the potential of ML algorithms to drug resistance to artemisinin in isolates of malaria parasite *Plasmodium falciparum*. Artemisin-based therapies are a first line of defense for treating malaria caused by *Plasmodium falciparum*. However, the emergence of resistant strains of *Plasmodium falciparum* has deemed it seemingly difficult to treat as the infection rates increase gradually. Identification of antiviral resistance genes can lead to the effective management of the disease. This Ensemble ML approach utilized several ML algorithms to create a robust prediction model. This model exhibited accurate prediction and specificity in identifying resistance genes in *P. falciparum*. The identification of essential genes which contribute to artemisinin resistance further holds great potential as drug targets to improve therapeutic strategies in combating antiparasitic resistance.

Another study incorporated the use of ML algorithms to predict artemisinin resistance based on transcription molecular biomarkers [120]. Based on the predictions of the ML model, Zhang *et al.* [120] identified three new biomarkers associated with artemisinin resistance in *Plasmodium falciparum* such as Pfmdr1, PF3D7_1372000, and UBC12, all of which have known functions in regulating the survival of *Plasmodium falciparum* and authors also suggested that, with future advances in therapeutic strategies, knowledge of essential genes in conferring artemisinin resistance can be used to develop more target-specific therapies to counter antiparasitic resistance. Table 5.5 provides some examples of ML algorithms for combating antiparasitic resistance.

5.5.4 AI in AMR Surveillance

AMR surveillance encompasses the monitoring of AMR emergence and spread of drug-resistant pathogens in real-time [126]. Traditional methods for AMR surveillance however is time consuming with a manual data input system and may not be completely reliable with questionable accuracy. AI and ML-based approaches provide a versatile approach in AMR surveillance as it confers the ability to comprehensively scan large scale genomic and clinical data. ML algorithms can be trained to predict indicative patterns of emerging AMR based on clinical and historical data and genetic patterns in microbes associated with AMR [127]. Based on approaches like pattern recognition, AI-based approaches may significantly aid in predicting the emergence of AMR even before it occurs, which is a critical step in AMR surveillance. ML models have been investigated in predicting AMR. ML-based approaches like support vector machine (SVM) and set covering machine (SCM) models have been used to analyze WGS to predict the resistance of *Actinobacillus pleuropneumoniae* to a few antimicrobial drugs (38). Both models were reported to have significant accuracy in predicting the AMR phenotypes of *A. pleuropneumoniae*, which substantiates the efficiency of ML models in monitoring AMR *via* available genomic data. Monitoring the spread of AMR among species is also a critical aspect of AMR surveillance. Environments like animal farms were recognized by Peng *et al.* [128] as having the optimum conditions for selection pressure to result in the development of AMR genes. The researchers thus incorporated an ML approach using WGS and gene-sharing network analysis to identify the cross-sharing of AMR genes among humans and animal livestock species [128]. The authors isolated *E. coli* isolates from farms and livestock environment and performed a pangenome analysis using WGS and gene network analysis of single-nucleotide polymorphisms (SNPs). Astoundingly, the authors found sharing of common AMR genes across human, poultry, and farm environment. This finding suggested a possible cross-transmission of *E. coli* among the different species and environment. The study highlights the importance of AMR surveillance to monitor the spread of AMR.

5.5.5   Rapid Diagnostics

The application of AI in healthcare and drug development, with a focus on real-time patient diagnosis for various complex diseases, aims to provide solutions for medical practitioners to rapidly diagnose critical conditions using these techniques [129]. AI can assist in improving rapid diagnostics by streamlining the process of antimicrobial susceptibility testing (AST). AST is a method of treatment regimen that is incorporated for an individual to identify which drug would have the most potent antibiotic activity and the required dosage. AST is an important aspect in regulating AMR progression as it reduces the risks of the development of AMR due to poor diagnosis or misuse of unnecessary drugs [130]. However, the current AST techniques are highly time consuming as it may take 16–24 h to see results, provide limited information, costly, and do not cover a broad spectrum [131]. AI algorithms can be modeled to overcome these limitations of current state of AST. Khaledi *et al.* [132] evaluated the efficiency of ML in molecular diagnostics to combat antibiotic resistance. The researchers conjugated machine learning approaches with datasets on transcriptomic and phenotypic data of clinical *Pseudomonas aeruginosa* isolates to precisely predict antibiotic resistance. These methods for molecular diagnostics can be easily incorporated to overcome deficiencies of culture-based methods in AST. AI models such as artificial neural networks have also been incorporated in conjugation with IR spectroscopy to significantly reduce the time for AST diagnosis from 24 to 3 h [133].

5.5.6   Combating Biofilm Through AI

Biofilms are highly antibiotic-resistant amalgamations of microbes that adhere to a surface and are enclosed in a protective extracellular substrate [134]. Biofilms that are able to adhere to any known surface pose a major threat in contamination and infection [135]. Biofilms pose a major threat to healthcare industries as they develop easily on medical devices like catheters, cause plant-related diseases in an agricultural setting, are responsible for about 60% of food-borne diseases conferring a major threat to the food industry, are responsible for the contamination of water distribution systems, contaminate marine-exposed objects like ship hulls and buoys, etc. [136]. The current standards of biofilm treatment include the application of anti-biofilm agents that disrupt pathways which regulate the formation of the biofilms. AI and ML models can thereby be incorporated to accelerate this discovery process (Figure 5.1).

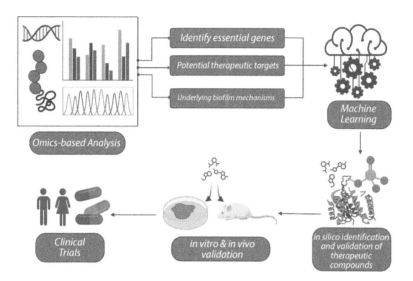

Figure 5.1 Schematic workflow of an AI-powered omics-based analysis and process to develop therapeutic interventions to combat biofilms.

Omics-based systems biology approaches to study biofilms, such as transcriptomics [137], transposon insertion sequencing [138], proteomics [139], and metabolomics [140], had been investigated previously to uncover metabolic pathways and essential genes required for the regulation of biofilms. This enormous data provides an insight to the biofilm mechanisms and highlight any cause of AMR emergence that is available for further screening by ML models. AI and ML models can be used to screen data obtained from the omics-based approaches to select potential targets and predict candidate molecules to target the same to effectively combat biofilm regulation. AI approaches such as molecular docking, quantitative structure–activity relationship (QSAR)-based modeling, and machine learning can be used to integrate omics data to uncover new solutions [24]. Molecular docking studies can be used to uncover the binding efficiency and orientation of anti-biofilm agents and biofilm proteins like QS protein, (p) ppGpp synthetases and essential biofilm regulatory proteins, etc.

An antibiotic-resistant, biofilm-forming bacterium *Streptococcus dysgalactiae* subsp. *dysgalactiae* (SDSD) was investigated in a study and evaluated how biofilm formation was regulated in SDSD [141]. Alves-Barroco *et al.* [141] identified a potential homolog of the regulatory protein BrpA in SDSD that expressed involvement in biofilm formation and used ML frameworks to perform high-throughput virtual screening to identify the found potential inhibitors of the BrpA protein and predicted five compounds with strong binding affinity to BrpA. Molecular docking was used to confirm the binding orientation and efficiency of the five compounds to the BrpA protein and found strong binding in the region of the hydrophobic cleft. The experiment strongly suggested how ML approaches can be used to identify proteins involved in biofilm regulation and also their ability to screen for potential inhibitors, which may lead to the development of a new treatment for biofilm-associated diseases.

ML algorithms can be used to identify features of anti-biofilm molecules to predict novel molecules based on known physico-chemical parameters. Di Luca *et al.* [142] highlighted the use of online databases such as BaAMPs as a comprehensive database to search for

Table 5.6 ML models employed for combating biofilms.

ML-algorithm(s) used	Purpose and application	Reference
Support vector machine (SVM), random forest (RF), multilayer perceptron (MLP), KStar, and M5Rules	ML model to predict and analyze the biofilm inhibitory activity of small molecules	[146]
Random forest (RF), non-linear support vector machine (SVM), gradient boosting (GB)	ML model to identify essential oils from Mediterranean plants with anti-biofilm activity against *Pseudomonas aeruginosa*	[147]
Principal component analysis (PCA), Bayesian optimization, logistic regression	ML to analyze chemical configuration of essential oils and identify their potential activity in biofilm inhibition against *Staphylococcus aureus* and *Staphylococcus epidermidis*	[148]
Random forest	Developed *Molib* using multiple ML models which can predict potential biofilm inhibitory chemical molecules	[145]
Random forest (RF), Logistic regression (LR), support vector (SV), gradient boosting (GB), decision tree (DT), and K-nearest neighbors (KNN)	Investigation of ML algorithms to predict anti-biofilm action of essential oils against *Pseudomonas aeruginosa* strains isolated from cystic fibrosis patients	[149]
Random forest	ML-aided cocktail assay for detection of biofilms using lanthanide nanoparticles	[150]
K-nearest neighbor, neural networks, support vector machine, naïve bayes classifier, random forest, and XGBoost	Developed ML framework TargIDe to predict protein targets of molecules with biofilm inhibitory activity against *Pseudomonas aeruginosa*	[151]
Support vector machine and Weka	Developed dPABBS for analysis of whole amino acid composition to identify anti-biofilm peptides and predict AMPs with potential to be repurposed for anti-biofilm therapy	[143]
Support vector machine	Developed Biofilm-*I*, an ML-based platform incorporating recursive regression and QSAR to predict the anti-biofilm efficiency of potential chemical compounds	[152]
Support vector machines (SVM), random forest (RF), extreme gradient boosting (XgBoost), multilayer perceptron (MLP) classifier	ML-algorithms to predict novel, potent anti-biofilm peptides by comprehensively scanning existing peptide databases	[153]

AMPs having a potent anti-biofilm activity, which can be a valuable tool for discovering anti-biofilm AMPs. A novel ML framework—dPABBs, which uses a combination of machine learning and bioinformatics techniques to predict anti-biofilm AMPs, was also developed by Sharma *et al.* [143]. The authors reported that the dPABBS model was ~95% accurate in predicting AMPs with anti-biofilm activity and also had the capability to predict novel anti-biofilm peptides. A QSAR-based ML model to identify AMPs with anti-biofilm activity towards methicillin-resistant *Staphylococcus aureus* (MRSA) biofilms was evaluated by Haney *et al.* [144]. The authors reported ~85% accuracy in predicting AMPs with anti-biofilm activity and highlighted the prediction of a peptide—3002, for its potent anti-biofilm activity a concentration eight times less than that of peptide 1018 and demonstrated significant *in vivo* activity in treating a chronic MRSA mouse infection model. The use of QSAR descriptors and chemo-informatics was also used to develop a hybrid RF algorithm—*Molib*, to predict agents with biofilm inhibitory activity [145].

These studies emphasize the capability of ML models to be incorporated in identifying key proteins of biofilm formation in microbes, screening for potential bio-film inhibitory molecules, and discovering novel agents to disrupt the biofilm regulation. Although the discovery of new molecules would require subsequent *in vitro* and *in vivo* biological experiments to determine their potency, efficacy, and feasibility for employment in clinical settings, AI- and ML-based approaches surely provides a fast track to accelerate the research and discovery process. Table 5.6 provides some examples of ML algorithms for combating biofilms.

5.6   Challenges Towards Practical Implementation

Despite being a robust aid in accelerating the research to combat AMR and in the discovery of novel antimicrobial, AI- and ML-based approaches still face a lot of challenges toward their practical implementation (Figure 5.2).

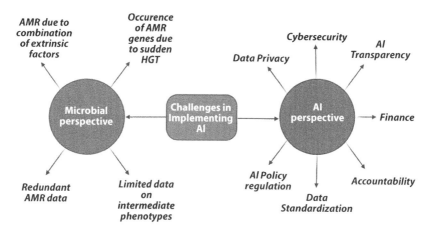

Figure 5.2 Challenges involved in the practical implementation of AI.

5.6.1 Challenges from a Microbial Perspective

The rising numbers of mutations due to various facets in the microbial populations tend to pose as a major threat in understanding the evolution of AMR [154]. Ali *et al.* [155] discussed this theme and how it affects the implementation of AI. AI models may find it difficult to understand the underlying mechanisms of resistance that may have occurred due to sudden environmental stress causing the occurrence of AMR genes due to horizontal gene transfer in the genome of a bacterial sub-population [156]. AI models would require a more updated set of genomic data conferring to these facets to overcome AMR. AI models may be unable to apprehend AMR generated by genetic combination due to extrinsic factors—for instance, a different subset of AMR emerges due to amalgamation of environmental factors such as metals with AMR genes in a microbial population, which may lead to a more resilient form of AMR [157]. It may be currently difficult for AI models to fully understand these mechanisms and may thus be unable to understand the emergence of AMR due to these multivariate factors. Current ML-based models classify AMR genes as susceptible and resistant. However, there is a need to classify the intermediate phenotype as well to fully optimize the antimicrobial discovery process [158]. Due to limited occurrence and availability of data regarding intermediate phenotypes, AI models may be difficult to train on those parameters, leading to inefficient data outputs. The lack of data availability and understanding of uncommon microbes associated with unusual environments also make it difficult to train AI models to predict AMR from these phenotypes [155]. Over-fitting due to the high complexity of ML models may include redundant AMR data, causing inefficient data production [159].

5.6.2 Challenges from AI Perspective

Apart from the microbial aspects, AI faces other challenges in its widespread application on a global scale. Data sharing is a valuable practice for combating AMR as the availability of high-quality datasets is critical for training a robust AI model. These datasets include clinical data, patient records, clinical trial data, genomics data, etc. However, the first barrier to AI implementation is data privacy, data security, and ethical concerns [160]. Data must first be properly de-identified to provide total anonymity for data privacy and confidentiality of patients and address subsequent cyber-security issues to efficiently share data [161]. Patrzyk *et al.* [162] emphasized the significance of data transparency, i.e., the ability to interpret an AI model from a human perspective [162]. AI must be transparent to be able to justify its predictions of diagnosis and treatment outcomes to uncover clinical insights [163]. Transparent AI models also give stakeholders and other users an insight and a potential to optimize and shortcomings for creating a more robust AI model. AI transparency also helps overcome discriminatory biases such as race or sex [161]. Since AI is seen as a separate entity by the FDA as compared to traditional methods in healthcare, the major question of accountability rises. If a patient suffers adverse effects due to AI-suggested treatments, since a traditional doctor–patient relation does not exist—who is liable to take blame for such adversities? A strong need for regulatory frameworks is required to address such issues. Data standardization is another challenge in AI implementation as healthcare and clinical data is highly heterogeneous and varies vastly from patient to patient [164]. Kruse *et al.* [164] emphasized the standing need to standardize and integrate a common format for AI models to allow robust performance to validate data from heterogeneous datasets. Financial burden is another challenge faced in the practical implementation of AI as there is a constant need for updating software and hardware. AI companies can also manipulate profits from clinical tests, drugs, and medical devices [161]. The role of regulatory agencies is also a key to implement AI. The regulatory frameworks are necessary to implement AI-related policies to develop regulatory standards for safely and robustly implementing AI in the healthcare setting [160].

5.6.3   Approval by Regulatory Bodies

AI has proven to be a vital tool in the field of healthcare. ML models are trained in order to predict individualized suggestions for patients and even deter the chances of AMR in them. Neural network approach in the healthcare field helps categorize patient information and can also identify the onset or susceptibility of patients to certain diseases [165]. The ability of AI to automatically analyze and process information makes it far more useful than using traditional approaches that often render ineffective. Governing challenges allied with AI include safety and good-quality healthcare to the patients, which is why explainable AI models are preferred as they can justify their decision-making strategy for an output based on the input data. Superior regulations are however necessary as AI models can auto-update/modify itself constantly to ascertain reliability. From the clinicians' point of view, there may be trust issues with the predicted output which results in clinicians dismissing the AI-suggested treatment plan. Although AI holds great potential in the healthcare field, without regulatory systems there would be a swift upsurge in the expansion and distribution of AI models that could be risky and defective because of incorrect and poor training data for AI models that will result in imprecise predictions, biases, medical flaws, and discernment [166, 167]—for instance, an AI model that was developed to predict potential pneumonia patients that could be discharged erroneously learnt that patients suffering from asthma had a lesser mortality risk. The AI model used this dataset to train itself and therefore suggested patients suffering from pneumonia and asthma to be admitted to ICUs. This highlights the importance of a clinician's judgment in assessing a patient at a preliminary level [168]. A governance model (GMAIH) which includes four elements—transparency, fairness, accountability, and trustworthiness—to address moral, governing, quality, and safety concerns was also suggested previously [167]. Deep learning algorithms employ the use of big datasets for training, prediction, and standardization. In order to train a model appropriately, data collection and data sharing from different geographical regions are also required, which creates issues concerning AI. Patients, in general, also show concerns as to how their confidential medical data is being used because breach of patient data is not only unethical but also creates a lack of trust between a clinician and his patients. One strategy to overcome this issue involves adopting a policy of broad consent from the patient where they may consent to the use of their medical records for secondary purposes while being guaranteed complete anonymity. Misinterpretation of data by an AI model is also a concern when it comes to patient safety. Manipulation of deep learning models can result in error-prone outputs, and this, in turn, can be dangerous to patients. Therefore, it is imperative for developers of AI models to put efforts into integrating AI into prevailing clinical settings as well as enable AI models to recognize and learn from errors. Employing proper parameter during this model development phase will automatically improve the safety of patients. In order to enable effective usage of software as a medical device (SaMD), the US Food and Drug Administration (FDA) has piloted a precertification program [168] as many AI-centric SaMD have been permitted in the field of healthcare. The FDA employs a balanced strategy to ensure the effectiveness and safety of SaMD while simultaneously reducing hindrances for developers to deploy SaMD. The World Health Organization (WHO) can take part in serving countries that adopt SaMD which lack a traditional governing process. The complexity in regulation also arises in the form of liability which mostly concerns with misinterpreted data by AI. The regulating strategies across the world are still unclear on whom to blame when there are errors in the output from AI software/devices [167]. This, however, depends on recognizing ethical issues during each AI operation stage and requires a standardized decision on how the risks will be dispersed throughout the society [168]. Morley *et al.* [169] proposed that challenge with AI cannot be solved by simply implementing rules and regulations. Often the issues arise at the hands of the developers who fail to adopt strategies to protect patient privacy and ignore cyber-security. Personal-level ability is one strategy to address these challenges. For issues that arise at the organizational level, improved control over design and interface is required to ascertain that healthcare professionals, patients, and artificial agents can network efficiently. For the proper execution and utilization of AI in healthcare at the institutional level, campaigns and professional accreditations can be given to individuals looking to use AI-based health tools. The challenges of AI in health can be modulated using appropriate governance models, but there remain certain open questions on what regulations and policies should cover and how they should be developed. One solution employs the use of a comprehensive strategy encompassing ethical concerns and different levels of abstraction (LoA)—individual, group, interpersonal, sectoral, institutional, and societal [169].

5.7 Conclusion and Future Scope

The fusion of AI and AMR emerges as a profound paradigm shift, heralding a new era in translational research to combat the emerging global AMR crisis. The essence of this chapter sheds light on assessing the vast potential that AI embraces in transfiguring clinical translational models—from understanding the mechanisms of AMR to the discovery of novel antimicrobials.

The potential of integrating AI algorithms has unveiled the intricate underlying mechanisms of AMR emergence by dissecting complex genomic datasets. Through methodologies like machine learning and deep learning, AI has transcended human limitations, revealing patterns and connections that eluded conventional approaches. This achievement stands as a testament to AI's ability to decipher the genomic code, providing invaluable insights that serve as the bedrock for targeted interventions.

One of the most remarkable facets of AI's engagement with AMR is its aptitude to reshape the trajectory of antimicrobial discovery. *In silico* predictive analysis powered by AI algorithms offers a palette of possibilities, expediting the identification of novel antimicrobial compounds. The development of novel antibiotics showcasing the power of AI can be exemplified by the discovery of *Halicin*. This leap beyond conventional trial-and-error methodologies holds the promise of confronting AMR head on by populating the arsenal of clinicians with a broader range of effective treatments and augments the horizons for exploration of the vast chemical space to foster drug innovation.

AI's contribution extends beyond the laboratory and into the realm of patient care. Through predictive modeling and integration of clinical data, AI possesses the acumen to guide clinicians toward tailored treatment decisions, minimizing the risk of AMR emergence. This, coupled with the augmentation of antibiotic stewardship programs, reflects AI's transformative role in safeguarding both individual and collective health.

Despite the accomplishment of substantial advancement by AI, practical implementation still faces its own set of challenges to develop robust AI models. Integration of AI into existing healthcare systems necessitates vigilant contemplation for factors such as data security, data standardization, and interoperability. Overcoming these challenges would entail interdisciplinary collaborations, regulatory provisions by governing bodies, and a robust committee to supervise ethical facets and responsible implementation. As the amalgamation of AI and AMR reaches new heights, our journey through this chapter divulges a harmonious union of knowledge and innovation, propelling healthcare and clinical settings towards a future where AI poses as a steadfast ally in deciphering the underlying enigmas of AMR, revolutionizing antimicrobial discovery, and safeguarding the very foundations of global health infrastructure.

So far, we have discussed the various applications of AI models in understanding the mechanisms of AMR and for antimicrobial discovery. Without ambiguity, one can be certain that AI presents an immense potential in revolutionizing the global fight against AMR. With the development of AI-powered tools against AMR, the foreseeable future can expect the discovery of several promising avenues and innovative strategies to fortify healthcare infrastructures. AI algorithms can compare vast datasets of genetic, genomic, and phenotypic data [49] which can offer a prediction insight regarding the resistance mechanisms of AMR. Using AI to study these datasets can potentially offer recognition of certain patterns and associations to AMR, which may be missed by the human eye. Further development and integration of newer datasets will certainly increase the robustness and accuracy of AI-enabled models in the identification of previously uncharacterized and novel mechanisms of AMR. AI techniques have significantly accelerated antimicrobial discovery as well. AI models are capable of leveraging vast datasets of chemical data, pharmacological data, etc., to guide the design of novel antibiotics with enhanced efficacy and improved pharmacological profiles with the potential of overcoming existing resistance mechanisms [25, 75]. As the global threat of AMR continues to rise, the discovery of novel antibiotics to overcome existing resistance mechanisms is of utmost necessity. Tailoring personalized medicine to individual patients can significantly improve clinical outcomes while mitigating the risks of emergence of AMR. Personalized treatment plans such as antibiotic selection and dosage can be created by integrating patient-specific genomic data, clinical history, etc. [17]. Biosensors and nanobiosensors have the potential to be developed for the real-time surveillance of AMR by detecting the presence of drug-resistant bacteria in clinical samples [170]. AI algorithms can be incorporated into these technologies to enhance their accuracy and speed, enabling healthcare providers to make informed decisions about treatment and infection control measures. AI algorithms can be implemented in surveillance models to monitor the emergence and spread of AMR on a global scale [38]. Early identification of resistance patterns due to facilitation of surveillance programs can assist in guiding necessary healthcare interventions and providing necessary public health policies.

AI-driven surveillance systems can help us navigate the evolving landscapes of AMR. AI holds a great promise as an ally for the future of healthcare. By harnessing the power of AI, we can advance our understanding of the underlying mechanisms of AMR, develop precision treatment strategies, and significantly expedite the process of new antimicrobial discovery. The design and production of vaccinations to combat resistant microbes can benefit from deep learning. It can aid in the development of more potent vaccinations by modeling the interactions between antigens and immune system components. Deep learning techniques can be used into multidisciplinary projects to address the complex problems brought on by antimicrobial resistance, improve patient outcomes, and strengthen global health security.

References

1. Dadgostar, P., Antimicrobial resistance: Implications and costs. *Infect. Drug Resist.*, 12, 3903–10, 2019, Available from: https://www.tandfonline.com/action/journalInformation?journalCode=didr20.

2. Khaznadar, O., Khaznadar, F., Petrovic, A., Kuna, L., Loncar, A., Kolaric, T.O. *et al.*, Antimicrobial resistance and antimicrobial stewardship: Before, during and after the COVID-19 pandemic. *Microbiol. Res.*, 14, 2, 727–740, 2023, Available from: https://www.mdpi.com/2036-7481/14/2/52/htm.

3. Morrison, L. and Zembower, T.R., Antimicrobial Resistance. *Gastrointest. Endosc. Clin. N. Am.*, 30, 4, 619–35, 2020 Oct 1.

4. De Oliveira, D.M.P., Forde, B.M., Kidd, T.J., Harris, P.N.A., Schembri, M.A., Beatson, S.A. *et al.*, Antimicrobial Resistance in ESKAPE Pathogens. *Clin. Microbiol. Rev.*, 33, 3, e00181-19, 2020, Available from: https://pubmed.ncbi.nlm.nih.gov/32404435/.

5. Schrader, S.M., Vaubourgeix, J., Nathan, C., Biology of antimicrobial resistance and approaches to combat it. *Sci. Transl. Med.*, 12, 549, 1–14, 2020 Jun 24.

6. Wong, C.H., Siah, K.W., Lo, A.W., Estimation of clinical trial success rates and related parameters. *Biostatistics*, 20, 2, 273–86, 2019 Apr 1.

7. Kaprou, G.D., Bergšpica, I., Alexa, E.A., Alvarez-Ordóñez, A., Prieto, M., Rapid Methods for Antimicrobial Resistance Diagnostics. *Antibiotics*, 10, 2, 209, 2021 Feb 20.

8. de Kraker, M.E.A., Stewardson, A.J., Harbarth, S., Will 10 Million People Die a Year due to Antimicrobial Resistance by 2050? *PloS Med.*, 13, 11, 1002184, 2016 Nov 1, Available from: https://journals.plos.org/plosmedicine/article?id=10.1371/journal.pmed.1002184.

9. George, A., Antimicrobial resistance, trade, food safety and security. *One Health*, 5, 6, 6–8, 2018 Jun 1, Available from: /pmc/articles/PMC5725214/.

10. Paphitou, N.I., Antimicrobial resistance: action to combat the rising microbial challenges. *Int. J. Antimicrob. Agents*, 42, 1, 25–8, 2013 Jun 1.

11. Harikumar, G. and Krishanan, K., The growing menace of drug resistant pathogens and recent strategies to overcome drug resistance: A review. *J. King Saud. Univ. Sci.*, 34, 4, 101979, 2022 Jun 1.

12. Wise, R., Blaser, M., Carrs, O., Cassell, G., Fishman, N., Guidos, R. *et al.*, The urgent need for new antibacterial agents. *J. Antimicrobial. Chemotherapy*, 66, 9, 1939–40, 2011 Sep 1, Available from: https://dx.doi.org/10.1093/jac/dkr261.

13. Doron, S. and Davidson, L.E., Antimicrobial Stewardship. *Mayo Clin. Proc.*, Nov 1, 86, 1113–23, 2011.

14. O'Neill, J., Review on antimicrobial resistance: tackling drug-resistant infections globally: final report and recommendations, in: *CABI, Global Health*, p. 80, 2016.

15. Nayyar, A., Gadhavi, L., Zaman, N., Machine learning in healthcare: review, opportunities and challenges, in: *Machine Learning and the Internet of Medical Things in Healthcare*, pp. 23–45, 2021 Jan 1.

16. Ament, S.A., Pearl, J.R., Cantle, J.P., Bragg, R.M., Skene, P.J., Coffey, S.R. *et al.*, Transcriptional regulatory networks underlying gene expression changes in Huntington's disease. *Mol. Syst. Biol.*, 14, 3, 7435, 2018 Mar 1, Available from: https://onlinelibrary.wiley.com/doi/full/10.15252/msb.20167435.

17. Feretzakis, G., Sakagianni, A., Loupelis, E., Kalles, D., Skarmoutsou, N., Martsoukou, M. *et al.*, Machine Learning for Antibiotic Resistance Prediction: A Prototype Using Off-the-Shelf Techniques and Entry-Level Data to Guide Empiric Antimicrobial Therapy. *Healthc. Inform. Res.*, 27, 3, 214–21, 2021 Jul 31.

18. Li, X., Xu, Y., Cui, H., Huang, T., Wang, D., Lian, B. *et al.*, Prediction of synergistic anti-cancer drug combinations based on drug target network and drug induced gene expression profiles. *Artif. Intell. Med.*, 83, 35–43, 2017 Nov.

19. Sethi, T., Maheshwari, S., Nagori, A., Lodha, R., Stewarding antibiotic stewardship in intensive care units with Bayesian artificial intelligence. *Wellcome Open Res.*, 3, 73, 2018 Jun 18.

20. James, S., Rao, S.V., Granger, C.B., Registry-based randomized clinical trials—a new clinical trial paradigm. *Nat. Rev. Cardiol.*, 12, 5, 312–6, 2015 May 17.

21. Lv, J., Deng, S., Zhang, L., A review of artificial intelligence applications for antimicrobial resistance. *Biosaf. Health*, 3, 1, 22–31, 2021 Feb 1.

22. Munita, J.M., Arias, C.A., Kudva, I.T., Zhang, Q., Mechanisms of Antibiotic Resistance. *MicrobiolSpectr.* 4, 2, 481–511, 2016 Mar 25, Available from: https://journals.asm.org/doi/10.1128/microbiolspec.VMBF-0016-2015.

23. Her, H.L. and Wu, Y.W., A pan-genome-based machine learning approach for predicting antimicrobial resistance activities of the Escherichia coli strains. *Bioinformatics*, 34, 13, 89–95, 2018 Jul 1, Available from: https://dx.doi.org/10.1093/bioinformatics/bty276.

24. An, A.Y., Choi, K.Y.G., Baghela, A.S., Hancock, R.E.W., An Overview of Biological and Computational Methods for Designing Mechanism-Informed Anti-biofilm Agents. *Front. Microbiol*, 12, 640787, 2021 Apr 13.

25. Stokes, J.M., Yang, K., Swanson, K., Jin, W., Cubillos-Ruiz, A., Donghia, N.M. *et al.*, A Deep Learning Approach to Antibiotic Discovery. *Cell*, 180, 4, 688–702.e13, 2020 Feb.

26. Vikramkumar, B.V. and Trilochan, Bayes and Naive Bayes Classifier, 1, 1–3, 2014 Apr 3, Available from: https://arxiv.org/abs/1404.0933v1.

27. Alpaydin, E., *Introduction to Machine Learning*, vol. 1, The MIT Press, United States, England, 2004.

28. Rezaei-hachesu, P., Samad-Soltani, T., Yaghoubi, S., GhaziSaeedi, M., Mirnia, K., Masoumi-Asl, H. *et al.*, The design and evaluation of an antimicrobial resistance surveillance system for neonatal intensive care units in Iran. *Int. J. Med. Inform.*, 115, 24–34, 2018 Jul 1.

29. Oonsivilai, M., Mo, Y., Luangasanatip, N., Lubell, Y., Miliya, T., Tan, P. *et al.*, Using machine learning to guide targeted and locally-tailored empiric antibiotic prescribing in a children's hospital in Cambodia. *Wellcome Open Res.*, 3, 131, 1–18, 2018 Oct 10.

30. Quinlan, J.R., Induction of decision trees. *Mach. Learn.*, 1, 1, 81–106, 1986, Available from: https://link.springer.com/article/10.1007/bf00116251.

31. Navada, A., Ansari, A.N., Patil, S., Sonkamble, B.A., Overview of use of decision tree algorithms in machine learning, in: *Proceedings - 2011 IEEE Control and System Graduate Research Colloquium, ICSGRC*, pp. 37–42, 2011.

32. Voermans, A.M., Mewes, J.C., Broyles, M.R., Steuten, L.M.G., Cost-Effectiveness Analysis of a Procalcitonin-Guided Decision Algorithm for Antibiotic Stewardship Using Real-World U.S.

Hospital Data. *OMICS*, 23, 10, 508–15, 2019 Oct 1, Available from: https://www.liebertpub.com/ doi/10.1089/omi.2019.0113.

33. Breiman, L., Random forests. *Mach. Learn.*, 45, 1, 5–32, 2001 Oct, Available from: https://link.springer.com/article/10.1023/A:1010933404324.

34. Ao, Y., Li, H., Zhu, L., Ali, S., Yang, Z., The linear random forest algorithm and its advantages in machine learning assisted logging regression modeling. *J. Pet Sci. Eng.*, 174, 776–89, 2019 Mar 1.

35. Pan, L., Liu, G., Lin, F., Zhong, S., Xia, H., Sun, X. *et al.*, Machine learning applications for prediction of relapse in childhood acute lymphoblastic leukemia. *Sci. Rep.*, 7, 1, 2017 Dec 1, Available from: https://pubmed.ncbi.nlm.nih.gov/28784991/.

36. Chandrasekaran, S., Cokol-Cakmak, M., Sahin, N., Yilancioglu, K., Kazan, H., Collins, J.J. *et al.*, Chemogenomics and orthology-based design of antibiotic combination therapies. *Mol. Syst. Biol.*, 12, 5, 872, 2016 May 1. Available from: https://onlinelibrary.wiley.com/doi/full/10.15252/msb.20156777.

37. Kecman, V., *Support Vector Machines – An Introduction*, vol. 7, 1, pp. 1–47, Berlin, Heidelberg, Germany, 2005 Apr 22, Available from: https://link.springer.com/chapter/10.1007/10984697_1.

38. Liu, Z., Deng, D., Lu, H., Sun, J., Lv, L., Li, S. *et al.*, Evaluation of Machine Learning Models for Predicting Antimicrobial Resistance of Actinobacillus pleuropneumoniae From Whole Genome Sequences. *Front. Microbiol.*, 11, 474876, 2020 Feb 6.

39. Lecun, Y., Bengio, Y., Hinton, G., Deep learning. *Nature*, 521, 7553, 436–444, 2015, Available from: https://www.nature.com/articles/nature14539.

40. Ii, T.C.S., Pullen, K.M., Olson, M.C., McNellis, M.E., Richardson, I., Hu, S. *et al.*, Morphological profiling of tubercle bacilli identifies drug pathways of action. *Proc. Natl. Acad. Sci. U.S.A.*, 117, 31, 18744–53, 2020, Available from: https://www.pnas.org/doi/abs/10.1073/pnas.2002738117.

41. Schürch, A.C. and van Schaik, W., Challenges and opportunities for whole-genome sequencing–based surveillance of antibiotic resistance. *Ann. N Y Acad. Sci.*, 1388, 1, 108–20, 2017 Jan 1, Available from: https://onlinelibrary.wiley.com/doi/full/10.1111/nyas.13310.

42. Ren, Y., Chakraborty, T., Doijad, S., Falgenhauer, L., Falgenhauer, J., Goesmann, A. *et al.*, Prediction of antimicrobial resistance based on whole-genome sequencing and machine learning. *Bioinformatics*, 38, 2, 325–34, 2022 Jan 3, Available from: https://dx.doi.org/10.1093/bioinformatics/btab681.

43. Arango-Argoty, G., Garner, E., Pruden, A., Heath, L.S., Vikesland, P., Zhang, L., DeepARG: A deep learning approach for predicting antibiotic resistance genes from metagenomic data. *Microbiome*, 6, 1, 1–15, 2018 Feb 1, Available from: https://microbiomejournal.biomedcentral.com/articles/10.1186/s40168-018-0401-z.

44. Hicks, S.A., Strümke, I., Thambawita, V., Hammou, M., Riegler, M.A., Halvorsen, P. *et al.*, On evaluation metrics for medical applications of artificial intelligence. *Sci. Rep.*, 121, 5979, 2022, Available from: https://www.nature.com/articles/s41598-022-09954-8.

45. Kavvas, E.S., Yang, L., Monk, J.M., Heckmann, D., Palsson, B.O., A biochemically-interpretable machine learning classifier for microbial GWAS. *Nat. Commun.*, 11, 1, 2580, 2020, Available from: https://www.nature.com/articles/s41467-020-16310-9.

46. Anahtar, M.N., Yang, J.H., Kanjilal, S., Applications of Machine Learning to the Problem of Antimicrobial Resistance: an Emerging Model for Translational Research. *J. Clin. Microbiol.*, 59, 7, 0126020, 2021 Jun 1, Available from: https://journals.asm.org/doi/10.1128/jcm.01260-20.

47. Vamathevan, J., Clark, D., Czodrowski, P., Dunham, I., Ferran, E., Lee, G. *et al.*, Applications of machine learning in drug discovery and development. *Nat. Rev. Drug Discov.*, 18, 6, 463–477, 2019, Available from: https://www.nature.com/articles/s41573-019-0024-5.

48. Ahmed, Z., Zeeshan, S., Mendhe, D., Dong, X., Human gene and disease associations for clinical-genomics and precision medicine research. *Clin. Transl. Med.*, 10, 1, 297–318, 2020 Mar 1, Available from: https://onlinelibrary.wiley.com/doi/full/10.1002/ctm2.28.

49. Ament, S.A., Pearl, J.R., Cantle, J.P., Bragg, R.M., Skene, P.J., Coffey, S.R. *et al.*, Transcriptional regulatory networks underlying gene expression changes in Huntington's disease. *Mol. Syst. Biol.*, 14, 3, 7435, 2018 Mar 26.

50. Costa, P.R., Acencio, M.L., Lemke, N., A machine learning approach for genome-wide prediction of morbid and druggable human genes based on systems-level data. *BMC Genomics*, 11, 5, 1–15, 2010 Dec 2, Available from: https://bmcgenomics.biomedcentral.com/articles/ 10.1186/1471-2164-11-S5-S9.

51. Medema, M.H., Blin, K., Cimermancic, P., De Jager, V., Zakrzewski, P., Fischbach, M.A. *et al.*, antiSMASH: rapid identification, annotation and analysis of secondary metabolite biosynthesis gene clusters in bacterial and fungal genome sequences. *Nucleic Acids Res.*, 39, 2, 339–46, 2011 Jul 1, Available from: https://dx.doi.org/10.1093/nar/gkr466.

52. Alcock, B.P., Raphenya, A.R., Lau, T.T.Y., Tsang, K.K., Bouchard, M., Edalatmand, A. *et al.*, CARD 2020: antibiotic resistome surveillance with the comprehensive antibiotic resistance database. *Nucleic Acids Res.*, 48, 1, 517–25, 2020 Jan 8, Available from: https://dx.doi. org/10.1093/nar/ gkz935.

53. Zankari, E., Hasman, H., Cosentino, S., Vestergaard, M., Rasmussen, S., Lund, O. *et al.*, Identification of acquired antimicrobial resistance genes. *J. Antimicrob. Chemother.*, 67, 11, 2640–4, 2012 Nov 1, Available from: https://dx.doi.org/10.1093/jac/dks261.

54. Gupta, S.K., Padmanabhan, B.R., Diene, S.M., Lopez-Rojas, R., Kempf, M., Landraud, L. *et al.*, ARG-annot, a new bioinformatic tool to discover antibiotic resistance genes in bacterial genomes. *Antimicrob. Agents Chemother.*, 58, 1, 212–20, 2014 Jan, Available from: https://journals. asm.org/doi/10.1128/aac.01310-13.

55. Manjula, M.S., Rachana, K.E., Naganeeswaran, S., Hemalatha, N., Karun, A., Rajesh, M.K., PRGPred: A platform for prediction of domains of resistance gene analogue (RGA) in Arecaceae developed by using machine learning algorithms. *J. BioSci. Biotechnol.*, 4, 3, 327–338, 2015.

56. Lakin, S.M., Kuhnle, A., Alipanahi, B., Noyes, N.R., Dean, C., Muggli, M. *et al.*, Hierarchical Hidden Markov models enable accurate and diverse detection of antimicrobial resistance sequences. *Commun. Biol.*, 21, 294, 2019, Available from: https://www.nature.com/articles/ s42003-019-0545-9.

57. Bonin, N., Doster, E., Worley, H., Pinnell, L.J., Bravo, J.E., Ferm, P. *et al.*, MEGARes and AMR++, v3.0: An updated comprehensive database of antimicrobial resistance determinants and an improved software pipeline for classification using high-throughput sequencing. *Nucleic Acids Res.*, 51, 1, 744–52, 2023 Jan 6, Available from: https://dx.doi.org/10.1093/nar/gkac1047.

58. Arango-Argoty, G.A., Guron, G.K.P., Guron, G.K.P., Garner, E., Riquelme, M.V., Heath, L.S. *et al.*, ARGminer: a web platform for the crowdsourcing-based curation of antibiotic resistance genes. *Bioinformatics*, 36, 9, 2966–73, 2020 May 1, Available from: https://dx.doi.org/10.1093/ bioinformatics/btaa095.

59. Tanoli, Z., Vähä-Koskela, M., Aittokallio, T., Artificial intelligence, machine learning, and drug repurposing in cancer. *Expert opinion on drug discovery*, 16, 9, 977–989, 2021, Available from: https://www.tandfonline.com/doi/ abs/10.1080/17460441.2021.1883585.

60. Prasad, K. and Kumar, V., Artificial intelligence-driven drug repurposing and structural biology for SARS-CoV-2. *Curr. Res. Pharmacol. Drug Discov.*, 2, 100042, 2021 Jan 1.

61. Melo, M.C.R., Maasch, J.R.M.A., de la Fuente-Nunez, C., Accelerating antibiotic discovery through artificial intelligence. *Commun. Biol.*, 4, 1, 1050, 2021, Available from: https://www. nature.com/articles/s42003-021-02586-0.

62. Mba, I.E. and Nweze, E.I., Focus: Antimicrobial Resistance: Antimicrobial Peptides Therapy: An Emerging Alternative for Treating Drug-Resistant Bacteria. *Yale J. Biol. Med.*, 95, 4, 445, 2022 Dec 1, Available from: /pmc/articles/PMC9765339/.

63. Yan, J., Bhadra, P., Li, A., Sethiya, P., Qin, L., Tai, H.K. *et al.*, Deep-AmPEP30: Improve Short Antimicrobial Peptides Prediction with Deep Learning. *Mol. Ther. Nucleic Acids*, 20, 882–94, 2020 Jun 5, Available from: http://www.cell.com/article/S2162253120301323/fulltext.

64. Porto, W.F., Irazazabal, L., Alves, E.S.F., Ribeiro, S.M., Matos, C.O., Pires, ÁS *et al.*, *In silico* optimization of a guava antimicrobial peptide enables combinatorial exploration for peptide design. *Nat. Commun.*, 9, 1, 1490, 2018, Available from: https://www.nature.com/articles/s41467-018-03746-3.

65. Bhadra, P., Yan, J., Li, J., Fong, S., Siu, S.W.I., AmPEP: Sequence-based prediction of antimicrobial peptides using distribution patterns of amino acid properties and random forest. *Sci. Rep.*, 8, 1, 2018, Available from: https://www.nature.com/articles/s41598-018-19752-w.

66. Singh, O., Hsu, W.L., Su, E.C.Y., Co-AMPpred for *in silico*-aided predictions of antimicrobial peptides by integrating composition-based features. *BMC Bioinf.*, 22, 1, 1–21, 2021 Dec 1, Available from: https://bmcbioinformatics.biomedcentral.com/articles/10.1186/s12859-021-04305-2.

67. Lv, H., Yan, K., Guo, Y., Zou, Q., Hesham, A.E.L., Liu, B., AMPpred-EL: An effective antimicrobial peptide prediction model based on ensemble learning. *Comput. Biol. Med.*, 146, 105577, 2022 Jul 1.

68. Lee, H., Lee, S., Lee, I., Nam, H., AMP-BERT: Prediction of antimicrobial peptide function based on a BERT model. *Protein Sci.*, 32, 1, 4529, 2023 Jan 1, Available from: https://onlinelibrary.wiley.com/doi/full/10.1002/pro.4529.

69. Mooney, C., Haslam, N.J., Pollastri, G., Shields, D.C., Towards the Improved Discovery and Design of Functional Peptides: Common Features of Diverse Classes Permit Generalized Prediction of Bioactivity. *PloS One*, 7, 10, 45012, 2012 Oct 8, Available from: https://journals.plos. org/plosone/article?id=10.1371/journal.pone.0045012.

70. Meher, P.K., Sahu, T.K., Saini, V., Rao, A.R., Predicting antimicrobial peptides with improved accuracy by incorporating the compositional, physico-chemical and structural features into Chou's general PseAAC. *Sci. Rep.*, 7, 1, 42362, 1–12, 2017, Available from: https://www.nature.com/articles/srep42362.

71. Landin, M. and Rowe, R.C., Artificial neural networks technology to model, understand, and optimize drug formulations. *Formulation Tools Pharm. Dev.*, 1, 7–37, 2013 Jan 1.

72. Ventola, C.L., The Antibiotic Resistance Crisis: Part 1: Causes and Threats. *Pharm. Ther.*, 40, 4, 277, 2015, Available from: /pmc/articles/PMC4378521/.

73. Talat, A. and Khan, A.U., Artificial intelligence as a smart approach to develop antimicrobial drug molecules: A paradigm to combat drug-resistant infections. *Drug Discov. Today*, 28, 4, 103491, 2023 Apr 1.

74. Dara, S., Dhamercherla, S., Jadav, S. S., Babu, C. M., Ahsan, M.J., Machine learning in drug discovery: A review. *Artificial Intell. Rev.*, 55, 3, 1947–1999, 2022.

75. Liu, G., Catacutan, D.B., Rathod, K., Swanson, K., Jin, W., Mohammed, J.C. *et al.*, Deep learning-guided discovery of an antibiotic targeting Acinetobacter baumannii. *Nat. Chem. Biol.*, 19, 11, 1342–1350, 2023 May 25, Available from: https://www.nature.com/articles/s41589-023-01349-8.

76. Dean, S.N. and Walper, S.A., Variational autoencoder for generation of antimicrobial peptides. *ACS Omega*, 5, 33, 20746–54, 2020 Aug 25, Available from: https://pubs.acs.org/doi/full/10.1021/acsomega.0c00442.

77. Wu, X., Wang, Z., Li, X., Fan, Y., He, G., Wan, Y. *et al.*, *In vitro* and *in vivo* activities of antimicrobial peptides developed using an amino acid-based activity prediction method. *Antimicrob. Agents Chemother.*, 58, 9, 5342–9, 2014, Available from: https://journals.asm.org/doi/10.1128/aac.02823-14.

78. Fitzgerald, J.B., Schoeberl, B., Nielsen, U.B., Sorger, P.K., Systems biology and combination therapy in the quest for clinical efficacy. *Nat. Chem. Biol.*, 2, 9, 458–66, 200, Available from: https://www.nature.com/articles/nchembio817.

79. Worthington, R.J. and Melander, C., Combination approaches to combat multidrug-resistant bacteria. *Trends Biotechnol.*, 31, 3, 177–84, 2013 Mar 19, Available from: http://www.cell.com/article/S0167779912002259/fulltext.

80. Cantrell, J.M., Chung, C.H., Chandrasekaran, S., Machine learning to design antimicrobial combination therapies: Promises and pitfalls. *Drug Discov. Today*, 27, 6, 1639–51, 2022 Jun 1.

81. Güvenç Paltun, B., Kaski, S., Mamitsuka, H., Machine learning approaches for drug combination therapies. *Brief Bioinform.*, 22, 6, 1–16, 2021 Nov 5. Available from: https://dx.doi.org/10.1093/bib/bbab293.

82. Julkunen, H., Cichonska, A., Gautam, P., Szedmak, S., Douat, J., Pahikkala, T. *et al.*, comboFM: leveraging multi-way interactions for systematic prediction of drug combination effects. *BioRxiv*, 09, 02, 278986, Sep 3; 2020, Available from: https://www.biorxiv.org/content/10.1101/2020.09.02.278986v1.

83. Preuer, K., Lewis, R.P.I., Hochreiter, S., Bender, A., Bulusu, K.C., Klambauer, G., DeepSynergy: predicting anti-cancer drug synergy with Deep Learning. *Bioinformatics*, 34, 9, 1538–46, 2018 May 1, Available from: https://dx.doi.org/10.1093/bioinformatics/btx806.

84. Ianevski, A., Giri, A.K., Gautam, P., Kononov, A., Potdar, S., Saarela, J. *et al.*, Prediction of drug combination effects with a minimal set of experiments. *Nat. Mach. Intell.*, 1, 12, 568–577, 2019, Available from: https://www.nature.com/articles/s42256-019-0122-4.

85. Jin, W., Stokes, J.M., Eastman, R.T., Itkin, Z., Zakharov, A.V., Collins, J.J. *et al.*, Deep learning identifies synergistic drug combinations for treating COVID-19. *Proc. Natl. Acad. Sci.*, 118, 39, 1–7, 2021 Sep 28. Available from: https://doi.org/10.1073/pnas.2105070118

86. Srinivasan, A., Antibiotic stewardship: Why we must, how we can. *Cleve Clin. J. Med.*, 84, 9, 673–9, 2017 Sep 1. Available from: https://www.ccjm.org/content/84/9/673.

87. Shrestha, J., Zahra, F., Cannady, J.R.P., Antimicrobial Stewardship. *StatPearls.*, 1, 1–15, 2022 Jun 23, Available from: https://www.ncbi.nlm.nih.gov/books/NBK572068/.

88. Magill, S.S., O'Leary, E., Ray, S.M., Kainer, M.A., Evans, C., Bamberg, W.M. *et al.*, Assessment of the Appropriateness of Antimicrobial Use in US Hospitals. *JAMA Netw. Open*, 4, 3, e212007, 2022 Mar 18.

89. Singh, N., Rogers, P., Atwood, C.W., Wagener, M.M., Yu, V.L., Short-course empiric antibiotic therapy for patients with pulmonary infiltrates in the intensive care unit: a proposed solution for indiscriminate antibiotic prescription. *Am. J. Respir. Crit. Care Med.*, 162, 2, 505–511, 2000.

90. Chang, A. and Chen, J.H., BSAC Vanguard Series: Artificial intelligence and antibiotic stewardship. *J. Antimicrob. Chemother.*, 77, 5, 1216–7, 2022 Apr 27, Available from: https://dx.doi.org/10.1093/jac/dkac096.

91. Beaudoin, M., Kabanza, F., Nault, V., Valiquette, L., Evaluation of a machine learning capability for a clinical decision support system to enhance antimicrobial stewardship programs. *ArtifIntell Med.*, 68, 29–36, 2016 Mar 1.

92. Cavallaroid, M., Moran, E., Collyer, B., Mccarthy, N.D., Greenid, C., Keeling, M.J., Informing antimicrobial stewardship with explainable AI. *PloS Digital Health*, 2, 1, 0000162, 2023 Jan 5, Available from: https://journals.plos.org/digitalhealth/article?id=10.1371/journal.pdig.0000162.

93. Cai, T., Anceschi, U., Prata, F., Collini, L., Brugnolli, A., Migno, S. *et al.*, Artificial Intelligence Can Guide Antibiotic Choice in Recurrent UTIs and Become an Important Aid to Improve Antimicrobial Stewardship. *Antibiotics*, 12, 2, 375, 2023 Feb 11, Available from: https://www.mdpi.com/2079-6382/12/2/375/htm.

94. Li, D., Wang, Y., Hu, W., Chen, F., Zhao, J., Chen, X. *et al.*, Application of Machine Learning Classifier to Candida auris Drug Resistance Analysis. *Front. Cell Infect. Microbiol.*, 11, 742062, 2021 Oct 15.

95. Fu, C., Zhang, X., Veri, A.O., Iyer, K.R., Lash, E., Xue, A. *et al.*, Leveraging machine learning essentiality predictions and chemogenomic interactions to identify antifungal targets. *Nat. Commun.*, 121, 6497, 2021, Available from: https://www.nature.com/articles/s41467-021-26850-3.

96. Delavy, M., Cerutti, L., Croxatto, A., Prod'hom, G., Sanglard, D., Greub, G. *et al.*, Machine Learning Approach for Candida albicans Fluconazole Resistance Detection Using Matrix-Assisted Laser Desorption/Ionization Time-of-Flight Mass Spectrometry. *Front. Microbiol.*, 10, 500387, 2020 Jan 14.

97. Badura, A., Krysiński, J., Nowaczyk, A., Buciński, A., Application of artificial neural networks to the prediction of antifungal activity of imidazole derivatives against Candida albicans. *Chemome. Intell. Lab. Syst.*, 222, 104501, 2022 Mar 15.

98. Leidner, F., Kurt Yilmaz, N., Schiffer, C.A., Deciphering Antifungal Drug Resistance in Pneumocystis jirovecii DHFR with Molecular Dynamics and Machine Learning. *J. Chem. Inf Model*, 61, 6, 2537–41, 2021 Jun 28, Available from: https://pubs.acs.org/doi/abs/10.1021/acs.jcim.1c00403.

99. Sharma, R., Shrivastava, S., Singh, S.K., Kumar, A., Saxena, S., Singh, R.K., Deep-AFPpred: identifying novel antifungal peptides using pretrained embeddings from seq2vec with 1DCNN-BiLSTM. *Brief Bioinform.*, 23, 1, 1–16, 2022 Jan 17, Available from: https://dx.doi.org/10.1093/bib/ bbab422.

100. Gao, Y., Tang, M., Li, Y., Niu, X., Li, J., Fu, C. *et al.*, Machine-learning based prediction and analysis of prognostic risk factors in patients with candidemia and bacteraemia: a 5-year analysis. *PeerJ.*, 10, 13594, 2022 Jun 15, Available from: https://peerj.com/articles/13594.

101. Strasfeld, L. and Chou, S., Antiviral Drug Resistance: Mechanisms and Clinical Implications. *Infect. Dis. Clin. North Am.*, 24, 2, 413–37, 2010 Jun 1.

102. Blassel, L., Tostevin, A., Villabona-Arenas, C.J., Peeters, M., Hué, S., Gascuel, O., Using machine learning and big data to explore the drug resistance landscape in HIV. *PLoSComput Biol.*, 17, 8, 1008873, 2021 Aug 1, Available from: https://journals.plos.org/ploscompbiol/article?id=10.1371/ journal.pcbi.1008873.

103. Zazzi, M., Incardona, F., Rosen-Zvi, M., Prosperi, M., Lengauer, T., Altmann, A. *et al.*, Predicting Response to Antiretroviral Treatment by Machine Learning: The EuResist Project. *Intervirology*, 55, 2, 123–7, 2012 Jan 1, Available from: https://dx.doi.org/10.1159/000332008.

104. Tarasova, O. and Poroikov, V., Machine Learning in Discovery of New Antivirals and Optimization of Viral Infections Therapy. *Curr. Med. Chem.*, 28, 38, 7840–61, 2021 May 5.

105. Ivanov, J., Polshakov, D., Kato-Weinstein, J., Zhou, Q., Li, Y., Granet, R. *et al.*, Quantitative structure–activity relationship machine learning models and their applications for identifying viral 3Clpro- And RDRP-targeting compounds as potential therapeutics for Covid-19 and related viral infections. *ACS Omega*, 5, 42, 27344–58, 2020 Oct 27, Available from: https://pubs.acs. org/doi/full/10.1021/acsomega.0c03682.

106. Kwofie, S.K., Broni, E., Teye, J., Quansah, E., Issah, I., Wilson, M.D. *et al.*, Pharmacoinformatics-based identification of potential bioactive compounds against Ebola virus protein VP24. *Comput. Biol. Med.*, 113, 103414, 2019 Oct 1.

107. Tian, Y., Zhang, S., Yin, H., Yan, A., Quantitative structure-activity relationship (QSAR) models and their applicability domain analysis on HIV-1 protease inhibitors by machine learning methods. *Chemom. Intell. Lab. Syst.*, 196, 103888, 2020 Jan 15.

108. Serafim, M.S.M., dos Santos Júnior, V.S., Gertrudes, J.C., Maltarollo, V.G., Honorio, K.M., Machine learning techniques applied to the drug design and discovery of new antivirals: A

brief look over the past decade. *Expert Opin. Drug Discov.*, 16, 9, 961–75, 2021, Available from: https://www.tandfonline.com/doi/abs /10.1080/17460441.2021.1918098.

109. Steiner, M.C., Gibson, K.M., Crandall, K.A., Drug Resistance Prediction Using Deep Learning Techniques on HIV-1 Sequence Data. *Viruses*, 12, 5, 560, 2020May 19. Available from: https://www.mdpi.com/1999-4915/12/5/560/htm.

110. Park, H., Lo-Ciganic, W.H., Huang, J., Wu, Y., Henry, L., Peter, J. *et al.*, Machine learning algorithms for predicting direct-acting antiviral treatment failure in chronic hepatitis C: An HCV-TARGET analysis. *Hepatology*, 76, 2, 483–91, 2022, Available from: https://journals.lww.com/hep/Fulltext/2022/08000/Machine_learning_algorithms_for_predicting.20.aspx.

111. Gawriljuk, V.O., Foil, D.H., Puhl, A.C., Zorn, K.M., Lane, T.R., Riabova, O. *et al.*, Development of Machine Learning Models and the Discovery of a New Antiviral Compound against Yellow Fever Virus. *J. Chem. Inf. Model*, 61, 8, 3804–13, 2021, Available from: https://pubs.acs.org/doi/abs/10.1021/acs.jcim.1c00460.

112. Brandt, P., Moodley, D., Pillay, A.W., Seebregts, C.J., De Oliveira, T., An investigation of classification algorithms for predicting HIV drug resistance without genotype resistance testing, in: *Lecture Notes in Computer Science (including subseries Lecture Notes in Artificial Intelligence and Lecture Notes in Bioinformatics)*, vol. 8315, pp. 236–53, 2014, Available from: https://link.springer.com/ chapter/10.1007/978-3-642-53956-5_16.

113. Chowdhury, A.S., Reehl, S.M., Kehn-Hall, K., Bishop, B., Webb-Robertson, B.J.M., Better understanding and prediction of antiviral peptides through primary and secondary structure feature importance. *Sci. Rep.*, 10, 1, 1–8, 2020, Available from: https://www.nature.com/articles/s41598-020-76161-8.

114. Alves, N.G., Mata, A.I., Luís, J.P., Brito, R.M.M., Simões, C.J.V., An Innovative Sequence-to-Structure-Based Approach to Drug Resistance Interpretation and Prediction: The Use of Molecular Interaction Fields to Detect HIV-1 Protease Binding-Site Dissimilarities. *Front. Chem.*, 8, 518214, 2020 Apr 29.

115. Salama, M.A., Hassanien, A.E., Mostafa, A., The prediction of virus mutation using neural networks and rough set techniques. *EURASIP J. Bioinform. Syst. Biol.*, 1, 1–11, 2016, Available from: https://bsb-eurasipjournals.springeropen.com/articles/10.1186/s13637-016-0042-0.

116. Shaltout, N., Rafea, A., Moustafa, A., Moustafa, M., ElHefnawi, M., Optimizing the Detection of Antiviral-Resistant Influenza-A Strains using Machine Learning, in: *Lecture Notes in Engineering and Computer Science*, p. 2226, 2016, Available from: https://fount.aucegypt.edu/faculty_journal_articles/1597.

117. Tao, S., Chen, Y., Wu, J., Zhao, D., Cai, H., Wang, L. *et al.*, VDDB: A comprehensive resource and machine learning tool for antiviral drug discovery. *MedComm – Future Medicine;*, 2, 1, 32, 2023, Available from: https://onlinelibrary.wiley.com/doi/full/10.1002/mef2.32.

118. Pawar, S.D., Freas, C., Weber, I.T., Harrison, R.W., Analysis of drug resistance in HIV protease. *BMC Bioinf.*, 19, 11, 1–6, 2018, Available from: https://bmcbioinformatics.biomedcentral.com/articles/10.1186/s12859-018-2331-y.

119. Ford, C.T., Janies, D., Antani, S.K., Jaeger, S., Burrows, J., Ensemble machine learning modeling for the prediction of artemisinin resistance in malaria. *F1000Research*, 9, 62, 1–3, 2020, Available from: https://f1000research.com/articles/9-62.

120. Zhang, H., Guo, J., Li, H., Guan, Y., Machine learning for artemisinin resistance in malaria treatment across *in vivo-in vitro* platforms. *iScience*, 25, 3, 103910, 2022, Available from: http://www.cell.com/article/S2589004222001808/fulltext.

121. Deelder, W., Benavente, E.D., Phelan, J., Manko, E., Campino, S., Palla, L. *et al.*, Using deep learning to identify recent positive selection in malaria parasite sequence data. *Malar. J.*, 20, 1, 1–9, 2021, Available from: https://malariajournal.biomedcentral.com/articles/10.1186/s12936-021-03788-x.

122. Neves, B.J., Braga, R.C., Alves, V.M., Lima, M.N.N., Cassiano, G.C., Muratov, E.N. *et al.*, Deep Learning-driven research for drug discovery: Tackling Malaria. *PLoSComput Biol;*, 16, 2, 1007025, 2020, Available from: https://journals.plos.org/ploscompbiol/article?id=10.1371/journal.pcbi.1007025.

123. Ashdown, G.W., Dimon, M., Fan, M., Terán, F.S.R., Witmer, K., Gaboriau, D.C.A. *et al.*, A machine learning approach to define antimalarial drug action from heterogeneous cell-based screens. *Sci. Adv.*, 6, 39, 1–8, 2020, Available from: https://www.science.org/doi/10.1126/sciadv.aba9338.

124. Jamal, S. and Scaria, V., Cheminformatic models based on machine learning for pyruvate kinase inhibitors of Leishmania mexicana. *BMC Bioinf.*, 14, 1, 1–7, 2013, Available from: https://bmc-bioinformatics.biomedcentral.com/articles/10.1186/1471-2105-14-329.

125. Kumari, M. and Chandra, S., *In silico* prediction of anti-malarial hit molecules based on machine learning methods. *Int. J. Comput. Biol. Drug Des.*, 8, 1, 40–53, 2015.

126. Iskandar, K., Molinier, L., Hallit, S., Sartelli, M., Hardcastle, T.C., Haque, M. *et al.*, Surveillance of antimicrobial resistance in low- and middle-income countries: A scattered picture. *Antimicrob. Resist. Infect. Control*, 10, 1, 1–19, 2021. Available from: https:// aricjournal.biomedcentral.com/articles/10.1186/s13756-021-00931-w.

127. McArthur, A.G. and Tsang, K.K., Antimicrobial resistance surveillance in the genomic age. *Ann. N Y Acad. Sci.*, 1388, 1, 78–91, 2017, Available from: https://onlinelibrary.wiley.com/doi/full/10.1111/ nyas.13289.

128. Peng, Z., Maciel-Guerra, A., Baker, M., Zhang, X., Hu, Y., Wang, W. *et al.*, Whole-genome sequencing and gene sharing network analysis powered by machine learning identifies antibiotic resistance sharing between animals, humans and environment in livestock farming. *PLoSComput Biol.*, 18, 3, 1010018, 2022, Available from: https://journals.plos.org/ploscomp-biol/ article?id=10.1371/journal.pcbi.1010018.

129. Kumar, S., Nayyar, A., Paul, A., *Swarm intelligence and evolutionary algorithms in healthcare and drug development*, vol. 1, pp. 0–168, Chapman & Hall, CRC Press, United States, 2019.

130. Hindler, J.F. and Munro, S., Antimicrobial Susceptibility Testing, in: *Clinical Microbiology Procedures Handbook*, Third Edition, pp. 2–3, 2022, 5.0.1-5.18.2.1, Available from: https://www.ncbi.nlm.nih.gov/books/NBK539714/.

131. Burnham, C.A.D., Leeds, J., Nordmann, P., O'Grady, J., Patel, J., Diagnosing antimicrobial resistance. *Nat. Rev. Microbiol.*, 15, 11, 697–703, 2017, Available from: https://www.nature.com/articles/nrmicro.2017.103.

132. Khaledi, A., Weimann, A., Schniederjans, M., Asgari, E., Kuo, T.H., Oliver, A. *et al.*, Predicting antimicrobial resistance in Pseudomonas aeruginosa with machine learning-enabled molecular diagnostics. *EMBO Mol. Med.*, 12, 3, 10264, 2020, Available from: https://onlinelibrary.wiley.com/doi/full/10.15252/emmm.201910264.

133. Lechowicz, Ł., Urbaniak, M., Adamus-Białek, W., Kaca, W., The use of infrared spectroscopy and artificial neural networks for detection of uropathogenic Escherichia coli strains' susceptibility to cephalothin. *Acta Biochim. Pol.*, 60, 4, 713–8, 2013. Available from: https://ojs.ptbioch.edu.pl/index.php/abp/article/view/2046.

134. Donlan, R.M., Microbial Life on Surfaces Emerging Infectious Diseases journal - CDC. *Emerg Infect. Dis.*, 8, 9, 881–90, September 2002, Available from: https://wwwnc.cdc.gov/eid/article/8/9/02-0063_article.

135. Hall-Stoodley, L., Costerton, J.W., Stoodley, P., Bacterial biofilms: From the Natural environment to infectious diseases. *Nat. Rev. Microbiol.*, 2, 2, 95–108, 2004, Available from: https://www.nature.com/articles/nrmicro821.

136. Muhammad, M.H., Idris, A.L., Fan, X., Guo, Y., Yu, Y., Jin, X. *et al.*, Beyond Risk: Bacterial Biofilms and Their Regulating Approaches. *Front. Microbiol.*, 11, 530515, 2020 May 21.

137. Alford, M.A., Baghela, A., Yeung, A.T.Y., Pletzer, D., Hancock, R.E.W., NtrBC Regulates Invasiveness and Virulence of Pseudomonas aeruginosa During High-Density Infection. *Front. Microbiol.*, 11, 533374, 2020 May 5.

138. Cameron, D.R., Shan, Y., Zalis, E.A., Isabella, V., Lewis, K., A genetic determinant of persister cell formation in bacterial pathogens. *J. Bacteriol*, 200, 17, 10-1128, 2018, Available from: https://journals.asm. org/doi/10.1128/jb.00303-18.

139. Suryaletha, K., Narendrakumar, L., John, J., Radhakrishnan, M.P., George, S., Thomas, S., Decoding the proteomic changes involved in the biofilm formation of Enterococcus faecalis SK460 to elucidate potential biofilm determinants. *BMC Microbiol*, 19, 1, 1–13, 2019, Available from: https://bmcmicrobiol.biomedcentral.com/articles/10.1186/s12866-019-1527-2.

140. Harrison, A., Hardison, R.L., Wallace, R.M., Fitch, J., Heimlich, D.R., Bryan, M.O. *et al.*, Reprioritization of biofilm metabolism is associated with nutrient adaptation and long-term survival of Haemophilus influenzae. *NPJ Biofilms Microbiomes*, 5, 1, 1–14, 2019, Available from: https://www.nature.com/articles/s41522-019-0105-6.

141. Alves-Barroco, C., Roma-Rodrigues, C., Balasubramanian, N., Guimarães, M.A., Ferreira-Carvalho, B.T., Muthukumaran, J. *et al.*, Biofilm development and computational screening for new putative inhibitors of a homolog of the regulatory protein BrpA in Streptococcus dysgalactiae subsp. dysgalactiae. *Int. J. Med. Microbiol.*, 309, 3–4, 169–81, 2019 May 1.

142. Di Luca, M., Maccari, G., Maisetta, G., Batoni, G., BaAMPs: the database of biofilm-active antimicrobial peptides. *Biofouling*, 31, 2, 193–199, 2015, Available from: https://www.tandfonline.com/doi/abs/10. 1080/08927014.2015.1021340.

143. Sharma, A., Gupta, P., Kumar, R., Bhardwaj, A., dPABBs: A Novel in silico Approach for Predicting and Designing Anti-biofilm Peptides. *Sci. Rep.*, 6, 1, 1–13, 2016, Available from: https://www.nature.com/articles/srep21839.

144. Haney, E.F., Brito-Sánchez, Y., Trimble, M.J., Mansour, S.C., Cherkasov, A., Hancock, R.E.W., Computer-aided Discovery of Peptides that Specifically Attack Bacterial Biofilms. *Sci. Rep.*, 8, 1, 1–12, 2018, Available from: https://www.nature.com/articles/s41598-018-19669-4.

145. Srivastava, G.N., Malwe, A.S., Sharma, A.K., Shastri, V., Hibare, K., Sharma, V.K., Molib: A machine learning based classification tool for the prediction of biofilm inhibitory molecules. *Genomics*, 112, 4, 2823–32, 2020 Jul 1.

146. Rajput, A., Bhamare, K.T., Thakur, A., Kumar, M., Anti-Biofilm: Machine Learning Assisted Prediction of IC50 Activity of Chemicals Against Biofilms of Microbes Causing Antimicrobial Resistance and Implications in Drug Repurposing. *J. Mol. Biol.*, 435, 14, 168115, 2023 Apr 20.

147. Artini, M., Patsilinakos, A., Papa, R., Bozović, M., Sabatino, M., Garzoli, S. *et al.*, Antimicrobial and Antibiofilm Activity and Machine Learning Classification Analysis of Essential Oils from Different Mediterranean Plants against Pseudomonas aeruginosa. *Molecules*, 23, 2, 482, 2018, Available from: https://www.mdpi.com/1420-3049/23/2/482/htm.

148. Patsilinakos, A., Artini, M., Papa, R., Sabatino, M., Garzoli, S. *et al.*, Machine Learning Analyses on Data including Essential Oil Chemical Composition and *In Vitro* Experimental Antibiofilm Activities against Staphylococcus Species. *Molecules*, 24, 5, 890, 2019, Available from: https://www.mdpi.com/1420-3049/24/5/890/htm.

149. Artini, M., Papa, R., Sapienza, F., Vrenna, G., Assanti, V.T.G. *et al.*, Essential Oils Biofilm Modulation Activity and Machine Learning Analysis on Pseudomonas aeruginosa Isolates from Cystic Fibrosis Patients. *Microorganisms*, 10, 5, 887, 2022, Available from: https://www.mdpi.com/2076-2607/10/5/887/htm.

150. Wang, J., Jiang, Z., Wei, Y., Wang, W., Wang, F., Yang, Y. *et al.*, Multiplexed Identification of Bacterial Biofilm Infections Based on Machine-Learning-Aided Lanthanide Encoding. *ACS Nano*, 16, 2, 3300–10, 2022, Available from:https://pubs.acs.org/doi/abs/10.1021/acsnano.1c11333.

151. Carneiro, J., Magalhães, R.P., de la Oliva Roque, V.M., Simões, M., Pratas, D., Sousa, S.F., TargIDe: a machine-learning workflow for target identification of molecules with antibiofilm activity against Pseudomonas aeruginosa. *J. Comput. Aided Mol.*, 37, 5, 265–78, 2023, Available from: https://link.springer.com/article/10.1007/s10822-023-00505-5.

152. Rajput, A., Bhamare, K.T., Thakur, A., Kumar, M., Biofilm-i: A Platform for Predicting Biofilm Inhibitors Using Quantitative Structure—Relationship (QSAR) Based Regression Models to Curb Antibiotic Resistance. *Molecules*, 27, 15, 4861, 2022, Available from: https://www.mdpi.com/1420-3049/27/15/4861/htm.

153. Bose, B., *Prediction of Novel Antibiofilm Peptides from Diverse Habitats using Machine Learning. Master's Theses*, Master's Theses, 2020, San Jose University, San Jose, USA, 2020, Available from: https://scholarworks.sjsu.edu/etd_theses/5137.

154. Marciano, D.C., Wang, C., Hsu, T.K., Bourquard, T., Atri, B., Nehring, R.B. *et al.*, Evolutionary action of mutations reveals antimicrobial resistance genes in Escherichia coli. *Nat. Commun.*, 13, 1, 1–13, 2022, Available from: https://www.nature.com/articles/ s41467-022-30889-1.

155. Ali, T., Ahmed, S., Aslam, M., Artificial Intelligence for Antimicrobial Resistance Prediction: Challenges and Opportunities towards Practical Implementation. *Antibiotics*, 12, 3, 523, 2023, Available from: https://www.mdpi.com/2079-6382/12/3/523/htm.

156. Olsen, I., Biofilm-specific antibiotic tolerance and resistance. *Eur. J. Clin. Microbiol. Infect. Dis.*, 34, 5, 877–86, 2015, Available from: https://link.springer.com/article/10.1007/s10096-015-2323-z.

157. Li, L.G., Xia, Y., Zhang, T., Co-occurrence of antibiotic and metal resistance genes revealed in complete genome collection. *ISME J.*, 11, 3, 651–62, 2016, Available from: https://www.nature.com/articles/ismej2016155.

158. Rodloff, A., Bauer, T., Ewig, S., Kujath, P., Müller, E., Susceptible, Intermediate, and Resistant – The Intensity of Antibiotic Action. *DtschArztebl Int.*, 105, 39, 657–662, 2008 Sep 26.

159. Ren, Y., Chakraborty, T., Doijad, S., Falgenhauer, L., Falgenhauer, J., Goesmann, A. *et al.*, Deep Transfer Learning Enables Robust Prediction of Antimicrobial Resistance for Novel Antibiotics. *Antibiotics*, 11, 11, 1611, 2022, Available from: https://www. mdpi.com/2079-6382/11/11/1611/htm.

160. He, J., Baxter, S.L., Xu, J., Xu, J., Zhou, X., Zhang, K., The practical implementation of artificial intelligence technologies in medicine. *Nat. Med.*, 25, 1, 30–6, 2019, Available from: https://www.nature.com/articles/s41591-018-0307-0.

161. Char, D.S., Shah, N.H., Magnus, D., Implementing Machine Learning in Health Care — Addressing Ethical Challenges. *New Engl. J. Med.*, 378, 11, 981–3, 2018. Available from: https://www.nejm.org/doi/10.1056/NEJMp1714229.

162. Patrzyk, P.M., Link, D., Marewski, J.N., Human-like machines: Transparency and comprehensibility. *Behav. Brain Sci.*, 40, 276, 2017, Available from: https://www.cambridge.org/core/journals/behavioral-and-brain-sciences/article/abs/humanlike-machines-transparency-and-comp rehensibility/5A1BCA43DEE578220D66B3089F8DED46.

163. National Science and Technology Council. (2016) The National Artificial Intelligence Research And Development Strategic Plan, Available from: www.nitrd.gov.

164. Kruse, C.S., Goswamy, R., Raval, Y., Marawi, S., Challenges and Opportunities of Big Data in Health Care: A Systematic Review. *JMIR Med. Inform*, 4, 4, 38, 2016, https://medinform.jmir.org/2016/4/e38;.

165. Davenport, T. and Kalakota, R., The potential for artificial intelligence in healthcare. *Future Healthc. J.*, 6, 2, 94–8, 2019, Available from: https://www.rcpjournals.org/content/futurehosp/6/2/94.

166. Abouhawwash, M., Tanwar, S., Nayyar, A., Naved, M., *Innovations in healthcare informatics: from interoperability to data*, p. 342, IET, USA, 2023.

167. Reddy, S., Allan, S., Coghlan, S., Cooper, P., A governance model for the application of AI in health care. *J. Am. Med. Inf. Assoc.*, 27, 3, 491–7, 2020, Available from: https://dx.doi.org/10.1093/jamia/ocz192.

168. Ahmad, O.F., Stoyanov, D., Lovat, L.B., Barriers and pitfalls for artificial intelligence in gastroenterology: Ethical and regulatory issues. *Tech. Innov. Gastrointest. Endosc.*, 22, 2, 80–4, 2020, Available from: http://www.tigejournal.org/article/S1096288319300750/fulltext.

169. Morley, J., Machado, C.C.V., Burr, C., Cowls, J., Joshi, I., Taddeo, M. *et al.*, The ethics of AI in health care: A mapping review. *Soc. Sci. Med.*, 260, 113172, 2020 Sep 1.

170. Pramanik, P.K.D., Solanki, A., Debnath, A., Nayyar, A., El-Sappagh, S., Kwak, K.S., Advancing Modern Healthcare with Nanotechnology, Nanobiosensors, and Internet of Nano Things: Taxonomies, Applications, Architecture, and Challenges. *IEEE Access*, 8, 65230–66, 2020.

6

Artificial Intelligence-Powered Molecular Docking: A Promising Tool for Rational Drug Design

Nabajit Kumar Borah, Yukti Tripathi, Aastha Tanwar, Deeksha Tiwari, Aditi Sinha, Shailja Sharma, Neetu Jabalia, Ruchi Jakhmola Mani, Seneha Santoshi and Hina Bansal*

Centre for Computational Biology and Bioinformatics, Amity Institute of Biotechnology, Amity University, Noida, Uttar Pradesh, India

Abstract

Molecular docking is a vital computational method for predicting how small molecules bind to target proteins, aiding drug discovery. It involves screening vast small molecule databases to identify potential drug candidates, relying on scoring functions to rank them. This interaction between proteins and ligands is the cornerstone of drug design. Integrating artificial intelligence (AI) algorithms has revolutionized this field, boosting efficiency and accuracy. This chapter explores various docking techniques, with a focus on AI-based methods. Neural networks, reinforcement learning, and evolutionary algorithms play pivotal roles, enhancing prediction accuracy and speed by utilizing deep learning models trained on extensive protein-ligand datasets. This integration has the potential to expedite drug discovery. Recognizing that AI is not a standalone solution, the chapter emphasizes the need for integration with other methodologies to achieve comprehensive drug discovery. It also addresses the challenges and limitations of AI in molecular docking, pointing toward future research directions. In summary, AI-driven advancements in molecular docking offer a promising pathway to accelerate drug discovery while recognizing the need for a holistic approach in the field.

Keywords: Artificial intelligence, molecular docking, deep learning model, quantitative structure–activity relationship, virtual screening, drug discovery

6.1 Introduction

Over the past three decades, chemical and biological scientists have faced a significant challenge: how to deliver therapeutics to the right patients with the greatest possible efficacy and the fewest possible risks. Another obstacle in the process of designing and developing new drugs was the expense and time required to produce the novel therapeutic agents. To overcome these difficulties, scientists from around the world used computational methods, also known as traditional methods like virtual screening and molecular docking [1].

Corresponding author: hinabansal@gmail.com

Abhirup Khanna, May El Barachi, Sapna Jain, Manoj Kumar and Anand Nayyar (eds.) *Artificial Intelligence and Machine Learning in Drug Design and Development*, (157–188) © 2024 Scrivener Publishing LLC

Technology advancements incorporate artificial intelligence algorithms in computer-aided drug design to do away with the difficulties of conventional drug design and development. Artificial intelligence is the umbrella term for supervised learning, unsupervised learning, and reinforcement learning, which are all subsets of machine learning. "Deep learning", the most common subset of ML, has been widely used in drug development. Predicting a ligand's ideal binding conformation within a receptor's binding site is the goal of molecular docking. In the past, docking algorithms used the inflexible models of the ligand and receptor and scoring functions based on physics. The lengthy and intricate processes involved in drug discovery and design also include choosing and validating the targets, screening of therapeutics, lead compound optimization, pre-clinical and clinical trials, and production processes, to name just a few [2].

Computer-aided modeling that utilizes artificial intelligence (AI) and machine learning (ML) concepts has become a useful tool for various components of the drug discovery and development process. The evaluation of drug toxicity, the study of physicochemical behavior, the discovery and verification of organic substances, target recognition, peptide synthesis, drug monitoring, and the evaluation of drug efficacy and efficiency are all included in this. These jobs can now be completed more quickly, more affordably, and with greater accuracy thanks to AI-powered computational modeling techniques [3]. This chapter aims to provide a comprehensive exploration of the integration of AI in molecular docking, a crucial step in the drug discovery pipeline. Traditional docking algorithms face challenges in terms of efficiency and accuracy. By incorporating AI techniques, such as ML and deep learning, into docking algorithms, these limitations can be overcome, paving the way for more effective drug discovery processes [4].

Objectives of the Chapter

The objectives of the chapter are:

- To present a comprehensive overview of AI techniques in drug discovery, emphasizing the role of computational modeling;
- To provide an in-depth understanding of the principles and fundamentals of molecular docking;
- To explore the integration of AI into molecular docking algorithms, showcasing different algorithms and its usage;
- To highlight various applications of AI in molecular docking, including chemical compound identification, target validation, toxicity evaluation, and drug monitoring;
- To discuss the challenges encountered in implementing AI in docking algorithms and propose potential solutions
- And, to identify and analyze potential future directions for the integration of AI in molecular docking.

By addressing these objectives, the chapter aims to contribute to the knowledge and understanding of researchers, practitioners, and enthusiasts in the field of drug discovery and computational modeling in the modern age.

Organization of the Chapter

The rest of chapter is organized as follows: Section 6.2 covers the basics of molecular docking which are then explained, covering the definition, ligand–receptor interactions, docking algorithms, and scoring functions. Section 6.3 is where the role of AI in molecular docking is explored, discussing how AI enhances the accuracy and efficiency of docking predictions, and diverse AI-based algorithms are presented, delving into the various machine learning and deep learning techniques used in molecular docking. Section 6.4 enlightens drug discovery. Section 6.5 discusses diverse machine learning algorithms for drug discovery. Section 6.6 discusses deep learning-oriented information. Section 6.7 highlights the AI-based toolkits used for drug discovery. Section 6.8 stresses on the applications of AI in molecular docking. Section 6.9 elaborates the challenges and limitations of AI-based molecular docking. And, finally, section 6.10 concludes the chapter with future scope.

6.2   Basics of Molecular Docking

A type of computational modeling technique is one which predicts the preferred binding orientation of a molecule (such as a ligand) to a different one (such as a receptor) when they interact and form a stable complex (Figure 6.1). This development has been brought about by the understanding that the interacting surfaces of cellular receptors are frequently flexible and chemically active and that these characteristics frequently play a crucial role in the biological effects of the small molecules or ligands that bind to these receptors. It is used to anticipate how drug candidates will bind to protein targets in order to forecast the drug's affinity and activity [1].

The main goal of molecular docking is to achieve an optimized conformation and computationally simulate the molecular identification process in order to reduce the free energy of the entire system.

The process of docking can be performed between the following:

a.   Protein/small ligand
b.   Protein/peptide
c.   Protein/protein
d.   Protein/nucleotide

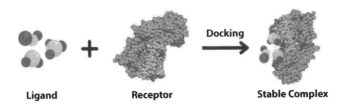

Figure 6.1 Illustration of molecular docking.

In silico chemo-biological approaches are the mainstay of contemporary drug discovery.

Docking has grown to be a crucial tool for both drug development and comprehending the interactions between chemical compounds and their molecular targets since it was first introduced in the middle of the 1970s. In fact, since its initial publication, various studies have described the use of molecular docking in the development of more accurate docking techniques and the identification of structural determinants necessary for efficient ligand–receptor binding [5].

6.2.1   Fundamental Process of Molecular Docking

The mechanics of molecular docking involves several steps as presented in Figure 6.2 [6].

A.   Preparation of ligand and receptor

Any unwanted molecules, such as solvent molecules or co-crystallized ligands, are eliminated from the crystal structure or three-dimensional models before the ligand and receptor molecules are ready. In most cases, the receptor is a protein, nucleic acid, or some other type of biomolecular target, whereas the ligand is typically a small organic molecule.

B.   Generation of search space

The area where the ligand is anticipated to bind to the receptor is represented by its binding site, and a search space is established around it. Experimental data can be used to determine this, or different algorithms can be used to predict it.

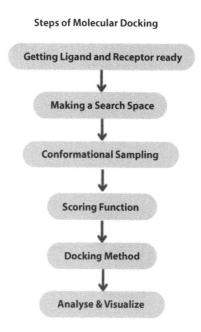

Figure 6.2 Key steps involved in docking.

C. Conformational sampling

Multiple conformations of the ligand are generated to explore the possible binding orientations. This can be achieved through techniques such as molecular dynamics simulations and systematic conformational search methods or by using pre-generated conformer libraries.

D. Scoring function

Using a scoring function, the different conformations of the ligands inside the binding site are ranked and assessed. The binding affinity or energy of the ligand–receptor complex is determined by the scoring function. The ranking function takes into account a number of variables such as hydrogen bonds, effect of solvation, van der Waals, and electrostatic interactions.

E. Docking algorithm

The best location for the ligand within the binding site is found using a docking algorithm, which explores the conformational space of the ligand and receptor. There are many algorithms available, including fast Fourier transform-based methods, Monte Carlo techniques, and Lamarckian genetic algorithms. To find the ideal docking solution, these algorithms combine random sampling, local optimization, and scoring.

F. Analysis and visualization

The most advantageous binding poses of a ligand within the receptor binding site are found after the step of docking simulation is finished. In order to better understand the binding mechanism and direct future optimization, visualization tools are used to examine how the ligand and receptor interact.

6.2.2   Essential Components of Molecular Docking

The success and accuracy of the molecular docking process depend on two basic components: search algorithms and scoring function.

A) Search algorithm

Theoretically, the search space is composed of all possible orientations and conformations of protein–ligand combinations. To fully explore the search space, it would be necessary to list every potential molecule distortion as well as every potential rotational and translational orientation of the ligand relative to the protein, at a particular level of granularity. With the available computational resources, this is, however, essentially impossible [7].

Some of the commonly used search algorithms are as follows: [8]

a. Exhaustive search: This algorithm generates and evaluates each potential binding pose, thoroughly exploring the entire conformational space. Although it ensures that the global minimum energy configuration will be found, the sheer number of possible configurations makes it computationally expensive and frequently impractical [9].

b. Genetic algorithms (GA): Genetic algorithms, which are inspired by biological evolution, use a population of potential solutions (individuals) that go through reproduction, crossover, and mutation to create new generations.

The selection process is influenced by each person's fitness, which serves as a representation of its binding energy. In addition to efficiently searching the conformational space, genetic algorithms provide a balance between exploration and exploitation.

c. Monte Carlo (MC) methods: Random sampling is used in Monte Carlo methods to investigate the conformational space. Algorithms like Metropolis Monte Carlo or simulated annealing are frequently employed in docking. By applying perturbations (rotations and translations) to the ligand, they start from an initial pose, and a random pose sample is taken from each new pose. The Metropolis criterion or a temperature schedule is used to decide whether to accept or reject a move.

d. Particle swarm optimization (PSO): It keeps a population of particles, each of which stands for a prospective resolution. The particles move through conformational space, updating their positions in accordance with their own knowledge and the current best solution. PSO algorithms are effective at efficiently navigating the search space and converging on the best answers.

e. Lamarckian genetic algorithm: This algorithm combines local search techniques with genetic algorithms. Like genetic algorithms, it begins with a population of individuals. Then, it refines each person's binding poses by using local search operators (like gradient-based optimization). This method combines the local refinement power of optimization methods with the global exploration capabilities of genetic algorithms.

Both the ligand and the receptor have been subjected to a variety of conformational search techniques such as the following:

1. Torsion searches involving rotatable bonds that are systematic or random
2. Computer simulations of atomic dynamics
3. "Evolve" new low-energy conformations using genetic algorithms

The algorithm should generate as many configurations as possible so that binding modes can be discovered through experimentation [6].

B) Scoring functions

Ranking the ligand positioning in relation to one another is made possible by the scoring function. In a perfect world, the score and the ligand's affinity for binding to the protein would be directly correlated, making the best-scoring ligands also the best binders. The most common type of scoring functions used in molecular mechanics are force field-based, knowledge-based, empirical, and machine learning-based (Figure 6.3).

The strength and power of the non-covalent interaction of two molecules after docking is predicted using scoring functions, which are quick, approximate mathematical techniques. Typically, there are two molecules involved: a biological target of the drug, such as a protein receptor, and a tiny organic chemical compound, such as a drug [10].

Three different expressions that are relevant to docking and drug design are used to determine scoring, namely:

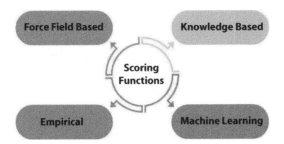

Figure 6.3 Most commonly used scoring functions.

    a. Docking search-based ranking of generated configurations.
    b. Ranking various ligands when screening proteins virtually.
    c. According to the binding affinity of ligand–receptor (selectivity and speci-
       ficity) against different proteins, the ligands are ranked [11].

Using force fields, a set of equations, and associated constants, force field-based scoring functions evaluate the electrostatic and van der Waals interactions between and within
the docked molecules. Other techniques for calculating the desolation energy between
ligands and receptors include combining molecular mechanics energies with the Poisson–
Boltzmann generalized Born and surface area continuum solvation methods [12].

Based on the interactions and forces counted for the docked molecules, including the
quantity of hydrogen bonds, rotatable bonds, hydrophobic interactions, and hydrophilic
interactions, empirically based scoring functions are calculated. Multiple linear regression
is used to fit the scoring function coefficients. The statistical mechanics analysis of liquids,
also referred to as the potential of mean force scoring functions, was the original source of
knowledge-based scoring functions.

In order to assess the fitness, a statistical potential function of protein–ligand pairs is
solved. The Protein Data Bank's collection of protein–ligand complex structures is used as
a training set or "knowledge base," in which the atoms of proteins and ligands are classified
into different types based on the environment of molecules, and the distance-dependent
potential of each potential pair is calculated based on the frequency of the atomic pair.

Machine learning is used to create a non-linear energy function for the dot structure
using a variety of descriptors, including hydrogen bonding, electrostatic interactions or
aromatic stacking, shape or surface characteristics, ligand molecular weight, and rotatable
bonds [13]. A branch of artificial intelligence called "machine learning" aims to replicate
human learning processes using data and algorithms.

6.2.3   Types of Molecular Docking

Numerous molecular docking techniques exist, which use either flexible or rigid ligand/
target combinations, depending on the objectives of the docking simulations [14]. These
may specifically include the following (Figure 6.4):

    a. Rigid docking
    b. Semi-flexible docking
    c. Flexible (soft) docking

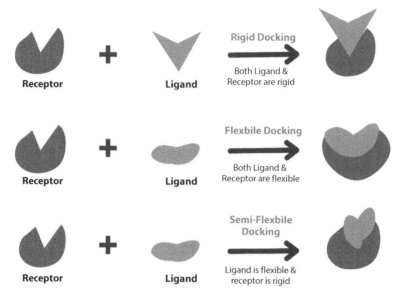

Figure 6.4 Types of docking.

6.2.3.1 Rigid Docking

Rigid docking, also known as rigid body docking, is a molecular docking technique that assumes both the ligand and receptor molecules maintain their rigid structures during the binding process. In this approach, the ligand is treated as a rigid entity, and its conformational flexibility is not considered. The docking algorithm explores the possible binding poses by exhaustively sampling the translational and rotational space of the ligand with respect to the receptor. The binding affinity between the ligand and receptor is typically evaluated using scoring functions that assess complementarity and interaction energies. Rigid docking is computationally faster compared to flexible docking methods but may overlook important conformational changes of the ligand and receptor upon binding [15].

6.2.3.2 Flexible Docking

Flexible docking, as the name suggests, incorporates the flexibility of the ligand or receptor (or both) into the docking process. It considers the conformational changes that may occur in the binding partners upon binding. Ligand flexibility can be accounted for by generating multiple conformations or by using conformational sampling algorithms such as molecular dynamics simulations or Monte Carlo techniques. Receptor flexibility is typically addressed by employing flexible side-chain modeling or through induced fit protocols. Flexible docking algorithms search the conformational space of the ligand and receptor simultaneously, exploring various binding poses and optimizing the binding affinity. However, the increased flexibility introduces additional computational complexity and may require more resources compared to rigid docking [16].

6.2.3.3   Semi-Flexible Docking

Also referred to as induced fit docking, it combines elements of both rigid docking and flexible docking approaches. It aims to capture the induced fit phenomenon, where the binding of a ligand induces conformational changes in the receptor or *vice versa*. In hybrid docking, an initial docking step is performed with the ligand and receptor assumed to be rigid, similar to rigid docking. The resulting complex is then subjected to energy minimization or molecular dynamics simulations to relax the structure and allow for conformational adjustments. After this step, a refinement stage is carried out, where the ligand and receptor flexibility are considered, and the binding poses are optimized further. Semi-flexible docking provides a balance between computational efficiency and accuracy, capturing the essential flexibility required for accurate binding prediction while avoiding the exhaustive sampling of the entire conformational space [17].

6.2.4   Common Tools and Software for Molecular Docking

The search for potential targets using a structural data bank and an evaluation method for ligands is necessary for the practical application of molecular docking. Numerous molecular docking tools and methodologies are available to achieve this. The computational tools are used to rank the potential ligands according to their ability to interact with the particular target candidates [1].

Various search algorithms, including genetic, molecular docking algorithms, Monte Carlo, and fragment-based algorithms, are used by docking tools that are widely used. Additional tools include GOLD, FlexX, DOCK, and ICM, which are primarily employed for the purpose of high-throughput docking simulations (Table 6.1) [18].

Using a hierarchical docking strategy, Glide (Grid-based Ligand Docking with Energetics) generates the top potential combinations or hits after completing its four main steps. These steps are as follows: [19]

1. Site point search in the receptor's active site.
2. Assigning the rough scores utilizing the greedy scoring, subset test, and diameter test.
3. Energy minimization using electrostatic grids and OPLA-AA.
4. Use the Glide Score Function.

New algorithms from academia and industry are quickly incorporated into high-end packages. As public domain software advances, it can now functionally compete with some commercial products. Computers double in speed every year and a half, while graphic displays advance in sophistication and usability at the same time. These factors collectively make molecular docking an essential component of drug design. It keeps expanding its function in innovative new methods like computational enzymology, genomics, and proteomic search engines [6].

Table 6.1 List of some common docking tools along with their algorithms.

Sr. no.	Software tool	Algorithm	Scoring term	Advantages	References
1.	Glide	Monte Carlo	Glide score	Lead optimization and lead discovery	[6]
2.	AutoDock	Lamarkian genetic algorithm	Empirical free energy function	Ability to adapt to user-defined input	[6]
3.	GOLD (Genetic Optimization for Ligand Docking)	Genetic algorithm	GoldScore, ChemScore, ASP (Astex Statistical Potential)	Atomic overlap between the ligand and the protein	[20]
4.	Surflex	Surflex dock search algorithm	Bohm's Scoring Function	Enhanced accuracy through the extension of force fields	[21]
5.	FlexX	Incremental reconstruction	Modified Bohm Scoring Function	Offers a variety of conformations	[6]
6.	ICM (Internal Coordinate Modeling)	Monte Carlo minimization	Virtual library screening scoring function	Allows two rigid helices to be arranged parallel by using side chain flexibility	[22]
7.	MVD (Molegro Virtual Docker)	Evolutionary algorithm	MolDock Score	High level of binding mode prediction accuracy	[23]
8.	Fred (Fast Rigid Exhaustive Docking)	Exhaustive search algorithm	Gaussian Scoring Function	A non-stochastic method to look at every position within the protein active site	[6]

(Continued)

Table 6.1 List of some common docking tools along with their algorithms. (*Continued*)

Sr. no.	Software tool	Algorithm	Scoring term	Advantages	References
9.	LigandFit	Monte Carlo method	LigScore, piecewise linear potential (PLP)	Produces high hit rates using LigScore	[6]
10.	FITTED (Flexibility Induced Through Targeted Evolutionary Description)	Genetic algorithm	Potential of mean force (PMF), drug score	Examines how water molecules affect protein–ligand complexes	[24]

6.3   Role of Artificial Intelligence in Molecular Docking

The National Institutes of Health (NIH) has emphasized that precision medicine is a new approach for "drug prevention or treatment that also considers the other variations in genetics, libertines, and environment." Compared to another method currently being used, this enables doctors and physicians to treat and recover diseases more accurately [25]. This needs to be made more powerful using extremely sophisticated techniques that can later be applied in an uncommon way to trained sets of data.

In order to produce successful results, the field of artificial learning uses the cognitive abilities of medical professionals in conjunction with biomedical and bioinformatics data. Artificial general intelligence, artificial narrow intelligence, and super intelligence are roughly the three categories into which artificial intelligence can be divided [26]. Artificial natural intelligence or ANI is currently under development with a target release date of the next 10 years. It has the capacity to create fresh data sets, examine them, discover relationships between them, and draw conclusions that are either meaningful or practical.

The most well-known pharmaceutical companies are utilizing deep learning, artificial intelligence, and ANI during their development process with the goal of identifying the distinct genetic mutations in a large set of data, and physicians can use it in a variety of medical science fields as a result [27].

By utilizing massive datasets, learning intricate patterns, and directing the search for ideal binding configurations, artificial intelligence techniques can enhance the precision and effectiveness of molecular docking.

The following sub-sections enlists some key areas where AI was integrated in the docking process.

6.3.1   ML-Based Scoring Functions

Recent advancements in machine learning regression models have led to the development of new scoring functions for virtual screening. These cutting-edge scoring functions have proven to be superior to traditional scoring methods, as demonstrated by Ain *et al.* [28] 2015. In a comprehensive evaluation conducted by Khamis and Gomma [29] (2015) both classical scoring functions (20 in total) and machine learning-based scoring functions (12 in total) were thoroughly examined. The findings revealed that the machine learning-based scoring functions outperformed the classical ones in terms of scoring power, which refers to the accuracy of predicting binding affinity, and ranking power, which relates to the ability to predict relative rankings.

The research conducted by Khamis and Gomaa [29] in 2015 clearly showcased the significant advantages of machine learning-based scoring functions over classical approaches. These machine learning methods exhibited superior performance in accurately predicting the binding affinities of proteins and their relative rankings. Ashtawy and Mahatrapa [30] further supported these findings, stating that scoring functions utilizing the random forests algorithm or enhanced regression trees often demonstrated the best performance. The introduction of new scoring functions based on advanced machine learning regression models has revolutionized virtual screening. These methods had surpassed traditional scoring functions in terms of accuracy and predictive power, as demonstrated by various studies. The utilization of machine learning algorithms such as random forests or enhanced regression trees has been particularly effective.

One crucial factor contributing to the success of these machine learning scoring functions is the availability of structural information on protein–ligand complexes in public databases. With the accumulation of this data, it has become possible to create more precise scoring functions that can accurately predict the binding affinities of specific proteins or protein families [31].

6.3.2   Pose Prediction or Protein–Ligand Interactions

Machine learning (ML) is a powerful approach used to predict the behavior of unknown ligands or proteins. It does this by analyzing the relationship between physicochemical properties and protein–ligand interactions, based on known protein–ligand complex structures. Dhakal *et al.* [32] (2021) highlighted the significance of ML in inferring statistical models for predicting the status of additional unknown ligands or proteins. By leveraging the known structures of protein–ligand complexes, ML algorithms learn patterns and correlations between physicochemical parameters and the interactions between proteins and ligands. This enables the ML model to make predictions about the interactions of new, uncharacterized protein–ligand pairs.

Yamanishi *et al.* [33] (2018) proposed a method that incorporates a kernel regression-based approach to infer protein–ligand interactions. The approach involves integrating various sources of information, including the chemical structure of ligands, the protein sequence information, and the drug–target complex network. By combining these data, the model identifies associations between drugs and target proteins, revealing the interactions between them.

Bleakley and Yamanishi [34] (2009) conducted BLM experiments, which employed supervised learning methods, to predict protein–ligand interactions. Similarly, Wang and Zeng [35] (2013) developed a method using restricted Boltzmann machines, a type of machine learning model, to predict different types of interactions, such as those between proteins and ligands.

Macari *et al.* [36] (2019) provided a comprehensive review of computational paradigms used to predict binding sites for proteins and small molecules. Authors compared various techniques, ranging from traditional geometrical methods to more recent machine learning strategies, analyzing their characteristics and results. This review shed light on the strengths and limitations of different approaches in predicting protein–ligand interactions and binding sites.

6.3.3   High-Throughput Virtual Screening

In the field of drug discovery, virtual screening plays a crucial role. It is divided into two main categories: receptor-based and ligand-based approaches. The receptor-based approach focuses on targeting specific receptors and improving lead compounds. It involves analyzing known active ligands to establish a quantitative relationship between their three-dimensional structure and activity (3D-QSAR). To apply this approach, knowledge of the 3D structures of the receptor and ligand molecules is essential. Molecular docking calculations are then performed to determine the binding sites and energies of different conformations. Receptor-based virtual screening is commonly used during the lead compound discovery phase [37].

High-throughput virtual screening (HTVS) is a method that analyzes the binding characteristics and affinities of potential compounds to a target receptor. By screening a large library of molecules, HTVS can identify promising compounds. This approach aids in the search for potential lead molecules from millions of compounds [38].

With the increasing challenges and costs associated with drug development, it is important to leverage advanced technologies. Medicinal chemists now utilize machine learning (ML)-based virtual screening (VS) to enhance high-throughput screening (HTS) and expedite early-stage drug development. ML-based VS improves the efficiency and productivity of identifying potential lead molecules from vast chemogenomic libraries [39].

6.4   Drug Discovery in the New Age

Drug discovery is a complex and methodical process that aims to identify appropriate compounds with the capability to become successful medications. The procedure entails the investigation and assessment of both tiny synthetic compounds and big biomolecules, such as proteins or antibodies, to determine their potential as medicines [40]. In 2021, the worldwide drug discovery industry was projected to be worth more than 55 billion USD. It is also estimated to surpass 120 billion dollars by the year 2030, expanding at a CAGR of around 10% in the late 2023s [41].

Developing medicinal drugs for the market is a lengthy and costly process that can cost billions of dollars. The feasibility of loss in the field of drug approval process is considerable, with over 91% of medicines in clinical trials that do not gain FDA clearance and reach the consumer market [42]. Drug discovery has evolved over three distinct periods. In the nineteenth century, it relied on chance discoveries by medicinal chemists. The early twentieth century saw the identification of new drug structures, leading to advancements in antibiotics. Towards the end of the century, technological innovations like molecular modeling and high-throughput screening (HTS) revolutionized the field [43]. In the twenty-first century, advancements in biotechnology and genomics have paved the way for the development of biopharmaceutical drugs using AI and ML algorithms.

Modern drug discovery has witnessed the rise of faster high-throughput screening (HTS) methods, which eliminate the need for human labor. However, HTS remains costly and demands abundant resources. Academic institutions often lack these resources, while pharmaceutical companies seek ways to avoid screening unpromising ligands. Consequently, computer-aided drug discovery (CADD) tools have gained significant attention in both academia and the pharmaceutical industry [44].

6.5   Drug Discovery Using Machine Learning (ML) Algorithms

ML algorithms have made significant contributions to the field of drug discovery, offering valuable tools for pharmaceutical companies. These algorithms have been harnessed to create predictive models that aid in determining the chemical, biological, and physical properties of compounds during the drug discovery process.

Broadly classifying, there are two types of ML algorithms, namely:

A. Supervised learning
Supervised learning entails training a model with labeled data which includes the desired outcome or target variable. Biological sequences (e.g., DNA, RNA, protein) can be classified into distinct functional categories using supervised learning algorithms, such as predicting protein function or finding disease-associated genetic variants. These models learn from labeled data in which sequences are linked to certain classes or labels, allowing the model to categorize fresh, unlabeled sequences [45].

In drug research, supervised learning algorithms may forecast quantitative attributes such as a compound's activity or potency against a certain target. These algorithms can develop prediction models to estimate the potential effectiveness of novel compounds by training on labeled datasets with known chemical actions [46].

B. Unsupervised learning
This method entails training an algorithm on unknown information with no stated goal variables. The objective is to find undetected trends, structures, or correlations in the data. Unsupervised learning methods are used in computational biology and drug discovery for tasks such as grouping, reducing dimensionality, and data exploration.

Clustering algorithms help identify groups or clusters of similar biological entities, such as genes or proteins based on shared characteristics. In drug discovery, clustering algorithms aid in grouping compounds with similar chemical structures or biological activities, facilitating the identification of chemical classes or target families [47]. Dimensionality reduction methods, such as PCA (principal component analysis) or t-SNE, are employed in bioinformatics to manage enormous amounts of data. These algorithms reduce the dimensionality of complex datasets while preserving essential information, enabling visualization and interpretation of the data [48].

The ML algorithms which are widely used are shown in Figure 6.5.

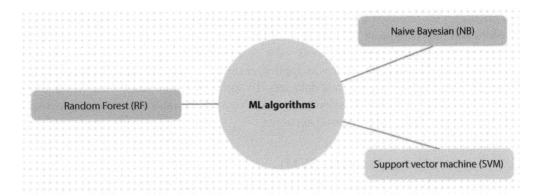

Figure 6.5 Widely used ML algorithms.

6.5.1   Random Forest (RF)

Random forest (RF) is a well-known method for massive data sets that contain numerous attributes. It simplifies the data by removing outliers and performs classification and designation based on relevant features specific to the algorithm. RF is commonly trained on large inputs and variables, making it accessible for data collected from multiple databases [49].

Ryu *et al.* [50] developed PredMS, a computer model that predicts whether tiny molecules are biologically either stable or unstable within individual liver microsomes. Using a random forest model and a database of metabolic stability data for 1,900+ compounds, PredMS achieved good prediction accuracy. PredMS was also tested on an external dataset of 60+ compounds and obtained promising results, with high accuracy, sensitivity, specificity, and positive predictive value.

This shows that PredMS may provide a reliable and beneficial method to evaluate the metabolite stability of small molecules, particularly in the early phases of the development and discovery of drugs. Researchers can utilize PredMS to make informed decisions about the potential viability and safety of compounds, helping streamline the drug discovery process.

6.5.2   Naive Bayesian (NB)

It is based on the principles of Bayesian probability theory and is particularly useful when dealing with large datasets and complex relationships between variables. Given the class label, the naive Bayesian approach assumes that all characteristics or parameters in the information set are distinct from one another. This simplifying assumption allows for efficient and straightforward calculations of probabilities.

As techniques for the classification for biological data, which typically includes noise and irrelevant information, NB algorithms have shown considerable potential. They provide a potential approach for predicting ligand–target communication, which might be a significant step ahead in finding leads. NB methods can play crucial roles in discovering possible leads and expediting the drug development process by efficiently handling noise and unrelated data [51].

Chen *et al.* [52] reported a database of molecules categorized as P-glycoprotein (P-gp) inhibitors and non-inhibitors. The effect of different physicochemical parameters on P-gp suppression was studied. Decision trees were constructed using a training set of compounds. A naive Bayesian classifier was applied, resulting in an average correct prediction of 80% for both the training and test data sets. To summarize, the study indicates that the developed models, including decision trees and a naive Bayesian classifier, can effectively predict whether a molecule with good accuracy.

6.5.3   Support Vector Machine (SVM)

SVMs are sophisticated algorithms for machine learning that have been utilized extensively in drug development for a variety of applications. SVM is important in drug research because of its ability to distinguish among inactive and active drugs, grade drugs within a database, and build models using regression [53].

Warmuth *et al.* [54] employed a machine learning approach termed "active learning" to pick batches of chemicals for testing. The "maximum margin hyperplane" of support vector machines (SVM) was utilized. A hyperplane is a border that divides active (target-binding) molecules from inactive ones. The aim was to find a hyperplane that was as far away from any labeled compound as feasible, maximizing the gap between the two classes. In terms of discovering molecules with binding activity, they discovered that tactics determined by the maximum margin hyperplane surpassed simpler methods.

In another case, the SVM approach outperformed three artificially generated neural networks, a function with a radial basis system, and a C5.0 decision tree model for predicting the inhibitory effects of dihydrofolate reductase with pyrimidines [55].

6.6   Drug Discovery Using Deep Learning (DL) Algorithms

Deep learning has emerged as an effective technique in bioinformatics, transforming how we analyze and interpret biological data. Deep learning algorithms may automatically learn detailed patterns and representations from complex biological information by exploiting artificial neural networks with numerous layers, resulting in better accuracy and predictive capabilities [56].

Deep learning has made important breakthroughs in bioinformatics, particularly in the processing of genetic data. Deep learning algorithms have been important in extracting relevant information from this plethora of genetic information generated by genomic sequencing technology [57].

Deep learning (DL) has emerged as a potent method within the field of machine learning, particularly in the era of big data. DL models have demonstrated their effectiveness and efficiency in handling large volumes of data, surpassing the predictive accuracy achieved by traditional machine learning methods. One key advantage of DL over conventional machine learning is its ability to efficiently process and extract valuable information from raw, unprocessed natural data.

DL models excel in discovering patterns within high-dimensional datasets, making them applicable across various domains. However, it is important to note that DL models heavily

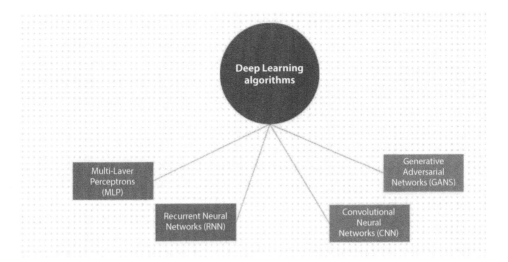

Figure 6.6 Deep learning algorithms.

rely on training data, and the quantity and quality of this data significantly impact the predictive capabilities of the trained model (Figure 6.6) [57].

6.6.1 Multilayer Perceptrons (MLPs)

MLPs are a type of artificial neural network (ANN) that is made up of numerous layers of linked artificial neurons or nodes. MLPs frequently play a role in machine learning applications such as regression, classification, and recognizing patterns.

An MLP's architecture is made up of an input layer, a couple of hidden layers, and a layer that provides output. Each layer is made up of engineered neurons (inspired by biological neurons), also called perceptrons or nodes. A graph with a directed acyclic pattern is formed when neurons in one layer are linked to neurons in subsequent layers in an MLP. Weights indicate the connections between neurons, which impact the strength of the link and impact the flow of information across the network [58].

MLPs are used to forecast the molecular makeup of biomolecules (proteins), usually for secondary structure prediction, fold identification, and tertiary structure prediction. MLPs may predict the molecular composition of unidentified proteins by using their amino acid sequences after being trained on existing structures of proteins and associated sequences. MLPs have demonstrated promising results in terms of enhancing the accuracy of predicting protein structure techniques, assisting in the understanding of protein function, and identifying therapeutic targets [59].

MLPs have been utilized to predict drug–drug interactions and target protein interactions. MLPs can estimate the probability of a potential medicine binding to a certain target by training them on known drug–target interaction data. MLPs are being used to prioritize possible drug–target combinations, aiding in the early phases of drug development by lowering the amount of time-consuming and costly clinical trials [60].

6.6.2   Recurrent Neural Networks (RNN)

Also referred to as RNNs are a type of artificial neural network that models data in succession by capturing temporal relationships and how data flow within a sequence. RNNs are establishing themselves as strong tools in bioinformatics for analyzing numerous types of biochemical data, such as the sequencing of DNA, RNA sequences, sequences of proteins, and time-series data gene expression data.

RNNs, as opposed to feedforward neural networks, use recurrent connections to allow information to be transmitted through each stage of the sequence to the subsequent one. An RNN's main component is a concealed state that stores information about past steps. The present input and the prior concealed state are merged to generate an outcome and update the state that is hidden at each step. Because of this recurring link, RNNs can process sequences of any length, making them suited for analyzing biological sequences of varying lengths [58].

Prediction of protein binding sites: RNNs can predict protein binding regions and how they interact with ligands. RNNs can recognize the sequence of amino acids and structural patterns related to binding sites *via* learning from existing protein–ligand combinations, assisting in the development of drugs and protein modification [61].

Time-series analysis of gene expression: RNNs can simulate the temporal changes of expression of gene data gathered through time-series investigations. RNNs may find patterns, discover gene regulation networks, and forecast future expression levels by capturing the connections between the expression of genes profiles at distinct time periods [62].

6.6.3   Convolutional Neural Networks (CNN)

CNNs have transformed bioinformatics by offering robust instruments for analyzing many forms of biological data such as sequences of DNA, protein sequences, genomic information, and medical image analysis. CNNs are exceptionally effective at detecting spatial and regional connections in these datasets, making them ideal for applications like sequence categorization, protein structure forecasting, variant calling, and clinical image analysis such as computed tomography [18].

The following are the major components of CNN architecture:

A. Convolutional layers: Each of these layers is made up of a number of adaptive filters or kernels that examine the input data for specific trends or features. Convolution is performed by each filter, which comprises element-wise multiplication and summing of the filter weights with the corresponding input area. Convolutional layers are in charge of collecting local spatial characteristics and mapping them.

B. Pooling layers: Pooling layers reduce the spatial dimensions of feature maps created by convolutional layers while keeping critical characteristics. Pooling methods such as maximum pooling and average pooling are commonly used to extract the most important information from local areas.

C. Fully connected layers: These layers are able to connect all of the neurons from the previous one with the next, allowing the extracted characteristics to be classified or regressed. Based on the learnt representations, fully linked layers capture global connections and generate final predictions.

One such example is the DeepSF deep 1D-convolution neural network, which was designed to classify protein sequences into known folds, providing critical insights into fold recognition and the sequence–structure relationship. The method automatically extracts fold-related properties, allowing for the classification of protein sequences of any length. Training and testing on curated datasets from SCOP1.75 resulted in an average accuracy of more than 70%, but experimenting on a separate data set using SCOP2.06 led to an accuracy of 73%. On CASP9-12 targets, DeepSF surpassed HHSearch, a top profile–profile alignment technique, in terms of fold detection accuracy. DeepSF's hidden feature extraction is immune to sequence modifications, deletions, insertions, and truncations, which makes it helpful for a variety of protein motif identification tasks like grouping, comparison, and ranking [63].

6.6.4   Generative Adversarial Networks (GANs)

It comprises deep learning algorithms made up of two separate neural nets: a generator and a discriminator. GANs were launched in 2014 by Ian Goodfellow and his colleagues and have received a lot of interest because of their capacity to produce lifelike and superior-quality artificial data.

GANs have shown usefulness in bioinformatics and drug discovery, assisting with tasks like protein structure formation, biochemical property estimation, and chemical synthesis. GANs provide a novel method for generating new data that matches the features of the original set of data, allowing researchers to investigate and analyze complicated biological systems [64].

Protein structure creation is one use of GANs in bioinformatics. Protein architectures are critical for comprehending how proteins work and interact with drug targets. However, determining protein structures experimentally is time-consuming and costly. By programming the generator network to generate topologies that closely match the empirically discovered structures, GANs may be utilized to build realistic protein structures. The discriminator network gives input on the quality of the created structures, assuring that they match the known structural properties of proteins [65].

GANs have also been used in medication development to create unique chemical structures with desired features. The GAN's generator network may be trained to generate compounds that are structurally comparable to existing medicines or that have certain properties linked to medicinal effectiveness or safety. GANs are a helpful tool for generating innovative drug candidates with better characteristics by examining the chemical environment and using the generator's capacity to produce varied and distinct compounds [66].

Furthermore, GANs have been used in drug creation from scratch, wherein the generator network constructs chemical structures with desirable features and the network of discriminators evaluates their drug likeness. This repetitive procedure of producing and assessing molecules enables chemical exploration and the detection of new compounds with desired features [67].

6.7   AI-Based Toolkits Used for Drug Discovery

Table 6.2 presents some ML tools used currently for drug design and development.

Deep learning (DL) has emerged as a powerful approach in various fields, including drug discovery. DeepChem uses deep learning methods to develop models that predict essential features of chemicals, such as activity against a certain target or toxicity. Models like these learn from enormous volumes of information and can reveal complicated patterns and correlations that older approaches may miss. Figure 6.7 explains the workflow of Deepchem.

Deep learning's capacity to automatically identify useful characteristics from unprocessed molecular data is one of its primary advantages in drug development. Deep learning models may acquire and adjust to the most useful interpretations directly from the data, rather than depending on predetermined descriptors or features. Deep learning models can capture delicate and detailed molecular properties that are essential to their biological function because of their flexibility. It can handle a variety of molecular data formats, such as 1D patterns (such as proteins or DNA patterns), 2D models (such as biochemical graphs), as well as 3D structures. This adaptability enables the combination of many forms of data to produce more accurate forecasts [68].

Table 6.2 Machine learning toolkits used widely for drug design and development.

S. no	ML tools	Function	Web Link
1	Alpha Fold	Protein fold prediction	https://alphafold.ebi.ac.uk/
2	DeepChem	Drug discovery	https://deepchem.io/
3	AMPL—atom modeling pipeline	Data preparation for drug discovery	https://github.com/ATOMconsortium/AMPL
4	Open Drug Discovery Toolkit (ODDT)	Molecular docking and prediction	https://pypi.org/project/oddt/0.1.9

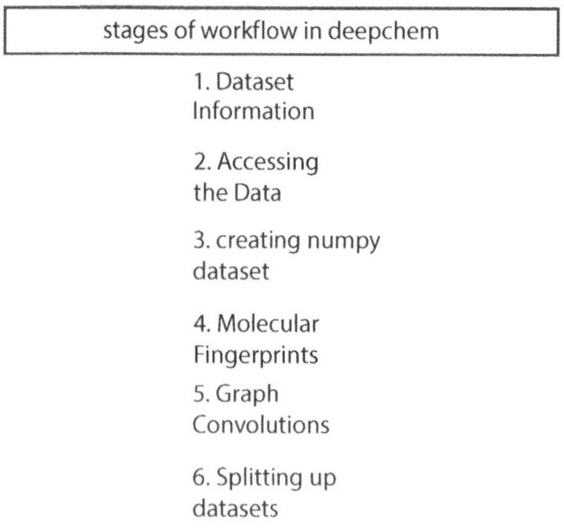

stages of workflow in deepchem

1. Dataset Information

2. Accessing the Data

3. creating numpy dataset

4. Molecular Fingerprints

5. Graph Convolutions

6. Splitting up datasets

Figure 6.7 Deepchem workflow chart.

6.8   Applications of AI in Molecular Docking

Traditional drug and vaccine development are difficult endeavours that seek to produce novel molecules with a variety of desirable characteristics [69]. As a result, developing drugs and vaccines is very expensive, time-consuming, and has a low success rate. In the vast molecular space, the efficient discovery of numerous plausible, unique, and new candidate molecules has been revolutionized by advancements in artificial intelligence (AI) and machine learning (ML)-based models, which has helped to resolve this conundrum [70].

The use of AI-powered molecular docking in drug development is becoming more prevalent thanks to advancements in docking algorithms, neural networking models, and the availability of open-access data on ligands and targets. Initially, molecular docking was primarily used to study the interactions between ligands and targets. However, in the modern era, the applications and scope of molecular docking have expanded and evolved [71].

6.8.1   Prediction of Drug–Target Interactions

Computational tools are being developed to predict the activities of new molecular targets for drug repurposing. These tools work alongside experimental drug–target discovery efforts, providing data on compound-target interactions. Machine learning (ML) models, for example, use the structures of drugs and targets to guide their predictions in a drug–target space. This approach helps in understanding the interactions between compounds and targets [72].

In addition, AI and ML methods have been employed to predict target activities for kinase inhibitors and other compound classes. Researchers have used multi-kernel learning and chemical fingerprints to forecast the affinities of compound kinase targets. Deep learning techniques, such as convolutional network models, have also emerged for predicting drug–target interactions (DTIs). These techniques improve our understanding of the factors influencing DTI prediction and enable computational drug repurposing [73].

Atom-wise, a biopharma company, utilizes 3D identification and prediction of small structures. They employed this method to identify active molecules for the Ebola virus and successfully developed two new drugs using artificial intelligence. These drugs have demonstrated greater effectiveness than previously available options. However, to ensure safety and other considerations, peer review and regulatory oversight are necessary before these drugs can be widely utilized [74].

6.8.2   Drug Repurposing

Discovering new therapeutic uses for existing drugs, developing drug candidates, and exploring natural products are exciting avenues in drug discovery. One promising approach is drug repurposing, which involves repurposing approved medications, candidates in development, or synthesized compounds for new therapeutic purposes. To expedite this process, docking, a virtual screening technique, allows for rapid screening of approved drugs, phytochemicals, or pre-synthesized compounds against specific targets of interest.

Innovative deep learning (DL) methodologies have revolutionized de novo drug design. State-of-the-art DL models like Generative Autoencoders (GAE) and Generative

Adversarial Networks (GAN) have transformed the way new molecules are designed [75]. Recently, generative models such as variational autoencoders (VAE) have been utilized to generate atom sequences, resulting in the production of diverse and distinct drug molecules [76]. These powerful autoencoders, encode molecules into a vector that captures crucial characteristics such as bond order, element properties, and functional groups [77]. This cutting-edge approach opens up new possibilities for innovative and unique drug design.

The COVID-19 pandemic has caused the world to realize the need for novel drug development at this historic time. This process has been greatly aided over the past year by AI/ML [78]. A computational drug discovery system typically has three components: target discovery, small molecule drug discovery, and clinical trial outcome predictors. The fusion of artificial intelligence and core chemistry in computational drug design holds tremendous promise for revolutionizing the field. Researchers are eagerly seeking high-quality research on drugs and clinical data to harness the full potential of this innovative approach [79]. By combining the power of artificial intelligence with deep insights from rigorous scientific investigations, computational drug design has the potential to unlock ground-breaking discoveries and transform the landscape of drug development. The quest for this cutting-edge synergy between AI and chemistry drives the pursuit of excellence in drug research and clinical investigations, pushing the boundaries of what is possible in the world of medicine.

Artificial intelligence (AI) facilitates the use of the continuously growing open-access information sources in databases of biological, chemical, and structural activity. Therefore, predictions of binding affinity of molecules are more precise [80]. In this text, pose generation and scoring have been handled by deep learning neural networks. In order to study the convolutional neural network, protein–ligand complexes were designed as three-dimensional cages. Similar to the machine learning models and other non-neural network algorithms, deep learning scoring functions have produced superior results [81]. AI-based ML makes predictions based on blind data by learning from the properties of the available data. These strategies might not be preferable to recently identified therapeutic targets because they have not undergone in-depth analysis and lack chemical, structural, and bioactivity data [82].

In order to predict binding affinities in classical scoring, predetermined function forms can be improved upon or replaced by machine learning algorithms. In virtual screening, these have also been used to distinguish between binders and non-binders [83]. Nonparametric learning, or machine learning, does not use predefined functions. Instead, results are extracted from the data used as input. The output could be continuous, similar to nonlinear regression. This then makes it possible for precise and varied scoring. The random forest (RF)-Score was among the first machine learning scoring methods to outperform conventional scoring methods. Additionally, support vector machines (SVM) and logistic regression were applied to enhance docking-based binding affinity prediction [84].

6.9 Challenges and Limitations of AI-Based Molecular Docking

The use of docking tools and the study's findings presents a number of challenges. Each program reportedly has its own restrictions and flaws. Programs therefore are unable to produce the same output as reliably [85]. Additionally, if the amount of chemical structure processed exceeds the capabilities of the developed software, the program might not function properly. As a result, it's crucial to continually validate and update the developed software in light of the information.

Among many, the most significant issues encountered while docking are:

1. Properties of ligands

By docking, it is impossible to determine whether a ligand will act as an agonist or an antagonist. Only the binding mode and affinities of a molecule to a receptor are revealed by docking studies. After the docking process, experiments in a lab should be performed to determine whether a molecule has agonist or antagonist properties [86]. This means that unless additional validations, such as lab experiments, are carried out, it is advised not to overinterpret docking results regarding the nature of the ligand . The way that ligands are prepared and their conformation play a role in the docking process. Prior to docking, molecules are ionized during the ligand preparation [84].

2. Accuracy of docking

During the initial phases of drug discovery and development, docking methods are commonly employed to find potential ligands. To understand how molecules interact with targets, a variety of programs are used. Despite these programs, *in vivo* testing of some molecules has not produced encouraging results [87]. Due to a variety of problems, docking results may need to be questioned. The first one has to do with how the protein structure is used. In the PDB, protein structures are typically found as complexes with ligands [88]. In order to dock the molecule under study, researchers remove the bound ligand from the protein structure. However, this process might have an impact on the docking output. The environment surrounding the binding site is the second crucial issue. To perform their functions, drug candidate molecules must bind to specific cell-based targets. Even when the docking results show strong binding in an *in silico* setting, they sometimes produce unexpected results when used *in vivo* [89].

3. Search and scoring functions

Docking is difficult because there are numerous ways that two molecules can be arranged in three dimensions (three degrees of freedom for translation and three for rotation). The search algorithm in use rotates and systematically transposes one molecule over the other to find every possible orientation between two molecules [87]. A search algorithm is capable of producing numerous solutions. According to their scores, the solutions are ranked. There is no single scoring function because different programs have different docking functions and scoring systems. Overall, there is still little relationship between experimental binding affinities and docking scores. Each docking algorithm makes use of a search tool and a scoring function [90].

To summarize, deep learning is establishing itself as a strong and transformational tool in the fields of bioinformatics and drug development. The use of algorithms based on deep learning has revolutionized the processing and interpretation of complicated biological data, resulting in substantial advances in the comprehension of the functioning of biological systems, predicting protein configurations, discovering sequence patterns, and aiding drug discovery.

ML algorithms have grown in importance in drug development. They allow us to work quicker and explore numerous various ideas that we would not have been able to achieve otherwise. These algorithms utilize data, but there are situations when we do not have much knowledge about the individual protein or target that we are examining. Because of lacking sufficient data to train the algorithms efficiently, getting reliable results might be difficult. Despite these limitations, ML is still a helpful tool in drug development and is helping us comprehend novel biological pathways and targets.

The potential for overfitting or underfitting is a common worry in algorithm prediction. Overfitting occurs when a model performs well on the training data but fails to generalize to new, unseen data. This happens when the model learns irrelevant or uncommon patterns during training, resulting in poor performance in real-world situations [91]. Various solutions, such as expanding the size of the sample and applying cross-validation, can be used to overcome these concerns. Techniques such as cross-validation are a frequently used approach that includes assessing the correctness of machine learning models using distinct data sets.

Deep learning models will continue to advance further as more data becomes accessible, resulting in significant discoveries in bioinformatics and medication discovery. With ongoing advances in deep learning frameworks, algorithms, and computational capabilities, we can expect even more accurate predictions, enhanced comprehension of complicated biological structures, and the discovery of novel insights that will drive advances in precision medicine and revolutionize drug discovery and development processes [92].

6.10   Conclusion and Future Scope

Molecular docking, a structure-based drug design technique, plays a vital role in predicting how small-molecule ligands interact with their target. Various powerful docking programs are used, and the selection depends on factors like availability, need, and computational resources. The integration of artificial intelligence (AI) and machine learning (ML) in drug discovery has revolutionized the field, particularly in challenging areas like central nervous system (CNS) diseases. AI/ML enables target identification, compound screening, lead optimization, therapy response prediction, and drug repurposing, leveraging vast amounts of biological data to enhance decision-making and accelerate the drug development process.

This chapter delves into the profound impact of AI on molecular docking. It covers the fundamentals of docking, introduces AI in drug discovery, and explores its integration into docking algorithms. The chapter also highlights diverse applications of AI in molecular docking, along with the challenges faced and future directions.

However, it is critical to recognize AI/ML's limits in computational biology and developing drugs. The reliance on excellent and well-curated datasets is one restriction, as the success of AI/ML models is strongly dependent on the accuracy and the diversity of the training data. Despite these limitations, ongoing research, algorithm advancements, and cooperation between researchers and companies hold a guarantee for overcoming these obstacles and realizing the full capacity of AI/ML in bioinformatics as well as drug search, eventually resulting in the discovery of improved treatments for diseases.

Future Directions

The future of drug discovery with AI and ML holds tremendous potential for advancements in several key areas, namely:

1. Augmented target recognition: AI and machine learning (ML) may enhance target identification even further by combining varied data sources such as genomes, proteomics, and transcriptomics to uncover novel therapeutic targets. Deep learning algorithms can analyze enormous amounts of omics data in order to reveal complicated disease causes and possible therapeutic targets [93].

2. Generative algorithm using GANs: AI and machine learning (ML) may be used to create generative algorithms that help study the results of CT images, PET/MRI scans, ultrasound, etc. [94].

3. Conventional drug development focuses mostly on single targets; however, many illnesses have complicated molecular pathways involving several targets. AI and machine learning can help in the creation of multi-target pharmaceuticals by optimizing their interactions with numerous proteins or pathways at the same time to create synergistic effects [95].

4. Personalized medicine: AI and machine learning algorithms may analyze patient data, such as genetic details and medical records, in order to anticipate how patients will react to certain medications. This personalized medicine strategy can assist in identifying patients who will probably reap the advantages of a certain medication while also reducing unwanted effects [95].

5. Real-world data integration: Results reported by patients may be combined with AI and ML models to acquire insights on drug efficacy and safety in real-world settings. This information can help improve after-market monitoring and allow for the early detection of adverse occurrences [96, 97].

The future scope of AI and ML in drug discovery is extensive and holds several promising avenues for exploration.

The continued development of comprehensible AI models will assure compliance with regulations and raise confidence in AI-driven drug development procedures. Accelerated chemical identification and increased precision of drug candidate selection will result from the integration of AI and ML approaches in high throughput testing and virtual drug screening [98]. Development of AI systems for *de novo* drug design could create new opportunities in creating unique and optimized medication for high-risk diseases like cancer, acquired immunodeficiency syndrome (AIDS), etc. [99].

Collaboration among academia, business, and regulatory authorities will be critical to realizing the potential of AI in drug research. Standardized principles and methods for development will ensure transparency, repeatability, and regulatory compliance [100]. This collaborative effort will facilitate the responsible and ethical application of artificial intelligence in the drug discovery process. Ethical considerations, such as protecting patient data privacy, ensuring transparency in algorithmic decision-making, and mitigating biases in computerized models, will remain a priority. By upholding ethical norms, the field can maintain public trust and harness its full benefits [101].

Overall, the future scope of the chapter on understanding molecular docking through artificial intelligence lies in the continuous advancements in AI algorithms, integration of big data, personalized medicine, drug combination optimization, high-throughput virtual screening, drug toxicity prediction, and ethical considerations. The field of AI-driven molecular docking holds great promise for transforming the drug discovery process and improving patient outcomes [102]. In conclusion, harnessing real-world data, better target identification, enabling personalized medicine, and improving drug design are just a few of the ways that the combination of AI and ML in drug discovery offers enormous promise to revolutionize the profession. Researchers and corporates should prioritize ethical norms at its utmost consideration. This will change the landscape of drug discovery.

References

1. Agarwal, S. and Mehrotra, R.J.J.C., An overview of molecular docking. *JSM Chem.*, 4, 2, 1024–1028, 2016.
2. Quazi, S. and Fatima, Z., Role of artificial intelligence and machine learning in bioinformatics: Drug discovery and drug repurposing, in: *Interdisciplinary Reviews: Computational Molecular Science*, pp. 182–197, IGI Global, 2021.
3. Gentile, F., Yaacoub, J.C., Gleave, J., Fernandez, M., Ton, A.T., Ban, F., Cherkasov, A., Artificial intelligence–enabled virtual screening of ultra-large chemical libraries with deep docking. *Nat. Protoc.*, 17, 3, 672–697, 2022.
4. Nayarisseri, A., Artificial intelligence, big data and machine learning approaches in precision medicine & drug discovery. *Curr. Drug Targets*, 22, 631–655, 2021.
5. Pinzi, L. and Rastelli, G., Molecular docking: shifting paradigms in drug discovery. *Int. J. Mol. Sci.*, 20, 18, 4331, 2019.
6. Chaudhary, K.K. and Mishra, N., A review on molecular docking: novel tool for drug discovery. *Databases*, 3, 4, 1029, 2016.
7. Guedes, I.A., de Magalhães, C.S., Dardenne, L.E., Receptor–ligand molecular docking. *Biophys. Rev.*, 6, 75–87, 2014.
8. García-Godoy, M.J., López-Camacho, E., García-Nieto, J., Del Ser, J., Nebro, A.J., Aldana-Montes, J.F., Bio-inspired optimization for the molecular docking problem: state of the art, recent results and perspectives. *Appl. Soft Comput.*, 79, 30–45, 2019.
9. Tripathi, A. and Misra, K., Molecular docking: A structure-based drug designing approach. *JSM Chem.*, 5, 2, 1042–1047, 2017.
10. Li, J., Fu, A., Zhang, L., An overview of scoring functions used for protein–ligand interactions in molecular docking. *Interdiscip. Sci.: Comput. Life Sci.*, 11, 320–328, 2019.
11. Farid, R., Day, T., Friesner, R.A., Pearlstein, R.A., New insights about HERG blockade obtained from protein modeling, potential energy mapping, and docking studies. *Bioorganic Med. Chem.*, 14, 9, 3160–3173, 2006.
12. Wójcikowski, M., Ballester, P. J., Siedlecki, P., Performance of machine-learning scoring functions in structure-based virtual screening. *Sci. Rep.*, 7, 1, 46710, 2017.
13. Zhong, F., Xing, J., Li, X., Liu, X., Fu, Z., Xiong, Z., Jiang, H., Artificial intelligence in drug design. *Sci. China Life Sci.*, 61, 1191–1204, 2018.
14. Fan, J., Fu, A., Zhang, L., Progress in molecular docking. *Quantitative Biol.*, 7, 83–89, 2019.

15. Raval, K. and Ganatra, T., Basics, types and applications of molecular docking: A review. *IP Int. J. Compr. Adv. Pharmacol.*, 7, 1, 12–16, 2022.

16. Wang, Y. and Zeng, J., Predicting drug-target interactions using restricted Boltzmann machines. *Bioinformatics*, 29, 13, 126–134, 2013.

17. Morris, C.J. and Corte, D.D., Using molecular docking and molecular dynamics to investigate protein-ligand interactions. *Modern Phys. Lett. B*, 35, 08, 2130002, 2021.

18. Kothari, D., Patel, M., Sharma, A.K., Implementation of grey scale normalization in machine learning & artificial intelligence for bioinformatics using convolutional neural networks, in: *2021 6th International Conference on Inventive Computation Technologies (ICICT)*, pp. 1071–1074, IEEE, 2021.

19. Panwar, U. and Singh, S.K., Atom-based 3D-QSAR, molecular docking, DFT, and simulation studies of acylhydrazone, hydrazine, and diazene derivatives as IN-LEDGF/p75 inhibitors. *Struct. Chem.*, 32, 337–352, 2020.

20. Verdonk, M.L., Chessari, G., Cole, J.C., Hartshorn, M.J., Murray, C.W., Nissink, J.W.M., Taylor, R., Modeling water molecules in protein– ligand docking using GOLD. *J. Med. Chem.*, 48, 20, 6504–6515, 2005.

21. Jain, A.N., Surflex: fully automatic flexible molecular docking using a molecular similarity-based search engine. *J. Med. Chem.*, 46, 4, 499–511, 2003.

22. Abagyan, R., Totrov, M., Kuznetsov, D., ICM—A new method for protein modeling and design: Applications to docking and structure prediction from the distorted native conformation. *J. Comput. Chem.*, 15, 5, 488–506, 1994.

23. Puspaningtyas, A.R., Molecular Docking Using Molegro Virtual Docker (Mvd) on Water Extract of Guava Fruit (Psidium Guajava, Linn) and Sweet Orange (Citrus Sinensis, Peels) as Inhibitor on Enzyme Tyrosinase as Positive Control of Whitening Agent. *Indonesian J. Appl. Chem.*, 15, 1, 106895, 2013.

24. Corbeil, C.R., Englebienne, P., Moitessier, N., Docking ligands into flexible and solvated macromolecules. 1. Development and validation of FITTED 1.0. *J. Chem. Inf. Modeling*, 47, 2, 435–449, 2007.

25. Lamb, M.L. and Jorgensen, W.L., Computational approaches to molecular recognition. *Curr. Opin. Chem. Biol.*, 1, 449–457, 1997.

26. Álvarez-Machancoses, Ó. and Fernández-Martínez, J.L., Using artificial intelligence methods to speed up drug discovery. *Expert Opin. Drug Discovery*, 14, 769–777, 2019.

27. Jiménez-Luna, J., Grisoni, F., Schneider, G., Drug discovery with explainable artificial intelligence. *Nat. Mach. Intell.*, 2, 573–584, 2020.

28. Ain, Q.U., Aleksandrova, A., Roessler, F.D., Ballester, P.J., Machine-learning scoring functions to improve structure-based binding affinity prediction and virtual screening. *Wiley Interdiscip. Reviews: Comput. Mol. Sci.*, 5, 405–424, 2015.

29. Khamis, M.A. and Gomaa, W., Comparative assessment of machine-learning scoring functions on PDBbind 2013. *Eng. Appl. Artif. Intell.*, 45, 136–151, 2015.

30. Ashtawy, Hossam, M., Mahapatra, N.R., A comparative assessment of predictive accuracies of conventional and machine learning scoring functions for protein-ligand binding affinity prediction. *IEEE/ACM Trans. Comput. Biol. Bioinf.*, 12, 335–347, 2015.

31. Zhang, B., Li, H., Yu, K., Jin, Z., Molecular docking-based computational platform for high-throughput virtual screening. *CCF Trans. High Perform. Computing*, 4, 63–74, 2022.

32. Dhakal, A., McKay, C., Tanner, J.J., Cheng, J., Artificial intelligence in the prediction of protein-ligand interactions: recent advances and future directions. *Briefings Bioinf.*, 23, 1, 476, 2022.

33. Yamanishi, Y., Araki, M., Gutteridge, A., Honda, W., Kanehisa, M., Prediction of drug-target interaction networks from the integration of chemical and genomic spaces. *Bioinformatics*, 24, 232–240, 2008.

34. Bleakley, K. and Yamanishi, Y., Supervised prediction of drug–target interactions using bipartite local models. *Bioinformatics*, 25, 2397–2403, 2009.

35. Wang, Y. and Zeng, J., Predicting drug-target interactions using restricted Boltzmann machines. *Bioinformatics*, 29, 126–134, 2013.

36. Macari, G., Toti, D., Polticelli, F., Computational methods and tools for binding site recognition between proteins and small molecules: from classical geometrical approaches to modern machine learning strategies. *J. Comput-Aided Mol. Des., 33*, 887–903, 2019.

37. Srinivasarao, M. and Low, P.S., Ligand-targeted drug delivery. *Chem. Rev., 117*, 12133–12164, 2017.

38. Dhasmana, A., Kashyap, V.K., Dhasmana, S., Kotnala, S., Haque, S., Ashraf, G.M., Jaggi, M., Yallapu, M.M., Chauhan, S.C., Neutralization of SARS-CoV-2 spike protein via natural compounds: A multilayered high throughput virtual screening approach. *Curr. Pharm. Design*, 26, 5300–5309, 2020.

39. Carpenter, K.A. and Huang, X., Machine learning-based virtual screening and its applications to alzheimer's drug discovery: A review. *Curr. Pharm. Design*, 24, 3347–3358, 2018.

40. Mohs, R.C. and Greig, N.H., Drug discovery and development: Role of basic biological research. *Alzheimer's & Dementia: Translational Research & Clinical Interventions, 3*, 4, 651–657, 2017, https://doi.org/10.1016/j.trci.2017.10.005.

41. Research, S., (n.d.). Global drug discovery market size, suppliers to 2030, Straitsresearch.com. Retrieved June 2023, from https://straitsresearch.com/report/drug-discovery-market#:~:text=Market%20Overview

42. Tollman, P., *A revolution in R&D: How genomics and genetics are transforming the biopharmaceutical industry*, ResearchGate, The Boston Consulting Group - Publications. 2001, unknown. https://www.researchgate.net/publication/245043093_A_Revolution_in_RD_How_Genomics_and_Genetics_are_Transforming_the_Biopharmaceutical_Industry.

43. Pina, A.S., Hussain, A., Ana, An historical overview of drug discovery. *Methods Mol. Biol., 5*, 3–12, 2010, https://doi.org/10.1007/978-1-60761-244-5_1.

44. Leelananda, Sumudu, P., Lindert, S., Computational methods in drug discovery. *12*, 2694–2718, 2016, https://doi.org/10.3762/bjoc.12.267.

45. Larrañaga, P., Calvo, B., Santana, R., Bielza, C., Galdiano, J., Inza, I., Lozano, J.A., Armañanzas, R., Santafé, G., Pérez, A., Robles, V., Machine learning in bioinformatics. *Brief. Bioinform., 7*, 1, 86–112, 2006, https://doi.org/10.1093/bib/bbk007.

46. Dara, S., Dhamercherla, S., Jadav, S.S., Babu, C.S., Ahsan, M.J., Machine learning in drug discovery: A review. *Artificial Intelligence Review, 55*, 1947–1999, 2021. https://doi.org/10.1007/s10462-021-10058-4.

47. Jafari, M., Wang, Y., Amiryousefi, A., Tang, J., Unsupervised learning and multipartite network models: A promising approach for understanding traditional medicine. *Front. Pharmacol., 11*, 2020, https://doi. org/10.3389/fphar.2020.01319.

48. Tsetsos, F., Drineas, P., Paschou, P., Genetics and population analysis. *Elsevier EBooks, 3*, 363–378, 2019, https://doi.org/10.1016/b978-0-12-809633-8.20114-3.

49. Zakariah, M., Classification of large datasets using Random Forest Algorithm in various applications: Survey. *International Journal of Engineering and Innovative Technology (IJJEIT)*, 4, 3, 2014.

50. Ryu, J.K., Lee, J.M., Lee, B.S., Song, J.D., Ahn, S., Oh, K.-S., PredMS: a random forest model for predicting metabolic stability of drug candidates in human liver microsomes. *Bioinformatics, 38*, 2, 364–368, 2021, https://doi.org/10.1093/bioinformatics/btab547.

51. Anagaw, A. and Chang, Y.-L., A new complement naïve Bayesian approach for biomedical data classification. *J. Ambient Intell. Humaniz. Comput., 10*, 3889–3897, 2019, https://doi.org/10.1007/s12652-018-1160-1.

52. Chen, L., Li, Y., Zhao, Q., Peng, H., Hou, T., ADME evaluation in drug discovery. 10. Predictions of p-glycoprotein inhibitors using recursive partitioning and naive bayesian classification techniques. *Mol. Pharmaceutics*, 8, 889–900, 2011, https://doi.org/10.1021/mp100465q.

53. Heikamp, K. and Bajorath, J., Support vector machines for drug discovery. *Expert Opin. Drug Discov.*, 9, 1, 93–104, 2014, https://www.tandfonline.com/doi/abs/10.1517/17460441.2014.866 943.

54. Warmuth, M.K., Liao, J., Rätsch, G., Mathieson, M., Putta, S., Lemmen, C., Active learning with support vector machines in the drug discovery process. *J. Chem. Inf. Comput. Sci.*, 43, 667–673, 2003, https://doi.org/10.1021/ci025620t.

55. Burbidge, R., Trotter, M., Buxton, B.F., Holden, S.B., Drug design by machine learning: support vector machines for pharmaceutical data analysis. *Comput. Chem.*, 26, 5–14, 2001, https://doi.org/10.1016/ s0097-8485(01)00094-8.

56. Zou, J., Huss, M., Abid, A., Mohammadi, P., Torkamani, A., Telenti, A., A primer on deep learning in genomics, in: *https://doi.org/10.1038/s41588-018-0295-5*, vol. 51, pp. 12–18, 2019.

57. Koumakis, L., Deep learning models in genomics; are we there yet? *Comput. Struct. Biotechnol. J.*, 18, 1466–1473, 2020, https://doi.org/10.1016/j.csbj.2020.06.017.

58. Min, S., Lee, B., Yoon, S., Deep learning in bioinformatics. *Brief. Bioinform.*, 18, 5, 851–869, 2016.

59. Wang, Z., Wang, Y., Xuan, J., Dong, Y., Bakay, M., Feng, Y., Clarke, R., Hoffman, E.A., Optimized multilayer perceptrons for molecular classification and diagnosis using genomic data. *Bioinformatics*, 22, 755–761, 2006.

60. Hapudeniya, M., Artificial neural networks in bioinformatics. *Sri Lanka J. Bio- Med. Inf.*, 1, 104, 2010, https://doi.org/10.4038/sljbmi.v1i2.1719.

61. Pollastri, G., Przybylski, D., Rost, B., Baldi, P., Improving the prediction of protein secondary structure in three and eight classes using recurrent neural networks and profiles. *Proteins*, 47, 228–235, 2002.

62. Monti, M., Fiorentino, J., Milanetti, E., Gosti, G., Tartaglia, G.G., Prediction of time series gene expression and structural analysis of gene regulatory networks using recurrent neural networks. *Entropy*, 24, 141–141, 2022, https://doi.org/10.3390/e24020141.

63. Hou, J., Adhikari, B., Cheng, J., DeepSF: deep convolutional neural network for mapping protein sequences to folds. *Bioinformatics*, 34, 1295–1303, 2018.

64. Blanchard, A.J., Stanley, C.B., Bhowmik, D., Using GANs with adaptive training data to search for new molecules. *J. Cheminform.*, 13, 1–8, 2021, https://doi.org/10.1186/s13321-021-00494-3.

65. Gao, W., Mahajan, S. P., Sulam, J., Gray, J.J., Deep learning in protein structural modeling and design. *Patterns*, 1, 100142–100142, 2020, https://doi.org/10.1016/j.patter.2020.100142.

66. Lan, L., You, L., Zhang, Z., Fan, Z., Zhao, W., Zeng, N., Chen, Y., Zhou, X., Generative adversarial networks and its applications in biomedical informatics. *Front. Public Health*, 8, 5253500, 2020, https://doi.org/10.3389/ fpubh.2020.00164.

67. Tripathi, S., Augustin, A., II, Dunlop, A., Sukumaran, R., Dheer, S., Zavalny, A., Haslam, O., Austin, T., Donchez, J., Tripathi, P.K., Kim, E.S., Recent advances and application of generative adversarial networks in drug discovery, development, and targeting. *Artificial Intelligence in the Life Sciences*, 2, 100045–100045, 2022, https://doi.org/10.1016/j.ailsci.2022.100045.

68. Ramsundar, B., *Molecular machine learning with DeepChem - ProQuest*, (Doctoral dissertation, Stanford University, 2018, Proquest.com, https://www. proquest.com/openview/9c0e-06a343233b48d962991d19873ed8/1?pq-origsite=gscholar&c- bl=18750&diss=y.

69. Zhao, T., Hu, Y., Peng, J., Cheng, L., DeepLGP: a novel deep learning method for prioritizing lncRNA target genes. *Bioinformatics*, 36, 16, 4466–4472, 2020, https://doi.org/10.1093/ bioinformatics/btaa428.

70. Wang, H., Liang, P., Zheng, L., Long, C., Li, H., Zuo, Y., eHSCPr discriminating the cell identity involved in endothelial to hematopoietic transition. *Bioinformatics, 37*, 2157–2164, 2021, https://doi. org/10.1093/bioinformatics/btab071.

71. Hecht, D. and Fogel, G., Computational intelligence methods for docking scores. *Curr. Comput. Aided-Drug Design, 5*, 56–68, 2009, https://doi.org/10.2174/157340909787580863.

72. Daina, A., Michielin, O., Zoete, V., SwissTargetPrediction: updated data and new features for efficient prediction of protein targets of small molecules. *Nucleic Acids Res., 47*, 357&ndash364, 2019, https://doi.org/10.1093/nar/gkz382.

73. Cichonska, A., Rousu, J., Aittokallio, T., Identification of drug candidates and repurposing opportunities through compound–target interaction networks. *Expert Opin. Drug Discovery, 10*, 1333–1345, 2015, https://doi.org/10.1517/17460441.2015.1096926.

74. Aljofan, M. and Gaipov, A. Drug discovery and development: the role of artificial intelligence in drug repurposing. *Future Med. Chem., 0*, 2024.

75. *druGAN: An Advanced Generative Adversarial Autoencoder Model for de Novo Generation of New Molecules with Desired Molecular Properties in Silico*, ACS Publications, 2017, https:// pubs.acs.org/doi/abs/10.1021/acs.molpharmaceut.7b00346.

76. Griffiths, R.-R. and Hernández-Lobato, J.M., Constrained Bayesian optimization for automatic chemical design using variational autoencoders. *Chem. Sci., 11*, 2, 577–586, 2020, https://doi. org/10.1039/c9sc04026a.

77. Prasad, K. and Kumar, V., Artificial intelligence-driven drug repurposing and structural biology for SARS-CoV-2. *Curr. Res. Pharmacol. Drug Discov., 2*, 100042, 2021, https://doi.org/10.1016/j. crphar.2021.100042.

78. Charoenkwan, P., Nantasenamat, C., Hasan, M.M., Manavalan, B., Shoombuatong, W., BERT4Bitter: a bidirectional encoder representations from transformers (BERT)-based model for improving the prediction of bitter peptides. *Bioinformatics, 37*, 17, 2556–2562, 2021, https:// doi.org/10.1093/ bioinformatics/btab133.

79. Chan, H.C.S., Shan, H., Dahoun, T., Vogel, H., Yuan, S., Advancing drug discovery via artificial intelligence. *Trends Pharmacol. Sci., 40*, 592–604, 2019, https://doi.org/10.1016/j. tips.2019.06.004.

80. Yang, X., Wang, Y., Byrne, R., Schneider, G., Yang, S., Concepts of artificial intelligence for computer-assisted drug discovery. *Chem. Rev., 119*, 10520–10594, 2019, https://doi.org/10.1021/ acs.chemrev.8b00728.

81. Jiménez, J., Škalič, M., Martínez-Rosell, G., De Fabritiis, G., KDEEP: Protein–Ligand absolute binding affinity prediction via 3D-Convolutional neural networks. *J. Chem. Inf. Modeling, 58*, 287–296, 2018, https://doi.org/10.1021/acs.jcim.7b00650.

82. Jamal, S., Khubaib, M., Gangwar, R., Grover, S., Grover, A., Hasnain, S.E., Artificial Intelligence and Machine learning based prediction of resistant and susceptible mutations in Mycobacterium tuberculosis. *Sci. Rep., 10*, 1, 5487, 2020, https://doi.org/10.1038/s41598-020-62368-2.

83. Li, H., Peng, J., Leung, Y., Leung, K. S., Wong, M. H., Lu, G., Ballester, P.J., The impact of protein structure and sequence similarity on the accuracy of machine-learning scoring functions for binding affinity prediction. *Biomolecules, 8*, 1, 12, 2018.

84. Muhammed, M.T. and Aki-Yalcin, E., Molecular docking: Principles, advances, and its applications in drug discovery. *Lett. Drug Design Discov., 21*, 3, 480–495, 2024, https://doi.org/10.217 4/1570180819666220922103109.

85. Huang, S.-Y., Comprehensive assessment of flexible-ligand docking algorithms: current effectiveness and challenges. *Briefings Bioinf., 19*, 982–994, 2017, https://doi.org/10.1093/bib/ bbx030.

86. Prinz, F., Schlange, T., Asadullah, K., Believe it or not: how much can we rely on published data on potential drug targets? *Nat. Rev. Drug Discov.*, 10, 712–712, 2011, https://doi. org/10.1038/ nrd3439-c1

87. Gupta, M., Sharma, R., Kumar, A., Docking techniques in pharmacology: How much promising? *Comput. Biol. Chem.*, 76, 210–217, 2018, https://doi.org/10.1016/j. compbiolchem.2018.06.005.

88. Rose, P.W., Prlić, A., Altunkaya, A., Bi, C., Bradley, A.R., Christie, C.H., Costanzo, L.D., Duarte, J.M., Dutta, S., Feng, Z., Green, R.K., Goodsell, D.S., Hudson, B., Kalro, T., Lowe, R., Peisach, E., Randle, C., Rose, A.S., Shao, C., Tao, Y.-P., The RCSB protein data bank: integrative view of protein, gene and 3D structural information. *Nucleic Acids Res.*, 45, 271–281, 2017, https://doi. org/10.1093/nar/gkw1000.

89. Pyrkov, T.V., Priestle, J.P., Jacoby, E., Efremov, R.G., Ligand-specific scoring functions: improved ranking of docking solutions. *SAR QSAR Environ. Res.*, 19, 91–99, 2008, https://doi. org/10.1080/10629360701844092.

90. Yadava, U., Search algorithms and scoring methods in protein-ligand docking. *Endocrinol. Metabolism Int. J.*, 6, 6, 359–367, 2018, https://doi.org/10.15406/emij.2018.06.00212.

91. Vamathevan, J., Clark, D., Czodrowski, P., Dunham, I., Ferrán, E.A., Lee, G.C., Li, B., Madabhushi, A., Shah, P.K., Spitzer, M., Zhao, S., Applications of machine learning in drug discovery and development. *Nat. Rev. Drug Discov.*, 18, 463–477, 2019, https://doi.org/10.1038/ s41573-019-0024-5.

92. Tripathi, M.K., Nath, A., Singh, T., Ethayathulla, A.S., Kaur, P., Evolving scenario of big data and Artificial Intelligence (AI) in drug discovery. *Mol. Divers.*, 25, 1439–1460, 2021, https://doi. org/10.1007/s11030-021-10256-w.

93. Vatansever, S., Schlessinger, A., Wacker, D., Kaniskan, H. Ü., Jin, J., Zhou, M.-M., Zhang, B., Artificial intelligence and machine learning-aided drug discovery in central nervous system diseases: State-of-the-arts and future directions. *Mol. Divers.*, 41, 1427–1473, 2021, https://doi. org/10.1002/ med.21764.

94. Sorin, V., Barash, Y., Konen, E., Klang, E., Creating artificial images for radiology applications using generative adversarial networks (GANs) – a systematic review. *Acad. Radiol.*, 27, 1175–1185, 2020a, https://doi.org/10.1016/j.acra.2019.12.024.

95. Peng, J., Jury, E.C., Dönnes, P., Ciurtin, C., Machine learning techniques for personalised medicine approaches in immune-mediated chronic inflammatory diseases: Applications and challenges. *Front. Pharmacol.*, 12, 720694, 2021, https://doi.org/10.3389/fphar.2021.720694.

96. Choudhury, A. and Asan, O., Role of artificial intelligence in patient safety outcomes: Systematic literature review. *JMIR Med. Inform.*, 8, 18599–18599, 2020, https://doi.org/10.2196/18599.

97. Ilmudeen, A. and Nayyar, A., Novel Designs of Smart Healthcare Systems: Technologies, Architecture, and Applications. *Machine Learning for Critical Internet of Medical Things*, 1, 125–151, 2022, https://doi.org/10.1007/978-3-030-80928-7_6.

98. Nayyar, A., Gadhavi, L., Zaman, N., Machine learning in healthcare: review, opportunities and challenges. *Mach. Learn. Internet Med. Things Healthcare*, 1, 23–45, 2021, https://doi. org/10.1016/b978-0-12-821229-5.00011-2.

99. Pramanik, P.K.D., Pareek, G., Nayyar, A., Security and Privacy in Remote Healthcare. *Telemedicine Technol.*, 1, 201–225, 2019, https://doi.org/10.1016/b978-0-12-816948-3.00014-3.

100. Pramanik, P.K.D., Solanki, A., Debnath, A., Nayyar, A., El-Sappagh, S., Kwak, K.-S., Advancing Modern Healthcare With Nanotechnology, Nanobiosensors, and Internet of Nano Things: Taxonomies, Applications, Architecture, and Challenges. *IEEE Access*, 8, 65230–65266, 2020, https://doi.org/10.1109/access.2020.2984269.

101. Pushkar, P., Ananth, C., Nagrath, P., F. Al-Amri, J., Nayyar, A., Mutation Prediction for Coronaviruses Using Genome Sequence and Recurrent Neural Networks. *Comput., Mater. & Contin.*, 73, 1, 1601–1619, 2022, https://doi.org/10.32604/cmc.2022.026205.
102. Venaik, A., Kumari, R., Venaik, U., Nayyar, A., The Role of Machine Learning and Artificial Intelligence in Clinical Decisions and the Herbal Formulations Against COVID-19. *Int. J. Reliable Qual. E-Healthcare*, 11, 1, 1–17, 2022, https://doi.org/10.4018/ ijrqeh.2022010107.

7

Revolutionizing Drug Discovery: The Role of AI and Machine Learning in Accelerating Medicinal Advancements

Anu Sayal[1]*, Janhvi Jha[2], Chaithra N.[2], Atharv Rajesh Gangodkar[2] and Shaziya Banu S.[2]

[1]School of Accounting and Finance, Taylor's Business School, Taylor's University, Selangor, Malaysia
[2]Department of CSE (AI & ML), JAIN (deemed to be University), Bangalore, Karnataka, India

Abstract

Historically, drug discovery was dominated by relentless scientific experiments and repetitive laboratory procedures. However, with the introduction of computational technologies and multidimensional data, this process has undergone significant transformation. This chapter emphasizes the pivotal role of AI, ML, DL, NLP, and robotics in contemporary drug development. AI, with its evolving intelligence, amplifies decision processes when supported by comprehensive data. The focus remains on the capabilities of ML, DL, and NLP in the pharmaceutical industry—from accurate drug interaction predictions to the formulation of specialized treatment methods. Robotics has emerged as a vital tool, streamlining the management and distribution of medications. By leveraging AI methodologies such as random forest, SVM, and others, it is feasible to predict drug outcomes, identify new pharmaceutical benefits, and foresee any adverse side effects. It is notable how AI is the cornerstone for innovations including personalized medications, digital drug analysis, original drug formulation, and data-driven predictions. While these technological breakthroughs signify a monumental evolution in drug discovery, there exist challenges like data gaps, unclear models, and ethical considerations. This chapter provides a comprehensive overview of the present drug discovery techniques, outlines prevalent challenges, and suggests potential solutions.

Keywords: Artificial intelligence, convolutional neural network, deep learning, drug discovery, machine learning, *de novo* design

7.1 Introduction

In an ever-evolving world, humanity continuously aims to assert control over evolution, especially when it enhances our overall well-being. Central to this objective are the spheres of pharmaceutical and medical research, diligently striving to produce compounds that alleviate human suffering. Historically, the pharmaceutical industry has navigated through a rigorous regulatory labyrinth to ensure the pinnacle of therapeutic product quality, yet

*Corresponding author: anu.sayal.07@gmail.com

Abhirup Khanna, May El Barachi, Sapna Jain, Manoj Kumar and Anand Nayyar (eds.) *Artificial Intelligence and Machine Learning in Drug Design and Development*, (189–222) © 2024 Scrivener Publishing LLC

our modern age has infused an overwhelming digitization of data within this field. While this digital influx holds vast potential, it simultaneously introduces monumental challenges, especially when leveraged to solve sophisticated clinical riddles [69].

Step in artificial intelligence (AI)—a shining solution in the vast expanse of data. Anchored in the ambition of replicating human thought processes, AI, equipped with a wide suite of intricate tools, is on the brink of redefining data analysis, all the while ensuring that human engagement remains integral. Encompassed within the broad objective of AI is machine learning (ML), a strategy that employs algorithms to sift through and decipher patterns from vast amounts of data. A notable branch of ML is deep learning (DL), which places a profound emphasis on artificial neural networks (ANNs) to emulate human cognitive functionality. The pharmaceutical domain is ripe with expectations, eagerly anticipating a future where AI and ML not only augment but also considerably elevate its capacity for innovation. Imagine a realm where colossal data repositories are rapidly unraveled, thus catalyzing the emergence of cutting-edge medications and refining therapeutic blueprints [70].

This chapter embarks on an expedition, with the purpose of delving into the nucleus of this imminent transformation. The exploration begins with an examination of the multifaceted applications of machine learning within the pharmaceutical sphere, touching upon the subtleties of deep learning in pharmacovigilance and the strengths of natural language processing in hastening drug production. As the chapter progresses, the main aim is to spotlight methodologies like genetic algorithms and feature selection, techniques inspired by evolution, that fine-tune potential therapeutic pathways. Furthermore, the chapter explores innovative modeling paradigms, such as random forests and Bayesian networks, poised to reshape personalized treatment approaches. Despite the promising horizon, the integration of AI into the pharmaceutical landscape is not without its hurdles. This chapter acknowledges the inherent challenges, ranging from data quality concerns to model transparency and ethical quandaries. Beyond merely identifying these challenges, the objective is to propose viable remedies and provide a forward-looking perspective.

Objectives of the Chapter

The following are the objectives of the chapter:

- To highlight the game-changing potential of artificial intelligence (AI), machine learning (ML), deep learning (DL), natural language processing (NLP), and robotics in modernizing the process of drug development and spearheading transformations in the pharmaceutical sector;
- To present a detailed picture of the numerous machine learning methodologies, inclusive of deep learning, NLP, feature selection, genetic algorithms, and clustering techniques and their critical roles in drug discovery, from predicting results to introducing innovative applications to optimizing medical solutions;
- To explore the diverse facets of AI's applications in pharmaceuticals, emphasizing domains like personalized medicine, drug reallocation, safety assessments, predictive analysis, and pioneering drug formulation;

- And, to comprehensively explore advanced techniques like random forests, SVM, Bayesian networks, ANN, and CNN provides clarity on the inner workings of drug prediction and its successful analysis. Simultaneously, the chapter confronts the complexities and obstacles associated with infusing AI into drug development, discussing challenges like data inconsistencies, model interpretability mysteries, and ethical dilemmas, and also proposes possible remedies for these concerns.

Organization of the Chapter

The rest of the chapter is organized as follows: Section 7.2 enlightens machine learning techniques in drug discovery. Section 7.3 highlights AI techniques for prediction and analysis of drugs. Section 7.4 elaborates AI for revolutionizing drug development, followed by challenges and solutions in Section 7.5. Finally, Section 7.6 concludes the chapter with future scope.

7.2   Machine Learning Techniques in Drug Discovery

7.2.1   Deep Learning in the Pharmaceutical Industry

When it comes to the development of novel pharmaceuticals, artificial intelligence (AI) networks and instruments employ fundamental paradigms. Deep learning (DL) technology, which employs neural networks known as artificial neural networks (ANN) and is thus a subset of machine learning (ML]) methodology, is crucial for accurately assessing and predicting a drug's affinity for specific targets. It can save time and money by expediting the medication formulation process with discretion and deliberation. Due to its superior performance compared to other methods utilized in the industry, DL is now widely accepted as the most important method for predicting bioactivity. Before a drug molecule is synthesized or manufactured in a laboratory, DL can be used to assess its therapeutic efficacy in a target-based drug development and creation process. Site-specific drug delivery (SSDD) is a smart localized and targeted delivery method used to enhance drug efficacy, reduce drug-related toxicity, and prolong the duration of action. SSDD guarantees the safety of a drug's contact with diseased tissue. In conjunction with computational methods, the SSDD system is used to improve the therapeutic efficacy of drug discovery, design, and fabrication [62].

New medicinal molecules have been found using cutting-edge deep learning algorithms. Deep learning research in this field is extensive. In particular, Gawehn *et al.* [31] discussed machine learning approaches for QSAR model determination. "Shallow" models use one layer of feature alterations and are simple. The research paper briefly introduced deep learning before covering deep neural networks. The study included RBMs, CNNs, and medicinal applications. Deep learning proved successful in chemoinformatics [57]. The machine learning model predicted chemical molecule properties using a recursive neural network. An ensemble of recursive neural networks resolved the discrepancy between undirected cyclic graphs (molecules) and guided acyclic graphs (recursive approaches). This notion explains water solubility. Despite the tiny training datasets, the outcomes were better than competing approaches [47, 97] and studied deep learning for pharmaceutical compound categorization.

Deep learning was used to predict aqueous solubility using four published datasets, a major achievement in pharmaceutical research. This technique outperformed other machine learning algorithms after 10-fold cross-validation. DL's cross-validation AUC exceeds 94.0 for predicting the compounds' epoxidation sites. It is uncertain how this methodology compares to other machine learning methods and if it can be used for prospective prediction. This approach should be properly investigated. Researchers have used route- and landmark-level data reduction methods in deep learning systems that use gene expression data to learn about drugs and therapeutic categories. The 10-factor cross-validation shows that deep neural networks outperform SVM-based internal testing. These findings show that repurposing pharmaceuticals using deep neural networks may be promising. Recent research used a 10-fold cross-validation analysis to assess machine learning methods for predicting drug release from polylactide-co-glycolide (PLGA) microspheres in drug formulation. Deep learning is performed similarly to random forest, single tree, and genetic algorithms. Drug-induced liver damage is a unique deep learning dataset [25, 67].

Academic research created the framework for deep learning or layered neural networks in machine learning applications. The first public deep learning application framework was Theano. The MILA lab at the famous University of Montréal released Theano, the first deep learning framework, in 2008 [102]. This system features a well-documented interface and a stable code base. Its use by the academic community has been consistent and ongoing. This framework is versatile like TensorFlow and efficient like the other frameworks. Its advanced design and graph approach for complex dataset calculations explain this. Google, Facebook, Microsoft, and NVIDIA have contributed to recent advances in this field. Hardware and software are integrated and supplied by one company. The acclaimed Google Brain Team created TensorFlow. Since November 2015, the architecture has influenced deep learning research. This area's development activity is unmatched, with 5,614 contributions on GitHub in the previous 6 months. Persistent networking is fascinatingly young. TensorFlow, like Theano, uses a graph-based computational architecture and distributes calculations among GPUs. This might streamline business software rollout. Mailing lists and enquiry forums like Stack Overflow show popular interest despite the lack of corporate funding. Early TensorFlow versions performed poorly, especially in convolutional neural network architecture creation [117]. The framework now matches other alternatives. TensorFlow's interoperability with Google's TPUs, specialized tensor processing hardware, is noteworthy. TensorFlow-based consumer solutions and their native operation on new hardware can reduce runtimes by 15× to 30×. TPUs helped AlphaGo beat Fan Hui and Lee Sedol [94]. Figure 7.1 shows a drug discovery deep learning word cloud.

7.2.2   Natural Language Processing (NLP) Methodologies for Drug Development

Natural language processing (NLP) is a sophisticated AI technique that enables the interpretation and analysis of written or spoken information generated by humans. By employing syntactic and semantic analysis, natural language processing enables us to delve deeply into text data. Over the past decade, NLP has made remarkable advancements, integrating

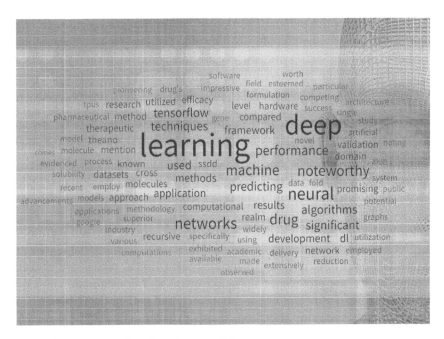

Figure 7.1 Drug discovery using deep learning: a word cloud.

itself seamlessly into our daily lives. NLP has become indispensable to modern life, from sifting emails and assisting voice-controlled virtual assistants to facilitate language translations, enabling digital phone conversations, and empowering text analytics [7].

The burgeoning field of natural language processing (NLP) has sparked a surge of interest in the analysis of text-based representations of biomolecules. This exciting area of research is rapidly evolving thanks to cutting-edge advancements in NLP techniques. The field of natural language processing (NLP) is an exciting area of research that utilizes a diverse range of techniques to sift through copious amounts of textual data with the aim of uncovering latent, unstructured knowledge. This advancement has the potential to enhance employment opportunities in fields where language, specifically textual data, is crucial for achieving comprehension. The study of language in bioinformatics and cheminformatics can be classified into three discrete groups. Firstly, there is the natural language, which is commonly English, utilized in scientific publications, patents, and websites. Secondly, there is the domain-specific language, which is established by a structured set of regulations derived from empirical data and characterizing human understanding of the subject matter, such as proteins and substances. Lastly, there are structured forms, including tables, ontologies, knowledge graphs, and databases. One of the key applications of natural language processing (NLP) techniques in the biomedical sector, commonly referred to as BioNLP, is the analysis and retrieval of textual data published in natural languages. It is common practice within the field of BioNLP to utilize knowledge graphs or relational databases as a means of effectively storing and distributing data obtained through various techniques [108, 121].

Due to the growth of medical data, artificial intelligence methods like NLP are becoming more useful in healthcare. Healthcare is hindered by 80% of medical data being disorganized and unanalyzed. NLP has great potential in healthcare and model-informed drug development (MIDD) since it makes dealing with and synthesizing natural language data easier. NLP replaces the manual curation of natural language data with large-scale, automated text and speech analysis [46]. MIDD aids drug development decision-making with quantitative models. MIDD maximizes and accelerates medication development by extracting information from structured (e.g., electronic health records) and unstructured (e.g., research materials) data using natural language processing (NLP) [112]. Figure 7.2 depicts NLP features. Model-based meta-analysis, illness progression modeling, patient–trial matching, pharmaceutical repurposing, biomarker discovery, and identification are included. NLP algorithms analyze academic literature to find links between chemical/drug entities, target proteins, and new disease-related pathways [55, 77]. NLP saves time and money by repurposing drugs for new uses. Natural language processing automates text mining from unstructured data, improving pharmaceutical safety. NLP accelerates clinical trial subject selection [7].

Deep learning has surpassed ML on a wide range of general-domain natural language processing (NLP) tasks, including language modeling, POS tagging, named entity recognition, paraphrase detection, and sentiment analysis. Clinical papers are challenging to handle because healthcare providers employ acronyms and nonstandard clinical vocabulary while document structure and organization vary, and patient data protection requires strict de-identification and anonymization. If these challenges could be overcome, additional research and innovation would improve clinical decision support, patient cohort verification of identity, patient engagement support, population health management, pharmacovigilance, personalized medicine, and clinical text summary. With regard poor test performance, memory network versions provide many knowledge sources for effective query responding and other NLP tasks that need complicated reasoning and inference. Visual cues are essential for natural language understanding. Computer vision and natural language processing researchers have recently focused on visual identification and caption

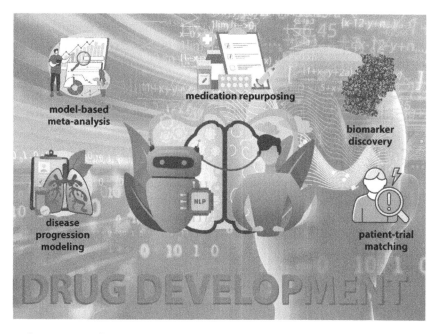

Figure 7.2 Characteristics of NLP-based language processing.

generation due to the challenge of autonomously understanding a picture and expressing it in natural language [3, 35].

Medical procedure medication injuries are called adverse drug events (ADEs). They cause undesirable consequences and long hospital stays, causing healthcare issues. ADEs cause millions of hospitalizations and unnecessary post-discharge consequences. Due to limited sample numbers and rigorous inclusion/exclusion criteria in pre-marketing randomized controlled trials (RCTs), identifying ADEs before a drug's launch is challenging. Natural language processing (NLP) can identify ADEs faster, more accurately, and more cost-effectively than human chart inspection and voluntary reporting. NLP algorithms search UMLS datasets for illnesses and drugs to make ADE predictions based on co-occurrence indicators. NLP algorithms can identify ADEs faster and more accurately than conventional methods [41].

7.2.3   Automated Management and Dispensing of Prescriptions Using Robotics

The automation of pharmacy has resulted in substantial cost savings and increased output. The pharmacy automation systems' primary objective is to maximize prescription throughput while minimizing operating expenses. By automating the pharmacy, pharmacists and technicians can save time by averting repetitive manual tasks. This permits them to spend more time providing direct patient care. In addition, pharmacists have more time for patient consultation and conversation, allowing them to gain a deeper understanding of their patients' circumstances and satisfy their healthcare requirements more effectively. In recent years, the demand for automated pharmacies has skyrocketed, especially at centralized fill pharmacies that distribute medications to various retail pharmacies. Enhancements to the robotic prescription dispensing system (RPDS) are necessary to enable automated pharmacies to process more prescriptions per hour in light of this expanding demand [39, 40].

The RPDS is comprised of a primary conveyance system, a pneumatic vial and cap delivery system, and medication dispensers contained within a hexagonal robotic unit. In drug dispensing devices, computers are used to store, count, and disseminate numerous capsule and tablet varieties. Based on the order type and routing parameters, a total of 65 containers are sent to the various filling stations *via* the conveyor system. Empty vials and caps are transferred onto a pneumatic vial and cap delivery system before being transported to robotics. Due to the high volume of prescriptions, the RPDS of a central fill pharmacy is frequently comprised of numerous robotic units, making the distribution and assignment of medication dispensers to these robotic units challenging [44].

Advanced optical character recognition (OCR) technology is utilized extensively in robotic applications such as the automated verification of prescriptions. Using this innovation, machines can accurately read and comprehend prescription information, ensuring that the individual's medication is safe and effective. If the human element is removed from the verification procedure, medication errors can be reduced significantly. OCR can readily connect to existing EHR and pharmacy databases when used to verify prescriptions. This enables the machines to compare the prescription to the patient's medical records, allergies, and current prescriptions to ensure that the substance is safe and appropriate. By promptly addressing contraindications and drug interactions, the likelihood of adverse reactions or consequences can be diminished. Automated prescription verification enhances patient safety and outcomes by reducing pharmaceutical errors. Medication errors can result in severe complications, including inadequate therapy and unwanted adverse effects. By having machines perform the verification process, patients have an additional safeguard against errors such as incorrect dosage, medication mix-ups, and illegible handwriting [95].

7.2.4   Feature Selection and Genetic Algorithm in Drug Discovery

In the field of informatics, the process of selecting molecular descriptors is known as "feature selection," and several machine learning techniques have been applied to this problem. There are three primary categories of employed methods: filter, wrapper, and embedding [54]. Filter techniques have the disadvantage of analyzing each feature separately without considering how well it performs in comparison to the other characteristics in the group. This issue may affect the following machine learning applications. A significant issue is that machine learning algorithms have a high temporal complexity to implement in wrapper and embedded techniques. The genetic algorithm, a type of genetic algorithm (GA), can be used to select features. Many GA-based feature selection approaches require the incorporation of a classification technique, such as a support vector machine (SVM), artificial neural network (ANN), k-nearest neighbor (KNN), or decision tree (DT), in order to properly evaluate each member of the population [96]. There is no means to describe the nature of the features' effect on the treated class, and all of the features identified by these methods are identical. In addition, these methods require extensive training periods for each separate set [50].

Holland's work on genetic algorithms was motivated by biological evolution's flexibility. These stochastic optimization methods are useful in chemometrics and drug development, where the problem space is often large. A genetic algorithm represents people as chromosomes. After initializing the first generation, each individual is objectively functionally evaluated for fitness. Parent selection, crossover, and mutation create descendants in the next phase. Steps 2 and 3 repeat until objective function convergence [104].

Structural alignment compares ligands that bind the target receptor to analyze their spatial and electrical requirements for pharmacophore recognition in receptors with unknown 3D structures. GAMMA, a GA-Newton optimizer program, offers adjustable molecular alignment. GAs automates small organic compound synthesis. SMILES strings calculate a scoring function that includes lipophilicity, electrical properties, and shape-related factors [24]. GAs construct combinatorial libraries by reproducing a similarity-measure fitness function template. Virtual combinatorial libraries often exceed experimental synthesis [84]. Selected building elements optimize production. GAs diminishes tripeptide library amines. They score in such a way that there is resemblance to a tripeptide target [91, 104].

Mathematicians have developed several strategies to find optimum permutations. Genetic algorithms (GAs) may change population size, number of surviving genomes, crossover, mutation, parent–child connection, and ranking function parameters. GAs are ideal for optimization issues requiring careful parameter selection due to their versatility. GA performance depends on search space structure. The building-block theory suggests that GAs can explore genomes for higher-order fitness schemes by merging "fit" building blocks or contiguous gene schemes. The GA statistically analyzes these building elements—atoms,

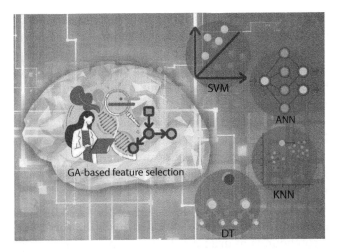

Figure 7.3 Algorithms in GA-based feature selection approach: SVM, ANN, KNN, and DT.

reagents, starting materials, and reactions. This generates combinatorial compound libraries using methodical building element arrays. Thus, a systematic SAR is expected. Optimizing predicts more active compounds with fewer samples [114]. The GA-based feature selection strategy utilizes the SVM, ANN, KNN, and DT algorithms as shown in Figure 7.3.

7.2.5   Clustering Algorithms for Drug Discovery

Fundamental to the drug discovery process is the effort to create innovative medications that specifically target disease-causing proteins. However, this is a protracted and difficult process, involving multiple stages from target identification to FDA approval. Unfortunately, the pharmaceutical industry confronts considerable uncertainty, with clinical trial failure rates that exceed 90% [1]. The potential for novel drug candidates to interact with unintended proteins, resulting in undesirable side effects, is a significant obstacle [38, 2]. Molecular dynamics (MD) is frequently used to evaluate the potency of ligand–protein interactions. The selection of specific protein conformations becomes ambiguous, however, when interacting with novel protein targets for which no prior knowledge exists. Although MD simulations are useful for concept validation and proof, they are incapable of revealing data patterns or characteristics that facilitate the preferential selection of target protein conformations. Therefore, sophisticated machine learning (ML) techniques are required to identify precise bindings, minimize pre-clinical lab trials, and reduce failure rates earlier in the drug discovery pipeline. For protein conformational selection, clustering-based ML techniques, such as RMSD clustering, PCCA+, and MCL, are extensively utilized. RMSD clustering creates clusters of protein conformations based on a user-defined threshold by calculating RMSD values using least-squares techniques. Utilizing a fuzzy clustering methodology, PCCA+ concentrates on aggregating the eigenvalues of protein conformational changes. MCL, a technique for clustering based on graphs, considers the probability of a random pedestrian following specific paths within the graph. These ML techniques provide valuable insights and instruments to improve the selection of protein conformations, thereby making drug discovery processes more efficient and effective [26, 27].

Chemoinformatics is an emerging discipline that encompasses all aspects of chemical data management and analysis. This application of informatics technologies to chemical problems is crucial to the identification and optimization of lead compounds during the drug development process. Cheminformatics expedites decision-making, increases the effectiveness of the drug discovery process, and reduces associated costs. Appropriate descriptors are used to represent the chemical data collection, followed by the application of data mining techniques to isolate the most promising chemicals. A number of stages are involved in the identification of a lead molecule, including the selection of compounds, the construction of a structure–activity relationship, the generation of a chemical library, and the prediction of pharmacological properties. Effectiveness, selectivity, bioavailability, safety, and scalability are among the characteristics described. Using clustering techniques including K-means, bisecting K-means, and Ward clustering, similar compounds are organized together and their activities are calculated. The success of these algorithms in identifying lead compounds in drug development applications is highly dependent on the application's accuracy requirements and the nature of the data collection [60]. Various drug discovery clustering approaches for the pharmaceutical industry are highlighted in Figure 7.4.

7.3   AI Techniques for Prediction and Analysis of Drugs

7.3.1   Random Forest (RF)

An approach to machine learning that is frequently employed in drug development is the random forest (RF) algorithm. It is a supervised learning technique that may be used to analyze and forecast several elements of drug development, including toxicity, chemical activity, and interactions with targets.

RF can be used in the drug development process for activities like virtual screening, which involves scanning huge datasets of chemicals to find prospective drug candidates. In order to uncover patterns and connections between various substances and their actions, RF models may be trained to utilize a wide range of chemical descriptors, molecular

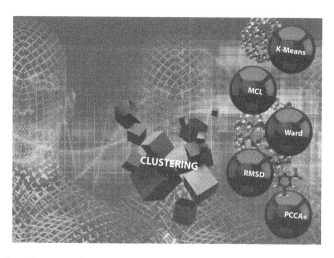

Figure 7.4 Various drug discovery clustering approaches.

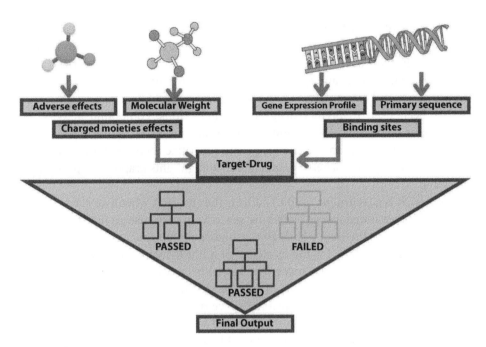

Figure 7.5 RF functioning.

characteristics, and biological factors. The chemicals that should be tested in additional experiments may then be ranked using these models.

The RF technique builds a collection of decision trees, each of which is trained using a different random subset of the data. The RF method combines each tree's forecast during the prediction stage to provide a final prediction. By using an ensemble technique, predictions are more accurate and resilient (refer to Figure 7.5).

RF provides a number of benefits for drug discovery. When compared to single decision trees, it is more resistant to overfitting and can handle high-dimensional data with many characteristics. RF could also throw insight into the significance of a trait, enabling researchers to point out the primary factors influencing a compound's activity and other properties.

7.3.2   Support Vector Machines (SVM)

An established machine learning strategy Drug prediction and other applications involving the identification of new drugs employ support vector machines (SVM). SVM, a supervised learning technique, may be used for tasks including predicting chemical activity, determining toxicity, and virtual screening.

Molecular descriptors, chemical characteristics, and biological traits are some examples of the drug information included in the labeled datasets used to train SVM models for drug prediction. Finding the ideal hyperplane to divide several classes of compounds in a feature space is the goal of SVM. This hyperplane increases the distance between the classes, enabling regression or classification.

A primary benefit of SVM is its ability to effectively deal with high-dimensional data. Because of the varied variety of chemical and biological characteristics, it can manage datasets with an extensive variety of attributes, which is prevalent in drug discovery. SVM is particularly renowned for its ability to withstand overfitting since it maximizes the margin between categories and concentrates on the most important support vectors.

SVM has been used to predict drug-target interactions, compound activity against particular targets or biological tests, and chemical toxicity. SVM algorithms can produce predictions about novel, unlabeled chemicals and prioritize them for future experimental assessment by learning from labeled data. Figure 7.6 highlights graphical representation of SVM working.

The kernel trick is a technique used to address the situation when two classes of objects cannot be linearly separated in a given feature space X. In such cases, a non-linear mapping φ is applied to project the data points into a higher-dimensional space H. This higher-dimensional space may allow for the existence of a linear hyperplane that can effectively separate positive and negative instances. The kernel trick overcomes the need for explicit mapping by utilizing kernel functions. These kernel functions enable the computation of inner products in the higher-dimensional space directly in the original feature space, thereby avoiding the computational cost associated with explicitly transforming the data. By leveraging the kernel trick, it becomes possible to efficiently perform classification or regression tasks even when dealing with complex, non-linear relationships between features and class labels.

7.3.3   Bayesian Network

Bayesian networks are used in medication prediction to represent the connections between variables and generate predictions based on probabilistic reasoning.

The variables A and B in the Bayes' Rule equation indicate the occurrences or propositions for which we are computing the probability. Let us decode A and B in the context of drug prediction:

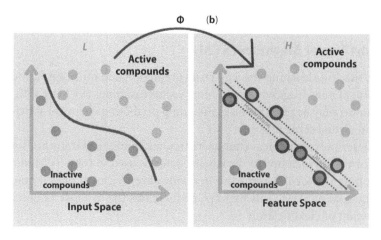

Figure 7.6 SVM working.

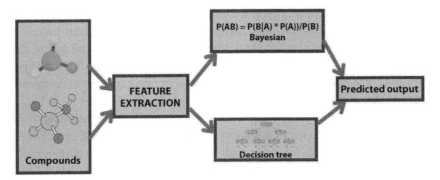

Figure 7.7 Working of Bayesian model.

The estimation of the probability of an event A (such as a molecule being active against a target or having a certain quality) given some evidence or observation B (such as experimental data, molecular traits, or prior knowledge) in drug prediction can often be used (refer Figure 7.7).

As a result, in the Bayes' Rule equation, "A" represents the event or proposition of interest in drug prediction, and "B" represents the evidence or observation pertinent to that event. Based on the observed evidence B, the equation allows us to update the estimation of event A over B.

The following Bayes' rule can be used for drug prediction:

$$P(A|B) = (P(B|A) * P(A)) / P(B)$$

where Bayes' rule allows us to calculate the posterior probability of event A given event B, based on the prior probability of A, the likelihood of B given A, and the evidence probability of B.

The joint probability can be estimated by:

$$P(A, B) = P(A) * P(B|A)$$

where the joint probability of events A and B is the probability of A multiplied by the conditional probability of B given A.

The conditional probability can be calculated by:

$$P(A|B) = P(A, B) / P(B)$$

where the conditional probability of event A given event B is calculated by dividing the joint probability of A and B by the probability of B.

7.3.4 ANN and CNN

It is common for pharmaceutical dosage forms to contain impurities that are similar in nature, although not necessarily identical. The choice of ANN is made because of its capacity to accurately identify and assess different characteristics, such as distinguishing and measuring closely related components. Researchers frequently use artificial neural networks (ANN) to detect and calibrate tryptophan, tyrosine, and histidine due to the similarities in their structures and spectra. By using artificial neural networks (ANN), it is possible to detect nonlinear correlations and determine the enantiomeric and chiral compositions of a sample with just one spectrophotometric measurement [5, 76, 78].

Using artificial neural networks (ANN) for computer-aided optimization to determine optimum gradient designs in chromatography has significant technical promise. ANNs can estimate retention durations to optimize high-performance liquid chromatography. This is done by correlating analyte capacity parameters with mobile phase composition and pH. ANNs may separate components regardless of solvent concentration or pH [61, 65].

Thus, artificial neural networks (ANN) may reduce technique optimization time and cost. ANNs can help find relationships in complicated mixed data sets [64]. Isolating the pharmaceutical ingredient or its byproduct makes assessing a drug's concentration in a physiological fluid more difficult than in a formulated state or solvent. For detecting the drug's binding site and defining the ideal storage conditions for future analysis, a deep learning artificial neural network (ANN) is advised. ANNs maximize extraction and estimation methods to choose internal standards [118].

Pharmacology and clinical practice make drug–drug interaction (DDI) detection problematic. Patients and society benefit from early clinical trial DDU detection. Drug–drug interactions (DDIs) are best identified using computational approaches. Similarity metrics like DDI, side-effect, structural, or a mix of these can identify drug–drug interactions (DDI). GNNs and KGNNs can predict drug–drug interactions (DDIs). Networks help identify, enhance, and test drugs in unstudied illnesses. Drug interactions are important since taking numerous drugs might aggravate side effects. ANNs, factor propagation over graph nodes, adjacency matrix factorization (AMF), and AMFP can predict drug–drug interactions (DDI). Drug Bank data may be used to train nodes retrospectively. Deep learning, notably Bi-LSTM and CNNs, has been used for DDI extraction [17, 86, 88].

Pharmaceutical research has several ANN applications. Pharmaceutical designers employ the aforementioned concepts. Analysis, effectiveness, and interactions are covered. Scientific proof and methodology are required by regulators for product development. This is key to attracting clients. Artificial neural networks (ANN) have saved the pharmaceutical sector time and money during product development. ANN technology also improves the efficacy, quality, and safety of medicines, benefiting patients. The artificial neural network (ANN) meets regulatory, industrial, and patient demands [14, 53].

Evaluation criteria for CNN: Using a multi-label classification method is an effective way to predict Drug–drug Interaction (DDI) occurrences with precision. To cover all possible results, predictions are classified into four groups: true positives (TP), false positives (FP), true negatives (TN), and false negatives (FN). In addition, the assessment of results frequently includes the use of precision and recall standards as dependable evaluation metrics. The definition of accuracy within a sample set is the proportion of true positive (TP) cases to the overall number of positive samples that have been classified. The definition of recall is the proportion of accurately identified positive samples to the overall number of positive samples present in a dataset.

$$\text{Precision} = \text{TP/TP+FP}$$

$$\text{Recall} = \text{TP/TP+FN}$$

Metrics like accuracy, F1-score, AUPR, and AUC are utilized to assess the performance of the algorithm.

The study employed various performance measures such as accuracy, F1-score, micro-averaged AUPR, and micro-averaged AUC. After gathering data from all participants, the metrics undergo micro-averaging [49].

CNN-DDI's efficacy is measured by cosine, Jaccard, and Gaussian feature similarity. To assess CNN-DDI performance, different similarity methods were used. Similarity measures reveal behavioral tendencies. Researchers used Jaccard similarity since the CNN-DDI is unaffected by the other two measures. CNN-DDI models that employ different feature types to show the superior performance of particular pharmaceutical categories and combinations are tested in the study. Drug categories performed best in the CNN-DDI model, with an AUPR score of 0.9139. Drug targets lowered scores to 0.8470. Medication categories rank best in all five measures. Thus, adding the medicine category to the CNN-DDI model yields good results. Instead of using one feature, CNN-DDI may benefit from numerous features. Four criteria yielded the greatest AUPR score of 0.9251. CNN-DDI's efficiency improves with each feature [28, 71].

CNN-DDI may anticipate DDI incidents, according to study. Modules that choose combinational information and create convolutional neural network predictions are the most popular method. Four pharmacological features reduce CNN input dimensions. Drug–drug interactions (DDI) are predicted using a deep convolutional neural network (CNN) model. The forecast module uses selection module input vectors. CNN was added to the forecasting module due to feature noise and its benefits. Convolutional Neural Networks (CNNs) excel in image classification, object identification, and picture segmentation, making them popular. Bioinformatics research is incorporating deep learning. CNN offers benefits over deep neural networks.

The convolutional layer can decrease the number of parameters by using sparse connections and shared parameters. The convolutional layer has the ability to extract information from both global and local features. Concerning the task of forecasting drug–drug interactions (DDIs). There is a strong correlation between drug classification and drug properties, including their overall properties and how they combine. To improve the ability to learn features. The current research utilizes CNN as a supervised model to extract information from integrated features with the aim of predicting DDIs. This study employs a prediction model that uses convolutional neural networks (CNNs). The model consists of five convolutional layers, two fully connected layers, and a softmax layer. Convolutional layers are primarily responsible for extracting sub-space features from input vectors. The model being analyzed has convolutional layers that display uniformity in kernel size. Each layer uses a kernel size of (3 1). In addition, it is noted that the quantity of filters used in each layer gradually rises as you progress from one layer to the following.

CNN-DDI algorithm as a new semi-supervised method employs a CNN structure to forecast drug–drug interactions. The process of extracting feature vectors involves identifying feature interactions from drug categories, targets, pathways, and enzymes. A new convolutional neural network model was introduced that predicted drug–drug interaction (DDI) events by utilizing feature representation. The predictor is composed of a SoftMax layer based on CNN, two fully connected layers, and five convolutional layers [87, 101, 115].

7.3.5   Development of Individualized Treatment Plans

Tissues, pictures, and genetic profiling have improved risk assessment, prognosis, and therapy. Computational technologies can assess and analyze patient changes that may affect treatment tactics. Computer-aided solutions provide high-quality diagnostic imaging. Several of these improvements appear to use moderate utility factors to improve multivariate prediction models. Large datasets fuel medical machine learning. Individualized treatment regimens can increase life expectancy since patients respond differently to therapy and drugs. Patient-specific care requires identifying the most important aspects to consider when choosing a treatment strategy. In this case, artificial intelligence—particularly machine learning—may be useful. Machine learning helps understand patient characteristics that affect medical therapy. Methodology can help predict a treatment intervention's success. Physicians may now perform more thorough patient observations using a large dataset of patient health information, genetic data, clinical history, and sensitivities. Technology has accelerated medical progress. AI is helping doctors spot trends, abnormalities, and other aberrations in patient data. Artificial intelligence can examine millions of clinical records to determine how a therapy method affects a gene [22, 92].

Artificial intelligence (AI) has been shown to be effective in reducing diagnostic errors, validating clinical judgment calls, and facilitating data extraction for clinicians and researchers in the context of clinical decision support systems [22]. Advancements in computational domains, including natural language processing (NLP), pattern recognition and identification, and unbiased forecasting, are expected to augment the capabilities of artificial intelligence (AI). The AI system is capable of ingesting and analyzing vast amounts of labeled or unlabeled data, subsequently discerning both the issue at hand and the corresponding resolution. A comprehensive comprehension of the interconnections between objects is crucial for accurate pattern recognition and identification [89].

In the context of developing a breast cancer prediction model, a multitude of mammograms can be utilized to facilitate the algorithm's learning process. The algorithmic approach is utilized to ascertain the potential malignancy or benignity of a biopsy outcome, and also to distinguish between regular and anomalous screening outcomes. Thus, this methodology can be employed to assess breast cancer with comparable accuracy as that of radiologists. The utilization of machine learning and deep learning techniques by the algorithm, which was trained on datasets of mammograms obtained from women diagnosed with breast cancer and the corresponding clinical health records [30, 59], has the potential to improve the precision of the results.

AI affects clinical trial treatment regimens. Clinical trials for novel cancer medicines usually start with "phase 0" and end with "phase IV." In [19], Atrius Health, an eastern Massachusetts healthcare provider, used its 20 years of data on 2.5 million patients to construct the application. AI assessed the data. Hypertension, type 2 diabetes, and hyperlipidemia—high cholesterol—were studied. We will next prepare a list of medicines and factors to consider when choosing the best prescription for a patient based on clinical treatment guidelines for each disease. The Atrius EHR patient information repository provides decision points for the next action. Patient visits were done for unmanaged medical conditions. During the following sessions, data on drug regimens, test results, comorbidities, and illness management status are collected. Next, disease-specific machine learning algorithms learn to distinguish valuable data pieces. Similar demographics and medical conditions constituted a precision cohort. Cohorts allow clinicians at the same institution to compare care results for individuals with comparable clinical features. The system can determine the best disease management strategies for the organization by comparing a patient to a cohort of patients with similar clinical characteristics and circumstances. Electronic data and clinical treatment suggestions showed that some treatment planning techniques are missed [45, 68, 99].

7.4   AI for Revolutionizing Drug Development

7.4.1   Personalized Medicine, Drug Repurposing, and Drug Safety Evaluation

The approach of drug repurposing, also known as drug repositioning, has been an effective strategy for finding solutions for rare diseases, especially when financial constraints may impede the creation of new drugs. Numerous diseases have been treated using individualized treatment. Herceptin, which is also called trastuzumab, is a drug used for treating breast cancer. The way it works is by focusing on the specific type of breast tumor that have an overexpression of HER-2 protein, which is present in around 30% of cases. The use of Gleevec (imatinib mesylate) has led to a remarkable increase in the 5-year survival rate of patients suffering from chronic myeloid leukemia, elevating it from a low 5% to an outstanding 95%. Zelboraf, also known as vemurafenib, is a drug that is prescribed for the treatment of melanoma. The advanced stages of this illness have a bleak outlook, with around 60% of individuals exhibiting the V600E mutation. A number of personalized therapy options have shown promise through treatment–biomarker combinations, including Erbitux-EFGR for colon cancer and Xalkori-ALK for lung cancer [36, 119].

Choosing an approved substance from a variety of options can be difficult, as it may involve significant research to limit the choices. Modern technological advancements are characterized by the prominent use of artificial intelligence (AI). The rapid availability of new potential candidates for medications is of great interest due to its ability to identify them, making them available for clinical trials. Once authorized, these drugs can be incorporated into medical systems. The use of artificial intelligence (AI) can speed up the process of finding new uses for existing medications to treat human diseases, including newly emerging ones such as COVID-19. The biomedical field now has access to a large amount of "big data" that includes biological, clinical, and open data like scientific articles and data repositories. This has resulted in a demand for new AI algorithms that can efficiently use these extensive data collections. Currently, there is a joint effort among pharmaceutical scientists, computer scientists, statisticians, and clinicians to utilize AI-based technologies to speed up the process of discovering and developing new treatments. The combination of big data and artificial intelligence (AI) can improve the effectiveness and efficiency of drug repurposing and medical decision-making based on real-world evidence for complex human diseases such as COVID-19 and Alzheimer's disease. The progress of AI tools is hindered by various obstacles, including the need to guarantee model security and interoperability, as well as address the diversity and below-par quality of data preserved by pharmaceutical firms. The precision of outcomes produced by upcoming AI models for drug repurposing is anticipated to be high. The models will have the ability to integrate different types and sources of information and will be interoperable across various deployment settings. Furthermore, these models will have the ability to be understood in relation to their internal mechanisms and will be able to withstand both interference and malicious attacks [100].

Recent advancements in computational methods have significantly improved the systematic process of medication repurposing. The process of *in silico* medication repurposing typically involves utilizing multiple sources of data, including electronic health records, genome-wide association studies, gene expression response profiles, route mappings, chemical structures, target binding assays, and other phenotypic profiling data. The aim is to repurpose existing medications for new therapeutic uses. Numerous extensive researches have been carried out on the subject of computational techniques. The research covers a wide variety of machine learning and artificial intelligence techniques, such as network propagation, matrix factorization and completion, and modern deep learning models [116].

7.4.1.1   Predictive Analytics and Precision Medicine

Precision medicine refers to a medical methodology that entails tailoring treatment plans for patients according to their unique circumstances, behaviors, and genetic makeup. The effectiveness of this specific procedure has been proven in accelerating the drug approval process and improving the success rates of clinical trials. The use of artificial intelligence (AI) to extract important information from vast medical data for diagnosis and treatment is a much-awaited advancement. The above statement is crucial in the field of precision medicine, which is a medical strategy that customizes treatment for each patient by utilizing extensive medical information, such as genomic data. The traditional approach to drug research and development is known for its substantial expenses, extended schedules, and notable uncertainties. Advancements in AI have the capability to aid in the development of technology-based solutions. Computer simulations are used to assess drug design, repositioning, and pharmacological combinations [10, 109]. The phase of drug design and clinical trials in the drug development pipeline has a significant rate of failure, as most drugs do not meet the required efficacy standards or have unforeseen side effects. Biomarkers possess the capability to provide novel understandings of the fundamental principles of biology and the progression of illnesses. The details provided can serve as a basis for developing novel drug therapies that are safer and more efficient. As an example, medications can be aimed at particular genetic variations, abnormal proteins, or related pathways that cause diseases [103].

A real-time digital doppelganger can talk to a physical thing. Industries use digital copies. Digital twins can transform healthcare and public health. Data analytics and modeling improve diagnostic, pharmacological effectiveness, and therapy in medical studies. Industrial and engineering firms employ digital twins increasingly. The unique method advances medicine, patient care, and public health. The FDA revealed in 2013 that many depression and cancer patients got substandard drugs, with 38%–75% reported cases. Randomized controlled trials reveal that comparable drugs affect people differently. Personalized medicine adapts treatments and prevention to each patient's genetics, lifestyle, and environment. Digital twins simulate individuals with distinct physiological and biomechanical properties to give personalized therapy. Organic methods are used. A completely functional digital clone of a person may not be possible due to the body's complexity and interconnectedness. Cell receptors and subcellular organelles may alter therapeutics. Digital human counterparts were created using molecular, genetic, and other data from healthy and sick persons [43, 56, 110].

Multiple sclerosis, a complex disease, produces most neurological disability in young individuals. Digital twins provide hope. The disease's intricacy and development make data analysis promising. Digital siblings can help develop genetic patient prototypes to test treatments. Genetics, environmental factors, sickness management costs, and medication side effects may help patients predict disease progression and treatment effectiveness. This technique considers all important patient health factors [79, 98]. Biopharmaceuticals are investigating digital twins for drug development. Subramanian models the liver using functions, diseases, and medications using ordinary differential equations. Healthy liver operations are correctly simulated. It simulates illness development and therapy. The hepatic twin model and experiments can explain drug-induced liver dysfunction [33].

AI technology is being studied as a cancer treatment core technology. Clinical radiography is using AI in medical equipment. Precision medicine requires accurate anticancer therapy efficacy predictions. To evaluate massive omics data, researchers used machine learning and deep learning [93]. In total, 23,427 tumors' CAA profiles were examined [18]. The goal was to discover tumor progression features like CAA order and CAAs that may indicate tissue-specific metastases. Deep neural network models and machine learning techniques were employed to find 31 CAAs that significantly affected the sensitivity of cell lines from 17 cancer types to 56 chemotherapeutic regimens in their study. Researchers found 1,024 potentially deadly medication interactions. CAAs outperform mutations and local deletions/amplifications in pharmaceutical response prediction, the study found. Cancer-associated fibroblasts (CAAs) can predict cancer prognosis, tumor development, metastasis, and therapy response, revolutionizing precision oncology. MK-0752 and gemcitabine were administered to pancreatic ductal cancer patients in [42]. The study was multicenter, nonrandomized Bayesian adaptive. The combination treatment was safe, and the phase II clinical trial dose was determined. Researchers proposed a Bayesian technique for phase I clinical trial dose in [85]. This method may identify the MTD using the posterior distribution of toxicity probability. After a cancer medication development phase I or phase II clinical trial, a proof-of-concept (PoC) study is common. A small group of patients is studied for clinical efficacy.

Predictive algorithms help cancer vaccine developers find hundreds to thousands of neoepitopes. Thus, a restricted collection of neoepitopes with the highest immunogenicity for the patient or target population's MHC alleles must be chosen. Diverse options should cover the tumor or pathogen's variety. The discrete optimization problem was initially solved using customized scoring techniques that considered important factors including neoepitope antigen coverage [106, 120].

Small molecule design benefits from AI. This technique's ability to obtain hidden representations that regulate these substances' operational features and use the geometric qualities of the embedding space has proved very beneficial. *In silico* identification and rejection of poor drug candidates allows efficient library creation for high-throughput drug testing. This may improve future clinical trials. Molecular dynamics is needed to improve created molecules because most generative models are taught end-to-end without considering physical plausibility. Like protein generative models, physics-informed networks may boost deep learning for *de novo* design. These networks restrict the latent space to physicochemical outcomes [103].

Bioinformatics and chemo-informatics employ AI extensively. They help find therapeutic chemicals. These domains study infectious agent behavior and pharmacokinetics, pharmacodynamics, and toxicity to construct multiscale models. Target-centric strategies are blamed for excessive turnover and low productivity in pharmaceutical R&D. As noted, global models are essential. Network system biology uses AI extensively. Understanding how genetic and epigenetic variables impact pharmaceutical reactions is critical [6, 74].

7.4.1.2　*Virtual Screening*

The pharmaceutical and biomedical sectors place great importance on the process of discovering new drugs. The typical method for drug discovery begins with identifying disease targets and then conducting high throughput screening (HTS) experiments to evaluate the bioactivity of the compound. This is a widely used approach. According to sources [111, 23], high-throughput screening (HTS) experiments are cost-effective and efficient as they utilize a wide range of protein resources, numerous synthesized compounds, and advanced laboratory bioactivity testing techniques. Virtual screening (VS) techniques are used to speed up the drug development process. The main purpose of virtual screening (VS) is to rank compounds according to their ability to bind to the target [12].

Researchers commonly use RMSD-based clustering as a technique to simplify data into more manageable and informative subsets before performing screening experiments. The ligand is expected to interact with several clusters of receptors that are both energetically stable and functional [16].

Professor Cheng's research expanded receptor-based pharmacophore modeling for virtual screening. This was achieved by integrating RMSD-based clustering information. Amaro *et al.* [4] described this investigation. Professor Cheng used RMSD-based clustering on snapshots from two 40-ns avian influenza N1 neuraminidase trajectories at 10-ps intervals. The apo and oseltamivir-complex forms were investigated [51]. This approach identified the best molecular dynamic simulation layouts. Simulation used N1 tetramer. Single-monomer protein chains were clustered [13], and 40-ns intervals simulated the tetramer. This quadrupled the monomer sampling to 160 ns. The simulation produced 16,000 structures for study. This computer-aided drug design (CADD) study has used longer molecular dynamics (MD) trajectories than others. Both apo and holo monomer MD simulations lasted 160 ns. A multi-copy molecular dynamics (MD) technique may be used with a four-monomer tetramer. This strategy enhances sampling efficiency over a single long trajectory [37]. Thus, receptor configuration space was thoroughly investigated. A researcher used root-mean-square deviation (RMSD) to cluster binding-site residues. The clusters have 10 apo and five holo structures. The study used AutoDock 4.0 to compare the core member structure of the top three clusters in the apo and holo sets with NCIDS1 [20]. After eight main screens, the weighted average of the docking scores throughout the whole representative set of the holo molecular dynamics trajectory determined the ligands' ranking. In total, 10 of 25 substances tested had Ki values below 500 M. Molecular dynamics structures alone revealed seven compounds. Simulation altered these structures' makeup. Simulations predicted that eight chemicals will partially bind to novel binding sites. Rearranging helped find findings that could have been missed [107]. According to the literature, artificial neural networks (ANNs) can classify virtual screens. Before quantitative structure–activity relationship (QSAR)-based artificial neural networks (ANN) were discovered to be better classifiers, random forest was utilized. Ligand-based virtual screening has largely employed ANNs. QSAR provides each compound's input data. This study employed active and inactive drug training data [8]. ANNs were used to find senescence-inducing compounds. Screening employed agonists and molecular description data. Screening a two-million-compound library yielded 247 compounds matching the model. The chemical was tested *in vitro* for development [52]. Target-based virtual screening (TBVS) and structure-based virtual screening (SBVS) are computational methods used to estimate the binding affinity and possible interactions between a variety of ligands and a molecular target. The ligands are arranged to maximize target affinity. Structure-based virtual screening (SBVS) requires a three-dimensional protein structure to comprehend chemical interactions [63].

Molecular docking is a preferred method for structure-based virtual screening (SBVS) due to its high accuracy, efficiency, and computational cost-effectiveness. The identification of compounds from the database is carried out through a process of categorization based on their respective affinities for receptor sites [90]. The present study employs score functions (SF) to rank molecules and compounds according to their receptor site affinity, thereby demonstrating a promising approach. The aforementioned procedures are employed to confirm the correlation between the receptor sites and the intended pharmaceutical agent. The integral role of the scoring function is evident in the docking procedure, as previously noted [29, 32]. The present study employs search algorithms to identify binding site conformations and ligand orientations. Upon successful implementation of the docking technique, the optimal conformations of the ligand are obtained and subsequently deposited in a realistic manner at the binding site. Various techniques are employed by search algorithms, including the verification of the chemistry and geometry of the pertinent molecules and atoms [81].

7.4.1.3 De Novo *Design*

De novo drug design uses computers to create new chemical structures from atomic building pieces. Drug development uses structure-based and ligand-based designs. These methods use a biological target's active site and known binders. Machine learning and other AI methods have enhanced medication discovery. Deep reinforcement learning combines neural network-based methods with reinforcement learning paradigms. Recurrent neural networks, convolutional neural networks, generative adversarial networks, and autoencoders have enabled *de novo* drug creation. Artificial intelligence (AI) uses machines to replicate human cognitive skills like learning and problem-solving. Algorithms and statistical models in machine learning (ML) allow machines to learn from data and make predictions or judgments without being programmed. Machine learning uses supervised, unsupervised, and reinforcement learning to help machines learn from data and improve. Machine learning aims to create intelligent machines that can execute difficult tasks and solve real-world challenges. Drug discovery results are predicted using ML. Deep learning develops and implements multilayer neural networks within machine learning (ML). Deep learning aims to make these networks computationally viable so they can handle and analyze big and complicated datasets more accurately and efficiently. Recurrent neural networks (RNNs), convolutional neural networks (CNNs), generative adversarial networks (GANs), and auto-encoders (AEs) have emerged due to data and computer capabilities [34, 66].

Reinforcement learning (RL) is a machine learning subfield that rewards good behavior and punishes bad. DRL has been used in medication development recently. DRL integrates reinforcement learning architectures with artificial neural networks. These methods have been successful in voice recognition, formal language understanding, visual representations, and musical creation, therefore they might alter drug discovery. Deep learning (DL) is a key subfield of artificial intelligence (AI) because it can mimic human performance in image recognition and natural language processing. Deep learning (DL) has been used in biology and healthcare to develop new analytical methods. Drug development uses deep learning (DL) to construct quantitative structure–activity relationship (QSAR) models that reliably predict molecular attributes like affinity and toxicity. Fully connected neural networks trained on chemical structure-derived molecular descriptors are being used in drug discovery deep learning. Deep reinforcement learning (DRL), which combines reinforcement learning and artificial neural networks, promises to find novel medications. *De novo* drug design DRL methods use a generator and a reinforcement learning-based agent. Most such methods use this strategy [105].

A deep neural network uses the model's many layers. Synthetic networks may use SMILES or molecular graphs in their input layers. SMILES encodes molecules using characters to describe atomic connection. To train the network, tokens representing pre-existing data like bioactive chemical inventory for a biological target are entered. Knowledge and decision cycles build output structures. The model selects the best vocabulary token at each level. The *de novo* drug design agent, a reinforcement framework virtual robot, manipulates molecules to improve their attributes. The generator, or artificial neural network, controls agent behavior. Examples of *de novo* design using AI include various deep reinforcement learning algorithms:

Recurrent neural networks (RNNs) have recurrent connections. Recurrent neural networks (RNNs) use inter-neuron connections to model the current state and retrieve input from prior stages of a sequence. Recurrent neural networks (RNNs) may analyze literary works or chemical structures in Simplified Molecular Input Line Entry System (SMILES) notation. Recurrent neural networks (RNNs) process actions linearly. Chemical principles generate *de novo* compounds. RNNs can identify Simplified Molecular Input Line Entry System (SMILES) string patterns.

De novo drug design using recurrent neural networks and reinforcement learning has yielded promising results. This approach uses a trained recurrent neural network (RNN) to find bioactive substances from a database like ChEMBL. In recurrent neural network (RNN) training, maximum likelihood estimates are used to predict the next token in a target sequence based on previously observed tokens. A recurrent neural network (RNN) can produce unique sequences that match its conditional probability distributions from target sequences like SMILES. Next, a policy that relates states' upcoming actions to their probability creates a *de novo* drug design agent. The agent's strategy now optimizes predicted reward by evaluating a series of acts in a state and the incentives obtained. Reinforcement learning has two policy-setting methods. Policy-based reinforcement learning generates and stores a decision policy representation in memory. Value-based reinforcement learning maintains a value function without policy. *De novo* drug development involves developing a SMILES string for a novel molecular entity in steps [11].

Improved episodic likelihood has trained algorithms to synthesize sulfur-free molecules. Other studies employ deep reinforcement learning and recurrent neural networks to identify novel medications. Deep reinforcement learning (DRL) for structural evolution (ReLeaSE) has been used to create chemical libraries with the right physicochemical and biological properties. Algorithmic patterns are deduced using an efficient stack-augmented recurrent neural network. SMILES strings are sentences in this implementation. The stack-RNN model uncovers the patterns that generate valid SMILES strings from letter sequences. SMILES strings integrate the generating and predicting aspects of the approach. A fragment-based deep reinforcement learning (DRL) strategy using RNN and RL was developed using an actor-centric model. Autonomous molecule creation with improved properties was the goal. This work seeks to create a model that optimizes freshly manufactured molecules by imitating the structural aspects of bioactive chemicals that interact with a specific target. Instead of thorough chemical space investigation, fragment-based optimization of a lead molecule is used to quickly find potential compounds.

RNNs created a multi-goal evolutionary *de novo* drug design technique. Transfer learning (TL) retrained the network with the most effective chemicals. As part of transfer learning, a model is first trained on a source task, then retrained on a corresponding target task. Transfer learning appears to improve task-specific model accuracy. Deep learning was used to train an LSTM recurrent neural network (RNN) to create new medicinal molecules. A model using LSTM-based RNN technology was trained to create large and accurate SMILES string libraries. Transfer learning (TL) was used to build compounds that resemble pharmaceuticals with bioactivities against a certain biological target to optimize the model. This method works in early pharmaceutical research when data is scarce. As is typical in fragment-based medication development, the generative model was used to improve a set of lead compounds derived from an active fragment [21].

The study integrated molecular descriptors into conditional recurrent neural network (RNN) construction. Without an encoder, this technique conditions the generation process using qualities from molecular structures or QSAR. Using a conditional seed, the RNN was trained to focus on the bioactive compounds of a biological target in the chemical domain. Novel negative log-likelihood diagrams were used to evaluate a probabilistic sequence generator's concentration. A convolutional neural network (CNN) trained on large chemical compound databases was used to build a new medication. This data-driven strategy generated novel molecules through *de novo* drug design. This study found that SMILES chemical sequences taught a recurrent neural network (RNN). The RNN learned grammatical rules to create legitimate SMILES and molecules with similar attributes to those used for training. We used a forward recurrent neural network (RNN) model and three bidirectional techniques—novelty, chemical biological relevance, and scaffold diversity—to evaluate compounds synthesized by a computer using the SMILES string synthesis method.

CNNs automatically extract important features from incoming data using many layers of transformation, convolution, and pooling processes. Convolutional neural networks (CNNs) have proven successful in image processing because they use a feature detector with a tight window over the input feature vector during both training and testing. This approach lets a convolutional neural network (CNN) learn input properties regardless of their feature vector location. Convolutional neural networks and two-dimensional chemical structure graphs make the DeepScaffold platform a powerful scaffold-based tool for *de novo* drug development. The current technique may create varied molecular structures using Bemis–Murcko scaffolds, cyclic skeletons, and scaffolds with particular side-chain property criteria. This technique allows generic chemical principles to incorporate new atoms and bonds into an existing scaffold. Molecular docking analyzed DeepScaffold output compounds' biological target affinity. This method appears promising for drug discovery and development. DeepGraphMolGen uses graph convolutional and recurrent neural networks to generate ideal molecules. This approach predicted properties and produced molecules using 2D graphs instead of SMILES strings. Graph theory-based medication development was invented. A simple decoding method and a resource-efficient graph convolutional design enhanced the graph generator for chemical synthesis [113].

Generative adversarial networks (GANs) train two neural networks. One network generates pictures, while the other detects fakes. These networks are trained simultaneously to increase GAN performance. The generator records the frequency distribution of real events to generate new data instances. A binary classifier, the discriminator distinguishes between manufactured and legitimate data. GANs have been used for text-to-image synthesis, super-resolution, and picture translation. A reinforced adversarial neural computer (RANC), a deep neural network (DNN) architecture based on GANs and reinforcement learning, generated new small-molecule organic molecules. Its explicit memory bank gives the RANC generator superior generating capabilities. This feature solves neural network adversarial problems. The study found that RANC can build structures with consistent distributions of major chemical descriptors and SMILES string lengths compared to the training dataset. The generative adversarial network (GAN)-based adversarial threshold neural computer (ATNC) uses reinforcement learning (RL) to develop drugs. An adversarial threshold filters the agent from the environment, which includes the discriminator and objective reward factions, and a differentiable neural computer generates. Molecule construction recently adopted internal diversity, clustering (IDC) as an objective reward function. This method increases molecular diversity. Recently created deep-learning system LatentGAN uses an autoencoder and GAN to generate new medicinal molecules. This technique worked well in both random and target-biased drug-like compound creation scenarios. This technique generates distinct molecules, unlike RNN-based models. The two strategies may be complimentary [75].

7.5   Challenges and Solutions

At present, the field of medicinal chemistry primarily employs empirical approaches and rigorous experimentation. The identification of compounds with the desired medicinal properties requires the testing of a significant number of substances using various methods. However, the employed techniques are commonly characterized by being laborious, expensive, and imprecise. Limitations in the quality of test compounds or the lack of accurate predictions regarding the *in vivo* functionality of medications may pose significant challenges. The implementation of AI-based algorithms, including supervised and unsupervised learning techniques, reinforcement, evolutionary, and rule-based algorithms, presents a promising avenue for addressing these issues. Oftentimes, the focus of these tactics revolves around the examination of extensive amounts of data that can be relevant in numerous settings. The utilization of these techniques is more favorable in making predictions, particularly in terms of the effectiveness and safety of potential novel therapeutic molecules, compared to conventional methods [58]. AI-based algorithms have the potential to identify new drug development targets, such as disease-related proteins or genetic pathways. The present study suggests that the utilization of this approach has the capacity to broaden the horizons of drug discovery beyond conventional techniques, thereby paving the way for the creation of novel and improved therapeutic agents. Historically, conventional methods employed in the field of pharmaceutical research have demonstrated a degree of efficacy, despite their dependence on trial-and-error experimentation and limited capacity to accurately forecast the actions of potentially novel bioactive compounds. The utilization of AI-based methodologies in drug discovery procedures holds promise for enhanced efficiency and accuracy, ultimately leading to the creation of more efficacious pharmaceuticals [15, 73].

The application of AI to the drug discovery process is subject to various limitations and challenges, despite its potential advantages. The lack of adequate information poses a significant challenge. AI-based techniques often necessitate vast amounts of data to be accurately trained. Insufficient data or low-quality data, or both, may compromise the quality and consistency of the results. The ethical implications of AI-based methods, particularly in regard to impartiality and prejudice, have been identified as a significant obstacle. Further elaboration on this topic will be provided below. If a machine learning system is trained on biased or unrepresentative data, it may result in inaccurate or unfair predictions. The utilization of artificial intelligence (AI) in the development of innovative pharmaceutical compounds raises significant ethical and legal inquiries. There exist several methodologies and approaches that can aid in overcoming the challenges faced by artificial intelligence in the domain of chemistry-based medicine. The utilization of data augmentation has been proposed as a potential resolution to this problem. This technique involves the augmentation of authentic data with synthetic data. The utilization of a larger and more diverse training dataset can enhance the quality and consistency of the outcomes produced by machine learning algorithms. Explainable artificial intelligence (XAI) techniques are being explored as a potential alternative to enhance the transparency and comprehensibility of machine learning (ML) predictions. The objective of XAI is to provide an explanation for the reasoning behind ML predictions. Understanding the underlying methods and assumptions of predictions is crucial in addressing concerns related to bias and fairness in AI-based techniques. The utilization of conventional experimental techniques remains pertinent, as contemporary AI-driven technologies are not capable of substituting the proficiency and discernment of human researchers. It is important to note that artificial intelligence (AI) is limited in its predictive capabilities, as it can only make predictions based on the data it has been trained on. Therefore, it is necessary for human experts to verify and interpret these predictions. In the field of drug development, there is potential for AI to enhance the process by integrating it with conventional experimental methods. The integration of artificial intelligence (AI) with human expertise has the potential to enhance the efficiency and speed of drug discovery and development. This approach leverages the predictive capabilities of AI in combination with the knowledge and experience of human researchers [9].

7.6   Conclusion and Future Scope

AI and ML have the potential to revolutionize the drug development process and accelerate the rate of medical progress. Several approaches and programs that demonstrate the potential of AI in this field were discussed in this book. Deep learning, natural language processing, feature selection, genetic algorithms, and clustering algorithms have aided the drug development process [31]. These strategies may aid in the development of effective medications by discovering novel compounds, predicting pharmacological properties, and enhancing treatment plans. Customized medicine, repurposing, and safety testing are a few examples of how artificial intelligence is transforming the pharmaceutical industry. Predictive analytics and precision medicine enable physicians to personalize treatment plans for each patient, thereby enhancing outcomes and reducing adverse effects. *De novo* design paves the way for the development of revolutionary new medications by enabling scientists to synthesize unique molecules with the required properties. With the assistance of random forests, support vector machines, Bayesian networks, artificial neural networks, and convolutional neural networks, it is possible to predict and analyze drug-related properties. These strategies facilitate the creation of treatment plans and the discovery of novel medications. There is a lot of room for expansion in the pharmaceutical industry's use of AI and ML. These problems include a lack of privacy and bias in the data, high-quality data, and readily interpretable complex models. The potential application of AI to drug development is intriguing. Data, technology, and partnerships between businesses and academic institutions will stimulate innovation. Exciting possibilities exist for AI to accelerate the discovery of new medications, improve the quality of outcomes, and lower healthcare costs. In conclusion, this chapter provides essential insights into how AI and machine learning have contributed to the revolution in drug development. By maximizing the potential of these technologies and overcoming existing obstacles, more effective and individualized remedies that will have a positive impact on patients around the globe can be developed.

Future Scope

The phenomenal advancement of AI and machine learning in the field of drug discovery presents a tremendous opportunity to revolutionize medical advancement. As scientists continue their research and application of these technologies, a number of promising directions and developments may emerge. Multiple data sets merged: In the near future, multiple data sources, including genomes, proteomics, metabolomics, and EHRs, will inevitably converge. By integrating and analyzing these multidimensional data to obtain a thorough understanding of disease causes, researchers will be able to design more targeted and effective medicines. Combined multi-omics strategies: Adopting the integration of multi-omics data would yield profound insights into disease pathways and patient characteristics. Multi-omics data comprises genomics, transcriptomics, epigenomics, and metabolomics. Algorithms based on artificial intelligence will be essential for elucidating complex relationships and devising patient-specific treatment plans [48].

Cutting-edge CNNs and RNNs are two examples of deep learning architectures that are ushering in a new era in the study of complex chemical structures and vast quantities of biological data. These complex structures will enable improved drug-target interaction prediction, identification of novel drug candidates, and optimization of drug design. In the future, understanding the reasoning behind AI models will be a top priority. We will attempt to develop AI algorithms that break down intricate deliberation into manageable segments. The regulatory approval process will be streamlined, and confidence in AI-driven drug development will increase. Automated and robotic procedures will play a significant role in the future of the pharmaceutical industry. Methods for high-throughput screening, robotic systems for chemical synthesis and analysis, and automated laboratory platforms will expedite experimentation and accelerate development [83].

The advancement of AI-driven drug discovery will rely heavily on the open sharing of data and the cooperation of academic institutions, private firms, and government organizations. Access to high-quality information, the creation of standardized methodologies, and the promotion of collaborative platforms are all ways to boost creativity and hasten the translation of results into actual therapeutic applications. Existing legal frameworks and moral restraints: As AI advances, it is crucial to provide equal focus to developing robust legal frameworks and ethical guidelines. Protecting patient privacy, ensuring data security, and supporting the right use of AI in drug research is crucial for gaining the public's trust and realizing the benefits of these groundbreaking findings [72, 80, 82].

References

1. (N.d.). Retrieved from https://www.uclahealth.org/clinical-trials
2. Akondi, V.S., Menon, V., Baudry, J., Whittle, J., Novel K-means clustering-based undersampling and feature selection for drug discovery applications, in: *2019 IEEE International Conference on Bioinformatics and Biomedicine (BIBM)*, IEEE, pp. 2771–2778, 2019, November.
3. Alsaffar, M., Yellowlees, P., Odor, A., Hogarth, M., The state of open source electronic health record projects: A software anthropology study. *JMIR Med. Inf.*, 5, 1, 5783, 2017.
4. Amaro, R.E., Minh, D.D., Cheng, L.S., Lindstrom, W.M., Olson, A.J., Lin, J.H., McCammon, J.A., Remarkable loop flexibility in avian influenza N1 and its implications for antiviral drug design. *J. Am. Chem. Soc.*, 129, 25, 7764–7765, 2007.
5. Azuaje, F., Artificial intelligence for precision oncology: Beyond patient stratification. *NPJ Precision Oncol.* 3, 1–5, 2019.
6. Berdigaliyev, N. and Aljofan, M., An overview of drug discovery and development. *Future Med. Chem.*, 12, 10, 939–947, 2020.
7. Bhatnagar, R., Sardar, S., Beheshti, M., Podichetty, J.T., How can natural language processing help model informed drug development?: A review. *JAMIA Open*, 5, 2, 43, 2022.
8. Bilsland, A.E., Liu, Y., Turnbull, A., Sumpton, D., Stevenson, K., Cairney, C.J., Keith, W.N., A novel pyrazolopyrimidine ligand of human PGK1 and stress sensor DJ1 modulates the shelterin complex and telomere length regulation. *Neoplasia*, 21, 9, 893–907, 2019.
9. Bittner, M., II and Farajnia, S., AI in drug discovery: Applications, opportunities, and challenges. *Patterns*, 3, 6, 1–2, 2022.
10. Boniolo, F., Dorigatti, E., Ohnmacht, A.J., Saur, D., Schubert, B., Menden, M.P., Artificial intelligence in early drug discovery enabling precision medicine. *Expert Opin. Drug Discov.*, 16, 9, 991–1007, 2021.
11. Burley, S.K., Berman, H.M., Bhikadiya, C., Bi, C., Chen, L., Di Costanzo, L., Zardecki, C., RCSB Protein Data Bank: Biological macromolecular structures enabling research and education in

fundamental biology, biomedicine, biotechnology and energy. *Nucleic Acids Res.*, 47, 1, 464–, 474, 2019.

12. Butkiewicz, M., Wang, Y., Bryant, S.H., Lowe Jr., E.W., Weaver, D.C., Meiler, J., High-throughput screening assay datasets from the pubchem database. *Chem. Inf.*, 3, 1, 1–12, 2017.

13. Caves, L.S., Evanseck, J.D., Karplus, M., Locally accessible conformations of proteins: Multiple molecular dynamics simulations of crambin. *Protein Sci.*, 7, 3, 649–666, 1998.

14. Chaithra, N., Jha, J., Sayal, A., Gupta, V., Gupta, A., A Paradigm Shift towards Computer Vision, in: *2023 International Conference on Device Intelligence, Computing and Communication Technologies (DICCT)*, IEEE, pp. 54–58, 2023, March.

15. Chen, R., Liu, X., Jin, S., Lin, J., Liu, J., Machine learning for drug-target interaction prediction. *Molecules*, 23, 9, 2208, 2018.

16. Cheng, L.S., Amaro, R.E., Xu, D., Li, W.W., Arzberger, P.W., McCammon, J.A., Ensemble-based virtual screening reveals potential novel antiviral compounds for avian influenza neuraminidase. *J. Med. Chem.*, 51, 13, 3878–3894, 2008.

17. Coley, C.W., Green, W.H., Jensen, K.F., Machine learning in computer-aided synthesis planning. *Accounts Chem. Res.*, 51, 5, 1281–1289, 2018.

18. Cook, N., Basu, B., Smith, D.M., Gopinathan, A., Evans, J., Steward, W.P., Jodrell, D., A phase I trial of the γ-secretase inhibitor MK-0752 in combination with gemcitabine in patients with pancreatic ductal adenocarcinoma. *Br. J. Cancer*, 118, 6, 793–801, 2018.

19. Cutter, G.R. and Liu, Y., Personalized medicine: The return of the house call? *Neurology: Clin. Pract.*, 2, 4, 343–351, 2012.

20. Dahl, G.E., Jaitly, N., Salakhutdinov, R., arXiv preprint, Multi-task neural networks for QSAR predictions, *Preprint*, 2014, arXiv:1406.1231.

21. Danziger, D.J. and Dean, P.M., Automated site-directed drug design: A general algorithm for knowledge acquisition about hydrogen-bonding regions at protein surfaces. *Proc. R. Soc. Lond. B. Biol. Sci.*, 236, 101–113, 1989.

22. Davenport, T.H., Hongsermeier, T., Mc Cord, K.A., Using AI to improve electronic health records. *Harvard Business Rev.*, 12, 1–6, 2018.

23. Deng, J., Lee, K.W., Sanchez, T., Cui, M., Neamati, N., Briggs, J.M., Dynamic receptor-based pharmacophore model development and its application in designing novel HIV-1 integrase inhibitors. *J. Med. Chem.*, 48, 5, 1496–1505, 2005.

24. Douguet, D., Thoreau, E., Grassy, G., A genetic algorithm for the automated generation of small organic molecules: drug design using an evolutionary algorithm. *J. Comput.-Aided Mol. Des.*, 14, 449–466, 2000.

25. Ekins, S., The next era: Deep learning in pharmaceutical research. *Pharm. Res.*, 33, 11, 2594–2603, 2016.

26. Ellingson, S.R., Miao, Y., Baudry, J., Smith, J.C., Multi-conformer ensemble docking to difficult protein targets. *J. Phys. Chem. B*, 119, 3, 1026–1034, 2015.

27. Evangelista Falcon, W., Ellingson, S.R., Smith, J.C., Baudry, J., Ensemble docking in drug discovery: How many protein configurations from molecular dynamics simulations are needed to reproduce known ligand binding? *J. Phys. Chem. B*, 123, 25, 5189–5195, 2019.

28. Fang, H.B., Chen, X., Pei, X.Y., Grant, S., Tan, M., Experimental design and statistical analysis for three-drug combination studies. *Stat. Methods Med. Res.*, 26, 3, 1261–1280, 2017.

29. Fischer, T., Gazzola, S., Riedl, R., Approaching target selectivity by *de novo* drug design. *Expert Opin. Drug Discov.*, 14, 8, 791–803, 2019.

30. Fleming, N., Computer-calculated compounds. *Nature*, 557, 7707, 55–7, 2018.

31. Gawehn, E., Hiss, J.A., Schneider, G., Deep learning in drug discovery. *Mol. Inf.*, 35, 1, 3–14, 2016.

32. Guedes, I.A., Pereira, F.S.S., Dardenne, L.E., Empirical scoring functions for structure-based virtual screening: Applications, critical aspects, and challenges. *Front. Pharmacol.*, 9, 1089, 2018.

33. Hamamoto, R., Suvarna, K., Yamada, M., Kobayashi, K., Shinkai, N., Miyake, M., Kaneko, S., Application of artificial intelligence technology in oncology: Towards the establishment of precision medicine. *Cancers*, 12, 12, 3532, 2020.

34. Kelly, J. E. and Hamm, S., Smart machines: IBM's Watson and the era of cognitive computing, Columbia University Press, 2013.

35. Hasan, S.A. and Farri, O., Clinical natural language processing with deep learning:. Methodologies and Applications, in: *Data Science for Healthcare*, pp. 147–171, 2019.

36. Hassan, M., Raza, H., Abbasi, M.A., Moustafa, A.A., Seo, S.Y., The exploration of novel Alzheimer's therapeutic agents from the pool of FDA approved medicines using drug repositioning, enzyme inhibition and kinetic mechanism approaches. *Biomed. Pharmacother.*, 109, 2513–2526, 2019.

37. Huey, R., Morris, G.M., Olson, A.J., Goodsell, D.S., A semiempirical free energy force field with charge-based desolvation. *J. Comput. Chem.*, 28, 6, 1145–1152, 2007.

38. Hughes, J.P., Rees, S., Kalindjian, S.B., Philpott, K.L., Principles of early drug discovery. *Br. J. Pharmacol.*, 162, 6, 1239–1249, 2011.

39. Ilmudeen, A. and Nayyar, A., Novel Designs of Smart Healthcare Systems: Technologies, Architecture, and Applications, in: *Machine Learning for Critical Internet of Medical Things: Applications and Use Cases*, pp. 125–151, Cham: Springer International Publishing, Germany, Switzerland, 2022.

40. Inje, B., Kumar, S., Nayyar, A., Swarm intelligence and evolutionary algorithms in disease diagnosis—introductory Aspects, in: *Swarm Intelligence and Evolutionary Algorithms in Healthcare and Drug Development*, vol. pp, pp. 1–18, Chapman and Hall/CRC, Florida, United States, 2019.

41. Jagannatha, A., Liu, F., Liu, W., Yu, H., Overview of the first natural language processing challenge for extracting medication, indication, and adverse drug events from electronic health record notes (MADE 1.0). *Drug Saf.*, 42, 99–111, 2019.

42. Jin, J., Liu, Q., Zheng, W., Shun, Z., Lin, T.T., Gao, L., Dong, Y., A Bayesian method for the detection of proof of concept in early phase oncology studies with a basket design. *Stat Biosci.*, 12, 167–179, 2020.

43. Kamel Boulos, M.N. and Zhang, P., Digital twins: from personalised medicine to precision public health. *J. Pers. Med.*, 11, 8, 745, 2021.

44. Khader, N., Lashier, A., Yoon, S.W., Pharmacy robotic dispensing and planogram analysis using association rule mining with prescription data. *Expert Syst. Appl.*, 57, 296–310, 2016.

45. Kola, I. and Landis, J., Can the pharmaceutical industry reduce attrition rates? *Nat. Rev. Drug Discovery*, 3, 8, 711–716, 2004.

46. Kong, H.J., Managing unstructured big data in healthcare system. *Healthcare Inf. Res.*, 25, 1, 1–2, 2019.

47. Korkmaz, S., Zararsiz, G., Goksuluk, D., MLViS: A web tool for machine learning-based virtual screening in early-phase of drug discovery and development. *PloS One*, 10, 4, 0124600, 2015.

48. Kumar, A., Krishnamurthi, R., Nayyar, A., Sharma, K., Grover, V., Hossain, E., A novel smart healthcare design, simulation, and implementation using healthcare 4.0 processes. *IEEE Access*, 8, 118433–118471, 2020.

49. Kusuhara, H., How far should we go? Perspective of drug-drug interaction studies in drug development. *Drug Metab. Pharmacokinetics*, 29, 3, 227–228, 2014.

50. Labjar, H., Al-Sarem, M., Kissi, M., Feature selection using a genetic algorithms and fuzzy logic in anti-human immunodeficiency virus prediction for drug discovery. *J. Inf. Technol. Manage.*,

14, 23–36, 2022. (Special Issue: 5th International Conference of Reliable Information and Communication Technology (IRICT 2020)).

51. Landon, M.R., Amaro, R.E., Baron, R., Ngan, C.H., Ozonoff, D., Andrew McCammon, J., Vajda, S., Novel druggable hot spots in avian influenza neuraminidase H5N1 revealed by computational solvent mapping of a reduced and representative receptor ensemble. *Chem. Biol. Drug Des.*, 71, 2, 106–116, 2008.

52. Liu, S., Alnammi, M., Ericksen, S.S., Voter, A.F., Ananiev, G.E., Keck, J.L., Gitter, A., Practical model selection for prospective virtual screening. *J. Chem. Inf. Model.*, 59, 1, 282–293, 2018.

53. Liu, S., Tang, B., Chen, Q., Wang, X., Drug-Drug Interaction Extraction via Convolutional Neural Networks. *Comput. Math Methods Med.*, 14, 6918381, 2016, Epub 2016/01/31. https://doi. org/10.1155/2016/6918381 PMID: 26941831.

54. Liu, X.Y., Liang, Y., Wang, S., Yang, Z.Y., Ye, H.S., A hybrid genetic algorithm with wrapper-embedded approaches for feature selection. *IEEE Access*, 6, 22863–22874, 2018.

55. Liu, Z., Roberts, R.A., Lal-Nag, M., Chen, X., Huang, R., Tong, W., AI-based language models powering drug discovery and development. *Drug Discov. Today*, 26, 11, 2593–2607, 2021.

56. Lloyd-Price, J., Abu-Ali, G., Huttenhower, C., The healthy human microbiome. *Genome Med.*, 8, 51, 2016.

57. Lusci, A., Pollastri, G., Baldi, P., Deep architectures and deep learning in chemoinformatics: the prediction of aqueous solubility for drug-like molecules. *J. Chem. Inf. Model.*, 53, 7, 1563–1575, 2013.

58. Mahapatra, B., Krishnamurthi, R., Nayyar, A., Healthcare models and algorithms for privacy and security in healthcare records, in: *Security and Privacy of Electronic Healthcare Records: Concepts, Paradigms and Solutions*, p. 183, 2019.

59. Mahmud, M., Kaiser, M.S., Hussain, A., Vassanelli, S., Applications of deep learning and reinforcement learning to biological data. *IEEE Trans. Neural Netw. Learn. Syst.*, 29, 6, 2063–2079, 2018.

60. Malhat, M.G., Mousa, H.M., El-Sisi, A.B., Clustering of chemical data sets for drug discovery, in: *2014 9th International Conference on Informatics and Systems (pp. DEKM-11)*, IEEE, 2014, December.

61. Mandlik, V., Bejugam, P.R., Singh, S., Application of artificial neural networks in modern drug discovery, in: *Artificial Neural Network Drug Design, Delivery Disposition*, pp. 123–139, Academic Press, 11, 3, 2016.

62. Meenakshi, D.U., Nandakumar, S., Francis, A.P., Sweety, P., Fuloria, S., Fuloria, N.K., Khan, S.A., Deep Learning and Site-Specific Drug Delivery: The Future and Intelligent Decision Support for Pharmaceutical Manufacturing Science, in: *Deep Learning for Targeted Treatments: Transformation in Healthcare*, pp. 1–38, 2022.

63. Meng, X.Y., Zhang, H.-X., Mezei, M., Cui, M., Molecular docking: a powerful approach for structure-based drug discovery. *Curr. Comp. Aided Drug Design*, 7, 2, 146–157, 2011.

64. Merk, D., Friedrich, L., Grisoni, F., Schneider, G., De novo design of bioactive small molecules by artificial intelligence. *Mol. Inf.*, 37, 1-2, 1700153, 2018.

65. Moingeon, P., Kuenemann, M., Guedj, M., Artificial intelligence-enhanced drug design and development: Toward a computational precision medicine. *Drug Discov. Today*, 27, 1, 215–222, 2022.

66. Mouchlis, V.D., Melagraki, G., Zacharia, L.C., Afantitis, A., Computer-aided drug design of β-secretase, γ-secretase and anti-tau inhibitors for the discovery of novel Alzheimer's therapeutics. *Int. J. Mol. Sci.*, 21, 3, 703, 2020.

67. Nayyar, A., Gadhavi, L., Zaman, N., Machine learning in healthcare: review, opportunities and challenges, in: *Machine Learning and the Internet of Medical Things in Healthcare*, vol. 1, pp. 23–45, 2021.

68. Ng, K., Kartoun, U., Stavropoulos, H., Zambrano, J.A., Tang, P.C., Personalized treatment options for chronic diseases using precision cohort analytics. *Sci. Rep.*, 11, 1, 1139, 2021.

69. Patel, V. and Shah, M., Artificial intelligence and machine learning in drug discovery and development. *Intell. Med.*, 2, 3, 134–140, 2022.

70. Paul, D., Sanap, G., Shenoy, S., Kalyane, D., Kalia, K., Tekade, R.K., Artificial intelligence in drug discovery and development. *Drug Discov. Today*, 26, 1, 80, 2021.

71. Percha, B. and Altman, R.B., Informatics confronts drug–drug interactions. *Trends Pharmacol. Sci.*, 34, 3, 178–184, 2013.

72. Pramanik, P.K.D., Nayyar, A., Pareek, G., WBAN: Driving e-healthcare beyond telemedicine to remote health monitoring: Architecture and protocols, in: *Telemedicine Technologies*, pp. 89–119, Academic Press, Cambridge, United States, 2019.

73. Pramanik, P.K.D., Pareek, G., Nayyar, A., Security and privacy in remote healthcare: Issues, solutions, and standards, in: *Telemedicine Technologies*, pp. 201–225, Academic Press, Cambridge, United States, 2019.

74. Pramanik, P.K.D., Solanki, A., Debnath, A., Nayyar, A., El-Sappagh, S., Kwak, K.S., Advancing modern healthcare with nanotechnology, nanobiosensors, and internet of nano things: Taxonomies, applications, architecture, and challenges. *IEEE Access*, 8, 65230–65266, 2020.

75. Pu, L., Naderi, M., Liu, T., Wu, H.C., Mukhopadhyay, S., Brylinski, M., eToxPred: a machine learning-based approach to estimate the toxicity of drug candidates. *BMC Pharmacol. Toxicol.*, 20, 1, 1–15, 2019.

76. Puri, M., Pathak, Y., Sutariya, V.K., Tipparaju, S., Moreno, W., *Artificial neural network for drug design, delivery and disposition*, Academic Press, Cambridge, United States, 2015.

77. Sadrieh, N., Brower, J., Yu, L., Doub, W., Straughn, A., Machado, S., Buhse, L., Stability, dose uniformity, and palatability of three counterterrorism drugs—human subject and electronic tongue studies. *Pharm. Res.*, 22, 1747–1756, 2005.

78. Santoshi, S. and Sengupta, D., Artificial intelligence in precision medicine: A perspective in biomarker and drug discovery, in: *Artificial Intelligence and Machine Learning in Healthcare*, pp. 71–88, 2021.

79. Sayal, A., Data Analytics: An Overview, in: *New Approaches to Data Analytics and Internet of Things Through Digital Twin*, pp. 1–27, 2023.

80. Sayal, A. and Pant, M., Examining the Moderating Effect of Green Product Knowledge on Green Product Advertising and Green Product Purchase Intention: A Study Using SmartPLS SEM Approach. *Int. J. Asian Business Inf. Manage. (IJABIM)*, 13, 1, 1–16, 2022.

81. Sayal, A., Singh, A.P., Aggarwal, D., Crisp and fuzzy EOQ model for perishable items with ramp type demand under shortages. *Int. J. Agricult. Stat. Sci.*, 14, 1, 441–452, 2018.

82. Sayal, A., Singh, A.P., Aggarwal, D., Optimisation of EOQ model with Weibull deterioration under crisp and fuzzy environment. *Int. J. Math. Model. Numer. Optim.*, 9, 4, 400–428, 2019.

83. Sayal, A., Singh, A.P., Chauhan, A., Crisp and fuzzy economic order quantity model with time dependent demand and permissible delay in payments. *Mater. Today: Proc.*, 46, 10933–10941, 2021.

84. Schneider, G., Lee, M.L., Stahl, M., Schneider, P., De novo design of molecular architectures by evolutionary assembly of drug-derived building blocks. *J. Comput. Aided Mol. Des.*, 14, 487–494, 2000.

85. Schumacher, T.N. and Schreiber, R.D., Neoantigens in cancer immunotherapy. *Science*, 348, 6230, 69–74, 2015.

86. Schwaller, P., Gaudin, T., Lanyi, D., Bekas, C., Laino, T., "Found in Translation": Predicting outcomes of complex organic chemistry reactions using neural sequence-to-sequence models. *Chem. Sci.*, 9, 28, 6091–6098, 2018.

87. Segura-Bedmar, I., Crespo, M., de Pablo-Sánchez, C., Martínez, P., Resolving anaphoras for the extraction of drug-drug interactions in pharmacological documents. *BMC Bioinf.*, 11, 2, 1–9, 2010.

88. Senior, A.W., Evans, R., Jumper, J., Kirkpatrick, J., Sifre, L., Green, T., Hassabis, D., Improved protein structure prediction using potentials from deep learning. *Nature*, 577, 7792, 706–710, 2020.

89. Sharma, K., Singh, H., Sharma, D.K., Kumar, A., Nayyar, A., Krishnamurthi, R., Dynamic models and control techniques for drone delivery of medications and other healthcare items in COVID-19 hotspots, in: *Emerging Technologies for Battling Covid-19: Applications and Innovations*, pp. 1–34, 2021.

90. Sharma, S. and Bhatia, V., Treatment of Type 2 diabetes mellitus (T2DM): Can GLP-1 Receptor Agonists fill in the gaps? *Array. Chem. Biol. Lett.*, 7, 4, 215–224, 2020.

91. Sheridan, R.P. and Kearsley, S.K., Using a genetic algorithm to suggest combinatorial libraries. *J. Chem. Inf. Comput. Sci.*, 35, 2, 310–320, 1995.

92. Shim, J., Hong, Z.Y., Sohn, I., Hwang, C., Prediction of drug–target binding affinity using similarity-based convolutional neural network. *Sci. Rep.*, 11, 1, 4416, 2021.

93. Shukla, A., Nguyen, T.H., Moka, S.B., Ellis, J.J., Grady, J.P., Oey, H., Duijf, P.H., Chromosome arm aneuploidies shape tumour evolution and drug response. *Nat. Commun.*, 11, 1, 449, 2020.

94. Siegismund, D., Tolkachev, V., Heyse, S., Sick, B., Duerr, O., Steigele, S., Developing deep learning applications for life science and pharma industry. *Drug Res.*, 68, 06, 305–310, 2018.

95. Soeny, K., Pandey, G., Gupta, U., Trivedi, A., Gupta, M., Agarwal, G., Attended robotic process automation of prescriptions' digitization. *Smart Health*, 20, 100189, 2021.

96. Srivastava, A.K., Singh, D., Pandey, A.S., Maini, T., A novel feature selection and short-term price forecasting based on a decision tree (J48) model. *Energies*, 12, 19, 3665, 2019.

97. Stephenson, N., Shane, E., Chase, J., Rowland, J., Ries, D., Justice, N., Cao, R., Survey of machine learning techniques in drug discovery. *Curr. Drug Metab.*, 20, 3, 185–193, 2019.

98. Subramanian, K., Digital twin for drug discovery and development—The virtual liver. *J. Indian Institute Sci.*, 100, 4, 653–662, 2020.

99. Tang, P.C., Miller, S., Stavropoulos, H., Kartoun, U., Zambrano, J., Ng, K., Precision population analytics: population management at the point-of-care. *J. Am. Med. Inf. Assoc.*, 28, 3, 588–595, 2021.

100. Tanoli, Z., Vähä-Koskela, M., Aittokallio, T., Artificial intelligence, machine learning, and drug repurposing in cancer. *Expert Opin. Drug Discov.*, 16, 9, 977–989, 2021.

101. Tari, L., Anwar, S., Liang, S., Cai, J., Baral, C., Discovering drug–drug interactions: a text-mining and reasoning approach based on properties of drug metabolism. *Bioinformatics*, 26, 18, 547–, 553, 2010.

102. Team, T.T.D., Al-Rfou, R., Alain, G., Almahairi, A., Angermueller, C., Bahdanau, D., Zhang, Y., arXiv preprint, Theano: A Python framework for fast computation of mathematical expressions, 2016. arXiv:1605.02688.

103. Telenti, A., Pierce, L.C., Biggs, W.H., Di Iulio, J., Wong, E.H., Fabani, M.M., Venter, J.C., Deep sequencing of 10,000 human genomes. *Proc. Natl. Acad. Sci.*, 113, 42, 11901–11906, 2016.

104. Terfloth, L. and Gasteiger, J., Neural networks and genetic algorithms in drug design. *DDT*, 6, 102–, 108, 2001.

105. Torjesen, I., Drug development: the journey of a medicine from lab to shelf. *Pharm. J.*, 12, 1–7, 2015.

106. Toussaint, N.C., Maman, Y., Kohlbacher, O., Louzoun, Y., Universal peptide vaccines–optimal peptide vaccine design based on viral sequence conservation. *Vaccine*, 29, 47, 8745–8753, 2011.

107. Tropsha, A., Best practices for QSAR model development, validation, and exploitation. *Mol. Inform.*, 29, 6–7, 476–488, 2010.

108. Venaik, A., Kumari, R., Venaik, U., Nayyar, A., The Role of Machine Learning and Artificial Intelligence in Clinical Decisions and the Herbal Formulations Against COVID-19. *Int. J. Reliable Qual. E-Healthcare (IJRQEH)*, 11, 1, 1–17, 2022.

109. Vignaux, P.A., Minerali, E., Lane, T.R., Foil, D.H., Madrid, P.B., Puhl, A.C., Ekins, S., The antiviral drug Tilorone is a potent and selective inhibitor of Acetylcholinesterase. *Chem. Res. Toxicol.*, 34, 5, 1296–1307, 2021.

110. Voigt, I., Inojosa, H., Dillenseger, A., Haase, R., Akgün, K., Ziemssen, T., Digital twins for multiple sclerosis. *Front. Immunol.*, 12, 669811, 2021.

111. Walters, W.P., Stahl, M.T., Murcko, M.A., Virtual screening—an overview. *Drug Discov. Today*, 3, 4, 160–178, 1998.

112. Wang, Y., Zhu, H., Madabushi, R., Liu, Q., Huang, S.M., Zineh, I., Model-informed drug development: current US regulatory practice and future considerations. *Clin. Pharmacol. Ther.*, 105, 4, 899–911, 2019.

113. Waszkowycz, B., Clark, D.E., Frenkel, D., Li, J., Murray, C.W., Robson, B., Westhead, D.R., PRO_LIGAND: an approach to de novo molecular design. 2. Design of novel molecules from molecular field analysis (MFA) models and pharmacophores. *J. Med. Chem.*, 37, 23, 3994–4002, 1994.

114. Weber, L., Evolutionary combinatorial chemistry: application of genetic algorithms. *Drug Discov. Today*, 3, 8, 379–385, 1998.

115. Yan, S., Jiang, X., Chen, Y., Text mining driven drug-drug interaction detection, in: *2013 IEEE International Conference on Bioinformatics and Biomedicine*, IEEE, pp. 349–354, 2013, December.

116. Zeng, X., Zhu, S., Liu, X., Zhou, Y., Nussinov, R., Cheng, F., deepDR: a network-based deep learning approach to *in silico* drug repositioning. *Bioinformatics*, 35, 24, 5191–5198, 2019.

117. zer0n. (n.d.). Retrieved from https://github.com/zer0n/deepframeworks

118. Zhavoronkov, A., Ivanenkov, Y.A., Aliper, A., Veselov, M.S., Aladinskiy, V.A., Aladinskaya, A.V., Aspuru-Guzik, A., Deep learning enables rapid identification of potent DDR1 kinase inhibitors. *Nat. Biotechnol.*, 37, 9, 1038–1040, 2019.

119. Zhou, Y., Wang, F., Tang, J., Nussinov, R., Cheng, F., Artificial intelligence in COVID-19 drug repurposing. *Lancet Digital Health*, 2, 12, 667–, 676, 2020.

120. Álvarez-Machancoses, Ó., DeAndres Galiana, E.J., Cernea, A., Fernandez-de la Vina, J., Fernández-Martínez, J.L., On the role of artificial intelligence in genomics to enhance precision medicine. *Pharmacogenomics Pers. Med.*, 13, 105–119, 2020.

121. Öztürk, H., Özgür, A., Schwaller, P., Laino, T., Ozkirimli, E., Exploring chemical space using natural language processing methodologies for drug discovery. *Drug Discov. Today*, 25, 4, 689–705, 2020.

Data Processing Method for AI-Driven Predictive Models for CNS Drug Discovery

Ajantha Devi Vairamani[1]*, Sudipta Adhikary[2] and Kaushik Banerjee[2]

[1]AP3 Solutions, Chennai, Tamil Nadu, India
[2]School of Law, Brainware University, Barasat, West Bengal, India

Abstract

In the challenging field of central nervous system (CNS) drug discovery, machine learning (ML) and artificial intelligence (AI) have recently come into their own as potent tools. This industry is infamous for its lengthy lead times and high failure rates. However, the combination of AI/ML and contemporary experimental technology has unlocked the potential to fundamentally alter how CNS illness treatments are created. Biomedical data's rapid expansion has made it possible for AI/ML-driven solutions to flourish. This chapter explores the revolutionary effects of AI/ML on the creation of CNS medications, demonstrates how AI/ML might quicken the creation of effective treatments for neurological diseases, particularly when it comes to predicting blood–brain barrier permeability, a key factor in medication development and shed insights on the current state of AI/ML-driven CNS drug discovery and its potential to address current methodological issues. The development of CNS drugs can be made much more successful and efficient by utilizing AI/ML, giving patients suffering from crippling neurological illnesses hope. The chapter concludes by highlighting the impressive advancements made in the discovery of CNS medicine powered by AI and ML and looks ahead to a bright future. Utilizing AI/ML capabilities, pharmaceutical companies and researchers are collaborating to make ground-breaking improvements that will give patients fresh hope.

Keywords: Artificial intelligence, machine learning, CNS disorder, drug design, drug discovery

8.1 Introduction

Multiple diseases with substantial economic and societal impacts can be traced back to central nervous system (CNS) disorders. The development of novel medications for CNS illnesses presents distinct obstacles despite significant advancement in our understanding of the structure and functioning of the CNS. These challenges add up to an average of 15–19 years for a CNS therapy to get from initial discovery to final regulatory approval [1]. There is a lot of information created throughout the process of creating a new medicine. The quantity of information about chemical reactions [2] and functional genomics has

---

*Corresponding author: ap3solutionsresearch@gmail.com

Abhirup Khanna, May El Barachi, Sapna Jain, Manoj Kumar and Anand Nayyar (eds.) *Artificial Intelligence and Machine Learning in Drug Design and Development*, (223–250) © 2024 Scrivener Publishing LLC

increased dramatically thanks to the developments in "omics" technology, high throughput screening (HTS), and chemical synthesis during the past few decades [3, 4]. Therefore, it has become a critical issue for CNS drug discovery to figure out how to effectively aggregate, correlate, and analyze the current large-scale data.

ML, a type of artificial intelligence (AI), has the potential to hasten pharmaceutical research by gleaning previously unknown insights from the mountain of complex data produced by the search for a cure. Recent years have seen widespread implementation of AI/ML-based methodologies across a variety of therapeutic domains, with state-of-the-art performance attained in tackling a wide range of drug development challenges. The most difficult area of drug discovery, central nervous system treatments, has also showed promise from such AI/ML algorithm applications. The potential of these technologies to uncover new therapies and repurpose established ones for CNS illnesses has only just begun to be explored. The chapter therefore examines the ways in which AI and ML have been applied to this exciting new field of drug research, enlightens how these technologies have been used to address challenges unique to the study of CNS illnesses. The process of creating drugs to treat conditions of the central nervous system (CNS) is difficult and complex, with lengthy timeframes and high attrition rates. Traditional drug discovery techniques have found it challenging to keep up with the volume and complexity of biomedical data that are being produced by contemporary experimental technology. The fusion of machine learning (ML) and artificial intelligence (AI) has emerged as a transformational force in pharmaceutical research as a reaction to these difficulties. With an emphasis on their uses, potential, and future possibilities, we intend to give an in-depth analysis of the function of AI/ML-driven approaches in CNS medicine discovery in this article.

8.1.1   Background Information

Biomedical research has experienced an exponential rise in the production of data from a variety of sources over the past few decades, including genomes, proteomics, metabolomics, and imaging investigations. Due to the difficulty of processing and gaining useful insights from such huge datasets using conventional approaches, the quantity of data for drug discovery brings both potential and challenges.

Application of AI/ML in drug development: AI/ML technologies have shown their ability to effectively analyze and understand massive amounts of biomedical data. They are capable of finding intricate patterns, making precise forecasts, and facilitating decision-making procedures that support the creation of new drugs.

Problem definition: Predicting the permeability of substances across the blood–brain barrier (BBB), a significant element impacting the success or failure of proposed CNS treatments, is the main difficulty in the development of CNS drugs. Traditional techniques for predicting BBB permeability take a lot of time and resources, which adds to the long development times for CNS drugs.

Objectives of the Chapter

The objectives of the chapter are as follows:

1. To present the underlying ideas behind AI algorithms and how they might be used to generate new drugs;

2. To discuss AI/ML in drug development at various stages: from target identification and characterization through virtual screening and lead development, a complete delve into the real-world uses of AI/ML in CNS drug research, and to highlight advanced applications of AI/ML in drug repurposing, drug synergy prediction, *de novo* drug design, and drug sensitivity prediction;

3. To analyze the advantages and drawbacks of AI/ML-aided drug discovery and to discuss potential difficulties and restrictions that should be taken into account when applying AI/ML to pharmaceutical research;

4. And, to highlight prospects for AI/ML in CNS drug discovery in the future regarding how multi-omics data can be integrated, how AI models can be improved, and how researchers and the pharmaceutical industry may work together to find faster ways to treat CNS conditions.

Organization of the Chapter

The rest of the chapter is organized as follows: Section 8.2 enlightens the role of artificial intelligence and machine learning in drug discovery. Section 8.3 highlights the role of AI/ML in CNS drug discovery. Section 8.4 illustrates the effect of AI/ML in CNS drug research. Section 8.5 focusses on prospects for AI/ML in CNS drug research in the future. Section 8.6 dives into the proposed methodology for data processing for CNS drug-likeness prediction. Finally, section 8.7 concludes the chapter with future scope.

8.2   The Role of AI And ML in Drug Discovery

Target identification, lead generation and optimization, and preclinical development are the three early drug discovery stages that have benefited from AI/ML application (Figure 8.1). To better understand the molecular mechanisms at play in diseases and therapeutic actions, researchers have turned to AI-based approaches in the field of target discovery. Predictive models of physicochemical features are generated using AI/ML methods in preclinical research to enhance absorption, distribution, metabolism, excretion, and toxicity (ADME-T) profiles.

The three phases of early drug discovery can all benefit from the application of AI/ML techniques, which offer a variety of tools to enhance decision making and speed up the process.

Figure 8.1 The use of AI and ML in the pharmaceutical R & D process.

8.2.1 Exposition of Machine Learning and Artificial Intelligence Algorithms

The models used in AI's construction of intelligent systems fall into one of several categories definable in terms of their respective learning methodologies. ML algorithms are often referred to as "AI," even though they are not the same thing. Therefore, it is best to define both terms at the outset. The FDA's definition of AI has been used throughout this evaluation. Brief explanations about the basic learning algorithms in the context of drug development is highlighted in Figure 8.2. Learning methods in the field of AI can be broken down into several major categories, including supervised, unsupervised, semi-supervised,

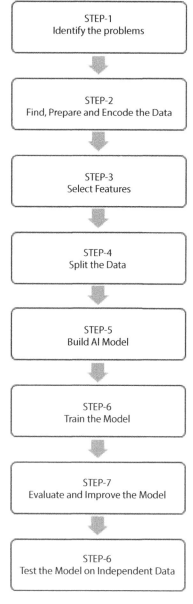

Figure 8.2 The stages involved in developing an AI model.

active, reinforcement, transfer, and multitask. These learning architectures employ several algorithms to carry out tasks like classification and grouping. Training an AI model is necessary, but not sufficient, for AI success. An effective AI workflow (i) defines a problem, (ii) cleans and organizes data, (iii) extracts characteristics from the data, (iv) chooses training and testing data sets, (v) creates a model, (vi) trains the model and evaluates its efficacy (*via* cross-validation), and (vii) applying the model for testing data sets to improve its performance. The fundamentals of creating an AI architecture is depicted in Figure 8.2.

The first phase is to precisely characterize the issue at hand (target, expected outcomes, etc.); the second is to collect, investigate, profile, format, and enhance the quality of the data; and the third is to transform the raw data into features and choose important features.

8.2.2   Molecular Fingerprints and Identifiers for Pre-Processing Data

Drug candidates with the desired beginning features are sought out, and from there, chemical structures with the desired effectiveness against the target molecule are produced. Such physical features can be quantified for chemical units and their biological target molecules using molecular descriptors and fingerprints. In contrast to simpler descriptors like molecular formulae or molecular structures, molecular fingerprints are more complicated descriptors that are represented as binary bit strings and can be used to identify a specific molecule [5, 6].

Chemical descriptors and molecular fingerprints: The use of chemical descriptors and molecular fingerprints is one of the fundamental foundations of AI/ML-driven drug development. Numerous ML-based applications [7, 8], including target molecule ranking, compound search based on structural similarity, virtual screening, QSAR analysis, and lead molecule ADME-T prediction, heavily rely on these quantitative representations of molecular structures.

Compound search and virtual screening: When it comes to the discovery of new drugs, the capacity to search for and evaluate compounds based on structural similarities is crucial [9–14]. The rapid scanning of large chemical databases by AI/ML algorithms makes it possible to identify prospective drug candidates with specified structural properties [15–18].

QSAR evaluation and ADME-T forecast: In order to establish relationships between the structural characteristics of substances and their biological activities, a quantitative structure–activity relationship (QSAR) study makes use of ML models. Additionally, AI/ML can forecast candidate compounds' ADME-T (absorption, distribution, metabolism, excretion, and toxicity) features, which help with early-stage drug optimization [19–22].

Several well-known programs make it easier to calculate chemical descriptors and molecular fingerprints in the context of drug discovery. Each of these programs has distinct abilities that affect how they are used in the drug development process. We highlight and discuss the most popular programs and their individual contributions to AI/ML-driven drug development throughout this chapter. Additionally, the analytical review of Chuang *et al.* [23] of AI-based techniques and their potential to enhance the predictive modeling of chemical bioactivities was well done. AI-based techniques provide intriguing prospects to improve the precision and effectiveness of drug development efforts by overcoming the limits of conventional molecular descriptors and fingerprints.

8.2.3   Use of Machine Learning and AI for Target Recognition

Modulating the activity of a target is a common strategy in drug discovery, with the goal of reversing a disease's progression [24]. The first step in drug development is typically the discovery of a novel target whose modulation promises therapeutic benefit and an acceptable risk profile. Once a goal has been recognized, it must be validated in *in vivo* models of the disease and, finally, in clinical trials. Therefore, finding effective therapeutic targets early on is crucial to the outcome of a drug development effort.

A desirable pharmacological target will be both amenable to therapeutic modification ("druggable") and relevant to the disease phenotype. High-throughput biomedical data have been continuously generated as a result of breakthroughs in biology and medicine, opening up new windows of opportunity for the early detection of prospective therapeutic targets. However, efficient methods are needed to analyze such massive multi-dimensional biological data in order to provide reliable predictions for target identification. AI and ML have appeared as an effective means for assessing the fast-expanding multiomics data for the purpose of locating possible therapeutic targets.

Two common uses of the phrase "target identification" in the literature are target discovery and target deconvolution [25]. It starts with the identification of a novel treatment target for a disease. The second method is "target fishing," in which a known active chemical is used to locate a target. Target discovery and deconvolution will be used in this context rather than just "target identification" to keep things clear.

Drug discovery: a theoretical framework for an AI platform: The first phase is to precisely characterize the issue at hand (target, expected outcomes, etc.); the second is to collect, investigate, profile, format, and enhance the quality of the data; and the third is to transform the raw data into features and choose important features.

Categories of Learning

Supervised learning: A predictive model trained on data points with known outcomes.
   Regression: The model finds outputs that are real variables.
   Classification: The model divides the input into classes or groups.

Algorithm

Naïve Bayes: A "probabilistic classifier" that determines the probability of the features occurring in each class by treating every feature independently to return the most likely class based on the Bayes rule.

Support vector machines: A discriminative classifier that outputs an optimal hyperplane to categorized new examples. The vectors that define the hyperplane are the support vectors.

Random forest: (1) As ensemble of simple tree predictors that vote for the most popular class for classification problems: In the regression problems, the tree responses are averaged to obtain an estimate of the dependent variables; (2) Over-fitting is less likely to occur as most decision trees are added to the forest.

K-nearest-neighbors: A nonparametric algorithm based on feature similarity by assuming that similar things exist in proximity. It is useful for classification study when there is little or no prior knowledge about the distribution data.

Artificial neural networks: A method that learns from input data based on layers of connected neurons consisting of input layers, hidden layers, and output layers.

Deep neural network:

1. A collection of neurons organized in a sequence of multiple layers.
2. Type of artificial neural network of several advantages (i.e., spatial relations and local receptive fields).
3. Learning can be supervised, unsupervised, and semi-supervised.
4. End-to-end learning and transfer learning are the major approaches performed by the deep neural network.

Autoencoders and generative adverse arial networks are the two specific forms of deep neural networks.

8.2.4   Applications of AI in the Early Phases of Drug Target Discovery

8.2.4.1   *Discovery of a Target*

Finding a novel target candidate is the first step to begin with in the drug development process. Next, the target's capacity to bind small molecule medicines (its "druggability") is evaluated, both experimentally and theoretically [26, 27]. Identifying specific molecules or biological processes that are important to the pathophysiology of a disease is the goal of target identification, a crucial stage in the drug development process. These targets represent prospective areas for therapeutic development intervention. The biological processes that make up the human body are exceedingly complex and varied; therefore, this period is fraught with difficulties. Researchers use a variety of techniques to find targets related to disease pathogenesis. To find possible candidates, they first go through the biomedical literature and experimental data. The capability of successfully targeting a particular molecule is then assessed for these potential targets through the druggability process. The evaluation takes into account factors like the target's accessibility, specificity, and chance of inducing a therapeutic response without harmful side effects.

The complexity of human diseases, however, necessitates increasingly sophisticated methods that include heterogeneous data and knowledge from multiple sources. It is difficult to identify precise biological pathways responsible for disease phenotypes since

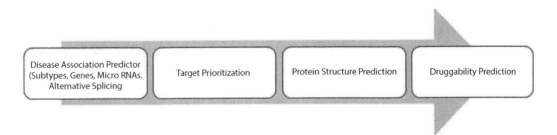

Figure 8.3 Target identification using AI. In order to expedite the development of disease related therapeutic targets, AI/ML algorithms can quickly assess all relevant data.

human diseases frequently originate from a combination of genetic, environmental, and lifestyle variables. The incorporation of AI/ML approaches has become a potent tool to address these difficulties in recent years. Large-scale and diversified datasets can be effectively analyzed and interpreted by AI/ML models, allowing researchers to see patterns and relationships that conventional approaches would overlook. Researchers can forecast prospective "reliable" therapeutic targets by utilizing AI/ML, which increases the effectiveness and efficiency of the target discovery process. The multi-step target identification process is depicted in Figure 8.3.

8.2.4.2   Deconvolution of the Target

After identifying substances that induce a desired phenotypic change, the next stage is target deconvolution, also known as target fishing. To better develop analogy, identify potential off-targets, and account for observed adverse effects, it is important to gain insight into the binding targets of compounds derived through phenotypic screens. However, the current experimental methods for target deconvolution require a lot of time, energy, and resources to complete. In order to cut back on the number of sources needed for the tests, researchers have applied computational approaches to deconvolution challenges. They found that "fuzzy" molecular representations, like pharmacophoric feature descriptors, were more effective than atomistic techniques in similarity searches and hence were the representations of choice. Their unsupervised SOM system grouped query compounds with unknown targets and drug-like molecules with known targets based on the similarity of their pharmacophoric properties. In addition, a target-fishing server called RF-QSAR was developed employing SAR models for potential targets that were ranked using an RF algorithm [28]. BANDIT, [29] is a novel target discovery tool that employs a Bayesian technique to incorporate six different data sets, including medication efficacies. Given its significance for side effect prediction and attempts at therapeutic repositioning, the prediction of drug–target interaction (DTI) has attracted increased attention in the discovery of the novel targets of medicines [30]. Data integration methodologies enabled by artificial intelligence and machine learning perform better than conventional approaches in categorizing positive and negative interactions, [31] enhancing the quality of expected interactions and speeding up the discovery of new DTI [32].

8.2.5   AI and ML in Drug Screening

Virtual screening (VS) alternatives have emerged as a result of the high cost and low hit rate of HTS, allowing for the rapid, low-cost screening of far larger chemical libraries [33, 34]. Using a number of methods, VS can determine which compounds are most likely to bind to a given protein. Structure-based VS (SBVS) and ligand-based VS (LBVS) are two major types of VS; the former employs target protein structures as input [35, 36], while the latter makes use of information on known inhibitors. Because molecules with similar structures tend to share comparable properties, LBVS can be thought of as a form of "analoging" [37] and can aid in the development of more accurate pharmacophore models [38]. Artificial intelligence and machine learning-based techniques have been used for both SBVS and LBVS to improve workflow performance. First, we will look at how AI/ML techniques are being used in SBVS, and then we will move on to how they are being used in LBVS.

8.2.5.1   Digital Ligand-Based Screening

SBVS methods (such as molecular docking) can be used when a 3D structure of a target is available. If the 3D structure of the protein of interest is unknown, however, only LBVS approaches will do. LBVS is founded on the idea that structurally identical ligands tend to have a similar activity, as opposed to molecular docking, which predicts the binding pose of ligands to the target protein by using the protein structure [39]. As a result, LBVS relies on data on active chemicals rather than the structure of the target protein. It is common practice in drug development to establish a panel of active compounds by subjecting molecules to biochemical or functional assays prior to determining the structure of the target protein. By comparing the potential ligands' structures to those of known active chemicals, the LBVS method can be used in these situations to identify new ligands. Finding a suitable similarity model that connects compound properties to test results is thus a significant task.

8.2.6   Prediction of QSAR

Molecular descriptors are used in quantitative structure–activity relationship (QSAR) models to reflect the physicochemical properties of compounds. These models are crucial to the process of optimizing drugs since they allow for an *in silico* first look at crucial characteristics including activity, selectivity, and toxicity [40–42]. This drastically cuts down the number of potential compounds that need to be investigated in animal studies. Depending on the chosen computational approach, QSAR models can use either a regression or a classification approach—AI/ML techniques (e.g., RF, [43] and SVM [44–46]). QSAR modeling has made heavy use of naive Bayesian [47–56] and ANN [57–67] (for a more in-depth description of their respective uses, see the Supplementary Materials). QSAR investigations typically use the RF method, which is widely regarded as the gold standard, for classification and regression purposes [68]. The Pqsar [69] technique for soluble epoxide hydrolase [70] and the Janus kinase 2 [71] model are only two examples of the many RF-based QSAR models that have been created. When comparing RF-based QSAR models to those based on SVMs and partial least squares, two popular linear modeling approaches, RF not only provides superior prediction performance but also facilitates an approachable chemical and biological interpretation [72].

8.2.6.1   Artificial Intelligence and Machine Learning for Physicochemical Property and ADME/T Prediction Physicochemical Property Forecasting

The likelihood of a drug's success in the clinic is heavily influenced by its physicochemical qualities, which reveal all facets of therapeutic activity. To effectively reach and interact with its targets, a potential small molecule medication must be both soluble and permeable. For the purpose of making predictions about important physicochemical qualities including water solubility, membrane permeability, and lipophilicity, scientists have turned to ML-driven techniques. In the Supplementary Material, we describe in depth each feature and talk about the ML-based algorithms that can predict things like water solubility, permeability through membranes, and lipophilicity. While advancements in ML models have allowed for a more accurate prediction of molecular properties, these gains have been hampered by the absence of common criteria for evaluating model performance. To combat this, the scientific community now has access to Molecule Net, a benchmark collection for molecular ML that can be used to train sophisticated models to learn molecular features [73]. Several ML techniques have been integrated into Molecule Net to facilitate model comparison and development. Recent research confirms GCN's exceptional performance [74].

8.2.7 Prediction of ADME-T

Evaluation of ADMET characteristics aids researchers in selecting promising drug candidates in the early stages of drug discovery. It is believed that half of all clinical failures can be attributed to ADMET characteristics [75]. In this setting, the availability of several drugs with documented pharmacokinetic properties during the past 40 years has allowed for significant development in *in silico* ADMET prediction models [76]. The goal of most prediction models is to establish a causal connection between a specific ADME-T feature and a specified set of molecular descriptors [77]. Structural warnings are the primary substructures responsible for specific toxicity; their discovery in given small compounds could be utilized to anticipate toxicity [78]. Classification models including DT, KNN, SVM, RF, and NN have been widely utilized for predicting the regulators of medication ADME/T characteristics. Beyond that, advancements have been made because DL models were introduced. Alchemite [79], a DL model, predicts ADME/T features by imputing heterogeneous drug discovery data.

8.2.8 Use of ANNs and MLs in Drug Discovery

For the purpose of achieving certain efficacy and safety profiles in a cost- and time-efficient manner, *de novo* drug design involves the generation of unique chemical entities with desired chemical and biological features from scratch. New chemical entities with desirable features can now be generated automatically using state-of-the-art AI/ML-based techniques. Due to these breakthroughs, research into the use of AI and ML in *de novo* discovery has surged in recent years. In particular, there is a lot of interest in AI/ML-powered generative molecular design. Here we provide a brief overview of the artificial intelligence and machine learning methods used in *de novo* drug discovery, with an emphasis on generative models. Those interested in this topic might read additional thorough works on the subject available in the literature [80, 81].

The chemical space is skewed toward what is already known since conventional methods for producing new chemical structures rely on predefined reaction or transformation principles. Generative models built using AI/ML are data-driven and rule-free, allowing them to create novel compounds that are not included in the training set. These generative models, in a nutshell, take in data, use that data to train an abstract representation, and then use that representation to generate new data instances [82]. These generative models then exhibit the full range of capabilities associated with AI systems, including the ability to solve problems, acquire knowledge through experience, and adapt to novel circumstances [83].

8.2.9 Predicting Medication Interactions Using Artificial Intelligence and Machine Learning

The goal of drug coadministration is to decrease toxicity, increase effectiveness, and forestall the development of resistance in the course of treatment. Synergistic, antagonistic, and additive drug combinations are the three main types. Synergy between medications occurs when the combined effect of multiple drugs is greater than the sum of their separate effects [84]. If medications have additive effects, it may be possible to use smaller doses of each treatment while still achieving the desired result. When two medications are combined antagonistically, their combined activity is less than the reaction to either drug used alone [85]. Last but not least, a medicine combination is said to be additive if the reaction to each individual drug does not cancel out or boost the effectiveness of the others [86]. It is difficult to develop a new drug combination regimen that can be transmitted to the clinic, despite the fact that combinatorial therapy provides advantages over monotherapy. Clinical evidence or high-throughput screening (HTS) of medication pairs at varying concentrations on cell lines has informed recommendations for the most effective therapeutic combinations to date. The former can put people at risk, while the latter cannot evaluate every possible combination [87]. In an effort to speed up traditional combinatorial therapy, AI/ML algorithms are being used to prioritize medication combinations and to explore the greater combinatorial space [88].

8.2.10 Role of AI and ML in Repurposing Existing Drugs

The entire process of creating a new treatment that is approved by the FDA can take anywhere from 10 to 17 years and can cost upwards of $2.6 billion [89]. However, the approval rate of new treatments has not increased despite the enormous cost of drug research and development [90]. The persistent use of the standard "one gene, one drug, one disease" paradigm in conventional drug development is likely a contributing factor to the low rate of approvals [91]. Since drug targets do not function independently of the biochemical system, it is necessary to examine each DTI in the context of the whole [92]. To further guide medication repurposing efforts, this method reveals previously unknown information about "off-target" consequences (i.e., side effects), resistance to precision medicine, and pharmacological mechanism of action.

8.3 Role of AI and ML in Central Nervous System (CNS)

Neurological conditions affecting the central nervous system (CNS) have major monetary and societal consequences. Complex brain anatomy and function, a lack of knowledge about the biology of CNS diseases, and the presence of the blood–brain barrier (BBB) all make the development of new medications for CNS diseases more difficult than for other diseases. Here we provide an overview of AI/ML-based methods for addressing issues like BBB permeability in central nervous system drug development (Figure 8.4).

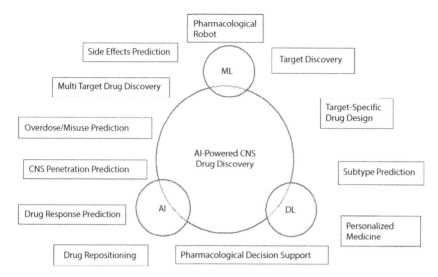

Figure 8.4 CNS disease treatment has benefited from advancements made possible by AI and ML.

8.3.1   Hypothesis on BBB Permeability

There has been enormous progress in our understanding of CNS diseases, but there are still significant obstacles to overcome in the development of innovative therapeutics for CNS diseases. Identifying targets in the central nervous system is challenging, but so is creating new compounds that can cross the blood–brain barrier. The blood–brain barrier (BBB) functions to keep harmful substances and fluctuations in blood chemistry (such as hormones, amino acids, and potassium) out of the brain. Low brain penetration is preferred for medications that have unwanted central nervous system (CNS) effects, yet high brain penetration is required for CNS-active drugs. Drug candidates' BBB permeability needs to be addressed early in the drug discovery process if success rates are to be increased in CNS drug discovery.

8.3.2   Benefits of Using AI and ML in Neurological Disease Drug Discovery

8.3.2.1   *Drug Discovery Using AI/ML for Neurological Illnesses*

Schizophrenia, a neuro-developmental condition with a lifetime prevalence of 0.30% to 0.66% [93], which often manifests before age 25 and persists throughout life, is a major contributor to the worldwide burden of disease [94]. There is currently no effective treatment for schizophrenia, despite the fact that its complicated pathophysiology has been studied for almost a century. As a result, novel medication treatments for schizophrenia require a departure from traditional research methods [95]. Recently, artificial intelligence and machine learning have been considered as a potentially useful tool in guiding schizophrenia diagnosis [96, 97], spotting heterogeneity [98, 99], and subtyping [100, 101].

8.3.2.2   The Use of ML and AI in the Search for Antidepressants

In psychiatric drug discovery, AI/ML-based approaches have been used for pharmacological decision assistance [102, 103]. Using the indicators revealed by the elastic net, researchers in a study of depression created a gradient boosting machine to foretell whether a patient on the antidepressant citalopram would experience symptomatic remission [104]. The escitalopram treatment arm of a separate clinical trial also benefited from this model's application [105]. Chekroud *et al.* [99] used the same model to classify patients into clusters based on their symptoms and then forecast how each cluster would react to therapy with a variety of antidepressants. A web-based program was developed to help doctors decide which medications would be most effective for a specific set of symptoms. However, the Chekroud *et al.* [100] model had its own shortcomings. The model does not quantify the extent to which an individual responds to antidepressants; rather, it just predicts whether or not a certain patient would respond to a given antidepressant. Since the model was developed for a single antidepressant, it cannot effectively choose the most helpful medications among the many options available to patients [108]. To overcome these constraints, Chang *et al.* [101] created a NN-based Antidepressant Response Prediction Network (ARP Net) model. ARP Net can predict how well a patient will respond to antidepressants, whether they will achieve clinical remission from depression, and how well they will respond to a combination of antidepressants by using a feature selection process that is both literature-based and data-driven.

8.3.2.3   The Use of AI and ML in Parkinson's Disease Medication Discovery

Over 1% of the population over 60 and up to 5% of those over 85 are diagnosed with Parkinson's disease (PD), making it the second most frequent age-related neurodegenerative ailment [106]. Parkinson's disease (PD) is a classic example of a complex disease due to the wide variety of motor and non-motor symptoms it can cause [105]. Movement control and cognitive decline, characterized by tremors and memory loss, are underpinned by a depletion of dopaminergic neurons in the substantia nigra, but this decrease is irreversible without treatment at this time [104, 105].

8.3.2.4   Applications of AI and ML in Alzheimer's Disease Medication Discovery

The incidence and severity of age-related illnesses have increased dramatically as life expectancy has risen. Alzheimer's disease (AD) is the most common kind of neurodegenerative illness in the elderly, and it causes a gradual decline in a variety of mental abilities, including memory [105]. Although the precise origin of Alzheimer's disease is still unknown, its characteristic neuropathological features—including neuronal and synaptic loss and/or dysfunction as well as extracellular Abeta plaques and intracellular neurofibrillary tangles—are widely recognized [106]. Most AD patients see only modest gains from the current medicines for the disease, which target cholinergic and glutamatergic neurotransmission to alleviate symptoms [107]. Therefore, innovative medicines that can stop or slow the start of disease, slow its progression, or alleviate patients' symptoms are desperately needed [108]. An insufficient understanding of AD pathogenesis, complicated ethology, and complex pathophysiology is a major hurdle to drug discovery efforts and is likely to blame for [108] failed AD medication attempts.

The recent years have seen a rise in the use of AI/ML-based models in Alzheimer's disease research, with their primary application being the diagnosis and prognosis of the disease through the processing of electronic health records and photographs [108]. However, there has been limited use of AI/ML methods in the search for effective treatments for AD. A small number of researchers, though, have hinted to AI/ML's promise as a tool in the search for treatments for AD. Potential therapeutic targets have been identified using ML methods alongside the characterization of amyloid fibrils. In order to predict AD-associated genes, HENA [109], a heterogeneous network-based data set, uses GCN to combine multiple types of data.

8.3.2.5   Medical Uses of AI and ML for Painkillers and Anesthetics

Both general anesthetics and pain relievers are classified as CNC medicines. Therapeutic decision making in anesthesia and pain management has become more reliant on autonomous and AI-based recommender systems in recent years. In particular, pharmacological robots have established themselves as indispensable tools in the anesthetic industry, as they provide individualized dosing of anesthetic drugs that helps patients maintain homeostasis even under deep sedation or general anesthesia [103].

8.4   The Effect of AI/ML on CNS Drug Research

Artificial intelligence (AI) and machine learning (ML) have had a dramatic impact on the study of drugs for the central nervous system (CNS), revolutionizing the entire drug development process and opening the door to more efficient treatments for CNS illnesses. The fusion of AI and ML technologies has solved major problems and opened up fresh possibilities for CNS drug research.

The following are some notable effects of AI/ML on CNS drug research:

- Speeded-up drug discovery: Researchers are now better able to identify prospective drug targets, forecast pharmacological actions, and effectively screen chemical libraries thanks to AI/ML systems' quick analysis of large amounts of biomedical data. The time and resources needed to find potential therapeutic candidates for CNS illnesses are greatly reduced by this expedited drug discovery process.
- Target identification and validation: By evaluating various omics data and discovering important biological targets connected to CNS illnesses, AI/ML-driven target identification has transformed CNS drug research. These algorithms more accurately rank prospective therapeutic targets, resulting in more targeted and efficient attempts to discover new drugs.
- Precision medicine and customized treatments: Precision medicine and customized treatments are made possible by AI/ML, which analyzes patient-specific data to forecast particular therapy responses. Based on a patient's genetic profile, medical history, and treatment response, this method enables

clinicians to customize CNS medication regimens, increasing treatment success and lowering side effects.

- Blood–brain barrier permeability prediction: Delivering drugs across the blood–brain barrier (BBB) is extremely difficult. Researchers can be directed toward substances with a higher likelihood of successfully reaching the CNS by using AI/ML models to estimate the permeability of therapeutic candidates across the BBB.

- Medication repurposing and polypharmacology: By examining current medication databases and discovering possible candidates with novel therapeutic indications, AI/ML algorithms have facilitated drug repurposing for CNS illnesses. The idea of polypharmacology, in which medications can have numerous targets, has also been clarified by AI/ML, enabling the creation of multi-targeted therapeutics for CNS illnesses.

- Drug–drug interaction prediction: AI/ML models can anticipate possible drug–drug interactions, assisting medical professionals in avoiding dangerous mixtures and enhancing treatment plans for patients with CNS diseases.

The identification of novel biomarkers and disease subtypes in CNS illnesses have been made possible by AI/ML analysis of multi-omics data. These biomarkers support the identification of diseases, the classification of patients, and the design of specialized treatments. Data challenges can be overcome since AI/ML algorithms are skilled at processing massive, heterogeneous information from a variety of sources, including genomes, proteomics, and imaging investigations. With the help of this skill, researchers have been able to combine and evaluate complex data to get new understanding of CNS illnesses.

Clinical trial designs can be improved by using AI/ML-driven algorithms, which can also be used to choose the right patient demographics and forecast trial results. Clinical trials for CNS medicines become more effective and productive as a result of this modification. In a nutshell AI and ML have significantly changed the way drug targets are found, compounds are screened, and treatments are tailored in CNS drug development. As these technologies develop and grow, they have the potential to spur revolutionary developments in the field of CNS therapies, giving patients with CNS illnesses renewed hope and a higher standard of living.

8.5   Prospects for AI/ML in CNS Drug Research in Future

As these technologies continue to develop and expand quickly, they hold enormous potential for the future of central nervous system (CNS) drug research. Different facets of CNS drug discovery and development are anticipated to undergo radical change as a result of the integration of AI/ML approaches.

The following are the potential applications of AI and ML to the study of CNS drugs:

- Precision medicine and personalized therapies: The potential for precision medicine in CNS drug development will increase as AI/ML models grow more advanced and capable of processing huge and diverse information. In order to precisely anticipate each patient's reaction to treatment, AI/ML algorithms will incorporate genomes, proteomics, metabolomics, and other patient-specific data [110]. This will make it possible for medical professionals to customize CNS medication regimens to each patient's particular genetic profile and illness features, leading to more efficient and individualized treatments.

- Integration of multi-omics data: The integration of multi-omics data combines genomes, transcriptomics, proteomics, and other -omics information, which is crucial for the future of AI/ML in CNS drug research. A comprehensive understanding of the intricate relationships underlying CNS illnesses will be made possible by systems biology-driven AI/ML methods. Researchers will discover new targets, pathways, and biomarkers by examining these interconnected networks, which will result in the creation of novel and targeted medicines.

- Medicine combination optimization: AI/ML methods are going to be very important for figuring out the best medicine combinations for CNS illnesses. AI/ML models will evaluate the synergistic effects of combining various medications to increase efficacy and decrease negative effects rather than only concentrating on single-target therapy. This method, often referred to as polypharmacology, will result in the creation of numerous targeted medicines that address the complex character of CNS illnesses.

- AI-designed drugs: AI/ML's predictive modeling capabilities will be used to create brand-new medications that are tailored to hit particular CNS targets. AI/ML algorithms will streamline the drug design process and broaden the chemical space investigated for CNS drugs by proposing novel chemical structures with desired pharmacological properties through generative models and reinforcement learning.

- Real-time decision support: In the future, AI/ML systems will assist healthcare professionals in making decisions in real-time as they treat patients with CNS illnesses. In order to improve treatment outcomes and patient safety, these systems will assess patient data, continually track treatment responses, and suggest adjustments in drug dosages or therapies based on dynamic patient profiles.

- Optimized clinical trial designs: Clinical trial designs will be optimized by means of augmented clinical trials, making CNS drug studies more effective and productive. By predicting patient reactions, identifying eligible patient populations, and optimizing dose regimens, AI/ML algorithms will help shorten the time and money needed for drug development and approval.

- Drug safety and toxicity prediction: For CNS drugs, the use of AI/ML models to forecast drug safety and toxicity profiles is expected to rise. AI/ML algorithms can predict probable side effects by examining data from preclinical studies and human clinical trials, allowing researchers to make well-informed decisions on drug candidates early in the development process.

- Translational research and data sharing: AI/ML will make it easier to integrate and analyze data collected at different stages of the drug discovery process, from preclinical research to clinical trials. Researchers, pharmaceutical companies, and regulatory authorities will work together more frequently and share data, hastening the development of viable CNS medicines based on AI/ML-driven discoveries.

In final analysis, there is a bright and promising future for AI/ML in the study of CNS drugs. These cutting-edge technologies have the power to completely alter the process of discovering and developing CNS drugs, ushering in a new era of precision medicine, individualized care, and creative therapeutic strategies. A safe and effective treatment for CNS illnesses will certainly be developed as AI/ML develops, giving hope to millions of sufferers around the world.

8.6   Proposed Methodology on Data Processing for CNS Drug-Likeness Prediction

The "Data Processing for CNS Drug-Likeness Prediction" approach is a collection of organized stages designed to provide a dataset for precise and thorough predictions about a compound's potential to effectively target the central nervous system (CNS). This process entails a number of steps, starting with the collection of data on orally available medications and their physicochemical characteristics. The term "CNS drugs" refers to a group of medications that can cross the blood–brain barrier (BBB). On top of this basis, the notion of CNS drug-likeness is broadened to include QSAR predictions, which relate molecular structure to biological activity. To ensure data integrity and improve predictive accuracy, the data preprocessing stage is crucial. This entails managing missing values, standardizing physicochemical attributes, curating data for QSAR predictions, and including ADME-T (absorption, distribution, metabolism, and excretion) concerns.

After that, the prepared dataset is divided into features, target variables (CNS drug status), and other variables important for QSAR and ADME-T predictions. Multiple prediction techniques, including neural network-based forecasts, QSAR modeling, and ADME-T evaluations, are based on this organized information. These hypotheses shed light on the possibility of drugs to successfully cross the BBB, display desired biological behaviors, and satisfy crucial ADME-T requirements.

Finally, a comprehensive understanding of each compound's aptitude for CNS drug targeting is provided by synthesizing the integrated predictions from these several approaches. This comprehensive viewpoint, which incorporates biological functions, pharmacokinetic factors, and molecular insights, improves the decision-making process in the development of CNS drugs.

Algorithm

The "Data Processing for CNS Drug-Likeness Prediction" methodology as shown in Figure 8.5 goes beyond the initial data preparation stage to take ADME-T and QSAR modeling into account, improving prediction accuracy and providing a comprehensive understanding of drug candidates' potential for CNS targeting.

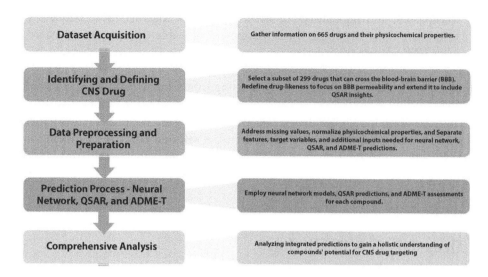

Figure 8.5 Proposed methodology on data processing for CNS drug-likeness prediction.

Step 1: Obtaining the dataset

Much like before, the procedure starts with gathering an extensive dataset of medications that are available orally together with their physicochemical characteristics. However, this enlarged methodology contains more information on biological activities and ADME-T characteristics, allowing for a more thorough analysis.

Step 2: Recognizing CNS drugs

Similar to earlier, a subset of medications having BBB-permeating potential are called "CNS drugs." These CNS medications are further described in this enlarged method by their QSAR and ADME-T characteristics, allowing for a multi-dimensional evaluation of their potential for CNS targeting.

Step 3: Defining CNS drug-likeness

The ability to cross the BBB is still emphasized by the concept of CNS drug-likeness. It now goes farther and includes QSAR predictions, giving information on the connection between molecular structure and biological activity.

Step 4: Preprocessing the data

Preprocessing now includes curation and organization of QSAR-related data, such as biological activity measurements, molecular descriptors, and features pertinent to ADME-T, in addition to managing null values and normalization.

Step 5: Data preparation for QSAR, ADME-T, and neural network models

Features, target variables (CNS drug status), and other variables needed for QSAR and ADME-T predictions are all separated out from the data. These many prediction features are taken into consideration by expanding the training and testing subgroups.

Step 6: Prediction process—neural network, QSAR, and ADME-T

This methodology now contains two further prediction procedures in addition to the initial neural network-based prediction method:

Modeling a QSAR models are created to forecast biological activities based on molecular structure using the extended dataset. These models shed light on the connection between molecular characteristics and CNS functioning.

ADME-T prognosis: Predicting the ADME-T characteristics of the CNS medicines is another aspect. This entails assessing the absorption, distribution, metabolization, and excretion of medications as well as taking toxicity into account.

Step 7: Integrating predictions

Each CNS drug's potential to target the central nervous system is depicted in detail using predictions from the neural network, QSAR models, and ADME-T evaluations. For a thorough analysis, this holistic method combines structural knowledge, biological functions, and pharmacokinetic characteristics [111].

Step 8: Comprehensive analysis' conclusion

An extensive analysis of the combined forecasts follows the approach. The ensuing insights offer a thorough evaluation of the drug-likeness of CNS compounds, taking into account chemical structure, biological activity, and ADME-T factors. By providing a more comprehensive viewpoint, this integrated understanding improves the decision-making process in the development of CNS drugs.

The "Data Processing for CNS Drug-Likeness Prediction" methodology, in conclusion, combines data preprocessing, neural network-based prediction, QSAR modeling, and ADME-T evaluations into a thorough methodology. This all-encompassing framework enables researchers to develop a comprehensive understanding of the potential of substances to successfully target the CNS, expediting drug development procedures and encouraging informed choices in the hunt for innovative CNS treatments.

8.7   Conclusion and Future Scope

Both general anesthetics and pain relievers are classified as CNC medicines. Therapeutic decision making in anesthesia and pain management has become more reliant on autonomous and AI-based recommender systems in recent years. Pharmacological robots have established themselves as indispensable tools in the anesthetic industry, as they provide individualized dosing of anesthetic drugs that helps patients maintain homeostasis even under deep sedation or general anesthesia. These robots calculate the best possible medicine dosage by analyzing a patient's data (from devices like EEG monitors, blood pressure monitors, heart rate monitors, etc.) and the pharmacokinetic properties of the drugs themselves.

In terms of therapeutic advancement, the application of AI technology to advance central nervous system (CNS) drug discovery is in its infancy. Below, we talk about the current restrictions and potential future possibilities for this developing sector. One of the biggest obstacles to implementing AI/ML in the drug development process for the central nervous system is the dearth of high-quality data. The information stored in public databases is often not directly comparable since it was gathered using different biological assays, methodologies, or experimental settings. Furthermore, there may be discrepancies between different data sets on the same topic. Thus, obtaining high-quality data by filtering the raw inputs is a necessary step before carrying out specific AI/ML operations. An additional difficulty in CNS drug research is the "black box" character of most next-generation AI platforms.

Artificial intelligence and machine learning are useful, but their outcomes are difficult to understand. Therefore, researchers have no way of knowing or explaining the model's underlying biological mechanisms or explaining the model's results. This further complicates the process of diagnosing and fixing such models when they fail for no apparent reason. As a result, it is crucial to find ways of unlocking DL's mysteries.

Many neurological disorders have no known treatment that can reverse the illness state, making it difficult to nominate new targets or medications for them. When there are not enough training examples for a drug discovery assignment, transfer learning technology can help by taking what is learned in one context and applying it to another. In the long run, however, data sharing among scientists offers the most promise for addressing data shortages. With the advent of faster machines like quantum computers, a system of widespread data sharing might greatly benefit the process of discovering new CNS drugs.

Here the next-generation AI architecture known as capsule networks can help out since it encloses CNNs in a single, interconnected module. In this first application of capsule networks to the field of drug development, they proved particularly effective at predicting the cardiotoxicity of drugs. Capsule networks are able to learn from diverse data sets while maintaining the data's inherent hierarchy due to its modular representation of CNNs. Despite pharmaco MRI's continued utility in neuropharmacology studies, its preclinical application is hindered by a number of issues. Recent advances in pharmaco fUS have made it possible to image brain activity with exceptional spatial and temporal resolution and without the use of anesthetic. Studies on the AD464 medication combination of donepezil and mefloquine and the ADHD medicine atomoxetine have shown that fUS imaging can be used to evaluate the dynamic characteristics of these CNS drugs. Scopolamine is a popular preclinical drug used to imitate AD, and their ML model was able to identify the "fingerprint" of drug-induced brain connection alterations in awake mice. As can be seen from these examples, AI/ML techniques have the potential to improve our understanding of the brain's drug action mechanism by allowing us to characterize treatment effects using unique neuroimaging data sets. To create effective medicines for treating CNS illnesses, it is crucial to first figure out how to get pharmaceuticals over the BBB. Despite its importance in preventing harmful substances from entering the central nervous system, the BBB is frequently misunderstood as merely a static barrier. Disruption of the BBB or problems with BBB transporters have both been linked to central nervous system illnesses. To date, AI/ML-based predictive algorithms have treated BBB as if it were unaffected by CNS diseases, assuming that it is a static entity. Therefore, a BBB penetrance prediction model that was trained on data from non-CNS disorders might not be applicable to a CNS condition. Including BBB alterations caused by disease in prediction models should lead to more accurate estimates of BBB permeability. This also opens up new possibilities for the application of AI and ML in the discovery of drugs for the central nervous system. Moreover, physiological events are usually influenced by their surroundings: The liver is a possible site for a receptor contact, but the brain is not. Such context-dependent nonlinear interactions and other unknown contributory elements are typically missed by AI/ML systems. Drug targets that are predicted by an AI/ML algorithm but which neuroscientists know are likely to have serious side effects in the brain or which generate compounds that cannot be synthesized are two examples. Many of these difficulties can only be overcome *via* the application of human judgment and a hypothesis-driven approach. The finest possible scientific outcomes can be ensured by the transfer of knowledge from human experts to AI systems.

As a result, the decision-making process in the development of CNS drugs will be aided by this hybrid of machine and mind [110]. The use of AI/ML algorithms in drug discovery is still in its infancy despite its revolutionary impact in other areas.

For this reason, we conclude with a comprehensive analysis of the most recent AI/ML-assisted drug development applications for the treatment of CNS illnesses. The exceptional success of AI/ML-based approaches in several scientific and technological disciplines has contributed to the explosive growth of these applications over the past couple of years. We foresee a bright future for AI/ML in CNS drug discovery as we move towards personalized medicine, especially in the following areas: (1) patient subtyping, (2) identification of key disease drivers, (3) prediction of cell type-specific drug response, (4) autonomous design of novel drugs, and (5) disease-specific BBB permeability testing. The existing shortcomings of AI and ML can be traced back to data and algorithmic restrictions. However, improvements in neuropharmacology will be possible if we apply artificial intelligence and machine learning techniques to the field.

References

1. Mohs, R.C. and Greig, N.H., Drug discovery and development: Role of basic biological research. *Alzheimer's & Dementia (New York, N. Y.)*, 3, 4, 651–657, 2017.
2. Papadatos, G., Gaulton, A., Hersey, A., Overington, J.P., Activity, assay and target data curation and quality in the ChEMBL database. *J. Comput.-Aided Mol. Design*, 29, 9, 885–896, 2015.
3. Wilson, B.J. and Nicholls, S.G., The Human Genome Project, and recent advances in personalized genomics. *Risk Manage. Healthc. Policy*, 8, 9–20, 2015.
4. David, L., Arús-Pous, J., Karlsson, J. *et al.*, Applications of deep learning in exploiting large-scale and heterogeneous compound data in industrial pharmaceutical research. *Front. Pharmacol.*, 10, 1303, 2019.
5. Todeschini, R., Wiese, M., Consonni, V., Handbook of molecular descriptors. *Angewandte Chemie (International Ed. English)*, 40, 10, 1977, 2001.
6. Dong, J., Cao, D.-S., Miao, H.-Y. *et al.*, ChemDes: An integrated web-based platform for molecular descriptor and fingerprint computation. *J. Cheminf.*, 7, 1, 60, 2015.
7. Cao, D.S., Zhou, G.H., Liu, S. *et al.*, Large-scale prediction of human kinase-inhibitor interactions using protein sequences and molecular topological structures. *Anal. Chim. Acta*, 792, 10–18, 2013.
8. Yee, S.W., Lin, L., Merski, M. *et al.*, Prediction and validation of enzyme and transporter off-targets for metformin. *J. Pharmacokinet. Pharmacodyn.*, 42, 5, 463–475, 2015.
9. Muegge, I. and Mukherjee, P., An overview of molecular fingerprint similarity search in virtual screening. *Expert Opin. Drug Discov.*, 11, 2, 137–148, 2016.

10. Cereto-Massague, A., Ojeda, M.J., Valls, C., Mulero, M., Garcia-Vallve, S., Pujadas, G., Molecular fingerprint similarity search in virtual screening. *Methods (San Diego, Calif.)*, 71, 58–63, 2015.

11. Willett, P., Similarity-based virtual screening using 2D fingerprints. *Drug Discov. Today*, 11, 23-24, 1046–1053, 2006.

12. Heikamp, K. and Bajorat, J., Fingerprint design and engineering strategies: Rationalizing and improving similarity search performance. *Future Med. Chem.*, 4, 15, 1945–1959, 2012.

13. Irwin, J.J., Gaskins, G., Sterling, T., Mysinger, M.M., Keiser, M.J., Predicted biological activity of purchasable chemical space. *J. Chem. Inf. Modeling*, 58, 1, 148–164, 2018.

14. Axen, S.D., Huang, X.P., Caceres, E.L., Gendelev, L., Roth, B.L., Keiser, M.J., A simple representation of three-dimensional molecular structure. *J. Med. Chem.*, 60, 17, 7393–7409, 2017.

15. Geppert, H., Vogt, M., Bajorath, J., Current trends in ligand-based virtual screening: Molecular representations, data mining methods, new application areas, and performance evaluation. *J. Chem. Inf. Modeling*, 50, 2, 205–216, 2010.

16. Berenger, F., Voet, A., Lee, X.Y., Zhang, K.Y., A rotation-translation invariant molecular descriptor of partial charges and its use in ligand-based virtual screening. *J. Cheminf.*, 6, 23, 2014.

17. Roy, K. and Mitra, I., Electro topological state atom (E-state) index in drug design, QSAR, property prediction and toxicity assessment. *Curr. Comput.-Aided Drug Des.*, 8, 2, 135–158, 2012.

18. Cao, D.-S., Xu, Q.-S., Liang, Y.-Z., Chen, X., Li, H.-D., Prediction of aqueous solubility of drug-like organic compounds using partial least squares, back-propagation network and support vector machine. *J. Chemometrics*, 24, 9, 584–595, 2010.

19. Viswanadhan, V.N., Rajesh, H., Balaji, V.N., Atom type preferences, structural diversity, and property profiles of known drugs, leads, and nondrugs: A comparative assessment. *ACS Combinatorial Sci.*, 13, 3, 327–336, 2011.

20. Khan, M.T., Predictions of the ADMET properties of candidate drug molecules utilizing different QSAR/QSP modelling approaches. *Curr. Drug Metab.*, 11, 4, 285–295, 2010.

22. Maltarollo, V.G., Gertrudes, J.C., Oliveira, P.R., Honorio, K.M., Applying machine learning techniques for ADME-Tox prediction: A review. *Expert Opin. Drug Metab. & Toxicol.*, 11, 2, 259–271, 2015.

23. Chuang, K.V., Gunsalus, L.M., Keiser, M.J., Learning molecular representations for medicinal chemistry. *J. Med. Chem.*, 63, 8705–8722, 2020.

24. Moffat, J.G., Vincent, F., Lee, J.A., Eder, J., Prunotto, M., Opportunities and challenges in phenotypic drug discovery: An industry perspective. *Nat. Rev. Drug Discov.*, 16, 8, 531–543, 2017.

25. Van den Broeck, W.M.M., Chapter 3. Drug targets, target identification, validation, and screening, in: *The Practice of Medicinal Chemistry*, 4th ed, C.G. Wermuth, D. Aldous, P. Raboisson, D. Rognan (Eds.), pp. 45–70, Academic Press, San Diego, CA, 2015.

26. Gashaw, I., Ellinghaus, P., Sommer, A., Asadullah, K., What makes a good drug target? *Drug Discov. Today*, 16, 23-24, 1037–1043, 2011.

27. Lindsay, M.A., Target discovery. *Nat. Rev. Drug Discov.*, 2, 10, 831–838, 2003.

28. Lee, K., Lee, M., Kim, D., Utilizing random Forest QSAR models with optimized parameters for target identification and its application to target-fishing server. *BMC Bioinf.*, 18, 16, 567, 2017.

29. Madhukar, N.S., Khade, P.K., Huang, L. *et al.*, A Bayesian machine learning approach for drug target identification using diverse data types. *Nat. Commun.*, 10, 1, 5221, 2019.

30. D'Souza, S., Prema, K.V., Balaji, S., Machine learning models for drug-target interactions: Current knowledge and future directions. *Drug Discov. Today*, 25, 4, 748–756, 2020. [DOI Link].

31. Monteiro, N. R., Ribeiro, B., Arrais, J. P., Drug-target interaction prediction: end-to-end deep learning approach. *IEEE/ACM Trans. Comput. Biol. Bioinf., 18*, 6, 2364–2374, 2020.

32. Nascimento, A.C., Prudêncio, R.B., Costa, I.G., A multiple kernel learning algorithm for drug-target interaction prediction. *BMC Bioinf.,* 17, 1–16, 2016.

33. Lionta, E., Spyrou, G., Vassilatis, D.K., Cournia, Z., Structure-based virtual screening for drug discovery: Principles, applications, and recent advances. *Curr. Topics Med. Chem.,* 14, 16, 1923–1938, 2014.

34. Ghosh, S., Nie, A., An, J., Huang, Z., Structure-based virtual screening of chemical libraries for drug discovery. *Curr. Opin. Chem. Biol.,* 10, 3, 194–202, 2006.

35. Acharya, C., Coop, A., Polli, J.E., Mackerell, A.D., Jr, Recent advances in ligand-based drug design: Relevance and utility of the conformationally sampled pharmacophore approach. *Curr. Comput.-Aided Drug Des.,* 7, 1, 10–22, 2011.

36. Maldonado, A.G., Doucet, J.P., Petitjean, M., Fan, B.-T., Molecular similarity and diversity in chemoinformatics: From theory to applications. *Mol. Diversity,* 10, 1, 39–79, 2006.

37. Johnson, M.A. and Maggiora, G.M., *Concepts and Applications of Molecular Similarity*, Wiley, United States, 1990.

38. Wang, T., Wu, M.B., Lin, J.P., Yang, L.R., Quantitative structure-activity relationship: Promising advances in drug discovery platforms. *Expert Opin. Drug Discov.,* 10, 12, 1283–1300, 2015.

39. Kumar, R., Chaudhary, K., Singh Chauhan, J. *et al.,* An *in-silico* platform for predicting, screening and designing of antihypertensive peptides. *Sci. Rep.,* 5, 12512, 2015.

40. Briard, J.G., Fernandez, M., de Luna, P., Woo, T.K., Ben, R.N., QSAR Accelerated discovery of potent ice recrystallization inhibitors. *Sci. Rep.,* 6, 26403, 2016.

41. Zakharov, A.V., Varlamova, E.V., Lagunin, A.A. *et al.,* QSAR modelling and prediction of drug-drug interactions. *Mol. Pharmaceutics,* 13, 2, 545–556, 2016.

42. Fang, X., Bagui, S., Bagui, S., Improving virtual screening predictive accuracy of Human kallikrein 5 inhibitors using machine learning models. *Comput. Biol. Chem.,* 69, 110–119, 2017.

43. Chen, J.J.F. and Visco, D.P., Jr, Developing an *in-silico* pipeline for faster drug candidate discovery: Virtual high throughput screening with the signature molecular descriptor using support vector machine models. *Chem. Eng. Sci.,* 159, 31–42, 2017.

44. Chen, J.J.F. and Visco, D.P., Jr, Identifying novel factor XIIa inhibitors with PCA-GA- SVM developed vHTS models. *Eur. J. Med. Chem.,* 140, 31–41, 2017.

45. Xia, X., Maliski, E.G., Gallant, P., Rogers, D., Classification of kinase inhibitors using a Bayesian model. *J. Med. Chem.,* 47, 18, 4463–4470, 2004.

46. Bender, A., Mussa, H.Y., Glen, R.C., Screening for dihydrofolate reductase inhibitors using MOLPRINT 2D, a fast fragment-based method employing the Naive Bayesian classifier: Limitations of the descriptor and the importance of balanced chemistry in training and test sets. *J. Biomol. Screen.,* 10, 7, 658–666, 2005.

47. Prathipati, P., Ma, N.L., Keller, T.H., Global Bayesian models for the prioritization of antitubercular agents. *J. Chem. Inf. Model.,* 48, 12, 2362–2370, 2008.

48. Ekins, S., Reynolds, R.C., Kim, H. *et al.,* Bayesian models leveraging bioactivity and cytotoxicity information for drug discovery. *Chem. Biol.,* 20, 3, 370–378, 2013.

49. Vijayan, R.S., Bera, I., Prabu, M., Saha, S., Ghoshal, N., Combinatorial library enumeration and lead hopping using comparative interaction fingerprint analysis and classical 2D QSAR methods for seeking novel GABA(A) alpha (3) modulators. *J. Chem. Inf. Model.,* 49, 11, 2498–2511, 2009.

50. Liu, L., Lu, J., Lu, Y. *et al.,* Novel Bayesian classification models for predicting compounds blocking hERG potassium channels. *Acta Pharmacol. Sin.,* 35, 8, 1093–1102, 2014.

51. Singh, N., Chaudhury, S., Liu, R., Abdul Hameed, M.D.M., Tawa, G., Wallqvist, A., QSAR classification model for antibacterial compounds and its use in virtual screening. *J. Chem. Inf. Model.*, 52, 10, 2559–2569, 2012.

52. Renault, N., Laurent, X., Farce, A. *et al.*, Virtual screening of CB (2) receptor agonists from Bayesian network and high-throughput docking: Structural insights into agonist-modulated GPCR features. *Chem. Biol. Drug Design*, 81, 4, 442–454, 2013.

53. Abdul Hameed, M.D., Ippolito, D.L., Wallqvist, A., Predicting rat and human pregnane X receptor activators using Bayesian classification models. *Chem. Res. Toxicol.*, 29, 10, 1729–1740, 2016.

54. Shi, H., Tian, S., Li, Y. *et al.*, Absorption, distribution, metabolism, excretion, and toxicity evaluation in drug discovery. Prediction of human pregnane X receptor activators by using naive Bayesian classification technique. *Chem. Res. Toxicol.*, 28, 1, 116–125, 2015.

55. Murcia-Soler, M., Pérez-Giménez, F., García-March, F.J. *et al.*, Artificial neural networks and linear discriminant analysis: A valuable combination in the selection of new antibacterial compounds. *J. Chem. Inf. Comput. Sci.*, 44, 3, 1031–1041, 2004.

56. Douali, L., Villemin, D., Cherqaoui, D., Neural networks: Accurate nonlinear QSAR model for HEPT derivatives. *J. Chem. Inf. Comput. Sci.*, 43, 4, 1200–1207, 2003.

57. Sabet, R., Fassihi, A., Hemmateenejad, B., Saghaei, L., Miri, R., Gholami, M., Computer-aided design of novel antibacterial 3-hydroxypyridine-4-ones: Application of QSAR methods based on the MOLMAP approach. *J. Comput.-Aided Mol. Design*, 26, 3, 349–361, 2012.

58. Fjell, C.D., Jenssen, H., Hilpert, K. *et al.*, Identification of novel antibacterial peptides by chemoinformatics and machine learning. *J. Med. Chem.*, 52, 7, 2006–2015, 2009.

59. Torrent, M., Andreu, D., Nogues, V.M., Boix, E., Connecting peptide physicochemical and antimicrobial properties by a rational prediction model. *PloS One*, 6, 2, 16968, 2011.

60. Sardari, S., Kohanzad, H., Ghavami, G., Artificial neural network modeling of antimycobacterial chemical space to introduce efficient descriptors employed for drug design. *Chemom. Intell. Lab. Syst.*, 130, 151–158, 2014.

61. Khatri, N., Lather, V., Madan, A., Diverse classification models for anti-hepatitis C virus activity of thiourea derivatives. *Chemom. Intell. Lab. Syst.*, 140, 13–21, 2015.

62. Hu, L., Chen, G., Chau, R.M., A neural networks-based drug discovery approach and its application for designing aldose reductase inhibitors. *J. Mol. Graph. Model.*, 24, 4, 244–253, 2006.

63. Patra, J.C. and Chua, B.H., Artificial neural network-based drug design for diabetes mellitus using flavonoids. *J. Comput. Chem.*, 32, 4, 555–567, 2011.

64. Myint, K.Z., Wang, L., Tong, Q., Xie, X.Q., Molecular fingerprint-based artificial neural networks QSAR for ligand biological activity predictions. *Mol. Pharm.*, 9, 10, 2912–2923, 2012.

65. Geanes, A.R., Cho, H.P., Nance, K.D. *et al.*, Ligand-based virtual screen for the discovery of novel M5 inhibitor chemotypes. *Bioorganic & Med. Chem. Lett.*, 26, 18, 4487–4491, 2016.

66. Ma, J., Sheridan, R.P., Liaw, A., Dahl, G.E., Svetnik, V., Deep neural nets as a method for quantitative structure-activity relationships. *J. Chem. Inf. Model.*, 55, 2, 263–274, 2015.

67. Martin, E.J., Polyakov, V.R., Tian, L., Perez, R.C., Profile-QSAR 2.0: Kinase virtual screening accuracy comparable to four-concentration IC50s for realistically novel compounds. *J. Chem. Inf. Model.*, 57, 8, 2077–2088, 2017.

68. Shamsara, J., A random forest model to predict the activity of a large set of soluble epoxide hydrolase inhibitors solely based on a set of simple fragmental descriptors. *Comb. Chem. & High Throughput Screen.*, 22, 555–569, 2019.

69. Simeon, S. and Jongkon, N., Construction of quantitative structure-activity relationship (QSAR) models to predict potency of structurally diverse Janus kinase 2 inhibitors. *Molecules*, 24, 23, 4393, 2019.

70. Wu, Z., Ramsundar, B., Feinberg, E.N. *et al.*, MoleculeNet: A benchmark for molecular machine learning. *Chem. Sci.*, 9, 2, 513–530, 2018.

71. Feinberg, E.N., Joshi, E., Pande, V.S., Cheng, A.C., Improvement in ADMET prediction with multitask deep featurization. *J. Med. Chem.*, 63, 16, 8835–8848, 2020.

72. Kola, I. and Landis, J., Can the pharmaceutical industry reduce attrition rates? *Nat. Rev. Drug Discovery*, 3, 8, 711–716, 2004.

73. Bhhatarai, B., Walters, W.P., Hop, C., Lanza, G., Ekins, S., Opportunities and challenges using artificial intelligence in ADME/Tox. *Nat. Mater.*, 18, 5, 418–422, 2019.

74. Shen, J., Cheng, F., Xu, Y., Li, W., Tang, Y., Estimation of ADME properties with substructure pattern recognition. *J. Chem. Inf. Model.*, 50, 6, 1034–1041, 2010.

75. Yang, H., Sun, L., Li, W., Liu, G., Tang, Y., *In silico* prediction of chemical toxicity for drug design using machine learning methods and structural alerts. *Front. Chem.*, 6, 30, 2018.

76. Irwin, B.W.J., Levell, J.R., Whitehead, T.M., Segall, M.D., Conduit, G.J., Practical applications of deep learning to impute heterogeneous drug discovery data. *J. Chem. Inf. Model.*, 60, 6, 2848–2857, 2020.

77. Schneider, G., Future de novo drug design. *Mol. Inf.*, 33, 6-7, 397–402, 2014.

78. Struble, T.J., Alvarez, J.C., Brown, S.P. *et al.*, Current and future roles of artificial intelligence in medicinal chemistry synthesis. *J. Med. Chem.*, 63, 8667–8682, 2020.

79. Schneider, G., Generative models for artificially-intelligent molecular design. *Mol. Inf.*, 37, 1-2, 1880131, 2018.

80. Greco, W.R., Faessel, H., Levasseur, L., The search for cytotoxic synergy between anticancer agents: A case of Dorothy and the ruby slippers? *J. Natl. Cancer Inst.*, 88, 11, 699–700, 1996.

81. Roell, K.R., Reif, D.M., Motsinger-Reif, A.A., An introduction to terminology and methodology of chemical synergy-perspectives from across disciplines. *Front. Pharmacol.*, 8, 158, 2017.

82. Gibbs, B.K. and Sourbier, C., Detecting the potential pharmacological synergy of drug combination by viability assays *in vitro*. *Methods Mol. Biol. (Clifton, N.J.)*, 1709, 129–137, 2018.

83. Mayr, A., Klambauer, G., Unterthiner, T., Hochreiter, S., DeepTox: Toxicity prediction using deep learning. *Front. Environ. Sci.*, 3, 80, 2016. https://doi.org/10.3389/ fenvs.2015.00080.

84. Madani Tonekaboni, S.A., Soltan Ghoraie, L., Manem, V.S.K., Haibe-Kains, B., Predictive approaches for drug combination discovery in cancer. *Briefings Bioinf.*, 19, 2, 263–276, 2018.

85. Avorn, J., The $2.6 billion pill—methodologic and policy considerations. *N. Engl. J. Med.*, 372, 20, 1877–1879, 2015.

86. Mullard, A., FDA drug approvals. *Nat. Rev. Drug Discov.*, 16, 2, 73–76, 2017.

87. Tan, S.Y. and Grimes, S., Paul Ehrlich (1854–1915): Man, with the magic bullet. *Singapore Med. J.*, 51, 11, 842–843, 2010.

88. Greene, J.A. and Loscalzo, J., Putting the patient back together—social medicine, network medicine, and the limits of reductionism. *N. Engl. J. Med.*, 377, 25, 2493–2499, 2017.

89. Mathers, C., The global burden of disease: 2004 update. *World Health Organization, 2008. (Available at: https://www.who.int/publications/i/item/9789241563710)

90. Hyman, S.E., Revolution stalled. *Sci. Trans. Med.*, 4, 155, 155cm111, 2012.

91. Kambeitz, J., Kambeitz-Ilankovic, L., Leucht, S. *et al.*, Detecting neuroimaging biomarkers for schizophrenia: A meta-analysis of multivariate pattern recognition studies. *Neuropsychopharmacology*, 40, 7, 1742–1751, 2015.

92. Rajula, H. S. R., Verlato, G., Manchia, M., Antonucci, N., Fanos, V., Comparison of conventional statistical methods with machine learning in medicine: Diagnosis, drug development, and treatment. *Medicina*, 56, 9, 455, 2020.

93. Schnack, H.G., Improving individual predictions: Machine learning approaches for detecting and attacking heterogeneity in schizophrenia (and other psychiatric diseases). *Schizophr. Res.*, 214, 34–42, 2019.

94. Tandon, N. and Tandon, R., Using machine learning to explain the heterogeneity of schizophrenia. Realizing the promise and avoiding the hype. *Schizophr. Res.*, 214, 70–75, 2019.

95. Talpalaru, A., Bhagwat, N., Devenyi, G.A., Lepage, M., Chakravarty, M.M., Identifying schizophrenia subgroups using clustering and supervised learning. *Schizophr. Res.*, 214, 51–59, 2019.

96. Mothi, S.S., Sudarshan, M., Tandon, N. *et al.*, Machine learning improved classification of psychoses using clinical and biological stratification: Update from the bipolar-schizophrenia network for intermediate phenotypes (B-SNIP). *Schizophr. Res.*, 214, 60–69, 2019.

97. Tian, S., Sun, Y., Shao, J. *et al.*, Predicting escitalopram monotherapy response in depression: The role of anterior cingulate cortex. *Hum. Brain Mapp.*, 41, 5, 1249–1260, 2019.

98. Koutsouleris, N., Kahn, R.S., Chekroud, A.M. *et al.*, Multisite prediction of 4-week and 52-week treatment outcomes in patients with first-episode psychosis: A machine learning approach. *Lancet Psychiatry*, 3, 10, 935–946, 2016.

99. Chekroud, A.M., Zotti, R.J., Shehzad, Z. *et al.*, Cross-trial prediction of treatment outcome in depression: A machine learning approach. *Lancet Psychiatry*, 3, 3, 243–250, 2016.

100. Chekroud, A.M., Gueorguieva, R., Krumholz, H.M., Trivedi, M.H., Krystal, J.H., McCarthy, G., Re-evaluating the efficacy and predictability of antidepressant treatments: A symptom clustering approach. *JAMA Psychiatry*, 74, 4, 370–378, 2017.

101. Chang, B., Choi, Y., Jeon, M. *et al.*, ARP Net: Antidepressant response prediction network for major depressive disorder. *Genes (Basel)*, 10, 11, 2019.

102. Reeve, A., Simcox, E., Turnbull, D., Ageing and Parkinson's disease: Why is advancing age the biggest risk factor? *Ageing Res. Rev.*, 14, 19–30, 2014.

103. Glaab, E., Computational systems biology approaches for Parkinson's disease. *Cell Tissue Res.*, 373, 1, 91–109, 2018.

104. Pinto, M., Fernandes, C., Martins, E. *et al.*, Boosting drug discovery for Parkinson's: Enhancement of the delivery of a monoamine oxidase-B inhibitor by brain-targeted PEGylated polycaprolactone-based nanoparticles. *Pharmaceutics*, 11, 7, 331, 2019.

105. Goedert, M. and Spillantini, M.G., A century of Alzheimer's disease. *Science*, 314, 5800, 777–781, 2006.

106. Taylor, J.P., Hardy, J., Fischbeck, K.H., Toxic proteins in neurodegenerative disease. *Science*, 296, 5575, 1991–1995, 2002.

107. Misra, S. and Medhi, B., Drug development status for Alzheimer's disease: Present scenario. *Neurol. Sci.*, 34, 6, 831–839, 2013.

108. Cummings, J.L., Morstorf, T., Zhong, K., Alzheimer's disease drug-development pipeline: Few candidates, frequent failures. *Alzheimer's Res. & Ther.*, 6, 4, 37, 2014.

109. Sügis, E., Dauvillier, J., Leontjeva, A. *et al.*, HENA, heterogeneous network-based data set for Alzheimer's disease. *Sci. Data*, 6, 1, 151, 2019.

110. Schneider, G., Mind and machine in drug design. *Nat. Mach. Intell.*, 1, 3, 128–130, 2019.

111. Nadar, S., Devi, A., Jain, R., Al-Turjman, F., Use of artificial intelligence in pharmacovigilance for social media network, in: *Leveraging Artificial Intelligence in Global Epidemics*, pp. 239–259, Academic Press, United States, 2021.

9

Machine Learning Applications for Drug Repurposing

Bancha Yingngam

Department of Pharmaceutical Chemistry and Technology, Faculty of Pharmaceutical Sciences, Ubon Ratchathani University, Ubon Ratchathani, Thailand

Abstract

Machine learning (ML) is revolutionizing drug repurposing, offering a more efficient, cost-effective approach to drug discovery by identifying new therapeutic uses for existing drugs. ML algorithms process large, complex biomedical datasets, find hidden patterns that reveal unexpected links between drugs and diseases, and predict potential side effects. This advancement holds significant promise for precision medicine and personalized healthcare. This chapter aims to explore the growing role of ML in drug repurposing, an emergent frontier that aims to identify new therapeutic uses for existing drugs, thereby accelerating the pace of medical innovation while mitigating cost and risk. The chapter discusses various case studies, demonstrating the application of ML in identifying drug–disease connections and predicting adverse drug reactions, significantly contributing to precision medicine. In addition, the chapter investigates the successes and challenges encountered in this nascent field, highlighting the potential of ML to modernize drug discovery. Emphasis is placed on the ethical and privacy concerns surrounding the use of patient data in ML models, urging the need for robust regulations. This comprehensive review serves as a practical guide for those at the intersection of pharmaceutical research, clinical practice, and computer sciences, advocating for the synergetic use of these fields in advancing healthcare.

Keywords: Artificial intelligence, biomedical data integration, drug discovery, drug repurposing, machine learning, precision medicine

List of Abbreviations

AI   artificial intelligence
GISTs   gastrointestinal stromal tumors
FDA   Food and Drug Administration
ML   machine learning
PDE5   phosphodiesterase type 5
RdRp   RNA-dependent RNA polymerase

Email: bancha.y@ubu.ac.th

Abhirup Khanna, May El Barachi, Sapna Jain, Manoj Kumar and Anand Nayyar (eds.) Artificial Intelligence and Machine Learning in Drug Design and Development, (251–294) © 2024 Scrivener Publishing LLC

9.1   Introduction

The prolonged and costly process of novel therapeutic drug discovery, which often exceeds a decade and costs billions, poses substantial challenges for the pharmaceutical industry [1]. As a result, more efficient strategies are needed, one of which is drug repurposing or repositioning. This strategy focuses on finding new uses for existing drugs and offers several advantages over traditional drug development pathways [2]. Repurposed drugs, having already undergone safety and bioavailability testing in humans, can reach clinical use for new indications faster, less expensively, and with higher success rates [3]. Their known safety profiles and pharmacokinetic and pharmacodynamic properties substantially lower the risk of failure [4]. Moreover, drug repurposing plays a crucial role in personalized medicine by facilitating tailored treatments based on a comprehensive understanding of individual disease mechanisms, thereby improving therapeutic success and patient outcomes [5].

The increasing rate of new disease discovery and the prevalence of untreatable orphan diseases underscores the importance of drug repurposing [6]. Creating new treatments from scratch is often untenable due to significant time and cost implications [7]. Drug repurposing, however, offers a quicker, more cost-effective alternative. The growing understanding of the genetic origins of illnesses reveals that many share molecular mechanisms [8]. Hence, a drug formulated for one disease might be useful for another with similar genetic or molecular traits. This notion aligns well with the shift toward precision medicine, which focuses on personalized treatments based on individual patient's genetic and molecular makeup [9]. Despite its promise, drug repurposing poses challenges, especially in identifying viable drug–disease combinations among the numerous possibilities [10]. Here advancements in machine learning (ML) and artificial intelligence (AI) play a transformative role [11]. The surge in available biomedical data, coupled with modern computational techniques, has birthed innovative methods for identifying promising drug–disease pairs [12]. ML algorithms excel at identifying complex data patterns, predicting outcomes, and revealing hidden relationships, making them aptly suited for tackling drug repurposing challenges [13].

Objectives of the Chapter

The objectives of this chapter are as follows:

(i)   To explore various machine learning (ML) techniques used in drug repurposing, ranging from traditional methods such as supervised and unsupervised learning to advanced approaches such as deep learning and reinforcement learning;

(ii)   To discuss the challenges encountered in applying ML to drug repurposing, including issues related to data availability, data quality, model interpretability, and the necessity for experimental validation of model predictions;

(iii)   And, to equip readers with a comprehensive understanding of how ML is revolutionizing drug repurposing, thereby contributing to a more efficient and personalized healthcare domain.

Organization of the Chapter

The rest of the chapter is organized as follows: Section 9.2, "Trends in ML Applications for Drug Repurposing", sets the stage by defining the problem statement and highlighting the crucial role of ML applications in drug repurposing. Following this, Section 9.3, "Understanding Drug Repurposing", undertakes a detailed examination of the necessity for drug repurposing, offering insights into its potential benefits and existing challenges. The subsequent Section 9.4, "Traditional Techniques in Drug Repurposing", investigates the conventional methodologies applied in drug repurposing, establishing a solid foundation for comprehending the ensuring role of ML. Section 9.5, "Modern Technologies in Drug Repurposing", presents an extensive introduction to the employment of ML techniques in the domain. This includes an in-depth discussion on data mining, bioinformatics, network pharmacology, and innovative applications of ML and AI in drug repurposing. Section 9.6 highlights diverse "Data Sources for Drug Repurposing", while Section 9.7 is devoted to "Case Studies: Applications of ML in Drug Repurposing". Section 9.8, "Challenges and Future Directions", identifies current limitations and obstacles in the field and proposes potential future developments. And, finally, section 9.9 concludes the chapter with future scope.

9.2 Trends in ML Applications for Drug Repurposing

Investigating trends in ML for drug repurposing promises substantial potential to accelerate therapeutic breakthroughs and improve patient care. Superior to traditional drug development in time and cost efficiency, this approach enhances the predictability of effective drug–disease pairings. Analyzing these trends offers valuable insights into how AI might revolutionize drug discovery, foster innovation, and personalize healthcare. This study also reveals challenges and opportunities in this field, directing future research, technology investments, and healthcare policies. Its significance lies in fostering precision medicine and advancing disease treatment strategies.

9.2.1 Global Research on ML Applications in Drug Repurposing

To fully understand the current trends in ML applications for drug repurposing, a literature review using the Scopus database is conducted. Chosen for its interdisciplinary reach and broad coverage of both technology- and healthcare-related academic literature, Scopus enabled a comprehensive overview of the field. The initial phase involved judicious keyword selection, including "artificial intelligence", "machine learning", "drug repurposing", and "drug repositioning". These keywords, representative of the study's central theme, ensured the precision of the research area in the search query. Boolean operators—namely, AND, OR, and NOT—were tactically employed to construct robust and comprehensive search queries. The query ("machine learning" OR "artificial intelligence") AND ("drug repurposing" OR "drug repositioning") was used to ensure that the retrieved literature intersected the domains of ML and drug repurposing. Further refinement of the search results was achieved through the application of relevant filters, including prioritizing more recent works to reflect current trends, limiting results to English-language publications for the convenience of review, and focusing on research and review articles while excluding non-peer-reviewed content. Following the procurement of the search results, a systematic review was conducted. This was followed by a comprehensive full-text review of the remaining papers, examining their methodologies, results, and conclusions. The final phase entailed backward and forward citation tracing on relevant papers, capturing a broader spectrum of research and ensuring that seminal works of significant influence were not overlooked. The data extracted from each paper were synthesized to identify discernible patterns, offering valuable insights into the contemporary trends in ML applications for drug repurposing.

Figure 9.1 depicts the publication trends associated with ML applications for drug repurposing. The data, extracted from the Scopus database, span from January 1, 2000 to July 23, 2023. The results identified 1,007 documents pertinent to this field in various formats. This includes 524 research articles, 274 review articles, 68 book chapters, 60 conference papers, 40 editorials, 15 notes, 9 conference reviews, 8 short surveys, 6 letters, 2 books, and 1 erratum. The publication trend during this period revealed two distinct phases. The initial phase began in 2009 and continued until 2017, after which an exponential growth phase was observed. The year 2022 marked a peak, with a record 265 documents published. While the data for 2023 are not yet complete, they already show a significant number of documents (109 as of July 23, 2023). These trends provide valuable insights into the evolving interest and research activities within the application of ML for drug repurposing. The initial phase, from 2009 to 2017, represents a period of exploration when the potential of ML in this area was gradually recognized and examined. The modest number of publications prior to 2018 indicates the relative infancy of this field during the early 2010s. The publication surge since 2018 signifies a significant growth in interest in the use of ML for drug repurposing, marking the start of the exponential phase. This trend could be attributed to factors such as the increasing accessibility and advancement of ML techniques, the growing recognition of their potential in drug discovery, and the emergent need for more efficient drug repurposing strategies. The significant increase in publications in 2022 further emphasizes the escalating importance and prevalence of this research area. Preliminary data for 2023 suggest sustained or potentially increasing interest, although definitive conclusions

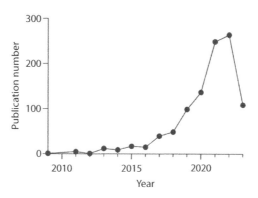

Figure 9.1 Publication trends of machine learning for drug repurposing from January 1, 2000, to July 23, 2023: A Scopus database analysis.

for this year will have to wait until year-end. Notably, research articles constitute more than half of the total documents (approximately 52%), indicating active and ongoing scientific exploration in this field. Review articles, which make up approximately 27% of the total, demonstrate a substantial level of summary and evaluation activity, often associated with mature and expanding fields. The current trend suggests that this research area will continue to grow and develop in the coming years. Further studies could investigate the impact of these publications and understand their influence on the field and the practical outcomes achieved to date.

The comprehensive analysis of the Scopus database pertaining to publication trends in ML for drug repurposing revealed geographical discrepancies in the quantity of research contributions. As illustrated in Figure 9.2, the study identified the top 10 contributing nations, collectively accounting for a substantial share of the global output. The United States spearheaded the research, producing 322 documents, followed by China and India, with 187 and 146 documents, respectively. Subsequent contributions were from the United Kingdom and Italy, with 97 and 53 documents, respectively. Canada produced 51 documents, Germany 47, and South Korea and Spain each contributed 37 documents. France completed the list with 28 documents. The remaining contributions came from various other countries. These findings highlight a concentration of research activities within certain nations, indicative of global trends in ML for drug repurposing research. The leadership of the United States underscores its robust research infrastructure and significant investments in the ML and drug discovery fields. The high output from China and India, ranking second and third, reflects their rapid advancements and investments in technology and healthcare research. The significant contributions from the United Kingdom and other European countries, such as Italy, Germany, Spain, and France, suggest an active research landscape, possibly bolstered by interinstitutional collaborations and extensive governmental and institutional support. The inclusion of Canada and South Korea among the top contributors emphasizes the global reach of this research field and the worldwide recognition of the potential of ML in drug repurposing. It is worth noting the geographical diversity of the contributors, spanning Western and Eastern countries, indicating wide-ranging interest

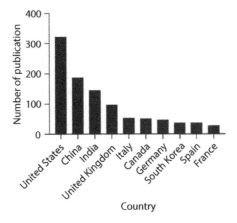

Figure 9.2 Distribution of publications on machine learning for drug repurposing among the top 10 countries from 1 January 2000 to 23 July 2023. The data are derived from a comprehensive analysis of the Scopus database.

in ML for drug repurposing. This diversity may foster varied perspectives and methodologies in the field, potentially stimulating innovation and advancement. However, the evident disparities in contributions among countries could highlight unequal resource access, variations in national research priorities, or infrastructural or policy-related constraints. Encouraging more equitable international collaboration is vital to spreading knowledge, sharing resources, and ensuring global advancement in using ML for drug repurposing. Future research could explore the impact of these publications by country and the collaborative networks between these nations to further understand the global landscape of ML for drug repurposing research.

9.2.2   Cluster Analysis of ML Applications in Drug Repurposing

In this section, VOS viewer tool is utilized to visualize and analyze significant bibliometric networks. This tool is known for its user-friendly interface, making it easier for researchers to identify and explore academic publishing trends. It facilitates the mapping of keywords, authors, and institutions, enabling the identification of trending topics, prolific authors, and influential institutions in a specific field [14, 15]. In this context, a keyword co-occurrence network analysis was carried out using the VOS viewer version 1.6.16 tool, providing critical insights into the research focus within the ML applications for the drug repurposing field (Figure 9.3). Out of 10,453 keywords, 1,999 met the minimum occurrence threshold of five. These keywords formed five distinct clusters, each signifying a specific research emphasis. Cluster 1 (green, 429 items) mainly concentrated on computational biology, data mining, drug–target interactions, and the drug discovery process. This suggests a strong emphasis on computational and ML algorithmic approaches in drug interactions, discovery and repurposing. Cluster 2 (red, 247 items) highlighted the use of ML to explore drug mechanisms of action at the molecular level (*via* gene expression). This indicates a drive to leverage ML technologies to deepen the understanding of drug action, potentially enhancing drug repurposing precision and efficacy. Cluster 3 (blue, 205 items) emphasized the use of ML for antiviral drugs, reflecting a consistent interest in utilizing computational methods to quicken and improve antiviral drug discovery and repurposing, possibly driven by the recent pandemic crisis (COVID-19). Cluster 4 (yellow, 184 items) focused on molecular docking and bioassays. This hints at a rising interest in using ML methodologies to supplement laboratory-based assessments and preclinical evaluations, which are crucial stages in drug development and repurposing. Finally, Cluster 5 (purple, 134 items) was characterized by an emphasis on applying AI and ML for clinical decision-making, clinical studies, and adverse outcome investigations. This underlines the potential of ML technologies to transform clinical practice, aid clinical research, and enhance the prediction and understanding of adverse drug reactions.

9.2.3   Research Trends in ML Applications for Drug Repurposing

As depicted in Figure 9.4, the application of ML for drug repurposing, particularly within the contexts of therapeutics and precision medicine, represents a significant and rapidly evolving research trend. This trend effectively integrates with the objectives of precision medicine, which seeks to deliver the right treatment to the right patient at the right time.

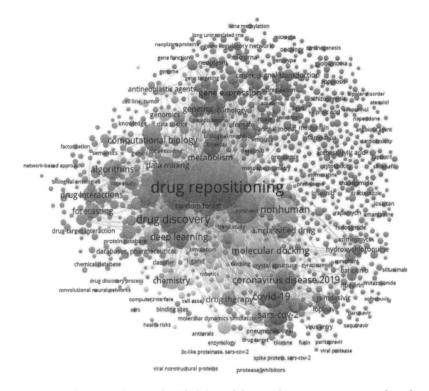

Figure 9.3 Clustering of research themes identified through keyword co-occurrence network analysis. The network was generated using VOS viewer v. 1.6.16 based on the literature included in Scopus spanning the period between 2000 and 2023. Each cluster represents a distinct research theme within the field of machine learning for drug repurposing.

A prime example of this trend is the repurposing of antiviral drugs for COVID-19 treatment, catalyzed by the urgency posed by the pandemic. Researchers have employed ML algorithms to scan the vast array of existing antiviral drugs to pinpoint potential treatments for COVID-19—for instance, ML algorithms can anticipate potential drug–target interactions based on the genetic sequence of SARS-CoV-2, the virus responsible for COVID-19, thereby identifying antiviral drugs that could inhibit the virus and expedite the development of effective treatments for this novel disease. In the realm of cancer research, ML is being utilized to analyze genetic, transcriptomic, proteomic, and pharmacological data to identify drugs that can be repurposed for specific types of cancer. These drugs could potentially target cancer-specific genetic or molecular aberrations, thereby providing more precise and effective treatments. In the case of diabetes and neurodegenerative disorders, ML is employed to predict patient responses to different treatments on the basis of their unique genetic, epigenetic and physiological profiles, facilitating the identification of potentially repurposable drugs for individual patients. Furthermore, in the field of rare or orphan diseases, ML has shown considerable promise in identifying potential treatments. The development of drugs for these conditions is often constrained due to a lack of financial incentives and small patient populations. Here drug repurposing serves as a time- and cost-efficient solution by identifying new uses for existing drugs. In summary, the trend of utilizing ML for drug repurposing in precision medicine holds significant potential to revolutionize

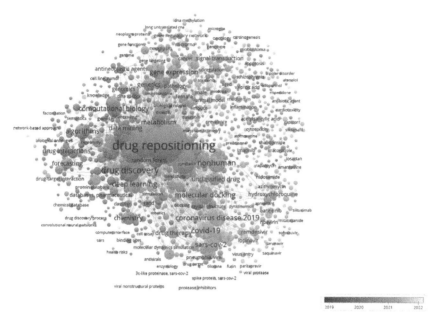

Figure 9.4 Research trends in the application of machine learning for drug repurposing, derived from keyword co-occurrence network analysis. This illustration was created using VOS viewer v. 1.6.16, utilizing literature from Scopus from the period between 2000 and 2023.

patient care, leading to more personalized and effective treatments, particularly for diseases that currently lack effective therapies. However, it is imperative to emphasize that while promising, this field is complex and challenging. Candidates for drug repurposing identified through ML must still undergo stringent preclinical and clinical testing to ascertain their safety and efficacy.

9.3   Understanding Drug Repurposing

The pharmaceutical industry is continuously in search of novel treatments for a range of diseases. The traditional method, known as *de novo* drug discovery, involves developing entirely new drugs. However, this approach is lengthy, costly, and risky. In contrast, drug repurposing is the practice of finding new uses for existing drugs. These drugs can already be on the market or be those that failed their initial target but have proven safe in phase I clinical trials [1]. The goal is to discover therapeutic uses beyond the original medical indication [2]. Drug repurposing has emerged as a promising and efficient alternative to traditional methods. Interestingly, approximately 30% of all drugs approved by the Food and Drug Administration (FDA) are repurposed, contributing significantly to the global pharmaceutical industry's total revenue (25%) [16–18]. To streamline this process further, bioinformatics-based tools have been developed for the rapid analysis of thousands of drugs. The comparative timeline of *de novo* drug discovery and drug repurposing is shown in Figure 9.5. *De novo* drug discovery involves initial discovery,

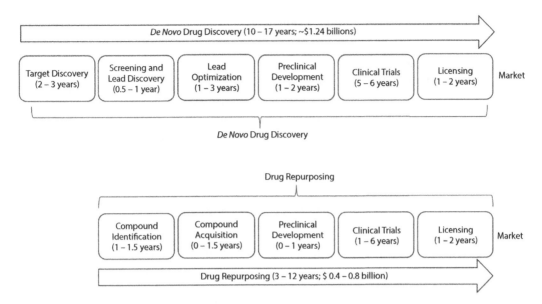

Figure 9.5 Comparative timeline illustrating the speed and efficiency of *de novo* drug discovery *versus* drug repurposing.

preclinical testing, clinical trials, and finally FDA approval [1]. This lengthy process can span years or even decades and costs an average of 1.2–2.8 billion dollars to bring a new drug to market [19, 20]. Conversely, drug repurposing significantly reduces the overall time required for approval of a new use (3–12 years), as these drugs have already passed several initial testing stages [21].

9.4 Traditional Techniques in Drug Repurposing

This section discusses the concept of drug repurposing and its growing relevance in modern medicine. Initially, the traditional methods of drug repurposing, such as serendipity, *in vitro* and phenotypic screening, side effect analysis, and off-label use are explored. The advantages and drawbacks of each technique are examined to provide a comprehensive understanding. The discussion then transitions to a growing trend: the shift from these traditional methods to data-driven approaches. Thanks to the rise of big data and ML, drug repositioning is experiencing a significant shift, opening new avenues for faster, more efficient, and potentially superior drug discovery.

9.4.1 Serendipity

Serendipity in drug repurposing is the unplanned discovery of a new application for a drug while it is being used or tested for its primary intended purpose. This less systematic approach often depends on chance or unexpected observations made by observant researchers or clinicians [22]. Despite the unpredictability of this method, serendipity has led to many significant breakthroughs in drug repurposing. Table 9.1 illustrates examples

Table 9.1 Examples of repurposing drugs approved for other indications based on the serendipity approach.

Drug name	Original indication	Indication	Description	Reference
Sildenafil (Viagra)	Angina (chest pain due to reduced blood flow to the heart)	Erectile dysfunction	During clinical trials for angina, male patients report improved erectile function, which led to the repurposing of sildenafil for erectile dysfunction.	[4]
Thalidomide	Sedative/morning sickness	Erythema nodosum leprosum and multiple myeloma	Initially withdrawn due to severe birth defects, it was later discovered to be effective in treating erythema nodosum leprosum, a skin condition associated with leprosy, and multiple myeloma, a type of cancer.	[4]
Minoxidil	Hypertension (high blood pressure)	Hair loss (alopecia)	Originally used to treat hypertension, minoxidil was repurposed for hair loss treatment after patients observed increased hair growth as a side effect.	[27, 28]
Propranolol	Angina and hypertension	Stage fright (performance anxiety)	Propranolol, a b-blocker used for cardiovascular conditions, was found to alleviate symptoms of stage fright due to its effect on the nervous system.	[4]
Aspirin	Pain relief	Prevention of heart attacks and strokes	Originally a pain reliever, aspirin was found to have anti-clotting properties that could prevent heart attacks and strokes, leading to its repurposing for these indications.	[4, 28]
Botulinum toxin (Botox)	Muscle spasms	Wrinkle reduction	Initially, used for treating muscle spasms, Botox was repurposed for cosmetic uses when patients noticed a reduction in wrinkles after treatment.	[4, 29]

of drugs repurposed based on the serendipity approach. The table lists the original and new uses of these drugs, providing a brief explanation of each repurposing process. In this case, an example of drug repurposing for the treatment of erectile dysfunction is discussed. Erectile dysfunction, the inability to achieve or maintain an erection sufficient for satisfactory sexual performance, is a prevalent condition affecting millions of men worldwide. The Massachusetts Male Aging Study suggests that approximately 52% of men aged 40 to 70 experience some form of erectile dysfunction [23]. Predictions suggest that the worldwide prevalence of erectile dysfunction will increase substantially by 2025, largely owing to an aging population and a rising incidence of conditions such as diabetes and cardiovascular disease, which are closely linked to erectile dysfunction. Current treatments include lifestyle changes, oral medications (such as sildenafil, vardenafil, or tadalafil), vacuum erection devices, penile injections, and penile implants. However, these treatments might not work for everyone and can have side effects. Therefore, drug repurposing can play a significant role in discovering new treatments for this condition. A significant example of successful drug repurposing is sildenafil (Figure 9.6), commonly known as Viagra [24]. Pfizer originally developed sildenafil in the late 1980s to treat angina pectoris (chest pain due to heart disease) and high blood pressure. It functions as a phosphodiesterase type 5 (PDE5) inhibitor, which blocks the PDE5 enzyme. In the context of angina and high blood pressure, the indication was to widen the blood vessels to improve blood flow to the heart [25]. However, during early 1990s clinical trials, sildenafil did not prove very effective for angina. Many male participants reported an unexpected side effect instead: improved erections. The drug enhanced blood flow not only to the heart but also to the penis, facilitating men's ability to achieve and maintain an erection. Recognizing this potential, Pfizer decided to repurpose the drug to treat erectile dysfunction. Following a series of additional clinical trials to confirm its efficacy and safety for this use, the FDA approved sildenafil in 1998. As the first oral medication approved for erectile dysfunction, sildenafil has since helped millions of men with the condition [26]. Sildenafil is now one of the most well-known treatments for erectile dysfunction, and its discovery fundamentally transformed the understanding and treatment of this condition.

Thalidomide serves as another notable example of drug repurposing. Initially, marketed as a sedative and morning sickness, the drug was withdrawn due to severe birth defects. However, it was subsequently found to be effective in treating erythema nodosum leprosum, a skin condition associated with leprosy, and multiple myeloma, a type of cancer. Additional instances of serendipitous drug repurposing can be found in the stories of

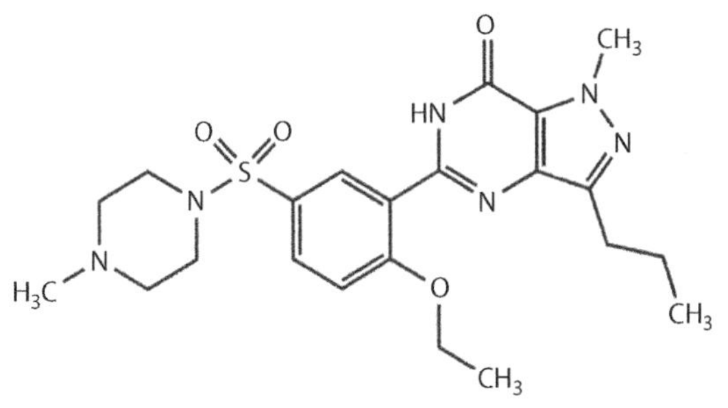

Figure 9.6 Chemical structure of sildenafil (ChemDraw 20.1.1).

minoxidil, propranolol, aspirin, and botulinum toxin (Botox), each with its own unique journey. These cases, from the accidental discovery of minoxidil's hair growth stimulation and propranolol's calming effects to the expanded roles of aspirin and Botox, highlight the unpredictable yet significant potential of drug repurposing [4]. However, it is important to note that despite these success stories, serendipity is neither a reliable nor scalable method due to its dependence on chance. Consequently, in the modern era, there has been a shift toward more systematic, scalable, and data-driven methods. These contemporary approaches can accelerate the drug repurposing process, increase efficiency and offer a more predictable path to discovery.

9.4.2 *In Vitro* Screening

In vitro screening is a fundamental technique traditionally employed in drug repurposing. The term *in vitro*, Latin for "in glass", refers to experiments conducted outside a living organism, typically in a controlled laboratory environment, such as a test tube or petri dish. This method entails screening existing drugs against cell lines (groups of cells that originate from a single cell and share the same genetic makeup) or biological targets associated with a disease of interest. The aim is to determine whether these drugs exhibit any potential activity against the disease. Numerous instances of successful drug repurposing have originated from *in vitro* screening. Azidothymidine (AZT), for instance, was initially developed as a cancer drug in the 1960s (Table 9.2). Through *in vitro* testing, it was found to inhibit human immunodeficiency virus (HIV) replication, paving the way for its repurposing for HIV treatment. AZT, also known as zidovudine, became the first approved antiretroviral drug for the treatment of HIV/AIDS following further testing [30].

Similarly, imatinib (Gleevec) was initially developed and approved for treating chronic myeloid leukemia, a type of blood cancer. This was due to its ability to inhibit a specific protein, BCR-ABL tyrosine kinase, that fuels the growth of these cancer cells. *In vitro* screening

Table 9.2 Examples of repurposed drugs approved for other indications based on the *in vitro* screening approach.

Original drug	Initial indication	*In vitro* observation	Repurposed indication	Reference
Azidothymidine (AZT)	Cancer	Inhibition of HIV (human immunodeficiency virus) replication in cell lines	HIV treatment	[30]
Imatinib (Gleevec)	Leukemia	Inhibition of certain protein tyrosine kinases in cancer cell lines	Gastrointestinal stromal tumors, other cancers	[32]
Disulfiram (Antabuse)	Alcohol dependence	Inhibition of cancer cell growth and viability in cell lines	Cancer (in experimental stages)	[34]

revealed that imatinib also inhibits other tyrosine kinases, including c-KIT, which is often overly active in gastrointestinal stromal tumors (GISTs), a rare cancer type. This led to the successful repurposing of imatinib for GIST treatment [31, 32]. Additionally, disulfiram (antabuse), originally approved for treating alcohol dependence, was shown to inhibit the growth and viability of cancer cells through *in vitro* screening experiments. This result indicated its potential repurposing for cancer treatment. This repurposing is still experimental, and more research is needed to determine its effectiveness and safety for this new use in humans [33].

Despite these successes, the *in vitro* screening approach has certain limitations. It can be an expensive and time-consuming process. Additionally, a drug's effectiveness in a test tube or petri dish does not necessarily translate to its effectiveness in a complex living organism. The drug must safely and effectively reach the target site in the body. *In vitro* processes often yield a high rate of false positives, wherein a drug appears to be effective *in vitro* but fails to demonstrate the same effect *in vivo*. For these reasons, while *in vitro* screening can generate valuable initial insights and hypotheses, it is typically just one aspect of a larger drug discovery and repurposing process. Positive *in vitro* results require validation through further testing, often involving *in vivo* studies in animal models followed by human trials.

9.4.3   Phenotypic Screening

Phenotypic screening is a traditional drug discovery and repurposing technique that has played a crucial role in identifying numerous therapeutic agents. Unlike target-based screening, which begins with a known biological target such as a protein or gene and seeks drugs that interact with it, phenotypic screening commences without a predefined target. This approach involves observing phenotypic changes—variations in the observable physical or biochemical characteristics of an organism resulting from the interaction between genotype and environment—elicited by a drug in a biological system. This system might be a cell line, a group of cells, tissue samples, or even an entire organism [35].

For instance, researchers might administer a drug to cancer cells and observe whether it inhibits their growth, or they could give the drug to a zebrafish or mouse and monitor the animal for any changes. In the context of drug repurposing, a phenotypic screening approach would involve testing an approved drug or a collection of approved drugs in disease models to observe any beneficial effects. If a drug induces a favorable change in phenotype, it may be considered for repurposing to treat the disease modeled. Phenotypic screening can identify drugs that are effective in complex biological systems, irrespective of the mechanism of action. This is particularly valuable in diseases where the underlying molecular mechanisms are not fully understood. However, a significant challenge with this method is that once a potential drug is identified, substantial effort is often required to decipher its mechanism of action, i.e., how it produces the observed effect. Additionally, phenotypic screening can be resource intensive, as it requires disease models and specialized assays. It may not always accurately represent the disease environment in humans, especially when using *in vitro* models. Amantadine serves as a notable example of a drug that was repurposed through phenotypic screening. Originally developed as an antiviral, it was found to alleviate symptoms of Parkinson's disease through observations of patient symptoms—a type of phenotype—and is now used as a treatment for this condition [36].

9.4.4 Side Effect Analysis

Side effect analysis is another method used in drug repurposing that involves monitoring the unforeseen effects of drugs on patients. While side effects are typically perceived as negative or unwanted, they can occasionally offer insights into additional therapeutic uses of a drug. The fundamental idea is that if a drug induces a specific effect in a patient, it could hint at the drug's interaction with a biological mechanism associated with that effect. Investigating these interactions can potentially reveal new applications for the drug—for example, minoxidil was initially approved to treat high blood pressure, but it was observed to stimulate hair growth, an unexpected side effect. This observation led to the successful repurposing of minoxidil as a topical treatment for hair loss. Today, it is widely sold under various brand names, including Rogaine [37]. However, the limitations of side effect analysis must be recognized. Side effects can be unpredictable and may not be beneficial or even desirable for all patients. Indeed managing or minimizing side effects is often necessary, as they can cause discomfort or pose health risks. Furthermore, not all side effects lead to beneficial new applications. Despite these challenges, with proper management, side effect analysis can significantly contribute to successful drug repurposing. The increasing availability of big data on drug effects, coupled with advancements in computational methods, indicates that systematic, large-scale analysis of side effects could unveil more opportunities for drug repurposing.

9.4.5 Biochemical Assay

Biochemical assays are tests performed to measure the presence or activity of a substance, such as a drug, within a biological sample, typically at the molecular level. In the context of drug repurposing, these assays are used to explore whether an existing drug can interact with a specific target protein or pathway implicated in a disease different from the one the drug was initially designed to treat—for example, if a protein is identified as a key contributor to a disease, a biochemical assay can be utilized to examine whether an existing drug can bind to that protein or inhibit its activity. This approach is based on the understanding that drugs produce their effects by interacting with specific molecules in the body, thereby modifying their behavior or function. If a drug is found to interact with a target associated with a different disease, it could potentially be repurposed to treat that disease. A prime example of successful drug repurposing using a biochemical assay is the case of imatinib. Initially developed to target a specific type of tyrosine kinase enzyme in chronic myeloid leukemia, biochemical assays revealed that imatinib also inhibits the activity of another tyrosine kinase associated with gastrointestinal stromal tumors. This led to the successful repurposing of imatinib for treating GISTs [38]. However, similar to other methods, the biochemical assay approach has limitations. It necessitates a comprehensive understanding of the disease's biology and the specific target, which is not always available for all diseases. Furthermore, while a drug may interact with a disease target in an assay, this does not guarantee that the drug will effectively fight the disease in a living organism. Given that assay conditions can significantly differ from conditions within the human body, the results derived from biochemical assays must always be validated through further preclinical and clinical tests.

9.4.6   Off-Label Use

Off-label use refers to the use of pharmaceutical drugs for an indication, age group, dosage, or route of administration that has not been officially approved [39]. Regulatory agencies such as the U.S. FDA and the European Medicines Agency (EMA) are responsible for approving drugs for specific indications. However, once a drug is approved, physicians are at liberty to prescribe it off-label if they deem it beneficial for their patients [40]. In the context of drug repurposing, off-label use can provide valuable insights into potential new applications for existing drugs. Physicians may observe that a drug, when used off-label, yields a beneficial effect on a condition or disease that differs from its original approved indication. This observation could prompt further research, potentially leading to formal approval for the new use.

A well-known instance of drug repurposing through off-label use is the case of aspirin. Originally developed for pain relief, physicians noticed its blood-thinning properties and began prescribing it off-label to prevent heart attacks and strokes. This off-label use was later supported by clinical studies, leading to its widespread use and official approval for this purpose. Nonetheless, off-label use is not without risks, as the drug has not undergone rigorous testing and regulatory review for off-label indications. This could lead to unforeseen risks or side effects. Therefore, off-label use should be grounded in substantial scientific evidence or informed clinical judgment. While regulatory bodies such as the FDA do not regulate medical practice and thus do not govern physicians' discretion to prescribe drugs off-label, they do monitor communication about off-label use by pharmaceutical companies, which is generally not allowed unless explicitly requested by healthcare professionals. Although off-label use can lead to successful drug repurposing, it is more of an opportunity that arises during medical practice than a systematic approach to drug repurposing.

9.5   Modern Technologies in Drug Repurposing

As the field of drug repurposing evolves, new technologies are being developed and applied to streamline the process. Advances in genomics, bioinformatics, ML, and AI are ushering in a systematic and efficient approach to identifying promising candidates for drug repurposing [9, 41]—for instance, genomics and bioinformatics have revolutionized our understanding of disease pathology. The sequencing of the human genome, coupled with advances in other "omics" technologies such as proteomics and metabolomics, allows us to compare genomic profiles between healthy and diseased individuals. These comparisons could potentially identify new drug targets. Bioinformatics tools then use these "omics" data to analyze and interpret biological information, potentially revealing drug–disease relationships that could be exploited for drug repurposing [42]. Significantly, ML, a subset of AI, comes into play here. ML algorithms can be trained to recognize patterns in large datasets, such as gene expression data, and predict how a drug might affect a disease based on those patterns. Furthermore, AI can process vast amounts of data to explore previously unknown connections between drugs and diseases. It can also predict potential side effects, drug-drug interactions, and patient responses, aiding in the evaluation of a candidate drug for repurposing [43].

Network pharmacology also plays a crucial role. This holistic approach considers the interaction network between drugs and biological systems. This method uses mathematical and computational tools to visualize and analyze these interactions, potentially revealing new targets for existing drugs and thus providing opportunities for drug repurposing [44]. Technological advances have also made high-throughput screening a viable option. This process enables the screening of large libraries of existing drugs against various biological targets or disease models quickly and cost-effectively. It identifies potential repurposing candidates more systematically and on a larger scale than traditional methods [45]. Finally, *in silico* modeling allows for the simulation of interactions between a drug and its potential targets. This enables researchers to predict a drug's effects without costly and time-consuming lab experiments, serving as a preliminary step in identifying potential drug repurposing candidates [46]. Despite the range of technological developments, this chapter will focus specifically on the application of ML in drug repurposing, while other technologies will not be discussed in detail.

9.5.1 Machine Learning

ML is a computational technique that employs algorithms to learn from data and make decisions or predictions without explicit programming. In essence, ML trains a model using large datasets, enabling it to autonomously discern patterns and relationships within the data. This learning process involves feeding an algorithm with training data, which it utilizes to construct a mathematical model. Once trained, this model can make predictions or decisions without human intervention by identifying similar patterns in new, unseen data [47]. ML finds extensive application in a variety of fields, including but not limited to finance, healthcare, marketing, and, increasingly, drug repurposing. Its ability to handle and learn from vast amounts of complex data and apply this knowledge to predict outcomes in new data [48, 49]. This characteristic makes it an excellent tool for tasks such as identifying potential drug candidates, predicting side effects, and uncovering new therapeutic uses for existing drugs. The essence of ML is iterative learning; with each exposure to more data, the model incrementally improves its predictive accuracy. This is similar to human learning, where repetition and experience enhance understanding and skill [50]. In the context of drug repurposing, ML introduces a new level of efficiency and accuracy, significantly bolstering our ability to find innovative and effective uses for existing drugs [5]. Nonetheless, to optimally utilize ML in drug repurposing, it is crucial to understand how it operates, how to interpret its results, and how to manage its limitations. These aspects will be further discussed in subsequent sections.

9.5.2 Machine Learning Methods in Drug Repurposing

This section provides an in-depth look at various ML methodologies employed in drug repurposing studies (Table 9.3). The aim is to highlight the diverse advantages and unique capabilities of these methods, underscoring their pivotal role in unveiling the potential new therapeutic applications of existing drugs. Additionally, it underscores the way ML algorithm complexity can enhance efficiency and predictive accuracy in drug repurposing endeavors.

Table 9.3 Comparison of machine learning techniques for drug repurposing.

Technique	Description	Example applications in drug repurposing	Advantages	Limitations	Reference
Supervised learning	This type of learning involves an algorithm that is trained on a labeled dataset. The algorithm learns a function that maps input data to output data.	It can be used to predict whether a drug can be repurposed based on its features. This is achieved by training the algorithm on a dataset where the labels indicate whether a drug was successfully repurposed.	It can provide accurate and reliable predictions when a large, high-quality labeled dataset is available.	It requires labeled training data. Additionally, it may not generalize well to unseen data if overfitting occurs.	[52]
Unsupervised learning	This type of learning involves an algorithm that is trained on an unlabeled dataset. The goal is to identify patterns or relationships in the data.	It can be used as cluster drugs based on their features, which can indicate potential new uses.	It can identify novel patterns or clusters in the data that may not be apparent with supervised learning.	It can be challenging to interpret the results or to know if the identified patterns are meaningful.	[53]
Semi-supervised learning	Uses both labeled and unlabeled data for training, typically a small amount of labeled data and a large amount of unlabeled data.	It can be used in predicting drug–target interactions or drug–disease associations when only a limited amount of labeled data is available.	Can make good use of data even when labels are scarce, often achieving a higher accuracy than either purely supervised or unsupervised methods.	Requires careful design to ensure that the learning from unlabeled data complements the learning from the labeled data.	[54]

(Continued)

Table 9.3 Comparison of machine learning techniques for drug repurposing. (*Continued*)

Technique	Description	Example applications in drug repurposing	Advantages	Limitations	Reference
Reinforcement learning	This involves an agent that learns to make decisions by taking actions in an environment to maximize some notion of cumulative reward.	It can be used in drug discovery and repurposing to navigate the vast space of possible drug molecules and biological targets.	It can optimize decisions over time and is well suited to problems where the optimal decision-making strategy is complex and not easily captured by traditional methods.	It can require significant computational resources and can be challenging to apply in situations where it is difficult to define a suitable reward function.	[55]
Deep learning	This is a type of ML that involves artificial neural networks with multiple layers	It can be used in a variety of drug repurposing tasks, such as predicting drug–target interactions, generating novel drug candidates, or integrating multimodal data for drug repurposing.	It can model complex, nonlinear relationships and can handle large and complex datasets, including image, text, and sequence data.	It requires large datasets and significant computational resources. The models can also be difficult to interpret.	[56]

Note: The exact details of how these techniques are implemented can vary widely based on the specific problem, dataset, and method used.

9.5.2.1 Supervised Learning

Supervised learning, a subset of ML, involves algorithm learning from labeled training data and then applying this learned relationship to new, unseen data. Each instance in the training dataset comprises an input vector (independent variables) and an expected output value (the label or dependent variable) [51]. The goal is to learn a mapping function from inputs to outputs that can predict outcomes from new data. Familiar supervised learning algorithms include linear regression for regression problems and logistic regression, k-nearest neighbor, support vector machines, and decision trees for classification problems [52]. In the context of drug repurposing, supervised learning plays several roles, such as predicting drug–target interactions and drug–disease associations, as well as classifying drugs based on therapeutic effects. Supervised learning can predict new drug–target interactions, which is often the first step in drug repurposing. The training data can consist of known drug–target pairs (positive examples) and noninteracting drug–target pairs (negative examples), with input features derived from both the drug (e.g., chemical structure, molecular properties) and the target (e.g., protein sequence, structural features). The labels indicate whether each drug–target pair interacts. Another application is predicting new drug–disease associations. Here known drug–disease pairs can serve as positive examples in the training data, with features encompassing drug properties and disease properties such as associated genes and symptoms. The labels indicate whether each drug is known to treat each disease. Supervised learning algorithms can also classify drugs based on their therapeutic effects using known classifications as labels. This enables the repurposing of drugs for new disease areas that require similar therapeutic effects. While these applications underline the potential of supervised learning, the method's success heavily relies on the availability of high-quality labeled training data. Nevertheless, given the availability of such data, supervised learning can serve as a powerful tool for predicting new uses for existing drugs, thereby expediting the drug repurposing process.

9.5.2.2   Unsupervised Learning

Unsupervised learning is a branch of ML designed to identify patterns in data without relying on labeled output values or rewards. It is particularly useful when there is minimal understanding of the outcomes to predict or when the focus is on uncovering the underlying data structure or distribution. Typical unsupervised learning techniques include clustering, aiming to group similar instances into clusters, and dimensionality reduction, with the objective of simplifying data without significant information loss [53]. In the sphere of drug repurposing, unsupervised learning can contribute in numerous ways, such as drug clustering, the discovery of drug–disease associations, the identification of drug side effects, and the determination of new drug classes. In drug clustering, unsupervised learning identifies groups of drugs exhibiting similar characteristics based on properties such as molecular structure, known targets, and side effects. Drugs in the same cluster may have comparable therapeutic effects, suggesting new uses based on their relatedness in the feature space. To discover drug–disease associations, unsupervised learning can unveil previously unknown correlations. Dimensionality reduction techniques can project high-dimensional drug and disease data into a lower-dimensional space. Subsequent clustering in this reduced space can identify potential drug–disease associations. Regarding drug side effect identification, unsupervised learning, by clustering drugs on the basis of reported side effects, can predict new, previously unidentified side effects. The predictions are based on the known side effects of other drugs in the same cluster. Unsupervised learning can also identify new drug classes based on various drug features, offering insights into potential novel uses of drugs. However, applying unsupervised learning to drug repurposing is not without challenges. The results can sometimes be ambiguous, and validating predictions often requires additional experimental data. Moreover, there is no assurance that patterns identified by unsupervised learning hold meaning in the drug repurposing context. Despite these challenges, unsupervised learning presents a robust tool for navigating and understanding complex drug data.

9.5.2.3   Semi-Supervised Learning

Semi-supervised learning utilizes a combination of labeled and unlabeled data for training, often involving a small volume of labeled data and a significantly larger quantity of unlabeled data. The methodology typically commences with producing an initial model using labeled data, followed by the application of this model to label the unlabeled data. The datasets are then combined to generate a revised model, a process capable of iterative repetition. This learning method becomes particularly beneficial when acquiring training labels is costly or time-consuming, which are common conditions in drug repurposing [54]. Several applications of semi-supervised learning in drug repurposing include drug–target interaction prediction, drug–disease association prediction, drug clustering, and novel class discovery. In drug–target interaction prediction, labeled data may consist of pairs of drugs and targets that are confirmed interactors (positive examples) or noninteractors (negative examples). The copious unlabeled data might comprise drug–target pairs with unknown interaction statuses. The semi-supervised learning model can predict additional drug–target interactions by learning from the labeled data and applying it to the unlabeled data. A similar approach is applied to drug–disease association prediction, where labeled data might include known drug–disease associations and unlabeled data might involve potential drug–disease pairs with unknown association status. Semi-supervised learning aids in predicting new associations, thereby facilitating the identification of new uses for existing drugs. For drug clustering and novel class discovery, semi-supervised learning can help cluster drugs based on various features. Labeled data could include drugs with known classifications, while unlabeled data could involve drugs with unknown classifications. The semi-supervised learning model can contribute to discovering new drug classes by assigning drugs to appropriate clusters. Semi-supervised learning often delivers superior predictive performance compared to either purely supervised or unsupervised learning methods, especially when labeled data are limited. However, its effectiveness is contingent upon the assumption that the distribution of unlabeled data mirrors that of labeled data, an assumption not always upheld in practice. Additionally, it is crucial to ensure that the introduction of unlabeled data does not inject bias or noise into the learning process.

9.5.2.4   Reinforcement Learning

Reinforcement learning works by training an algorithm to make a sequence of decisions, with the goal of maximizing some notion of cumulative reward. In this process, the agent takes actions in a certain state, which transitions it to a new state and yields a reward (or penalty). The goal of the agent is to learn a policy, which is a strategy that prescribes the best action to take in every state, to maximize the cumulative reward over time [55]. In drug repurposing, reinforcement learning can be used in multitarget drug design or in optimizing treatment regimens. Some potential roles of reinforcement learning include navigating chemical space, optimizing drug combinations, personalized treatment regimens, and drug synthesis pathways. For navigating chemical space, reinforcement learning can be used to navigate the vast and complex chemical space of drug-like molecules. The agent can be set to explore this space and identify promising drug candidates for further investigation. The agent's actions could involve making modifications to a molecular structure, and the rewards could be based on various predicted properties of the molecules, such as drug-likeness, synthetic accessibility and predicted efficacy against a target. With respect to optimizing drug combinations, reinforcement learning can also be used to optimize combinations of drugs for repurposing. The actions in this case might involve selecting drugs to include in a combination, and the rewards could be based on predicted synergistic effects or the minimization of side effects. In the case of personalized treatment regimens, reinforcement learning can be used to personalize treatment regimens for patients based on their individual characteristics and responses to treatment. The actions could involve selecting drugs and dosages at each stage of treatment, and the rewards could be based on measures of patient health and well-being. In addition, in drug development and repurposing, reinforcement learning can be used to identify optimal synthesis pathways for drug-like molecules, reducing the time and cost of drug production. There are challenges even though reinforcement learning holds great promise for drug repurposing. Reinforcement often requires significant computational resources, and the design of suitable reward functions can be difficult. Additionally, ensuring that the reinforcement learning agent explores the environment sufficiently without making too many mistakes (the exploration *versus* exploitation tradeoff) can be a tricky balance.

9.5.3   Deep Learning

Deep learning, a subset of ML, uses neural networks with several layers—hence the term "deep"—for more complex analyses. Deep learning techniques can automatically extract features from raw data, making them particularly useful in analyzing complex biological data such as image or text data [56]. Deep learning methods such as convolutional neural networks for image data, recurrent neural networks for sequential data, and deep belief networks for biological network data, among others, have found applications in drug repurposing. Table 9.4 summarizes the deep learning techniques for drug repurposing and delineates four distinct deep learning methodologies and their roles in drug repurposing. Convolutional neural networks, known for their proficiency in analyzing grid-like data, can be harnessed to examine grid representations of molecular structures, aiding in the prediction of drug–target interactions and drug properties. Recurrent neural networks, specialized in processing sequential data, can be employed on sequence representations of drug compounds and target proteins, enabling accurate drug–target interaction predictions. Autoencoders, a type of unsupervised neural network, are capable of learning compact representations of drug-like molecules and can subsequently generate potential new drug compounds, while generative adversarial networks serve as an adversarial system where the generator produces new molecular structures and the discriminator ensures that these structures resemble existing drug compounds, thus effectively generating new drug-like molecules. These techniques all have significant potential in drug repurposing, given ample data and computational resources, along with careful task design and result validation.

In the context of drug repurposing, deep learning can be particularly valuable due to its ability to automatically learn meaningful representations from raw data. Some specific roles that deep learning can play in drug repurposing include predicting drug–target interactions, predicting drug–disease associations, generating new drug candidates, predicting drug side effects, and multimodal learning. For predicting drug–target interactions, deep learning can automatically extract useful features from the raw molecular structures of drugs and proteins, which can be used to predict drug–target interactions—for instance, conventional neural networks can be applied to grid representations of molecular structures, while recurrent neural networks can be applied to sequence representations. Similar to predicting drug–target interactions, deep learning can be used to predict drug–disease associations. The features learned by the deep network can capture complex relationships between drugs and diseases that might be missed by simpler methods. For generating new

Table 9.4 Deep learning techniques for drug repurposing.

Technique	Description	Application in drug repurposing	Reference
Convolutional neural networks (CNNs)	CNNs are neural networks that are especially effective for processing grid-like data, such as images.	CNNs can be used to analyze grid representations of molecular structures to predict drug–target interactions or drug properties.	[57]
Recurrent neural networks (RNNs)	RNNs are designed to recognize patterns in sequential data, making them effective for processing time series or text.	RNNs can be applied to the sequence representations of drug compounds and target proteins to predict drug–target interactions.	[58]
Autoencoders	Autoencoders are unsupervised neural networks that learn to compress input data into a lower-dimensional representation and then reconstruct the original data from this compressed representation.	Autoencoders, especially variational autoencoders (VAEs), can be used to learn a compact representation of drug-like molecules and then generate new potential drug compounds.	[59]
Generative adversarial networks (GANs)	GANs consist of two neural networks, a generator and a discriminator, which compete with each other. The generator tries to produce data that looks like the real data, while the discriminator tries to distinguish the real data from the fake data.	GANs can be used to generate new drug-like molecules, where the generator produces new molecular structures, and the discriminator ensures that these new structures resemble known drug compounds.	[60]

drug candidates, generative models, such as variational autoencoders and generative adversarial networks, can be trained on the molecular structures of known drugs and then used to generate the structures of potential new drugs. These new drugs can then be tested *in silico* or *in vivo* for their therapeutic effects, potentially leading to new drug repurposing opportunities. Concerning predicting drug side effects, by training on large databases of known drug side effects, deep learning models can learn to predict the potential side effects of novel or repurposed drugs. In addition, deep learning models can manage multiple types of input data simultaneously (e.g., drug chemical structures, target protein sequences, and patient genetic profiles). This can lead to a more comprehensive understanding of the drug repurposing landscape. Deep learning models require substantial amounts of labeled data and considerable computational resources. There are also often "black boxes", making their predictions difficult to interpret. Furthermore, ensuring the generalizability of deep learning models to new data can be a challenge, especially given the diversity and complexity of biological systems. However, with careful application and interpretation, deep learning holds great promise for drug repurposing.

9.5.4   Software Tools for Machine Learning in Drug Repurposing

Drug repurposing is not without challenges, as it requires the assimilation and analysis of vast and complex biological, chemical, and clinical data to explore potential new drug–disease associations. This is where ML, specifically software tools designed for ML, plays a pivotal role. These tools can efficiently process and learn from large-scale, high-dimensional data, making them particularly adept at identifying patterns and relationships that might be difficult or impossible for humans to discern. Such insights can then guide the identification of promising drug repurposing candidates. Software tools for ML provide an array of functionalities needed for these tasks. They include algorithms for different types of learning (supervised, unsupervised, semi-supervised, reinforcement, and deep learning), data preprocessing tools, model evaluation techniques, visualization tools, and more. With these capabilities, they enable researchers to operationalize complex ML workflows for drug repurposing, from the initial stages of data exploration and preprocessing to model training, validation, and deployment. Moreover, several of these tools are open-source and have large and active user communities. This means that they are continuously tested, updated, and expanded by researchers worldwide, ensuring that they stay at the forefront of methodological advancements in ML. Their widespread use also implies that they come with extensive documentation and tutorials, making them accessible even to researchers who might be new to ML.

Table 9.5 shows a list of the software tools for ML in drug repurposing and provides a comprehensive list of tools that are particularly useful in implementing ML techniques in drug repurposing efforts. Starting with scikit-learn, it is a highly versatile tool for Python, offering a wide array of algorithms for classification, regression, and clustering, hence supporting a range of learning techniques, including supervised, unsupervised, and semi-supervised learning. DeepChem, a Python library, is purpose-built for computer-aided drug design and includes native integration with other ML frameworks such as TensorFlow and PyTorch, facilitating deep learning, supervised learning, and reinforcement learning techniques. RDKit is an open-source chemoinformatics tool used for the chemoinformatic analysis of molecular structures and provides ML functionalities through its integration with scikit-learn, primarily supporting supervised and unsupervised learning. TensorFlow and PyTorch are open-source platforms that offer comprehensive support for a wide range of ML tasks. Both of these tools are particularly known for their capabilities in deep learning, but they also provide robust support for other learning paradigms, such as supervised, semi-supervised, and reinforcement learning. Keras is a high-level neural network API that enables quick and easy model design and experimentation. It is built to run on top of TensorFlow, CNTK, or Theano, and it is primarily used for deep learning and supervised

Table 9.5 Software tools for machine learning in drug repurposing.

Software tool	Description	Machine learning techniques supported
scikit-learn	A free software ML library for Python. It features various algorithms for classification, regression, and clustering.	Supervised learning, unsupervised learning, semi-supervised learning
DeepChem	An open-source Python library designed specifically for computer-aided drug design. It integrates with other ML frameworks like TensorFlow and PyTorch.	Deep learning, supervised learning, reinforcement learning
RDKit	An open-source cheminformatics software that provides tools for the chemoinformatic analysis of molecular structures. It includes ML functionalities through integration with scikit-learn.	Supervised learning, unsupervised learning
TensorFlow	An open-source platform for ML that supports a wide range of tasks. TensorFlow includes high-level APIs for defining and training ML models as well as tools for deploying models in production.	Deep learning, supervised learning, semi-supervised learning, reinforcement learning
PyTorch	A Python-based scientific computing package serving as a replacement for NumPy to use the power of GPUs. It is also a deep learning platform that provides maximum flexibility and speed.	Deep learning, supervised learning, reinforcement learning
Keras	A high-level neural network API, written in Python, and capable of running on top of TensorFlow, CNTK, or Theano. It was developed with a focus on enabling fast experimentation.	Deep learning, supervised learning
Weka	A collection of ML algorithms for data mining tasks written in Java, containing tools for data preprocessing, classification, regression, clustering, association rules, and visualization.	Supervised learning, unsupervised learning, semi-supervised learning

learning applications. Finally, Weka is a Java-based collection of ML algorithms for data mining tasks. It provides a plethora of tools for data preprocessing, classification, regression, clustering, association rules, and visualization. It is useful for a variety of learning techniques, such as supervised, unsupervised, and semi-supervised learning. Each of these tools offers its own unique capabilities, and often, their usage overlaps, offering the flexibility to use them in conjunction to meet the specific requirements of any drug repurposing project.

9.6   Data Sources for Drug Repurposing

The successful application of ML in drug repurposing heavily depends on the availability of comprehensive, accurate, and relevant data. Various data sources, which can be broadly categorized into biomedical databases and clinical data sources, are essential for fueling ML algorithms. In this section, some of these critical data sources that are currently being utilized in the field of drug repurposing are discussed.

9.6.1   Biomedical Databases

Biomedical databases, which include genomic, proteomic, and chemoinformatics data, are rich resources that can be leveraged in drug repurposing (Table 9.6). They provide a vast amount of structured data that can be used for building and training ML models.

Table 9.6 Summary of datasets used in machine learning for drug repurposing.

Dataset name	Source	Availability	Content
ChEMBL (www. ebi.ac.uk/ chembl)	European Bioinformatics Institute (EBI)	Open source	A manually curated database of bioactive molecules with drug-like properties. It contains information on approximately 2.2 million compounds and over 11K targets.
DrugBank (www. drugbank.ca)	University of Alberta	Open source and commercial	A unique bioinformatics and cheminformatics resource that combines detailed drug data with comprehensive drug target information. It covers 13K drugs.
PubChem (https:// pubchem.ncbi. nlm.nih.gov/)	National Center for Biotechnology Information (NCBI)	Open source	A free database of chemical structures of small organic molecules and information on their biological activities. This database contains approximately three million compounds.
BindingDB (https://www. bindingdb. org/rwd/bind/ index.jsp)	University of California, San Diego	Open source and commercial	Public, web-accessible database of measured binding affinities for biomolecules, genetically or chemically modified biomolecules, and synthetic compounds.
PDB (protein data bank) (https://www. rcsb.org/)	Worldwide Protein Data Bank	Open source	An archive of information about the 3D shapes of proteins, nucleic acids, and complex assemblies to help students and researchers understand aspects of biomedicine and agriculture.

9.6.1.1   Genomic Databases

Genomic databases hold vast promise as essential resources in drug repurposing efforts. They house comprehensive genomic data, including genetic sequences, gene expression, and mutations, which are crucial in understanding disease pathways and drug mechanisms of action—for instance, databases such as the Human Genome Project, The Cancer Genome Atlas, and GenBank have revolutionized the field by offering rich, high-quality, and open-access genomic data. ML algorithms trained on these large-scale datasets have succeeded in identifying novel drug–disease associations and predicting potential therapeutic candidates—for example, utilizing genomic data from these resources, ML models have pointed toward repurposing antidiabetic drugs such as metformin for cancer treatment and neurodegenerative diseases. Moreover, these databases promote the integration of genomic data with other omics data (such as proteomics and metabolomics), leading to a holistic understanding of disease biology and drug interactions, which could enable more robust and precise drug repurposing. Therefore, genomic databases stand as pivotal cornerstones in the data-driven landscape of future drug repurposing endeavors.

9.6.1.2   Proteomic Databases

Protein databases such as the Universal Protein Resource (UniProt), Protein Data Bank (PDB), and Human Protein Atlas (HPA) provide information about protein structures, functions, and interactions. Analyzing these data can help identify potential drug targets—for example, UniProt is a comprehensive resource for protein sequence and annotation data. It is a collaboration between the European Bioinformatics Institute (EBI), the Swiss Institute of Bioinformatics (SIB), and the Protein Information Resource (PIR). UniProt provides several databases, with the UniProt Knowledgebase (UniProtKB) being the central hub containing functional information on proteins with accurate, consistent, and rich annotation. In addition, UniProt offers a variety of tools and resources to analyze protein sequences and structures, predict protein function, and perform complex queries. It is widely used in bioinformatics for protein analysis in the development of new drugs. PBD is an open-access digital database that collects 3D structural data for large biological molecules, such as proteins and nucleic acids. The data, obtained primarily from X-ray crystallography and nuclear magnetic resonance spectroscopy, are used by scientists to understand the functions of these molecules, to design drugs and to engineer new proteins. The PBD archive is maintained by the Worldwide Protein Data Bank, an international consortium that ensures that the PDB maintains uniform data standards, data quality, and worldwide accessibility. In addition, the HPA is a Swedish-based program initiated in 2003 with the aim of mapping all human proteins in cells, tissues, and organs using the integration of various omics technologies, including antibody-based imaging, mass spectrometry-based proteomics, transcriptomics, and systems biology. All the data in the HPA are open access to allow scientists both in academia and industry to freely access the data for exploration of the human proteome. HPA provides a wide range of information, including protein expression profiles, protein interactions, and the specific subcellular locations of proteins. These resources can be invaluable in the discovery of potential drug targets and the development of therapeutic strategies.

9.6.1.3   Chemoinformatics Databases

Chemoinformatics databases are instrumental resources for drug repurposing, offering detailed information on the chemical structures, properties, and bioactivities of numerous compounds. Noteworthy databases, such as PubChem, ChEMBL, and DrugBank, provide vast and accessible chemical data that fuel ML algorithms in drug repurposing efforts—for instance, these databases have contributed to the development of models capable of predicting drug–target interactions, thereby guiding the identification of new therapeutic uses for existing drugs. A notable example includes the repurposing of antihistamines for the treatment of neurodegenerative diseases, guided by chemoinformatics data analyzed by ML models. Moreover, these databases facilitate the integration of chemical data with biological and clinical data, allowing for a comprehensive understanding of drug–disease interactions. As such, chemoinformatics databases form an integral part of the data-driven landscape of drug repurposing, enabling ML algorithms to harness chemical information for the discovery of novel therapeutic avenues.

9.6.2   Clinical Data Sources

Clinical data sources provide real-world evidence of drug performance, patient health outcomes, and disease progression patterns. They include electronic health records, clinical trial databases, and adverse event databases (Table 9.7).

9.6.2.1   Electronic Health Records (EHR)

Electronic health records (EHRs) constitute a rich, patient-centric data source, playing a crucial role in the future direction of drug repurposing. EHRs, which capture comprehensive patient histories, including diagnoses, treatments, and outcomes, provide a goldmine of real-world clinical data for ML algorithms [61]. By training on these data, ML models

Table 9.7 Summary of clinical datasets used in machine learning for drug repurposing.

Dataset	Description	Use in machine learning for drug repurposing
Electronic health records	Detailed patient records containing diagnostics, treatments, and outcomes	Identification of real-world patterns of drug use and effects to suggest new therapeutic uses
Clinical trial databases (e.g., ClinicalTrials.gov)	Comprehensive information on past and ongoing clinical trials	Analyzing patterns of drug performance in diverse patient populations and various conditions to suggest new indications
Adverse event databases (e.g., FAERS)	Comprehensive insights into the side effects of drugs postmarketing	Understanding drug–target interactions and safety profiles to suggest new uses and assess their risks of repurposing

can identify patterns that suggest new therapeutic uses for existing drugs [27] —for example, by mining EHR data, ML models identified that patients with diabetes who were taking the drug metformin had a lower incidence of cancer, hinting at the potential anticancer properties of metformin. Furthermore, EHRs facilitate the study of drug–disease associations in diverse and large patient populations, enhancing the generalizability and robustness of repurposing predictions. However, the successful use of EHRs for drug repurposing also requires stringent data privacy protections and the handling of data heterogeneity and quality. Thus, with adequate data governance, EHRs are set to become a critical component in the data-driven future of drug repurposing.

9.6.2.2   Clinical Trial Databases

Clinical trial databases are an essential resource for data-driven drug repurposing efforts. These databases, which include platforms such as ClinicalTrials.gov and the World Health Organization's International Clinical Trials Registry Platform, provide extensive information about past and ongoing clinical trials, including trial design, patient populations, interventions, and outcomes. ML models trained on these data can identify patterns suggesting new indications for existing drugs—for instance, by analyzing data from clinical trial databases, ML algorithms have suggested that antidepressants could be repurposed for the treatment of chronic pain. Furthermore, these databases provide valuable information on drug safety and adverse events, which are critical for assessing the viability of drug repurposing candidates. It is worth noting, however, that the successful application of these databases also requires careful handling of data quality and standardization. In summary, clinical trial databases serve as a vital link in the chain of drug repurposing, offering an expansive view of drug performance in diverse patient populations and across various conditions.

9.6.2.3   Adverse Event Databases

Adverse event databases are indispensable tools for drug repurposing, as they provide critical data on the safety profiles of drugs and can sometimes hint at potential new uses. These databases, such as the FDA's Adverse Event Reporting System (FAERS) and the WHO's VigiBase, offer comprehensive insights into the side effects of postmarketing drugs. ML models can utilize this information to understand drug–target interactions and their potential unexpected consequences—for instance, ML algorithms analyzing adverse event databases have suggested repurposing drugs used for treating diabetes to target cardiovascular diseases, as side effects indicated a modulation of cardiovascular risk factors. Importantly, these databases also provide a crucial safety checkpoint, helping to identify drugs that, although possibly effective for a new indication, might carry too much risk owing to severe adverse events. Therefore, despite their initial purpose of tracking drug safety, adverse event databases hold immense potential for informing future directions of drug repurposing, making them a key part of the ecosystem of data-driven drug discovery.

9.7 Case Studies: Applications of Machine Learning in Drug Repurposing

This section discusses a few notable instances when ML has been employed for the purpose of drug repurposing. These examples can provide insight into the significant implications and possibilities of this technology in a practical context.

9.7.1 Cancer Treatment

Due to its widespread prevalence and high mortality rate, cancer therapy is crucial. It is a complicated disease characterized by unregulated cell proliferation and dissemination in numerous body parts. Thus, cancer drug repurposing is crucial for various reasons. An application of ML in the field of drug repurposing pertains to the utilization of approved drugs for the treatment of cancer—for instance, aspirin and celecoxib have been extensively studied for their potential roles in the prevention and treatment of colorectal cancer, among other types of cancer. Originally intended as pain relievers and anti-inflammatory drugs (with aspirin being a nonsteroidal anti-inflammatory drug and celecoxib being a selective cyclooxygenase-2 inhibitor), research has demonstrated that they also possess anticancer effects. The anticancer effect of aspirin is thought to stem from several mechanisms. Aspirin inhibits the enzyme cyclooxygenase (COX), which is involved in the production of prostaglandins. These prostaglandins promote inflammation, a process that can contribute to the development and progression of cancer. Therefore, by inhibiting COX, aspirin may help reduce cancer risk and progression. Another mechanism of action involves aspirin's well-known antiplatelet effects, which may also contribute to its anticancer properties. Platelets are believed to protect circulating tumor cells from the immune system and facilitate metastasis. By inhibiting platelet activation, aspirin might slow cancer spread. The long-term use of aspirin has been associated with a decreased risk of colorectal cancer in various observational studies. Some research suggests that aspirin might also decrease the risk of other types of cancer, such as breast and prostate cancer, although the evidence is not as robust as for colorectal cancer. Celecoxib, currently approved for the treatment of arthritis and acute pain, has also been investigated for its potential anticancer effects. This is because COX-2 is often overexpressed in various types of cancer, including colorectal cancer. There are a few ways it may work. Similar to aspirin, by inhibiting COX-2, celecoxib may help reduce inflammation and decrease the proliferation of cancer cells. Some studies suggest that celecoxib might induce apoptosis (programmed cell death) in cancer cells. Additionally, celecoxib might inhibit angiogenesis (the formation of new blood vessels), a process essential for tumor growth and metastasis. It is important to note that while both aspirin and celecoxib show promise in the prevention and treatment of colorectal and other cancers, they also have potential side effects, such as gastrointestinal bleeding. Therefore, their routine use for cancer prevention is not currently recommended for everyone. Decisions about using these drugs for cancer prevention should be made on an individual basis, considering the person's risk of cancer, potential side effects, and overall health.

In addition, Madugula *et al.* [62] reported the combination of ML techniques and structure–activity relationship (SAR) predictions to analyze a dataset of 1,671 approved drugs for potential repurposing. The researchers applied principal component analysis and k-means clustering to two-dimensional molecular descriptors of the drugs, resulting in nine distinct clusters. Using the predicted activity spectra of substances tool, the team predicted biological activities for these drugs to identify potential new uses. The results showed that each cluster contained drugs with similar structures but with varying therapeutic indications, suggesting the potential for repurposing these drugs based on their predicted high biological activities. In total, the researchers identified 66 drugs that, despite structural similarities, have different therapeutic uses and could therefore be repurposed for one or more indications of other drugs in the same cluster. Additionally, 1,423 drugs were identified for potential repurposing for 366 new indications. Within the cancer category, a substantial number of drugs have been identified for repurposing in many therapeutic areas. Specifically, there are 136 drugs for anticarcinogenic purposes, 125 drugs for preneoplastic disorders, eighty-four drugs for antimetastatic effects, 37 drugs for antileukemic properties, 27 drugs for antimutagenic purposes, and 24 drugs for conditions related to antineoplastic antimetabolites. Thus, this research demonstrates the utility of an integrated machine learning and SAR analysis approach in drug repurposing, providing valuable insights into the structural and activity relationships of approved drugs.

9.7.2   Antiviral Treatment

Viruses, microscopic pathogens capable of infecting almost all life forms, can cause a variety of diseases in humans, ranging from mild ailments such as the common cold to severe conditions such as HIV/AIDS, Ebola, and COVID-19 [63–65]. Viruses are highly prevalent in human populations, and according to the World Health Organization (WHO), millions of people worldwide suffer from viral infections each year. Among the most widespread viral diseases are respiratory infections, hepatitis, HIV/AIDS, influenza, and, more recently, coronavirus infections. The need for drug repurposing in antiviral treatment arises from several factors. New viral diseases, such as SARS, MERS, Zika, and COVID-19, have emerged rapidly in recent years, surpassing traditional drug discovery rates [66]. Additionally, viral mutations and drug resistance are vital factors to consider, as frequent mutations can lead to resistance to antiviral drugs [67]. In such cases, drug repurposing can offer quicker access to treatment options.

Several compelling case studies highlight the potential of ML for identifying new therapeutic uses for antiviral drugs—for example, Shahabadi *et al.* [68] conducted a study to investigate potential drug repurposing options for treating COVID-19, acknowledging the effectiveness of vaccines but also recognizing the associated risks and the necessity for a range of new drug molecules. The research focused on the role of RNA-dependent RNA polymerase (RdRp), which is known to be instrumental in viral replication. Using molecular modeling, docking, and dynamic simulation, the study repurposed five FDA-approved drugs—bexarotene, diiodohydroxyquinoline, abiraterone, cetilistat, and remdesivir—against RdRp. The effectiveness of these drugs was gauged in comparison with remdesivir, a known antiviral that inhibits RdRp. The findings suggested that these selected drugs exhibited significant potential for development as RdRp inhibitors. With further validation, these drugs could potentially be used for COVID-19 treatment.

In addition, the recent COVID-19 pandemic has also seen the application of ML for drug repurposing [65]. Scientists have used ML models to analyze large datasets, including the genome of the virus, patient clinical data, and existing antiviral drugs. They found that several existing drugs, including some antimalarial and antiviral drugs, could potentially be effective in treating COVID-19 patients [63]. These studies highlight the speed and efficiency of ML in repurposing drugs, especially in urgent, global health crises [58] —for instance, Wang *et al.* [69] used a network-based drug repurposing approach to identify effective treatments for COVID-19, specifically for patients in various stages of the disease. Utilizing computational prediction methods that integrate the public clinical transcriptome and experimental data, this research identified 51 drugs that could potentially regulate proteins interacting with SARS-CoV-2. Several notable drug candidates were discussed. Lovastatin was found to cause differential gene expression in the clinical transcriptome of mild COVID-19 patients. Estradiol cypionate, a hormone-related drug, was noted to be effective for treating patients with severe COVID-19. Another drug, erlotinib, was found to target viral proteins interacting with cytokines and cytokine receptors, which could affect the virus's attachment and invasion processes. Additionally, lovastatin and testosterone were identified as having the potential to block the angiotensin system, thereby potentially suppressing SARS-CoV-2 infection. The study concluded by highlighting its success in identifying viable drug candidates for treating COVID-19 patients at various stages of the disease and in providing a comprehensive understanding of potential drug mechanisms.

Moreover, Kamboj *et al.* [70] conducted a study to predict repurposed drugs for hepatitis C virus infection, which can lead to viral hepatitis and hepatocellular carcinoma. Despite the clinical use of direct-acting antivirals, they fail in 5–10% of cases, emphasizing the need for new antivirals. The authors developed an anti-hepatitis C virus platform using ML and quantitative structure–activity relationship methodologies, selecting relevant molecular descriptors and fingerprints with a recursive feature elimination algorithm. They developed predictive models using several ML techniques and validated their accuracy by achieving Pearson's correlation coefficients ranging from 0.80 to 0.92 during 10-fold cross-validation, with similar performance observed on independent datasets. The models were then used to identify potential repurposed drugs, with molecular docking further validating the selected candidates. Several drugs, including naftifine, butalbital, vinorelbine, epicriptine, pipecuronium, trimethaphan, olodaterol, and vemurafenib, were identified as promising candidates for repurposing against the hepatitis C virus. The study underscored these drugs' potential in the development of new antiviral treatments for the hepatitis C virus. Thus, these case studies showcase ML's profound impact on drug repurposing, demonstrating its ability to expedite the discovery process and potentially save countless lives by identifying novel therapeutic uses for existing antiviral drugs.

9.7.3 Antidiabetic Treatment

Diabetes is a major global health concern. It is a chronic condition that affects the way the body processes blood sugar and comes in two main forms: type 1 diabetes (an autoimmune condition where the body does not produce insulin) and type 2 diabetes (where the body becomes resistant to insulin or does not produce enough). There is also gestational diabetes, which affects some women during pregnancy. According to the International Diabetes Federation, approximately 537 million adults (20–79 years old) were living with diabetes in 2021, and this number is predicted to rise to 783.2 million by 2045 [71]. Diabetes is a leading cause of heart disease, stroke, blindness, kidney failure, and lower limb amputation [72]. While several treatments are available for diabetes, they do not work for everyone, and many patients struggle to achieve optimal blood glucose control. New drugs could provide more treatment options and improve outcomes for these patients. Given the scale and severity of the diabetes epidemic, drug discovery and repurposing are crucial to providing new treatment options, improving patient outcomes, and reducing healthcare costs. ML is a potent tool for identifying new therapeutic applications for antidiabetic drugs, as illustrated by several significant case studies. Notably, an ML model trained on genomic, phenotypic, and clinical data, for example, pinpointed the antidiabetic drug metformin as a potential therapeutic for cancer, leading to numerous ongoing clinical trials investigating metformin's anticancer properties. The study by Rashid *et al.* [72] was aimed at identifying potential new treatments for type 2 diabetes through drug repurposing. The research focused on finding drugs that can inhibit the enzyme α-glucosidase, which is involved in carbohydrate metabolism. By slowing carbohydrate metabolism, blood sugar levels can be better controlled in people with type 2 diabetes. Hence, researchers looked at FDA-approved drugs to find potential inhibitors of α-glucosidase. They used a refined and optimized target protein, introducing missing residues and minimizing clashes, to identify the potential inhibitor. Using AutoDock Vina, the researchers analyzed binding affinities and root-mean-squared deviation (RMSD) values, which measure the difference between values predicted by a model and the values actually observed. Based on these analyses, two compounds, trabectedin and demeclocycline, were selected as potential α-glucosidase inhibitors. These compounds were further analyzed through a molecular dynamics (MD) simulation to study the stability and specific interactions between the receptor (α-glucosidase) and ligand (the drug). The docking score, RMSD values, pharmacophore studies, and MD simulations suggested that trabectedin and demeclocycline could be potential inhibitors of α-glucosidase, potentially outperforming existing standard inhibitors. Trabectedin, in particular, showed significant effectiveness *in vitro*, with an IC_{50} (a measure of the effectiveness of a substance in inhibiting a specific biological or biochemical function) of 1.263 ± 0.7 µM. However, the researchers concluded that further investigation is needed to determine the safety of these drugs for *in vivo* use in treating type 2 diabetes. This study's findings suggest that drug repurposing could potentially offer new ways to manage type 2 diabetes, a disease that is rapidly increasing in prevalence worldwide.

9.7.4   Neurodegenerative Disease Treatment

Neurodegenerative diseases are a broad group of disorders characterized by the progressive degeneration of the structure and function of the nervous system. They include conditions such as Alzheimer's disease, Parkinson's disease, Huntington's disease, and amyotrophic lateral sclerosis, among others. Many of these diseases are becoming more common as the global population ages, and they impose a significant burden on patients. The current situation with neurogenerative diseases is becoming more prevalent—for instance, the Alzheimer's Association estimates that approximately 6.2 million Americans aged 65 and older will be living with Alzheimer's disease in 2021. Without significant medical breakthroughs, this number could rise to nearly 14 million by 2060. The growing prevalence and impact of neurodegenerative diseases, coupled with the lack of effective treatments, make

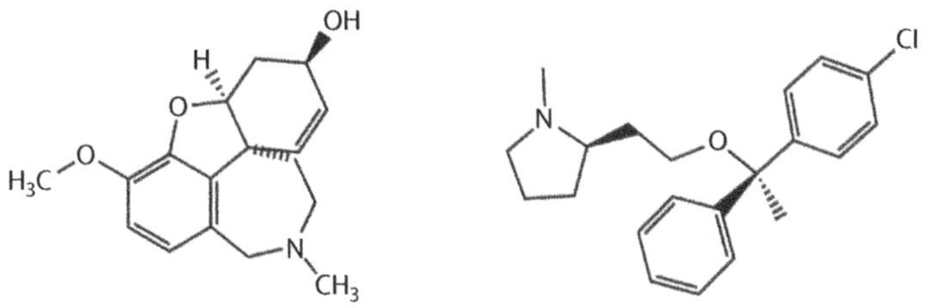

Figure 9.7 Chemical structures of galantamine (left) and clemastine (right) (ChemDraw 20.1.1).

drug repurposing a promising strategy to expedite the discovery of novel treatments for these conditions.

Galantamine (Figure 9.7), originally derived from the snowdrop plant (*Galanthus nivalis* L., Amaryllidaceae family), was initially used in the 1950s and 1960s as an anesthetic adjunct and treatment for polio and various muscular disorders due to its neuromuscular junction transmission-enhancing properties. Galantamine's action as an acetylcholinesterase inhibitor was discovered later. Acetylcholinesterase is an enzyme that breaks down acetylcholine, a neurotransmitter in the brain that is crucial for memory and learning. By inhibiting this enzyme, more acetylcholine is available in the brain, which can potentially improve cognitive function. Thus, galantamine was repurposed for Alzheimer's disease, a neurodegenerative disorder characterized by progressive memory loss and cognitive decline. In Alzheimer's disease, the neurons that produce acetylcholine degenerate, leading to reduced acetylcholine levels in the brain. By blocking the action of acetylcholinesterase, galantamine helps to increase the levels of acetylcholine, thereby improving communication between nerve cells and potentially improving or maintaining cognitive function. In the United States, the FDA approved galantamine for the treatment of mild to moderate Alzheimer's disease in 2001. Since then, it has been widely used as part of the symptomatic treatment of this condition. However, while galantamine can help manage the symptoms of Alzheimer's disease, it does not cure the disease or stop its progression. As Alzheimer's disease advances, neuron loss continues, and eventually, the amount of acetylcholine decreases to a level that galantamine and similar drugs can no longer effectively compensate for.

ML applications in drug repurposing have displayed considerable potential in tackling neurodegenerative diseases, as evidenced by several impactful case studies. One prominent example includes the use of ML in the identification of potential therapeutic uses of the antihistamine drug clemastine (Figure 9.7) for multiple sclerosis. ML models trained on genomic and clinical data flagged clemastine as a candidate for repurposing, an insight subsequently confirmed through clinical trials. In another instance, ML models have been deployed to explore the repurposing of the cancer drug nilotinib for the treatment of Parkinson's disease and other neurodegenerative disorders. The models leveraged complex biochemical and patient-derived data to uncover potential neuroprotective effects of nilotinib, a discovery currently under clinical validation. Finally, ML has guided the repurposing of the diabetes drug metformin for the treatment of Alzheimer's disease, capitalizing on comprehensive genetic, epigenetic, and phenotypic data to reveal metformin's potential as a neuroprotective agent. These instances highlight how ML can uncover novel therapeutic avenues in neurodegenerative diseases, demonstrating its promise in accelerating drug repurposing and potentially providing new hope for patients suffering from these debilitating conditions.

9.7.5 Hair Loss Treatment

Androgenetic alopecia, also known as male-pattern baldness or female-pattern hair loss, is the most common type of hair loss in both men and women. In men, androgenetic alopecia can start as early as the late teens, and the risk increases with age. By the age of 50, approximately 30–50% of men experience some degree of hair loss [73]. This condition is characterized by a receding hairline and thinning of hair at the temples and crown of the head. In women, this type of hair loss usually presents as more diffuse, with general thinning over the entire scalp, but the frontal hairline is typically preserved. It often becomes noticeable later in life than it does in men, usually after andropause [74]. The American Academy of Dermatology estimates that approximately 40% of women will have visible hair loss by the time they reach age 40. Several factors influence the likelihood of developing androgenetic alopecia, including genetics and levels of androgens, the sex hormones that play a role in male traits and reproductive activity. Overall, androgenetic alopecia affects a significant proportion of the population, particularly older adults. It often leads to psychological distress and reduced quality of life, underscoring the importance of effective treatments for this condition [75].

Minoxidil and finasteride are two well-known examples of successful drug repurposing for the treatment of hair loss or androgenetic alopecia (Figure 9.8). Initially, minoxidil was developed as a treatment for hypertension. As an antihypertensive vasodilator, it helps relax and widen blood vessels to lower blood pressure. However, during the clinical trials for hypertension, a notable side effect was observed: the drug appeared to cause hair growth [37]. Given this unexpected effect, scientists began to investigate minoxidil's potential as a

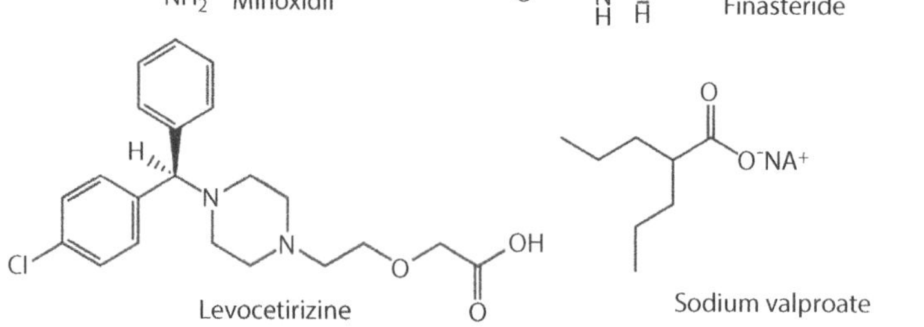

Figure 9.8 Chemical structures of minoxidil, finasteride, levocetirizine, and sodium valproate (ChemDraw 20.1.1).

treatment for hair loss. While minoxidil's precise mechanism for promoting hair growth is still not fully understood, it is believed to prolong the growth phase of hair follicles and increase blood flow to the scalp. As a result of these studies, topical minoxidil, applied directly to the scalp, was approved by the FDA as a treatment for hair loss in the 1980s. It is now widely recognized and used as a hair growth product.

Furthermore, finasteride was developed to treat benign prostatic hyperplasia, a condition involving an enlarged prostate. Finasteride works by inhibiting fiveα-reductase, an enzyme that converts testosterone to dihydrotestosterone. Dihydrotestosterone is a hormone known to contribute to both benign prostatic hyperplasia and hair loss; it can shrink hair follicles, leading to thinner, shorter hair and eventually hair loss [76]. During clinical trials for benign prostatic hyperplasia, patients reported an unexpected side effect of hair growth. Scientists then recognized finasteride's potential to treat hair loss. Following further research, the FDA approved a lower-dose finasteride tablet for the treatment of male-pattern hair loss in 1997.

Levocetirizine provides another instance of ML application in drug repurposing [77]. Typically, this medication is a third-generation nonsedating antihistamine primarily utilized to ease allergy symptoms such as runny nose, sneezing, and itchy eyes or throat. Its mode of action involves attaching to G protein-coupled receptors in the cell membrane, which leads to a decrease in the secretion of allergy-associated inflammatory substances. As the R-enantiomer of cetirizine, levocetirizine exhibits enhanced bioavailability and up to 95% plasma binding. It has a low propensity for tissue accumulation, limited cardiotoxicity, and minor sedative effects [78]. Recent research by Rossi *et al.* [79] discovered that applying 1% cetirizine to the area of hair loss increased hair density. Additionally, a separate study performed on human dermal papilla cells indicated that levocetirizine blocked the PGD2-GPR44 (active prostaglandin) pathway and stimulated the AKT signaling pathway, leading to *in vitro* hair growth and proliferation [80]. Furthermore, a study conducted by Wen *et al.* [81] examined the effects of levocetirizine on hair growth and verified its ability to support hair preservation.

In addition, sodium valproate, chemically known as 2-propyl pentanoate, is the sodium salt of valproic acid. It is a histone deacetylase inhibitor that is widely used for the treatment of conditions such as epilepsy, migraines, bipolar disorders, and various seizure disorders [82]. Frequently observed side effects of ingesting valproate include weight gain, tremors, hepatic dysfunction, gastrointestinal issues, thrombocytopenia, and metabolic acidosis. While topical application of this drug has demonstrated efficacy in promoting hair growth, this hair regrowth property of sodium valproate is attributed to the initiation of the anagen phase and the stimulation of the Wnt/β-catenin pathway, which plays a crucial role in the differentiation of stem cells in follicular keratinocytes and the formation of hair follicles. Therefore, sodium valproate presents a potential candidate for repurposing its use for androgenetic alopecia treatment [83].

9.8 Future of Machine Learning in Drug Repurposing

In recent years, ML has increasingly been utilized to streamline and expedite drug repurposing processes owing to its ability to analyze intricate datasets and predict outcomes. While the initial progress is encouraging, the full potential of this technological revolution is just starting to unfold. The sub-sections of this text will explore the projected evolution of ML in the domain of drug repurposing. The discussion will cover a variety of influential factors, including advancements in computational power, developments in ML models, and strategies for improved data integration. It will also explore the movement toward greater transparency and modifications to regulatory frameworks. In addition to highlighting these progressive elements, this discourse will tackle the inherent challenges in this field, underscoring the critical role of strategic collaborations and the practice of open science in surmounting these hurdles. In this context, the aim is to create a comprehensive perspective on a future where ML has a substantial impact on drug repurposing. Such a transformative shift could lead to significant improvements in patient outcomes globally, emphasizing the transformative potential of ML in this pivotal healthcare domain.

9.8.1   Advanced Machine Learning Techniques

The continued evolution of ML techniques and their application in drug repurposing seems certain. As computational power improves and the understanding of ML methodologies expands, there will be increasingly sophisticated models. Such models are projected to skillfully navigate the multidimensional, heterogeneous and intricate landscape of biological and clinical data, potentially revealing patterns and relationships that currently elude existing algorithms. Among the advanced techniques, deep learning models stand out for their remarkable capacity to learn from complex datasets—for example, convolutional neural networks are particularly adept at analyzing molecular structures, while recurrent neural networks effectively process sequential data such as genetic sequences. Furthermore, the introduction of transformer-based models marks a significant advancement in biomedical text data analysis, enhancing our understanding and prediction of drug–disease relationships.

In the near future, it is anticipated that there will be a shift in drug repurposing toward more unsupervised learning techniques. While supervised learning models, which are reliant on labeled data, have been broadly applied, their usage can be limited. In contrast, unsupervised learning can identify hidden patterns within unlabeled data, which may lead to its greater adoption in future drug repurposing initiatives. Techniques such as clustering and dimensionality reduction can assist in uncovering novel drug–disease associations. Graph neural networks also show promise. Given the inherent network nature of biological systems, graph neural networks can accurately model these systems. They represent drugs and diseases as nodes and interactions as edges, thereby potentially illuminating new uses for existing drugs. The incorporation of reinforcement learning introduces an exciting direction for drug repurposing. This ML technique enables models to learn optimal strategies through trial and error. By simulating the drug discovery process, reinforcement learning models can identify promising candidates for drug repurposing more efficiently and cost-effectively. Finally, transfer learning represents another promising approach. This technique repurposes a model trained on one task for a related task, allowing it to leverage knowledge from extensive datasets, such as genomic data. It can then apply this knowledge to tasks where data are scarce or expensive to acquire, thereby enhancing the accuracy and feasibility of drug repurposing initiatives.

9.8.2 Interdisciplinary Approaches

The future of ML in drug repurposing is expected to thrive on interdisciplinary approaches, where ML interfaces with multiple domains to harness their collective strengths. Integrating bioinformatics with ML can enhance the analysis of complex biological data, promoting the discovery of novel drug–disease relationships. Combining chemoinformatics with ML can lead to the development of predictive models capable of efficiently screening large libraries of drugs for new therapeutic uses. Furthermore, the intersection of pharmacology and ML can foster a deeper understanding of drug–target interactions, mechanisms of action, and side effects, thereby informing effective drug repurposing strategies. Combining clinical medicine with ML can empower clinicians with data-driven insights, facilitating informed decisions about potential drug repurposing based on individual patient profiles. Finally, as ML is increasingly applied to sensitive health data, it is crucial to consider ethical and legal aspects. An interdisciplinary collaboration between ML scientists, ethicists, and legal scholars can help construct robust frameworks for patient privacy, data security, and the ethical use of ML in drug repurposing [84]. Therefore, the future of ML in drug repurposing is envisaged as a collaborative journey across various disciplines, aiming to unlock the full potential of ML and usher in a new era of efficient and effective drug repurposing.

9.8.3 Improved Data Quality and Availability

The future of ML in drug repurposing is inextricably linked to the quality and availability of data. As ML algorithms rely on vast datasets for training and validation, advancements in data collection, standardization, and sharing protocols are of paramount importance. Harnessing real-world data from electronic health records, genomic databases and patient registries can provide a robust foundation for ML models, enabling the extraction of nuanced insights for drug repurposing. Moreover, improvements in data quality, such as standardized data entry, better handling of missing data, and robust privacy protection protocols, can augment the reliability and generalizability of ML models [85]. Additionally, fostering an environment of data sharing and open science can accelerate discoveries, enabling researchers worldwide to build upon each other's work and expedite the drug repurposing process. Therefore, in the future landscape of ML for drug repurposing, ensuring improved data quality and broadening data availability stand as critical facets that could significantly enhance the efficiency and effectiveness of drug repurposing strategies.

9.8.4 Integration with Clinical Trials and Healthcare Systems

The integration of ML with clinical trials and healthcare systems emerges as a key direction that can revolutionize the discovery and repurposing of drugs—for instance, ML has the potential to enrich the design and execution of clinical trials, a critical step in the drug repurposing process. ML can help identify suitable patient populations for trials, predict patient responses based on their genetic and clinical profiles, and optimize trial design for efficiency and effectiveness. Predictive models can help determine the probability of trial success, enabling more strategic decision-making in trial planning. Next, the integration of

ML with healthcare systems enables access to real-world data, including electronic health records, insurance claim data, patient registries, and even data from wearable devices. ML algorithms can mine this rich dataset to identify patterns suggestive of potential new uses for existing drugs. Moreover, ML can aid in monitoring drug safety and efficacy in a real-world setting postmarketing, providing valuable feedback for future drug repurposing.

9.9　Conclusion and Future Scope

Drug repurposing, or drug repositioning, involves discovering new therapeutic uses for already existing drugs. This strategy has the potential to conserve time and resources compared to the *de novo* drug discovery process, as repositioned drugs have already undergone numerous toxicity and safety tests. The integration of ML with drug repurposing represents a significant advancement in pharmaceutical research, reshaping the landscape of drug discovery with enhanced efficiency, speed, and precision. This chapter explores the multifaceted roles of ML in drug repurposing, highlighting its tremendous potential to uncover previously unknown drug–disease relationships, predict adverse effects, and assimilate disparate data types. A range of learning methods—supervised, unsupervised, semi-supervised, and reinforcement learning—along with the sophisticated capabilities of deep learning allow ML to pioneer innovative approaches in drug repurposing. By merging these computational strategies with traditional drug repurposing techniques, researchers can magnify their capabilities and expedite the discovery process. This interdisciplinary synergy can illuminate new therapeutic possibilities, thereby combating challenging diseases and enhancing patient outcomes. Despite these prospects, the journey faces challenges, including issues of data quality and availability, model interpretability, and validation. These issues must be addressed to ensure the responsible and effective use of ML in drug repurposing. Furthermore, ethical considerations, specifically those related to data privacy and fairness in predictions, require careful scrutiny. However, the potential benefits overwhelmingly surpass these challenges, positioning ML as a promising tool in drug repurposing. The amalgamation of ongoing technological advancements, expanding data volumes, and escalating computational power sets the stage for substantial progress in the field. The advancement of ML in drug repurposing is in its nascent stages, and the future appears promising. It is an exhilarating time to be involved in this field. This chapter testifies to the transformative potential of ML in the sphere of drug repurposing.

References

1. Yingngam, B., New Drug Discovery, in: *Multidisciplinary Applications of Natural Science for Drug Discovery and Integrative Medicine*, M. Aslam and M. Ahmad (Eds.), pp. 134–184, IGI Global, Pennsylvania, United States, 2023, https://doi.org/10.4018/978-1-6684-9463-9.ch005.
2. Pillai U, J., Ray, A., Maan, M., Dutta, M., Repurposing drugs targeting metabolic diseases for cancer therapeutics. *Drug Discov. Today*, 28, 9, 103684, 2023, https://doi.org/10.1016/j.drudis.2023.103684.

3. Donlin, M.J. and Meyers, M.J., Repurposing and optimization of drugs for discovery of novel antifungals. *Drug Discov. Today*, *27*, 7, 2008–2014, 2022, https://doi.org/10.1016/j.drudis.2022.04.021.

4. Ahmed, F., Samantasinghar, A., Soomro, A.M., Kim, S., Choi, K.H., A systematic review of computational approaches to understand cancer biology for informed drug repurposing. *J. Biomed. Inf.*, *142*, 104373, 2023, https://doi.org/10.1016/j.jbi.2023.104373.

5. Cavalla, D. and Crichton, G., Drug repurposing: Known knowns to unknown unknowns–Network analysis of the repurposome. *Drug Discov. Today*, *28*, 7, 103639, 2023, https://doi.org/10.1016/j.drudis.2023.103639.

6. Zhu, C., Xia, X., Li, N., Zhong, F., Yang, Z., Liu, L., RDKG-115: Assisting drug repurposing and discovery for rare diseases by trimodal knowledge graph embedding. *Comput. Biol. Med.*, *164*, 107262, 2023, https://doi.org/10.1016/j.compbiomed.2023.107262.

7. Murthannagari, V.R., Gonna Nandhi Krishnan, G., Manu, K.V., Jayachandraiah, C.T., Mandadhi Rajendra, P.K., Ahmed, S.S., Exploring the potential challenges for developing generic orphan drugs for rare diseases: A survey of us and european markets. *Value Health Regional Issues*, *35*, 87–94, 2023. https://doi.org/10.1016/j.vhri.2023.01.003.

8. Zanon, D., Musazzi, U.M., Cirino, M., Bennati, G., Casiraghi, A., Maximova, N., Minghetti, P., Cases of drug repositioning in children's orphan drugs: Licenced drugs versus unlicenced magistral preparations. *J. Drug Deliv. Sci. Technol.*, *82*, 104349, 2023, https://doi.org/10.1016/j.jddst.2023.104349.

9. Pan, X., Yun, J., Coban Akdemir, Z.H., Jiang, X., Wu, E., Huang, J.H., Yi, S.S., AI-DrugNet: A network-based deep learning model for drug repurposing and combination therapy in neurological disorders. *Comput. Struct. Biotechnol. J.*, *21*, 1533–1542, 2023, https://doi.org/10.1016/j.csbj.2023.02.004.

10. Jara, M.O. and Williams Iii, R.O., The challenge of repurposing niclosamide: Considering pharmacokinetic parameters, routes of administration, and drug metabolism. *J. Drug Deliv. Sci. Technol.*, *81*, 104187, 2023, https://doi.org/10.1016/j.jddst.2023.104187.

11. Gupta, R., Kumari, S., Senapati, A., Ambasta, R.K., Kumar, P., New era of artificial intelligence and machine learning-based detection, diagnosis, and therapeutics in Parkinson's disease. *Ageing Res. Rev.*, *90*, 102013, 2023, https://doi.org/10.1016/j.arr.2023.102013.

12. Mittal, P., Goyal, R., Kapoor, R., Gautam, R.K., Chapter 4 - Artificial intelligence (AI) and machine learning in the treatment of various diseases, in: *Computational Approaches in Drug Discovery, Development and Systems Pharmacology*, R.K. Gautam, M.A. Kamal, P. Mittal (Eds.), pp. 139–158, Academic Press, London, United Kingdom, 2023, https://doi.org/10.1016/B978-0-323-99137-7.00010-1.

13. Rajput, A., Bhamare, K.T., Thakur, A., Kumar, M., Anti-Biofilm: Machine Learning Assisted Prediction of IC50 Activity of Chemicals Against Biofilms of Microbes Causing Antimicrobial Resistance and Implications in Drug Repurposing. *J. Mol. Biol.*, *435*, 14, 168115, 2023, https://doi.org/10.1016/j.jmb.2023.168115.

14. van Eck, N.J. and Waltman, L., Software survey: VOSviewer, a computer program for bibliometric mapping. *Scientometrics*, *84*, 2, 523–538, 2010, https://doi.org/10.1007/s11192-009-0146-3.

15. Yingngam, B. and Atta ur, R., Chapter 11 - Modern solvent-free microwave extraction with essential oil optimization and structure-activity relationships. *Stud. Nat. Prod. Chem.*, *77*, 365–420, 2023, https://doi.org/10.1016/B978-0-323-91294-5.00011-7.

16. Pillaiyar, T., Meenakshisundaram, S., Manickam, M., Sankaranarayanan, M., A medicinal chemistry perspective of drug repositioning: Recent advances and challenges in drug discovery. *Eur. J. Med. Chem.*, *195*, 112275, 2020, https://doi.org/10.1016/j.ejmech.2020.112275.

17. Krishnamurthy, N., Grimshaw, A.A., Axson, S.A., Choe, S.H., Miller, J.E., Drug repurposing: a systematic review on root causes, barriers and facilitators. *BMC Health Serv. Res.*, 22, 1, 970, 2022, https://doi.org/10.1186/s12913-022-08272-z.

18. Botella, L.M., Drug repurposing as a current strategy in medicine discovery. *Medicina Familia. SEMERGEN*, 48, 8, 101790, 2022, https://doi.org/10.1016/j.semerg.2022.03.003.

19. Hua, Y., Dai, X., Xu, Y., Xing, G., Liu, H., Lu, T., Zhang, Y., Drug repositioning: Progress and challenges in drug discovery for various diseases. *Eur. J. Med. Chem.*, 234, 114239, 2022, https://doi.org/10.1016/j.ejmech.2022.114239.

20. Issa, N.T., Stathias, V., Schürer, S., Dakshanamurthy, S., Machine and deep learning approaches for cancer drug repurposing. *Semin. Cancer Biol.*, 68, 132–142, 2021, https://doi.org/10.1016/j.semcancer.2019.12.011.

21. Madrid, P.B. and Chang, P.Y., Accelerating space radiation countermeasure development through drug repurposing. *Life Sci. Space Res.*, 35, 30–35, 2022, https://doi.org/10.1016/j.lssr.2022.07.002.

22. Oh, H., Prevot, T.D., Newton, D., Sibille, E., From serendipity to rational drug design in brain disorders: *in silico, in vitro*, and *in vivo* approaches. *Curr. Opin. Pharmacol.*, 60, 177–182, 2021, https://doi.org/10.1016/j.coph.2021.07.012.

23. Ostfeld, R.J., Allen, K.E., Aspry, K., Brandt, E.J., Spitz, A., Liberman, J., Freeman, A.M., Vasculogenic Erectile Dysfunction: The Impact of Diet and Lifestyle. *Am. J. Med.*, 134, 3, 310–316, 2021, https://doi.org/10.1016/j.amjmed.2020.09.033.

24. Talevi, A., 2.34 - Drug Repurposing, in: *Comprehensive Pharmacology*, T. Kenakin (Ed.), pp. 813–824, Elsevier, Amsterdam, Netherlands, 2022, https://doi.org/10.1016/B978-0-12-820472-6.00108-0.

25. Giuliano, F., Joussain, C., Denys, P., Laurin, M., Behr-Roussel, D., Assaly, R., Intracavernosal onabotulinumtoxina exerts a synergistic pro-erectile effect when combined with sildenafil in spontaneously hypertensive rats. *J. Sexual Med.*, 19, 6, 899–906, 2022, https://doi.org/10.1016/j.jsxm.2022.03.213.

26. Sangkum, P., Sirisopana, K., Matang, W., Phengsalae, Y., Lertsithichai, P., Ketsuwan, C., Kongchareonsombat, W., Efficacy of the orally disintegrating strip sildenafil for the treatment of erectile dysfunction: A prospective, randomized trial. *Sexual Med.*, 9, 6, 100453, 2021, https://doi.org/10.1016/j.esxm.2021.100453.

27. Shuey, M.M., Lee, K.M., Keaton, J., Khankari, N.K., Breyear, J.H., Walker, V.M., Edwards, T.L., A genetically supported drug repurposing pipeline for diabetes treatment using electronic health records. *eBioMedicine*, 94, 104674, 2023, https://doi.org/10.1016/j.ebiom.2023.104674.

28. Ajmeera, D. and Ajumeera, R., Drug repurposing: A novel strategy to target cancer stem cells and therapeutic resistance. *Genes Dis.*, 11, 1, 148–175, 2024, https://doi.org/10.1016/j.gendis.2022.12.013.

29. Kandasamy, M., Perspectives for the use of therapeutic Botulinum toxin as a multifaceted candidate drug to attenuate COVID-19. *Med. Drug Discov.*, 6, 100042, 2020, https://doi.org/10.1016/j.medidd.2020.100042.

30. Kumbhar, N.M., Aparna, M.A., Nimal, S.K., Shewale, P., Barale, S., Gacche, R., Chapter 17 - New targets for old drugs: drug repurposing approach for accelerating the drug discovery engine with minimum financial inputs, in: *New Horizons in Natural Compound Research*, S.N. Meena, V. Nandre, K. Kodam, R.S. Meena (Eds.), pp. 315–349, Academic Press, London, United Kingdom, 2023, https://doi.org/10.1016/B978-0-443-15232-0.00021-7.

31. Syamprasad, N.P., Madje, N., Bachannagari, J., Jannu, A.K., Jain, S., Tene, K., Chella, N., Niclosamide nanocrystal for enhanced *in-vivo* efficacy against gastrointestinal stromal tumor via regulating EGFR/STAT-3/DR-4 axis. *J. Drug Deliv. Sci. Technol.*, 81, 104221, 2023, https://doi.org/10.1016/j.jddst.2023.104221.

32. Baalbaki, N., Duijvelaar, E., Said, M.M., Schippers, J., Bet, P.M., Twisk, J., Bartelink, I.H., Pharmacokinetics and pharmacodynamics of imatinib for optimal drug repurposing from cancer to COVID-19. *Eur. J. Pharm. Sci.*, *184*, 106418, 2023, https:// doi.org/10.1016/j. ejps.2023.106418.

33. Scrima, S., Tiberti, M., Ryde, U., Lambrughi, M., Papaleo, E., Comparison of force fields to study the zinc-finger containing protein NPL4, a target for disulfiram in cancer therapy. *Biochim. Biophys. Acta (BBA) - Proteins Proteomics*, *1871*, 4, 140921, 2023, https:// doi.org/10.1016/j. bbapap.2023.140921.

34. Banerjee, P., Geng, T., Mahanty, A., Li, T., Zong, L., Wang, B., Integrating the drug, disulfiram into the vitamin E-TPGS-modified PEGylated nanostructured lipid carriers to synergize its repurposing for anti-cancer therapy of solid tumors. *Int. J. Pharm.*, *557*, 374–389, 2019, https:// doi.org/10.1016/j.ijpharm.2018.12.051.

35. Lipinski, C.A. and Reaume, A.G., High throughput *in vivo* phenotypic screening for drug repurposing: Discovery of MLR-1023 a novel insulin sensitizer and novel Lyn kinase activator with clinical proof of concept. *Bioorg. Med. Chem.*, *28*, 9, 115425, 2020, https://doi.org/10.1016/j. bmc.2020.115425.

36. Vaz, R.L., Sousa, S., Chapela, D., van der Linde, H.C., Willemsen, R., Correia, A.D., Afonso, N.D., Identification of antiparkinsonian drugs in the 6-hydroxydopamine zebrafish model. *Pharmacol. Biochem. Behav.*, *189*, 172828, 2020, https://doi.org/10.1016/j. pbb.2019.172828.

37. He, H., Duo, H., Hao, Y., Zhang, X., Zhou, X., Zeng, Y., Li, B. (2023). Computational drug repurposing by exploiting large-scale gene expression data: Strategy, methods and applications. *Comput. Biol. Med.*, *155*, 106671, 2023, https://doi.org/10.1016/j. compbiomed.2023.106671.

38. Lu, T., Chen, C., Wang, A., Jiang, Z., Qi, Z., Hu, Z., Liu, J., Repurposing cabozantinib to GISTs: Overcoming multiple imatinib-resistant cKIT mutations including gatekeeper and activation loop mutants in GISTs preclinical models. *Cancer Lett.*, *447*, 105–114, 2019, https://doi. org/10.1016/j.canlet.2019.01.024.

39. Van Norman, G.A., Off-label use vs off-label marketing of drugs: Part 1: off-label use—patient harms and prescriber responsibilities. *JACC: Basic to Trans. Sci.*, *8*, 2, 224–233, 2023, https:// doi.org/10.1016/j.jacbts.2022.12.011.

40. Skånland, S.S. and Cieślar-Pobuda, A., Off-label uses of drugs for depression. *Eur. J. Pharmacol.*, *865*, 172732, 2019, https://doi.org/10.1016/j.ejphar.2019.172732.

41. Afief, A.R., Irham, L.M., Adikusuma, W., Perwitasari, D.A., Brahmadhi, A., Cheung, R., Integration of genomic variants and bioinformatic-based approach to drive drug repurposing for multiple sclerosis. *Biochem. Biophysics Rep.*, *32*, 101337, 2022, https://doi. org/10.1016/j. bbrep.2022.101337.

42. Irham, L.M., Adikusuma, W., Perwitasari, D.A., Dania, H., Maliza, R., Faridah, I.N., Cheung, R., The use of genomic variants to drive drug repurposing for chronic hepatitis. *Biochem. Biophysics Rep.*, *31*, 101307, 2022, https://doi.org/10.1016/j.bbrep.2022.101307.

43. Urbina, F., Puhl, A.C., Ekins, S., Recent advances in drug repurposing using machine learning. *Curr. Opin. Chem. Biol.*, *65*, 74–84, 2021, https://doi.org/10.1016/j. cbpa.2021.06.001.

44. McGovern, A.J. and Barreto, G.E., Network pharmacology identifies IL6 as an important hub and target of tibolone for drug repurposing in traumatic brain injury. *Biomed. Pharmacother.*, *140*, 111769, 2021, https://doi.org/10.1016/j.biopha.2021.111769.

45. Bhatti, M.S., Asiri, Y., II, Uddin, J., El-Seedi, H.R., Musharraf, S.G., Repurposing of pharmaceutical drugs by high-throughput approach for antihypertensive activity as inhibitors of angiotensin-converting enzyme (ACE) using HPLC-ESI-MS/MS method. *Arab. J. Chem.*, *14*, 8, 103279, 2021, https://doi.org/10.1016/j.arabjc.2021.103279.

46. Gurung, A.B., *In silico* structure modelling of SARS-CoV-2 Nsp13 helicase and Nsp14 and repurposing of FDA approved antiviral drugs as dual inhibitors. *Gene Rep.*, 21, 100860, 2020, https://doi.org/10.1016/j.genrep.2020.100860.

47. Durgam, R., Devarakonda, N., Nayyar, A., Eluri, R., Improved genetic algorithm using machine learning approaches to feature modelled for microarray gene data, in: *Soft Computing for Security Applications: Proceedings of ICSCS 2021*, Springer, Singapore, pp. 859–872, 2022, https:// doi.org/10.1007/978-981-16-5301-8_60.

48. Nayyar, A., Gadhavi, L., Zaman, N., Machine learning in healthcare: Review, opportunities and challenges, in: *Machine Learning and the Internet of Medical Things in Healthcare,* K.K. Singh, M. Elhoseny, A. Singh and A.A. Elngar (Eds.), pp. 23–45, Academic Press, London, United Kingdom, 2021, https://doi.org/10.1016/B978-0-12-821229-5.00011-2.

49. Solanki, A., Kumar, S., Nayyar, A. (Eds.), *Handbook of Research on Emerging Trends and Applications of Machine Learning*, IGI Global, Pennsylvania, United States, 2020, https://doi.org/10.4018/978-1-5225-9643-1.

50. Kumar, S., Nayyar, A., Paul, A., *Swarm intelligence and evolutionary algorithms in healthcare and drug development*, CRC Press, New York, United States, 2019, http://dx.doi.org/10.1201/9780429289675.

51. Alzubi, J., Nayyar, A., Kumar, A., Machine learning from theory to algorithms: An overview. *J. Physics: Conf. Ser.*, 1142, 012012, 2018, https://doi. org/10.1088/1742-6596/1142/1/012012.

52. Lim, P.K., Julca, I., Mutwil, M., Redesigning plant specialized metabolism with supervised machine learning using publicly available reactome data. *Comput. Struct. Biotechnol. J.*, 21, 1639–1650, 2023, https://doi.org/10.1016/j.csbj.2023.01.013.

53. Cui, C., Li, Y., Liu, S., Wang, P., Huang, Z., The unsupervised machine learning to analyze the use strategy of statins for ischaemic stroke patients with elevated transaminase. *Clin. Neurol. Neurosurg.*, 232, 107900, 2023, https://doi.org/10.1016/j.clineuro.2023.107900.

54. Mahayni, A., Rostami, B., Ponce, A.C., Alkhouli, M.A., Semisupervised machine learning on intraoperative hemodynamic recordings predicts multiple clinical outcomes at 1 and 2 years following mitral valve transcatheter edge to edge repair. *J. Am. Coll. Cardiol.*, 81, 8, 4024, 2023, https://doi.org/10.1016/S0735-1097(23)04468-6.

55. Lazebnik, T., Data-driven hospitals staff and resources allocation using agent-based simulation and deep reinforcement learning. *Eng. Appl. Artif. Intell.*, 126, 106783, 2023, https://doi.org/10.1016/j.engappai.2023.106783.

56. Zhou, Y., Huang, Z., Jiang, Q., Wei, J., Li, W., Yang, W., Huang, J., Deep learning in preclinical antibody drug discovery and development. *Methods*, 218, 57–71, 2023, https://doi.org/10.1016/j.ymeth.2023.07.003.

57. Deepthi, K., Jereesh, A.S., Yuansheng, L., A deep learning ensemble approach to prioritize antiviral drugs against novel coronavirus SARS-CoV-2 for COVID-19 drug repurposing. *Appl. Soft Computing*, 113, 107945, 2021, https://doi.org/10.1016/j.asoc.2021.107945.

58. Ahmed, F., Soomro, A.M., Chethikkattuveli Salih, A.R., Samantasinghar, A., Asif, A., Kang, I.S., Choi, K.H., A comprehensive review of artificial intelligence and network based approaches to drug repurposing in Covid-19. *Biomed. Pharmacother.*, 153, 113350, 2022, https://doi.org/10.1016/j.biopha.2022.113350.

59. Liu, Z., Chen, X., Carter, W., Moruf, A., Komatsu, T.E., Pahwa, S., Tong, W., AI-powered drug repurposing for developing COVID-19 treatments, in: *Reference Module in Biomedical Sciences*, Elsevier, Amsterdam, Netherlands, 2022, https://doi.org/10.1016/B978-0-12-824010-6.00005-8.

60. Tripathi, S., Augustin, A., II, Dunlop, A., Sukumaran, R., Dheer, S., Zavalny, A., Kim, E., Recent advances and application of generative adversarial networks in drug discovery, development, and targeting. *Artif. Intell. Life Sci.*, 2, 100045, 2022, https://doi. org/10.1016/j.ailsci.2022.100045.

61. Kumar, A., Krishnamurthi, R., Nayyar, A., Sharma, K., Grover, V., Hossain, E., A novel smart healthcare design, simulation, and implementation using healthcare 4.0 processes. *IEEE Access*, 8, 118433–118471, 2020, https://doi.org/10.1109/ACCESS.2020.3004790.

62. Madugula, S.S., John, L., Nagamani, S., Gaur, A.S., Poroikov, V.V., Sastry, G.N., Molecular descriptor analysis of approved drugs using unsupervised learning for drug repurposing. *Comput. Biol. Med.*, 138, 104856, 2021, https://doi.org/10.1016/j.compbiomed.2021.104856.

63. Gunturu, L.N., Dornadula, G., Nimbagal, R.N., Chapter 3 - Reconsideration of drug repurposing through artificial intelligence program for the treatment of the novel coronavirus, in: *Artificial Intelligence in Healthcare and COVID-19*, P. Chatterjee and M. Esposito (Eds.), pp. 45–68, Academic Press, London, United Kingdom, 2023, https://doi.org/10.1016/B978-0-323-90531-2.00009-6.

64. Kumar, N. and Acharya, V., Machine intelligence-guided selection of optimized inhibitor for human immunodeficiency virus (HIV) from natural products. *Comput. Biol. Med.*, 153, 106525, 2023, https://doi.org/10.1016/j.compbiomed.2022.106525.

65. Sharma, K., Singh, H., Sharma, D.K., Kumar, A., Nayyar, A., Krishnamurthi, R., Dynamic models and control techniques for drone delivery of medications and other healthcare items in covid-19 hotspots, in: *Emerging Technologies for Battling Covid-19: Applications and Innovations*, F. Al-Turjman, A. Devi, A. Nayyar (Eds.), pp. 1–34, Cham, Switzerland, Springer International Publishing, Germany, 2021, https://doi.org/10.1007/978-3-030-60039-6_1.

66. Zivkovic, M., Bacanin, N., Venkatachalam, K., Nayyar, A., Djordjevic, A., Strumberger, I., Al-Turjman, F., COVID-19 cases prediction by using hybrid machine learning and beetle antennae search approach. *Sustain. Cities Soc.*, 66, 102669, 2021, https://doi.org/10.1016/j.scs.2020.102669.

67. Ekpenyong, M.E., Edoho, M.E., Udo, I.J., Etebong, P., II, Uto, N.P., Jackson, T.C., Obiakor, N.M., A transfer learning approach to drug resistance classification in mixed HIV data- set. *Inf. Med. Unlocked*, 24, 100568, 2021, https://doi.org/10.1016/j.imu.2021.100568.

68. Shahabadi, N., Zendehcheshm, S., Mahdavi, M., Khademi, F., Repurposing FDA- approved drugs cetilistat, abiraterone, diiodohydroxyquinoline, bexarotene, and remdesivir as potential inhibitors against RNA dependent RNA polymerase of SARS-CoV-2: A comparative *in silico* perspective. *Inf. Med. Unlocked*, 36, 101147, 2023, https://doi.org/10.1016/j. imu.2022.101147.

69. Wang, X., Wang, H., Yin, G., Zhang, Y.D., Network-based drug repurposing for the treatment of COVID-19 patients in different clinical stages. *Heliyon*, 9, 3, 14059, 2023, https://doi.org/10.1016/j.heliyon.2023.e14059.

70. Kamboj, S., Rajput, A., Rastogi, A., Thakur, A., Kumar, M., Targeting non-structural proteins of hepatitis C virus for predicting repurposed drugs using QSAR and machine learning approaches. *Comput. Struct. Biotechnol. J.*, 20, 3422–3438, 2022, https:// doi.org/10.1016/j.csbj.2022.06.060.

71. Sun, H., Saeedi, P., Karuranga, S., Pinkepank, M., Ogurtsova, K., Duncan, B.B., Magliano, D.J., IDF Diabetes Atlas: Global, regional and country-level diabetes prevalence estimates for 2021 and projections for 2045. *Diabetes Res. Clin. Pract.*, 183, 109119, 2022, https://doi. org/10.1016/j.diabres.2021.109119.

72. Rashid, R.S.M., Temurlu, S., Abourajab, A., Karsili, P., Dinleyici, M., Al-Khateeb, B., Icil, H., Drug repurposing of FDA compounds against α-glucosidase for the treatment of type 2 diabetes: Insights from molecular docking and molecular dynamics simulations. *Pharmaceuticals*, 16, 4, 555, 2023, https://doi.org/10.3390/ph16040555.

73. Asfour, L.C.W. and Sinclair, R., *Male androgenetic alopecia*, [Updated 2023 Jan 25] (2023, July 15). https://www.ncbi.nlm.nih.gov/books/NBK278957/.

74. Elshall, A.A., Ghoneim, A.M., Abd-elmonsif, N.M., Osman, R., Shaker, D.S., Boosting hair growth through follicular delivery of Melatonin through lecithin-enhanced Pickering emulsion

stabilized by chitosan-dextran nanoparticles in testosterone induced androgenic alopecia rat model. *Int. J. Pharmaceutics*, *639*, 122972, 2023; https:// doi.org/10.1016/j.ijpharm.2023.122972.

75. Chen, S., Xie, X., Zhang, G., Zhang, Y., Comorbidities in Androgenetic Alopecia: A Comprehensive Review. *Dermatol. Ther.*, *12*, 10, 2233–2247, 2022; https://doi.org/10.1007/s13555-022-00799-7.

76. Prieto Santamaría, L., Ugarte Carro, E., Díaz Uzquiano, M., Menasalvas Ruiz, E., Pérez Gallardo, Y., Rodríguez-González, A., A data-driven methodology towards evaluating the potential of drug repurposing hypotheses. *Comput. Struct. Biotechnol. J.*, *19*, 4559–4573, 2021; https://doi.org/10.1016/j.csbj.2021.08.003.

77. Albash, R., El-Dahmy, R.M., Hamed, M., II, Darwish, K.M., Alahdal, A.M., Kassem, A.B., Fahmy, A.M., Repurposing levocetirizine hydrochloride loaded into cationic ceramide/phospholipid composite (CCPCs) for management of alopecia: Central composite design optimization, *in- silico* and *in-vivo* studies. *Drug Deliv.*, *29*, 1, 2784–2795, 2022, https://doi.org/10.1080/10717544.2022.2108939.

78. Kanei, A., Asano, K., Kanai, K., Furuta, A., Sasaki, K., Suzaki, H., Inhibitory action of levocetirizine on the production of eosinophil chemoattractants RANTES and eotaxin *in vitro* and *in vivo*. *In Vivo*, *28*, 4, 657–666, 2014.

79. Rossi, A., Campo, D., Fortuna, M.C., Garelli, V., Pranteda, G., De Vita, G., Carlesimo, M., A preliminary study on topical cetirizine in the therapeutic management of androgenetic alopecia. *J. Dermatolog. Treat.*, *29*, 2, 149–151, 2018, https://doi.org/10.1080/09546634.2017.1341610.

80. Abo Dena, A.S. and Abdel Gaber, S.A., *In vitro* drug interaction of levocetirizine and diclofenac: Theoretical and spectroscopic studies. *Spectrochim. Acta A Mol. Biomol. Spectrosc.*, *181*, 239–248, 2017, https://doi.org/10.1016/j.saa.2017.03.043.

81. Wen, S., Wei, J., Bao, J., Guo, T., Zheng, W., Zhuang, X., Lin, Y., Effect of levocetirizine hydrochloride on the growth of human dermal papilla cells: a preliminary study. *Ann. Palliat. Med.*, *9*, 2, 308–317, 2020, https://doi.org/10.21037/apm.2020.01.15.

82. Marques, V.D., Hackbart, B.A., Guilhoto, L.M., Duarte, J.T.C., Peixoto-Santos, J.E., Yacubian, E.M.T., Bittar Guaranha, M.S., Minimum effective sodium valproate dose in genetic generalized epilepsies. *Seizure*, *108*, 53–59, 2023, https://doi.org/10.1016/j.seizure.2023.04.009.

83. Badria, F.A., Fayed, H.A., Ibraheem, A.K., State, A.F., Mazyed, E.A., Formulation of sodium valproate nanospanlastics as a promising approach for drug repurposing in the treatment of androgenic alopecia. *Pharmaceutics*, *12*, 9, 866, 2020, https://doi.org/10.3390/pharmaceutics12090866.

84. Pramanik, P.K.D., Pareek, G., Nayyar, A., Chapter 14 - security and privacy in remote healthcare: issues, solutions, and standards, in: *Telemedicine Technologies*, H.D. Jude and V.E. Balas (Eds.), pp. 201–225, Academic Press, London, United Kingdom, 2019, https://doi.org/10.1016/B978-0-12-816948-3.00014-3.

85. Mahapatra, B., Krishnamurthi, R., Nayyar, A., Healthcare models and algorithms for privacy and security in healthcare records, in: *Security and privacy of electronic healthcare records: Concepts, paradigms and solutions*, vol. 183, 2019, http://dx.doi.org/10.1049/PBHE020E_ch8.

10

Personalized Drug Treatment: Transforming Healthcare with AI

Abhirup Khanna[1] and Sapna Jain[2]*

[1]School of Computer Science, University of Petroleum and Energy Studies, Dehradun, Uttarakhand, India
[2]Cluster of Applied Sciences (Chemistry), University of Petroleum and Energy Studies, Energy Acres, Dehradun, Uttarakhand, India

Abstract

AI-enabled personalized drug treatment has the potential to revolutionize healthcare by tailoring drug therapies for individual patients, taking into account their unique characteristics, genetics, and medical history. The chapter talks about the foundations of AI in healthcare, including an overview of machine learning algorithms, data sources for personalized treatment, and the importance of personalized treatment in modern healthcare. It delves into the area of data collection and analysis process, discussing methods for data pre-processing, feature selection, and model training, as well as the challenges and considerations associated with data analysis in personalized drug treatment. Furthermore, the chapter highlights various case studies in AI-based personalized drug treatment, showcasing examples of how AI has been successfully applied in the treatment of different diseases, such as cancer, cardiovascular diseases, and mental health disorders. The case studies provide insights into the benefits and limitations of personalized drug treatment. Regulatory considerations and ethical and legal bindings associated with the use of personalized drug treatment are also discussed in the chapter. Overall, the chapter serves as a valuable resource for researchers, clinicians, and policymakers interested in the field of personalized medicine and the integration of AI in drug treatment.

Keywords: Artificial intelligence, precision medicine, biomarkers, pharmacogenetics, deep learning, machine learning

10.1 Introduction

In recent years, the field of medicine has witnessed significant growth and advancements in the application of artificial intelligence (AI). AI has emerged as a powerful tool that has the potential to revolutionize various aspects of healthcare, ranging from diagnosis and treatment to drug discovery and patient care. Deep learning algorithms, a subset of AI, have demonstrated remarkable accuracy in interpreting medical images such as X-rays, CT scans, and MRIs [1, 2]. These algorithms can aid radiologists in detecting and diagnosing diseases with greater precision, leading to faster and more accurate diagnoses.

*Corresponding author: sapnaj22@gmail.com

Abhirup Khanna, May El Barachi, Sapna Jain, Manoj Kumar and Anand Nayyar (eds.) Artificial Intelligence and Machine Learning in Drug Design and Development, (295–320) © 2024 Scrivener Publishing LLC

AI has the potential to accelerate the process of drug discovery [3]. Developing new medications traditionally involves a lengthy and costly process. AI algorithms can analyze vast amounts of biomedical data, including genomic and proteomic data, to identify potential drug candidates and predict their efficacy. Another significant application of AI in medicine is in personalized treatment and precision medicine. By analyzing large datasets of patient information, including genetic data and medical records, AI algorithms can identify patterns and correlations that can guide treatment decisions. This approach enables healthcare providers to tailor treatment plans to individual patients, taking into account their unique characteristics and genetic profiles, ultimately leading to more effective and targeted therapies. Pharmacogenomics is the study of how an individual's genetic makeup, specifically their genes and their variations, can affect their response to drugs [4]. It combines pharmacology (the study of drugs) with genomics (the study of genes and their functions) to understand how genetic differences among individuals can influence their response to medications. The field of pharmacogenomics aims to identify genetic factors that can contribute to variations in drug response, including drug efficacy, safety, and adverse reactions. By studying these genetic factors, researchers can gain insights into why individuals may respond differently to the same medication and develop personalized treatment plans based on a person's genetic profile. The information obtained from pharmacogenomic studies can be used to optimize drug selection and dosage for individual patients, enhancing the effectiveness of treatments while minimizing the risk of adverse reactions. It can also aid in predicting an individual's likelihood of developing certain drug-related complications. Pharmacogenomics has the potential to revolutionize healthcare by enabling the practice of precision medicine.

Pharmacogenomics and precision medicine are closely related and interconnected concepts [5]. Pharmacogenomics is a key component of precision medicine, which is an approach to healthcare that seeks to tailor medical treatments and interventions to individual patients based on their unique characteristics, including their genetic makeup. Precision medicine recognizes that individuals differ in their responses to medications due to genetic variations, environmental factors, lifestyle choices, and other factors. Pharmacogenomics plays a significant role in precision medicine by providing insights into how an individual's genetic profile influences their response to specific drugs. By integrating pharmacogenomic information into clinical practice, healthcare providers can make more informed decisions about drug selection, dosing, and treatment strategies. Pharmacogenomic testing can identify genetic markers that are associated with drug efficacy, toxicity, and metabolism. This information allows healthcare professionals to personalize treatment plans, selecting the most effective medication and dosage for each patient based on their genetic profile—for example, if a patient has a genetic variant that affects how their body metabolizes a particular drug, pharmacogenomic testing can reveal this information. Armed with this knowledge, the healthcare provider can adjust the dosage or choose an alternative medication to achieve the desired therapeutic effect while minimizing the risk of adverse reactions. Precision medicine goes beyond pharmacogenomics and encompasses other aspects, such as molecular profiling, biomarkers, and advanced diagnostics. It aims to deliver the right treatment to the right patient at the right time based on comprehensive patient data, including genetic information.

Objectives of the Chapter

The objectives of the chapter are as follows:

- To understand the fundamentals of AI in healthcare;
- To explore data sources and collection methods for personalized treatment;
- To investigate data analysis techniques in personalized drug treatment;
- To examine case studies demonstrating AI's impact on personalized drug treatment;
- And, to discuss regulatory and ethical considerations in AI-enabled personalized medicine.

Organization of the Chapter

The rest of the chapter is organized as follows: Section 10.2 enlightens cheminformatics. Section 10.3 highlights data sources, followed by precision medicine vs. personalized drug treatment in Section 10.4. Section 10.5 highlights AI-enabled personalized drug treatment. Section 10.6 stresses on ethical considerations in AI-enabled personalized drug treatment followed by benefits and limitations of AI enabled personalized drug treatment in Section 10.7. Section 10.8 enlightens case studies. Finally, section 10.9 concludes the chapter with challenges and opportunities.

10.2   Cheminformatics

Cheminformatics has its roots in the early days of computational chemistry when researchers first began to use computers to model the structures and properties of molecules. Over time, cheminformatics has evolved to encompass a wide range of computational methods, from simple database searches to complex machine learning algorithms. The goal of cheminformatics is to help researchers make sense of large amounts of chemical data and to use that data to make predictions about the properties and behaviour of new molecules. This includes everything from predicting the toxicity of a new drug candidate to designing new materials with specific properties [6]. There are different methods for chemical structure representation (Figure 10.1). The preference to choose the method depends on the application, requirement, and level of features required to define the molecular structure.

10.2.1   Chemical Data and Databases

One of the key components of cheminformatics is chemical data and databases. Chemical data can take many forms, including chemical structures, properties, and reactions. Chemical databases are collections of chemical data that have been organized and indexed for easy searching and analysis. There are many different chemical databases available, each with its own strengths and weaknesses. Some databases are focused on specific areas of chemistry, such as drug discovery or materials science, while others are more general in scope.

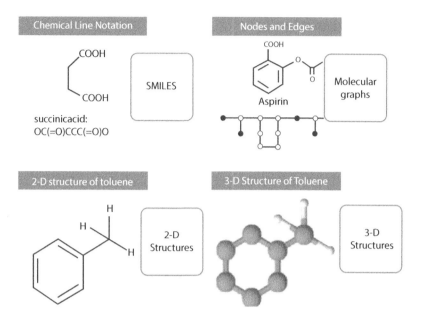

Figure 10.1 Types of chemical structure representation.

10.2.2   Chemical Structure Representation

One of the most important aspects of cheminformatics is the representation of chemical structures. Chemical structures can be represented in many different ways, including line drawings, 2D depictions, and 3D models. Each representation has its own advantages and disadvantages, depending on the application. In addition to visual representations, chemical structures can also be represented using various symbolic notations, such as SMILES and InChI. These notations provide a standardized way of representing chemical structures that can be easily stored and analyzed by computer programs.

10.2.3   Chemical Property Prediction

One of the most important applications of cheminformatics is the prediction of chemical properties. This includes everything from predicting the solubility and toxicity of new molecules to predicting their biological activity. There are many different methods for predicting chemical properties, ranging from simple rule-based methods to complex machine learning algorithms. These methods can be trained on large datasets of chemical data to learn patterns and relationships between chemical structures and properties.

10.2.4   Chemical Reaction Prediction

Another important application of cheminformatics is the prediction of chemical reactions. This involves predicting the products of a chemical reaction based on the starting materials and reaction conditions. There are different methods for predicting chemical reactions, ranging from simple rule-based methods to complex quantum mechanical simulations.

These methods can be used to design new synthetic routes for the production of complex molecules as well as to understand the mechanisms of chemical reactions.

10.2.5   Drug Discovery and Design

Perhaps the most well-known application of cheminformatics is in the field of drug discovery and design. Cheminformatics is used to identify new drug candidates, predict their properties and biological activity, and optimize their structure to improve their efficacy and safety. This involves everything from screening large databases of compounds to identify potential drug candidates, to using computational methods to design new molecules with specific properties. Cheminformatics plays a critical role in every stage of the drug discovery and development process, from target identification to clinical trials.

10.2.6   Materials Science

In addition to drug discovery and design, cheminformatics is also widely used in the field of materials science. Cheminformatics is used to design new materials with specific properties, such as electronic conductivity, mechanical strength, and thermal stability. This involves everything from screening large databases of compounds to identify potential materials candidates, to using computational methods to design.

10.3   Data Sources

To enable AI-based precision drug treatment, several data sources are typically required. There are many organizations with their own databases, few of them are available for free access whilst other are licensed based or under copy rights. The data bases have millions of compounds however we can retrieve a structure in few seconds or we cannot find virtual molecules in them. The current requirement and development is availability of virtual molecules that have not been synthesized so far but could be synthesized easily. The addition of these virtual molecules brings the number of molecular structures to count of billions. There is different software that can be used to draw structures, to be included in various scientific report writing (Table 10.1). The software provides a proper representation of a molecule that brings a real value in cheminformatics and computational chemistry. The drawn structure can be stored in a database for subsequent retrieval and search based on its chemical structure. These sources provide crucial information about patients, diseases, treatments, and outcomes. The following is a list of common data sources used in AI-based precision drug treatment:

1. Electronic health records (EHRs): EHRs contain comprehensive patient health information, including medical history, diagnoses, lab results, medications, and treatment plans. These records provide a valuable source of data for AI algorithms to analyze patient characteristics and treatment outcomes.
2. Genomic data: Genomic data, including DNA sequences, gene expression profiles, and genetic variations, play a significant role in precision medicine.

Table 10.1 Details of software.

Software	Developer(s)	Operating system	Features
Chimera	PerkinElmer	Windows and macOS	• One of the most popular software programmes for creating chemical structures • Provides an intuitive user interface along with a full complement of tools for building and altering chemical structures
MarvinSketch	ChemAxon	Windows 7 and upper versions	• It offers a variety of tools and an intuitive user interface • MarvinSketch is a standalone programme that can also be incorporated into several cheminformatics platforms
RDKit	GitHub and SourceForge	Windows and macOS	• A molecule drawing feature is part of the open-source cheminformatics software package known as RDKit • Python scripts are used to allow users to programmatically draw chemical structures • Used manipulating molecules, looking for substructures, and describing molecules
ChemDoodle	iChemlabs	Windows, macOS, and Linux.	• Chemical sketching and visualization programme • Provides a variety of tools for creating and altering structures
ACD/ChemSketch	ACD/Labs	Windows	• Free programme that lets you draw chemical structures in both 2D and 3D • It has tools for making IUPAC names, predicting chemical properties, and calculating properties based on structure
BKChem	BedaKosata	Windows, macOS, and Linux.	• An open-source chemical sketching programme • It offers a straightforward and lightweight interface for building chemical structures and enables the import and export of a wide range of file formats
JChemPaint	ChemAxon	Windows, Linux	• It supports a number of file formats and provides a variety of drawing tools • Can be used as stand-alone programme or incorporate it into other cheminformatics platforms

Understanding a patient's genetic makeup can help identify specific biomarkers and genetic targets that influence treatment responses.

3. Clinical trials data: Clinical trials provide data on the safety, efficacy, and side effects of drugs and treatments. This data is crucial for training AI algorithms to predict the effectiveness of different drugs for specific patient populations.

4. Biobanks and biorepositories: Biobanks store biological samples such as tissues, blood, and cells collected from patients. These samples can be used to analyze molecular characteristics, genetic mutations, and other biomarkers that aid in tailoring drug treatments.

5. Pharmacogenomic data: Pharmacogenomics focuses on how genetic variations influence an individual's response to drugs. Pharmacogenomic data helps in determining optimal drug dosages and identifying potential drug interactions or adverse reactions based on genetic profiles.

6. Real-time monitoring data: Real-time monitoring data, collected through wearable devices, sensors, or mobile apps, can provide continuous information about a patient's health parameters, vital signs, activity levels, and treatment adherence. This data can assist in personalized treatment decisions.

7. Medical imaging data: Medical imaging data, such as X-rays, CT scans, MRI images, and pathology slides, can provide valuable insights into disease progression and response to treatment. AI algorithms can analyze these images to identify patterns, detect abnormalities, and guide treatment decisions.

8. Literature and research databases: Scientific literature and research databases contain a vast amount of information on diseases, drug interactions, treatment guidelines, and clinical studies. Accessing these resources helps AI algorithms stay up to date and incorporate the latest medical knowledge.

9. Health outcome data: Health outcome data, such as patient-reported outcomes, quality of life measures, and disease progression data, provide insights into the effectiveness of different treatments. This information helps AI models understand the impact of treatments on patients' well-being.

10. Demographic and socioeconomic data: Demographic and socioeconomic data, including age, gender, ethnicity, income, and education, can help identify health disparities and understand how different populations may respond to specific treatments.

It is important to note that the availability and integration of these data sources may vary depending on the healthcare setting, data privacy regulations, and research collaborations. Ensuring data privacy, security, and compliance with ethical guidelines are critical aspects when utilizing these data sources for AI-based precision drug treatment.

10.4 Precision Medicine vs. Personalized Drug Treatment

Precision medicine and personalized drug treatment are often used interchangeably, but there are slight differences between the two concepts [7–9]. Precision medicine is an approach to healthcare that takes into account individual variations in genes, environment, and lifestyle to tailor medical treatments and interventions. It aims to identify the most effective treatment options for specific patient subgroups or even individual patients. Precision medicine encompasses a wide range of factors beyond genetics, including molecular profiling, biomarkers, and clinical data. It seeks to deliver the right treatment to the right patient at the right time, based on a comprehensive understanding of the patient's characteristics. On the other hand, personalized drug treatment focuses specifically on tailoring drug therapies to individual patients based on their unique characteristics, including genetic information. It emphasizes the use of genetic testing and pharmacogenomics to determine the most appropriate drug selection, dosage, and treatment strategy for an individual. Personalized drug treatment recognizes that people respond differently to medications due to genetic variations, and it seeks to optimize drug therapy by using this genetic information. In essence, personalized drug treatment is a subset or a specific application of precision medicine that focuses specifically on optimizing drug therapy based on individual genetic factors. It utilizes pharmacogenomic information to tailor drug treatments to maximize effectiveness and minimize adverse reactions for each patient. While precision medicine encompasses a broader scope, including various aspects of healthcare beyond drug therapy, personalized drug treatment zooms in on the individualized approach to drug selection and dosing based on genetic information. Figures 10.2 - 10.4 represent the outcomes of the literature survey conducted across various themes involving drug design and development using machine learning and AI.

10.4.1 Survey Results

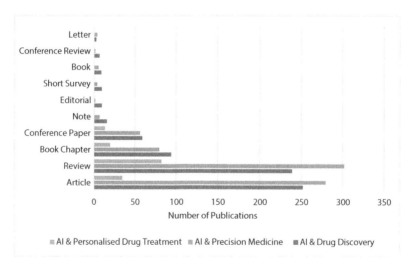

Figure 10.2 Scopus analysis for document type distribution.

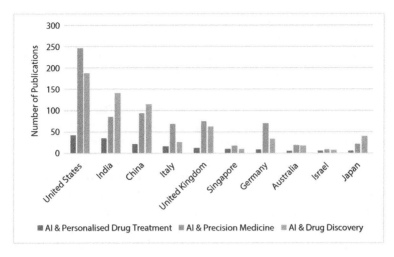

Figure 10.3 Publication landscape: comparative analysis of countries/regions.

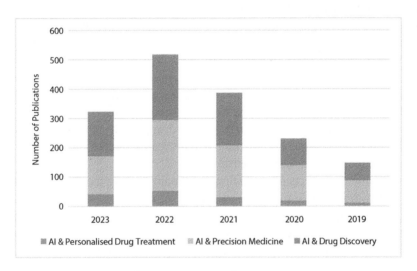

Figure 10.4 Temporal evolution of publications: Scopus analysis.

10.4.2   Importance of Personalized Drug Treatment

The following points highlights the importance of Personalized Drug Treatment:

- Enhanced treatment efficacy: Every individual responds differently to medications due to genetic variations, physiological differences, and other factors. Personalized drug treatment takes into account these individual variations, allowing healthcare providers to select medications and treatment strategies that are most likely to be effective for each patient. By tailoring treatment to the individual's unique characteristics, personalized drug treatment can improve treatment outcomes and increase the likelihood of a successful response to therapy.
- Minimized adverse reactions: Adverse drug reactions can range from mild to severe and can be caused by various factors, including genetic predispositions.

Personalized drug treatment helps identify individuals who may be at higher risk for adverse reactions based on their genetic profiles or other clinical factors. By considering this information, healthcare providers can select medications and dosages that minimize the risk of adverse events, ensuring patient safety and well-being.

- Optimized resource utilization: Personalized drug treatment can help optimize healthcare resources by reducing trial-and-error prescribing and unnecessary medication use. By tailoring treatment to the individual, healthcare providers can avoid prescribing medications that are unlikely to be effective or may cause adverse reactions. This approach minimizes healthcare costs associated with ineffective treatments, reduces the burden on healthcare systems, and allows resources to be allocated more efficiently.

- Prevention of treatment resistance: Some patients may develop resistance to certain medications over time, resulting in a loss of treatment effectiveness. Personalized drug treatment can help identify patients who may be prone to developing resistance or have specific genetic markers associated with treatment resistance. By using this information, healthcare providers can select alternative treatment options or adjust the medication regimen to overcome resistance and maintain treatment efficacy.

- Patient-centered care: Personalized drug treatment places the patient at the center of healthcare decision-making. It recognizes the uniqueness of each individual and tailors treatment plans to their specific needs, preferences, and genetic makeup. This patient-centered approach can improve patient satisfaction, engagement, and adherence to treatment plans, leading to better health outcomes and overall well-being.

- Advancement of precision medicine: Personalized drug treatment is a fundamental component of precision medicine, an approach that aims to deliver targeted therapies based on individual characteristics. By incorporating personalized drug treatment into healthcare practices, precision medicine can be advanced, leading to more effective and precise treatments across a wide range of diseases and conditions.

AI-enabled personalized drug treatment refers to the use of artificial intelligence (AI) techniques and technologies to optimize drug therapies on an individualized basis. It involves leveraging AI algorithms and computational models to analyze vast amounts of patient's data, including genetic information, clinical records, biomarkers, and other relevant factors, to guide and personalize drug treatment decisions.

Some key benefits of AI-enabled personalized drug treatment are as follows:

- Data analysis and pattern recognition: AI algorithms can process and analyze large datasets, identifying patterns, correlations, and associations that may be challenging for humans to detect. This includes analyzing genomic data, molecular profiles, patient histories, and treatment outcomes to identify relationships between genetic variations and drug responses.

- Predictive modeling and risk assessment: AI models can be trained to predict an individual's response to specific drugs based on their genetic profile and other relevant factors. These models can estimate the likelihood of treatment efficacy, adverse reactions, or other treatment outcomes, enabling healthcare professionals to make informed decisions.

- Treatment optimization and decision support: AI algorithms can assist healthcare providers in selecting the most appropriate medication, dosage, and treatment plan for each patient based on their unique characteristics. By considering genetic information, drug–drug interactions, comorbidities, and other factors, AI-enabled systems can suggest personalized treatment options and provide decision support tools for healthcare professionals.
- Real-time monitoring and adaptation: AI can enable continuous monitoring of patients during treatment, integrating real-time data such as physiological parameters, biomarker levels, and patient-reported outcomes. This data can be analyzed to assess treatment response, identify early signs of adverse reactions, and trigger treatment adjustments or interventions as needed.
- Clinical trial optimization: AI algorithms can aid in the design and optimization of clinical trials by identifying patient subgroups likely to respond well to specific treatments. This can improve trial efficiency, increase the chances of successful outcomes, and accelerate the development of new personalized therapies.

AI-enabled personalized drug treatment holds great promise for improving patient outcomes, reducing adverse reactions, and optimizing drug therapies. By leveraging AI's computational power and data analysis capabilities, healthcare providers can make more precise treatment decisions based on individual patient characteristics, leading to more effective and safer medication regimens.

10.5   AI Models for Healthcare

The following are the AI models for healthcare:

1. Convolutional neural networks (CNNs): CNNs have shown great success in analyzing medical imaging data, such as X-rays, CT scans, and MRIs. They can automatically learn hierarchical representations and detect patterns or anomalies in medical images, aiding in disease diagnosis and treatment planning.
2. Recurrent neural networks (RNNs): RNNs are effective in processing sequential data, such as patient medical records or time-series data. They can capture temporal dependencies and longitudinal information, enabling personalized treatment prediction, disease progression modeling, and adverse event detection.
3. Generative adversarial networks (GANs): GANs are used for generating synthetic data that resembles real patient data distributions. This synthetic data can help augment limited datasets and improve model generalization. GANs have been employed in areas like generating synthetic medical images or imputing missing patient information.
4. Variational autoencoders (VAEs): VAEs are generative models that can learn latent representations of data, capturing underlying patterns and variations.

They have been applied in precision medicine for tasks such as patient stratification, identifying disease subtypes, and generating personalized treatment recommendations.

5. Transformer models: Transformer models, such as the popular bidirectional encoder representations from transformers (BERT), have shown success in natural language processing tasks. They have been applied to extract valuable information from clinical text data, including electronic health records, medical literature, and patient reports, enabling personalized treatment recommendation and decision support.

10.5.1   Personalized Drug Treatment Using AI for Cancer

Personalized drug treatment using AI for cancer involves harnessing the power of artificial intelligence to tailor cancer treatments to individual patients based on their specific characteristics, including genetic information, tumor profiles, treatment history, and clinical data [10–12]. This approach aims to optimize treatment effectiveness, minimize adverse effects, and improve patient outcomes in the context of cancer therapy. The key aspects of personalized drug treatment using AI for cancer are as follows:

- Genomic analysis: AI algorithms can analyze the genetic profile of a patient's tumor to identify specific mutations or biomarkers that may be driving cancer growth. By understanding the genetic alterations present in the tumor, AI can help determine targeted therapies that are likely to be effective against those specific molecular targets.
- Treatment prediction and selection: AI models can leverage data from previous patient cases, clinical trials, and scientific literature to predict the likelihood of response to different cancer treatments for an individual patient. These models can help guide treatment decisions by suggesting the most effective therapies or combinations based on the patient's unique characteristics.
- Drug discovery and repurposing: AI techniques such as machine learning and deep learning can be used to analyze large volumes of biological and chemical data to identify new potential drug candidates or repurpose existing drugs for specific cancer types. AI can facilitate the identification of novel molecular targets, optimize drug design, and accelerate the drug discovery process.
- Treatment monitoring and adaptation: AI-enabled systems can continuously monitor the patient's response to treatment by analyzing various data sources, including imaging scans, biomarker measurements, and clinical data. AI algorithms can detect early signs of treatment efficacy or resistance, enabling healthcare professionals to modify the treatment plan in real time to maximize effectiveness.
- Clinical decision support: AI can provide decision support tools for oncologists and other healthcare professionals, offering evidence-based treatment recommendations based on a patient's specific characteristics and the latest research findings. This can help clinicians navigate complex treatment decisions and consider personalized options that may lead to better outcomes.

- Predictive prognosis and survival analysis: AI models can analyze patient data to predict disease progression, recurrence risk, and overall survival rates. These predictions can assist in treatment planning and enable clinicians to develop personalized follow-up and surveillance strategies.

10.5.2   Personalized Drug Treatment Using AI for Cardiovascular Diseases

Personalized drug treatment using AI for cardiovascular diseases involves leveraging artificial intelligence techniques to optimize the selection and dosing of medications for individual patients with cardiovascular conditions [13, 14]. By considering a patient's unique characteristics, including genetic factors, medical history, biomarkers, and clinical data, AI can assist in tailoring drug treatments to maximize efficacy, minimize side effects, and improve patient outcomes in the context of cardiovascular disease management. The key aspects of personalized drug treatment using AI for cardiovascular diseases are as follows:

- Risk assessment and prediction: AI algorithms can analyze patient data, including medical records, lifestyle factors, genetic information, and biomarkers, to assess an individual's cardiovascular risk. By considering multiple variables, AI models can provide personalized risk predictions, aiding healthcare professionals in identifying patients who may benefit from pharmacological interventions and preventive measures.
- Treatment optimization and drug selection: AI can analyze large datasets, including clinical trial data, electronic health records, and scientific literature, to identify patterns and associations between patient characteristics and treatment responses. AI models can help guide healthcare providers in selecting the most appropriate medications, doses, and treatment strategies for individual patients based on their unique profiles, increasing the likelihood of positive outcomes.
- Adverse event prediction and mitigation: AI algorithms can analyze patient data to identify potential risks for adverse drug events, such as drug–drug interactions or drug-induced side effects. By flagging these risks, AI can assist healthcare professionals in making informed decisions about drug selection, dosing, and monitoring strategies to minimize the occurrence of adverse events.
- Treatment monitoring and adjustment: AI-enabled systems can continuously monitor patient data, including physiological parameters, biomarkers, and patient-reported outcomes, to assess treatment response and adjust medication regimens in real time. This dynamic monitoring allows for personalized treatment adaptations, ensuring that patients receive the most effective and appropriate drug therapies throughout their cardiovascular disease management.
- Clinical decision support: AI can provide decision support tools to healthcare professionals, offering evidence-based treatment recommendations based on a patient's specific cardiovascular condition, comorbidities, and individual characteristics. These tools can assist in navigating complex

treatment decisions, considering personalized options, and integrating the latest research findings into clinical practice.

10.5.3   Personalized Drug Treatment Using AI for Mental Health

Personalized drug treatment using AI for mental health involves utilizing artificial intelligence techniques to optimize the selection and management of medications for individuals with mental health conditions. By considering a patient's specific characteristics, including their symptoms, medical history, genetic factors, biomarkers, and treatment response data, AI can assist in tailoring drug treatments to improve efficacy, minimize side effects, and enhance overall mental health outcomes [15, 16].

- Symptom assessment and prediction: AI algorithms can analyze patient-reported symptoms, electronic health records, and other relevant data to assess the severity and progression of mental health conditions. By identifying patterns and correlations, AI models can help predict symptom trajectories and aid in determining the most appropriate medication interventions.
- Treatment response prediction: AI techniques can analyze data from previous treatment outcomes, clinical trials, and patient-specific factors to predict an individual's response to different medications. These models can consider genetic information, biomarkers, and other relevant variables to provide insights into the likelihood of treatment efficacy, enabling healthcare professionals to make informed decisions about medication selection.
- Side effect prediction and management: AI algorithms can analyze patient data to identify potential risks for medication side effects and adverse drug reactions. By considering factors such as genetics, medication interactions, and patient characteristics, AI models can help healthcare providers proactively manage and mitigate side effects, ultimately improving medication tolerability and patient adherence.
- Treatment optimization and medication selection: AI-enabled systems can analyze large datasets, including electronic health records and scientific literature, to identify patterns and associations between patient characteristics and treatment responses. This information can assist healthcare professionals in selecting the most appropriate medications, doses, and treatment strategies for individual patients, improving the likelihood of positive outcomes and minimizing trial-and-error prescribing.
- Personalized medication management: AI can assist in monitoring and adjusting medication regimens over time. By analyzing real-time patient data, including self-reported symptoms, biomarkers, and treatment adherence, AI algorithms can provide recommendations for optimizing medication dosing, scheduling, and combinations, tailored to the individual's evolving mental health needs.
- Clinical decision support: AI can provide decision support tools to aid healthcare professionals in treatment decisions for mental health conditions. These tools can integrate patient-specific data with evidence-based guidelines and

research findings, assisting clinicians in selecting appropriate medications and personalized treatment plans.

10.6   Ethical Considerations in AI-Enabled Personalized Drug Treatment

AI systems often operate as black boxes, meaning that their decision-making processes are not easily understandable or explainable to humans [17]. This lack of transparency raises concerns about accountability and the potential for AI systems to make decisions that have significant impacts on individuals' lives without proper justification. Developing AI systems that are transparent and can provide explanations for their decisions is crucial to building trust and ensuring accountability [18]. Privacy and data protection are central ethical concerns in AI. AI systems require vast amounts of data to learn and make accurate predictions. However, the collection, storage, and use of personal data raise privacy concerns. It is essential to establish robust data protection policies and frameworks to safeguard individuals' privacy rights and ensure that their data is used in a responsible and secure manner. AI-enabled personalized drug treatment brings about various ethical considerations that need to be carefully addressed. Some of the key ethical considerations include the following:

- Privacy and data security: AI relies on accessing and analyzing large amounts of patient data, including sensitive genetic and medical information. It is essential to ensure robust data privacy and security measures to protect patient confidentiality and prevent unauthorized access or misuse of personal health information.
- Informed consent: Patients should be adequately informed about the use of AI in their treatment and the potential implications. Informed consent should include transparent explanations about data usage, potential risks, and benefits of AI-enabled personalized drug treatment. Patients should have the right to make informed decisions and have control over the use of their data.
- Algorithm bias and fairness: AI algorithms can be influenced by biases in the data used for training, leading to potential biases in treatment recommendations. It is crucial to identify and address any biases to ensure fair and equitable treatment recommendations that do not disproportionately affect certain patient populations or perpetuate healthcare disparities.
- Transparency and explainability: AI algorithms can be complex and difficult to interpret. There is a need for transparency and explainability in AI-enabled personalized drug treatment to ensure that healthcare providers and patients can understand the basis for treatment recommendations. The ability to explain how decisions are made by AI systems is crucial for trust, accountability, and enabling informed decision-making.
- Accountability and liability: Determining responsibility and liability in AI-enabled personalized drug treatment can be challenging. In cases where AI systems are involved in treatment decisions, it is necessary to clarify the

roles and responsibilities of healthcare professionals, developers, and regulatory bodies. Clear frameworks should be established to address issues of accountability and potential liability for errors or adverse outcomes.

- Equity and access: AI-enabled personalized drug treatment should be designed and implemented in a way that ensures equitable access for all patients. It is important to consider disparities in access to healthcare resources, including AI technologies, and address potential challenges to ensure that personalized treatments are accessible to diverse populations.

- Continuous monitoring and validation: AI algorithms used in personalized drug treatment should be continuously monitored and validated to ensure their accuracy, reliability, and effectiveness. Regular updates and rigorous evaluation should be conducted to maintain the quality and safety of AI-enabled systems.

- Human oversight and clinical judgment: While AI can provide valuable insights and support in personalized drug treatment, it should always be complemented by human expertise and clinical judgment. The final treatment decisions should remain in the hands of healthcare professionals, who should use AI recommendations as tools to inform their decision-making rather than relying solely on automated systems.

Addressing these ethical considerations requires collaboration between healthcare professionals, AI developers, regulators, and policymakers. Ethical guidelines and frameworks should be established to ensure responsible and accountable use of AI in personalized drug treatment, while safeguarding patient rights, privacy, and well-being.

10.7   Benefits and Limitations of AI-Enabled Personalized Drug Treatment

AI-enabled personalized drug treatment offers several benefits in healthcare, but it also has certain limitations. The key benefits and limitations are listed as follows:

10.7.1   Benefits

- Improved treatment efficacy: By leveraging AI algorithms to analyze large datasets and patient-specific information, personalized drug treatment can enhance treatment effectiveness. AI can identify patterns, genetic markers, and treatment responses to guide healthcare providers in selecting the most appropriate medications and dosages for individual patients, leading to improved treatment outcomes.

- Enhanced safety and adverse event reduction: Personalized drug treatment using AI can help identify patients who may be at a higher risk for adverse drug reactions or side effects. By considering genetic factors, drug–drug interactions, and individual patient characteristics, AI can aid in minimizing the occurrence of adverse events, improving patient safety, and optimizing medication regimens.

- Optimization of resource utilization: AI-enabled personalized drug treatment can help optimize healthcare resources by reducing trial-and-error prescribing and unnecessary medication use. By tailoring treatments to individual patients, healthcare providers can avoid prescribing medications that are unlikely to be effective or may cause adverse reactions. This approach can minimize healthcare costs associated with ineffective treatments and allocate resources more efficiently.

- Accelerated treatment development: AI algorithms can analyze vast amounts of biomedical data, including genetic and molecular information, to identify new potential drug candidates or repurpose existing drugs. AI can assist in drug discovery, optimization, and repurposing efforts, potentially speeding up the development of novel therapies and expanding treatment options for patients.

10.7.2   Limitations

- Data availability and quality: AI relies on large and high-quality datasets for training and validation. The availability and quality of data, including genetic profiles, electronic health records, and treatment outcomes, can vary across different healthcare settings. Limited or biased data can affect the accuracy and generalizability of AI models, potentially leading to suboptimal treatment recommendations.

- Algorithm bias and interpretability: AI algorithms may be susceptible to biases present in the data used for training, potentially resulting in biased treatment recommendations. Additionally, some AI models, such as deep learning models, can be challenging to interpret and explain. Lack of transparency and interpretability may raise concerns regarding the trustworthiness and accountability of AI-enabled personalized drug treatment systems.

- Ethical and privacy concerns: The use of AI in personalized drug treatment raises ethical considerations related to data privacy, informed consent, algorithm fairness, and equity of access. Safeguarding patient privacy, ensuring informed consent, and addressing biases and disparities are critical for maintaining ethical standards in AI-enabled healthcare.

- Validation and generalizability: AI models used in personalized drug treatment require rigorous validation and testing to ensure their accuracy, reliability, and generalizability across diverse populations and healthcare settings. The generalizability of AI models can be challenging due to variations in patient characteristics, healthcare practices, and data availability across different populations and geographical regions.

- Human expertise and clinical judgment: AI should be considered as a supportive tool for healthcare professionals rather than a replacement for human expertise and clinical judgment. The final treatment decisions should always be made by healthcare providers, who should interpret and contextualize AI-generated recommendations within the broader clinical context.

To fully leverage the benefits of AI-enabled personalized drug treatment and overcome its limitations, ongoing research, development, and collaboration among healthcare professionals, AI experts, policymakers, and regulatory bodies are necessary.

10.8   Case Studies

10.8.1   Project CancerLinQ

Project CancerLinQ is an initiative developed by the American Society of Clinical Oncology (ASCO) to harness the power of big data and analytics to improve cancer care and outcomes [19]. CancerLinQ aims to create a robust and comprehensive learning health system that collects, aggregates, and analyzes real-world cancer data from various sources to generate meaningful insights and support evidence-based decision-making. The primary goal of CancerLinQ is to gather data from electronic health records (EHRs) and other structured and unstructured sources to create a vast database of oncology patient information. This includes information on patient demographics, disease characteristics, treatment regimens, and outcomes. By aggregating and harmonizing these diverse data sources, CancerLinQ creates a comprehensive and longitudinal view of patients' journeys through cancer care. The data collected through CancerLinQ is de-identified and securely stored to protect patient privacy. It undergoes rigorous data cleaning, normalization, and quality control processes to ensure accuracy and reliability. Once the data is processed and transformed into a usable format, it is subjected to advanced analytics and machine learning techniques to derive insights and knowledge. These insights can then be utilized to the following:

1. Identify and promote evidence-based best practices: By analyzing real-world data, CancerLinQ aims to identify patterns and trends in cancer care, enabling healthcare providers to access evidence-based best practices and make informed treatment decisions.
2. Quality improvement and benchmarking: CancerLinQ supports quality improvement initiatives by providing healthcare providers with benchmarking data and performance metrics. It allows them to compare their practice patterns and outcomes to those of their peers, facilitating continuous improvement in cancer care delivery.
3. Research and clinical trials: The vast dataset within CancerLinQ provides a valuable resource for research purposes. It can support the identification of research questions, patient cohorts, and potential participants for clinical trials, fostering scientific advancements in oncology.
4. Real-time decision support: CancerLinQ aims to provide healthcare providers with real-time decision support tools that integrate with electronic health records. These tools can offer personalized treatment recommendations, guidelines, and clinical pathways based on the latest evidence and insights derived from the CancerLinQ database.

By leveraging the power of big data and analytics, CancerLinQ aims to transform cancer care by promoting a learning health system that continually evolves and improves based on real-world evidence. It strives to enhance the quality, efficiency, and effectiveness of cancer care delivery, ultimately improving patient outcomes and the overall quality of cancer care.

10.8.2   Project Atomwise

Project Atomwise is a drug discovery platform that utilizes artificial intelligence (AI) and machine learning to accelerate the process of identifying potential drug candidates for various diseases [20]. It combines advanced algorithms and high-performance computing with a vast database of molecular structures and drug data to predict the binding affinity between small molecules and target proteins. The core technology of Atomwise revolves around molecular docking simulations, where the AI algorithms analyze the three-dimensional structures of target proteins and small molecules to predict their binding interactions. By leveraging large-scale computational power and deep learning techniques, Atomwise can evaluate millions of potential drug candidates in a fraction of the time and cost compared to traditional drug discovery methods.

The key aspects of Project Atomwise include the following:

1. Virtual screening: Atomwise uses its AI platform to perform virtual screening of vast chemical libraries, including both known drugs and novel compounds, to identify potential candidates that have the potential to bind to specific target proteins implicated in diseases.
2. Structure-based design: Atomwise's algorithms analyze the structures of both the target protein and the small molecules to predict their binding affinity and interaction. This information helps researchers design and optimize drug candidates with improved potency and selectivity.
3. Therapeutic areas: Atomwise's technology can be applied to various therapeutic areas, including infectious diseases, oncology, neurology, and rare diseases. It has been used to discover potential drug candidates for conditions such as Ebola, multiple sclerosis, Parkinson's disease, and more.
4. Collaboration: Atomwise collaborates with academic institutions, pharmaceutical companies, and biotech firms to discover and develop new drugs. Through partnerships, Atomwise applies its AI platform to specific drug discovery projects, providing valuable insights and support to accelerate the development of novel therapeutics.

The potential benefits of Project Atomwise are as follows:

1. Speed and efficiency: By leveraging AI and computational methods, Atomwise can rapidly screen and evaluate a large number of potential drug candidates, significantly accelerating the drug discovery process. This speed and efficiency can potentially reduce the time and cost required to develop new treatments.
2. Expanded chemical space exploration: Atomwise's approach enables the exploration of a vast chemical space, including both known and novel compounds. This expands the possibilities for discovering unique and innovative drug candidates that may have been overlooked using traditional methods.

3. Target-specific drug design: Atomwise's technology focuses on specific target proteins implicated in diseases, allowing for targeted drug design and increased precision in treatment development. This approach increases the likelihood of identifying effective therapies with better therapeutic outcomes.

However, it is important to note that Atomwise's predictions and findings still need to be experimentally validated and tested in preclinical and clinical settings. The AI models are built on available data and may be subject to limitations and biases based on the data used for training. Collaboration with domain experts and rigorous validation processes are essential to ensure the reliability and safety of the discovered drug candidates.

10.8.3   Project BenevolentAI

Project BenevolentAI is a research and technology initiative that harnesses artificial intelligence (AI) and machine learning to accelerate drug discovery and development as well as the advancement of biomedical research [21]. The project aims to leverage AI-driven approaches to unlock valuable insights from vast amounts of scientific data and apply them to various disease areas. The key aspects of Project BenevolentAI include:

1. Knowledge graph: BenevolentAI has developed a proprietary knowledge graph that integrates and connects vast amounts of structured and unstructured data from scientific literature, clinical trials, patents, and other sources. This comprehensive knowledge graph serves as a foundation for AI-driven analyses and insights generation.
2. Drug discovery and repurposing: BenevolentAI applies AI algorithms and machine learning techniques to analyze the knowledge graph and identify potential drug candidates for various diseases. By exploring patterns and relationships within the data, the project aims to discover new therapeutic targets and repurpose existing drugs for alternative indications.
3. Disease understanding: BenevolentAI aims to improve the understanding of diseases by leveraging AI-driven approaches to analyze molecular and clinical data. By uncovering hidden connections and patterns, the project seeks to gain insights into disease mechanisms, identify biomarkers, and understand patient subpopulations, facilitating precision medicine approaches.
4. Data-driven hypothesis generation: Project BenevolentAI uses AI algorithms to generate hypotheses for scientific research and drug development. By analyzing and synthesizing data from different sources, the project aims to identify novel connections and propose potential research directions, accelerating the discovery of new treatments.
5. Collaboration: BenevolentAI collaborates with academic institutions, pharmaceutical companies, and research organizations to apply its AI-driven platform to specific drug discovery projects and research initiatives. Through partnerships, the project aims to combine expertise and resources to accelerate scientific advancements and improve patient outcomes.

The potential benefits of Project BenevolentAI are as follows:

1. Accelerated drug discovery: By leveraging AI and machine learning, BenevolentAI aims to accelerate the drug discovery process, reducing the time and cost required to identify and develop new therapies. The project's AI-driven analyses and insights generation can help identify promising drug candidates and optimize their design.
2. Repurposing existing drugs: BenevolentAI focuses on repurposing existing drugs for new indications. By analyzing the wealth of available data, the project aims to identify potential uses for approved drugs, enabling faster development and reduced costs compared to starting from scratch.
3. Precision medicine and patient stratification: By analyzing molecular and clinical data, BenevolentAI aims to contribute to precision medicine approaches. The project seeks to identify biomarkers and patient subpopulations to guide personalized treatment strategies, enhancing therapeutic outcomes.
4. Knowledge integration and insights generation: The integration of diverse scientific data into the knowledge graph allows BenevolentAI to generate valuable insights and identify connections that may have been previously overlooked. This can lead to novel scientific discoveries and new approaches for disease understanding and treatment.

As with any AI-driven project, it is essential to validate the findings and insights generated by BenevolentAI through rigorous experimental and clinical studies. Collaboration with domain experts and adherence to ethical and regulatory standards are crucial to ensure the reliability and safety of the discovered drug candidates and research findings.

10.8.4 Project Deep Genomics

Project Deep Genomics is an initiative that combines artificial intelligence (AI) and genomics to advance the understanding and treatment of genetic diseases. The project aims to leverage AI-driven approaches to analyze genomic data, identify disease-causing genetic variants, and predict the impact of these variants on biological processes [22]. The ultimate goal is to accelerate the development of targeted therapies and precision medicine interventions. The key aspects of Project Deep Genomics include the following:

1. Genomic data analysis: Deep Genomics focuses on analyzing large-scale genomic datasets, including sequencing data from patients with genetic diseases and population-level genomic data. AI algorithms are applied to identify genetic variants and analyze their potential functional consequences, enabling researchers to understand the underlying genetic mechanisms of diseases.
2. AI-driven variant interpretation: The project utilizes deep learning techniques to interpret the functional impact of genetic variants. AI models are trained to predict the effects of variants on gene expression, protein structure, and molecular interactions. This enables researchers to prioritize and understand the significance of disease-associated genetic variants.

3. Disease modeling and mechanistic understanding: Deep Genomics aims to model and simulate the effects of genetic variants within biological systems. By integrating genomic data with molecular and cellular models, the project seeks to elucidate the mechanisms through which genetic variants contribute to disease development. This can provide insights into disease pathways, potential therapeutic targets, and the design of targeted interventions.

4. Drug discovery and development: Project Deep Genomics utilizes AI algorithms to screen and identify potential drug candidates. By considering the genomic context and predicted effects of genetic variants, the project aims to identify novel therapeutic targets and repurpose existing drugs for specific genetic diseases. This approach can expedite the drug discovery process and improve treatment options for patients with genetic disorders.

5. Precision medicine and patient stratification: Deep Genomics contributes to the field of precision medicine by integrating genomic data with clinical and phenotypic information. By understanding the genetic basis of diseases, the project aims to stratify patients based on their genetic profiles, enabling personalized treatment approaches and optimizing therapeutic outcomes.

The benefits of Project Deep Genomics are as follows:

1. Enhanced understanding of genetic diseases: By leveraging AI and genomics, Deep Genomics can provide insights into the underlying genetic mechanisms of diseases. This understanding can lead to improved disease classification, identification of novel disease-associated genes, and a deeper understanding of disease heterogeneity.

2. Accelerated drug discovery: AI-driven approaches can accelerate the identification of potential drug candidates by integrating genomic data and disease models. Deep Genomics aims to expedite the discovery and development of targeted therapies, enabling faster translation of research findings into clinical applications.

3. Precision medicine approaches: Deep Genomics contributes to the development of precision medicine by integrating genomic data into clinical decision-making. This allows for personalized treatment strategies based on a patient's genetic profile, increasing the likelihood of therapeutic success and minimizing adverse reactions.

4. Insights into disease mechanisms: The integration of AI and genomics can provide insights into the molecular mechanisms underlying genetic diseases. This knowledge can contribute to the development of new biomarkers, diagnostic tools, and therapeutic interventions.

10.9   Conclusion, Challenges, and Opportunities

As with any AI-driven project, it is important to validate the findings and predictions generated by Deep Genomics through experimental and clinical studies. Collaborations with domain experts, adherence to ethical guidelines, and data privacy considerations are crucial for responsible and effective implementation of AI-driven genomics research. AI-enabled personalized drug treatment has made significant strides in improving patient care, but there are still several challenges and opportunities for further development in this field.

Here are some key challenges and opportunities.

The challenges are as follows:

1. Data quality and availability: Access to high-quality, diverse, and comprehensive patient data, including genomic information, electronic health records, and real-world data, remains a challenge. Ensuring data accuracy, standardization, and interoperability across different healthcare systems is crucial for robust AI-enabled personalized drug treatment.

2. Ethical and legal considerations: Protecting patient privacy, ensuring informed consent, and addressing ethical considerations related to data usage and algorithm fairness are ongoing challenges. The development of robust ethical guidelines and regulatory frameworks is essential to maintain patient trust and ensure responsible use of AI in personalized drug treatment.

3. Algorithm bias and interpretability: Addressing bias and ensuring fairness in AI algorithms is critical to prevent unintended consequences and disparities in treatment recommendations. Enhancing interpretability and explainability of AI models can improve trust, facilitate clinical adoption, and enable healthcare providers to make informed decisions based on AI-generated insights.

4. Validation and clinical adoption: Validating the performance and effectiveness of AI-enabled personalized drug treatment approaches through rigorous clinical studies and real-world evidence is necessary for wider adoption. Demonstrating the clinical utility, safety, and cost-effectiveness of these approaches is crucial to gain acceptance from healthcare providers, regulatory bodies, and payers.

5. Integration with clinical workflow: Seamless integration of AI-enabled tools and recommendations into existing clinical workflows is essential for widespread adoption. Ensuring compatibility with electronic health record systems and providing user-friendly interfaces that align with clinicians' needs and preferences are key challenges.

The opportunities are as follows:

1. Precision medicine advancements: AI-enabled personalized drug treatment has the potential to significantly advance precision medicine approaches. By integrating genomic information, biomarkers, and clinical data, AI can support the identification of patient subgroups, optimize treatment selection, and predict treatment response, leading to more targeted and effective therapies.

2. Real-time monitoring and adaptive treatment: AI can enable real-time monitoring of patients' health data, including biomarkers, imaging, and patient-reported outcomes. This allows for adaptive treatment strategies,

where therapies can be adjusted in real-time based on individual patient responses and evolving disease conditions.

3. Combination therapies and drug repurposing: AI algorithms can identify potential synergistic effects and optimal combinations of drugs, as well as repurpose existing drugs for new indications. This can expand treatment options, accelerate drug development, and potentially reduce costs associated with new drug discovery.

4. Patient empowerment and shared decision-making: AI-enabled personalized drug treatment can empower patients by providing them with access to their own health data, treatment options, and personalized recommendations. This facilitates shared decision-making between patients and healthcare providers, improving patient engagement and satisfaction.

5. Multimodal data integration: Integrating diverse data sources, including genomics, proteomics, imaging, and clinical data, holds promise for a comprehensive understanding of disease mechanisms and treatment response. AI can analyze and integrate these multimodal datasets to generate more accurate and holistic personalized treatment recommendations.

6. Collaborative research and data sharing: Opportunities exist for collaborative research and data sharing among healthcare institutions, researchers, and pharmaceutical companies. Establishing data sharing platforms and fostering collaborations can facilitate larger-scale analyses, improve AI models, and enhance the generalizability of personalized drug treatment approaches.

Addressing these challenges and capitalizing on the opportunities requires interdisciplinary collaboration, regulatory support, ongoing research and development, and the active involvement of stakeholders including healthcare providers, patients, researchers, and policymakers. By overcoming these challenges and leveraging the opportunities, AI-enabled personalized drug treatment can continue to advance and revolutionize patient care in the near future.

References

1. Suzuki, K., Overview of deep learning in medical imaging. *Radiological Phys. Technol.*, 10, 3, 257–273, 2017.
2. Kim, M., Yun, J., Cho, Y., Shin, K., Jang, R., Bae, H.J., Kim, N., Deep learning in medical imaging. *Neurospine*, 16, 4, 657, 2019.
3. Paul, D., Sanap, G., Shenoy, S., Kalyane, D., Kalia, K., Tekade, R.K., Artificial intelligence in drug discovery and development. *Drug Discov. Today*, 26, 1, 80, 2021.
4. Pirmohamed, M., Pharmacogenomics: current status and future perspectives. *Nat. Rev. Gen.*, 24, 6, 350–362, 2023, January 27. https://doi.org/10.1038/s41576-022-00572-8
5. Chenoweth, M.J., Giacomini, K.M., Pirmohamed, M., Hill, S.L., van Schaik, R.H., Schwab, M., Tyndale, R.F., Global pharmacogenomics within precision medicine: challenges and opportunities. *Clin. Pharmacol. Ther.*, 107, 1, 57–61, 2020.
6. Wishart, D.S., Introduction to cheminformatics. *Curr. Protoc. Bioinf.*, 18, 1, 2007, June. https://doi.org/10.1002/0471250953.bi1401s18

7. Denny, J.C. and Collins, F.S., Precision medicine in 2030—seven ways to transform healthcare. *Cell*, 184, 6, 1415–1419, 2021.

8. Manzari, M.T., Shamay, Y., Kiguchi, H., Rosen, N., Scaltriti, M., Heller, D.A., Targeted drug delivery strategies for precision medicines. *Nat. Rev. Mater.*, 6, 4, 351–370, 2021.

9. Ho, D., Quake, S.R., McCabe, E.R., Chng, W.J., Chow, E.K., Ding, X., Zarrinpar, A., Enabling technologies for personalized and precision medicine. *Trends Biotechnol.*, 38, 5, 497–518, 2020.

10. Han, H.J., Ekweremadu, C., Patel, N., Advanced drug delivery system with nanomaterials for personalised medicine to treat breast cancer. *J. Drug Deliv. Sci. Technol.*, 52, 1051–1060, 2019.

11. Catanese, S. and Lordick, F., Targeted and immunotherapy in the era of personalised gastric cancer treatment. *Best Pract. Res. Clin. Gastroenterol.*, 50, 101738, 2021.

12. Mazurakova, A., Samec, M., Koklesova, L., Biringer, K., Kudela, E., Al-Ishaq, R.K., Golubnitschaja, O., Anti-prostate cancer protection and therapy in the framework of predictive, preventive and personalised medicine—comprehensive effects of phytochemicals in primary, secondary and tertiary care. *EPMA J.*, 13, 3, 461–486, 2022.

13. Shen, L., Shen, K., Bai, J., Wang, J., Singla, R.K., Shen, B., Data-driven microbiota biomarker discovery for personalized drug therapy of cardiovascular disease. *Pharmacol. Res.*, 161, 105225, 2020.

14. Bertsimas, D., Orfanoudaki, A., Weiner, R.B., Personalized treatment for coronary artery disease patients: a machine learning approach. *Health Care Manage. Sci.*, 23, 482–506, 2020.

15. Drake, R.E., Cimpean, D., Torrey, W.C., Shared decision making in mental health: prospects for personalized medicine. *Dialogues Clin. Neurosci.*, 11, 4, 455–463, 2009.

16. Hickie, I.B., Scott, E.M., Cross, S.P., Iorfino, F., Davenport, T.A., Guastella, A.J., Scott, J., Right care, first time: a highly personalised and measurement-based care model to manage youth mental health. *Med. J. Aust.*, 211, 3–, 46, 2019.

17. Safdar, N.M., Banja, J.D., Meltzer, C.C., Ethical considerations in artificial intelligence. *Eur. J. Radiol.*, 122, 108768, 2020.

18. Keskinbora, K.H., Medical ethics considerations on artificial intelligence. *J. Clin. Neurosci.*, 64, 277–282, 2019.

19. Rubinstein, S.M. and Warner, J.L., CancerLinQ: origins, implementation, and future directions. *JCO Clin. Cancer Inf.*, 2, 1–7, 2018.

20. Home Page. (n.d.). Atomwise. https://www.atomwise.com/

21. BenevolentAI | AI Drug Discovery | AI Pharma. (n.d.). BenevolentAI (AMS: BAI). https://www.benevolent.com/

22. Home | Deep Genomics. (n.d.). Deep Genomics. https://www.deepgenomics.com/

11

Process and Applications of Structure-Based Drug Design

Shanmuga Sundari M.*, Sree Aiswarya Thotakura, Mounika Dharmana, Priyanka Gadela
and Mayukha Mandya Ammangatambu

BVRIT HYDERABAD College of Engineering for Women, Hyderabad, India

Abstract

Structure-based drug design (SBDD) is a methodology used in drug discovery to design and develop new drugs based on the three-dimensional structure of the biological target, usually a protein. The process involves the identification of a target protein, determining its structure through experimental methods such as X-ray crystallography or NMR spectroscopy, and then the design molecules that can bind to and modulate the activity of the protein. The SBDD process can be broken down into multiple steps to reach the final design. Initially, data collection and structural determination are performed to define the design. Then, virtual screening and hit optimization are carried out to define the internal molecules of the structure. In the end, the selection process is carried out with clinical trials. Through SBDD, drugs can be developed to interact with specific protein targets, reducing the potential of unintended side effects and enhancing the efficiency of the treatment. SBDD has several advantages over traditional drug discovery methods, including a higher success rate in identifying lead compounds and reduced risk of toxicity. SBDD has led to the discovery of clinically approved drugs and has the potential to revolutionize the way we develop new medicines.

Keywords: Artificial intelligence, drug design, medicinal process, precision, structure-based drug design (SBDD)

11.1 Introduction

Structure-based drug design (SBDD) [1] is a potent and adaptable method for finding new drugs that has the potential to hasten the identification of novel treatments for a variety of ailments. The foundation of SBDD is the idea that knowing the three-dimensional structure of a target protein or enzyme is essential for creating medications that bind to it with a high degree of specificity and affinity. Drugs can be created *via* SBDD to interact with particular protein targets, lowering the possibility of side effects that are not intended and increasing the effectiveness of the treatment.

Corresponding author: sundari.m@bvrithyderabad.edu.in

Abhirup Khanna, May El Barachi, Sapna Jain, Manoj Kumar and Anand Nayyar (eds.) *Artificial Intelligence and Machine Learning in Drug Design and Development*, (321–368) © 2024 Scrivener Publishing LLC

The process of SBDD typically involves several steps as shown in Figure 11.1, including target identification, protein structure determination, and virtual screening. Target identification is the process of identifying a protein or enzyme that is involved in a disease process and is typically based on a combination of biological and computational approaches. Once a target has been identified, protein structure determination is used to determine the three-dimensional structure of the protein [2], usually by X-ray crystallography or nuclear magnetic resonance (NMR) spectroscopy. Once the protein structure has been established, chemicals that are likely to bind to the protein with a high affinity and specificity can be found *via* molecular docking and virtual screening. In order to improve the binding interactions between the drug candidate and the target protein, molecular dynamics simulations can be performed.

SBDD has several advantages over traditional drug discovery methods, including higher potency and selectivity, fewer off-target effects, and reduced development times and costs. Many successful drugs have been developed using SBDD, including the HIV protease inhibitors and the anti-cancer drug Gleevec.

SBDD has numerous applications in drug discovery, including in the development of drugs for cancer, infectious diseases, and metabolic disorders—for example, SBDD has been used to develop new inhibitors of cancer-associated proteins such as p53, Bcl-2, and PI3K, and to identify new antibiotics that target bacterial enzymes involved in cell wall synthesis. In addition, SBDD has been used to design drugs for metabolic disorders such as diabetes and obesity, by targeting key enzymes involved in glucose and lipid metabolism.

Finally, SBDD is a promising strategy for drug discovery that has the potential to hasten the creation of novel treatments for a variety of ailments. As computational power and data analytics continue to increase, SBDD is likely to play a bigger role in the fight against illness.

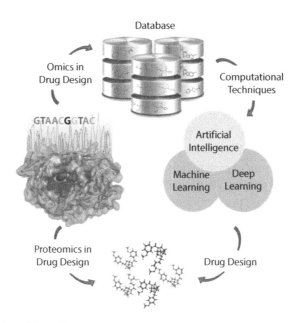

Figure 11.1 Structure-based drug discovery process.

11.1.1 Overview of the Drug Discovery Process

Drug development is an intricate and iterative process with many stages, each of which is essential to the creation of safe and efficient medicines. The steps involved in the drug discovery process are detailed as follows:

1. Target identification: Finding a target protein or enzyme that is implicated in a disease process is the first step in the drug discovery process. This is typically done through a combination of biological and computational methods, including genomics, proteomics, and bioinformatics. Once a target has been identified, the next step is to validate its potential as a drug target.

2. Hit identification: Once a target has been identified and validated, the next step is to identify potential drug candidates that bind to the target. High-throughput screening (HTS), which involves testing huge libraries of compounds for activity against the target, is often used to do this. Alternatively, virtual screening can be used to computationally screen large libraries of compounds for potential drug candidates.

3. Hit-to-lead optimization: The compounds identified in the hit identification stage are known as hits, and they often have low potency and selectivity. The goal of the hit-to-lead optimization stage is to identify compounds with higher potency and selectivity through medicinal chemistry approaches, such as structure–activity relationship (SAR) analysis, and to optimize their pharmacological properties, such as their solubility, bioavailability, and toxicity.

4. Lead optimization: Once a lead compound has been identified with good potency, selectivity, and pharmacological properties, the next step is to optimize its drug-like properties through further medicinal chemistry approaches. To enhance the compound's pharmacokinetic features, such as its absorption, distribution, metabolism, and excretion (ADME), this entails iterative cycles of design, production, and testing.

5. Preclinical development: Before a drug candidate can move to clinical trials, it must undergo preclinical development. This include examining the drug candidate's pharmacokinetics, effectiveness, and safety in animal models. Toxicology research is also done at this stage to find any potential side effects of the drug candidate.

6. Clinical development: If a drug candidate passes preclinical testing, it can proceed to clinical trials. Clinical development involves testing the drug candidate in human subjects in three phases of clinical trials. Phase I trials examine the drug candidate's pharmacokinetics and safety in a small group of healthy volunteers, whereas phase II and III trials examine the drug candidate's efficacy and safety in larger patient populations.

In summary, the drug discovery process involves a series of iterative stages that are aimed at identifying and optimizing drug candidates with high potency, selectivity, and safety. Each stage involves a range of techniques and methods, and the entire process can take several years and cost billions of dollars.

11.1.2   Importance of Structure-Based Drug Design

The 3D structure of a protein or enzyme target is used in the rational drug discovery process known as "structure-based drug design" (SBDD) to create and improve therapeutic candidates. This approach has become increasingly important in recent years because it allows researchers to design drugs with higher potency and selectivity, which can lead to improved efficacy and safety in patients.

The ability to comprehend the molecular underpinnings of the interaction between the drug candidate and the target protein or enzyme is one of the primary benefits of SBDD. By studying the 3D structure of the target, researchers can identify key binding sites and design compounds that fit tightly into these sites, leading to higher potency and selectivity. In addition, SBDD can be used to design drugs that specifically target disease-causing mutations or variants of the target protein or enzyme, it has a special application in the treatment of genetic illnesses.

Another advantage of SBDD is that it can reduce the risk of off-target effects, which can be a significant problem with traditional drug discovery approaches. By designing drugs that specifically target the disease-causing protein or enzyme, SBDD can minimize the potential for unintended interactions with other proteins or enzymes in the body, leading to a lower chance for aftereffects.

Due to its potential to cut down on the time and resources needed for hit identification and optimization, SBDD is also a financially advantageous method of drug development. Researchers can speed up the drug discovery process and decrease the number of compounds that need to be synthesized and tested by employing computational approaches to screen vast libraries of compounds and create new therapeutic candidates.

Overall, it is impossible to emphasize the significance of structure-based drug design in drug discovery. This strategy continues to be an important area of study in the pharmaceutical industry and has produced a number of significant medications, such as HIV protease inhibitors. SBDD is anticipated to get even more potent in the future as computational techniques, like as machine learning and artificial intelligence, continue to evolve, making it possible to create safer and more potent medications for a variety of conditions.

11.1.3   Historical Background and Milestones

The origins of structure-based drug design (SBDD) can be traced back to the discovery of the three-dimensional structures of myoglobin and hemoglobin using X-ray crystallography [3] in the late 1950s and early 1960s as shown in Figure 11.2. This breakthrough in the field of structural biology opened up new avenues for researchers to understand how molecules interact with each other and paved the way for the development of SBDD.

SBDD is a computational approach that involves using the three-dimensional structure as shown in Figure 11.3 of a target protein to design small molecules that can interact with it and modulate its activity. The goal is to identify compounds that bind to the target protein with high affinity and specificity, leading to the development of new drugs that can be used to treat a variety of diseases.

In the early days of SBDD, researchers relied on manual methods to design molecules that could bind to a target protein. However, with the development of powerful computational

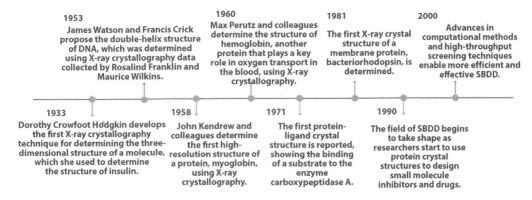

1953

James Watson and Francis Crick propose the double-helix structure of DNA, which was determined using X-ray crystallography data collected by Rosalind Franklin and Maurice Wilkins.

1960

Max Perutz and colleagues determine the structure of hemoglobin, another protein that plays a key role in oxygen transport in the blood, using X-ray crystallography.

1981

The first X-ray crystal structure of a membrane protein, bacteriorhodopsin, is determined.

2000

Advances in computational methods and high-throughput screening techniques enable more efficient and effective SBDD.

1933

Dorothy Crowfoot Hodgkin develops the first X-ray crystallography technique for determining the three-dimensional structure of a molecule, which she used to determine the structure of insulin.

1958

John Kendrew and colleagues determine the first high-resolution structure of a protein, myoglobin, using X-ray crystallography.

1971

The first protein-ligand crystal structure is reported, showing the binding of a substrate to the enzyme carboxypeptidase A.

1990

The field of SBDD begins to take shape as researchers start to use protein crystal structures to design small molecule inhibitors and drugs.

Figure 11.2 Timeline of the historical milestones of drug design.

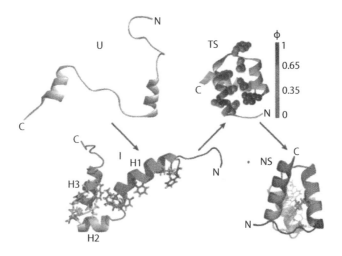

Figure 11.3 Three-dimensional structure of myoglobin.

tools and algorithms, it has become possible to perform high-throughput virtual screening of large compound libraries to identify potential drug candidates.

The development of virtual screening and docking approaches during the 1970s and 1980s was made possible by improvements in computer technology and molecular modeling strategies. These technologies allowed researchers to screen enormous databases of chemicals to find prospective therapeutic candidates. In the early days, these methods were limited by the available computational power, and the accuracy of the predictions was often poor. However, as computers became faster and more powerful and as new algorithms and scoring functions were developed, virtual screening and docking methods became increasingly reliable and accurate.

SBDD saw further progress in the 1990s and 2000s with the advent of fragment-based drug design (FBDD). Finding low-affinity substances or fragments [4] that can bind to the target protein or enzyme is the key step in this strategy. These fragments are then optimized through iterative cycles of design and testing, leading to the development of high-affinity drug candidates. FBDD has been shown to be a highly effective approach to drug discovery, leading to the development of drugs such as vemurafenib, which targets the BRAF V600E mutation in melanoma.

With the advent of new computational techniques like machine learning and artificial intelligence that can quicken the drug discovery process and increase prediction accuracy, the area of SBDD has advanced in recent years. New treatments for a variety of illnesses, including cancer, infectious diseases, and neurological problems, have also been developed using SBDD.

Overall, the development of novel methods and procedures that enable the design of more potent and specific medications as shown in Figure 11.4 is reflected in the historical backdrop and milestones of SBDD as well as an increasing knowledge of the significance of protein structure in drug discovery. SBDD is projected to continue to be a crucial area of research in drug discovery thanks to advancements in computational techniques and technology, resulting in the creation of safer and more efficient medicines for a variety of ailments.

Organization of the Chapter

The rest of the chapter is organized as follows: Section 11.2 highlights steps involved in structure-based drug design. Section 11.3 illustrates the tools and techniques used in structure-based drug design. Section 11.4 discusses applications, followed by other examples in Section 11.5. Section 11.6 enlightens with regard the advantages and limitations of structure-based drug design. Section 11.7 elaborates case studies and examples, followed by future outlook and implications in 11.8. Section 11.9 discusses the potential impact on healthcare and drug development. And, finally, section 11.10 concludes the chapter with future scope.

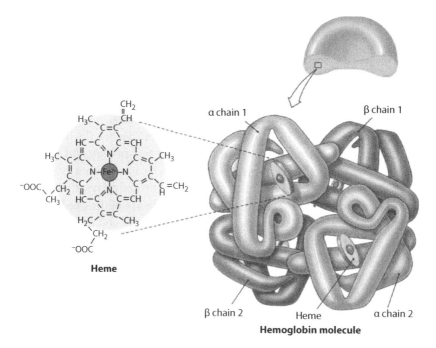

Figure 11.4 Structure of hemoglobin.

11.2   Structure-Based Drug Design: Steps

The technique of creating tiny compounds with high affinity and specificity to bind to a target protein, known as structure-based drug design, paves the way for the creation of potent medications. In this procedure, the 3D structure of the target protein and the interactions between the protein and a possible therapeutic molecule are determined using computational and experimental techniques [5].

Structure-based medication design aims to maximize potency and selectivity while minimizing toxicity and other undesirable side effects by optimizing the properties of the therapeutic molecule. Structure-based drug design often entails a number of phases, each of which is essential to the creation of a potent therapeutic candidate.

11.2.1   Target Identification and Validation

The initial step in structure-based drug design is the identification and validation of targets. It involves the identification of a specific protein or enzyme that is involved in a disease process and can be targeted by a drug molecule. This protein or enzyme is referred to as the target, and it must be validated to ensure that it is a suitable target for drug development.

Target identification typically involves a combination of experimental and computational methods. Experimental methods may include techniques such as genetic screening, high-throughput screening, and biochemical assays. Techniques like molecular docking, homology modeling, and molecular dynamics simulations are examples of computational methods.

Once a target has been identified, it must be validated to ensure that it is a suitable target for drug development. This typically involves demonstrating that the target is involved in the disease process, that inhibiting the target will result in a therapeutic effect, and that the target can be selectively inhibited without causing toxic side effects.

Validation may involve a combination of *in vitro* and *in vivo* experiments. *In vitro* experiments may include cell-based assays and biochemical assays, while *in vivo* experiments may include animal studies and clinical trials.

Getting structural information [6] about the target is the next step in structure-based drug design after the target has been determined and validated. Typically, this entails analyzing the target's three-dimensional structure using methods like X-ray crystallography or NMR spectroscopy. The resulting structure offers a thorough perspective of the target, including information on its active site and other crucial characteristics.

Using this structural knowledge, pharmacological compounds can be created that bind to the target with a high degree of specificity and affinity. In order to forecast how various medicinal compounds would interact with the target, researchers frequently employ computational techniques like molecular docking.

The target activity of the developed therapeutic compounds as shown in Figure 11.5 can subsequently be evaluated *in vitro* after being synthesized. The potency, selectivity, and pharmacokinetic features of the compounds may be further improved utilizing structure-based drug design strategies if they exhibit potential action.

In order to assess the safety and efficacy of the optimized therapeutic compounds, animal models and clinical studies may be used. Drug molecules may be further developed for usage in humans as therapeutic agents if they are determined to be secure and efficient.

11.2.2 Structure Determination of Target Protein

The next stage in structure-based drug design is to ascertain the target protein's three-dimensional structure [7] after it has been discovered and validated. This is an essential step because the target protein's structure reveals crucial details about its function and makes it possible to pinpoint potential drug-binding sites.

A few methods that can be used to figure out the structure of a protein are X-ray crystallography, nuclear magnetic resonance (NMR) spectroscopy, and cryo-electron microscopy (cryo-EM). The most popular technique for determining protein structures in structure-based medication creation is X-ray crystallography. In this technique, the protein is crystallized and then exposed to X-rays, which cause the crystal's atoms to diffract the light and produce a diffraction pattern. The locations of the atoms in the protein can be calculated from this pattern.

Once the target protein's structure has been established, it can be utilized to pinpoint possible drug-binding sites. This is usually accomplished through the use of computational techniques, including molecular docking, which entails the virtual screening of sizable drug molecule libraries to find those with the ability to attach to the target protein. In order to improve predictions of potential binding sites and comprehend the dynamic behavior of the protein and its interactions with drug molecules, molecular dynamics simulations can also be performed.

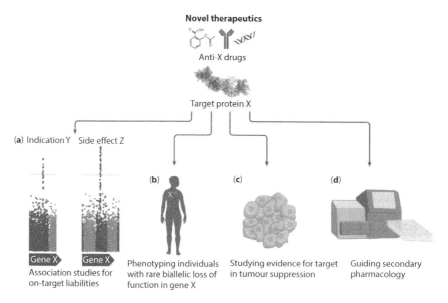

Figure 11.5 Safety measures for therapeutic compounds.

The design and optimization of therapeutic compounds can also be influenced by the structure of the target protein. Researchers can utilize computational techniques to create and optimize therapeutic compounds that bind to the target protein with high affinity and selectivity by analyzing the structure of the target protein and its interactions with drug molecules. This entails iteratively designing and optimizing therapeutic molecules based on their interactions with the target protein using computer-aided drug design (CADD) techniques [8] like molecular dynamics simulations and structure-based optimization.

Following the determination of the target protein's structure, small molecule medicines that selectively attach to the protein and alter its function can be designed. A drug's qualities can be optimized to increase its efficacy, specificity, and safety using the protein's 3D structure to find possible drug-binding sites.

In general, a crucial step in the development of structure-based drugs is figuring out the structure of the target protein. It enables the discovery of possible drug molecule binding sites and offers crucial information about the protein's function. Designing and improving therapeutic compounds with high affinity and selectivity using this knowledge will increase the likelihood that clinical trials will be successful.

11.2.3 Virtual Screening of Compounds

Virtual screening is a computational technique used in the drug discovery process to identify potential drug candidates from a large library of compounds. It involves the use of computational tools to predict the binding affinity of compounds to a target protein or enzyme, allowing researchers to prioritize compounds for further experimental testing.

There are two main types of virtual screening: ligand-based and structure-based. In ligand-based virtual screening, the focus is on identifying compounds that have similar structural and chemical features to known active compounds. This is done by comparing the 2D or 3D structures of compounds using molecular descriptors or fingerprints. The advantage of this approach is that it can identify compounds that are structurally distinct from known active compounds, allowing for the discovery of novel chemical scaffolds. However, it requires the availability of active compounds with known structures for comparison.

In structure-based virtual screening, the focus is on identifying compounds that bind to a specific site on the target protein or enzyme. This is done by generating a 3D model of the target protein or enzyme and using docking algorithms to predict the binding modes of compounds to the target. The advantage of this approach is that it can identify compounds that are structurally distinct from known active compounds, and it can also identify compounds that bind to allosteric or less well-characterized binding sites. However, it requires the availability of a high-quality 3D structure of the target protein or enzyme.

Virtual screening can be performed on large libraries of compounds, ranging from millions to billions of compounds. The compounds can be obtained from commercial vendors or synthesized in-house. Once the virtual screening is complete, the compounds are ranked based on their predicted binding affinity, and the top-ranked compounds are selected for experimental testing.

Experimental testing typically involves biochemical and biophysical assays to confirm the binding affinity of the compounds to the target protein or enzyme, as well as cell-based assays to evaluate the compounds' activity and selectivity in cellular contexts. The most promising compounds are then further optimized using medicinal chemistry techniques, such as scaffold hopping as shown in Figure 11.6 and structure–activity relationship analysis, to improve their potency, selectivity, and pharmacokinetic properties.

In summary, virtual screening is a powerful computational tool used in the drug discovery process to identify potential drug candidates from large libraries of compounds. It requires a combination of computational and experimental techniques and expertise in medicinal chemistry, biochemistry, and pharmacology.

11.2.4   Hit Selection and Optimization

In the drug discovery process, hit selection and optimization [9] are crucial phases, particularly in the initial stages of lead identification and development. Using high-throughput screening (HTS) or virtual screening techniques, the aim of hit selection is to find a small number of compounds that exhibit activity against the target of interest.

In order to quickly find active compounds, HTS entails screening sizable libraries of compounds using automated techniques like microtiter plates or microarrays. On the other side, virtual screening entails the use of computer techniques to find substances that are anticipated to bind to the target protein or enzyme. Molecular docking and scoring approaches, which simulate the binding of tiny molecules to the target protein and evaluate the binding energy and conformation of each ligand, can be used to do this.

Once hits are identified, the next step is to optimize them for potency, selectivity, and drug-like properties. Hit optimization can be done using a variety of approaches, such as medicinal chemistry, structure–activity relationship (SAR) analysis, and scaffold hopping.

Medicinal chemistry involves modifying the chemical structure of the hit compound to improve its potency, selectivity, and pharmacokinetic properties. This can be done by introducing new functional groups, modifying the core structure of the molecule, or changing the stereochemistry of the compound. In order to pinpoint structural elements that are crucial for activity, SAR analysis includes studying the connection between the hit compound's

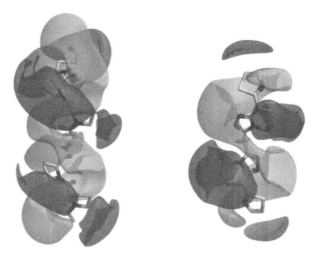

Figure 11.6 Scaffold hopping.

structure and its biological activity. The creation of novel analogues with enhanced activity can be guided by this information. Scaffold hopping involves identifying new chemical scaffolds or frameworks that are structurally distinct from the hit compound but can still bind to the target protein with high affinity. This approach can lead to the identification of novel chemical entities with improved activity and selectivity.

Overall, hit selection and optimization are critical steps in the drug discovery process, as they help to identify compounds with high potential for further development into drug candidates. These steps require a combination of experimental and computational methods, as well as expertise in medicinal chemistry, biochemistry, and pharmacology, to successfully identify and optimize lead compounds for further development.

11.2.5   Lead Optimization and Development

The last stages of the drug discovery process before clinical trials are lead optimization and development. The objective of lead optimization is to further enhance the lead compound's discovered qualities from the hit optimization stage. The lead compound must be optimized for pharmacokinetic properties such as solubility, bioavailability, metabolic stability, and toxicity. The lead compound should also be optimized for potency and selectivity, which can be achieved through further medicinal chemistry modifications, SAR analysis, and scaffold hopping.

Lead optimization also involves the evaluation [10] of the lead compound's pharmacological properties, such as its mechanism of action, mode of binding to the target, and selectivity against other targets. This can be done using a range of experimental techniques, such as enzyme assays, cell-based assays, and animal models.

Once the lead compound has been optimized, it can be developed further for clinical trials. This involves the synthesis of larger quantities of the lead compound, formulation development to create a drug product suitable for clinical use, and preclinical studies to evaluate the compound's safety and efficacy. Preclinical studies typically include pharmacokinetic studies, toxicology studies, and efficacy studies in animal models of the disease.

Once the preclinical studies are completed and the lead compound has demonstrated sufficient safety and efficacy, it can proceed to clinical trials. Human clinical trials are carried out to assess the efficacy, pharmacokinetics, safety, and tolerability of the medication candidate. Clinical trials are normally undertaken in three phases, each including a greater number of patients and a more thorough assessment of the safety and efficacy of the drug candidate.

In conclusion, lead optimization and development are crucial steps in the drug discovery process since they include enhancing the lead compound's potency, selectivity, and pharmacokinetics while also assessing its pharmacological characteristics. These phases demand knowledge of medicinal chemistry, biochemistry, pharmacology, and clinical development in addition to a combination of experimental and computational techniques.

11.3   Tools and Techniques Used in Structure-Based Drug Design

A novel strategy for drug development called structure-based drug design (SBDD) uses computational techniques to create compounds that can interact directly with a target protein or enzyme. This strategy can aid in the discovery of lead compounds that are more likely to bind to the target protein, improving the likelihood of creating medications that work better and have fewer adverse effects.

X-ray crystallography, a major method in SBDD, is employed to ascertain the target protein's three-dimensional structure. In this method, protein crystals are grown, and then X-rays are used to create a diffraction pattern that can be used to solve the structure. Researchers can utilize computational techniques to build and improve tiny compounds that can interact with the protein in a certain way once the structure is determined.

Molecular docking, which makes use of computer algorithms to forecast the binding mechanism and affinities of small compounds to the target protein, is another crucial SBDD approach. In order to find the optimum match and calculate the binding energy, docking algorithms produce many conformations of the small molecule and dock them into the protein binding site. Large libraries of compounds can be screened using these methods to find those with the highest binding affinity to the target protein.

Another method employed in SBDD is homology modelling, which creates a three-dimensional model of the target protein in the absence of the experimental structure. This method aligns the target protein sequence to a template protein structure made from a known protein structure, then creates a model of the target protein based on the alignment. The creation and improvement of tiny compounds that can interact with the protein can then be done using this paradigm.

Molecular dynamics simulations are also an important technique in SBDD, which can provide insights into protein–ligand binding kinetics and thermodynamics. This technique involves simulating the motion and behavior of the target protein and ligand over time using a force field to simulate the interactions between atoms. This can help researchers understand the dynamics of protein–ligand interactions and identify key features that contribute to binding affinity.

Overall, SBDD as shown in Figure 11.7 is an interdisciplinary field that integrates computational and experimental methods to design and optimize small molecules that can interact with specific target proteins or enzymes. These methods and tools can be used to find and improve drug candidates that have greater binding affinity and lower toxicity, which could ultimately result in the creation of more potent treatments for a number of disorders.

11.3.1   X-Ray Crystallography

A powerful technique for determining the three-dimensional structure of macromolecules like proteins and nucleic acids is X-ray crystallography. This method entails generating crystals of the target macromolecule, subjecting the crystals to X-rays, and studying the diffraction pattern to ascertain the macromolecule's structure.

The first step in X-ray crystallography [11] is to obtain a pure sample of the macromolecule of interest. The sample is then crystallized using methods such as vapor diffusion or liquid-liquid diffusion. The crystals are typically grown in small glass plates or plastic trays and can take several days to several weeks to grow, depending on the molecule and the conditions used.

Once the crystals are grown, they are mounted on a thin fibre or loop and placed in a beam of X-rays. The X-rays diffract off the atoms in the crystal lattice, creating a diffraction

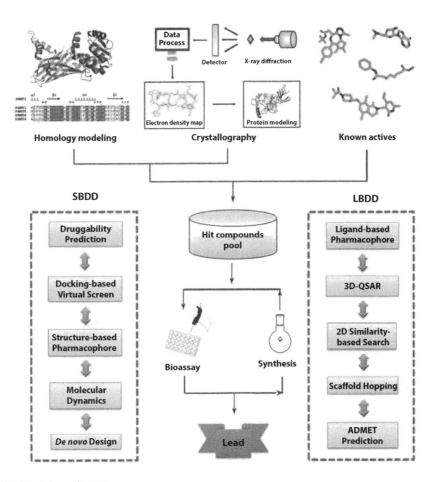

Figure 11.7 Workflow of SBDD.

pattern that is captured by a detector. The location of the atoms in the crystal lattice is then determined by examining the diffraction pattern.

It takes several steps to extract the macromolecule's structure from the diffraction pattern, which is a complicated operation. The intensities of the diffraction spots are first extracted from the diffraction pattern, and these intensities are then utilised to determine the phases of the diffracted waves. The electron density map, which is created by computing the phases and intensities, is then utilised to create a model of the macromolecule.

The process can be divided into three main stages:

- Data collection
- Structure determination
- Model refinement

Data collection involves exposing the crystal to a beam of X-rays and collecting the diffraction pattern generated by the X-rays. The diffraction pattern is a complex pattern of spots, each of which corresponds to the scattering of X-rays off the atoms in the crystal. The intensity and position of the spots in the diffraction pattern are recorded using a detector.

In the next stage, structure determination, the intensities and positions of the spots in the diffraction pattern are used to calculate the electron density of the molecule. The electron density is a three-dimensional map of the distribution of electrons within the crystal lattice, which reflects the positions of the atoms in the molecule.

The phases of the diffracted waves must be ascertained in order to calculate the electron density map. However, the phase information cannot be directly measured from the diffraction pattern. Instead, it is inferred by using a mathematical technique called phase determination. There are several methods for phase determination, including molecular replacement, multiple isomorphous replacement, and single-wavelength anomalous dispersion.

The electron density map can be computed using the Fourier transformation once the phases have been identified. The positions of the atoms in the molecule are revealed by the electron density map, but the lengths and angles of the bonds between them are not. The electron density map is analysed using molecular modelling methods to obtain the bond angles and lengths.

In the final stage of model refinement [12], the initial model is refined and validated using a variety of methods, including refinement against experimental data, molecular dynamics simulations, and validation against other experimental data. The refined model is then used to study the molecular structure and function of the macromolecule, as well as in the design of small molecules that can interact with the molecule.

The process requires sophisticated computational methods and can take several months or even years to complete for a complex molecule. However, the results of X-ray crystallography can be utilised to build medications that specifically target particular protein targets and can offer insights into the molecular basis of function.

Structural biology and drug development both rely heavily on X-ray crystallography as a technique. Numerous proteins and nucleic acids have had their structures determined, revealing information on their functions and modes of action. X-ray crystallography is frequently employed in structure-based drug design (SBDD) in the drug discovery process to create and improve small molecule inhibitors that can interact with a particular protein target.

Despite its power and utility, X-ray crystallography has some limitations. It needs the presence of a pure sample of the targeted macromolecule, and for some compounds, growing crystals might be challenging. Additionally, the technique is limited to static structures and cannot provide information on dynamic processes or conformational changes in the molecule. However, with advances in technology and methodology, X-ray crystallography continues to be a valuable tool in structural biology and drug discovery.

11.3.2   NMR Spectroscopy

The three-dimensional structure of macromolecules in solution can be ascertained using the potent technique of nuclear magnetic resonance (NMR) spectroscopy, which is employed in structural biology and drug development. NMR spectroscopy, which is different from X-ray crystallography in that it doesn't require the sample to be crystallized, can reveal details on the dynamics and flexibility of the molecule in solution.

The magnet, radiofrequency transmitter and receiver, as well as the computer system required to handle and analyze the data, are all shown as parts of an NMR spectrometer.

A sample inserted into a magnet, which produces a powerful magnetic field that aligns the atoms' nuclei. After that, radiofrequency waves are used to irradiate the sample, causing the nuclei to absorb energy and shift to a higher energy state. The NMR spectrometer can pick up radiofrequency waves that the nuclei produce when they revert to their initial state.

The process of determining the structure of a macromolecule by NMR spectroscopy [13] as shown in Figure 11.8 involves several steps, including:

- Protein expression and purification: The first step in the process is to express and purify the protein of interest. The protein is typically produced using recombinant DNA technology and then purified using various chromatography techniques to obtain a high-purity sample.
- Isotopic labeling: The protein is then labeled with stable isotopes, typically ^{15}N, ^{13}C, or ^{2}H. This is done to generate a potent NMR signal that may be utilized to investigate the structure and dynamics of the protein.
- Sample preparation: The labeled protein is dissolved in a solution, typically containing deuterated water, to reduce the signal from the solvent. This ensures that the NMR spectra obtained from the sample are dominated by signals from the protein and not from the solvent.
- NMR data collection: The sample will next be subjected to multidimensional NMR tests to produce a number of spectra. The most often utilized studies provide details on the chemical shifts and spin-spin couplings of the labelled

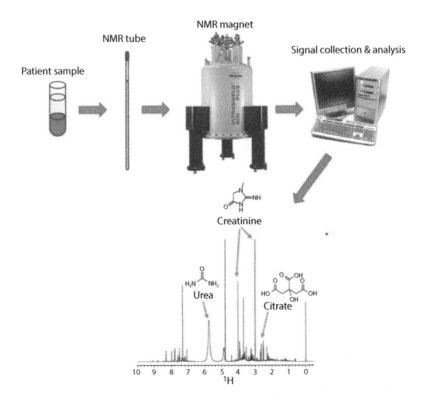

Figure 11.8 NMR spectroscopy.

atoms in the protein through 2D homonuclear and heteronuclear correlation spectroscopy.

- Spectral analysis: The tests' NMR spectra reveal a lot of knowledge about the protein's chemical and physical characteristics. The positions and intensities of the peaks in the spectra give information on the separations between pairs of atoms in the molecule, the angles between bonds, and the orientation of functional groups. The peaks in the spectra correspond to the resonant frequencies of the labelled atoms in the protein.
- Data processing: The spectral data obtained from the experiments are processed using specialized software programs that can extract distance and angle restraints from the data.
- Molecular modeling: The restraints obtained from the spectral data are then used to generate an ensemble of structures that fit the data. This is typically done using molecular modeling techniques, such as simulated annealing or molecular dynamics simulations, which calculate the lowest-energy conformations that satisfy the restraints.
- Structure validation: Once a set of structures has been generated, they are validated using various techniques, such as Ramachandran plots, which show the distribution of the backbone dihedral angles in the protein, and R-factors, which measure the agreement between the calculated and observed data.
- Structure refinement: The structures are refined further by adjusting the model parameters to improve the fit between the calculated and observed data.

Overall, NMR spectroscopy is a multi-step, iterative procedure that can be used to determine the structure of macromolecules. It calls for proficiency in both experimental and computational methods.

However, Structure determination is more difficult using NMR spectroscopy because it lacks direct phase information, unlike X-ray crystallography. Instead of using a single static structure to fit the NMR data, researchers frequently employ computational techniques to construct ensembles of structures that do so.

The capacity to provide information on the dynamics and flexibility of the molecule in solution is one of the key benefits of NMR spectroscopy. By analyzing the line widths and relaxation times of the NMR spectra, researchers can determine the mobility of different regions of the protein and gain insights into the molecular mechanisms of function. This information can be particularly useful in drug discovery, as it can help identify potential binding sites and aid in the design of small molecules that can interact with the protein.

Despite its many advantages, NMR spectroscopy also has some limitations. One of the main limitations is the relatively low resolution compared to X-ray crystallography, which can make it difficult to determine the precise position of individual atoms within the molecule. Additionally, the technique is sensitive to the quality of the sample and can require large quantities of labeled protein.

In conclusion, NMR spectroscopy is an effective method for determining the three-dimensional structure of macromolecules in solution, which is employed in structural biology and drug development. The technique can help in the creation of tiny compounds that can interact with particular protein targets and offers useful information about the dynamics and flexibility of the molecule. Although the method has significant drawbacks, scientists frequently combine many methods to get a more comprehensive understanding of the molecular structure and function.

11.3.3 Homology Modeling

A computational method called homology modelling, commonly referred to as comparative modelling, predicts the three-dimensional structure of a protein from its amino acid sequence and the structure of a homologous protein [14] that is already known. This method is frequently used in molecular biology research and structure-based drug design to anticipate the structure of proteins whose structures have not yet been determined experimentally.

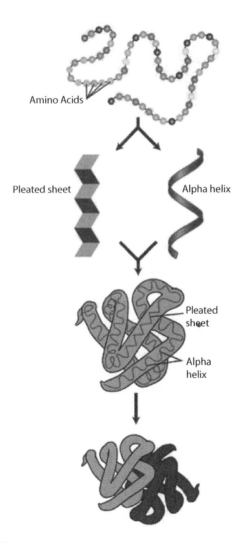

Figure 11.9 Homology modeling.

Homology modeling as shown in Figure 11.9 comprises a number of phases. First, the target protein's amino acid sequence is either created by sequencing or taken from a database. Second, based on how closely its sequence resembles that of the target protein, a template protein with a known structure is chosen. Usually, the target protein's closest relative that has a known structure is chosen as the template protein.

Sequence alignment methods are then used to align the target protein sequence with the template protein structure. A sequence alignment is produced as a result, demonstrating how the amino acid residues in the target protein sequence and the template protein structure correlate. The spatial information is subsequently transferred from the template protein to the target protein using sequence alignment.

Sequence alignment is followed by the real homology modelling procedure. For homology modelling, a range of software programs are available, and the majority of them create a three-dimensional model of the target protein using the concepts of molecular mechanics and molecular dynamics simulations. The target protein's corresponding amino acids are gradually substituted for those in the template protein to create the model, which is then refined, and its conformation optimized using energy minimization methods.

Once a homology model is generated, it undergoes several validation and refinement procedures to ensure its accuracy and reliability. These procedures aim to correct any errors in the model and improve its quality.

One of the first validation procedures is energy minimization, which involves optimizing the conformation of the protein to minimize the potential energy of the model. This is done to ensure that the model has a stable and energetically favorable structure. This procedure typically involves using molecular mechanics simulations to relax the structure and correct any steric clashes or bond angles that are unfavorable.

In order to optimize the packing of the protein structure, side-chain optimization, another refinement method, involves changing the orientation of the amino acid side chains in the model. This procedure is critical for ensuring that the side chains are in the most favorable positions and do not cause steric clashes with neighboring residues.

Structural refinement is also an important step in the validation process. This procedure involves adjusting the backbone and side chain torsion angles in the model to improve the fit of the protein structure with the experimental data. This can be done using molecular dynamics simulations or other optimization techniques.

After refinement, the homology model is evaluated using several quality measures, such as the Root Mean Square Deviation (RMSD), MolProbity score, and Ramachandran plot analysis. The RMSD measures [15] the overall difference between the homology model and the experimental structure, with a lower value indicating a better fit. The MolProbity score evaluates the overall quality of the model and identifies potential errors or clashes. The Ramachandran plot analysis evaluates the backbone torsion angles in the model and identifies regions that are in unfavorable conformations.

The study of homology has transformed drug discovery and structural biology. Numerous protein structures, including those linked to diseases like cancer, Parkinson's, and Alzheimer's, have been predicted using this method. Thanks to improvements in computational algorithms, the accessibility of high-resolution structural data, and the creation of better validation and refinement procedures, homology modeling's accuracy and dependability have considerably increased over time.

11.3.4 Molecular Docking

A computer method called molecular docking is used in the structure-based drug design process to forecast the binding mechanism and affinities of a ligand to a receptor. This technique is used to find possible therapeutic candidates that might bind to the receptor with high affinity by predicting the structure of a complex formed between a ligand and receptor.

Molecular docking can be broken down into a number of phases, each of which improves the precision and dependability of the outcome. The steps that make up the molecular docking process are as follows:

Creation of ligand and receptor structures: The creation of ligand and receptor structures is the initial step in molecular docking as shown in Figure 11.10. The receptor structure is typically determined using experimental methods like X-ray crystallography or NMR spectroscopy, while the ligand structure is typically retrieved from a database or synthesized based on the target molecule. Then, in order to optimize their geometry and reduce energy, the structures are prepared utilizing software tools.

Identifying the binding site: Finding the receptor's binding site or pocket where the ligand is most likely to bind is the next step. The experimental data can be analyzed to find this, or computational methods that anticipate the binding site based on the receptor's structure and electrostatic characteristics can be used.

Ligand conformational sampling: Ligands are usually flexible and can adopt different conformations, so it is necessary to sample multiple conformations to identify the optimal binding mode. This is achieved by generating a set of conformers using software tools such as molecular dynamics simulations or conformational searching algorithms.

Generation of docking poses: For the ligand in the binding site, the docking program generates a number of poses, each of which represents a different orientation and conformation

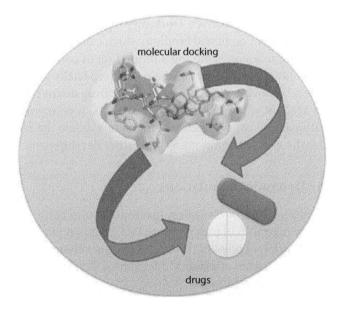

Figure 11.10 Molecular docking.

of the ligand. Each pose's binding energy is assessed by the docking algorithm using a scoring formula, and postures are prioritized based on their energy values.

Post-processing and analysis: The final step is to analyze the results and select the best docking pose(s) for further analysis. This entails utilizing molecular graphics software to visualize the docking position in order to pinpoint the crucial residues involved in the interaction between the ligand and receptor. Using post-docking optimization strategies, the docking poses can be further honed, and the outcomes can be verified using experimental methods like X-ray crystallography or NMR spectroscopy.

The quality of the ligand and receptor structures, the choice of docking program and scoring function, and the flexibility of the ligand and receptor all affect how accurately molecular docking predictions turn out. Numerous methods, including ensemble docking, protein flexibility, and the use of different docking programs, have been developed to increase the accuracy of docking predictions.

Molecular docking [16] has several advantages and limitations in the field of drug discovery. The ability to anticipate the binding affinity of a large number of ligands to a receptor using molecular docking is one of its key benefits. It is also versatile, allowing for the study of different types of molecules, including proteins, nucleic acids, and small molecules. Furthermore, molecular docking generates results quickly, which can be useful for selecting compounds for further experimental testing and prioritizing compounds for further optimization and lead identification. Additionally, molecular docking can provide insights into the molecular interactions between the ligand and receptor, which can be useful for designing more potent and selective compounds.

However, there are a number of limitations to molecular docking that need to be considered when interpreting the findings. Limited accuracy is one of the key drawbacks because it depends on a number of variables, including the calibre of the input structures, the choice of the docking programme, and the scoring mechanism. Additionally, docking programmes struggle to correctly anticipate the binding affinity of ligands, particularly for big and flexible ligands. Furthermore, molecular docking tends to overestimate the binding affinity of ligands, leading to false positives. Docking programs also often do not accurately account for the effects of solvent on ligand binding, which can be significant in many cases. Finally, molecular docking relies on sampling a limited set of conformations of the ligand and receptor, which can limit the accuracy of the results, especially for flexible ligands.

In conclusion, molecular docking is a valuable tool for drug discovery, but its limitations should be taken into account when interpreting the results. It is important to use a combination of computational and experimental methods to validate the results of molecular docking and optimize the selected compounds for further development.

11.3.5   Molecular Dynamics Simulations

The movements and interactions of biological macromolecules at the atomic level can be predicted and studied using molecular dynamics (MD) simulations [17], a computational technique that has been widely applied in the field of drug development. These simulations, which are based on the principles of classical mechanics, reveal details about the system under investigation's temporal evolution.

A macromolecule's initial structure, often acquired from X-ray crystallography, NMR spectroscopy, or homology modelling, is the basis for MD simulations. The structure is then neutralized using counter ions to maintain overall neutrality before being solvated in the suitable solvent environment, which is usually water. The system is given a force field, which describes the bonding, van der Waals, electrostatic, and solvation forces that interact with the atoms.

The simulation is then carried out by integrating the equations of motion for each atom over time. Depending on how complex the system is and the resources that are available for calculation, the simulation time scale can be anywhere from nanoseconds to microseconds or longer. The output of the simulation includes the trajectory of the system over time, including the positions, velocities, and energies of the atoms.

Numerous biological systems, such as proteins, nucleic acids, lipids, and carbohydrates, have been studied using MD simulations. These simulations can provide valuable insights into the conformational dynamics, stability, and function of these molecules, as well as the interactions with ligands, such as drugs or other small molecules.

One of the advantages of MD simulations is that they can provide information about the structural flexibility of macromolecules, which is important for understanding their biological function and for drug discovery. MD simulations can also be used to study the thermodynamics and kinetics of binding between ligands and their targets, which is critical for the design of potent and specific drugs.

However, MD simulations also have some limitations. One of the key drawbacks is that the simulations' accuracy depends on the force field's quality and the parameters that are selected for them. The precision of the underlying experimental data and the approximations used in the modelling determine the precision of the force field. The choice of simulation parameters, such as the length of the simulation and the size of the time step, can also affect the accuracy and reliability of the simulation results.

Another limitation of MD simulations is that they can be computationally expensive and time-consuming, especially for large and complex systems. The scale and complexity of the systems that can be examined *via* MD simulations may be constrained as a result. Additionally, MD simulations are limited by the available computing power, which may limit the length and number of simulations that can be performed.

In conclusion, MD simulations as shown in Figure 11.11 are a valuable tool for drug discovery [18], providing a detailed understanding of the dynamics and interactions of biological macromolecules at an atomic level. The simulations can be computationally expensive and time-consuming, and their accuracy and dependability are dependent on the force field's quality and the parameters that are selected. Therefore, a combination of computational and experimental methods should be used to validate the results and optimize the design of drug candidates for further development.

11.4 Applications

11.4.1 Kinase Inhibitors

Kinase inhibitors are a class of drugs that are designed to block the activity of enzymes called kinases. Cell signaling, which is important for regulating a number of biological activities including cell growth, proliferation, differentiation, and survival, involves kinases. Numerous illnesses, such as cancer, inflammatory disorders, and metabolic problems, have

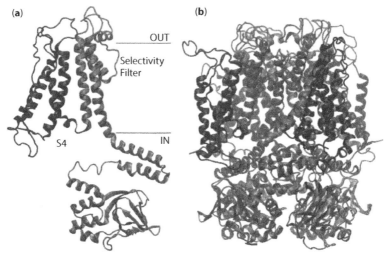

(a)

OUT

Selectivity Filter

S4

IN

• Voltage Sensor Domain
• Pore Domain
• Carboxy-Terminal Domainipsum

(b)

Figure 11.11 Molecular dynamics simulations.

been linked to abnormal kinase activity. As a result, a key focus of drug discovery efforts has been the creation of kinase inhibitors.

Kinase inhibitor's function [19] by attaching to the kinase enzyme's active site and preventing it from performing its function. This stops the kinase from phosphorylating its target proteins, which is required for the activation of downstream signaling cascades. Kinase inhibitors can stop the aberrant signaling pathways that support the emergence of illness by blocking the activity of particular kinases.

Kinase inhibitors come in a variety of forms, including covalent, allosteric, and ATP-competitive inhibitors. Inhibitors that compete with ATP for binding to the kinase active site are called ATP-competitive inhibitors. These inhibitors block ATP from binding by attaching to a pocket in the kinase enzyme that is close to the site. On the other hand, allosteric inhibitors attach to a location on the kinase enzyme other than the active site yet nonetheless have an impact on the enzyme's activity. Covalent inhibitors are made to attach to the kinase enzyme and create an irreversible covalent link, which inhibits the enzyme's function.

Several cancers, including chronic myelogenous leukemia (CML), non-small cell lung cancer, and breast cancer, have showed promise when treated with kinase inhibitors. For instance, the BCR-ABL kinase, which is in charge of the emergence of CML, is the target of the kinase inhibitor imatinib. Imatinib has been demonstrated to cause remission in CML patients by blocking BCR-ABL.

However, kinase inhibitors are not without their limitations. Because kinases play a role in numerous physiological processes, inhibiting a particular kinase can have unintended consequences. Additionally, some malignancies may become resistant to kinase inhibitors, necessitating the creation of alternative medications that focus on alternate pathways or modes of action. However, kinase inhibitors continue to play a significant role in the treatment of many diseases, and research into the creation of more potent and selective kinase inhibitors is ongoing.

11.4.2 Enzyme Inhibitors

Enzyme inhibitors are molecules that are designed to block the activity of enzymes, which are proteins that catalyze biochemical reactions in the body. Enzymes are critical for many biological processes, including metabolism, signaling, and DNA replication. Therefore, enzyme inhibitors can be used to treat a wide range of diseases by selectively blocking specific enzymes that are involved in the development or progression of a particular disease.

There are several different types of enzyme inhibitors, including uncompetitive, non-competitive, and competitive inhibitors. Competitive inhibitors occupy the enzyme's active site, blocking the substrate from adhering. By attaching to a region other than the active site, non-competitive inhibitors alter the structure of the enzyme and stop it from catalyzing the activity. Non-competitive inhibitors attach to the enzyme-substrate complex and prevent the product from being released.

Infectious infections [20], cancer, and metabolic problems are just a few of the conditions that can be treated using enzyme inhibitors—for example, protease inhibitors are a class of enzyme inhibitors that are used to treat viral infections, such as HIV and hepatitis C, by blocking the activity of viral proteases. Dihydrofolate reductase is an enzyme involved in DNA synthesis, and chemotherapy medicines like methotrexate serve as enzyme inhibitors to decrease its activity. Methotrexate can destroy quickly dividing cancer cells by blocking dihydrofolate reductase.

However, enzyme inhibitors can also have side effects, particularly if they are non-selective and block the activity of multiple enzymes. Unwanted consequences like toxicity or a disruption of regular biological processes may result from this. Therefore, the design of enzyme inhibitors requires a balance between efficacy and safety.

Structure-based drug design (SBDD) methods are frequently used to create enzyme inhibitors, which entail studying the three-dimensional structure of the enzyme and creating compounds that are expected to bind to the enzyme and suppress its activity. SBDD can be used to forecast potential toxicities or off-target effects, as well as to improve the binding affinity and selectivity of enzyme inhibitors.

11.4.3 G Protein-Coupled Receptor (GPCR) Ligands

A vast family of membrane proteins known as G protein-coupled receptors (GPCRs) play key roles in a variety of physiological functions including neurotransmission, taste, smell, and vision. Approximately 30% of all medications that the FDA has approved are FDA-approved target GPCRs. Molecules that attach to GPCRs and influence their activity are known as GPCR ligands.

Agonists, antagonists, and allosteric modulators are some of the several categories of GPCR ligands based on how they work. While antagonists bind to the GPCR and stop it from being activated by endogenous ligands or agonists, agonists are substances that bind to the GPCR and activate its signaling pathway. The activity of the receptor is modified by chemicals known as allosteric modulators, which bind to a region on the GPCR that is different from the agonist binding site.

GPCR ligands have diverse structures, and they can interact with the receptor in multiple ways. Some GPCR ligands, such as catecholamines, bind to a site on the receptor that is located in the transmembrane domain. Other GPCR ligands, the extracellular domain of the receptor has a place where ligands, including peptides, can bind.

GPCR ligands are used to treat a variety of illnesses, such as pain, schizophrenia, asthma, and hypertension. One class of GPCR antagonists, beta-blockers, for instance, works by inhibiting the action of beta-adrenergic receptors to treat hypertension. By engaging the opioid receptors in the central nervous system, opioid receptor agonists like morphine are used to relieve pain.

Due to the complexity of their structures and numerous binding sites, GPCRs present a difficult problem for the production of ligands. The creation and improvement of GPCR ligands have been made significantly easier through the use of structure-based drug design (SBDD) approaches. Based on the three-dimensional structure of GPCRs, SBDD uses computational techniques to forecast the binding mechanism of ligands to these receptors. This method can be used to find ligands that have better potency, selectivity, and pharmacokinetic characteristics.

11.4.4   Antibodies and Vaccines

Antibodies and vaccines are both important tools for preventing and treating infectious diseases. The immune system makes antibodies, which are proteins, in reaction to an infection or a vaccination. Vaccines are biological preparations that contain either weakened or killed pathogens, or parts of the pathogen, which stimulate the immune system to produce antibodies without causing disease.

Antigens, which are chemicals on the surface of pathogens, are recognized and bound to by antibodies, which are highly specialized proteins. By neutralizing or eliminating pathogens from the body, antibodies either prevent them from infecting cells or flag them for eradication by other immune cells. By activating the complement system, a collection of proteins that aid in the eradication of diseases, antibodies can also improve the clearance of pathogens.

The immune system is stimulated by vaccines to create antibodies in response to a particular infection. Pathogens that are alive, wounded, or dead, as well as pathogen components like proteins or carbohydrates, are all included in vaccines. After receiving an injection of a vaccine, the immune system recognizes the pathogen or any of its components as foreign and develops an immunological response, creating antibodies that can neutralize the pathogen if it is subsequently encountered. To sustain protection over time, some vaccines necessitate booster injections.

Both antibodies and vaccines can be used to prevent and treat infectious diseases. Antibodies can be produced in the laboratory and administered to individuals who have been exposed to a pathogen, to help clear the infection or prevent the disease from becoming severe. This approach is known as passive immunization. Vaccines, on the other hand, are a preventive measure that can be used to protect individuals from future infections. Vaccines are administered to healthy individuals to stimulate their immune system to produce antibodies before they are exposed to a pathogen.

The development of antibodies and vaccines requires a deep understanding of the pathogen and the immune response. Modern approaches to vaccine development use a combination of genetic engineering, protein chemistry, and computational modeling to design and optimize vaccines that are safe, effective, and can be produced on a large scale.

11.5 Other Examples

Structure-based drug design (SBDD), which has been used in a variety of therapeutic areas, has emerged as a crucial tool in the drug development process. Here are some further SBDD application examples:

11.5.1 Anti-Cancer Drugs

Anti-cancer pharmaceuticals work to cure cancer by preventing cancer cells from proliferating and multiplying. Depending on how these medications work, they can be divided into various categories. Chemotherapeutic medicines [21], which are cytotoxic treatments that destroy rapidly dividing cells, including cancer cells, are one of the main groups of anti-cancer medications. Alkylating agents, antimetabolites, and topoisomerase inhibitors, among other subcategories, are only a few examples of the other classifications that chemotherapy medications can be divided into.

Designing pharmaceuticals that may kill cancer cells only while leaving healthy cells unharmed is one of the difficulties in creating potent anti-cancer medications. Structure-based drug design (SBDD) has been used to find and create medications that target particular proteins that are overexpressed or altered in cancer cells as a solution to this problem. For instance, the growth and survival of many cancer cells are dependent on the activity of particular kinases, like EGFR, HER2, and ALK. Kinase inhibitors that can stop the action of these proteins and cause cancer cells to die have been created using SBDD.

In addition to kinase inhibitors, SBDD has been used to design drugs that target other proteins implicated in cancer cell survival and development, including proteases, histone deacetylases, and DNA repair enzymes, among others. By designing drugs that can selectively target these proteins, SBDD can help to develop anti-cancer drugs that are more effective and less toxic than traditional chemotherapeutic agents.

The creation of imatinib, a kinase inhibitor that targets the BCR-ABL protein, which is overexpressed in cells with chronic myelogenous leukemia (CML), is one of the most successful examples of SBDD in the development of anti-cancer medications. High response rates and better survival rates for CML patients have been made possible by imatinib, which has revolutionized the treatment of this illness.

In conclusion, SBDD has established itself as a crucial instrument in the development of anti-cancer medications and has the potential to speed up drug discovery and enhance the efficacy of cancer therapies.

11.5.2 Anti-Viral Drugs

Anti-viral drugs are medications that are used to treat viral infections by targeting the replication of the virus. Depending on how these medications work, they can be divided into various categories. Nucleoside/nucleotide analogues, which resemble the structural components of DNA or RNA [22] and can prevent viral reproduction by reducing viral polymerase activity, are one of the principal classes of anti-viral medications.

Protease inhibitors are a different class of anti-viral medications that can prevent viral proteases from digesting viral proteins during viral replication. The fusion inhibitors, which can stop the fusing of viral and cellular membranes, and the neuraminidase inhibitors, which can stop the action of viral neuraminidase and stop the release of new virions from infected cells, are further classes of anti-viral medications.

To develop effective anti-viral drugs, it is important to identify and target specific viral proteins or enzymes that are essential for viral replication. This is where structure-based drug design (SBDD) can be particularly useful. SBDD can aid in the identification of prospective therapeutic targets and the development of medications that can bind to these targets and limit their activity by leveraging knowledge about the structural details of viral proteins and enzymes.

The creation of protease inhibitors for HIV/AIDS treatment is one of the best instances of SBDD in anti-viral medication development. SBDD was used to create the protease inhibitors ritonavir, lopinavir, and darunavir, which have revolutionized the treatment of HIV/AIDS and increased survival rates while reducing the emergence of drug resistance.

SBDD has also been used to develop anti-viral drugs for the treatment of other viral infections, such as hepatitis C, influenza, and herpes simplex virus, among others. By using SBDD to design drugs that can selectively target viral proteins and enzymes, researchers can develop drugs that are more effective and less toxic than traditional anti-viral drugs.

Overall, SBDD has emerged as a crucial tool in the research and development of anti-viral medications, with the potential to hasten the discovery of novel pharmaceuticals and enhance the efficacy of anti-viral therapies.

11.5.3   Neurological Disorders

A collection of illnesses known as neurological disorders impact the nervous system, which includes the brain, spinal cord, and nerves. Numerous variables, including as genetics, infections, environmental factors, and way of life decisions, might contribute to the development of these disorders. Numerous bodily processes, including mobility, sensation, cognition, and behavior, can be impacted by neurological illnesses.

There are numerous varieties of neurological illnesses [23], such as:

1. Neurodegenerative disorders: These conditions are characterized by the gradual loss of brain neurons, which impairs cognitive and motor function. Examples include Alzheimer's, Parkinson's, and Huntington's disorders.
2. Epilepsy and seizure disorders: These conditions are characterized by aberrant brain electrical activity that can cause convulsions or seizures.
3. Stroke: When blood flow to the brain is disrupted, brain cells are damaged or killed, which results in a stroke.
4. Multiple sclerosis: This condition results in harm to the myelin sheath that surrounds nerve fibers, leading to a variety of symptoms such as muscle weakness, vision problems, and difficulty with coordination.

5. Neuromuscular disorders: These are disorders that affect the muscles and the nerves that control them, leading to symptoms such as muscle weakness, cramping, and difficulty with movement.

It can be difficult to develop effective treatments for neurological illnesses since the nervous system is so complex and tricky to target with medication. However, medications that can target particular proteins and enzymes implicated in neurological illnesses have been created using structure-based drug design (SBDD), resulting in the creation of new therapeutics.

For instance, the Alzheimer's disease enzyme acetylcholinesterase, which is involved in the breakdown of the neurotransmitter acetylcholine, has been the target of medications developed using SBDD. Drugs like donepezil and rivastigmine can help Alzheimer's patients with their cognitive function by blocking this enzyme.

Similarly, SBDD has been used to develop drugs that target specific ion channels and receptors involved in epilepsy and seizure disorders, leading to the development of drugs such as gabapentin and pregabalin.

Overall, SBDD has the potential to accelerate the discovery of new treatments for neurological disorders, improving the quality of life for millions of people around the world who suffer from these conditions.

11.5.4 Cardiovascular Diseases

Cardiovascular diseases (CVDs) [24] are a collective term for conditions affecting the heart and blood vessels as shown in Figure 11.12. These include, among other things, diseases including coronary artery disease, cardiac failure, arrhythmias, and stroke. High blood pressure, high cholesterol, smoking, obesity, diabetes, and a sedentary lifestyle are risk factors for CVDs, which are the leading cause of death and disability worldwide.

Using medications that specifically target certain proteins and enzymes involved in cardiovascular function is one of the key strategies for treating CVDs. Drugs that can specifically target these proteins and enzymes have been created using the structure-based drug design (SBDD) method, making them more efficient and secure for the treatment of CVDs.

Examples of drugs developed using SBDD for the treatment of CVDs include:

1. Statins: Statins are medications that specifically target the HMG-CoA reductase enzyme, which is important in the liver's production of cholesterol. Statins can lower blood cholesterol levels and lower the risk of coronary heart disease by blocking this enzyme.

2. ACE inhibitors and ARBs: Drugs that target the renin-angiotensin-aldosterone system (RAAS), which is important in controlling blood pressure and fluid balance, including ACE inhibitors and angiotensin receptor blockers (ARBs). These medications can assist in bringing down blood pressure and lowering the risk of heart failure.

3. Beta blockers: Beta blockers are drugs that target beta-adrenergic receptors, which are involved in regulating heart rate and blood pressure. Beta blockers can lower blood pressure and heart rate by inhibiting these receptors, which lowers the risk of heart failure and other CVDs.

4. Calcium channel blockers: Calcium channel blockers are medications that specifically target calcium channels in the heart and blood vessels, lowering the amount of calcium that enters these cells and blood pressure to drop.

SBDD has also been used to develop drugs that target other proteins and enzymes involved in CVDs, such as inhibitors of PCSK9 for the treatment of hypercholesterolemia and antithrombotic agents for the prevention of blood clots.

Overall, SBDD has the potential to hasten the development of novel medications for the treatment of CVDs, thereby enhancing the outlook and standard of living for millions of people worldwide who are afflicted with these conditions.

11.6 Advantages and Limitations of a Structure-Based Drug Design

11.6.1 Advantages of Rational Drug Design

The process of developing a medicine that can interact with a certain target molecule, such as an enzyme or receptor, to have the desired therapeutic effect is known as rational drug design. This method of drug discovery has significant advantages over other approaches because it is predicated on the understanding of the structure and function of the target molecule.

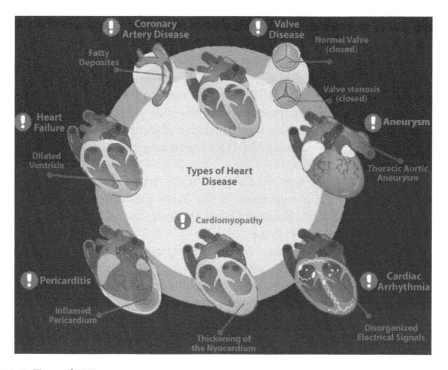

Figure 11.12 Types of CVDs.

The advantages of rational drug design are as follows:

1. Higher accuracy and specificity: Since rational drug design is based on actual knowledge of the structure and function of the target molecule, it is a more precise and focused method. This method allows researchers to design drugs that are specific to the target molecule and reduce the risk of off-target effects. The specificity of the drug also means that the drug can be designed to have minimal side effects, making it more desirable for clinical use.

2. Faster drug development: Rational drug design can accelerate the drug development process by allowing researchers to focus on specific targets and design drugs with greater efficiency. Drug development can be expedited and made less expensive with this method. To produce medications, for instance, rational drug design can be employed that have a similar structure to an existing drug but with improved specificity, bioavailability, or pharmacokinetics.

3. Higher success rate: Due to its foundation in a thorough knowledge of the structure and function of the target molecule, rational drug design has a better success rate in producing potent medications. It is more likely that a drug will be successful if it is created so that it can interact with a particular target molecule, according to researchers. Numerous effective pharmaceuticals, including statins and HIV protease inhibitors, have been created as a result of this strategy.

4. Ability to target new disease targets: Rational drug design can be used to target disease targets that were previously difficult to treat—for example, some diseases are caused by protein-protein interactions that are difficult to target using traditional drug discovery methods. Rational drug design can be used to design drugs that can disrupt these interactions and lead to the development of new treatments for these diseases.

5. Lower toxicity: Rational drug design can be used to design drugs that have lower toxicity. By designing drugs that are specific to the target molecule, researchers can reduce the risk of off-target effects that can cause toxicity. This method can also be used to create medications with slower metabolisms, giving them a longer half-life and less toxicity.

6. Increased understanding of the disease: By revealing information about the structure and operation of the target molecule, rational medication design can improve our understanding of the illness. By understanding how the target molecule contributes to the disease, researchers can design drugs that specifically target the molecule and provide a more effective treatment.

7. Rational and targeted drug design: A logical and focused approach to drug creation is possible with structure-based drug design. By analyzing the structure of a target molecule, researchers can identify binding sites and design drugs that specifically interact with the target. This targeted approach can reduce the risk of off-target effects, leading to drugs that are more specific and effective.

8. Speed and efficiency: By lowering the amount of time and money required for medication development, structure-based drug design can hasten the identification of new drugs. By using computational methods to predict the

structure of the target molecule, researchers can quickly identify potential drug candidates and optimize their properties, such as potency and selectivity.

9. Overcoming drug resistance: Drugs that can overcome drug resistance can be created *via* structure-based drug design. By analyzing the structure of the target molecule, researchers can identify mutations that may cause resistance to existing drugs and design drugs that can overcome these mutations.

10. New drug targets: Using structure-based medication design, one can determine new drug targets that were previously unknown or difficult to target using traditional drug discovery methods. By analyzing the structure of a target molecule, researchers can identify binding sites and design drugs that can interact with the target.

11. Improved pharmacokinetics: Using structure-based medication design, drugs are designed with improved pharmacokinetic properties, such as bioavailability, half-life, and solubility. By analyzing the structure of the target molecule and the drug, researchers can optimize the drug's properties to improve its efficacy and reduce toxicity.

12. Reduced experimental costs: Structure-based drug design can reduce experimental costs by allowing researchers to prioritize drug candidates that are most likely to be effective. By using computational methods to predict the structure of the target molecule and the drug, researchers can prioritize candidates for experimental validation, reducing the cost and time required for drug development.

11.6.2 Limitations and Challenges

Despite its advantages, structure-based drug design (SBDD) has several limitations and challenges that researchers must overcome to develop effective drugs.

The following are the most significant limitations and challenges of SBDD:

1. Limited availability of protein structures: SBDD's performance is reliant on the availability of high-quality structures of the target protein. However, obtaining high-quality protein structures can be challenging, particularly for membrane proteins, which play critical roles in many diseases. Moreover, even if a protein structure is available, it may not be in the relevant conformation or state required for drug design.

2. Dynamic nature of protein structures: Protein structures are not static but are rather dynamic and can adopt multiple conformations. This dynamic nature makes it difficult to design drugs that can bind specifically to the target protein, particularly if ligand interaction results in conformational changes in the protein. Consequently, it is essential to comprehend the conformational dynamics of the target protein while creating efficient medicines.

3. Ligand optimization challenges: While SBDD allows for the rational design of drugs, designing drugs that have optimal binding affinity, selectivity, and pharmacokinetic properties can be challenging. For instance, designing drugs with high selectivity for the target protein and minimal off-target effects is difficult because many proteins have similar structures and binding sites.

Moreover, designing drugs with optimal pharmacokinetic properties, such as bioavailability and half-life, requires a deep understanding of the drug's physicochemical properties.

4. Cost and time-consuming: SBDD is a lengthy and expensive procedure, especially if the target protein structure is not available or is difficult to crystallize. Additionally, SBDD requires a multidisciplinary team with expertise in structural biology, chemistry, and computational methods, which can be challenging to assemble.

5. Limited scope of application: SBDD is primarily effective for designing drugs that target specific protein targets. However, many diseases are caused by complex networks of protein-protein interactions, making it challenging to design drugs that can disrupt these interactions effectively.

6. Challenges with membrane proteins: Membrane proteins play critical roles in many diseases, and they are often challenging to study and crystallize. The hydrophobic nature of membrane proteins makes them difficult to solubilize and crystallize, limiting the availability of high-quality structures for SBDD.

7. Limited flexibility of target protein structures: The foundation of SBDD is the idea that the target protein structure is constant and does not change significantly upon ligand interaction. In truth, though, a lot of proteins are adaptable and capable of considerable conformational changes in response to ligand interaction. This limitation can impact the accuracy of SBDD predictions, particularly for flexible protein targets.

8. Limited understanding of the binding mechanism: SBDD is dependent on the accurate understanding of the binding mechanism between the drug and the target protein. However, in many cases, the binding mechanism is not fully understood, which can limit the success of SBDD. In addition, some drugs may bind to multiple sites on the target protein, which can complicate the design of selective compounds.

9. False negatives and false positives: SBDD relies on computational algorithms to predict the interactions between the drug and target protein. However, these predictions are not always accurate, leading to false negatives or false positives. False negatives occur when a drug that could have been effective is discarded due to a failure to identify a potential binding site. False positives occur when a drug that is predicted to be effective fails in experimental validation.

10. Limitations in designing allosteric modulators: Drugs known as allosteric modulators bind to a different location on the target protein, causing a conformational shift that alters the protein's action. It can be difficult to create medications that bind specifically to the allosteric site because the allosteric site may not be structurally well-defined. This makes it difficult to build allosteric modulators.

11. Limited predictability of drug toxicity: SBDD primarily focuses on identifying drugs that interact with the target protein. However, drugs that interact with other proteins or biomolecules may cause off-target effects, leading to toxicity. Predicting the toxicity of drugs can be challenging because it

depends on the drug's pharmacokinetic properties and other factors that may be difficult to predict computationally.

12. Inability to consider post-translational modifications: PTMs which are chemical alterations that happen after protein production such as phosphorylation or glycosylation. PTMs can affect protein structure and function, making them important targets for drug discovery. However, predicting the effects of PTMs on protein structure can be challenging, limiting the ability of SBDD to design drugs that target modified proteins.

13. Lack of understanding of disease mechanisms: Understanding the target protein's structure and function is essential for SBDD. However, many diseases are complex and involve multiple pathways and interactions. Limited understanding of disease mechanisms can make it challenging to identify relevant protein targets and design effective drugs.

14. Regulatory challenges: Regulatory agencies have strict requirements for drug safety and efficacy, which can make it challenging to get approval for new drugs. SBDD requires a significant investment in resources and time, and the risk of failure is high. This can make it challenging to justify the investment required to develop drugs using SBDD.

11.6.3   Comparison with Other Drug Discovery Methods

The following points highlights the comparison of SBDD with other drug discovery methods:

1. High-throughput screening (HTS): In order to find molecules that bind to a biological target, HTS entails testing huge libraries of compounds against the target. This approach does not rely on prior knowledge of the target structure, making it useful for identifying drugs that target novel or poorly understood targets. However, HTS can be expensive and time-consuming, and it can produce false positives and false negatives.

2. Phenotypic screening: Phenotypic screening involves testing compounds in cellular or animal models to identify molecules that affect a particular phenotype, such as cell death or growth. This method is helpful for finding medications that alter intricate pathways because it does not require knowledge of the target protein. However, phenotypic screening can be difficult to interpret, and it may not be clear how the drug is working.

3. Fragment-based drug design (FBDD): FBDD involves screening small fragments of compounds against a target protein and then growing or linking the fragments to develop more potent compounds. This approach can be useful for identifying novel chemical scaffolds and can lessen the quantity of substances that must be synthesized and screened. However, FBDD requires expertise in synthetic chemistry, and it may not be effective for targets with large, flat binding sites.

4. Natural product-based drug discovery: This approach involves screening natural products, such as plants or fungi, for their biological activity. Natural products often have complex chemical structures and can be useful for

identifying drugs that target complex pathways. However, natural products can be difficult to isolate, synthesize, and optimize for drug development.

5. Combinatorial chemistry: Combinatorial chemistry is a method used to generate large libraries of compounds with diverse chemical structures. The method involves the synthesis of multiple compounds in parallel, using automated systems. Combinatorial chemistry is often used to produce extensive libraries of chemicals for HTS in the early stages of drug discovery. However, the method has limitations, as it may result in a large number of inactive or toxic compounds.

6. Rational drug design (SBDD): Drugs are created using the SBDD approach, which bases its work on the target protein's three-dimensional structure. The method involves the use of structural and biophysical data to guide the design of compounds that specifically target the protein. SBDD has the advantage of being able to design compounds with increased potency, selectivity, and safety profiles, but it requires high-quality structural information and expertise in structural biology and computational chemistry.

7. Virtual screening: Virtual screening includes testing vast libraries of chemicals against a target protein using computational techniques. By using this method, fewer compounds will need to be synthesized and screened in order to find those that are anticipated to bind to the target protein. Virtual screening, on the other hand, is less accurate than SBDD because it relies on compound binding affinities that are predicted without a thorough understanding of the structure of the target protein.

8. Antibody-based drug discovery: Antibody-based drug discovery involves identifying monoclonal antibodies that bind to the target protein and modulate its activity. This approach can be used to target proteins that are difficult to modulate with small molecules, such as membrane-bound proteins. However, antibody-based drugs can be expensive to manufacture and may have limited tissue penetration.

9. Fragment-based lead discovery (FBLD): In FBLD, libraries of tiny molecular fragments are screened to find substances that bind to a target protein, and then using these fragments as building blocks to design larger, more potent compounds. FBLD is similar to FBDD, but it typically involves using smaller and more diverse fragment libraries. FBLD can be useful for identifying novel chemical scaffolds and can be combined with SBDD to design more potent and selective compounds. However, FBLD requires expertise in synthetic chemistry and may not be effective for targets with large binding sites or for proteins that are difficult to express or purify.

10. AI-assisted drug discovery: AI-assisted drug discovery involves using machine learning algorithms and other computational tools to analyze large datasets and predict the properties of drug candidates. SBDD and other drug discovery techniques can be combined with AI-assisted drug discovery to speed up the process and find new drug candidates. The effectiveness of AI-assisted drug discovery, however, is still in its infancy and is reliant on the caliber and variety of the data utilized to train the algorithms.

11. Repurposing existing drugs: Repurposing existing drugs involves identifying new uses for drugs that are already approved for other indications. This approach can be faster and less expensive than traditional drug discovery methods, as the safety and pharmacokinetic properties of the drug are already established. However, repurposed drugs may have limited efficacy or may cause unexpected side effects, and it can be challenging to identify new uses for drugs that were not originally designed to target a particular disease pathway.

11.7   Case Studies and Examples

11.7.1   Discovery of HIV Protease Inhibitors

Structure-based drug design (SBDD) has the potential to result in the creation of life-saving medications, as demonstrated by the discovery of HIV protease inhibitors [25]. HIV protease is a viral enzyme that is important for the virus' reproduction, making it a prime candidate for treatment development. However, early attempts to design inhibitors of HIV protease using traditional methods were largely unsuccessful.

In the late 1980s, researchers at Merck Sharp & Dohme (MSD) recognized the potential of SBDD in drug discovery and began a project to develop HIV protease inhibitors using this approach. The first step was to obtain the crystal structure of HIV protease, which was a challenging task given the large size and high flexibility of the protein. However, using a combination of X-ray crystallography and computational methods, the three-dimensional structure of the HIV protease was discovered by the researchers, who used this knowledge to create possible inhibitors.

The initial inhibitors identified using SBDD were relatively weak, with low potency and poor pharmacokinetic properties. However, the researchers at MSD continued to refine their approach, enhancing the inhibitors' potency and selectivity through iterative rounds of structural discovery, inhibitor creation, and biological testing [26]. The result was a series of compounds that were highly effective at inhibiting HIV protease and had good pharmacokinetic properties.

The first HIV protease inhibitor to be approved by the US FDA was saquinavir, developed by Roche in 1995. However, saquinavir had limited bioavailability and required frequent dosing, making it less than ideal for long-term treatment. In contrast, the HIV protease inhibitors developed by MSD as shown in Figure 11.13, including indinavir, ritonavir, and nelfinavir, had superior pharmacokinetic properties and were effective at suppressing viral replication in clinical trials.

One of the key advantages of SBDD in the discovery of HIV protease inhibitors was its ability to identify compounds that selectively targeted the viral protease without affecting human proteases. In order to minimize adverse effects and lower the possibility of drug interactions, selectivity was essential. In order to increase the inhibitors' binding affinity for the target protein, researchers were also able to modify the inhibitors' shape and electrostatic characteristics using SBDD.

A significant advancement in the field of drug development, the finding of HIV protease inhibitors utilizing SBDD has helped save countless lives. HIV protease inhibitors are now

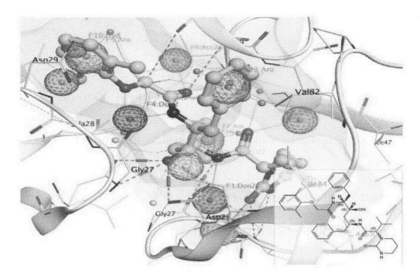

Figure 11.13 HIV protease inhibitors.

a crucial component of combination antiretroviral therapy for the treatment of HIV/AIDS, and research into the creation of new and improved inhibitors is still ongoing. Structure-based drug design has been shown to be effective in modern medicine through the application of this technique in the development of HIV protease inhibitors as well as the discovery of medications for other disorders.

11.7.2 Development of HER2 Kinase Inhibitors

Another illustration of how structure-based drug design (SBDD) can result in the discovery of fresh medications for the treatment of cancer is the development of HER2 kinase inhibitors. Transmembrane protein HER2 (human epidermal growth factor receptor 2) is over-expressed in a number of cancer forms, including breast, ovarian, and gastric cancer. HER2 overexpression is associated with aggressive tumor growth and poor prognosis, making it an attractive target for drug discovery.

In the early 2000s, researchers at GlaxoSmithKline (GSK) recognized the potential of SBDD in developing HER2 kinase inhibitors [27] and began a project to identify potent and selective inhibitors. The first step was to obtain the crystal structure of the HER2 kinase domain, which was a challenging task given the high flexibility of the protein. However, using a combination of X-ray crystallography and computational methods, the three-dimensional structure of the HER2 kinase domain was identified by the researchers, and they used this knowledge to develop possible inhibitors.

The initial inhibitors identified using SBDD were relatively weak, with low potency and poor pharmacokinetic properties. In order to increase the efficacy and selectivity of the inhibitors, the researchers at GSK continued to hone their strategy through repeating cycles of structural determination, inhibitor design, and biological testing. The result as shown in Figure 11.14(a–c) was a series of compounds that were highly effective at inhibiting HER2 kinase and had good pharmacokinetic properties.

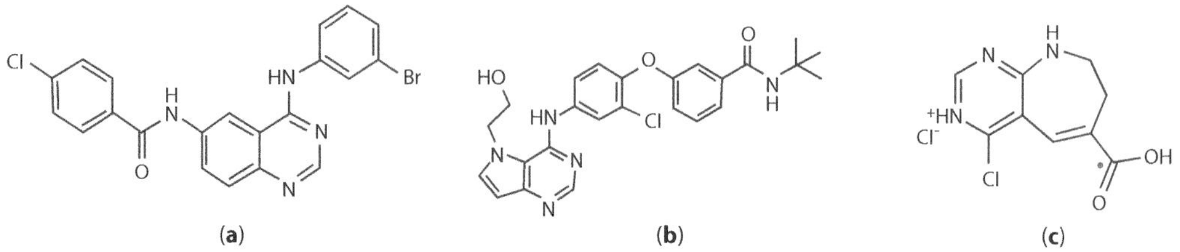

Figure 11.14 (a) Anilino quinazoline derivative. (b) Pyridopyrimidine derivative. (c) Pyrimidoazepine derivatives.

The HER2 kinase inhibitor lapatinib, created by GSK in 2007, was the first to receive FDA approval in the US. Breast cancer patients who are HER2-positive are treated with lapatinib, a dual HER2 and EGFR kinase inhibitor, in combination with other anticancer medications. A significant step forward in the field of cancer drug discovery, the development of lapatinib utilizing SBDD cleared the path for the creation of further HER2 kinase inhibitors.

Finding compounds that specifically targeted HER2 kinase without impacting other kinases was one of the main benefits of SBDD in the creation of HER2 kinase inhibitors. In order to minimize adverse effects and lower the possibility of drug interactions, selectivity was essential. In order to increase the inhibitors' binding affinity for the target protein, researchers were also able to modify the inhibitors' shape and electrostatic characteristics using SBDD.

Significant advancements in the treatment of HER2-positive breast cancer and other cancers have resulted from the development of lapatinib and other HER2 kinase inhibitors. However, the development of resistance to HER2 kinase inhibitors remains a significant challenge, and ongoing research is focused on identifying new inhibitors and combination therapies to overcome this resistance.

The development of HER2 kinase inhibitors using SBDD is a prime example of how this approach can lead to the discovery of effective drugs for the treatment of cancer. With the use of SBDD, scientists were able to enhance the inhibitors' shape and electrostatic characteristics in order to increase their binding affinity for the target protein, producing extremely effective and selective inhibitors. The development of SBDD for the discovery of medications for various diseases was spurred by the success of lapatinib and other HER2 kinase inhibitors in treating HER2-positive breast cancer.

11.7.3 Design of Influenza Neuraminidase Inhibitors

Influenza virus is a major public health concern due to its ability to cause seasonal epidemics and occasional pandemics. An important target for the creation of antiviral medications to cure and prevent influenza illness is the neuraminidase (NA) enzyme. In this case study, we will look at the creation and optimization of NA inhibitors as shown in Figure 11.15 using structure-based drug design (SBDD).

GlaxoSmithKline (GSK) produced zanamivir, the first NA inhibitor to be authorized for clinical use, in 1999. A competitive inhibitor of NA, zanamivir binds to the enzyme's active site and prevents it from cleaving sialic acid off host cells' surfaces, preventing the release of

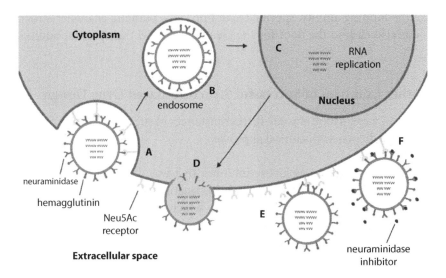

Figure 11.15 Influenza neuraminidase inhibitors.

viral particles. To maximize zanamivir's binding affinity for NA, X-ray crystallography and computational techniques were used in its development.

Despite zanamivir's effectiveness, Gilead Sciences created the second-generation NA inhibitor oseltamivir because to its low bioavailability and need for inhalation treatment. Oseltamivir, a prodrug, is converted to its active form, a competitive inhibitor of NA, in the liver. Similar to zanamivir, oseltamivir was created utilizing X-ray crystallography to direct the optimization of the inhibitor's binding affinity for NA.

While zanamivir and oseltamivir were effective against most strains of influenza, The advent of drug-resistant variations made it clear that new NA inhibitors were required. The third-generation NA inhibitor peramivir, which was authorized for clinical use in 2014, was created *via* SBDD. Peramivir is a transition-state analogue NA inhibitor with excellent affinity and specificity for the enzyme. Peramivir's geometry, electrostatic characteristics, and hydrogen bonding interactions with NA were all optimized throughout design utilizing X-ray crystallography and computational techniques [28].

In addition to peramivir, other NA inhibitors have been developed using SBDD, including laninamivir, which is used in Japan and Korea, and baloxavir marboxil, which was approved for clinical use in 2018. Baloxavir marboxil is a cap-dependent endonuclease inhibitor that targets the early stages of viral replication and has shown promise against drug-resistant strains of influenza.

The success of SBDD in the design of NA inhibitors is due to its ability to identify and optimize compounds that target the active site of NA with high specificity and affinity. X-ray crystallography is a critical tool for understanding the three-dimensional structure of NA and its interactions with inhibitors, whereas the binding affinity and selectivity of putative inhibitors are predicted using computational approaches.

Highly potent antiviral medications for the treatment and prevention of influenza infection have been created as a result of the design of NA inhibitors utilizing SBDD. The discovery of antiviral drugs has undergone a radical change as a result of SBDD's capacity to optimize the binding affinity, specificity, and pharmacokinetic characteristics of inhibitors. This has also cleared the door for the creation of novel therapies for additional viral disorders.

11.7.4   Other Examples of Successful Structure-Based Drug Design

In this case study, we will look at some further instances of successful SBDD that resulted in the creation of medicines with clinical approval.

1. Imatinib: It is a tyrosine kinase inhibitor that was developed by Novartis to treat chronic myeloid leukemia (CML). Imatinib functions by attaching to the Bcr-Abl fusion protein's active site, which is in charge of the leukemia cells' unchecked multiplication.

The Bcr-Abl kinase domain crystal structure and a computational strategy to improve the inhibitor's binding affinity and selectivity served as the foundation for the creation of imatinib. Imatinib as shown in Figure 11.16, which has a high percentage of patient response and long-term survival, was approved by the FDA in 2001 and has completely changed the way CML is treated.

2. Raltegravir: It is an HIV integrase inhibitor that was developed by Merck. In order to stop viral DNA from being incorporated into the host genome, raltegravir binds to the active site of the integrase enzyme.

The crystal structure of the HIV integrase enzyme and a computational strategy to maximize the binding affinity and selectivity of the inhibitor served as the foundation for the creation of raltegravir. Raltegravir as shown in Figure 11.17 has been proven to be extremely successful at treating HIV infection with few side effects, and the FDA authorized it in 2007.

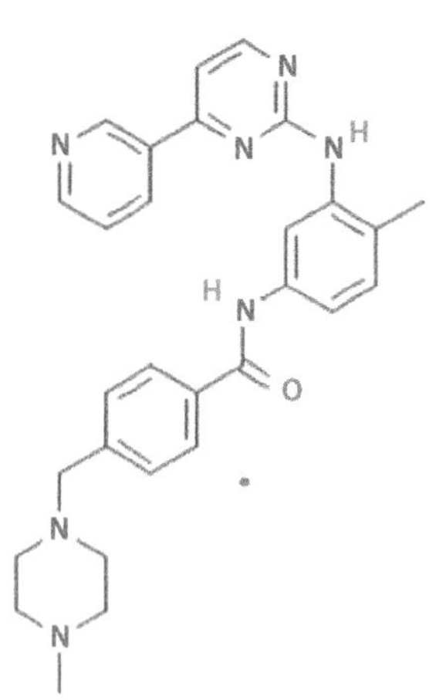

Figure 11.16 Chemical structure depiction of imatinib.

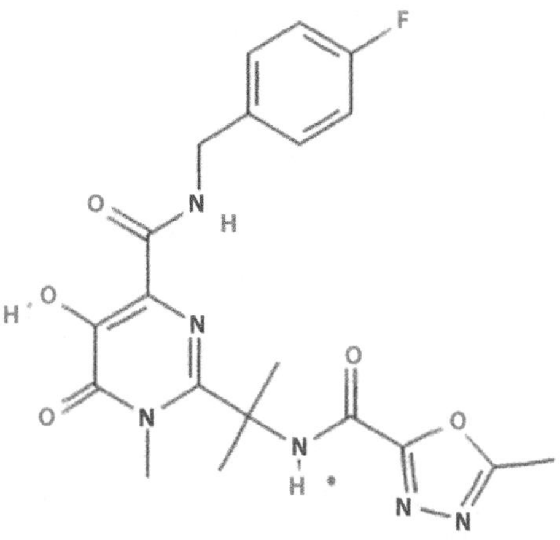

Figure 11.17 Chemical structure depiction of raltegravir.

3. Venetoclax: It is a Bcl-2 inhibitor that was developed by AbbVie and Roche to treat chronic lymphocytic leukemia (CLL). Venetoclax works by binding to the BH3-binding groove of Bcl-2, which is responsible for preventing apoptosis in cancer cells. The Bcl-2 protein crystal structure and a computational method to enhance the inhibitor's binding affinity and selectivity served as the foundation for the creation of venetoclax.

Venetoclax, as shown in Figure 11.18, was approved by the FDA in 2016 and has shown remarkable efficacy in treating CLL, with high response rates and durable remissions.

4. Osimertinib: It is a third-generation EGFR inhibitor which AstraZeneca created as a non-small cell lung cancer (NSCLC) treatment. Osimertinib functions by irreversibly attaching to mutant versions of the EGFR protein, which are in charge of promoting NSCLC cell growth and proliferation.

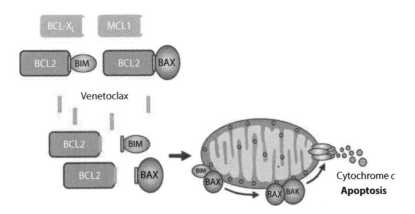

Figure 11.18 Mechanism of action of venetoclax.

Osimertinib as shown in Figure 11.19 was created using a computational method to enhance the inhibitor's binding affinity and selectivity and the EGFR protein crystal structure. Osimertinib was approved by the FDA in 2015 and has been shown to be highly effective in treating NSCLC, with minimal side effects.

11.8   Future Outlook and Implications

SBDD also has numerous implications for the future of personalized medicine [29]. By designing drugs that target specific macromolecules involved in disease processes, researchers can develop therapies that are tailored to individual patients, based on their unique genetic and molecular profiles. This personalized approach to drug development has the potential to revolutionize the management of difficult conditions like cancer and neurodegenerative disorders, by enabling targeted and effective therapies that minimize side effects and maximize patient outcomes.

The future of SBDD looks bright, with continued advances in technology and computing power enabling researchers to explore the structure and function of macromolecules in ever greater detail. With the potential to revolutionize drug discovery and personalized medicine, SBDD is poised to have a big impact on how healthcare is going to develop.

11.8.1   Emerging Trends and Technologies

Structure-based drug design is a discipline that is (SBDD) which is constantly evolving, driven by advances in technology and computing power. Here are some emerging trends and technologies that are likely to have a significant impact on the future of SBDD:

- Cryo-EM (cryo-electron microscopy): Cryo-EM is a technique that involves flash-freezing biological samples to preserve their native structure, and then imaging them with an electron microscope. The resulting images can be used to create 3D models of the sample at near-atomic resolution, providing

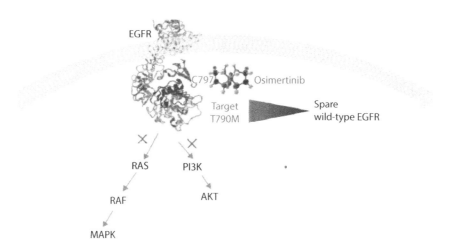

Figure 11.19 Chemical structure of osimertinib.

valuable insights into the structure and function of biological macromolecules. Cryo-EM has revolutionized the study of complex biological systems, and is becoming increasingly popular in drug discovery, particularly for difficult-to-target proteins such as membrane proteins.

- Machine learning (ML) and artificial intelligence (AI): These are rapidly advancing fields that involve developing algorithms that can learn from and make predictions on large datasets. In drug discovery, AI and ML algorithms are being used to analyze large amounts of data on drug targets, compounds, and clinical outcomes, in order to identify potential drug candidates with high efficacy and specificity. These algorithms can also be used to optimize drug candidates and predict their pharmacokinetic properties, reducing the time and cost required for drug development.

- Fragment-based drug design (FBDD): In order to boost affinity and selectivity, FBDD entails developing tiny, low-affinity molecules that bind to particular areas of a target protein. This approach has become increasingly popular in recent years, particularly for challenging targets such as protein-protein interactions and allosteric sites. By focusing on small fragments rather than large compounds, FBDD can also reduce the risk of toxicity and improve the pharmacokinetic properties of drug candidates.

- High-throughput screening (HTS): HTS is a technique that involves testing large numbers of compounds against a target protein, with the aim of identifying potential drug candidates. Advances in automation and robotics have made HTS more efficient and cost-effective, enabling researchers to screen larger numbers of compounds and targets. HTS is particularly useful for identifying hits against novel drug targets, and for optimizing drug candidates through iterative screening and optimization.

- Drug design *via* computer simulation: Drug design *via* computer simulation involves using computational methods to design and optimize drug candidates, based on their predicted interactions with a target protein. This strategy can greatly cut down on the time and money needed for drug development by allowing researchers to screen large numbers of compounds and predict their pharmacokinetic properties without the need for laborious and expensive laboratory experiments. *In silico* drug design can also be used to identify potential drug targets and predict the efficacy of existing drugs against new targets.

- Targeting RNA: RNA has emerged as an important drug target, particularly for diseases such as cancer and genetic disorders. Advances in SBDD methods and technologies are enabling researchers to design drugs that target RNA with high specificity and efficacy, opening up new avenues for drug discovery. RNA-targeting drugs can be designed to modulate gene expression, splicing, or translation and can be used to treat a variety of illnesses, such as those currently considered "undruggable" using conventional small molecule drugs.

These emerging trends and technologies are likely to shape the future of SBDD, enabling researchers to design drugs with higher efficacy and specificity, and to target previously intractable diseases and drug targets. These technologies do, however, come with some difficulties and restrictions, such as the necessity for precise medication toxicity prediction and the expense and length of time associated with drug development. However, SBDD's continuous growth will probably have a big impact on healthcare in the future by making it possible to create more efficient and individualized treatments for a variety of ailments.

11.8.2   Integration with Other Drug Discovery Methods

Structure-based medication design is an effective method for the rational design of new drugs with improved potency and specificity. However, it is not a standalone method and can be integrated with other drug discovery methods to accelerate the process of drug discovery. Integration with other drug discovery methods enables researchers to leverage the strengths of each method to develop more effective and specific drugs for a variety of diseases.

Structure-based drug design can be used with a number of drug discovery techniques, including high-throughput screening, rational design, fragment-based drug discovery, and microfluidic-based screening. Researchers can find substances that attach to the target of interest with high affinity and specificity by combining several strategies, and then optimize their structures using structure-based drug design to improve their pharmacological properties. This integration of methods enables researchers to accelerate the drug discovery process and develop drugs that have a higher probability of success in clinical trials.

Furthermore, integration with other drug discovery methods allows researchers to overcome a few of the drawbacks of designing drugs based on structure, such as the need for high-resolution structures and the difficulty in predicting the effects of mutations. By combining multiple methods, researchers can increase the chances of identifying successful drug candidates and minimize the risk of failure in the later stages of drug development.

Structure-based drug design has been integrated with various other drug discovery methods to improve the efficiency and success rates of drug development.

Some of the methods with which structure-based drug design has been integrated are as follows:

- Phenotypic screening: In phenotypic screening, compounds are screened based on their ability to affect a particular phenotype or disease state. This approach involves the use of cell-based assays or animal models to identify compounds that exhibit a desired functional effect. The identified compounds can then be optimized using medication design with a focus on structure to increase potency and selectivity. By integrating structure-based drug design with phenotypic screening, researchers can design compounds that not only bind to the target of interest but also exhibit the desired functional effect.
- Fragment linking: By joining two or more tiny molecule fragments, a bigger compound that binds to the desired target is created. This process is known as fragment linking. Using this method, it is possible to create substances that attach to various places on the target molecule, producing highly effective and targeted medication candidates. The best fragments for linking can be found *via* structure-based drug design. The linker can then be created, and

the structure of the final product can be optimized for better pharmacological effects.

- Directed evolution: Directed evolution involves generating libraries of mutated proteins or enzymes that have altered functional properties using genetic engineering techniques. By combining directed evolution with structure-based drug design, researchers can generate proteins or enzymes that bind to specific ligands with high affinity and specificity. Then, these enzymes or proteins can be utilized as potential therapeutic targets or as a means of drug discovery. It is also possible to use structure-based drug design to enhance the binding specificity and affinity of newly produced proteins or enzymes.

- Rational design: Rational design involves the use of computational methods to design compounds with desired properties. Rational drug design can be used in conjunction with structure-based drug design to create substances that bind to the target of interest with high affinity and specificity. Compounds that suit the target's binding site and interact with it in a particular way can be created using computational techniques like molecular docking, molecular dynamics simulations, and quantum mechanics calculations. The pharmacological properties of the developed molecules can then be enhanced utilizing structure-based drug design.

- Microfluidic-based screening: Microfluidic-based screening involves the process of screening libraries of compounds using microfluidic devices to determine whether they can bind to an interest target. High-throughput screening can be accomplished with little reagent use thanks to the exact control that microfluidic devices offer over the reaction conditions. Researchers can find compounds with high affinity and specificity for the target of interest by combining structure-based drug design with microfluidic-based screening. The selected compounds can then have their pharmacological properties improved through structure-based drug design.

Overall, the effectiveness and success rates of medication development have significantly increased as a result of the incorporation of structure-based drug design with other drug discovery techniques. Researchers can create and optimise drug candidates with desired pharmacological qualities by combining multiple methodologies such as phenotypic screening, fragment linking, directed evolution, rational design, and microfluidic-based screening with structure-based drug design. These integrated methodologies have also helped in the development of new therapeutic targets and fresh insights into the molecular causes of disease. As technology continues to advance, the integration of structure-based drug design with other drug discovery methods is expected to become increasingly important in the development of safe and effective drugs.

11.9 Potential Impact on Healthcare and Drug Development

Structure-based drug design's methods and applications have the power to completely alter the pharmaceutical and healthcare industries. With the ability to design drugs that specifically target disease-causing proteins, researchers can potentially develop more effective and safer drugs with fewer side effects. This has the potential to significantly improve the lives of patients and reduce the burden of diseases on healthcare systems.

The creation of more potent cancer treatments is one of the potential effects of structure-based drug design. With the ability to design drugs that specifically target cancer cells and spare healthy cells, patients may experience fewer side effects and a higher quality of life. In addition, with the ability to design drugs that target specific mutations in cancer cells, researchers can potentially develop personalized treatments for each patient.

The creation of novel antibiotics is a potential side effect of structure-based drug design. New medicines are desperately needed to treat infections because of the surge of bacteria that are resistant to current antibiotics. By designing drugs that specifically target bacterial proteins, researchers can potentially develop more effective antibiotics with fewer side effects. This has the potential to significantly improve public health by reducing the prevalence of antibiotic-resistant infections.

In addition to cancer treatments and antibiotics, structure-based drug design has the potential to impact many other areas of healthcare—for example, it could lead to the creation of novel therapies for neurological conditions including Alzheimer's and Parkinson's, by targeting the proteins associated with these diseases. It could also lead to the development of new treatments for viral infections, such as HIV and influenza, by targeting viral proteins.

Medication development may be significantly impacted by structure-based medication design. Researchers may be able to shorten the time and expense involved in drug development by creating medications that selectively target disease-causing proteins. This is because drugs can be designed with a higher likelihood of success in clinical trials, reducing the need for extensive testing and development of multiple drug candidates.

Another potential impact of structure-based drug design on drug development is the ability to repurpose existing drugs for new uses. By understanding the structure of disease-causing proteins, researchers can potentially identify existing drugs that could be effective in treating other diseases. The time and expense involved in developing new drugs could be greatly reduced as a result, increasing patient access to medicines.

Using structure-based drug design, it is possible to create medications that are extremely targeted to their target, which is one of the main advantages. Researchers can create medications that exactly fit into the target protein's active site by understanding the molecular structure of the protein. This leads to drugs that have high potency and selectivity, meaning they are effective at low doses and have fewer off-target effects.

The capacity to create medications using structure-based drug design is another benefit for targets that were previously considered "undruggable." With conventional small molecule medications, it has proven challenging to target some proteins, such as transcription factors. The creation of novel therapeutic classes, including stapled peptides, that can target these previously difficult proteins has been made possible by structure-based drug design.

Additionally, structure-based medication design may dramatically shorten drug development's time and expense. By designing drugs with high specificity and potency, fewer compounds need to be screened in preclinical studies. This can lower the cost of producing new pharmaceuticals and accelerate the drug development process.

Structure-based drug design also has implications for personalized medicine. By designing drugs that target specific proteins or mutations, it may be possible to develop drugs that are tailored to an individual's genetic makeup. This could lead to the development of drugs that are more efficient and produce fewer side effects.

Despite the potential benefits of structure-based drug design, there are also challenges that need to be addressed. One challenge is the limited availability of high-quality protein structures for drug design. This limits the ability of researchers to design drugs for many targets, particularly those that are not well characterized.

Another challenge is the potential for off-target effects. Structure-based medication design has the potential to have a large impact on both drug development and healthcare through its methods and applications. This highlights the importance of careful screening and testing of drug candidates to ensure their safety and efficacy.

Overall, Structure-based medication design has the potential to have a large impact on both drug development and healthcare through its methods and applications. With the ability to design drugs that specifically target disease-causing proteins, researchers can potentially develop more effective and safer treatments for patients. However, there are also challenges that need to be addressed to fully realize the potential of this approach.

11.9.1 Research Directions

Structure-based drug design (SBDD) has made great progress, but much more has to be done before its full potential as a tool for drug discovery can be realized. Therefore, a call to action is necessary for further research and development in this area.

Some of these are as follows:

1. Increased investment: Governments, private companies, and funding agencies should increase their investment in research and development of SBDD and related technologies. This can help to accelerate the pace of discovery and bring new drugs to market more quickly.
2. Collaboration: Researchers, pharmaceutical companies, and other stakeholders should collaborate more closely to share data, resources, and expertise. This can help to break down silos and accelerate progress in drug discovery.
3. Advanced technology: Advances in technologies like X-ray crystallography, NMR spectroscopy, and cryo-EM should be further developed and improved so that drug targets can be structurally determined more precisely and effectively.
4. Innovation: Researchers should continue to explore new and innovative approaches to drug discovery, such as artificial intelligence, machine learning, and quantum computing, to accelerate progress and improve the effectiveness of drug development.
5. Ethical considerations: With the increased potential for personalized medicine, it is important to consider the ethical implications of SBDD and related technologies. Researchers and policymakers should work together to ensure that these technologies are developed and used in a responsible and ethical manner.

Overall, continued investment, collaboration, and innovation in the field of SBDD have the potential to transform drug discovery and improve the lives of millions of people around the world.

11.10 Conclusion and Future Scope

In conclusion, a potent approach for creating new medications that can selectively target disease-causing proteins is structure-based drug design (SBDD). It offers many advantages over traditional drug discovery methods, including a higher success rate in identifying lead compounds and a reduced risk of toxicity. By identifying and targeting specific proteins involved in disease pathways, SBDD has the ability to completely change how we create new medications and has aided in the development of many therapies that have received clinical approval.

However, the success of SBDD depends on accurate structural determination of the target protein and efficient screening of compound libraries. The continuous development of SBDD will depend on continued investment in cutting-edge technologies including cryo-EM, NMR spectroscopy, and X-ray crystallography. Collaboration between researchers, pharmaceutical companies, and funding agencies will also be crucial to accelerate progress and bring new drugs to market more quickly.

Overall, SBDD represents a promising approach to drug discovery that can significantly improve the lives of patients suffering from a wide range of diseases. As we continue to refine and improve this methodology, we have the potential to develop more effective and targeted drugs that can improve the health and well-being of millions of people around the world.

Looking to the future, there are several exciting developments in the field of SBDD that hold promise for advancing drug discovery even further. One key area of research is the use of artificial intelligence (AI) and machine learning algorithms to analyze and interpret large amounts of data from experimental and computational sources. This approach has the potential to greatly increase the efficiency and accuracy of drug discovery by identifying new drug targets, predicting drug efficacy and toxicity, and optimizing lead compounds.

Another important area of research is the development of new techniques for characterizing the dynamic behavior of proteins, including their conformational changes and interactions with other molecules. This will require the use of advanced experimental methods such as time-resolved crystallography and cryo-electron microscopy as well as the development of new computational tools for analyzing these complex data sets.

References

1. Kumar, A., Krishnamurthi, R., Nayyar, A., Sharma, K., Grover, V., Hossain, E., A novel smart healthcare design, simulation, and implementation using healthcare 4.0 processes. *IEEE Access*, 8, 118433–118471, 2020.
2. Kaur, T., Bhandari, D.D., Sharma, R., Cloud Computing: A relevant Solution for Drug Designing using different Software's, in: *2021 Sixth International Conference on Image Information Processing (ICIIP)*, vol. 6, pp. 375–378, IEEE, 2021, November.

3. Huang, H.J., Tsai, F.J., Chung, J.G., Tsai, C.H., Hsu, Y.M., Ho, T.Y., Chen, C.Y.C., Drug design for XRCC4 *in silico*, in: *2009 2nd International Conference on Biomedical Engineering and Informatics*, pp. 1–4, IEEE, 2009, October.

4. Nayyar, A., Gadhavi, L., Zaman, N., Machine learning in healthcare: Review, opportunities and challenges, in: *Machine Learning and the Internet of Medical Things in Healthcare*, pp. 23–45, 2021.

5. Pal, R., Misra, G., Mathur, P., *In silico* screening of small molecule modulators of zika virus proteins, in: *2017 7th International Conference on Cloud Computing, Data Science & Engineering-Confluence*, pp. 381–386, IEEE, 2017, January.

6. Srinivasu, N., Satyanarayana, K.V.V., Murthy, N.G.K., Structure based drug design studies on CDK2 amino pyrazole inhibitors using autodock tools. *2014 Conference on IT in Business, Industry and Government (CSIBIG)*, Indore, India, pp. 1–5, 2014, doi: 10.1109/CSIBIG.2014.7056965.

7. Sadjad, B. and Zsoldos, Z., Toward a robust search method for the protein-drug docking problem. *IEEE/ACM Trans. Comput. Biol. Bioinf.*, 8, 4, 1120–1133, 2010.

8. Pramanik, P.K.D., Solanki, A., Debnath, A., Nayyar, A., El-Sappagh, S., Kwak, K.S., Advancing modern healthcare with nanotechnology, nanobiosensors, and internet of nano things: Taxonomies, applications, architecture, and challenges. *IEEE Access*, 8, 65230–65266, 2020.

9. Law, R., Barker, O., Barker, J.J., Hesterkamp, T., Godemann, R., Andersen, O., Whittaker, M., The multiple roles of computational chemistry in fragment-based drug design. *J. Comput.-Aided Mol. Des.*, 23, 459–473, 2009.

10. Pramanik, P.K.D., Pareek, G., Nayyar, A., Security and privacy in remote healthcare: Issues, solutions, and standards, in: *Telemedicine Technologies*, pp. 201–225, Academic Press, United States, 2019.

11. Choudhury, C., Murugan, N.A., Priyakumar, U.D., Structure-based drug repurposing: Traditional and advanced AI/ML-aided methods. *Drug Discov. Today*, 27, 7, 1847–1861, 2022.

12. Odoemelam, C.S., Percival, B., Wallis, H., Chang, M.W., Ahmad, Z., Scholey, D., Wilson, P.B., G-Protein coupled receptors: Structure and function in drug discovery. *RSC Adv.*, 10, 60, 36337–36348, 2020.

13. Lin, X., Li, X., Lin, X., A review on applications of computational methods in drug screening and design. *Molecules*, 25, 6, 1375, 2020.

14. Mahapatra, B., Krishnamurthi, R., Nayyar, A., Healthcare models and algorithms for privacy and security in healthcare records, in: *Security and Privacy of Electronic Healthcare Records: Concepts, Paradigms and Solutions, 183*, 2019.

15. Yu, W., Weber, D.J., MacKerell Jr., A.D., Computer-aided drug design: An update, in: *Antibiotics: Methods and Protocols*, pp. 123–152, Springer US, New York, NY, 2022.

16. Crampon, K., Giorkallos, A., Deldossi, M., Baud, S., Steffenel, L.A., Machine-learning methods for ligand–protein molecular docking. *Drug Discov. Today*, 27, 1, 151–164, 2022.

17. Aminpour, M., Montemagno, C., Tuszynski, J.A., An overview of molecular modeling for drug discovery with specific illustrative examples of applications. *Molecules*, 24, 9, 1693, 2019.

18. Traboulsi, H., Khedr, M.A., Al-Faiyz, Y.S., Elgorashe, R., Negm, A., Structure-based epitope design: Toward a greater antibody–SARS-CoV-2 RBD affinity. *ACS Omega*, 6, 47, 31469–31476, 2021.

19. D'Souza, S., Prema, K.V., Balaji, S., Machine learning models for drug–target interactions: Current knowledge and future directions. *Drug Discov. Today*, 25, 4, 748–756, 2020.

20. Ghosh, A.K. and Gemma, S., *Structure-based design of drugs and other bioactive molecules: Tools and strategies*, John Wiley & Sons, United States, 2014.

21. Doma, M. K., Padmanandam, K., Tambvekar, S., Kumar, K., Abdualgalil, B., Thakur, R. N., Artificial intelligence-based breast cancer detection using WPSO. *Int. J. Oper. Res. Inf. Syst. (IJORIS)*, 13, 2, 1–16, 2022.

22. Batool, M., Ahmad, B., Choi, S., A structure-based drug discovery paradigm. *Int. J. Mol. Sci.*, 20, 11, 2783, 2019.

23. Ramesh, S., Vallinayagam, S., Rajendran, K., Rajendran, S., Rathinam, V., Ramesh, S., Computer-aided drug designing–modality of diagnostic system, in: *Biomedical Signal Processing for Healthcare Applications*, pp. 195–218, CRC Press, United States, 2021.

24. Mahapatra, M.K. and Karuppasamy, M., Fundamental considerations in drug design, in: *Computer Aided Drug Design (CADD): From Ligand-Based Methods to Structure-Based Approaches*, vol. pp. 17–55, Elsevier, The Netherlands, 2022.

25. Ilmudeen, A. and Nayyar, A., Novel designs of smart healthcare systems: Technologies, architecture, and applications, in: *Machine Learning for Critical Internet of Medical Things: Applications and Use Cases*, pp. 125–151, Springer International Publishing, Cham, Germany, 2022.

26. Jadala, V.C., Pasupuleti, S.K., Yellamma, P., Deep Learning analysis using ResNet for early detection of cerebellar ataxia disease, in: *2022 International Conference on Advancements in Smart, Secure and Intelligent Computing (ASSIC)*, pp. 1–6, IEEE, 2022, November.

27. Yazhini, A., Chakraborti, S., Srinivasan, N., Protein structure, dynamics and assembly: Implications for drug discovery, in: *Innovations and Implementations of Computer Aided Drug Discovery Strategies in Rational Drug Design*, pp. 91–122, 2021.

28. Fischer, A., Smiesko, M., Sellner, M., Lill, M.A., Decision making in structure-based drug discovery: Visual inspection of docking results. *J. Med. Chem.*, 64, 5, 2489–2500, 2021.

29. Padmanandam, K., Rajesh, M. V., Upadhyaya, A. N., Chandrashekar, B., Sah, S., Artificial intelligence biosensing system on hand gesture recognition for the hearing impaired. *Int. J. Oper. Res. Inf. Syst. (IJORIS)*, 13, 2, 1–13, 2022.

12

AI-Based Personalized Drug Treatment

Shanmuga Sundari M.*, **Harshini Reddy Penthala, Akshita Mogullapalli**
and Mayukha Mandya Ammangatambu

BVRIT HYDERABAD College of Engineering for Women, Hyderabad, India

Abstract

Precision medicine, also known as AI-based personalized drug therapy, seeks to tailor treatment plans for individuals based on their genetics, medical history, lifestyle, and more. AI algorithms analyze vast datasets containing genetic information, medical records, and relevant data to identify patterns and predict a patient's response to specific treatments. This approach empowers healthcare professionals to make informed decisions, optimizing treatment effectiveness while avoiding potentially harmful or ineffective options. AI-based personalized drug therapy offers numerous advantages. By customizing treatment strategies for each patient, it enables doctors to deliver more effective and personalized care, ultimately improving patient outcomes and quality of life. In the realm of oncology, particularly lung cancer treatment, AI plays a pivotal role. Researchers have developed AI tools that analyze genetic data from lung cancer patients, identifying disease-causing mutations. By leveraging this data, AI algorithms predict the most suitable treatments for each patient based on their tumor-specific mutations. Clinical trials have shown promising results, highlighting the potential of this approach to enhance personalized cancer treatment. Overall, AI-based personalized drug therapy has the potential to revolutionize medicine by enabling physicians to offer targeted, efficient, and individualized care to their patients.

Keywords: Artificial intelligence, clinical trials, disease prediction, drug treatment, genetics, medicine

12.1 Introduction

Personalized medicine is an emerging field that aims to provide patients with individualized medical care tailored to their unique traits, such as their genetic makeup, lifestyle, and other factors. One of the key areas of personalized medicine is personalized drug treatment, which involves the use of drugs and other treatments that are customized to a patient's specific needs.

In recent years, the integration of artificial intelligence (AI) into personalized drug treatment has shown significant potential in enhancing patient outcomes, reducing side effects, and improving the overall efficiency of healthcare systems [1]. AI algorithms can analyze

---

Corresponding author: sundari.m@bvrithyderabad.edu.in

Abhirup Khanna, May El Barachi, Sapna Jain, Manoj Kumar and Anand Nayyar (eds.) *Artificial Intelligence and Machine Learning in Drug Design and Development*, (369–406) © 2024 Scrivener Publishing LLC

vast amounts of data, including genomic data, medical history, and lifestyle factors, to identify the most effective drug treatments for individual patients.

The use of AI in personalized drug treatment has several advantages over traditional methods of drug development and treatment. First, AI algorithms can analyze large amounts of data to identify patterns and correlations that may not be apparent to human researchers. This can help healthcare professionals to develop more accurate and effective treatment plans that are tailored to each patient's unique needs.

Second, AI-based drug treatment can help to reduce the risk of adverse side effects by identifying drugs that are less likely to cause harmful reactions in individual patients. This can lead to better patient outcomes and lower healthcare costs, as patients will require fewer follow-up appointments and hospital visits.

Third, AI algorithms can assist in identifying drugs that are most likely to be effective for individual patients, thereby reducing the need for trial-and-error approaches to drug treatment. This can also help to reduce the overall cost of treatment, as it can assist healthcare professionals in identifying the most cost-effective drugs and dosages for individual patients.

Despite the potential benefits of AI-based drug treatment, there are also several challenges that must be addressed—for example, AI algorithms may require large amounts of data to make accurate predictions, which can be challenging in some cases, particularly for rare diseases [2]. There are also ethical considerations around the use of patients' data and the potential for bias in algorithmic decision-making.

AI-based personalized drug treatment is an exciting area of research that has significant potential to improve patient outcomes, reduce healthcare costs, and enhance the overall efficiency of healthcare systems. As technology continues to advance and more data becomes available, it is likely that AI algorithms will become an increasingly important tool in the development and delivery of personalized drug treatments.

12.1.1   Background on Personalized Medicine

It is a medical strategy which involves tailoring medical treatment strategies to the unique requirements and traits of particular individuals. The concept of personalized medicine has gained increasing consideration in current times is because of the advances in technology, particularly in genomic sequencing. By analyzing a patient's genetic makeup, healthcare providers can develop targeted and effective treatments that are specific to the individual patient.

The idea of personalized medicine has been around for decades, but the field did not really start to take off before the Human Genome Project was finished in 2003. A worldwide research project called the Human Genome Project was set out to lay out the whole human genome [3]. A comprehensive map of the human genome was made available to scientists after the project's completion in 2003.

Since the finishing of the Human Genome Project, there was a significant increase in the availability of genomic data, which has allowed researchers to identify genetic variations that may contribute to disease. With this information, healthcare providers can develop targeted treatments that are specific to the individual patient—for example, a patient with

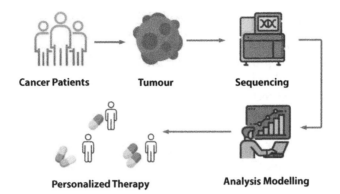

Figure 12.1 Background process on personalized medicine.

a specific genetic variation that increases their risk of developing a certain disease can be given a treatment that specifically targets that genetic variation.

In addition to genomic data, healthcare providers can also use information about a patient's lifestyle and medical history to build customized therapy strategies. By taking a holistic approach to healthcare, healthcare providers can develop treatment plans that are customized to the particular demands and characteristics of every patient.

The improvement of customized drug has the potential to revolutionize field of healthcare by providing more effective and targeted treatments for individual patients. By customizing treatments to particular necessities of every patient, healthcare providers can reduce the danger of adverse drug reactions and enhance victim results.

However, Figure 12.1 explains the challenges associated with personalized medicine, including the cost of genomic sequencing and the need for specialized expertise to analyze and interpret genomic data. Despite these difficulties, personalized medicine has the power to revolutionize the healthcare industry and enhance the results for patients. Personalized medicine is anticipated to become a more significant component of healthcare as technology develops.

12.1.2   Overview of AI in Drug Treatment

In recent years, AI has grown in significance as a tool for drug therapy. AI systems can examine enormous volumes of data to find trends and forecast the effectiveness of various therapies. Artificial intelligence (AI) models can be used to analyze medical data and find the most suitable pharmacological therapies for specific patients.

Drug discovery is one of the main uses of AI in drug treatment. Huge data sets can be analyzed by AI algorithms to find prospective medication candidates that might be useful in treating particular conditions [4]. This can aid in accelerating the drug development process and lowering the cost of creating new medications.

AI is able to create individualized strategies for therapy for each individual. AI models can determine the best suitable therapy for each patient by examining their genetic make-up, lifestyle, and medical history. This may lessen the possibility of negative drug reactions while also enhancing patients' results.

12.1.3 Importance of Personalized Drug Treatment

The subject of medicinal drug therapy is undergoing significant shifts due to artificial intelligence (AI), which is providing creative methods to advance drug discovery, drug development, and personalized medicine. Machine learning, natural language processing, computer vision, and other technologies are all included under the broad concept of artificial intelligence (AI). These tools have the potential to be used to examine huge quantities of information and spot trends which can be challenging for people to notice.

AI is utilized in the field of drug therapy to identify new therapeutic targets, develop fresh pharmaceuticals, and enhance existing treatments. One of the most intriguing uses of AI in medication therapy [5] is personalized medicine. By examining large datasets containing genomic and clinical data, AI can help medical professionals create customised treatment plans that are tailored to the needs of each patient.

An additional domain where AI is significantly influencing on drug treatment is drug repurposing. Drug repurposing involves identifying existing drugs that may be effective in treating new conditions. By analyzing large datasets of genomic and clinical data, AI can help identify potential new uses for existing drugs, reducing the duration and expense involved in creating new medications. AI is also being used to develop more effective clinical trial designs; this may assist with decreasing the amount of effort and expense involved in bringing new medications to trade. Research study designs can be improved for better patients' results and decrease the length of time and expenditure involved with clinical trials by utilizing AI to discover patients who will be more probable to get well with a specific treatment.

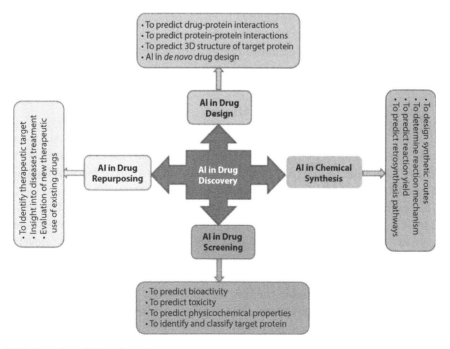

Figure 12.2 Overview of AI in drug discovery.

Overall, AI is offering exciting new opportunities to improve drug discovery and development, and personalized medicine. While there are still challenges associated with implementing AI in drug treatment, the potential benefits of AI are substantial and have the ability to transform the healthcare industry, despite the requirement for enormous data and specialized expertise. Figure 12.2 depicts the overall drug analysis using AI.

Organization of the Chapter

The rest of the chapter is organized as follows: Section 12.2 illustrates how AI can improve drug treatment. Section 12.3 enlists techniques used in AI-based drug treatment. Section 12.4 highlights case studies and examples. Section 12.5 discusses the challenges and limitations of AI-based drug treatment, followed by future outlook and implications in Section 12.6, and finally Section 12.7 concludes the chapter with future scope.

12.2   How AI Can Improve Drug Treatment?

By providing alternatives to enhance drug research and improvement as well as personalized therapy, artificial intelligence (AI) is revolutionizing the subject of drug treatment. Machine learning, natural language processing, and computer vision are examples of artificial intelligence (AI) techniques that can analyze enormous volumes of data and spot patterns that are challenging [6] for people to notice. This makes it possible for medical professionals to create more personalized treatment programmes that are more efficient for each patient as well as to find novel drug targets and solutions for a variety of illnesses.

Figure 12.3 explores how AI can improve drug treatment by examining some of the key areas where AI is being applied, including drug development and research, personalized medicine, design of a clinical study, and drug repurposing. In addition, some of the challenges associated with implementing AI in drug treatment, and the probable consequences of AI for future of medical care is also discussed. Overall, AI is offering exciting

Figure 12.3 Pharmaceutical areas with an AI footprint.

new opportunities to improve patients' results and reduce healthcare expenses and has the ability to transform the field of drug treatment.

12.2.1   Predicting Drug Efficacy

Predicting drug efficacy using AI has the potential to improve drug treatment. AI algorithms can be trained on large datasets of patient information, including genomic data, clinical data, and drug response data, to find trends and forecast which drugs are likely to be effective for a particular patient.

This approach, known as precision medicine, has the ability to enhance the patients' results by tailoring treatments to each individual patient [7]. By using AI to predict drug efficacy, clinicians can select treatments that are more likely to be effective and decrees the impact of adverse drug reactions.

AI has the potential to create new medications and find prospective therapeutic targets. AI systems are able to discover prospective pharmacological targets and create medications that specifically target these targets through processing enormous quantities of data on the mechanisms of illness. This approach, known as AI-driven drug discovery, has the potential to significantly reduce the time and cost associated with drug development and increases the availability of treatments for patients.

In addition, AI can be used to optimize drug dosing and reduce the risk of toxicity. By analyzing patients' data, including genetic data and drug response data, AI algorithms can identify optimal drug dosing regimens that minimize the risk of adverse reactions. This has the ability to enhance patients' results by reducing the risk of side effects and improving treatment efficacy.

Recent studies have shown promising results in using AI to predict drug efficacy—for example, a team of researchers used machine learning algorithms to predict drug sensitivity in cancer patients based on genomic and clinical data. Their models were able to accurately predict drug sensitivity for several cancer drugs, which could potentially lead to more personalized cancer treatment.

In another study, researchers used AI algorithms to analyze large amounts of chemical and biological data to identify potential new drug targets for cancer treatment [8]. Researchers were able to identify several promising targets that were previously unknown, demonstrating the potential of AI to accelerate drug discovery.

AI has also shown potential in predicting adverse drug reactions, which can improve patient safety. By analyzing huge volumes of data, like electronic health records and drug databases, AI algorithms can identify patterns and risk factors for adverse reactions. This can help healthcare providers create many decisions that are informed about prescribing medications and decrease the impact of unfavorable reactions for patients.

Furthermore, AI can potentially improve the efficiency of clinical trials by identifying patients who are most probable to react to a specific treatment. By analyzing patients' data and biomarkers, AI algorithms can identify patient subgroups that are more likely to benefit from a particular treatment. This can lead to more efficient and cost-effective clinical trials and ultimately accelerate the development of new treatments.

Figure 12.4 explains the efficacy of drug predictions. Overall, the potential impact of AI on drug treatment is significant. It may increase drug efficacy and safety, quicken the

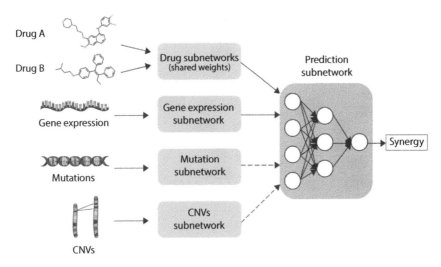

Figure 12.4 Prediction of drug efficacy.

drug development process, and cut down on the time and expense of clinical studies. It is probable that medical research and pharmacological therapy will advance even further as AI grows and gets better.

12.2.2   Identifying Patient Subgroups

Identifying patient subgroups is an important aspect of personalized medicine, and AI has the potential to improve drug treatment by identifying patients' groupings are most probable to react to a particular treatment [9]. Traditional methods of identifying patient subgroups involve analyzing patient characteristics, such as age, gender, and medical history, and using statistical methods to identify subgroups that share similar characteristics.

AI can improve upon these methods by analyzing large and complex datasets to identify subgroups that may not be apparent through traditional statistical methods. AI algorithms can identify patterns and relationships in the data that may be missed by human analysis, and can identify subgroups based on a wide range of factors, including genetic markers, biomarkers, and other molecular data.

One example of AI being used to identify patient subgroups is in the treatment of cancer. Cancer is a complex disease with many different subtypes, and different subtypes may respond differently to treatment. AI can analyze data on a large number of genetic and molecular factors to identify subgroups of patients with similar disease characteristics and treatment responses [10]. This can help researchers develop personalized treatments for each patient based on their individual characteristics.

AI can also be used to identify subgroups of patients who are more likely to experience side effects or adverse reactions to a particular treatment. Figure 12.5 explains the grouping system of drug usage. By analyzing data on patient characteristics, treatment history, and other factors, AI algorithms can identify patients who may be at a higher risk for adverse events. This can assist medical professionals in adjusting therapies to lower patient risks and making more knowledgeable decisions about alternatives to therapy.

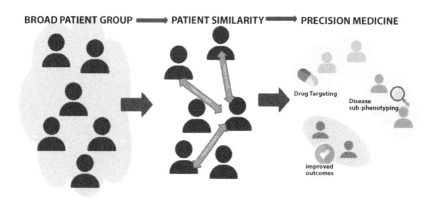

Figure 12.5 Identifying patient sub-groups.

Identifying patient subgroups with AI can also help reduce healthcare costs. By identifying patients who are unlikely to respond to a particular treatment, healthcare providers can avoid prescribing expensive medications that may not benefit the patient. This can also help prevent unnecessary adverse reactions and lower the possibility of negative responses.

AI may assist to recognize patients who are more vulnerable of developing certain diseases. By analyzing patients' data [11], including genetic information, lifestyle factors, and medical history, AI algorithms can detect patients who are at a higher danger of developing diseases like diabetes, tumors, and cardiovascular disease. This can allow healthcare providers to intervene earlier with preventive measures and personalized treatments.

Another potential benefit of using AI to identify patient subgroups is the ability to optimize clinical trial design. Clinical studies can be scheduled to involve groups of patients who are most probable to react positively to a specific therapy, which could improve their chances of success. This can also assist in decreasing the duration and expenses associated with clinical trials, as fewer patients may be needed to achieve statistically significant results.

Finally, artificial intelligence can assist in enhancing patients' results by discovering novel, earlier undiscovered therapeutic targets. AI methods are able to find prospective therapeutic targets that could have gone unnoticed by conventional approaches by analyzing vast volumes of data and spotting trends. This may result in the creation of fresh remedies for ailments that were once thought to be incurable, enhancing the wellbeing and outcomes of patients.

Drug therapy and patients' results could be considerably improved by using AI to recognize patient subgroups. Locating the patients who are probable to answer to a particular treatment, healthcare providers can personalize treatments, reduce healthcare costs, and improve clinical trial design. Additionally, AI can assist in the discovery of new therapeutic targets, resulting in the creation of fresh medications for diseases that were not curable in the past.

12.2.3   Tailoring Dosages

AI has the potential to improve drug treatment by tailoring dosage to individual patients based on a range of factors as listed below:

1. Personalized medicine: AI can examine huge volumes of patients' data, including genetic and clinical data, to find which patients are probable to get advantage from a particular drug and what the optimal dose for them might be. This can assist in minimizing the impact of side effects and maximizing the effectiveness of the drug.
2. Real-time monitoring: AI can view victims to detect changes in their condition and adjust the dosage accordingly. This can help ensure that patients receive the proper amount of dose at the exact duration and minimize the risk of adverse effects.
3. Adaptive dosing: AI can use feedback from patient responses to the drug to adapt the dosage over time, optimizing the dose for each patient based on their individual response. This can help maximize the effectiveness of the drug while minimizing the risk of adverse effects.
4. Population health management: AI can analyze data from large patient populations to identify trends and patterns that can assist in forecasting the patients who are more probable to side effects and which patients are likely to benefit from a particular drug. This might aid medical professionals in making better dosage and treatment decisions.

AI has the ability to improve drug treatment by tailoring dosage to individual patients, monitoring patients in real time, adapting dosing over time, and analyzing large datasets to inform population health management. This can help maximize the effectiveness of drugs while minimizing the danger of side effects, which leads to best patients' results.

12.2.4   Minimizing Adverse Effects

AI has the ability to transform drug treatment and minimize adverse effects by helping researchers and clinicians identify the most effective and safe treatments for patients.
Here are some ways that AI can improve drug treatment:

1. Predictive modeling: AI models can evaluate vast volumes of information to discover patterns which can predict how a drug will affect patients. By using machine learning algorithms to analyze large datasets, AI can identify which patients are most probable to get advantage from a particular drug and which patients may be at risk of experiencing adverse effects.
2. Personalized medicine: AI can help tailor drug treatments to individual patients based on their biological makeup, health history, and other factors. This will help identify the most effective and safe treatments for each patient, minimizing the risk of adverse effects.
3. Drug discovery: AI can assist in the rapid discovery process of a drug by identifying potential drug candidates and predicting how they will interact

with the human body. This can reduce the need for animal testing and human trials, which can be time-consuming and costly.

4. Drug repurposing: AI can help identify existing drugs that could be repurposed for new uses. This can save time and money by avoiding the need to develop new drugs from scratch and can also minimize the risk of adverse effects since these drugs have already been tested in humans.

Overall, AI has the potential to revolutionize drug treatment by helping to find the most useful and safe treatments for sufferers, minimizing the risk of adverse effects and speeding up the drug discovery process.

12.2.5   Streamlining Drug Development

AI can improve drug treatment by streamlining the drug development process in the following ways:

1. Target identification: AI can analyze large datasets to identify new drug targets that have the potential to be effective against a specific disease. This can hasten the discovery process of a drug by reducing the need for trial-and-error experiments.
2. Lead optimization: Once a drug target has been identified, AI can help optimize the chemical structure of potential drug candidates to maximize their effectiveness and safety. AI can evaluate huge volumes of information to forecast the activity and toxicity of different drug candidates, allowing researchers to prioritize the most promising candidates for further testing.
3. Clinical trial design: AI can help design more efficient clinical trials by identifying the most appropriate patient population and optimizing the trial design to minimize the number of patients needed. This can lower the price of clinical trials and expedite the medication development process.
4. Regulatory approval: AI can help streamline the regulatory approval process by analyzing data from clinical trials and identifying potential safety concerns or areas where additional data may be needed [12]. This can help drug developers address potential issues early on and reduce the likelihood of delays in the approval process.

Overall, AI has the potential to improve drug treatment by streamlining the drug development process, reducing costs, and accelerating the availability of new treatments for patients.

12.3   Techniques Used in AI-Based Drug Treatment

AI is speeding up in transforming the study of drug discovery and development. AI-based drug treatment involves utilizing various techniques such as ML, NLP, deep learning, and computer vision to analyze vast amounts of data and generate insights that can lead to the discovery of novel drug candidates and personalized treatment options for patients.

These techniques are utilized to analyze many kinds of data, including genetic data, biomedical literature, clinical study data, and patient records, among others. The resulting

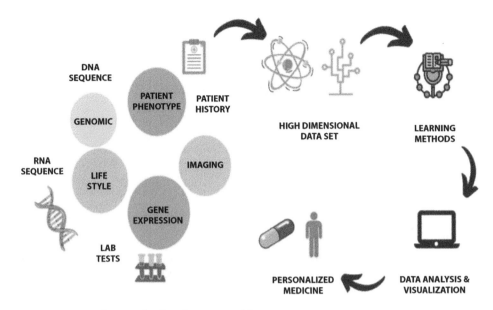

Figure 12.6 Process of personalized medicine using AI.

insights can aid in the identification of drug targets, the design of clinical trials, the prediction of drug efficacy and toxicity, and the development of personalized treatment plans.

AI-based drug development has a lot of potential for enhancing patients' results and cutting the time and expenses spent on traditional pharmaceutical discovery and development processes, which is explained in Figure 12.6.

12.3.1   Machine Learning in AI-Based Drug Treatment

ML prototypes are utilized in order to detect patterns in information and enhance performance without explicit programming. This technology has a big impact on how drug treatment approaches are created. Drug discovery, drug repurposing, and clinical trials are only a few of the steps of drug development where machine learning techniques are frequently applied.

Drug discovery: In order to forecast the efficacy and safety of possible medication candidates, machine learning algorithms may analyze enormous volumes of data from many sources, such as chemical structures, gene expression data, and clinical data [13]. This could hasten the process of discovering new drugs and lower the price of developing new ones.

Drug repurposing: Machine learning can be used to find novel applications for already-approved medications. Machine learning models can find medications that have the potential to treat novel diseases or ailments by analyzing information from various places, such as EHRs and public databases.

Clinical trials: The design and analysis of clinical trials can be enhanced by machine learning. A clinical trial's ideal patient population can be found using machine learning models, which can also be used to forecast patient outcomes and find potential trial-affecting variables.

Real-world evidence: Using machine learning, real-world data, like electronic health records, may be analyzed to find trends and insights that can help with drug development

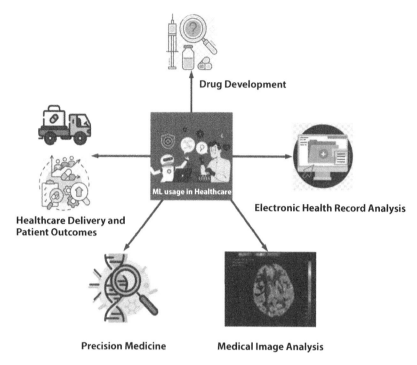

Figure 12.7 Usage of ML in healthcare.

and patient care. Real-world data can give important insights on the efficacy and security of medications in practical settings.

Challenges: Data privacy, bias, and interpretability are just a few of the issues that machine learning in drug treatment must deal with. Researchers are creating new methods and frameworks for moral and responsible AI in healthcare to solve these problems.

Drug development is a complex and time-consuming process that involves several stages, each of which requires significant resources and expertise. Here are the typical steps of drug development as presented in Figure 12.7:

1. Discovery and target identification: This is the first step in drug development, where scientists try to identify a potential target in the body that could be used to treat a particular disease or condition. This could involve studying the biology of the disease, conducting genetic or molecular analyses, or screening large databases of potential drug targets.

2. Lead discovery: Once a target has been identified, researchers start to look for compounds that could interact with the target in a specific way. This could involve testing large libraries of existing drugs or creating new molecules from scratch.

3. Lead optimization: After identifying a promising compound, researchers begin to optimize its properties to maximize its effectiveness and minimize any potential side effects. This could involve modifying the molecule's structure or testing different dosages and delivery methods.

4. Preclinical testing: Before a drug can be tested on humans, it must go through a rigorous series of preclinical tests to ensure its safety and effectiveness. This could involve testing the drug in animals to evaluate its toxicity, pharmacokinetics, and efficacy.

5. Clinical trials: If a drug passes preclinical testing, it can move on to clinical studies, which are typically conducted in three steps, namely:

   Step I: Trials are the first step in the testing of a medication to determine its safety and pharmacokinetics in a small sample of healthy volunteers.
   Step II: Trials test the medication on a greater number of patients in order to determine its effectiveness and the best dosages.
   Step III: To verify the medication's effectiveness and safety under actual use, trials test it on a greater number of patients.

6. FDA approval: If a drug passes all three phases of clinical studies, it may be sent for endorsement to the Food and Drug Administration (FDA). The FDA evaluates the drug's safety and efficacy and decides whether to approve it for use in the general population.

7. Post-marketing surveillance: Even after a drug is approved, it may be necessary to conduct further studies to monitor its safety and effectiveness in real-world conditions. This could involve collecting data on adverse events or monitoring the drug's long-term effects.

Drug development is a long and complex process that involves several stages, from discovery and lead optimization to preclinical testing, clinical trials, and FDA approval. Each stage requires significant resources and expertise, and only a small percentage of drugs that enter the pipeline will ultimately make it to the market.

Machine learning is a potent method used in AI-based medication therapy that has the potential to revolutionize patient care and drug development. Machine learning algorithms can find patterns and insights that help guide drug discovery, medication development, and personalized treatment by analyzing massive datasets. To ensure that the advantages of machine learning in drug treatment are realized while minimizing the hazards, it also faces difficulties that must be resolved.

Virtual screening is a type of machine learning technology used in drug development. To find molecules that are most likely to bind to particular therapeutic targets, a procedure known as virtual screening is utilized. In order to anticipate novel interactions between drugs and targets, machine learning algorithms can be trained on vast datasets of previously known drug–target interactions. By lowering the number of compounds that need to be examined in the lab, this can expedite the drug discovery process and save time and money.

Drug repurposing also makes use of machine learning. To do this, current medications must be given new therapeutic applications. To forecast potential medication–disease interactions, machine learning algorithms can be trained on massive datasets of pharmacological characteristics and illness indications. By locating medications that are currently permitted for use in humans, this can save time and resources during the process of producing drugs.

ML is utilized in clinical trials to enhance patient selection and pinpoint patient subgroups that are most likely to respond to a given treatment. Large datasets of patients' data can be used to train machine learning algorithms and predict which patients would respond best to a given treatment. By lowering the quantity of participants required to provide statistically significant results, this can increase the effectiveness of clinical trials.

Therefore, machine learning is a potent technology that is revolutionizing the creation and administration of medications [14]. It is a useful tool in drug discovery, drug repurposing, and clinical trials due to its capacity to learn patterns from data and enhance its performance over time.

12.3.2   Natural Language Processing (NLP) in AI-Based Drug Treatment

Machines can comprehend and evaluate human language thanks to a type of AI known NLP. Due to its ability, it helps computers to analyze massive amounts of text-based data, including electronic health records and scholarly literature, pharmacological therapy is becoming more and more relevant.

Adverse event monitoring is one of the most crucial uses of NLP in medication therapy. Adverse events are unfavorable side effects that develop during pharmacological therapy. To find patterns and trends in adverse occurrences, NLP algorithms can be trained on massive datasets of adverse event reports. This can assist drug regulators in identifying possible drug safety risks and in taking appropriate measures to safeguard the public's health.

Electronic health records are also analyzed using NLP to look for any drug interactions. When two or more medications interact in ways that could be dangerous to the patient, this is referred to as a drug–drug interaction. To find probable drug–drug interactions and inform healthcare professionals, NLP algorithms can be trained on big datasets of electronic health records.

In order to enhance drug discovery and the identification of new drug targets, NLP is also being used to analyze scientific literature.

Large databases of scientific papers can be used to train NLP algorithms to find new drug targets and extract pertinent data about possible drug targets.

NLP is a useful technique in the field of drug therapy that is revolutionizing how medical professionals and drug regulators interpret text-based data. As a result of its capacity to comprehend and interpret human language, machines are now able to enhance drug discovery by spotting drug–drug interactions, potential safety issues with medications, and other issues.

12.3.3   Deep Learning in AI-Based Drug Treatment

Artificial intelligence known as "deep learning" is built on neural networks. The structure and operation of the human brain serve as the basis for the mathematical models known as neural networks. Large datasets of organized and unstructured data can be used to train deep learning algorithms so that they can discover patterns and make predictions.

Image analysis is one of the most significant uses of deep learning in drug treatment. Large amounts of complicated picture data are generated by medical picturing technologies like MRI, CT, and PET examinations. Datasets can be used to train deep learning algorithms to find patterns and make predictions. Deep learning algorithms, for instance, can be used to spot tumors in medical photos or to forecast how a disease will develop based on the changes in those images over time.

Deep learning is additionally being applied to the analysis of electronic health records to find patterns in patients' data that can be used to enhance patient outcomes [15]. Large quantities of electronic health record data can be used to train deep learning algorithms to find patterns connected to specific illnesses or treatments. This can assist healthcare professionals in making better judgments regarding patient care.

Deep learning is an effective tool in medication therapy that is revolutionizing how medical professionals and drug developers interpret difficult data. Machines are now able to identify new drug targets, analyze medical pictures, forecast patient outcomes, and enhance patient care thanks to their capacity to learn patterns from massive amounts of organized and unstructured data.

There are several examples of how deep learning in AI-based drug treatment is being used in the healthcare industry.

One example is in the field of medical imaging. Deep learning models can evaluate huge amounts of medical images generated by MRI, CT, and PET scans to detect patterns that can be used to diagnose diseases and monitor disease progression—for instance, deep learning algorithms can identify subtle changes in brain MRI scans to detect early signs of Alzheimer's disease or forecast the probability of a patient having a certain type of cancer based on CT scan images.

Another example is the analysis of EHRs to identify patterns in patients' data that can be utilized to enhance patients' results. Deep learning prototypes are trained on large datasets of EHRs to identify risk factors and predict outcomes for specific illnesses or treatments—for example, a deep learning algorithm trained on EHR data could assist in discovering patients at more danger for heart disease and recommend personalized treatment plans to reduce their risk.

Drug development is another area where deep learning is being used. Deep learning models can examine large volumes of information on chemical structures and biological processes to find new drug targets and forecast the effectiveness of potential drugs—for example, a deep learning algorithm trained on data on the molecular structure of a specific protein could identify potential drugs that could bind to that protein and inhibit its activity, leading to the development of new treatments for diseases such as cancer or Alzheimer's.

Overall, deep learning in AI-based drug treatment is transforming how healthcare professionals diagnose and treat diseases, develop new drugs, and improve patient outcomes. We may anticipate even more fascinating advancements in the healthcare industry as technology develops.

12.3.4   Other AI Techniques Used in AI-Based Drug Development

There are various more AI approaches that are employed in the creation of pharmaceuticals along with ML, deep learning, and NLP. Figure 12.8 presents the different algorithms used in drug analysis. These methods consist of expert systems, genetic algorithms, Bayesian networks, and reinforcement learning. Each of these methods has certain advantages and can

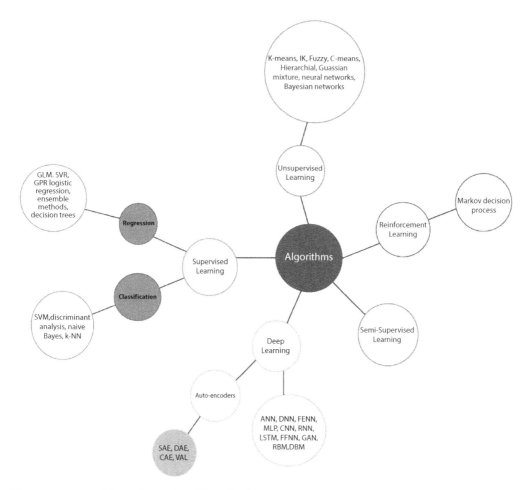

Figure 12.8 AI models used in AI-based drug development.

be applied to various problems in drug development. These methodologies will probably play a bigger role in the creation of novel, more potent medicinal therapies as AI develops.

12.3.4.1   Reinforcement Learning

Reinforcement learning is another subfield of AI that has the potential to improve drug treatment. Reinforcement learning is a type of machine learning that is inspired by the way humans learn from experience. It involves training a model to make decisions based on feedback received from the environment.

In the context of drug treatment, reinforcement learning can be used to identify the best dosage of a drug for a patient. This involves the patient's medical history, current condition, and other factors that may influence how they respond to a drug. The goal is to find the right balance between efficacy and side effects.

One example of reinforcement learning in drug treatment is the work being done by researchers at the University of California, San Francisco. They have developed a system that uses reinforcement learning to identify the optimal dosage of warfarin, a blood-thinning medication. The system takes into account a patient's age, weight, medical history, and other factors to determine the appropriate dose. The system was tested on a group of patients and was found to be more accurate than traditional dosing methods.

Another example is the work being done by researchers a university in North Carolina. They have developed a system that uses reinforcement learning to identify the optimal dose of an antibiotic for treating infections. The system takes into account a patient's medical history, the type of infection, and other factors to determine the appropriate dose. The system was tested on a group of patients and was found to be more accurate than traditional dosing methods.

While reinforcement learning shows promise for improving drug treatment, there are also challenges that need to be addressed [16]. One challenge is the availability of high-quality data. Reinforcement learning models need a huge volume of information to get knowledge from, and in many cases, this data may not be readily available.

Another challenge is the interpretability of the models. Reinforcement learning algorithms are often viewed as "black boxes" because it can be difficult to understand how they arrive at their decisions. Because of this, it may be challenging for physicians and patients to believe the model's suggestions.

Despite these challenges, reinforcement learning has the potential to improve drug treatment and help patients receive more personalized care. As more research is done in this area, we can expect to see more examples of successful applications of reinforcement learning in drug treatment.

12.3.4.2   *Bayesian Networks*

Bayesian networks are another technique used in AI-based drug treatment. They are a type of probabilistic graphical model that can represent the probability of certain events occurring based on the probability of other related events. Bayesian networks have been used in various fields, including medicine and healthcare, to forecast the probability of some conditions based on the presence or absence of other symptoms or risk factors.

In drug treatment, Bayesian networks can be used to forecast the probability of a patient responding positively or negatively to a particular treatment depending on various aspects like age, gender, health history, genetics, and other relevant factors. Bayesian networks can be utilized to predict adverse reactions to certain drugs.

One of the major benefits of Bayesian networks is the ability to handle uncertainty and incomplete information. Since medical data can be complex and incomplete, Bayesian networks can make predictions even when there is missing or incomplete data, using probabilities and statistical inference. This can help physicians and researchers make more informed decisions about drug treatments and improve patient outcomes.

For example, a study published in the Journal of Medical Internet Research explored the use of Bayesian networks to predict the success of treatment with antidepressants for people with serious depression. The researchers used information from EHRs to develop a Bayesian network model that incorporated aspects like age, gender, health history, and drug dosage. The model was able to accurately predict treatment response in 74% of patients, demonstrating the potential of Bayesian networks in improving drug treatment outcomes.

However, there are also some limitations to the use of Bayesian networks in drug treatment. One challenge is the necessity of perfection, accurate information to train and validate the model. Inaccurate or incomplete data can lead to inaccurate predictions and potentially harmful outcomes for patients.

Additionally, Bayesian networks can be complex and difficult to interpret, which may limit their practical use in a clinical setting [17]. Physicians and healthcare providers may require specialized training to effectively use Bayesian network models and understand their predictions.

In conclusion, Bayesian networks are a promising technique in AI-based drug treatment that can help improve patient outcomes by predicting treatment responses and potential side effects. While there are challenges to their implementation, further research and development in this area could lead to significant improvements in drug treatment and patient care.

12.3.4.3   *Genetic Algorithms*

Genetic algorithms are a type of AI-based optimization technique that has potential applications in drug development and treatment. These algorithms are inspired by the process of natural selection and evolution and use a set of computational rules to generate new generations of solutions to a problem, which can then be evaluated and improved upon.

In the context of drug treatment, genetic models can be utilized to enhance the drug component structure or to identify the best dosage for a patient. By generating a large number of possible solutions and testing them against a set of criteria, genetic algorithms can quickly identify the most promising candidates for further development.

One of the key benefits of genetic algorithms is their potential to explore a large search space efficiently. This is particularly useful in drug development, where the number of potential compounds that could be synthesized and tested is incredibly large. By using genetic algorithms to narrow down the pool of candidates, researchers can save time and resources and focus on developing the most promising drug candidates.

There have been several successful applications of genetic algorithms in drug development—for example, a study published in the Journal of Medicinal Chemistry used genetic algorithms to optimize the design of drug molecules targeting a specific protein involved in cancer. The researchers were able to identify several compounds with improved binding affinity compared to existing drugs, suggesting that this approach could be useful for developing more effective cancer treatments.

Another study published in PLOS One used a genetic algorithm to optimize the dosage of a drug used to treat rheumatoid arthritis. By considering a range of patient-specific factors, such as age, weight, and disease severity, the algorithm was able to identify an optimal dose that was more effective at reducing symptoms than the standard dose.

Despite the potential benefits of genetic algorithms in drug development, there are also some challenges and limitations to consider. One of the main limitations is the complexity of the search space. In order for genetic algorithms to be effective, the problem must be well defined and the evaluation criteria must be clear. In addition, genetic algorithms require significant computational resources, which may not be available to all researchers.

In conclusion, genetic algorithms are a promising tool for optimizing drug development and treatment. By exploring a large search space efficiently, these algorithms can help researchers identify the most promising candidates for further development. While there are still some challenges to overcome, the potential benefits of this approach make it a study of active research and development in the field of AI-based drug treatment.

12.3.4.4 Expert Systems

Expert systems, called knowledge-based systems, are a subset of artificial intelligence that is intended to simulate the judgmental skills of a human specialist in a certain field. In the field of drug treatment, expert systems can be used to assist healthcare providers in making more accurate diagnoses, selecting appropriate treatment options, and predicting patient outcomes.

Expert systems in drug treatment typically consist of a knowledge base, which contains information about the domain of interest, and an inference engine, which uses this information to make recommendations or predictions based on patients' data. The knowledge base may include information about drug interactions, side effects, contraindications, and dosages as well as patient-specific data like age, gender, weight, and health history.

One of the expert systems in drug treatment is the MYCIN system; this was created in the 1970s to help medical professionals identify and treat bacterial illnesses [18]. MYCIN used a rule-based approach to identify the most likely bacterial pathogen based on patient symptoms and laboratory data and then recommend appropriate antibiotic therapies.

More recent examples of expert systems in drug treatment include the Oncology Expert Advisor, which uses a decision tree approach to recommend treatment options for breast cancer patients based on their individual tumor characteristics, and the Clinical Pharmacogenetics Implementation Consortium (CPIC), which gives the guidelines for recommending medicines based on a patient's genetic profile.

Expert systems have several advantages in the field of drug treatment. They can help healthcare providers make more accurate diagnoses and treatment decisions, reduce the risk of adverse drug events, and improve patient outcomes. They can also assist in standardizing treatment protocols and reducing variability in healthcare delivery.

However, expert systems also have some limitations. They require a significant amount of domain-specific knowledge to be effective and may be less effective in cases where patients' data is incomplete or inconsistent. Additionally, they may be subject to biases or errors in the knowledge base or inference engine, which can lead to incorrect recommendations.

Despite these limitations, expert systems have the potential to have a significant impact in the future of drug treatment. As more data becomes available and machine learning algorithms become more advanced, expert systems may be able to make increasingly accurate predictions and recommendations. They may also be able to integrate with other AI-based technologies such as natural language processing and computer vision to provide a more comprehensive approach to drug treatment.

AI systems called expert systems are created to emulate the judgments of human experts. Expert systems can be used to help in the decision-making for both drug developers and healthcare professionals during the drug development process—for instance, based on patient characteristics and other considerations, an expert system can be used to prescribe medicine dosages or treatment plans.

12.4   Case Studies and Examples

In this section, various case studies and examples of AI-based drug treatment are explored. In recent years, there has been a lot of interest in the application of AI to the discovery and development of new drugs. AI-based platforms and algorithms have demonstrated great potential in accelerating the drug development process, identifying novel drug candidates, and optimizing treatment strategies for better patient outcomes.

Several examples, including Genomic Health's Oncotype DX, IBM Watson for Drug Discovery, BenevolentAI's drug discovery platform, PathAI's AI-powered pathology platform, Atomwise's AI-based drug discovery platform, and *In silico* Medicine's AI-based drug discovery platform are discussed. Each case study and example will showcase how AI is revolutionizing the drug discovery and development process, ultimately improving patient outcomes.

12.4.1   Genomic Health's Oncotype DX

Oncotype DX from Genomic Health is a ground-breaking genomic test used to forecast the possibility of a return of breast cancer and the potential advantages of chemotherapy. The test calculates a recurrence score based on the activation of 21 genes in breast cancer cells and can be used to direct therapy choices. The Oncotype DX test, which was created using machine learning algorithms, has revolutionized the way that breast cancer is treated by offering more precise and individualized recommendations based on each patient's particular genetic profile.

Machine learning in drug therapy must address a number of concerns, such as data protection, bias, and interpretability. To address these issues [19], researchers are developing new approaches and frameworks for moral and responsible AI in healthcare. The application of machine learning in AI-based drug therapy is a powerful technique that has the ability to enhance patient care and pharmaceutical research. By evaluating enormous datasets, machine learning algorithms can reveal patterns and insights that assist direct drug discovery, medication development, and individualized treatment. It also faces challenges that must be overcome in order to ensure that the benefits of machine learning in drug therapy are realized while minimizing the risks.

The effectiveness of the Oncotype DX test has been greatly attributed to the use of machine learning algorithms in its creation. To find the most significant genes and patterns linked to recurrence, the algorithm employed in the test was trained using data from hundreds of breast cancer patients. In order to find patterns and relationships that are not immediately obvious to the human eye, the computer may analyze gene expression data from breast cancer patients.

It has been demonstrated that the Oncotype DX test enhances therapeutic choices and lowers the need for chemotherapy in low-risk patients. The test gives personalized therapy recommendations based on the particular genetic profile of each patient by analyzing gene expression data using machine learning. Additionally, the test can spot people at high risk that might benefit from more forceful therapies.

Utilizing genetic tests, such as Oncotype DX, is a significant advancement in personalized medicine that has the potential to enhance patient outcomes and lower medical expenses.

These tests can offer more precise and individualized therapy suggestions by analyzing massive volumes of genomic data using machine learning, thus improving patient outcomes.

Other genetic tests for cancers including prostate and colon have been developed as a result of the success of Oncotype DX. Similar machine learning algorithms are used in these tests to analyze gene expression data and offer individualized therapy recommendations based on each patient's particular genetic profile.

Over a million individuals with breast cancer worldwide have utilized the Oncotype DX test to help them decide which treatments to pursue. Important medical organizations involving the National Comprehensive Cancer Network and the American Society of Clinical Oncology additionally support it.

In conclusion, the creation of Genomic Health's Oncotype DX test made use of machine learning algorithms to produce more individualized and accurate treatment recommendations based on a patient's particular genetic profile, which has revolutionized the treatment of breast cancer. It has been demonstrated that the test helps with treatment choices and lowers the need for chemotherapy in low-risk patients. Another genetic test for another form of cancer has been created as a result of the success of Oncotype DX. This represents a significant advancement in personalized medicine with the ability to enhance patients' results and lower healthcare costs.

12.4.2   IBM Watson for Drug Discovery

It is an artificial intelligence-based platform designed to help researchers speed up drug discovery and development by analyzing vast amounts of biomedical data. The platform combines ML, NLP, and other AI techniques to help researchers identify promising drug candidates and accelerate the drug discovery process.

As shown in Figure 12.9, IBM Watson for Drug Discovery works by analyzing large amounts of structured and unstructured data from a variety of sources, such as scientific papers, patents, clinical trials, and other biomedical databases. The platform uses natural

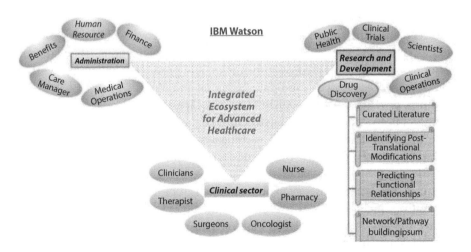

Figure 12.9 IBM Watson for drug discovery.

language processing to extract relevant information from these sources, such as information on genes, proteins, and pathways involved in diseases and potential drug targets.

Once the platform has identified potential drug targets, it uses machine learning algorithms to analyze data from various sources, such as chemical structures, genomic data, and clinical data, to predict the efficacy and safety of potential drug candidates. The platform also uses deep learning algorithms to analyze large datasets and discover trends and insights which can be utilized to enhance drug development and patient care.

One of the key benefits of IBM Watson for Drug Discovery is its ability to decrease the duration and expenses of drug development. By automating the drug discovery steps and analyzing huge volumes of information, the platform can identify promising drug candidates much faster than traditional methods. This can help accelerate the development of new treatments and bring them to market more quickly.

IBM Watson for Drug Discovery has already been used in several drug development initiatives. In one study, the platform was used to identify a promising drug candidate for a rare form of cancer called multiple myeloma. The drug candidate was identified by analyzing genomic and proteomic data from patient samples and was found to be effective in preclinical studies.

Another study used IBM Watson for Drug Discovery to identify potential drug targets for Parkinson's disease. The platform analyzed data from scientific papers, clinical trials, and other biomedical databases to identify genes and proteins that are involved in the disease. Depending on the results, the platform discovered many potential drug targets that are currently being investigated.

Overall, IBM Watson for Drug Discovery is a powerful tool in drug discovery that can help researchers identify promising drug candidates and accelerate the drug development process. By leveraging AI and machine learning techniques, the platform can evaluate large volumes of biomedical information and gives awareness that can lead to the improvement of new therapies for a variety of illnesses. As the platform continues to evolve and improve, it has the ability to revolutionize the study of drug discovery and bring new treatments to patients more quickly and efficiently.

12.4.3   BenevolentAI's Drug Discovery Platform

BenevolentAI is an artificial intelligence (AI)-based drug discovery platform that intends to use AI to hasten the discovery and development of novel medications. The platform analyses enormous volumes of biomedical information and produces perceptions which might be used to find prospective drug candidates using ml and nlp.

The platform developed by BenevolentAI has the capacity to process and analyze significant amounts of both structured and unstructured data. The platform can extract pertinent data from a variety of data sources, such as clinical trials, scientific papers, and patents, and analyze the data to find prospective therapeutic targets and forecast the effectiveness of new drug candidates.

The platform developed by BenevolentAI has been employed in a number of drug development initiatives, including the search for fresh therapies for ALS and Parkinson's disease. In one study, the platform was used to find a brand-new Parkinson's disease medication candidate that is now being further investigated.

THE RIGHT DRUG TARGET
Hypopthesis generation
and target identification

THE RIGHT FOUNDATIONS
Benevolent Knowledge Graph
including algorithmically
derived new knowledge

THE RIGHT DRUG
AI-Augmented
molecular design

THE RIGHT PATIENT
Patient stratification and
better clinical trials

Figure 12.10 Benevolent AI's drug discovery platform.

The platform's application in the search for novel medications for uncommon disorders serves as another illustration of its capabilities. Due to the dearth of viable medicines for many rare disorders, conventional drug discovery strategies can be difficult to use [20]. Utilizing information from a variety of sources, like patient history and scholarly articles, BenevolentAI's platform can suggest prospective therapeutic candidates and gauge their effectiveness.

The platform developed by BenevolentAI has the potential to enhance patient recruiting and clinical trial design. The platform can assist create more successful and efficient clinical trials by analyzing patient records and clinical trial data to identify patient populations most likely to benefit from a given medication.

Overall, BenevolentAI's drug discovery platform, as shown in Figure 12.10, has the ability to completely change the way drugs are discovered and developed by enabling researchers to examine enormous amounts of biomedical data and produce insights that can lead to the identification of novel drug candidates and better patient outcomes. The platform has already been employed in a number of successful drug discovery efforts, and as it is improved and enhanced, its capabilities are certain to grow.

12.4.4   Other Examples of AI-Based Drug Treatment

Artificial intelligence (AI) is changing the way drug treatment is being developed and implemented. AI-based drug treatment is using machine learning algorithms and deep learning techniques to analyze large datasets to identify patterns and prescriptions that can enhance pharmaceutical research and support for patients. In addition to the examples of Genomic Health's Oncotype DX, IBM Watson for Drug Discovery, and BenevolentAI's drug discovery platform, various additional examples of AI-based drug treatment that are worth exploring are listed as follows:

1. Atomwise
Atomwise is a drug discovery company that uses AI to accelerate the discovery of novel small molecules for drug development. The company uses deep learning to analyze large

datasets of molecular structures to identify drug candidates that have the potential to treat various diseases. Atomwise's AI-based platform has been used to identify potential drugs for Ebola, multiple sclerosis, and even COVID-19.

Atomwise's AI platform can analyze over 10 million molecular structures per day, significantly reducing the duration and expenses of traditional processes of discovering the drugs. The company also collaborates with researchers and pharmaceutical companies to identify potential drug targets and develop new treatments for various diseases.

2. *Insilico* Medicine

Insilico Medicine is a drug discovery company that uses AI to develop new treatments for cancer, Alzheimer's disease, and other age-related diseases. The company uses deep learning algorithms to analyze large datasets of gene expression data and identify potential drug targets.

Insilico Medicine has developed an AI platform that can predict the efficacy of potential drug candidates and identify the most promising candidates for clinical trials. The platform has been used to identify potential drug candidates for cancer, Alzheimer's disease, and other age-related diseases.

Additionally, the business shortens and lowers the expense of clinical studies in order to speed up the medication development process. *Insilico* Medicine's AI platform can predict the efficacy of potential drug candidates and reduce the need for expensive and time-consuming clinical trials.

3. Recursion Pharmaceuticals

Recursion Pharmaceuticals is a drug discovery company that uses AI to discover potential drug patients for various diseases. The company uses deep learning algorithms to analyze large datasets of gene expression information to find possible medication targets.

Recursion Pharmaceuticals' AI platform is capable of locating prospective treatment candidates for a range of illnesses, including uncommon genetic problems [21]. For a number of illnesses, including CF, muscular atrophy of the spine, and Tay–Sachs syndrome, the business has found promising therapeutic candidates.

Recursion Pharmaceuticals' AI platform has the potential to accelerate the process of drug discovery and speed up and lower the price of clinical trials. The platform can identify potential drug candidates for various diseases; this may result in the creation of novel remedies and improvement of patient outcomes.

4. Deep Genomics

Deep Genomics is a drug discovery company that uses AI to develop new treatments for genetic diseases. The company uses deep learning algorithms to analyze large datasets of genetic information to discover possible targets for drugs.

Deep Genomics' AI platform can identify potential drug candidates for various genetic diseases, including Huntington's disease and cystic fibrosis. The platform can also predict the efficacy of potential drug candidates and identify the most promising candidates for clinical trials.

Deep Genomics' AI platform has the potential to significantly improve the drug discovery process for genetic diseases. The platform can identify potential drug candidates and predict their efficacy, which can reduce the time and cost of clinical trials and lead to the development of new treatments for genetic diseases.

5. PathAI

PathAI is a medical technology company that uses AI to improve the accuracy of pathology diagnoses. The company uses deep learning algorithms to analyze large datasets of pathology images to identify potential diagnoses.

PathAI's AI platform can significantly improve the accuracy of pathology diagnoses, which can lead to more accurate treatment plans and improved patient outcomes. The platform has been used to identify potential assessment for several kinds of illnesses, such as cervical cancer and prostate tumors. Pathological diagnosis and help pathologists identify cancer subtypes with greater precision. The platform has already been used to analyze biopsy samples from sufferers possessing prostate, lung, or breast cancer, with promising results. In one study, the platform was able to accurately identify breast cancer subtypes in 99% of cases compared to 79% accuracy by human pathologists.

A further instance of an AI-based drug treatment method is the utilization of machine learning to personalize cancer treatment. The CancerLinQ platform, developed by the American Society of Clinical Oncology, uses ML models to evaluate the data from EHRs and identify the best cancer therapy options for every patient. The software can help oncologists make better treatment decisions through examining data from millions of patients to find patterns and clues.

In addition to improving treatment decisions, AI-based drug treatment can also assist in decreasing the duration and expenses of drug development—for example, the *Insilico* Medicine platform uses machine learning algorithms to design new drug candidates based on the desired properties of a target molecule. By simulating the interactions between molecules and predicting the efficacy and safety of new drug candidates, the platform can help researchers identify promising drug candidates more quickly and efficiently than traditional drug development methods.

AI-based drug treatment is also being used to enhance drug safety and decrease the danger of side effects. The Vigilance AI platform uses machine learning models to evaluate information from EHRs and identify potential drug–drug interactions and adverse events. By discovering these problems at the beginning, doctors might go with measures to enhance protection for patients and avoid unfavorable occurrences.

Overall, AI-based drug treatment has the ability to transform the way drugs are discovered, developed, and prescribed. By examining vast volumes of information and identifying trends and insights which would be difficult or impossible for humans to detect, AI platforms can accelerate drug development, improve treatment decisions, and enhance patient outcomes. As AI technology continues to improve and evolve, the possibilities for AI-based drug treatment are virtually limitless.

12.5   Challenges and Limitations of AI-Based Drug Treatment

AI-based drug treatment has the potential to revolutionize the drug development process by increasing efficiency and accuracy [22]. However, there are several challenges and limitations that need to be addressed before AI-based drug treatment can become widely adopted in the pharmaceutical industry. One of the main challenges is the quality and availability of data used in AI-based drug treatment.

12.5.1　Data Quality and Availability

The quality and availability of data used in AI-based drug treatment are crucial for the accuracy of the models and predictions. The precision of the algorithms based upon the standards and amount of the information utilized to train them. Inaccurate or incomplete data can lead to unreliable predictions and models, which can have serious consequences in drug development.

Figure 12.11 explains the various challenges in AI treatment. One of the main challenges in AI-based drug treatment is the availability of high-quality data. The data used in drug development is often complex, heterogeneous, and dispersed across different sources. This makes it difficult to find and extract relevant data, and even when relevant data is found, it may not be of sufficient quality or quantity for use in AI-based drug treatment.

Data quality is also a major issue in AI-based drug treatment. Inaccurate or incomplete data can lead to inaccurate predictions and models—for example, if the information utilized to learn a prototype is biased or incomplete, the model may make incorrect predictions or fail to identify important patterns and relationships.

Another challenge is the lack of standardization and interoperability of data. Data from different sources may be formatted differently, use different terminology, or have different levels of granularity. This can make it difficult to combine and analyze data from different sources, leading to inconsistencies and inaccuracies in the models and predictions.

To address these challenges, efforts are being made to improve the quality and availability of data used in AI-based drug treatment. These efforts include initiatives to standardize and harmonize data formats and terminologies, improve data sharing and interoperability, and enhance data quality through data curation and validation.

Data quality and availability are major challenges in AI-based drug treatment. Efforts are being made to improve the quality and availability of data used in AI-based drug treatment,

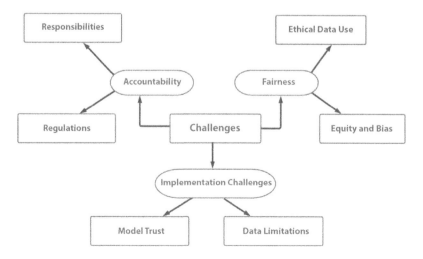

Figure 12.11 Challenges of AI-based drug treatment.

but more work needs to be done to ensure that the data used in drug development is of sufficient quality and quantity for use in AI-based drug treatment.

12.5.2   Ethical Considerations

There are ethical considerations related to AI-based drug treatment, including issues related to data privacy, bias, and accountability.

Data Privacy: Data privacy is one of the main moral issues surrounding AI-based medicine treatment. In order to create algorithms and make forecasts, AI needs a lot of data. This data may contain private information, such as genetic data and medical history, in the context of pharmacological therapy. To keep the patients' trust in the medical system, the confidentiality of the patients must be safeguarded.

The use of AI in drug treatment raises concerns about data breaches, unauthorized access to patients' data, and the potential misuse of this data. Regulations such as the GDPR in the European Union and the HIPAA in the USA provide some protection for patients' data. However, these regulations may not be sufficient to protect a patient's privacy in the era of AI-based drug treatment.

Bias: Bias is a further ethical issue with regard to AI-based pharmacological treatment. The data that AI algorithms are educated on determines how objective they are. Algorithms for AI will be discriminatory if the data utilized to generate them is prejudiced. Forecasts that are incorrect and erroneous may result from this bias.

In the case of drug treatment, bias can lead to incorrect predictions about the effectiveness of certain medications in specific patient populations. This can result in suboptimal treatment outcomes and harm to patients. It is crucial to make sure that the data utilized

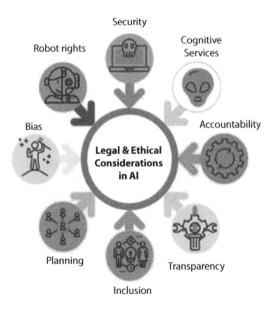

Figure 12.12 Ethical considerations.

to create AI algorithms is inclusive of all patients and avoids reinforcing pre-existing preju-
dices. Figure 12.12 explains the different ethical considerations of AI-based drugs.

Accountability: Utilizing AI in drug treatment also increases the aspects about accountability. Traditional drug development involves a clear chain of responsibility, with researchers, regulators, and pharmaceutical companies all held accountable for the protection and
effectiveness of new medications. However, the utilization of AI in drug treatment blurs
these lines of responsibility.

AI algorithms are often black boxes, making it difficult to understand how decisions
are made. This lack of transparency makes it challenging to assign responsibility for suboptimal treatment outcomes or adverse events. The responsibility for ensuring the safety
and efficacy of AI-based drug treatment must be clearly defined, with all stakeholders held
accountable for their role in the process.

AI-based drug treatment has the potential to revolutionize healthcare, but it is essential
to consider the ethical implications of this technology. Protecting patient privacy, avoiding
bias, and ensuring accountability are all essential considerations when using AI in drug
treatment. These challenges must be addressed to ensure that AI-based drug treatment is
safe, effective, and equitable for all patients.

12.5.3   Regulatory Hurdles

The regulatory landscape for AI-based drug treatment is complex and constantly evolving. Regulatory bodies around the world are grappling with how to regulate AI-based drug
development, given the unique challenges that AI poses to traditional regulatory frameworks. Some of the key regulatory hurdles in AI-based drug treatment are discussed below:

1. Lack of clear regulatory guidance: The regulatory landscape for AI-based
   drug treatment is still in its infancy. Many regulatory bodies have yet to issue
   clear guidance on the use of AI in drug development, leaving companies to
   navigate an uncertain regulatory landscape. This lack of clear guidance can
   slow down the medication manufacturing procedure and increase the difficulty for companies to bring new drugs to the market.
2. Validation of AI algorithms: AI-based drug treatment relies heavily on the
   use of algorithms to determine prospective therapeutic targets and gauge the
   effectiveness of new medications. However, there is currently no standardized
   approach to validate these algorithms, making it difficult to determine their
   accuracy and reliability. This lack of standardization can lead to inconsistencies in the medication manufacturing procedure and enhance difficulty to
   compare the effectiveness of different AI-based drug development programs.
3. Data privacy and security: AI-based drug treatment requires the use of
   huge volumes of people information, which increases worries about safety
   and confidentiality of data. Regulatory bodies around the world have implemented strict data protection regulations to ensure that patients' data is
   handled securely and confidentially. Companies developing AI-based drug
   treatments must comply with these regulations to ensure that patients' data
   is handled appropriately.

4. Ethical considerations: The utilization of AI in drug development improves a number of ethical considerations, such as the potential for bias in algorithmic decision-making and the need for transparency in the drug development process. Regulatory bodies must consider these ethical issues when developing regulatory frameworks for AI-based drug treatment to prove that the utilization of AI in drug development is ethically sound.

5. Interpretability of AI algorithms: AI models can be complex to interpret, that makes it difficult to comprehend how they make their projections. The regulatory approval procedure may take longer for AI-based drug treatments since it may be demanding to assess their safety and effectiveness.

The adoption of AI in drug development has the ability to revolutionize the drug development process, leading to the development of more effective medications. However, the regulatory hurdles concern to guarantees the secure and effective use of AI in medication development, and effective use of AI-based drug treatments [23]. Regulatory bodies around the world must work together to develop clear and standardized regulatory frameworks for AI-based drug treatment, taking into account the unique challenges that AI poses to traditional regulatory frameworks. This will help to ensure that the benefits of AI in drug development are realized while minimizing the risks to patient safety and data privacy.

12.5.4 Integration with Existing Healthcare Systems

The incorporation of AI-based drug treatment with existing healthcare systems has the potential to revolutionize patient care. However, this integration also poses several challenges and limitations that need to be addressed to ensure effective implementation.

1. Data interoperability: The integration of AI-based drug treatment with existing healthcare systems requires interoperability between different systems to ensure seamless data exchange. However, healthcare systems often use proprietary formats, making data interoperability difficult. The lack of interoperability can result in data silos, making it challenging to extract insights from data. Additionally, data quality issues, such as incomplete or inaccurate data, can affect the accuracy of AI-based drug treatment.

2. Workflow management: Integrating AI-based drug treatment with existing healthcare systems requires careful workflow management to make certain instruments based on AI are used effectively. The workflow must be designed to make certain instruments based on AI are integrated seamlessly into existing clinical workflows. Healthcare professionals need to be trained on how to use AI-based tools effectively, and the workflow must be designed to ensure that the right data is fed into the AI-based tools to generate accurate insights.

3. Regulatory compliance: The integration of AI-based drug treatment with existing healthcare systems requires adherence to legal requirements like the HIPAA. HIPAA mandates that patients' data must be protected and kept confidential. Any AI-based tool that handles patients' data must comply with HIPAA regulations to ensure patient privacy and data security.

4. Integration with electronic health records (EHRs): EHRs are central to healthcare systems, and integrating AI-based drug treatment with EHRs is crucial for effective integration. EHRs contain a wealth of patients' data that can be used to train AI-based tools, and integrating AI-based drug treatment with EHRs can help generate more accurate insights. However, integrating AI-based drug treatment with EHRs requires overcoming challenges related to data interoperability and workflow management.

5. Cost: Integrating AI-based drug treatment with existing healthcare systems requires significant investments in hardware, software, and training. AI-based drug treatment requires high-performance computing infrastructure, which can be expensive to set up and maintain. Additionally, healthcare professionals need to be trained on how to use AI-based tools effectively, which can be time-consuming and costly.

6. Trust and acceptance: The integration of AI-based drug treatment with existing healthcare systems requires building trust and acceptance among healthcare professionals and patients. Healthcare professionals must be convinced that AI-based tools can generate accurate insights and improve patient outcomes. Patients must be assured that their data is being used in a secure and ethical manner. Building trust and acceptance requires transparency and clear communication about the benefits and limitations of AI-based drug treatment.

The integration of AI-based drug treatment with existing healthcare systems poses significant challenges related to data interoperability, workflow management, regulatory compliance, integration with EHRs, cost, and trust and acceptance. Overcoming these challenges requires collaboration between healthcare professionals, AI experts, and regulatory bodies to ensure that AI-based drug treatment is integrated seamlessly into existing healthcare systems. Despite these challenges, the potential benefits of AI-based drug treatment are significant, and the integration of AI-based drug treatment with existing healthcare systems is essential for improving patient outcomes and advancing drug discovery.

12.6   Future Outlook and Implications

AI-based drug treatment is a rapidly evolving a sector that has the power to transform medical care. As we have seen in the previous sections, AI can assist to boost drug discovery, improve patient outcomes, and lower medical expenses [24]. The potential impact of AI on healthcare is immense, and it is important to understand the opportunities and challenges that lie ahead.

The prospective effects of AI-based drug treatment on healthcare will be covered in this section. We'll look at how AI can save costs, expand access to care, and enhance patient outcomes. Everyone is additionally going to look at some of the difficulties that must be resolved before AI in healthcare can completely realize its potential.

12.6.1 Potential Impact on Healthcare

The potential impact of technology on healthcare is vast and far-reaching. With the continuous advancements in technology, the healthcare industry has been transformed, and it is expected to undergo even more radical changes in the coming years. One of the primary way's technology is poised to transform healthcare is through the use of electronic health records (EHRs). EHRs allow healthcare professionals to access patients' data easily and securely from any location, making it easier to diagnose and treat illnesses. EHRs also enable healthcare professionals to track patient's progress, monitor medication use, and identify potential adverse effects.

Another significant potential impact of technology on healthcare is telemedicine. Telemedicine allows healthcare providers to diagnose and treat patients remotely, eliminating the need for patients to travel to a healthcare facility physically. Telemedicine has already shown promising results in rural fields; it is anticipated to continue to gain prominence in the upcoming years, especially in locations where there is a dearth of healthcare professionals.

The use of wearables is another potential impact of technology on healthcare. Wearables such as fitness trackers and smartwatches can monitor vital signs and track physical activity levels, allowing healthcare providers to monitor patients remotely [25]. Wearables can also detect possible health problems before they occur significant problems, enabling healthcare providers to intervene early.

AI is also poised to revolutionize healthcare. AI can quickly evaluate a lot of information, making it easier to identify patterns and predict potential health issues. AI can also assist healthcare providers in making diagnoses and developing treatment plans, improving patient outcomes.

In addition to the above, technology is also poised to transform healthcare in several other ways—for example, 3D printing technology can be utilized to make prosthetics and other medical devices quickly and cheaply, improving patient access to critical medical supplies. Robotics technology can be used to perform surgical procedures with more precision, reducing the danger of complications and improving patients' results.

However, despite the significant potential impact of technology on healthcare, there are also potential downsides to consider—for example, the increased use of technology in healthcare could lead to a loss of personal connection between patients and healthcare providers. Additionally, there are concerns about data confidentiality and safety, as the increasing use of EHRs and other technology could potentially lead to data breaches.

To summarize the potential impact of technology on healthcare is vast and far-reaching. From electronic health records and telemedicine to wearables and AI, technology is poised to revolutionize the healthcare industry. However, it is essential to consider the potential downsides of increased technology use in healthcare and work to mitigate these risks. With careful planning and implementation, the healthcare industry can leverage technology to enhance the victims' results and deliver most effective care.

AI has the ability to transform medical care in various types [26]. Here are some of the potential advantages of AI-based drug treatment:

1. Faster drug discovery: One of the biggest benefits of AI-based drug treatment is the speed with which new drugs can be discovered. Huge amounts of data

can be examined by AI, which can also spot trends that would be challenging, if not unattainable, for people to notice. Because of this, the creation of new medications to cure diseases that are currently untreated can be sped up.

2. More personalized medicine: AI may evaluate patient records to find trends and forecast results. This translates into the ability to customise treatments for every patient, resulting in greater results and fewer adverse effects. By avoiding unneeded treatments, personalized medicine can also lower healthcare expenditures.

3. Improved diagnosis: AI can help to improve the accuracy of diagnoses by analyzing patient information and identifying trends which may not be apparent to doctors. This means that patients can be diagnosed earlier and with greater accuracy, leading to good results.

4. Remote patient monitoring: AI is utilized to monitor patients remotely, allowing doctors to track patients' progress and intervene if necessary. This can help to reduce hospital readmissions and improve patient outcomes.

5. Increased access to care: AI-based drug treatment can help to increase access to care by allowing healthcare providers to reach more patients in rural or backward areas. Telemedicine and remote monitoring can aid to lower the cost of healthcare and enhance patients' results.

12.6.2   Opportunities for Research and Development

Artificial intelligence (AI) has been hailed as a transformative technology for drug discovery and research, along with the entire healthcare industry. The utilization of AI in the discovery of drugs has already resulted in some notable successes, and the potential for further advances is vast. In this section, the opportunities for research and development that AI-based drug treatment offers is explored.

Another benefit of AI-based drug treatment is the ability to identify new therapeutic targets that were previously unknown or not feasible for exploration. AI can analyze large volumes of information from a variety of sources, including scientific literature, clinical trials, and electronic health records, to identify potential targets for drug development. By examining trends and associations in the data, AI algorithms can suggest new approaches for treating complex diseases.

Another significant opportunity for AI-based drug treatment is the ability to personalize medicine for individual patients. AI models can examine patient information to detect genetic or other biomarkers that are associated with a particular disease or condition. This information can then be used to tailor treatment plans for each and every patient, improving results and reducing adverse effects.

AI-based drug treatment also holds promise for improving clinical trial design and accelerating the drug development process. By analyzing data from previous clinical trials [27], AI algorithms can identify factors that may have contributed to the failure of a trial or the limited efficacy of a drug. This information can be used to design more effective trials and to develop more targeted drugs.

In addition to these opportunities, AI-based drug treatment also offers the potential for more efficient and cost-effective drug development. By streamlining the process of drug discovery and development, AI can lower the duration and resources required to bring a fresh drug to market. This could have significant implications for healthcare systems around the world, particularly in countries where access to expensive medications is limited.

Despite these opportunities, there are also challenges and limitations to AI-based drug treatment. One significant challenge is the need for standard data. AI models are only as good as the information they are learned on, and poor-quality or biased data can lead to inaccurate or unreliable results. Ensuring that data is accurate, comprehensive, and representative is therefore essential for the success of AI-based drug treatment.

Another challenge is the need for ethical considerations in the use of AI-based drug treatment. As with any new technology, there are concerns about the potential for misuse or unintended consequences—for example, there may be concerns about privacy and data security as well as the potential for AI algorithms to reinforce existing biases or inequalities in healthcare.

Regulatory hurdles are also a significant challenge for AI-based drug treatment. As with any new drug, AI-based drugs will need to go through rigorous testing and approval processes before they can be brought to the market. However, these processes may not be designed to accommodate the unique features of AI-based drug treatment, such as the use of complex algorithms and the need for ongoing data analysis.

Integration with existing healthcare systems is also a challenge for AI-based drug treatment. Healthcare systems are often complex and fragmented, with multiple stakeholders involved in patient care. Integrating AI-based drug treatment into these systems will require significant coordination and investment, as well as changes to existing policies and procedures.

Despite these challenges, the future outlook for AI-based drug treatment is positive. With ongoing advances in AI technology, as well as increased investment and collaboration across the healthcare industry, there is tremendous potential for AI-based drug treatment to transform the way we discover and develop new drugs, personalize medicine, and improve patient outcomes. By addressing the challenges and limitations of this approach, we can unlock its full potential and make a more effective and equable healthcare system for all.

12.6.3   Implications for Patients and Providers

Artificial intelligence (AI) has the ability to revolutionize healthcare in a variety of types, involving drug discovery, diagnosis, and treatment. AI-based drug treatment, in particular, has the potential to benefit patients and providers in a number of ways. However, there are also a number of ethical, legal, and practical implications that must be considered as AI-based drug treatment becomes more prevalent in healthcare.

One of the primary implications of AI-based drug treatment for patients and providers is the potential for personalized medicine. With the potential to evaluate large volumes of patient information, AI models can identify biomarkers and other factors that may be unique to individual patients. This, in turn, can lead to the development of more effective and targeted therapies for a several of conditions, including cancer, cardiovascular disease, and neurological disorders.

Another potential benefit of AI-based drug treatment is the ability to improve patient outcomes while reducing healthcare costs. By developing more targeted treatments and decreasing the need for trial and error in drug development processes, AI-based drug treatment has the potential to reduce the expenses of development of drug and improve the speed and efficiency of clinical trials [28]. Additionally, by discovering the effective therapies for individual patients, AI-based drug treatment may help to reduce hospitalizations, emergency room visits, and other costly healthcare interventions.

However, there are also a number of ethical and legal implications of AI-based drug treatment that must be considered—for example, there are aspects about confidentiality and data safety, as patients' data must be collected, stored, and analyzed in order to develop effective AI algorithms. There are also concerns about bias and fairness, as AI algorithms may be developed based on biased data or may have unintended consequences for certain groups of patients.

Another potential ethical concern is the ability for AI-based drug treatment to be used in ways that are not aligned with the interests of patients or the public—for instance, AI models may be utilized to develop drugs that are profitable but not necessarily effective or safe or may be used to justify higher drug prices based on the perceived value of personalized medicine.

In addition to these ethical and legal implications, there are also practical considerations that must be taken into account as AI-based drug treatment becomes more prevalent in healthcare—for example, there may be challenges associated with integrating AI algorithms into existing healthcare systems and workflows, and there may be a need for new regulations and guidelines to ensure the safety and efficacy of AI-based drug treatments.

Despite these challenges and limitations, the future outlook for AI-based drug treatment is promising. As technology continues to advance and more data becomes available, AI algorithms will become increasingly sophisticated and accurate. Additionally, as the benefits of personalized medicine become more widely recognized, there will likely be an increasing demand for AI-based drug treatments.

Overall, the implications of AI-based drug treatment for patients and providers are complex and multifaceted. While there are a number of challenges and limitations that must be addressed, the potential benefits of personalized medicine and more efficient drug development are significant. As such, it is important for policymakers, healthcare providers, and other stakeholders to work together to ensure that AI-based drug treatment is developed and used in a way that is safe, effective, and aligned with the interests of patients and the public.

12.7 Conclusion and Future Work

In recent years, personalized medicine has gained significant attention in the healthcare industry. It is a revolutionary approach that concerns an environmental circumstance, a person's lifestyle, and their genetic composition to provide a tailored treatment plan. Artificial intelligence (AI) has emerged as a crucial tool in this field, enabling healthcare providers to predict drug efficacy, identify patient subgroups, tailor dosages, minimize adverse effects, and streamline drug development.

AI techniques such as machine learning, natural language processing, and deep learning have shown promising results in improving drug treatment outcomes—for instance, genomic profiling company Genomic Health's Oncotype DX uses AI to predict a patient's response to cancer treatment. IBM Watson for Drug Discovery and BenevolentAI's drug discovery platform are other examples of AI-based drug treatment [29]. These technologies leverage big data analytics and computational power to identify novel drug targets and predict the safety and efficacy of drugs.

However, the implementation of AI-based drug treatment faces challenges and limitations such as data quality and availability, ethical considerations, regulatory hurdles, and integration with existing healthcare systems. For AI to reach its full potential, regulatory agencies must establish clear guidelines on data privacy, safety, and ethical considerations. Moreover, healthcare providers must integrate AI technologies with existing healthcare systems to ensure smooth patient care delivery.

In conclusion, AI-based drug treatment has enormous potential to transform the healthcare industry by providing personalized, safe, and effective treatments. However, its success depends on addressing the challenges and limitations that currently exist. Further research and development in this field will help to unlock its full potential, resulting in improved patient outcomes and lower healthcare expenses.

12.7.1   Summary of Key Points

In summary, AI-based drug treatment has the ability to revolutionize the pharmaceutical industry and enhance patients' results. The key points to consider include the utilization of AI techniques like ML and NLP to analyze vast amounts of biomedical data [30], leading to the identification of novel drug candidates and more efficient clinical trial designs.

Moreover, there are ethical and regulatory challenges to consider, such as the need to ensure data quality and availability, maintain patient privacy and confidentiality, and comply with existing regulatory frameworks. Additionally, integration with existing healthcare systems is a critical consideration for the successful adoption and implementation of AI-based drug treatment.

The future of drug treatment is promising, with opportunities for research and development leading to the development of more effective and personalized treatments. The implications for patients and providers are vast, with the ability to enhance health results, lower expenses, and improve the overall quality of care.

12.7.2   Implications for the Future of Drug Treatment

The implications of AI-based drug treatment on the future of medicine are vast and far-reaching. The use of AI in drug discovery and development has the ability to transform the type we approach medical care by providing more personalized and targeted treatment options. AI can identify new drug candidates more efficiently and quickly than traditional methods, potentially speeding up the drug development process and reducing costs.

In addition, AI can assist healthcare professionals in making better judgments on the treatment of patients. Healthcare workers can examine a lot of patients' data by using machine learning algorithms and find trends or risk factors that may have previously gone unnoticed. This can lead to earlier detection of diseases and more effective treatment plans.

Another significant implication of AI in drug treatment is the ability to enhance patients' results. With the ability to predict a patient's response to a particular drug or treatment plan, healthcare providers can tailor their approach to each individual, leading to more effective and efficient care.

However, there are also challenges to consider in implementing AI-based drug treatment. Data quality and availability, ethical considerations, regulatory hurdles, and incorporation with pre-existing medical systems are all potential obstacles that must be addressed. As with any new technology, there is also a learning curve and potential for error or misinterpretation of data.

Despite these challenges, the potential benefits of AI-based drug treatment are too great to ignore. With continued research and development, AI has the ability to transform the approach to drug discovery, patient care, and the overall healthcare system.

12.7.3   Further Research and Development

There is a call to action for further studies and development in this study, with the need to continue exploring the potential of AI-based drug treatment and overcoming the challenges that exist to ensure its successful integration into the healthcare system. With continued progress, AI-based drug treatment has the potential to transform the way we approach drug discovery and treatment, ultimately benefiting patients and providers alike.

As we have seen, AI-based drug treatment has the ability to transform the field of medicine by increasing the speed and accuracy of drug discovery and development. However, there are still many challenges and limitations that these must be handled in order to completely realize the potential benefits of this technology.

In light of this, there is a necessity for further studies and development in this region. This includes developing more advanced AI algorithms that can better analyze and interpret complex biological data, as well as improving the quality and availability of data used in drug discovery.

There is also a need for greater collaboration between researchers, pharmaceutical companies, and regulatory bodies to ensure that AI-based drug treatment is improved and implemented in an ethical and accountable manner. This includes addressing concerns around data privacy, patient consent, and ensuring that AI-based drug treatment does not exacerbate existing health disparities.

Furthermore, it is important to continue investing in the training and education of healthcare professionals to make sure that they have the abilities and information required to successfully implement AI-based drug treatment into their procedures.

Overall, the potential benefits of AI-based drug treatment are vast, but it is important that we approach this technology with caution and a commitment to responsible development and implementation. By doing so, we can help ensure that AI-based drug treatment is used to improve the victims' results and advance the area of healthcare as a whole.

References

1. Kumar, A., Krishnamurthi, R., Nayyar, A., Sharma, K., Grover, V., Hossain, E., A novel smart healthcare design, simulation, and implementation using healthcare 4.0 processes. *IEEE Access*, 8, 118433–118471, 2020.
2. Kaur, T., Bhandari, D.D., Sharma, R., Cloud Computing: A relevant Solution for Drug Designing using different Software's, in: *2021 Sixth International Conference on Image Information Processing (ICIIP)*, vol. 6, pp. 375–378, IEEE, 2021, November.

3. Huang, H.J., Tsai, F.J., Chung, J.G., Tsai, C.H., Hsu, Y.M., Ho, T.Y., Chen, C.Y.C., Drug design for XRCC4 *in silico*, in: *2009 2nd International Conference on Biomedical Engineering and Informatics*, pp. 1–4, IEEE, 2009, October.

4. Nayyar, A., Gadhavi, L., Zaman, N., Machine learning in healthcare: Review, opportunities and challenges, in: *Machine Learning and the Internet of Medical Things in Healthcare*, pp. 23–45, 2021.

5. Pal, R., Misra, G., Mathur, P., *In silico* screening of small molecule modulators of zika virus proteins, in: *2017 7th International Conference on Cloud Computing, Data Science & Engineering-Confluence*, pp. 381–386, IEEE, 2017, January.

6. Srinivasu, N., Satyanarayana, K.V.V., Murthy, N.G.K., Structure based drug design studies on CDK2 amino pyrazole inhibitors using autodock tools. *2014 Conference on IT in Business, Industry and Government (CSIBIG)*, pp. 1–5, Indore, India, 2014, doi: 10.1109/CSIBIG.2014.7056965.

7. Sadjad, B. and Zsoldos, Z., Toward a robust search method for the protein-drug docking problem. *IEEE/ACM Trans. Comput. Biol. Bioinf.*, 8, 4, 1120–1133, 2010.

8. Pramanik, P.K.D., Solanki, A., Debnath, A., Nayyar, A., El-Sappagh, S., Kwak, K.S., Advancing modern healthcare with nanotechnology, nanobiosensors, and internet of nano things: Taxonomies, applications, architecture, and challenges. *IEEE Access*, 8, 65230–65266, 2020.

9. Law, R., Barker, O., Barker, J.J., Hesterkamp, T., Godemann, R., Andersen, O., Whittaker, M., The multiple roles of computational chemistry in fragment-based drug design. *J. Comput.-Aided Mol. Des.*, 23, 459–473, 2009.

10. Hariyono, P., Dwiastuti, R., Yusuf, M., Salin, N.H., Hariono, M., 2-phenoxyacetamide derivatives as SARS-CoV-2 main protease inhibitor: *In silico* studies. *Results Chem.*, 4, 100263, 2022.

11. Pramanik, P.K.D., Pareek, G., Nayyar, A., Security and privacy in remote healthcare: Issues, solutions, and standards, in: *Telemedicine Technologies*, pp. 201–225, Academic Press, United States, 2019.

12. Choudhury, C., Murugan, N.A., Priyakumar, U.D., Structure-based drug repurposing: Traditional and advanced AI/ML-aided methods. *Drug Discov. Today,*, 27, 7, 1847–1861, 2022.

13. Odoemelam, C.S., Percival, B., Wallis, H., Chang, M.W., Ahmad, Z., Scholey, D., Wilson, P.B., G-Protein coupled receptors: Structure and function in drug discovery. *RSC Adv.*, 10, 60, 36337–36348, 2020.

14. Lin, X., Li, X., Lin, X., A review on applications of computational methods in drug screening and design. *Molecules*, 25, 6, 1375, 2020.

15. Mahapatra, B., Krishnamurthi, R., Nayyar, A., Healthcare models and algorithms for privacy and security in healthcare records, in: *Security and Privacy of Electronic Healthcare Records: Concepts, Paradigms and Solutions,* 183, 2019.

16. Yu, W., Weber, D.J., MacKerell Jr., A.D., Computer-aided drug design: An update, in: *Antibiotics: Methods and Protocols*, pp. 123–152, Springer US, New York, NY, 2022.

17. Crampon, K., Giorkallos, A., Deldossi, M., Baud, S., Steffenel, L.A., Machine-learning methods for ligand–protein molecular docking. *Drug Discov. Today*, 27, 1, 151–164, 2022.

18. Aminpour, M., Montemagno, C., Tuszynski, J.A., An overview of molecular modeling for drug discovery with specific illustrative examples of applications. *Molecules*, 24, 9, 1693, 2019.

19. Traboulsi, H., Khedr, M.A., Al-Faiyz, Y.S., Elgorashe, R., Negm, A., Structure-based epitope design: Toward a greater antibody–SARS-CoV-2 RBD affinity. *ACS Omega*, 6, 47, 31469–31476, 2021.

20. D'Souza, S., Prema, K.V., Balaji, S., Machine learning models for drug–target interactions: Current knowledge and future directions. *Drug Discov. Today*, 25, 4, 748–756, 2020.

21. Ghosh, A.K. and Gemma, S., *Structure-based design of drugs and other bioactive molecules: Tools and strategies*, John Wiley & Sons, New Jersey, United States, 2014.

22. Doma, M. K., Padmanandam, K., Tambvekar, S., Kumar, K., Abdualgalil, B., Thakur, R. N., Artificial intelligence-based breast cancer detection using WPSO. *Int. J. Oper. Res. Inf. Syst. (IJORIS)*, 13, 2, 1–16, 2022.

23. Batool, M., Ahmad, B., Choi, S., A structure-based drug discovery paradigm. *Int. J. Mol. Sci.*, 20, 11, 2783, 2019.

24. Ramesh, S., Vallinayagam, S., Rajendran, K., Rajendran, S., Rathinam, V., Ramesh, S., Computer-aided drug designing–modality of diagnostic system, in: *Biomedical Signal Processing for Healthcare Applications*, pp. 195–218, CRC Press, United States, 2021.

25. Mahapatra, M.K. and Karuppasamy, M., Fundamental considerations in drug design, in: *Computer Aided Drug Design (CADD): From Ligand-Based Methods to Structure-Based Approaches*, vol. pp, pp. 17–55, Elsevier, The Netherlands, 2022.

26. Ilmudeen, A. and Nayyar, A., Novel designs of smart healthcare systems: Technologies, architecture, and applications, in: *Machine Learning for Critical Internet of Medical Things: Applications and Use Cases*, pp. 125–151, Springer International Publishing, Cham, Germany, New York City, 2022.

27. Jadala, V.C., Pasupuleti, S.K., Yellamma, P., Deep Learning analysis using ResNet for early detection of cerebellar ataxia disease, in: *2022 International Conference on Advancements in Smart, Secure and Intelligent Computing (ASSIC)*, pp. 1–6, IEEE, 2022, November.

28. Yazhini, A., Chakraborti, S., Srinivasan, N., Protein structure, dynamics and assembly: Implications for drug discovery, in: *Innovations and Implementations of Computer Aided Drug Discovery Strategies in Rational Drug Design*, pp. 91–122, 2021.

29. Fischer, A., Smiesko, M., Sellner, M., Lill, M.A., Decision making in structure-based drug discovery: Visual inspection of docking results. *J. Med. Chem.*, 64, 5, 2489–2500, 2021.

30. Padmanandam, K., Rajesh, M. V., Upadhyaya, A. N., Chandrashekar, B., Sah, S., Artificial intelligence biosensing system on hand gesture recognition for the hearing impaired. *Int. J. Oper. Res. Inf. Syst. (IJORIS)*, 13, 2, 1–13, 2022.

13

AI Models for Biopharmaceutical Property Prediction

Bancha Yingngam

Department of Pharmaceutical Chemistry and Technology, Faculty of Pharmaceutical Sciences, Ubon Ratchathani University, Ubon Ratchathani, Thailand

Abstract

Accurate and reliable prediction of drug properties is crucial in the biopharmaceutical industry because they directly impact drug efficacy and safety. However, the traditional experimental methods used to determine these properties are often expensive, time-consuming, and impractical, hindering efficient drug discovery and development. In recent years, machine learning (ML) and artificial intelligence (AI) techniques have gained popularity for predicting biopharmaceutical properties. This chapter aims to provide a comprehensive overview of AI models in biopharmaceutical property prediction. It covers key areas such as the critical importance of accurate prediction, traditional challenges, introduction to AI models, their underlying principles, advantages, challenges, recent advances, and future directions. The chapter consolidates the latest advancements in AI models tailored for predicting biopharmaceutical properties and explores alternative approaches, integrates AI techniques, and offers a focused and comprehensive overview. It discusses recent advances in ML and AI models, including deep learning and ensemble models, and their potential applications in drug discovery and development. Additionally, it addresses future directions and challenges in developing and implementing AI models for biopharmaceutical property prediction. In summary, this chapter presents a novel contribution by consolidating the latest advancements in AI models specifically designed for predicting biopharmaceutical properties.

Keywords: Artificial intelligence, machine learning, biopharmaceuticals, property prediction, validation, big data

List of Abbreviations

ADME	absorption, distribution, metabolism, and excretion
AI	artificial intelligence
CNNs	convolutional neural networks
DDIs	drug-drug interactions
GPCRs	G protein-coupled receptors

Email: bancha.y@ubu.ac.th

Abhirup Khanna, May El Barachi, Sapna Jain, Manoj Kumar and Anand Nayyar (eds.) *Artificial Intelligence and Machine Learning in Drug Design and Development*, (407–450) © 2024 Scrivener Publishing LLC

HTS	high-throughput screening
LSTM	long short-term memory
MD	molecular dynamics
ML	machine learning
MLP	multilayer perceptron
PBD	Protein Data Bank
PCA	principal component analysis
QM/MM	quantum mechanics/molecular mechanics
ReLU	rectified linear unit
RNNs	recurrent neural networks
SVMs	support vector machines

13.1   Introduction

The discovery and development of drugs play a critical role in modern healthcare by providing essential treatments for various diseases [1, 2]. One of the important strategies is biopharmaceutical property prediction. Biopharmaceuticals are a class of drugs that are produced using living organisms, such as bacteria, yeast, or mammalian cells [3]. These drugs are also sometimes called biologics. Unlike traditional small-molecule drugs that are chemically synthesized, biopharmaceuticals are produced using recombinant DNA technology, which involves inserting the genetic material that codes for the desired therapeutic protein into the cells of a living organism [4]. Biopharmaceuticals can be used to treat a wide range of diseases, including cancer, autoimmune disorders, and infectious diseases. They can be designed to target specific proteins or cells in the body, making them highly targeted and often more effective than traditional small-molecule drugs. Biopharmaceuticals can also be modified to improve their stability and reduce their immunogenicity or the likelihood of triggering an immune response in the body [5]. Examples of biopharmaceuticals include monoclonal antibodies, which are used to treat cancer and autoimmune disorders, and therapeutic proteins, such as insulin and growth hormone, which are used to treat diabetes and growth disorders. Other examples include vaccines, which are used to prevent infectious diseases, and gene therapies, which are used to treat genetic disorders (Figure 13.1). Biopharmaceuticals are a rapidly growing segment of the pharmaceutical industry, and they represent a major area of innovation in drug development [3]. They offer the potential for more effective and targeted treatments for a wide range of diseases, and they are likely to play an increasingly important role in the future of medicine [4].

There are various biopharmaceutical products available in the market and under development to treat various diseases and conditions. Some examples of biopharmaceutical products currently being used are Humira (adalimumab), a drug that treats rheumatoid arthritis, psoriasis, Crohn's disease, and other inflammatory conditions, manufactured by AbbVie Inc.; Rituxan (rituximab), used to treat non-Hodgkin's lymphoma and other cancers, manufactured by Genentech, Inc.; Avastin (bevacizumab), which inhibits the growth of blood vessels that supply tumors and treats cancer, manufactured by Genentech, Inc.; Herceptin (trastuzumab) targets the HER2 protein that is overexpressed in some types of

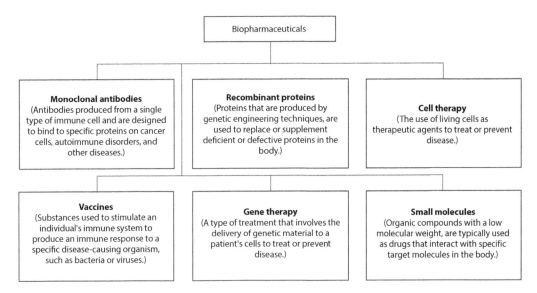

Figure 13.1 Categories of biopharmaceuticals.

breast cancer and is manufactured by Genentech, Inc.; and Keytruda (pembrolizumab), which blocks PD-1, a protein that suppresses the immune system's ability to attack cancer cells and is manufactured by Merck & Co., Inc. In addition, there are some upcoming biopharmaceutical products, such as aducanumab, currently under development by Biogen, Inc. for the treatment of Alzheimer's disease by targeting beta-amyloid protein, tanezumab, currently under development by Pfizer Inc. and Eli Lilly and Company for the treatment of chronic pain by targeting nerve growth factor, and erenumab, a drug approved for migraine prevention that targets calcitonin gene-related peptide, being developed by Amgen Inc. and Novartis AG.

Biopharmaceutical properties encompass the physical, chemical, and biological traits of drugs or biopharmaceutical products that dictate their pharmacological and therapeutic effects. These properties comprise factors such as solubility, permeability, stability, bioavailability, absorption, distribution, metabolism, excretion, toxicity, and efficacy [2]. Biopharmaceutical properties can significantly impact drug pharmacokinetics and pharmacodynamics and ultimately determine the therapeutic efficacy and safety profile of drugs. Precise prediction of biopharmaceutical properties is crucial in drug discovery and development, as it can help identify promising drug candidates, optimize drug design, and reduce the time and cost of clinical trials.

Despite its importance, predicting the biopharmaceutical properties of drug candidates remains a primary obstacle in drug development. Traditional experimental approaches to determining these properties are expensive, time-consuming, and sometimes impractical, creating a need for accurate and reliable predictive methods [6]. The emergence of machine learning (ML) and artificial intelligence (AI) techniques, however, has revolutionized the field of drug discovery and development by enabling the rapid and accurate prediction of biopharmaceutical properties [7, 8]. AI refers to the ability of machines or computer systems to perform tasks that typically require human intelligence, such as learning, reasoning, problem solving, and decision making [2]. AI systems are designed to process vast amounts of data, recognize patterns, and make predictions or decisions based on those data. AI can be broadly classified into two types: narrow or weak AI and general or strong AI. General AI refers to AI systems that can perform any intellectual task that a human can do. Several techniques and algorithms are used in AI, such as ML, deep learning, natural language processing, and computer vision. AI has numerous applications across various fields, including healthcare, finance, transportation, manufacturing, and entertainment. In healthcare, for example, AI can be used for disease diagnosis, drug discovery, medical image analysis, and personalized medicine.

AI/ML techniques are capable of analyzing large datasets and identifying patterns that may be difficult to detect through traditional experimental methods, resulting in a significant reduction in the time and cost associated with drug development [9–13]. ML/AI algorithms can learn from vast datasets and create predictive models that accurately forecast the properties of new drug candidates [7, 14–16]. Additionally, in the era of personalized medicine, where drugs can be tailored to individual patients based on their specific genetic and physiological characteristics, the prediction of biopharmaceutical properties has become increasingly vital. Precise prediction of biopharmaceutical properties can aid in the development of personalized drug therapies optimized for individual patients, resulting in better treatment outcomes and improved patient satisfaction. As a result, various AI models for biopharmaceutical property prediction have been developed, showing promising results.

Objectives of the Chapter

The objectives of the chapter are as follows:

(i) To provide an overview of the underlying principles, advantages, and challenges of AI models for biopharmaceutical property prediction;

(ii) To discuss recent advances in ML and AI models, such as deep learning and ensemble models, highlighting their applications in drug discovery and development;

(iii) To examine case studies of AI models for biopharmaceutical property prediction and their success in improving drug development;

(iv) To present the limitations and future challenges in the development and implementation of AI models for biopharmaceutical property prediction;

(v) And, to suggest future research directions that could improve the accuracy and applicability of AI models in drug discovery.

Organization of the Chapter

The rest of the chapter is organized as follows: Section 13.2 covers AI models used in predicting biopharmaceutical properties. Section 13.3 discusses recent advances in AI models for biopharmaceutical property prediction, including deep learning and ensemble models. It also compares different AI models and highlights successful applications. Section 13.4 presents a case study on the successful use of AI models in COVID-19 vaccine development. Section 13.5 critiques current research on the applications of AI for biopharmaceutical property prediction. Section 13.6 examines the potential impact of AI models, identifies challenges and limitations, and suggests future research directions to enhance the accuracy and applicability of AI models in drug discovery. Finally, Section 13.7 concludes the chapter with a future scope.

13.2   AI Models for Biopharmaceutical Property Prediction

AI has rapidly become a buzzword in the tech industry and beyond and is often used interchangeably with terms such as machine learning, deep learning, and data science. While these fields are related, they are not interchangeable, and understanding the differences and correlations between them is important [10–12]. This section explores the definitions of these terms, their similarities, and their differences to provide a clear understanding of each field's unique contribution to the development of intelligent systems.

As demonstrated in Figure 13.2, AI is a broad field that encompasses a range of techniques and technologies aimed at creating machines that can perform tasks that typically require human intelligence, such as visual perception, speech recognition, decision-making, and language translation. ML is a subset of AI that involves the use of algorithms and statistical models to enable machines to improve their performance on a task based on data inputs without being explicitly programmed. In other words, ML algorithms enable machines to learn from data and improve their performance over time. Deep learning is a type of ML that uses artificial neural networks to learn from data. These neural networks are composed of layers of interconnected nodes that can identify patterns in data inputs and make predictions based on those patterns. Deep learning has enabled breakthroughs in image and speech recognition, natural language processing, and other fields that involve complex data. Data science is an interdisciplinary field that involves the use of statistical and computational methods to extract insights and knowledge from data. It encompasses a

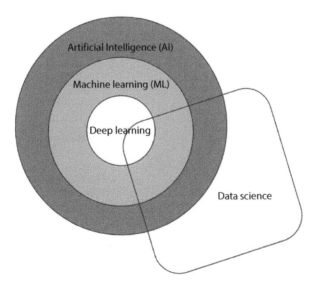

Figure 13.2 The correlations and differences between artificial intelligence, machine learning, deep learning, and data science.

range of techniques, including data mining, ML, and statistical analysis, and involves skills in programming, mathematics, and domain expertise. Thus, AI is the broadest field that aims to create intelligent machines, while ML is a subfield of AI that focuses on developing algorithms that can learn from data. Data science is an interdisciplinary field that combines statistical and computational methods to extract insights from data. While there is a significant overlap between these fields, each has its own unique goals and techniques.

AI models for predicting biopharmaceutical properties should consider data collection and preparation, feature selection, AI algorithm selection, model validation and evaluation, model interpretation and explainability, and integration with experimental methods [17, 18]. These processes are essential for developing accurate and reliable AI models. Figure 13.3 demonstrates that the process involves using ML and deep learning algorithms to analyze data on biopharmaceutical properties and make predictions based on patterns in the data.

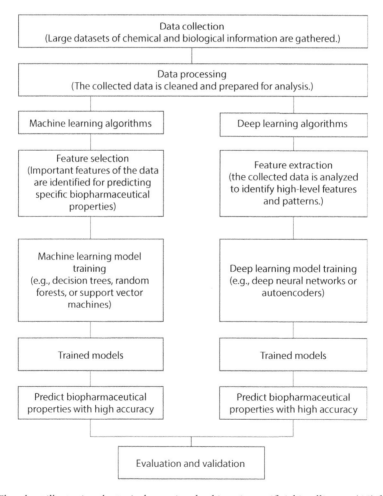

Figure 13.3 Flowchart illustrating the typical steps involved in using artificial intelligence (AI) for biopharmaceutical property prediction, including data collection, preprocessing, algorithm selection, model training, optimization, validation, and deployment.

Data collection is the first step, and it involves gathering data on the properties of bio-pharmaceuticals, such as their chemical structure, biological activity, pharmacokinetics, toxicity, and other relevant properties. The data can come from various sources, such as the literature, databases, and experimental studies [19]. The collected data need to be pre-processed to ensure that they are suitable for analysis by ML algorithms. This involves tasks such as data cleaning, normalization, feature selection, and data augmentation.

After data preprocessing, the appropriate ML algorithm for the specific prediction task needs to be selected. The choice of algorithm will depend on the type of data, the size of the dataset, and the prediction task. Common ML algorithms used for biopharmaceutical property prediction include random forests, support vector machines, and neural networks [19, 20]. Once the algorithm has been selected, the model needs to be trained using the preprocessed data. During training, the algorithm learns to recognize patterns in the data and make predictions based on those patterns.

Model performance is evaluated using a validation dataset and measured using metrics such as accuracy, precision, and recall. The model may need to be optimized to improve its performance. This can involve adjusting hyperparameters, changing the model architecture, or adding new features to the dataset. Once the model has been trained and optimized, it is validated using a test dataset to ensure that it can accurately predict the properties of new biopharmaceuticals.

Finally, the model is deployed for use in real-world applications, such as drug discovery or toxicity prediction. The model can be integrated into software tools, web applications, or other platforms to provide predictions and insights to researchers and developers [8]. Overall, following these steps is crucial for developing AI models that are accurate, reliable, and interpretable.

13.2.1 Types of ML Models for Biopharmaceutical Property Prediction

ML algorithms have emerged as powerful tools for biopharmaceutical property prediction. ML algorithms can learn from patterns and relationships within the data without being explicitly programmed, making them an ideal approach for analyzing large and complex datasets [7, 19, 21]. Supervised learning and unsupervised learning are the two main categories of machine learning models used for predicting biopharmaceutical properties (Figure 13.4) [8, 20, 22]. However, reinforcement learning is not typically used for biopharmaceutical property prediction because it is better suited for tasks that involve agent–environment interaction and immediate feedback, such as robotics, game theory, and self-driving vehicles. In contrast, biopharmaceutical property prediction involves analyzing and predicting properties based on data without direct interaction with an environment. Therefore, other types of machine learning models, such as supervised and unsupervised learning, are more appropriate for biopharmaceutical property prediction.

Supervised learning models are applicable when labeled datasets are available, indicating that the input data are already matched with the corresponding output data (i.e., the property of interest). The primary objective of supervised learning is to develop a model that can precisely predict the output based on new input data that are unseen. In biopharmaceutical property prediction, supervised learning models are usually employed for predicting characteristics such as toxicity, solubility, and bioavailability. Examples of supervised learning models include decision trees, random forests, support vector machines, and Bayesian networks.

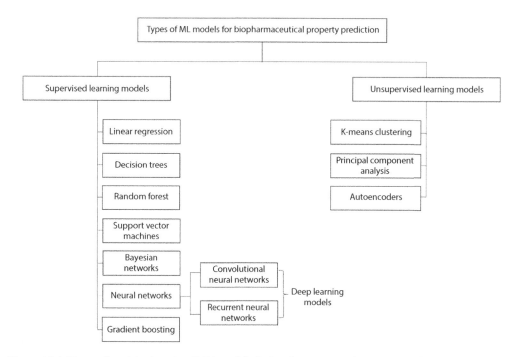

Figure 13.4 Types of machine learning (ML) models for biopharmaceutical property prediction: supervised learning and unsupervised learning.

On the other hand, unsupervised learning models are used when input data are unlabeled or there is no known output. The objective of unsupervised learning is to detect patterns or structures within the input data without any previous knowledge of the output. In biopharmaceutical property prediction, unsupervised learning models are utilized to identify groups of compounds with comparable properties or to decrease the dimensionality of input data. Examples of unsupervised learning models include K-means clustering, principal component analysis (PCA), and autoencoders. Both supervised and unsupervised learning models have advantages and limitations, and their preference depends on the type of problem and the availability and quality of data—for instance, supervision may be constrained by the quality of the labels or the bias in the data. Unsupervised learning models can be used when there are no labeled data available or when the relationship between the input and output is not well defined, but they may suffer from a lack of interpretability and generalization to new data.

13.2.1.1   Supervised Learning Models

1) Linear regression
One of the most commonly used supervised learning models is linear regression. Linear regression models predict continuous numerical values, such as biopharmaceutical properties, based on relevant input features. In machine learning, regression models establish a relationship between a dependent variable (also known as the target or outcome variable) and one or more independent variables (also known as features or predictors).

The model assumes a linear relationship between the input features and the output property and estimates the coefficients of a linear equation that best represents this relationship by minimizing the difference between predicted and actual output values in the training dataset.

The relationship between data points and the regression line in a regression model is crucial to understanding the accuracy of the model's predictions. As shown in Figure 13.5, the regression line is a line that best fits the data points in a scatter plot, representing the relationship between the independent and dependent variables. The regression line is created using a mathematical algorithm that minimizes the distance between the line and the actual data points. This process is known as "fitting" the data. The line represents the best estimate of the relationship between the variables based on the observed data.

Once trained, the model can predict the output property of new data by inputting the values into the linear equation. If the new data point is close to the regression line, the model's prediction is likely to be accurate. However, if the data point is far from the regression line, the prediction may be less accurate. The accuracy of the regression model depends on the quality of the data used to create the model. The more data points used to create the model, the more accurate it is likely to be. Additionally, the quality of the data is important. If the data are noisy or contain outliers, the regression line may not accurately represent the true relationship between the variables, and the model's predictions may be less accurate. Although linear regression is simple and effective, care must be taken to select appropriate input features to avoid overfitting or underfitting. It can be extended to more complex models, such as polynomial regression or multiple linear regression.

2) Decision trees

Decision trees are a type of ML algorithm that can be employed for biopharmaceutical property prediction. They use a tree-like structure consisting of a sequence of binary decisions to predict the target variable based on input feature values. Decision trees are known for their easy interpretability and visualization. They can be represented graphically, with each node denoting a decision based on a specific molecular feature and each branch representing the

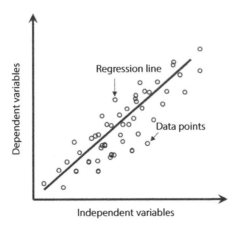

Figure 13.5 Linear regression in machine learning for predicting biopharmaceutical properties.

possible outcomes of that decision. This graphical representation enables researchers to comprehend how the model is making predictions and which molecular features are most influential for predicting a particular property. Moreover, decision trees can manage both categorical and continuous input features, making them an appropriate choice for biopharmaceutical property prediction, where there could be various types of molecular features to consider—for instance, Leski *et al.* [22] applied the RuleFit algorithm, a decision tree ML algorithm, to determine the top attributes that define the specificity of degenerate crRNAs to elicit collateral nuclease activity. The algorithm takes into account the total number of mismatches (0–4) as well as the space of mismatches and their proximity to the 5′ end of the spacer. By analyzing these attributes, RuleFit can identify which crRNAs are most likely to be effective in detecting diverse RNA targets. Despite their advantages, decision trees have some limitations when used for biopharmaceutical property prediction—for instance, they are prone to overfitting, where the model learns to fit the training data too closely and performs poorly on new, unseen data. Additionally, decision trees may encounter difficulties in dealing with nonlinear relationships between input features and output predictions.

3) Random forests

Random forests are an extension of decision trees that utilize an ensemble of decision trees instead of a single decision tree to make predictions. A random forest can be trained on a dataset of molecular structures and their associated properties. The random forest algorithm generates multiple decision trees based on different subsets of the data and combines their predictions to make a final prediction for a new chemical compound. Compared to a single decision tree, random forests are less prone to overfitting, as they create multiple decision trees based on different subsets of the data. This approach enables a random forest to capture a broader range of patterns in the data and produce more accurate predictions on new, unseen data [20]. However, random forests can be computationally expensive and require more resources than a single decision tree. Additionally, random forests can struggle with extrapolation, which is when the model performs poorly on data that fall outside the range of the training data.

4) Support vector machines

Support vector machines (SVMs) are based on the idea of finding a hyperplane that separates the data into different classes, such as compounds with high or low solubility. An SVM can be trained on a dataset of molecular structures and their associated properties. The SVM algorithm finds the hyperplane that best separates the compounds with high solubility from those with low solubility and uses this hyperplane to make predictions about the solubility of new chemical compounds. The advantages of SVMs are that they are effective in handling high-dimensional input data and can handle both linear and nonlinear relationships between the input features and output predictions. SVMs can also be used for both classification and regression tasks, making them versatile for biopharmaceutical property prediction [23]. Nevertheless, a limitation of SVMs is that they can be sensitive to the choice of hyperparameters, such as the kernel function used to transform the data into a higher-dimensional space and the regularization parameter that controls the balance between model complexity and overfitting. Additionally, SVMs can be computationally expensive for large datasets.

5) Bayesian networks

Bayesian networks represent a probabilistic graphical model that can capture complex relationships between different variables. The Bayesian network algorithm uses the principles of Bayesian statistics to model the joint probability distribution of the input variables and output predictions. This allows the algorithm to make predictions about the probability of the studied biopharmaceutical properties having a certain property, given the values of the input variables. Bayesian networks have advantages in that they can handle both discrete and continuous input variables, making them well suited for biopharmaceutical property prediction where there may be a mixture of different types of molecular features to consider [24]. Bayesian networks can also capture complex relationships between variables, such as nonlinear or nonmonotonic relationships, which may be difficult to model using other ML algorithms [25]. However, Bayesian networks can be computationally expensive to train and require large amounts of data to achieve high accuracy. Additionally, the performance of a Bayesian network is highly dependent on the prior probabilities chosen for the variables, which can be difficult to specify accurately in practice.

6) Neural networks

Neural networks are a type of artificial intelligence model that are increasingly being used for biopharmaceutical property prediction. Neural networks consist of layers of interconnected nodes that work together to process input data and generate output predictions. These models are designed to mimic the structure and function of the human brain, with the goal of learning from input data and making accurate predictions on new, unseen data [8, 19]. In the context of biopharmaceutical property prediction, neural networks can be trained on large datasets of chemical structures and their corresponding properties. These models can then be used to predict the properties of new chemical compounds based on their molecular structure. Neural networks can be used to predict a wide range of biopharmaceutical properties [14].

Neural networks have a significant advantage in their ability to capture complex nonlinear relationships between input data and output predictions [26]. Specifically, they can identify subtle correlations between specific molecular features and biopharmaceutical properties that are difficult or even impossible for humans to detect. Additionally, neural networks are capable of making accurate predictions even in the presence of noise and variability in the input data. In the context of biopharmaceutical property prediction, there may be intricate and nonlinear relationships between the chemical structure of a molecule and its biopharmaceutical properties. Traditional statistical methods may not be able to capture these relationships because they often assume linear relationships between the input and output parameters. Neural networks, however, can identify subtle and complex nonlinear correlations, enabling accurate predictions of biopharmaceutical properties for new chemical compounds [26].

However, like any AI model, neural networks have limitations and challenges that must be considered carefully—for example, neural networks can be prone to overfitting, where the model becomes too complex and fits the training data too closely, resulting in poor generalization to new data. Additionally, neural networks can be difficult to interpret, making it challenging to understand how the model makes its predictions. It is also worth noting that training neural networks can be computationally expensive, especially for large datasets with many input features. Despite these challenges, neural networks have shown great promise in predicting biopharmaceutical properties, and ongoing research is focused on improving the performance and interpretability of these models. Like any AI model, careful attention to model design, data quality, and validation procedures is crucial for achieving reliable and accurate predictions.

Deep learning is a subfield of ML that uses multilayered neural networks to model complex relationships in data. Its ability to capture complex patterns and correlations in large and diverse datasets has led to its increasing application in biopharmaceutical property prediction. In this context, deep learning models can be trained on large databases of chemical structures and their associated properties and then used to predict the properties of new chemical compounds based on their molecular structure [18].

One of the main advantages of deep learning is its ability to automatically extract features from raw data, which can be particularly useful in biopharmaceutical property prediction where there may be many complex molecular features to consider. Moreover, deep learning models are highly scalable and can handle large datasets, making them well suited for applications in drug discovery and development. Nonetheless, there are also challenges and limitations associated with deep learning in biopharmaceutical property prediction—for instance, deep learning models can be computationally expensive to train, requiring substantial computing power and time. Additionally, deep learning models can be prone to overfitting, where the model learns to fit the training data too closely and performs poorly on new, unseen data. Some popular neural network algorithms used in pharmaceutical sciences can be summarized in the following details.

6.1) Multilayer perceptron

A multilayer perceptron (MLP) is a type of feedforward neural network that consists of multiple layers of interconnected nodes or neurons. As depicted in Figure 13.6, an MLP architecture typically consists of an input layer, one or more hidden layers, and an output layer. Each layer contains a set of neurons, which are interconnected by weighted connections. The input layer receives input features, which are typically normalized or standardized to ensure that they have a similar scale. The hidden layers perform nonlinear transformations of the input features, while the output layer generates predicted output values. Each neuron in the MLP receives inputs from the previous layer and applies a nonlinear activation function to the weighted sum of those inputs. The activation function introduces nonlinearity to the model, which enables it to learn complex relationships between the input features

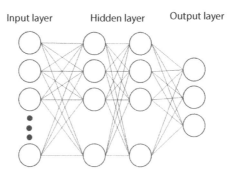

Figure 13.6 The architecture of a multilayer perceptron-based artificial neural network for machine learning.

and the output values. The most commonly used activation functions in MLPs are the sigmoid function, which maps inputs to a range between 0 and 1, and the rectified linear unit (ReLU) function, which returns the input if it is positive and 0 otherwise. Other activation functions, such as the hyperbolic tangent (tanh) function, can also be used. During training, the MLP learns the optimal weights for each connection between the predicted and actual output values. This is typically done using an optimization algorithm such as stochastic gradient descent. The architecture of an MLP can be customized based on the specific problem and data at hand. The number of hidden layers, the number of neurons in each layer, and the choice of activation functions can all be adjusted to optimize the model's performance. However, care must be taken to avoid overfitting the model to the training data by using regularization techniques such as dropout or L1/L2 regularization. MLPs have been used for a wide range of applications in pharmaceutical sciences, such as drug design, toxicity prediction, and protein structure prediction [27]. Navabhatra *et al.* [19] used this technology to predict the behavior of nanostructured lipid carriers containing 5-*O*-caffeoylquinic acid-rich *Cratoxylum formosum* leaf extract for skin application. The significance of using an MLP in this study was that it was a versatile technology that can handle complex and nonlinear relationships related to formulation processes without a prior model option. In other words, the MLP can learn and adapt to the data and problem at hand, making it a powerful tool for modeling complex systems. This flexibility makes MLPs a popular choice in various fields, including pharmaceutical sciences, where complex relationships between variables are common. Therefore, MLPs can provide valuable insights into biopharmaceutical property predictions and other related areas.

6.2) Convolutional neural networks

Convolutional neural networks (CNNs) are highly effective in processing data with a grid-like topology, such as images, audio signals, or even 2D molecular structures. CNNs are designed to automatically learn and extract features from input data without the need for manual feature engineering. The basic building block of a CNN is the convolutional layer, which applies a set of filters (also known as kernels) to the input data to extract features at different locations in the data. The filters are typically small matrices of weights that are learned during training to detect specific patterns in the input data. In biopharmaceutical property prediction, CNNs have been used to analyze various types of images, including protein structures, cell images, and histopathological images. In protein structure prediction, CNNs can be used to identify specific structural motifs and predict the stability and binding affinity of protein–ligand complexes. In cell image analysis, CNNs can be used to identify different cell types and structures, as well as detect abnormal cells or structures that may be indicative of disease. In histopathological image analysis, CNNs can be used to classify tissue samples and detect cancerous cells or tumors.

As shown in Figure 13.7, the architecture of a CNN typically consists of multiple convolutional layers, followed by one or more connected layers. The convolutional layers extract features from the input data by convolving the input data with a set of learned filters. The resulting feature maps are then passed through a nonlinear activation function, such as the ReLU, to introduce nonlinearity into the model. The fully connected layers then take the extracted features and use them to make predictions about the input data.

CNNs can also be augmented with additional layers, such as pooling layers and dropout layers, to improve their performance and reduce overfitting. Pooling layers downsample the

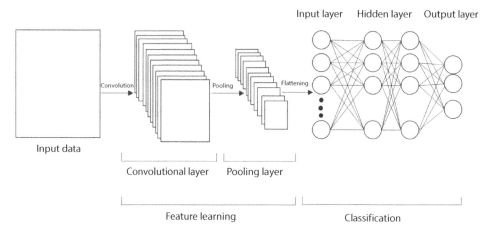

Figure 13.7 The architecture of the convolutional neural network for machine learning.

feature maps by taking the maximum or average value within a certain region of the map, reducing the dimensionality of the data and increasing computational efficiency. Dropout layers randomly drop out a certain percentage of the neurons in the network during training, preventing the network from relying too heavily on any one feature and reducing overfitting [28]. Finally, the output is passed through fully connected layers that perform classification or regression tasks [29]. CNNs have found widespread use in various applications in the pharmaceutical sciences, such as virtual screening, drug design, and protein structure prediction. They have been used to predict drug compound activity based on molecular structure and to identify potential drug targets based on protein structure information. CNNs have also been employed to screen large chemical databases for drug candidates with high affinity and selectivity for specific protein targets [28–30].

6.3) Recurrent neural networks

Recurrent neural networks (RNNs) are specialized for processing sequential data and can handle input sequences of variable lengths, such as molecular sequences or time series data. RNNs have the unique capability to maintain a memory of previous inputs through recurrent connections, which enables them to capture dependencies between input data at different time steps. This makes them suitable for modeling sequential data where the current output depends on previous inputs [31]. The basic architecture of an RNN consists of a single recurrent neuron that is connected to itself as well as to the input and output layers (Figure 13.8). This neuron receives an input vector at each time step, which is combined with its previous state using a set of weights. The resulting weighted sum is then passed through an activation function to produce the current output and update the state of the neuron. In practice, RNNs are often implemented using a variant called the long short-term memory (LSTM) network, which addresses some of the issues with the basic RNN architecture, such as the vanishing gradient problem. LSTMs have a more complex architecture that includes multiple recurrent neurons with gating mechanisms that regulate the flow of information through the network. These gates allow LSTMs to selectively remember or forget previous inputs based on their relevance to the current output, enabling them to capture

Input layer   Hidden layer   Output layer

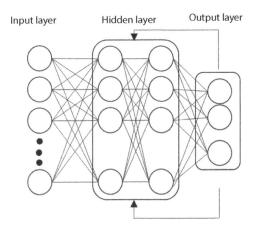

Figure 13.8 The architecture of recurrent neural networks for machine learning.

long-term dependencies in sequential data. In drug discovery, RNNs have been used to model the interactions between drug molecules and target proteins as well as predict the binding affinity and potency of candidate compounds. RNNs have also been used in gene expression analysis, where they can be used to model the complex regulatory networks that govern gene expression patterns. By analyzing large-scale gene expression datasets, RNNs can help identify new drug targets and biomarkers and shed light on the underlying biological mechanisms that contribute to disease [31].

Thus, the abovementioned algorithms work by identifying patterns in large datasets of molecular structures and their corresponding properties and using these patterns to make predictions on new, unseen data. One advantage of ML algorithms is that they are generally easier to interpret than more complex models such as neural networks and deep learning—for example, decision trees can be visualized to show how the model makes predictions based on specific molecular features. However, there are also limitations and challenges associated with ML algorithms for biopharmaceutical property prediction—for example, these models can be sensitive to the quality and completeness of the input data and can be prone to overfitting if the model is too complex or the training dataset is too small. Additionally, ML models can struggle with nonlinear relationships between input features and output predictions [19]. Despite these challenges, ML algorithms are a valuable tool for biopharmaceutical property prediction, and ongoing research is focused on developing new algorithms and improving their performance and accuracy. Ultimately, the successful application of ML in drug discovery and development will require careful attention to model design, data quality, and validation procedures.

13.2.1.2   Unsupervised Learning Models

1) K-means clustering
K-means clustering is used for clustering and grouping similar data points based on their similarities. The algorithm iteratively assigns data points to one of the K clusters, where K is a predefined number of clusters. The assignment is based on the similarity between the data

points and the centroids (center points) of the clusters. The centroids are updated in each iteration based on the mean of the data points assigned to the clusters. The algorithm stops when the centroids no longer change or after a predefined number of iterations. Once the clusters are formed, the properties of the compounds within each cluster can be analyzed to identify similarities and differences [19]. K-means clustering is a widely used unsupervised learning algorithm for biopharmaceutical property prediction, but it requires the selection of an appropriate number of clusters (K) and careful consideration of the input features to avoid irrelevant or noisy data.

2) Principal component analysis
PCA is commonly used for reducing the dimensionality of large datasets. In biopharmaceutical property prediction, PCA can be applied to identify patterns or structures in the data, which can help to understand the underlying relationships between input features and properties. PCA works by transforming the original dataset into a new coordinate system that maximizes the variance of the data along each axis. This new coordinate system is defined by a set of principal components, which are linear combinations of the original features. The first principal component represents the direction in which the data vary the most, while the second principal component is orthogonal to the first and represents the second highest variation. The number of principal components retained after the transformation is typically chosen based on the amount of variance in the data that needs to be explained. By reducing the dimensionality of the dataset, PCA can help to identify the most important features that contribute to the variation in the data and to visualize the data in a lower-dimensional space. PCA is a powerful tool for exploring large datasets and identifying trends and patterns that may be useful for predicting biopharmaceutical properties. However, it is important to keep in mind that the interpretation of the principal components may not always be straightforward and that the relationship between the input features and the properties may not be fully captured by the reduced dataset.

3) Autoencoders
Autoencoders are a type of neural network that is commonly used for compressing and decompressing data. In this network, the encoder component reduces the dimensionality of the input data and creates a compressed representation, while the decoder component reconstructs the original input data from the compressed representation [32]. The encoder network comprises one or more hidden layers that map the input data to a smaller representation, while the decoder network comprises one or more hidden layers that map the compressed representation back to the original input space. The weights of the network are adjusted to minimize the reconstruction error between the input data and its reconstruction during training [33, 34]. Autoencoders have been utilized in various applications in the pharmaceutical sciences, such as drug design and molecular property prediction [33]—for instance, autoencoders have been employed to create new drug molecules with desired properties. By encoding a vast dataset of known molecules, the network can learn to generate new molecules with similar properties. Moreover, autoencoders have been utilized to forecast the properties of molecules based on their structural features, such as their molecular weight, polarity, and bioactivity [34].

13.2.2   Data Sources for AI Models

One critical factor in developing accurate AI models for biopharmaceutical property prediction is the availability of high-quality data sources [35]. The following are some common data sources used for AI models in biopharmaceutical property prediction:

1) Experimental data
Experimental data from laboratory experiments, such as molecular properties and drug–target interactions, are often used as training data for AI models. These data can come from various sources, including high-throughput screening, *in vitro* assays, and clinical trials [19, 26].

2) Public databases
Several public databases provide large datasets for use in AI models. These include molecular structure databases, gene expression data, and drug–target interactions, among others. Examples of public databases include PubChem (https://pubchem.ncbi.nlm.nih.gov/), ChemBL (https://www.ebi.ac.uk/chembl/), and Gene Expression Omnibus (GEO) (https://www.ncbi.nlm.nih.gov/geo/).

3) Literature data
The scientific literature provides a wealth of information about molecular properties, drug targets, and other relevant data for AI models. Researchers can use text mining techniques to extract this information from the literature and use it to train AI models.

4) Computational simulations
Computational simulations, such as molecular dynamics simulations and quantum mechanics calculations, can provide valuable data for AI models. These simulations can provide detailed information about molecular structures and properties that may be difficult or expensive to obtain experimentally.

5) Electronic health records
Electronic health records (EHRs) contain information about patient health outcomes and drug treatments. These data can be used to train AI models to predict drug efficacy and toxicity.

It is important to note that using multiple data sources can help improve the accuracy and robustness of AI models in biopharmaceutical property prediction. However, it is essential to carefully evaluate and preprocess the data to ensure its quality and relevance to the research question at hand.

13.2.3   Popularly Used Software to Develop AI Models

These are just a few examples of commercial software that is popularly used to develop AI for pharmaceutical science applications. Some of the commercial software that are popularly used to develop AI for pharmaceutical science applications are detailed below. Other popular software include R, Python, TensorFlow, and Caffe. The choice of software depends on the specific application and the expertise of the user.

KNIME is a software platform that offers a graphical user interface (GUI) for developing workflows in data analytics, ML, and AI. It is designed to simplify the process of building predictive models and performing data analysis by providing an intuitive visual interface. The platform offers a wide range of prebuilt nodes, which are functional blocks that can be combined to perform various tasks, such as data cleaning, feature extraction, and model building. These nodes can be easily integrated with a variety of data sources, including public databases, experimental data, and literature data, to create comprehensive workflows for biopharmaceutical property prediction. The flexibility and versatility of KNIME are significant advantages that set it apart as a leading platform for data analytics, ML, and AI. KNIME supports a wide range of programming languages, including R and Python, which allows users to incorporate custom scripts and algorithms into their workflows. In addition, KNIME offers extensive documentation and an active community of users who share knowledge and provide support. The platform has proven useful in various pharmaceutical applications, including drug discovery and development, where it can be used to build predictive models for identifying potential drug targets, optimizing drug candidate properties, and predicting drug toxicity. KNIME's ability to handle large and diverse datasets, along with its flexibility and ease of use, makes it a valuable tool for researchers in the pharmaceutical industry.

13.2.3.1   SAS

SAS is a powerful and widely used commercial software suite that provides a comprehensive range of tools for data analytics, ML, and AI. SAS is particularly well suited for handling large, complex datasets and is widely used in the pharmaceutical industry for a variety of applications. One key advantage of SAS is its ability to handle multiple data sources and types, including structured, unstructured, and semistructured data. This makes it an ideal platform for data preparation, cleaning, and manipulation, as well as for performing exploratory data analysis and statistical modeling. SAS provides a wide range of statistical analysis tools and techniques, including regression analysis, hypothesis testing, and Bayesian analysis. These tools are particularly valuable for analyzing clinical trial data, where complex statistical models are often required to analyze the results. SAS also offers a range of ML algorithms, including decision trees, neural networks, and support vector machines, which can be used for predictive modeling in drug discovery and development. In addition to its analytical capabilities, SAS also offers robust tools for data visualization and reporting, which can be used to communicate insights and results to stakeholders. The SAS has also been widely used for regulatory compliance in the pharmaceutical industry, where it is used to analyze safety and efficacy data and generate regulatory reports.

13.2.3.2   MATLAB

MATLAB is a programming language and development environment that provides an extensive range of toolboxes and functions for numerical computation, data analysis, visualization, and ML. The platform's ML capabilities are particularly noteworthy, with a wide range of algorithms and techniques available for use, including deep learning, reinforcement learning, and computer vision. MATLAB is a popular tool in the pharmaceutical industry, with applications in drug discovery, toxicity prediction, and personalized medicine. In drug discovery, MATLAB can be used to develop predictive models for identifying potential drug targets and optimizing drug candidate properties. In toxicity prediction, MATLAB can be used to analyze large datasets and build models for predicting the potential toxicity of compounds. In personalized medicine, MATLAB can be used to analyze genomic data and develop models for predicting a patient's response to a particular treatment.

13.2.3.3   IBM Watson

IBM Watson is a powerful and versatile cloud-based AI platform that offers a range of tools and services to support various aspects of the pharmaceutical industry. Its natural language processing capabilities allow for efficient analysis of large volumes of unstructured data, such as scientific literature and electronic health records. Watson's ML algorithms can be used for tasks such as drug discovery, identifying potential drug targets, and predicting drug efficacy and toxicity. Additionally, IBM Watson has prebuilt models that enable quick and accurate predictions of drug interactions and adverse events, which can help improve patient safety in clinical trials and postmarket surveillance. The platform also offers a range of APIs and developer tools, allowing for customized solutions to be built on top of its existing infrastructure.

13.2.3.4   Accelrys

Accelrys is a comprehensive and commercial software suite that provides scientific informatics solutions for various areas, including drug discovery, biotechnology, and materials science. The platform is known for its wide range of molecular modeling, simulation, and analysis tools that can be used to support pharmaceutical research and development. Accelrys is widely used in the pharmaceutical industry to optimize drug formulations, facilitate regulatory compliance, and accelerate drug discovery and development. Additionally, the platform is equipped with a range of prebuilt models and workflows that can be customized to meet specific research needs, making it a valuable tool for pharmaceutical scientists and researchers.

13.2.4   Applications of AI Models for Predicting Specific Biopharmaceutical Properties

In recent years, AI has emerged as a promising tool for predicting biopharmaceutical properties. With the help of ML algorithms, AI models can be trained to analyze large amounts of data and identify patterns that can be used to predict specific properties of biopharmaceuticals [8]. Below are some of the applications of AI models for predicting specific biopharmaceutical properties.

13.2.4.1   Drug Solubility Prediction

Drug solubility is a critical factor that affects drug delivery and bioavailability. Poorly soluble drugs can have limited absorption and bioavailability, resulting in inadequate therapeutic effects. On the other hand, highly soluble drugs can have rapid absorption and distribution, leading to potential toxicity or adverse effects. AI models use ML algorithms to analyze the chemical structure of a drug and predict its solubility in different solvents. This approach can save time and resources compared to traditional experimental methods for solubility determination. Moreover, AI models can consider a wide range of chemical properties that can affect solubility, such as hydrogen bonding, molecular weight, and polarity. By predicting drug solubility, AI models can guide drug formulation strategies, such as selecting appropriate solvents, cosolvents, or surfactants to improve solubility and bioavailability [36].

13.2.4.2 Protein-Ligand Binding Affinity Prediction

AI models can predict the binding affinity between a protein and a ligand by analyzing their structures and physicochemical properties. ML algorithms can learn from large datasets of protein-ligand complexes and identify the features that contribute to the binding affinity, such as hydrogen bonds, hydrophobic interactions, and electrostatic interactions. AI models can accurately and efficiently predict the binding affinity of protein-ligand complexes by utilizing relevant features such as structure, physicochemical properties, and electrostatic interactions. The application of AI models to predict protein-ligand binding affinity has several implications for drug discovery and development—for instance, AI models can be used to screen large libraries of compounds and identify potential drug candidates that have high binding affinity and specificity to the target protein. Additionally, they can optimize the properties of existing drugs by predicting the binding affinity of new analogs and derivatives. Moreover, AI models can provide mechanistic insights into the mode of action of drugs by identifying the key interactions between the drug and the target protein [37].

13.2.4.3 Stability Prediction

The stability of biopharmaceuticals is a critical parameter that can affect their efficacy and safety. Biopharmaceuticals are complex molecules that can be affected by various environmental factors, such as temperature, pH, and agitation. Therefore, predicting the stability of biopharmaceuticals under different conditions is essential for designing stable formulations that can maintain their integrity and activity during storage and administration. AI models can predict the stability of biopharmaceuticals by analyzing their structures, physicochemical properties, and environmental factors. By learning from large datasets of biopharmaceuticals that have undergone stability testing under various conditions, ML algorithms can identify features that contribute to their stability, such as electrostatic interactions, hydrophobicity, and disulfide bonds. Utilizing these features, AI models can predict the stability of newly developed biopharmaceuticals accurately and rapidly under different environmental conditions. The application of AI models in this field has significant implications for drug development and manufacturing [38]—for instance, AI models can optimize the formulation of biopharmaceuticals by predicting the stability of different excipients and additives. They can also be used to screen for potential degradation pathways and identify strategies to prevent or mitigate degradation. In addition, AI models enable real-time monitoring of biopharmaceutical stability during manufacturing and storage, allowing for early detection of stability issues and ensuring product quality and safety.

For example, Narayanan *et al.* [38] employed ML algorithms to expedite the design of biopharmaceutical formulations and emphasized the need to optimize the stability and developability characteristics of biological drugs, which can be influenced by variables such as protein sequence and buffer composition. Authors introduced the Bayesian optimization algorithm as a robust tool for forecasting the performance of various formulations based on previous experimental data, thus reducing the number of experiments required to identify optimal formulations. Their study's primary conclusion was that ML algorithms can notably hasten the design process and enhance drug development efficiency.

13.2.4.4 *Aggregation Prediction*

Aggregation is a common problem that can occur in biopharmaceuticals, such as therapeutic proteins and monoclonal antibodies, during manufacturing, storage, and administration. Aggregation can result in reduced efficacy, immunogenicity, and safety of biopharmaceuticals and cause adverse reactions in patients. Therefore, predicting and mitigating the aggregation of biopharmaceuticals is essential for their development and clinical use. AI models are capable of predicting the likelihood of biopharmaceuticals to aggregate by analyzing their sequence, structure, and physicochemical properties. Through the use of ML algorithms, patterns and features that may influence the aggregation of biopharmaceuticals, including hydrophobicity, charge, and conformational stability, can be identified. The prediction of the aggregation propensity of biopharmaceuticals using AI models is essential in selecting and optimizing biopharmaceutical candidates that possess high stability and low aggregation propensity [39].

Furthermore, AI models can aid in the design of strategies to prevent the aggregation of biopharmaceuticals, such as the optimization of formulation conditions, the use of stabilizing excipients, or the modification of the sequence or structure of the biopharmaceutical to enhance stability. Lai *et al.* [39] reported the use of ML to predict therapeutic antibody aggregation rates and viscosity at high concentrations (150 mg/mL). The models developed using ML can predict antibody stability, which is essential for pharmaceutical development. The study also highlighted the use of ML to identify the most relevant features for aggregation and viscosity. The main findings of the study suggested that ML can accurately predict antibody stability, and larger datasets can improve the predictive models. However, due to the limited availability of high-concentration therapeutic antibody aggregation and viscosity data, further research is needed in this area.

13.2.4.5 *Immunogenicity Prediction*

Immunogenicity is a critical factor that can affect the safety and efficacy of biopharmaceuticals. Biopharmaceuticals, such as therapeutic antibodies, recombinant proteins, and gene therapies, are often derived from biological sources and can be recognized as foreign by the patient's immune system. This recognition can trigger an immune response that can neutralize or clear the biopharmaceutical, reducing its therapeutic effects or causing adverse reactions [40]. AI models are capable of predicting the immunogenicity of biopharmaceuticals through the analysis of their sequence, structure, and interaction with the immune system. By utilizing ML algorithms, these models can identify crucial patterns and features that may impact the immunogenicity of biopharmaceuticals, including T-cell and B-cell epitopes, antigen presentation, and posttranslational modifications [41]. This predictive ability can provide valuable guidance in selecting and optimizing biopharmaceutical candidates that possess low immunogenicity and high efficacy [42]. Additionally, AI models can assist in designing strategies to reduce the immunogenicity of biopharmaceuticals. Such strategies may involve modifications to the sequence or structure of the biopharmaceutical, the use of immunosuppressive drugs, or the selection of patients with low immunogenicity risk profiles [43].

13.3 Recent Advances in AI Models for Biopharmaceutical Property Prediction

Based on recent literature reviews and surveys, it is evident that research in the field of AI models for biopharmaceutical property prediction is rapidly growing and evolving. Many recent studies have been dedicated to developing and refining AI models for predicting specific biopharmaceutical properties, while others have explored the use of ML techniques for drug discovery and repurposing. There is also a growing interest in multitask learning approaches, which can simultaneously predict multiple biopharmaceutical properties, as well as the use of transfer learning to improve model generalizability. Additionally, researchers are increasingly focusing on incorporating biological data into AI models, such as gene expression data and protein structure data, to better capture the complex interactions between drugs and biological systems.

13.3.1 Deep Learning and Ensemble Models

Deep learning and ensemble models have emerged as promising approaches for biopharmaceutical property prediction. Deep learning is a subfield of ML that uses neural networks with multiple layers to extract complex features from large datasets. Ensemble models, on the other hand, combine the predictions of multiple models to improve accuracy and reduce the risk of overfitting [35].

One popular deep learning approach for biopharmaceutical property prediction is the use of convolutional neural networks (CNNs). CNNs are particularly well suited for processing complex inputs such as molecular structures, as they can learn to recognize important features and patterns within the data. Several studies have shown that CNNs can accurately predict a range of biopharmaceutical properties, including solubility, permeability, and toxicity [36]. Another promising approach is the use of recurrent neural networks (RNNs), which are designed to process sequential data such as time-series or text data. In the context of biopharmaceutical property prediction, RNNs have been used to predict the bioactivity of compounds and the likelihood of drug–drug interactions [44]. Ensemble models, such as random forests and gradient boosting machines, have also been successfully used for biopharmaceutical property prediction. These models combine the predictions of multiple simpler models to improve accuracy and reduce the risk of overfitting. Ensemble models are particularly useful when dealing with complex datasets that contain many features, as they can help identify the most important features for predicting a given property.

Deep learning and ensemble models are powerful approaches for predicting biopharmaceutical properties. These models need careful tuning and validation to ensure their accuracy and reliability. Nonetheless, they have the potential to significantly improve drug discovery and development efforts. They can predict the properties of not only monoclonal antibodies and therapeutic proteins but also small molecules, peptides, and other biologics. By accurately predicting these properties, AI models can help select and optimize potential drug candidates, reduce the time and cost of drug development, and increase the chances of success in clinical trials. Furthermore, these models can be employed for drug repurposing, enabling the identification of new uses for existing drugs on the basis of their predicted properties.

13.3.2   Comparison of Different AI Models

To identify the most suitable AI model for a biopharmaceutical property prediction task, it is essential to compare different models and understand their strengths and limitations. Popular commercial AI models used for this purpose include Schrödinger's Maestro Suite, Biovia's Discovery Studio, and Genedata's Screener, which use a combination of ML algorithms such as support vector machines, random forests, and deep neural networks. However, it is crucial to evaluate these models based on their accuracy, user-friendliness, speed and scalability, cost, transparency, and interpretability. Table 13.1 summarizes the strengths and weaknesses of each model, and researchers should choose a model that best meets their project's specific needs.

13.3.2.1   Schrödinger's Maestro Suite

Schrödinger's Maestro Suite is a comprehensive software platform that offers a wide range of computational tools for drug discovery and biopharmaceutical research. It comprises a suite of tools for molecular visualization, simulation, and analysis, along with advanced computational algorithms for drug design and biopharmaceutical property prediction. One of its key features is the Schrödinger suite of molecular dynamics (MD) simulation tools that enable researchers to simulate the behavior and movement of molecules in different environments, such as in solution or in complex with a target protein. These simulations can predict properties such as binding affinities, binding kinetics, and protein–ligand interactions, which are crucial in drug discovery. Moreover, the Maestro suite provides several tools for structure-based drug design that utilize the 3D structure of a protein target to design small molecules that can bind to it. These tools help optimize the binding affinity, selectivity, and pharmacokinetic properties of potential drug candidates and predict the absorption, distribution, metabolism, excretion, and toxicity (ADMET) properties of compounds. Additionally, the Maestro suite offers a host of other advanced computational algorithms for biopharmaceutical property prediction, including homology modeling, virtual screening, and quantum mechanics/molecular mechanics (QM/MM) simulations. Its advanced algorithms and user-friendly interface make it a popular choice for researchers in academia and industry.

Table 13.1 Comparison of the three commercial AI models used for biopharmaceutical property prediction.

Strengths and weaknesses	Commercial AI models		
	Schrödinger's maestro suite	Biovia's discovery studio	Genedata's screener
Accuracy and reliability	Offers high accuracy and reliability due to its use of physics-based modeling combined with ML.	Offers high accuracy and reliability, thanks to its use of a wide range of ML techniques and validated models.	Uses ML algorithms and predictive models that have been validated on large datasets, ensuring high accuracy and reliability.
User-friendliness	Has a user-friendly interface that allows for easy navigation and visualization of results.	Has a similar interface to other software in the Biovia suite, making it easy for researchers familiar with the platform to use.	Has a simple interface that allows for easy data import and export, making it easy to integrate into existing workflows.
Speed and scalability	Provides fast and scalable predictions, thanks to its optimized algorithms and parallel processing capabilities.	Offers fast predictions and can be scaled up to handle large datasets.	Is designed for high-throughput screening and can handle large datasets quickly and efficiently.
Cost	A premium product and can be quite expensive, with licensing fees and support costs.	Similarly priced and may require additional modules or add-ons to access certain features.	Pricing varies based on the specific needs of the user, but it is generally considered more affordable than the other two models.
Transparency and interpretability	Allows users to explore the underlying physics-based models and ML algorithms, providing transparency and interpretability.	Has a similar approach to transparency and interpretability, allowing users to understand how the models are constructed and how predictions are made.	Has limited transparency into the underlying models but provides tools for users to explore the results and identify potential outliers or errors.

13.3.2.2   Biovia's Discovery Studio

Biovia's Discovery Studio is a software platform designed for computational modeling and simulation in drug discovery and biopharmaceutical research. It provides a suite of tools and workflows that enable researchers to study and predict the properties of molecules, proteins, and biological systems. Discovery Studio includes a wide range of computational tools for biopharmaceutical property prediction, such as molecular docking, virtual screening, molecular dynamics simulations, and pharmacophore modeling. These tools can be used to predict properties such as ADMET of potential drug candidates.

In addition, Discovery Studio's intuitive user interface is a standout feature, as it allows researchers to easily perform complex computational workflows. The platform's graphical interface enables users to both construct and visualize molecular structures, while the drag-and-drop workflow builder empowers them to create elaborate computational pipelines without requiring programming expertise. Furthermore, Discovery Studio provides access to an extensive library of scientific databases and literature, which researchers can draw upon to enhance their predictions and analyses. Additionally, the platform has built-in integrations with key scientific databases, including the Protein Data Bank (PDB), which stores structural information for proteins and other macromolecules.

13.3.2.3   Genedata's Screener

Genedata's Screener is a software platform designed for high-throughput screening (HTS) and data analysis in drug discovery and biopharmaceutical research. Its suite of tools and workflows enables researchers to analyze large amounts of screening data quickly and accurately. The platform uses advanced algorithms, such as ML, statistical analysis, and data visualization, to predict properties such as potency, selectivity, and efficacy of potential drug candidates.

Screeners are known for their seamless integration with various laboratory automation and screening technologies, including imaging systems, liquid handlers, and plate readers. This integration allows researchers to automate their screening process, improving accuracy and efficiency. The platform offers advanced visualization and data analysis tools, allowing researchers to quickly identify and prioritize promising drug candidates. Additionally, Screener includes integrated statistical analyses and customizable visualization tools that enable researchers to explore their data from multiple perspectives.

13.3.3   Successful Application of AI Models

The utilization of AI models for the prediction of biopharmaceutical properties has resulted in several successful applications. The following are some examples of such successful applications.

13.3.3.1   G Protein-Coupled Receptor Modeling

Protein-coupled receptors (GPCRs) are pivotal in cell signaling and serve as significant targets for drug development due to their involvement in various physiological processes [45]. Illustrating the structural components and functional characteristics of these essential cell membrane proteins, a GPCR diagram typically encompasses the following key elements (Figure 13.9):

1) Cell membrane: Depicting the lipid bilayer surrounding cells, the diagram represents the cell membrane.
2) GPCR structure: The GPCR is visualized as a transmembrane protein that spans the cell membrane. It comprises a single polypeptide chain that weaves in and out of the membrane, forming seven α-helical segments known as transmembrane domains (TM1–TM7).
3) Extracellular loop: The diagram displays the extracellular loop regions, which connect the transmembrane segments on the outer side of the cell membrane. These loops play a role in ligand binding and receptor activation.
4) Intracellular loop: The diagram also portrays the intracellular loops situated on the inner side of the cell membrane. These loops contribute to GPCR signaling and interact with intracellular signaling molecules.
5) N-terminus and C-terminus: The N-terminus refers to the GPCR region located on the extracellular side of the cell membrane, while the C-terminus is positioned on the intracellular side.
6) Ligand binding site: The diagram identifies the ligand binding site, typically depicted as a pocket formed by the transmembrane domains. This is where specific ligands, such as biopharmaceutical molecules or neurotransmitters, bind to activate GPCRs.
7) G protein coupling: GPCRs are renowned for their interaction with G proteins, which act as molecular switches. The diagram may incorporate a

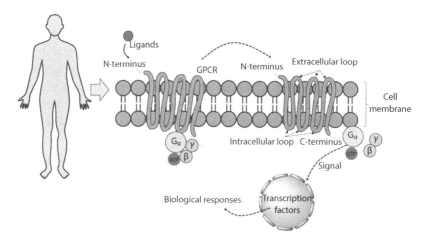

Figure 13.9 Structural components and functional aspects of G protein-coupled receptors (GPCRs). This diagram illustrates the key elements of GPCRs, including the cell membrane, GPCR structure, extracellular and intracellular loops, N-terminus and C-terminus, ligand binding site, G protein coupling, and signaling pathways. GPCRs play a crucial role in cell signaling and are important targets for drug development. The diagram also includes the abbreviations GDP (guanosine diphosphate) and GTP (guanosine triphosphate) to indicate the nucleotides involved in GPCR-associated signaling cascades.

representation of the G protein associated with the intracellular side of the GPCR, illustrating the interaction between the receptor and the G protein.

8) Signaling pathways: GPCR signaling pathways involve the activation of downstream signaling cascades.

These elements in the diagram provide an overview of the structural components and functional aspects of GPCRs, highlighting their role in cellular signaling and their interactions with ligands and G proteins [46, 47].

GPCR modeling involves the use of computational methods to predict the interactions between potential drug candidates and GPCRs. By accurately predicting the binding properties of compounds to GPCRs, researchers can identify potential drug candidates with high binding affinity, selectivity, and efficacy, as well as reduce the cost and time associated with traditional drug discovery methods. GPCR modeling can also help researchers better understand the mechanisms of GPCR activation and signal transduction, which can inform the development of new therapeutic strategies—for example, researchers at the University of California, San Francisco, developed a deep learning model that accurately predicted the binding affinities of compounds to GPCRs (https://mccammon.ucsd.edu/).

13.3.3.2   Protein–Ligand Binding

Protein–ligand binding modeling plays a crucial role in biopharmaceutical prediction, as it enables researchers to comprehend how potential drug compounds interact with their target proteins at a molecular level. This modeling helps researchers simulate and predict the binding properties of potential drug compounds to target proteins, which offers insights into the structure-activity relationships (SARs) of compounds and allows for the optimization of their properties for better drug efficacy and safety. Moreover, the modeling technique can aid in predicting the pharmacokinetics and pharmacodynamics of drug candidates, such as their absorption, distribution, metabolism, and elimination (ADME) properties. This information is indispensable for drug development because it facilitates the selection of the most promising compounds for further testing and enables the optimization of their properties for better therapeutic outcomes—for example, researchers at Pfizer developed an ML model that predicted the binding affinity of compounds to a protein target with high accuracy.

13.3.3.3   Pharmacokinetics Modeling

Pharmacokinetics (PK) modeling is an essential component of biopharmaceutical prediction because it helps researchers understand how drugs are absorbed, distributed, metabolized, and eliminated in the body. Pharmacokinetics models can predict how different factors, such as the route of administration, dosing frequency, and drug formulation, affect drug concentration over time in the blood and other tissues. This information is critical for determining optimal dosing regimens and ensuring that drugs reach their intended targets in the body while minimizing the risk of toxicity—for example, researchers at the University of Manchester developed an ML model that accurately predicted the PK properties of compounds in different species.

13.3.3.4   Toxicity Prediction

Toxicity prediction models can be used to identify compounds that may cause organ toxicity, such as liver or kidney damage, or other side effects, such as cardiovascular or neurological toxicity. These models can also help predict the potential for drug–drug interactions that may cause toxicity when two or more drugs are administered together. The ability to predict toxicity is especially critical in the early stages of drug development, when there is limited information available on the safety of the drug. By identifying potential toxicity issues early, researchers can optimize the drug's properties to reduce the risk of adverse effects and increase the likelihood of success in clinical trials.

13.3.3.5   Drug–Drug Interaction Prediction

Drug–drug interactions (DDIs) occur when the effect of one drug is altered by the presence of another drug in the body. DDIs can lead to adverse reactions, reduced efficacy of a drug, or even toxicity and can be a significant concern for patient safety in the use of multiple medications. In biopharmaceutical prediction, it is important to predict potential DDIs to ensure the safety and efficacy of drug candidates. AI models can be used to predict potential DDIs based on the molecular structures of the drugs and their interactions with enzymes, transporters, and receptors in the body. By predicting potential DDIs at an early stage of drug development, researchers can optimize drug properties to minimize the risk of adverse interactions and improve the safety and efficacy of drug candidates. Additionally, predicting potential DDIs can help identify drug–drug pairs that may require dose adjustment or monitoring and can inform healthcare professionals about the risk of DDIs when prescribing multiple medications to patients—for example, researchers at the University of California, San Diego, developed a deep learning model that accurately predicted drug–drug interactions in a large dataset of drugs.

These are just a few examples of how AI models have been successfully used in biopharmaceutical property prediction. With the increasing availability of large datasets and advances in ML algorithms, AI models are expected to play an increasingly important role in drug discovery and development.

13.4   Case Study: COVID-19 Vaccines

The COVID-19 pandemic has spurred an unprecedented global effort to develop effective vaccines against the SARS-CoV-2 virus [48]. AI has played a crucial role in designing COVID-19 vaccines by accelerating the discovery and development process [49]. The use of AI has enabled scientists to identify vaccine targets more quickly, design vaccine candidates more efficiently, and predict vaccine efficacy more accurately. Several companies around the world have applied AI algorithms to develop COVID-19 vaccines [50]—for example, Moderna is an American biotechnology company that developed one of the first COVID-19 vaccines authorized for emergency use by the US FDA. Moderna used AI algorithms to help design its vaccine by analyzing the virus's genomic sequence and predicting the most effective vaccine components. Pfizer/BioNTech is a collaboration between the American pharmaceutical company Pfizer and the German biotechnology company BioNTech. Companies have used AI algorithms to help design their vaccines by predicting the most effective vaccine components and optimizing vaccine formulation. *Insilico* Medicine is a Hong Kong-based biotechnology company that uses AI algorithms to identify potential drug candidates for COVID-19 treatment. The company used ML algorithms to predict the efficacy of various drugs in treating COVID-19. BenevolentAI is a UK-based pharmaceutical company that uses AI algorithms to identify potential drug candidates for COVID-19 treatment. The company used ML algorithms to analyze vast amounts of scientific literature and identify potential drug targets. Exscientia is a UK-based drug discovery company that uses AI algorithms to identify potential drug candidates for COVID-19 treatment. The company used ML algorithms to analyze vast amounts of scientific data and predict the most effective drug candidates. Atomwise is a US-based drug discovery company that uses AI algorithms to identify potential drug candidates for COVID-19 treatment. The company used ML algorithms to predict the efficacy of various drugs in treating COVID-19.

Based on the above-mentioned factors, some ways in which AI has been used in designing COVID-19 vaccines is summarized in sub-sections from 13.4.1 to 13.4.5.

13.4.1   Identifying Vaccine Targets

AI has been used to analyze the genetic sequence of the SARS-CoV-2 virus and identify potential vaccine targets. The first step in identifying vaccine targets is to analyze the genome of the virus. AI algorithms can analyze the genetic sequence of the virus and identify potential vaccine targets based on the structure and function of viral proteins. ML algorithms can also predict how the virus is likely to evolve over time and identify potential targets that are less likely to mutate. Once potential vaccine targets have been identified, AI algorithms can be used to predict the 3D structure of the viral proteins. Predicting the protein structure is important because it allows researchers to identify the specific regions of the protein that are most likely to elicit an immune response. AI algorithms can be used to simulate the interactions between viral proteins and human immune system proteins. This allows researchers to predict which parts of the viral protein will be most effective at eliciting an immune response. AI algorithms can identify conserved regions of viral proteins that are less likely to mutate over time. Targeting these conserved regions can increase the likelihood that the vaccine will remain effective even as the virus evolves. Finally, AI algorithms can be used to prioritize vaccine targets on the basis of their likelihood of success. ML algorithms can analyze large datasets of immunological data to predict which targets are most likely to elicit a strong immune response and provide protection against the virus.

13.4.2   Designing Vaccine Candidates

AI algorithms can predict the antigenic sites or the parts of the virus that will trigger an immune response and help design vaccine candidates accordingly. Rational vaccine design uses AI to determine the best vaccine formulation to generate a robust immune response. This process involves selecting the most effective antigens, adjuvants, and delivery systems based on computational models that predict the behavior of the vaccine candidate. AI can be used in synthetic biology to design and engineer antigens or other vaccine components. This process involves generating large numbers of potential antigens, selecting the most promising candidates using computational models, and engineering them to optimize their efficacy and safety. AI can be used to predict which parts of a viral protein will be most effective at generating an immune response. This can be used to design peptide-based vaccines that contain short fragments of the viral protein rather than the whole protein. AI can be used to design RNA-based vaccines that contain a genetic code that instructs cells to produce viral proteins. This process involves selecting the most effective viral proteins, predicting the optimal RNA sequence to produce those proteins, and optimizing the delivery system for the RNA vaccine.

13.4.3   Predicting Vaccine Efficacy

AI can be used to model the immune response to a vaccine candidate by predicting how different immune cells and proteins interact with the vaccine components. This can help predict the effectiveness of the vaccine candidate in generating an immune response and protecting against infection. AI algorithms can predict how well antibodies will bind to the viral proteins targeted by the vaccine candidate. This can help predict the strength of the immune response generated by the vaccine and the level of protection it is likely to provide. AI can be used to analyze large datasets of immunological and genetic data to predict how a vaccine candidate is likely to perform in different populations. This can help identify populations that may have a weaker immune response to the vaccine and may require a different vaccine formulation. AI can be used to predict the safety of a vaccine candidate by analyzing large datasets of clinical trial data and adverse event reports. This can help identify potential safety concerns before the vaccine is approved for use.

13.4.4   Optimizing Vaccine Formulations

AI has been used to optimize the formulation of vaccine candidates by predicting how different formulations will affect vaccine stability and efficacy. AI algorithms can predict how different vaccine components, such as antigens and adjuvants, will interact with antibodies in the immune system. By understanding these interactions, scientists can optimize the vaccine formulation to generate the most effective immune response. Rational vaccine design, which uses computational models to predict the behavior of vaccine components, can help scientists optimize vaccine formulation. This process involves selecting the most effective antigens, adjuvants, and delivery systems based on computational models that predict the behavior of the vaccine candidate. AI can be used to screen large numbers of potential vaccine components to identify the most promising candidates. By using ML algorithms to analyze large datasets of screening data, scientists can identify vaccine components that are most likely to generate an effective immune response. AI can be used to optimize the dosing and delivery of vaccines to maximize their effectiveness. By analyzing data on how different vaccine components behave in the body, AI algorithms can predict the most effective dosing and delivery strategies for each vaccine candidate [51].

13.4.5   Accelerating Clinical Trials

AI has been used to accelerate the clinical trial process by predicting which patients are most likely to respond to the vaccine candidate. Earning algorithms can analyze electronic health records and identify patients who meet specific criteria for the trial, such as age, medical history, and current medications. AI can be used to optimize the design of clinical trials, including the selection of endpoints, patient inclusion and exclusion criteria, and statistical analysis plans. By using AI algorithms to analyze large datasets, researchers can identify the most effective trial design that can accelerate the development process. AI can be used to predict trial outcomes based on previous clinical trial data and other factors. This can help researchers identify the most promising drug candidates and optimize the trial design to maximize the chance of success. AI can be used to monitor patient safety during clinical trials by analyzing patient data in real time [52]. This can help identify potential adverse events more quickly and accurately and enable researchers to take appropriate action to ensure patient safety. AI can be used to analyze large amounts of clinical trial data more efficiently and accurately. ML algorithms can identify patterns and trends in the data that may be missed by traditional statistical methods, allowing researchers to identify potential drug efficacy more quickly.

13.5   Current Research in Applications of AI for Biopharmaceuticals

To provide information on the current research in applications of AI for biopharmaceutical property prediction, the Scopus database (https://www.scopus.com) with the following keywords and Boolean operators: "biopharmaceutical" AND "prediction" AND "machine learning" is used. The search is limited to articles published only in English between January 1, 2010 and May 5, 2023. The search returned 36 research articles, 5 review articles, 3 book chapters, and 3 conference papers. Only 36 research articles in the bibliometric analysis are included and rest are excluded.

Bibliometric analysis reveals several key trends in this field. The use of AI in biopharmaceutical property prediction is a growing area of research, with a significant increase in the number of publications in recent years. As shown in Figure 13.10, there has been

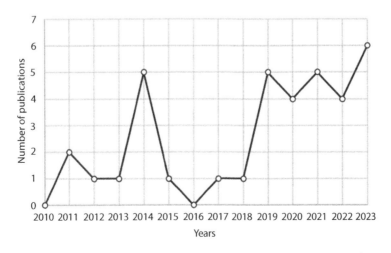

Figure 13.10 Trends in publications based on research articles between 1 January 2010 and 5 May 2023 on biopharmaceutical property prediction using artificial intelligence (AI).

a clear increase in the number of research articles on this topic between 2010 and 2023, with some fluctuations. In 2010, there were no published research articles on the topic, but since then, the number has steadily increased. The number of research articles published in 2011 and 2012 was relatively low, with only two and one, respectively. In 2013, the number remained the same, with only one article published. However, in 2014, there was a significant increase, with five articles published, marking the beginning of an upward trend. In 2015, the number of published articles dropped to one, but in 2016, there were no published articles. However, the upward trend resumed in 2017, with one article published, and in 2018 and 2019, there was a slight increase, with one and five articles published, respectively. The year 2020 saw a significant increase in the number of research articles published on the topic to four articles, and this trend continued in 2021, with five articles published. In 2022, the number of published articles remained relatively stable, with four articles. However, in 2023, there will be a marked increase in the number of published articles, with six articles, indicating that the trend of growth in the number of publications on this topic is continuing. Overall, the trend in publications based on research articles between 2010 and 2023 shows a steady increase with some fluctuations. This indicates a growing interest in the topic and suggests that there will be continued research in this area in the coming years.

Based on the documents' affiliation, the number of documents could be ranked from highest to lowest as follows: Astra Zeneca (three papers), University College of London (three papers), Amgen Incorporated (two papers), Chungbuk National University (two papers), University of Kansas (two papers), UCL School of Pharmacy (two papers), Universitate für Bodenkulfur Wien (two papers), Austrian Center of Industrial Biotechnology (two papers), Satara College of Pharmacy (one paper), and Laboratorios Fox (one paper). By country, the United States had the highest number of documents, followed by China, India, the United Kingdom, Austria, the Czech Republic, South Korea, Sweden, and Argentina.

One of the most notable trends identified in the analysis is the growing use of ML algorithms for predicting biopharmaceutical properties. These algorithms are utilized to predict crucial drug properties, leading to better drug development and performance. The analysis indicates a significant surge in the number of publications focused on using ML for biopharmaceutical property prediction.

Another trend highlighted in the analysis is the increasing use of deep learning algorithms for predicting biopharmaceutical properties. These algorithms are used to analyze large datasets of chemical and biological information and predict drug properties with high accuracy. The analysis shows a steady rise in the number of publications focused on using deep learning for biopharmaceutical property prediction.

Additionally, the analysis reveals a trend toward utilizing AI for predicting drug–target interactions. Researchers are employing ML algorithms to predict which drugs are likely to interact with specific targets, resulting in more efficient drug development. The number of publications in this area is growing steadily, reflecting the growing significance of AI in drug–target interaction prediction.

Finally, the analysis identifies a trend toward using AI for predicting drug toxicity. Researchers are utilizing ML algorithms to predict potential drug toxicity and identify potential safety issues before drugs are approved for use. The number of publications on this topic is also increasing steadily, indicating that AI is becoming an increasingly vital tool in drug safety assessment.

13.6 Future Directions and Challenges

13.6.1 Potential Impact of AI Models

Al models have the potential to significantly impact biopharmaceutical property prediction by enabling faster, more accurate, and more cost-effective drug discovery and development. Biopharmaceutical properties are crucial factors that determine a drug's efficacy and safety profile. However, predicting these properties is a complex and time-consuming process that often relies on expensive experimental methods. Algorithmic models can help overcome these challenges by leveraging large amounts of data to predict biopharmaceutical properties with high accuracy—for example, ML algorithms can be trained on large datasets of chemical structures and their corresponding biopharmaceutical properties to learn the underlying relationships between structure and function. Once trained, these models can be used to predict the properties of new chemical compounds, allowing researchers to quickly identify promising drug candidates and prioritize their development.

One area where AI models have already demonstrated success is in predicting drug solubility. Solubility is a critical factor in drug development, as poorly soluble drugs are often associated with low bioavailability and reduced efficacy. However, predicting solubility can be challenging, as it depends on a wide range of factors, including molecular structure, temperature, and pH. By using ML algorithms to analyze large datasets of chemical structures and their solubility profiles, accurately predicted solubility models can be built for new compounds.

Al models can also be used to predict other biopharmaceutical properties, such as permeability, metabolism, and toxicity—for example, ML algorithms are used to predict a drug's absorption, distribution, metabolism, and excretion (ADME) profile, which is critical for understanding a drug's pharmacokinetics and potential toxicity. By using AI models to predict these properties early in the drug development process, the time and cost of developing new drugs can be reduced, increasing the likelihood of success.

13.6.2 Potential Challenges and Limitations of AI Models

AI models can revolutionize many industries, including biopharmaceuticals, it is important to consider the challenges and limitations that they face. There are several potential challenges and limitations to AI models that should be considered.

13.6.2.1 Data Quality and Bias

Data quality and bias are two significant concerns that can affect the accuracy and reliability of AI models. Poor-quality data can lead to misleading and inaccurate predictions, resulting in incorrect decisions and adverse consequences. One common issue is bias in the data used to train AI models—for example, if a dataset used to train an AI model only includes data from a particular population or region, it may not generalize well to other populations or regions, leading to biased predictions. Incomplete or inaccurate data in the dataset can also contribute to biased predictions, as the AI model learns patterns from incomplete or incorrect data. Therefore, it is essential to perform data cleaning and preprocessing to ensure data quality and reduce bias in AI models. Additionally, using diverse datasets from multiple sources can help overcome the limitations of bias in data and improve the generalization of AI models to different populations and regions.

13.6.2.2   Interpretability

The lack of interpretability in AI models is a significant concern for many researchers, particularly in domains where the decisions made by the model can have significant consequences, such as in biopharmaceuticals. Without interpretability, it can be challenging to identify the factors that drive the model's predictions, and it can be difficult to identify and correct errors. Moreover, a lack of interpretability can make it challenging to trust the predictions made by the model, which is particularly problematic when the model is used to make decisions that can significantly impact human health. Several approaches have been proposed to improve interpretability, such as visualization techniques, simpler models, and model-agnostic approaches such as LIME or SHAP. However, these approaches have limitations, and more research needs to be done to develop more effective methods for improving interpretability in AI models.

13.6.2.3   Overfitting and Underfitting

As AI models and ML continue to become more prevalent, it is important to address the challenges of overfitting and underfitting. These challenges can significantly impact the performance of models. Overfitting occurs when the model is too complex and memorizes the training data, resulting in poor performance on new data. This can be prevented by using techniques such as regularization, early stopping, and data augmentation. On the other hand, underfitting occurs when the model is too simple and cannot capture the complexity of the data, resulting in poor performance on both the training and test data. Underfitting can be addressed by using more complex models or larger datasets. However, finding optimal performance requires a balance between model complexity and the amount of training data. This is known as the bias-variance trade-off. The goal is to find a model that has low bias and low variance and that can generalize well to new, unseen data.

13.6.2.4   Generalizability

Generalizability is a critical aspect of any AI model. It refers to the model's ability to perform well on new, unseen data that are not included in the training or testing datasets. Even if a model achieves high accuracy on the training and test data, it may not be able to generalize well to new data. This can occur if the model is overfitting to the training data, memorizing the data rather than learning general patterns that can be applied to new data. Poor generalizability often results from the model's exposure to a restricted set of data during its training and testing phases. This limitation may arise due to biased or nonrepresentative training data that do not reflect the real-world data the model is intended to operate on. To overcome this, it is crucial to use a diverse and representative dataset for training the model. Furthermore, it is essential to evaluate the model's performance on a separate validation dataset that is distinct from the training and testing datasets. Poor generalizability can also result from new data that differ significantly from the data used to train the model.

Such a situation may arise when the model is applied in an environment different from the one in which it was trained or when there are changes in the data distribution over time. To address this, it is crucial to monitor the model's performance over time and retrain the model with new data as necessary.

13.6.2.5 *Ethical Considerations*

As AI models become increasingly prevalent in various sectors, ethical considerations regarding their use have gained significant attention. One of the primary concerns is privacy, as AI models can collect and process vast amounts of personal data, raising questions about who has access to these data and how it is utilized [53, 54]. Additionally, another ethical consideration revolves around transparency [55], as AI models can be opaque and challenging to interpret, making it difficult to understand how decisions are being made, especially in high-stakes situations such as healthcare or criminal justice. To address this, researchers are working on developing explainable AI models that provide insight into how decisions are being made.

13.6.3 Areas for Future Research and Development in the Field

The development of AI models for biopharmaceutical property prediction faces several challenges and future directions. These challenges include the need for diverse and extensive datasets, interpretable models, and reliable model validation protocols. An area of study that could be explored is combining experimental methods with AI models to forecast biopharmaceutical properties—for example, AI models can help optimize experimental design, reduce the number of experiments needed, or guide experimental validation with predictions. Another promising direction is the development of hybrid models that combine different AI techniques [8], such as ML and deep learning, with computational methods such as molecular dynamics simulations or quantum mechanics calculations to capture complex molecular interactions and provide more reliable and accurate predictions. There are numerous opportunities for future research and development in the realm of AI models dedicated to predicting biopharmaceutical properties.

The following are some potential areas that could be explored further.

13.6.3.1 *Multitask Learning*

Multitask learning is a promising approach to improving the accuracy of biopharmaceutical property prediction. Currently, most AI models in this field are designed to predict a single property. However, this can be limiting since multiple properties of a drug often interrelate—for example, solubility and bioavailability are closely linked, as the solubility of a drug molecule can affect its bioavailability. By considering multiple properties simultaneously, the interrelationships between different properties can be better captured, leading to more accurate predictions. Multitask learning involves training a single AI model to predict multiple properties simultaneously rather than training separate models for each property. This approach has several advantages. First, it can reduce the amount of training data needed, as the model can learn to recognize common patterns across multiple properties. Second, it can help to avoid overfitting, where a model becomes too specialized for a specific property, by encouraging the model to learn general features that are relevant to multiple properties. Another benefit of multitasking is that it can lead to more efficient model training and deployment. By sharing common layers between different tasks, the model can be trained more quickly and with fewer parameters, reducing the computational burden. Moreover, once trained, the model can predict multiple properties in a single pass, rather than having to run separate predictions for each property.

13.6.3.2   Incorporating Biological Data

Incorporating biological data into AI models for biopharmaceutical property prediction has the potential to significantly enhance their accuracy and usefulness. While current models mainly focus on the chemical properties of drugs, the importance of biological data in predicting drug efficacy and safety is increasingly recognized. One significant advantage of incorporating biological data is its ability to capture the complex interactions between drugs and biological systems—for example, gene expression data can provide insights into how drugs interact with specific biological pathways, while protein structure data can identify potential drug targets and inform drug design. Moreover, the integration of biological data with AI models can help overcome the limitations of current models. While chemical properties are essential in understanding drug behavior, they do not necessarily capture all the factors that influence drug efficacy and safety. By integrating biological data, AI models can better capture the complex interplay between drugs, biological systems, and disease states. However, several challenges come with incorporating biological data into AI models. Biological data are often more complex and challenging to interpret than chemical data, and their analysis and integration may require specialized expertise. Despite these challenges, incorporating biological data is becoming increasingly feasible with the advancement of technology and data analysis methods. Furthermore, the integration of biological data into AI models has the potential to lead to significant improvements in drug development and patient outcomes, making it a promising direction for future research.

13.6.3.3   Improving Interpretability

Improving the interpretability of AI models for biopharmaceutical property prediction is an important goal. Currently, many models, such as deep neural networks, are black boxes, meaning that it is difficult to understand how they are making predictions. This lack of transparency can make it challenging to identify and correct potential errors, which is particularly concerning in the context of drug development, where accuracy is critical. To enhance interpretability in AI models for biopharmaceutical property prediction, researchers can employ various visualization techniques. Attention maps, for instance, can be utilized to identify the key areas of an image that significantly influence the prediction, while saliency maps can help identify the most relevant features of an input data point. These techniques enable researchers to better understand how the model is making its predictions, which can be crucial in identifying potential errors or biases. By improving interpretability, AI models can become more reliable and trustworthy tools in drug development and clinical decision-making. An alternative approach to enhancing interpretability is to employ simpler models that are easier to comprehend. Decision trees, for example, can furnish a lucid and comprehensible framework for making predictions, enabling researchers to track the decision-making process step by step. In addition, linear models and rule-based models can also provide insights into how a model is making predictions and help identify potential errors. Moreover, incorporating domain knowledge into the model can help improve its interpretability. By incorporating expert knowledge into the model, researchers can better understand the relationships between different features and the underlying biological mechanisms. This can lead to more accurate predictions and improved interpretability.

13.6.3.4   Transfer Learning

Transfer learning is a promising approach to improving the accuracy of biopharmaceutical property prediction models when data are limited or unavailable. With transfer learning, a pretrained model can be fine-tuned on a smaller, more targeted dataset, allowing it to learn the specific features of the new data. This approach can be particularly useful in drug discovery, where the number of available compounds is limited and the cost of experimental testing is high—for instance, a model trained on a large dataset of drug-like molecules can be fine-tuned on a smaller dataset of compounds with specific properties of interest, such as high bioavailability or low toxicity. This fine-tuning process can help the model better capture the unique characteristics of the target compounds, leading to more accurate predictions. Transfer learning can also be used to improve the performance of models when data are limited—for example, a model trained on a large dataset of molecules from related chemical families can be fine-tuned on a smaller dataset of structurally similar compounds, even if the new dataset is relatively small. This approach can help leverage the information learned from the larger dataset to improve predictions on the smaller dataset while reducing the risk of overfitting. Moreover, transfer learning can help accelerate model development, as pretrained models can be readily applied to new problems, reducing the time and cost of training new models from scratch.

13.6.3.5   Addressing Ethical Concerns

The use of AI models in biopharmaceutical property prediction raises ethical concerns, particularly regarding privacy, transparency, and accountability [49]. Further research is needed to develop methods that ensure fairness and unbiasedness in these models and address concerns about the use of personal data in drug discovery and development. Standardization and transparency in AI model development and implementation are also necessary. To ensure reproducibility and transparency, it is important to establish standard validation protocols, share datasets, and publish model details and parameters. While AI models have the potential to revolutionize biopharmaceutical property prediction, more research should focus on developing accurate and interpretable models, integrating AI with experimental approaches, and ensuring transparency and reproducibility in model development and implementation.

According to the author, several case studies can explore ethical concerns related to the use of AI in this field. These case studies shed light on the potential ethical implications and challenges that arise when utilizing AI models for biopharmaceutical property prediction.

1) Privacy and data security

A compelling case study can delve into the various aspects involved in addressing the ethical considerations surrounding the privacy and security of patient data used to train AI models [56]. It would examine how organizations safeguard sensitive information and maintain confidentiality while harnessing large datasets for predictive modeling. The case study explores measures such as implementing stringent access controls, employing encryption techniques, and adhering to industry-standard security protocols to ensure robust data protection. It would also scrutinize the ethical frameworks and guidelines followed by organizations to mitigate the risk of data breaches and unauthorized access. This case study provides valuable insight into effectively addressing privacy and data security concerns in AI-driven healthcare applications while balancing data utilization and patient privacy.

2) Bias and fairness

A thought-provoking case study can be conducted to delve into the intricate ethical issues linked to bias within AI models. It would focus on instances where AI algorithms inadvertently perpetuate biases in drug discovery and development, potentially resulting in inequitable health-care outcomes. By highlighting such instances, the case study emphasizes the significance of actively developing robust methods and techniques to effectively identify and mitigate biases within AI models. It would examine how biases can arise from skewed training data, algorithmic design choices, or systemic disparities within healthcare systems. The ethical implications of these biases, particularly the harm caused to marginalized or underrepresented patient populations, should be emphasized. The case study underscores the need for comprehensive approaches to mitigate bias, including data preprocessing techniques, algorithmic audits, and rigorous evaluation frameworks, to ensure fairness in AI-driven drug discovery and development. Collaborative efforts among researchers, healthcare professionals, policymakers, and regulators to establish guidelines and best practices should also be explored. This case study provides valuable insights into the ethical dimensions of bias in AI models and fosters discussions and actions toward promoting fairness and equity in healthcare applications.

3) Regulatory compliance

A comprehensive case study can delve into the multifaceted challenges of regulatory compliance when implementing AI models in the biopharmaceutical industry. It thoroughly examines the ethical considerations surrounding regulatory frameworks and emphasizes the need for robust guidelines to ensure the responsible and ethical use of AI models. The case study elucidates the complexities and regulatory compliance within the biopharmaceutical sector, taking into account the evolving nature of AI technologies and their impact on traditional regulatory paradigms. It explores the ethical dilemmas arising from the integration of AI models in drug discovery, development, and postmarketing surveillance. The case study sheds light on the potential benefits and risks associated with AI implementation, emphasizing the importance of striking a balance between innovation and patient safety. Challenges faced by regulatory bodies in overseeing and evaluating AI models, including transparency, interpretability, and algorithmic bias, will be examined. Additionally, the case study highlights the significance of collaborative efforts among industry stakeholders, regulatory agencies, and policymakers to establish comprehensive guidelines and frameworks that ensure the ethical and responsible use of AI models. It would delve into the development of specialized regulatory pathways tailored to AI-driven technologies, considering the unique considerations and potential risks they present. By providing real-world examples and insights into the complexities of regulatory compliance in the context of AI models in the biopharmaceutical industry, this case study fosters a deeper understanding of the ethical dimensions involved. It would serve as a catalyst for discussions and initiatives aimed at developing adaptable and future-proof regulatory frameworks that effectively address the challenges while promoting the ethical integration of AI technologies in healthcare.

4) Human oversight and decision-making

An insightful case study can comprehensively explore the vital role of human oversight and decision-making in the context of AI systems, highlighting the ethical responsibilities entrusted to healthcare professionals. This study delves into the complexities surrounding the integration of AI technologies in healthcare and emphasizes the need for critical evaluation and validation of AI outputs by human experts. The case study examines the ethical considerations related to human oversight, emphasizing the importance of healthcare professionals as key stakeholders in the AI-driven decision-making process. It would explore scenarios where AI systems provide recommendations or predictions and the subsequent responsibility of healthcare professionals to exercise their expertise and judgment in reviewing and validating those outputs. Furthermore, the case study highlights the potential risks and limitations associated with overreliance on AI systems, such as algorithmic bias, lack of interpretability, or unforeseen errors. It would emphasize the ethical imperative for healthcare professionals to remain vigilant and cautious in their decision-making process, considering AI outputs as valuable tools rather than absolute determinants of patient care. The case study also underscores the ethical responsibilities of healthcare professionals to continuously update their knowledge and skills to effectively navigate the evolving landscape of AI technologies. It discusses the importance of ongoing education and training programs that equip healthcare professionals with the necessary expertise to critically assess and interpret AI outputs within their specific domains.

13.7   Conclusion and Future Scope

AI models have shown great potential for predicting biopharmaceutical properties, providing accurate and reliable predictions that can accelerate drug discovery and development. However, there are still challenges that need to be addressed, including the need for more diverse and high-quality data, better understanding and interpretation of the models, and ensuring their transparency and interpretability. Despite these challenges, the rapid advances in AI models and technologies offer exciting opportunities to further improve the accuracy and efficiency of biopharmaceutical property prediction.

Looking to the future, it is anticipated that AI models will increasingly play an important role in biopharmaceutical property prediction, particularly as the amount and complexity of available data continue to grow. In addition, more collaboration between academia, industry, and regulatory agencies to develop standardized and transparent frameworks for evaluating and validating AI models in drug development. The development of more specialized and context-specific AI models that can better handle the complexity of biopharmaceutical data, such as those arising from cell and gene therapies, personalized medicine, and complex diseases, is also anticipated. Additionally, there will be a greater focus on the interpretability and explainability of AI models to ensure that their predictions can be understood and trusted by stakeholders. This will require the development of new techniques and tools for visualizing and explaining the behavior of AI models, as well as the incorporation of ethical and social considerations into their design and deployment. By fostering cooperative efforts across various fields, the advancement and integration of AI models for predicting biopharmaceutical properties can be furthered. Ultimately, this can facilitate the discovery and development of safer and more efficient drugs, ultimately benefiting patients who require them.

References

1. Arden, N.S., Fisher, A.C., Tyner, K., Yu, L.X., Lee, S.L., Kopcha, M., Industry 4.0 for pharmaceutical manufacturing: Preparing for the smart factories of the future. *Int. J. Pharm.*, *602*, 120554, 2021, https://doi.org/10.1016/j.ijpharm.2021.120554.

2. Mökander, J., Sheth, M., Gersbro-Sundler, M., Blomgren, P., Floridi, L., Challenges and best practices in corporate AI governance: Lessons from the biopharmaceutical industry. *Front. Comput. Sci.*, *4*, 1068361, 2022, https://doi.org/10.3389/fcomp.2022.1068361.

3. Marschall, L., Taylor, C., Zahel, T., Kunzelmann, M., Wiedenmann, A., Presser, B., Herwig, C., Specification-driven acceptance criteria for validation of biopharmaceutical processes. *Front. Bioeng. Biotechnol.*, *10*, 1010583, 2022, https://doi.org/10.3389/ fbioe.2022.1010583.

4. Sankar, S., O'Neill, K., Bagot D'Arc, M., Rebeca, F., Buffier, M., Aleksi, E., Spirio, L., Clinical use of the self-assembling peptide rada16: A review of current and future trends in biomedicine. *Front. Bioeng. Biotechnol.*, *9*, 679525, 2021. https://doi.org/10.3389/ fbioe.2021.679525.

5. Muthukumaran, J. and Jha, N.K., Sustainability in biopharmaceutical industry. *J. Crit. Rev.*, *7*, 1, 718–722, 2020, https://doi.org/10.31838/jcr.07.01.138.

6. Walsh, I., Myint, M., Nguyen-Khuong, T., Ho, Y.S., Ng, S.K., Lakshmanan, M., Harnessing the potential of machine learning for advancing "quality by design" in biomanufacturing. *MAbs*, *14*, 1, 2013593, 2022, https://doi.org/10.1080/19420862.2021.2013593.

7. Kolluri, S., Lin, J., Liu, R., Zhang, Y., Zhang, W., Machine learning and artificial intelligence in pharmaceutical research and development: A review. *AAPS J.*, *24*, 1, 19, 2022, https:// doi.org/10.1208/s12248-021-00644-3.

8. Yang, C.T., Kristiani, E., Leong, Y.K., Chang, J.S., Big data and machine learning driven bioprocessing – Recent trends and critical analysis. *Bioresour. Technol.*, *372*, 128625, 2023, https://doi.org/10.1016/j.biortech.2023.128625.

9. Puranik, A., Dandekar, P., Jain, R., Exploring the potential of machine learning for more efficient development and production of biopharmaceuticals. *Biotechnol. Progr.*, *38*, 6, e3291, 2022, https://doi.org/10.1002/btpr.3291.

10. Kumar, S., Nayyar, A., Paul, A. (Eds.), *Swarm Intelligence and Evolutionary Algorithms in Healthcare and Drug Development*, CRC Press, New York, United States, 2019, http://dx.doi.org/10.1201/9780429289675.

11. Alzubi, J., Nayyar, A., Kumar, A., Machine learning from theory to algorithms: An overview. *J. Phys. Conf. Ser.*, *1142*, 012012, 2018, https://doi. org/10.1088/1742-6596/1142/1/012012.

12. Zivkovic, M., Bacanin, N., Venkatachalam, K., Nayyar, A., Djordjevic, A., Strumberger, I., Al-Turjman, F., COVID-19 cases prediction by using hybrid machine learning and

beetle antennae search approach. *Sustain. Cities Soc.*, 6, 102669, 2021, https://doi.org/10.1016/j. scs.2020.102669

13. Nayyar, A., Gadhavi, L., Zaman, N., Machine learning in healthcare: Review, opportunities and challenges, in: *Machine Learning and the Internet of Medical Things in Healthcare*, pp. 23–45, 2021, https://doi.org/10.1016/B978-0-12-821229-5.00011-2.

14. Durgam, R., Devarakonda, N., Nayyar, A., Eluri, R., Improved genetic algorithm using machine learning approaches to feature modelled for microarray gene data, in: *Soft Computing for Security Applications: Proceedings of ICSCS 2021*, pp. 859–872, Springer, Singapore, 2022, https:// doi.org/10.1007/978-981-16-5301-8_60.

15. Solanki, A., Kumar, S., Nayyar, A. (Eds.), *Handbook of Research on Emerging Trends and Applications of Machine Learning*, IGI Global, Pennsylvania, United States, 2020, https://doi. org/10.4018/978-1-5225-9643-1.

16. Sahu, A., Mishra, J., Kushwaha, N., Artificial intelligence (AI) in drugs and pharmaceuticals. *Comb. Chem. High Throughput Screen.*, 25, 11, 1818–1837, 2022, https:// doi.org/10.2174/1386 20732566621120715394.

17. Zhao, J., Yan, W., Yang, Y., DeepTP: A deep learning model for thermophilic protein prediction. *Int. J. Mol. Sci.*, 24, 3, 2217, 2023, https://doi.org/10.3390/ ijms24032217.

18. Cerchia, C. and Lavecchia, A., New avenues in artificial-intelligence-assisted drug discovery. *Drug Discov. Today*, 28, 4, 103516, 2023, https://doi.org/10.1016/j.drudis.2023.103516.

19. Navabhatra, A., Brantner, A., Yingngam, B., Artificial neural network modeling of nano-structured lipid carriers containing 5-O-caffeoylquinic acid-rich *Cratoxylum formosum* leaf extract for skin application. *Adv. Pharm. Bull.*, 12, 4, 801–817, 2022, https://doi. org/10.34172/ apb.2022.082.

20. Huang, F., Xiong, H., Chen, S., Lv, Z., Huang, J., Chang, Z., Catani, F., Slope stability prediction based on a long short-term memory neural network: Comparisons with convolutional neural networks, support vector machines and random forest models. *Int. J. Coal Sci. Technol.*, 10, 1, 18, 2023, https://doi.org/10.1007/s40789-023-00579-4.

21. Rathore, A.S., Nikita, S., Thakur, G., Mishra, S., Artificial intelligence and machine learning applications in biopharmaceutical manufacturing. *Trends Biotechnol.*, 41, 4, 497–510, 2023, https://doi.org/10.1016/j.tibtech.2022.08.007.

22. Leski, T.A., Spangler, J.R., Wang, Z., Schultzhaus, Z., Taitt, C.R., Dean, S.N., Stenger, D.A., Machine learning for design of degenerate Cas13a crRNAs using lassa virus as a model of highly variable RNA target. *Sci. Rep.*, 13, 1, 6506, 2023, https://doi.org/10.1038/ s41598-023-33494-4.

23. Azari, H., Nazari, E., Mohit, R., Asadnia, A., Maftooh, M., Nassiri, M., Avan, A., Machine learning algorithms reveal potential miRNAs biomarkers in gastric cancer. *Sci. Rep.*, 13, 1, 6147, 2023, https://doi.org/10.1038/s41598-023-32332-x.

24. Feng, D., Svetnik, V., Liaw, A., Pratola, M., Sheridan, R.P., Building quantitative structure-activity relationship models using bayesian additive regression trees. *J. Chem. Inf. Model.*, 59, 6, 2642–2655, 2019, https://doi.org/10.1021/acs.jcim.9b00094.

25. Mazhar, K., Mohamed, S., Patel, A.J., Veith, S.B., Roberts, G., Warwick, R., Raseta, M., Bayesian networks identify determinants of outcomes following cardiac surgery in a UK population. *BMC Cardiovasc. Disord.*, 23, 1, 70, 2023, https://doi.org/10.1186/s12872-023-03100-6.

26. Yingngam, B., Navabhatra, A., Rungseevijitprapa, W., Prasitpuriprecha, C., Brantner, A., Comparative study of response surface methodology and artificial neural network in the optimization of the ultrasound-assisted extraction of diarylheptanoid phytoestrogens from curcuma comosa rhizomes. *Chem. Eng. Process. - Process Intensification*, 165, 108461, 2021, https:// doi.org/10.1016/j.cep.2021.108461.

27. Chiappini, F.A., Allegrini, F., Goicoechea, H.C., Olivieri, A.C., Sensitivity for multivariate calibration based on multilayer perceptron artificial neural networks. *Anal. Chem.*, 92, 18, 12265–12272, 2020, https://doi.org/10.1021/acs.analchem.0c01863.

28. Wang, S., Liaw, A., Chen, Y.M., Su, Y., Skomski, D., Convolutional neural networks enable highly accurate and automated subvisible particulate classification of biopharmaceuticals. *Pharm. Res.*, *40*, 1447–1457, 2023, https://doi.org/10.1007/s11095-022-03438-0.

29. Riba, J., Schoendube, J., Zimmermann, S., Koltay, P., Zengerle, R., Single-cell dispensing and 'real-time' cell classification using convolutional neural networks for higher efficiency in single-cell cloning. *Sci. Rep.*, *10*, 1, 1193, 2020, https://doi.org/10.1038/s41598-020-57900-3.

30. Zhao, H., Che, C., Jin, B., Wei, X., A viral protein identifying framework based on temporal convolutional network. *Math. Biosci. Eng.*, *16*, 3, 1709–1717, 2019, https://doi.org/10.3934/mbe.2019081.

31. Goulet, D.R., Yan, Y., Agrawal, P., Waight, A.B., Mak, A.N.S., Zhu, Y., Codon optimization using a recurrent neural network. *J. Comput. Biol.*, *30*, 1, 70–81, 2023, https://doi.org/10.1089/cmb.2021.0458.

32. Rafique, F., Fu, L., Mai, R., LSTM autoencoders based unsupervised machine learning for transmission line protection. *Electr. Power Syst. Res.*, *221*, 109432, 2023, https://doi.org/10.1016/j.epsr.2023.109432.

33. Mahdavi, M., Choubdar, H., Rostami, Z., Niroomand, B., Levine, A.T., Fatemi, A., Merrikhi, Y., Hybrid feature engineering of medical data via variational autoencoders with triplet loss: A COVID-19 prognosis study. *Sci. Rep.*, *13*, 1, 2827, 2023, https://doi.org/10.1038/s41598-023-29334-0.

34. Hauptmann, T. and Kramer, S., A fair experimental comparison of neural network architectures for latent representations of multi-omics for drug response prediction. *BMC Bioinf.*, *24*, 1, 45, 2023, https://doi.org/10.1186/s12859-023-05166-7.

35. Mandair, D., Reis-Filho, J. S., Ashworth, A., Biological insights and novel biomarker discovery through deep learning approaches in breast cancer histopathology. *NPJ Breast Cancer,* 9, 1, 21, 2023.

36. Sarkar, C., Das, B., Rawat, V.S., Wahlang, J.B., Nongpiur, A., Tiewsoh, I., Sony, H.T., Artificial intelligence and machine learning technology driven modern drug discovery and development. *Int. J. Mol. Sci.*, *24*, 3, 2026, 2023, https://doi.org/10.3390/ ijms24032026.

37. Dhakal, A., McKay, C., Tanner, J.J., Cheng, J., Artificial intelligence in the prediction of protein-ligand interactions: Recent advances and future directions. *Brief. Bioinf.*, *23*, 1, bbab476, 2022, https://doi.org/10.1093/bib/bbab476.

38. Narayanan, H., Dingfelder, F., Condado Morales, I., Patel, B., Heding, K.E., Bjelke, J.R., Arosio, P., Design of biopharmaceutical formulations accelerated by machine learning. *Mol. Pharmaceutics*, *18*, 10, 3843–3853, 2021, https://doi.org/10.1021/acs.molpharmaceut.1c00469.

39. Lai, P.-K., Gallegos, A., Mody, N., Sathish, H.A., Trout, B.L., Machine learning prediction of antibody aggregation and viscosity for high concentration formulation development of protein therapeutics. *mAbs*, *14*, 1, 2026208, 2022, https://doi.org/10.1080/19420862.2022.2026208.

40. Duhazé, J., Hässler, S., Bachelet, D., Gleizes, A., Hacein-Bey-Abina, S., Allez, M., ... Broët, P., A machine learning approach for high-dimensional time-to-event prediction with application to immunogenicity of biotherapies in the ABIRISK cohort. *Front. Immunol.,* 11, 608, 520845, 2020.

41. Doneva, N., Doytchinova, I., Dimitrov, I., Predicting immunogenicity risk in biopharmaceuticals. *Symmetry*, *13*, 3, 388, 2021, https://doi.org/10.3390/sym13030388.

42. Yang, X., Zhao, L., Wei, F., Li, J., DeepNetBim: Deep learning model for predicting HLA-epitope interactions based on network analysis by harnessing binding and immunogenicity information. *BMC Bioinf.*, *22*, 1, 231, 2021, https://doi.org/10.1186/s12859-021-04155-y.

43. Mattei, A.E., Gutierrez, A.H., Martin, W.D., Terry, F.E., Roberts, B.J., Rosenberg, A.S., De Groot, A.S., *In silico* immunogenicity assessment for sequences containing unnatural amino acids: A method using existing *in silico* algorithm infrastructure and a vision for future enhancements. *Front. Drug Discov.*, *2*, 952326, 2022, https://doi.org/10.3389/ fddsv.2022.952326.

44. Nagy, B., Galata, D.L., Farkas, A., Nagy, Z.K., Application of artificial neural networks in the process analytical technology of pharmaceutical manufacturing—A review. *AAPS J.*, *24*, 4, 74, 2022, https://doi.org/10.1208/s12248-022-00706-0.

45. Paki, R., Nourani, E., Farajzadeh, D., Classification of G protein-coupled recpetors using attention mechanism. *Gene Rep.*, *21*, 100882, 2020, https://doi.org/10.1016/j.genrep.2020.100882.

46. Duc, N.M., Kim, H.R., Chung, K.Y., Structural mechanism of G protein-coupled receptor. *Eur. J. Pharmacol.*, *763*, 214–222, 2015, https://doi.org/10.1016/j. ejphar.2015.05.016.

47. Kunselman, J. M., Lott, J., Puthenveedu, M. A., Mechanisms of selective G protein–coupled receptor localization and trafficking. *Curr. Opin. Cell Biol.,* 71, 158–165, 2021.

48. Sharma, A., Virmani, T., Pathak, V., Sharma, A., Pathak, K., Kumar, G., Pathak, D., Artificial intelligence-based data-driven strategy to accelerate research, development, and clinical trials of COVID vaccine. *BioMed. Res. Int.*, *2022*, 7205241, 2022, https://doi.org/10.1155/2022/7205241.

49. Goodarzian, F., Navaei, A., Ehsani, B., Ghasemi, P., Muñuzuri, J., Designing an integrated responsive-green-cold vaccine supply chain network using internet-of-things: Artificial intelligence-based solutions. *Ann. Oper. Res.*, *328*, 531–575, 2023, https://doi.org/10.1007/s10479-022-04713-4.

50. Sharma, K., Singh, H., Sharma, D.K., Kumar, A., Nayyar, A., Krishnamurthi, R., Dynamic models and control techniques for drone delivery of medications and other healthcare items in covid-19 hotspots, in: *Emerging Technologies for Battling Covid-19: Applications and Innovations*, F. Al-Turjman, A. Devi, A. Nayyar (Eds.), Germany, Springer International Publishing, Cham, Switzerland, 2021, https://doi.org/10.1007/978-3-030-60039-6_1.

51. Liu, G., Carter, B., Bricken, T., Jain, S., Viard, M., Carrington, M., Gifford, D.K., Computationally optimized SARS-CoV-2 MHC class I and II vaccine formulations predicted to target human haplotype distributions. *Cell Syst.*, *11*, 2, 131–144.e136, 2020, https://doi.org/10.1016/j.cels.2020.06.009.

52. Zame, W.R., Bica, I., Shen, C., Curth, A., Lee, H.-S., Bailey, S., van der Schaar, M., Machine learning for clinical trials in the era of COVID-19. *Stat. Biopharm. Res.*, *12*, 4, 506–517, 2020, doi: 10.1080/19466315.2020.1797867.

53. Van Campen, L.E., Poplazarova, T., Therasse, D.G., Turik, M., Kelman, A., Rossetti, A., Fortson, W., Considerations for applying bioethics norms to a biopharmaceutical industry setting. *BMC Med. Ethics*, *22*, 1, 31, 2021, https://doi.org/10.1186/s12910-021-00600-y.

54. Mahapatra, B., Krishnamurthi, R., Nayyar, A., Healthcare models and algorithms for privacy and security in healthcare records, in: *Security and Privacy of Electronic Healthcare Records: Concepts, Paradigms and Solutions*, p. 183, 2019, http://dx.doi.org/10.1049/PBHE020E_ch8.

55. Kumar, A., Krishnamurthi, R., Nayyar, A., Sharma, K., Grover, V., Hossain, E., A novel smart healthcare design, simulation, and implementation using healthcare 4.0 processes. *IEEE Access*, 8, 118433–118471, 2020, https://doi.org/10.1109/ACCESS.2020.3004790.

56. Pramanik, P.K.D., Pareek, G., Nayyar, A., Chapter 14 - Security and privacy in remote healthcare: Issues, solutions, and standards, in: *Telemedicine Technologies*, H.D. Jude and V.E. Balas (Eds.), pp. 201–225, Academic Press, London, United Kingdom, 2019, https://doi.org/10.1016/B978-0-12-816948-3.00014-3.

Deep Learning Tactics for Neuroimaging Genomics Investigations in Alzheimer's Disease

Mithun Singh Rajput[1]*, Jigna Shah[1], Viral Patel[2], Nitin Singh Rajput[3] and Dileep Kumar[4,5]

[1]Department of Pharmacology, Institute of Pharmacy, Nirma University, Ahmedabad, Gujarat, India
[2]Department of Pharmaceutics, Ramanbhai Patel College of Pharmacy, Charotar University of Science and Technology (CHARUSAT), Changa, Gujarat, India
[3]Department of Information and Communication Technology, School of Technology, Pandit Deendayal Energy University, Gandhinagar, Gujarat, India
[4]Poona College of Pharmacy, Department of Pharmaceutical Chemistry, Bharati Vidyapeeth (Deemed to be University), Pune, Maharashtra, India
[5]UC Davis Comprehensive Cancer Center, Department of Entomology and Nematology, University of California Davis, CA, USA

Abstract

Alzheimer's disease (AD) is a neurodegenerative condition that is hallmarked by senile dementia, worsens over time, and has no proven treatment. It causes a decline in cognitive abilities. Effective automated procedures are required for early prediction and diagnosis since it is imperative to stop the progression of the disease. The creation of precise computer diagnostic systems was made possible by the nature of several aspects of neural data, which were primarily retrieved from neuroimaging with computer-aided algorithms. In the field of computer vision, deep learning, a high-tech machine learning strategy, has demonstrated exceptional ability in identifying detailed structures in complicated, high-dimensional data. Presently, a rising body of research suggests that deep learning techniques can act as a crucial pillar for the diagnosis, categorization, and prediction of AD. In order to develop targeted therapies, it is crucial to comprehend the genetic aetiology of AD. Several researchers had tried to find possible biomarkers for future therapy by using machine learning techniques to analyze the expressed genes in AD patients. Technology advancements in genomic research, like genome-wide association studies (GWAS), which enable the identification of polymorphisms and have been extensively used in investigations of AD, have identified certain genes as significant clinical risk factors for AD. In addition, a number of deep learning models are currently being used in research investigations to distinguish AD from normal controls and/or to distinguish AD from mild cognitive impairment in light of the most recent developments in neuroimaging and genetics. The chapter enlightens many studies that apply deep learning algorithms to predict AD using genomes or neuroimaging data along with the supportive tactics. On the basis of combining both neuroimaging and genome data, pertinent integrative neuroimaging genomics studies that make use of deep learning techniques to forecast AD have been discussed. The limitations of the most recent deep learning combined with neuroimaging and genomics AD investigations have also been described. Lastly,

---

Corresponding author: mithun.sgsits@gmail.com

Abhirup Khanna, May El Barachi, Sapna Jain, Manoj Kumar and Anand Nayyar (eds.) Artificial Intelligence and Machine Learning in Drug Design and Development, (451–472) © 2024 Scrivener Publishing LLC

a summary of the research findings, challenges, and future directions for integrating deep learning methods into therapeutic settings is deliberated.

Keywords: Alzheimer's disease, deep learning, diagnosis, genomics, machine learning, neuroimaging

14.1   Introduction

Alzheimer's disease (AD) is a neurological condition that causes memory loss by causing brain atrophy and ultimately the death of brain cells [1]. The illness can be split into two subcategories: early-onset AD and late-onset AD, according to Herrera-Espejo *et al.* (2019) [2]. The early-onset disease is predominantly a hereditary condition, with a heritability of 92% to 100% and 35% to 60% of early-onset patients having affected first-degree relatives [3]. The majority of early-onset AD patients are diagnosed between the ages of 45 and 60 [4], while early-onset AD patients often have their first symptoms between 30 and 65 [4]. In contrast to early-onset AD, late-onset AD primarily affects the elderly (often those over the age of 65) and occurs in 90%–95% of cases [5]. A more complex disorder caused by both hereditary and environmental causes, late-onset AD looks to be more difficult to treat.

Memory loss, delusions, confusion, and disorientation are some of the cognitive deficits that accompany AD progression. A few factors that cause AD include inflammation, mitochondrial malfunction, shrinking of blood vessels and muscles, and the generation of free radicals [6]. The possibility of creating novel, focused medicines for the treatment of AD is highlighted by the apparent important genetic component of AD. The blood–brain barrier (BBB) integrity is disrupted by the Apolipoprotein E (APOE) gene which results in the progression of AD, as per the findings of the National Institute on Ageing [7]. However, not all cases of AD are caused by this gene. Understanding the specific root cause of AD is complicated by the unidentified gene–gene/environment interactions. Recent research found a strong correlation between the development of AD and neurodegenerative comorbidities and mutations in the APP, CD33, and BIN1 genes [8].

Applications of Computational Science in Artificial Intelligence (AI-ASCAI) provides technical solutions to enhance the design of smart technology, healthcare, and environmental sustainability [9]. The biological, medical, and pharmaceutical sectors have made extensive use of the ever-expanding smart-enabled data-generating technology in healthcare. Artificial intelligence now plays a variety of functions in the healthcare paradigm as it interacts with numerous applications, tools, structures, services, and technology. In the battle against different diseases, machine learning, artificial intelligence, and computer-based molecular docking analysis (CBMDA's) studies have been carried out [10]. It is essential to increase the focus of the study on the innovative design of healthcare systems in this field given that the majority of current research links IoT and big data analytics applications in smart healthcare [11]. Numerous computational techniques have recently been suggested for enhancing diagnosis or discovering new gene candidates linked to AD. For many common difficult diseases and symptoms, GWAS studies are a well-recognized strategy for recognizing genetic sections of interest [12]. The investigations are unique in that they analyze data from a sizable population with a large number (i.e., over 100K) of loci (i.e., SNPs) spread throughout the human genome. A change in biological function caused by a variation at particular loci may result in disease. By examining genotypes created from individuals with and without the desired feature, such variance can be found [13].

Clinical diagnosis benefits greatly from computer-aided systems since classifying medical images is a challenging undertaking. The most popular methods for diagnosing neurodegenerative illnesses include computed tomography (CT), structural magnetic resonance imaging (MRI), and positron emission tomography (PET) [14]. The speed and clarity of a CT scan are both impressive. Computer vision has drawn more and more attention in the diagnosis of AD as a result of the quick development of artificial intelligence. A prominent subset of machine learning called "deep learning" has the potential to overcome the limitations of more conventional approaches. Deep learning technology, which has recently gained ground in the field of medical imaging, has been effectively used to automatically extract characteristics from medical pictures in order to complete AD identification [15]. Genome-wide association studies (GWAS) employ a statistical approach to identify population-based genetic risk variation for human diseases and traits by taking into account one single nucleotide polymorphism (SNP) at a time across the entire genome [16]. Nonetheless, profound learning has not yet been utilized to perform GWAS, as it is trying because of the purported high-aspect low-example size (HDLSS) issue, which is known to influence phenotype prediction utilizing genetic variation [17]. The utilization of feature reduction approaches is common to determine this issue [18], yet to include feature reduction with help of high-layered genomic information is likewise difficult because of an NP-difficult matter [19]. Therefore, it is necessary to develop deep learning frameworks to identify genetic variants using whole-genome data. With technology advancements in genomic research, like GWAS, which enable the identification of polymorphisms in investigations of AD, the identification of certain genes as significant clinical risk factors for AD is essential.

Objectives of the Chapter

The objectives of this chapter are:

- To discuss about deep learning tactics in the prediction, classification, and diagnosis of AD;
- To portray phenotype classification using deep learning,
- To explain deep learning-based prediction of altered genes and mRNA levels in AD;
- And, to comprehend studies that apply deep learning algorithms to predict AD using genomes or neuroimaging data along with the supportive tactics.

Organization of the Chapter

The rest of the chapter is organized as follows: Section 14.2 elaborates the pathophysiology of Alzheimer's disease. Section 14.3 enlightens deep learning tactics in the prediction, classification, and diagnosis of AD, followed by Section 14.4 discussing the deep learning-based identification of genetic variants. Section 14.5 elaborates the deep learning-based prediction of altered genes and mRNA levels in AD. Section 14.6 stresses on deep learning with neuroimaging and genomics in Alzheimer's disease. Section 14.7 discusses the limitations and challenges in Deep Learning based neuroimaging genomics investigations in Alzheimer's disease, followed by Section 14.8 stressing on future prospects for applying deep learning techniques in Alzheimer's disease treatment environments. Finally, Section 14.9 concludes the chapter with future scope.

14.2   Pathophysiology of Alzheimer's Disease

Alzheimer's disease (AD), the most prevalent form of dementia in senior individuals, is a neurological condition that progresses and cannot be reversed. According to Rajput *et al.* (2020b) [20], AD is characterized by a significant deterioration of the brain's structural components, appearance of intra- and extracellular neurofibrillary tangles (NFT), and loss of neuronal cells in particular cortical and subcortical locations. The various hallmarks of AD are depicted in Figure 14.1.

Amyloid β-peptide: Amyloid β-peptide (Aβ) (composed of 40–42 amino acids) is regarded as being essential to the development of AD and making up the majority of amyloid plaques. A big amyloid-precursor protein (APP), which is catalyzed by β- and γ-secretases, serves as the starting point for the proteolytic process that produces these peptides. The levels of Aβ, particularly $A\beta_{1-42}$, rise in the brains of AD patients, and a number of lines of evidence point to the possibility that these A peptides cause neuronal death, which causes neurodegeneration and cognitive failure [21]. In culture, increasing free radicals, lipid peroxidation, intracellular Ca^{2+} concentrations, cell damage, and apoptosis are just a few of the neurodegenerative processes that might interact with A to cause neurodegeneration [22].

The amyloid beta peptide (A), which includes 40–42 amino acids and is the major component of amyloid plaques, is thought to be crucial for the onset of AD. The proteolytic process that results in these Aβ peptides begins with a large amyloid-precursor protein (APP), which is catalyzed by β- and γ-secretases. According to many lines of evidence and increased levels of Aβ, particularly $A\beta_{1-42}$, in the brains of AD patients, these Aβ peptides cause neuronal apoptosis, which leads to neurodegeneration and cognitive failure [21]. According to Eckert *et al.* (2003) [22], Aβ can promote neurodegeneration in culture by causing a

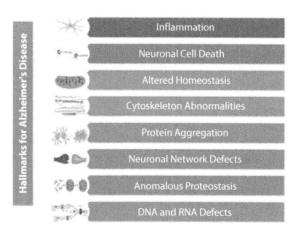

Figure 14.1 Hallmarks of Alzheimer's disease.

complex combination of neurodegenerative processes that include cell damage and apoptosis induction, lipid peroxidation, free radical production, and neuroinflammation.

Pro-inflammatory cytokines: The inflammatory cytokines interleukin-1 (IL-1) and tumor necrosis factor (TNF-α), inducible NO synthase (iNOS), and cyclooxygenase-2 (COX-2) are all upregulated as a result of Aβ inducing the production of pro-inflammatory cytokines through the nuclear factor b (NF-B) signaling pathway [23]. Aβ increases the production of pro-inflammatory cytokines through the nuclear factor B (NF-B) signaling pathway, which upregulates the associated inflammatory cytokines such as interleukin-1 (IL-1) and tumor necrosis factor (TNF-α), inducible NO synthase (iNOS), and cyclooxygenase-2 (COX-2).

These pro-inflammatory chemicals speed up the development of neurodegenerative disorders and contribute to brain damage. On the other hand, neuroprotective mechanisms exist in neuronal cells to guard against oxidative stress. The transcription factor nuclear factor erythroid 2-related factor 2 (Nrf2) regulates the redox state of the cell during times of oxidative stress. Under normal conditions, Nrf2 is localized in the cytoplasm by the ubiquitin–proteasome pathway and the actin-binding protein Kelch-like ECH associating protein 1 (Keap1). To transactivate the antioxidant response element (ARE) in the promoter of antioxidant genes like heme oxygenase (HO-1), glutamate-cysteine ligase catalytic (c-GCLC), quinine oxidoreductase 1 (NQO-1), and superoxide dismutase (SOD), Nrf2 enters the nucleus in response to various stimuli, such as oxidative stress [24]. In many disease situations, particularly oxidative stress, the Nrf2-ARE signaling pathway is regarded as a defensive molecular mechanism [25]. Therefore, one of the promising methods to prevent AD may be to decrease the Aβ-mediated oxidative cell death.

Neurofibrillary tangles: Numerous neurodegenerative diseases, including AD and frontotemporal dementia with Parkinsonism linked to chromosome 17 (FTDP-17), include NFT that are common, which are brought on by tau gene mutations [26]. Pairs of helical filaments (PHF) and small, twisted ribbons make up the filamentous aggregates that make up NFT. These are formed of the tau protein, which is connected with microtubules [27]. Both healthy and extra, pathogenic tau phosphorylation sites can be found in these filaments. Tau phosphorylation occurs along with tau dissociation from microtubules and tau localization from axons to cell bodies and dendrites. Pathological increases in this pool of soluble tau and structural changes to the normally unfolded tau are the first important steps in the production of the more insoluble pathological tau filaments. Both the co-expression of mutant amyloid precursor protein and intracerebral microinjections of A into P301L mutant tau transgenic mice considerably speed up the rate of NFT formation in mice [28]. These findings demonstrated a mechanistic link between Aβ toxicity and NFT production. Targeting the NFT creation process may therefore be one of the most effective ways to prevent AD. According to Wischik *et al.* (2008) [29], two tau aggregation inhibitors considerably slow down disease development and cognitive function deterioration in people. It is becoming clear that developing novel AD treatments may depend on the development of medicines that can stop tau aggregation.

Genetics: The development of late-onset AD has been associated with almost 2,000 genes over the past 20 years, but associations between late-onset AD and genes other than APOE were only confirmed in two sizable genome-wide association studies in 2009. In a research, in addition to APOE, described relationships between genetic markers in three additional genes with late-onset AD. Clusterin (CLU), complement receptor 1 (CR1), and phosphati-dylinositol-binding clathrin assembly protein (PICALM) are the other genes [30].

Other: Apart from Aβ toxicity, NFT formation, and genetic causes, many factors contribute to the pathogenesis of AD, *viz.*, synaptic and neural network deficits, abnormal proteostasis, and altered energy homeostasis related to mitochondrial dysfunction and DNA and RNA defects [31].

14.3   Deep Learning Tactics in the Prediction, Classification, and Diagnosis of AD

Artificial intelligence (AI), which includes machine learning (ML), analyzes the complex relationships between different data variables. Reinforcement learning, supervised learning, and unsupervised learning are the three categories into which these algorithms fall [32]. Pre-processing stages and appropriate architecture design must be guaranteed in order to recruit ML algorithms [33]. Feature mining, feature selection, data dimension reduction, and algorithm selection based on the features are typically required when using ML to sort studies. Such needs might be satisfied by specialized knowledge and optimization, which might be time-consuming and lacking in reproduction [33]. In order to surpass these constraints, AD research has made use of deep learning (DL), a particular type of ML approaches. According to LeCun *et al.* (2018) [34], DL is a subclass of ML that derives features using a hierarchical learning approach in which representations are inexorably disclosed from raw data. In order to comprehend both low-level and high-level data descriptions, DL algorithms employ numerous, deep layers made up of the perceptron algorithm, allowing them to develop richer conceptions of inputs. In addition to simplifying diverse sorts of data, this eliminates the need for manually constructed structures and enables DL structures to automatically find previously unidentified models. Modified variations of these systems have been successfully applied in the sectors of engineering and medicine [35].

In the context of thorough, multidimensional analysis of medical pictures, DL utilizes first-hand data obtained by neuroimaging to build features *via* on-the-fly learning in research on neurodegenerative diseases. Convolutional neural networks (CNN), for example, are employed in DL techniques to demonstrate quicker development than popular ML techniques [36]. DL methods are playing an increasingly important role in neurological research, tackling issues in numerous sub-domains. The first focus of DL development was on dividing and sorting the images. Due to the large amount of neuroimaging data generated by manual analysis, such functions are only suitable for DL. Gradually, using neuroimaging data for a variety of tasks like early detection and classification, DL approaches are employed to effectively map the brain and related areas. These days, AD risk is determined *via* DL-based diagnostic investigations that consider specific data kinds, laboratory results, and pictures. Given these facts, many alternative models have been addressed for examining neuroimaging data utilizing DL methods for the early prediction, classification, and diagnosis of AD [15]. DL has the power to significantly alter how medicine is practised. Data has been obtained by researchers from a variety of places, including hospitals, research labs, and Internet databases like EMIF-AD, NIFD, ROAD, etc. It is believed that MRI and

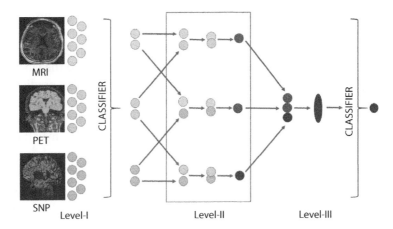

Figure 14.2 The fusion framework of a three-level AI network for the prediction, classification and diagnosis of Alzheimer's disease using MRI, PET, and SNP data. For each modality separately, Level-I represents latent representations (high-level features). Using the high-level features from Level-I, Level-II creates joint latent feature representations for each pair of modality combinations (e.g., MRI and PET, MRI and SNP, PET and SNP). Additionally, by combining the Level-II learnt joint latent feature representations, Level-III displays the diagnostic labels (Zhou *et al.*, 2019) [37].

PET data as well as CNN could be used to predict and diagnose AD. Fusion approaches [37] (Figure 14.2) have demonstrated accuracy levels of up to 96%, 99%, and 99.5% for AD prediction, classification, and diagnosis, respectively, in a partial available neuroimaging data set [15].

14.4   Deep Learning-Based Identification of Genetic Variants

Improvements in illness diagnosis and prognosis as well as the discovery of therapeutic targets are among the primary objectives of human genetics [38]. To do this, it is essential to have a thorough understanding of the genetic architecture of illnesses, more precisely, to know every genetic factor that contributes to a particular disease outcome and what makes those factors unique [39]. Single-nucleotide variations (SNVs) and significant structural alterations, including copy number variations, translocations, and inversions, can both occur in the human genome [40]. The most well-known and important genetic risk modulators for AD are common SNVs in APOE (apolipoprotein E) [41].

14.4.1   Deep Learning-Based Fragmentation of Genome Data

To analyze and understand genetic data, deep learning has been extensively used in genomics and bioinformatics. Many genomic techniques, including variant calling, *de novo* assembly, and regulatory element discovery, depend on the fragmentation of genome data [42]. Deep learning methods can be used to speed up the fragmentation procedure and increase the precision and effectiveness of downstream analysis [42].

Convolutional neural networks (CNNs) are a popular method for fragmenting genomic data. CNNs have demonstrated their efficacy in detecting local sequence dependencies and patterns [43]. They do not need to rely on manually created features because they can learn features straight from the raw DNA sequence data [43]. DNA sequences recorded as one-hot encoding or other appropriate encodings can be used as the input to the CNN model [44]. It is possible to train the CNN model using labeled data, where the labels denote the borders or breakpoints of the genetic segments. The model can reliably predict breakpoints in unseen genome data because during training it learns to recognize the sequence patterns connected to breakpoints [45]. By moving a fixed-size window along the sequence and estimating the likelihood of a breakpoint at each site, the trained CNN may then be used to fragment the genome data [45].

CNNs were originally applied to a sequence analysis of general text by Collobert *et al.* (2011) [46]. Few studies have, however, applied CNN-based methods to biological sequences [44]. These investigations [47] make use of CNNs that were trained directly from unprocessed DNA sequences—for instance, DeepBind uses CNNs to identify novel sequence motifs that predict the specificities of DNA and RNA binding sites [48]. Di Gangi *et al.* (2017) [49] determined the nucleosome location in sequences using recurrent neural networks (RNNs) and CNNs. According to Zhou and Troyanskaya (2015) [50], DeepSEA employs CNNs to predict the chromatin consequences of sequence changes with single-nucleotide sensitivity. Danq directly predicts non-coding function from sequences using the CNN and RNN frameworks [51]. According to Kelly *et al.* (2016), Basset employs CNNs to pinpoint the functional properties of DNA sequences, such as accessibility and protein binding. Meanwhile, CNNProm makes use of CNNs to anticipate prokaryotic and eukaryotic promoters [52]. According to Umarov and Solovyev (2017) [53], CNNProm outperforms other promoter prediction programmes in terms of accuracy.

A different approach is to use recurrent neural networks (RNNs) or its variants, such as long short-term memory (LSTM) or gated recurrent units (GRUs) [54–56]. Connections over a distance and sequential patterns in genomic data can be captured using RNNs. When anticipating breakpoints, they can analyze the DNA sequence data sequentially while taking the context into account [57]. RNNs may be trained using labeled data, much like CNNs, and then used to break up genomic sequences [55]. Genome data analysis has also been utilizing transformer-based models, such as those employed in natural language processing applications [58]. Transformers have demonstrated promising results in tasks like DNA sequence categorization and variant calling, efficiently capturing both local and global dependencies in genome sequences [59]. They may be utilized for fragmentation by forecasting breakpoints in the genomic data after being trained using labeled data [58] (Figure 14.3).

It is important to note that the properties of the genomic data and the current fragmentation job determine which unique deep learning architecture should be used [43]. To accommodate deep learning models for fragmented genomic data, researchers have investigated different topologies and adjustments [42]. Deep learning-based methods have the prospective to increase the precision and effectiveness of genome data fragmentation, allowing for improved downstream analytics in genomics and bioinformatics research [42].

14.4.2   Phenotype Classification Using Deep Learning

According to Orgogozo *et al.* (2015) [60], phenotypes are observable qualities or characteristics of an organism that are the outcome of the interaction between its genetic make-up

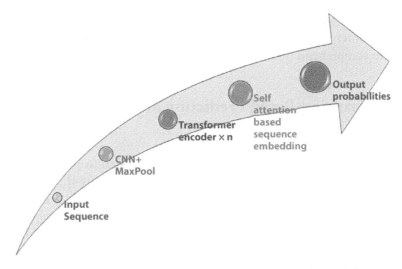

Figure 14.3 An example of a transformer model used in bioinformatics, together with the TransEPI frameworks (Shuang *et al.*, 2023) [58].

(genotype) and the environment. Deep learning algorithms are used in phenotypic classification to categorize or classify phenotypes according to particular traits or attributes [61]. Data collection, data processing, model design, model training, model assessment, and model deployment are all steps in the phenotypic classification process that uses deep learning [61, 62] (Figure 14.4).

Being aware of the fact that the effectiveness of deep learning for phenotypic classification relies on the availability and caliber of labeled training data, the selection of suitable features or representations, the design of the model architecture, and the optimization of

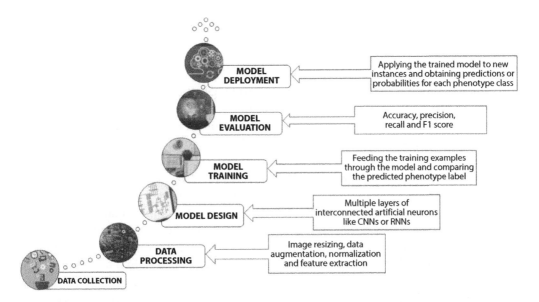

Figure 14.4 Phenotypic classification process using deep learning.

hyperparameters [63] is important. Deep learning models for phenotypic categorization can be difficult to interpret and explain since they frequently operate as "black boxes," making it difficult to comprehend the logic behind their predictions [61].

14.5　Deep Learning-Based Prediction of Altered Genes and mRNA Levels in AD

When several biomarkers or gene expression data's are utilized to predict the risk of AD, machine learning techniques are widely suggested as a solution [64]. In gene expression datasets, where the number of genes is often in the tens of thousands and generated from a few hundred samples, the "curse of dimensionality" affects machine learning methods. Datasets collected for AD research usually include this range of sampling [65]. Researchers typically merge many datasets to create a larger dataset with more samples since machine learning requires a greater number of samples [64]. Machine learning studies on gene expression data frequently start by eliminating superfluous genes or selecting differentially expressed genes to reflect the samples.

The need for feature engineering is decreased and, in many cases, eliminated by deep learning, a branch of machine learning [66]. CNNs are among the deep learning techniques whose effectiveness in categorizing pictures has been demonstrated even with less data [67]. Deep learning frameworks have been applied to genetic research to examine molecular phenotypes that foretell the consequences of noncoding mutations [42], differential gene expression [68], and possible transcription factor binding sites [69]. To predict chromatin properties like transcription factor binding or DNase hypersensitivity from DNA sequences, these programmes leverage CHIP-Seq or DNase-Seq data as training data. Deep learning has recently been used to analyze gene regulation and capture mutations, suggesting its potential to further our understanding of epigenetic control [70]. Additionally, CRISPR guide RNAs are designed by utilizing deep learning-based gene characteristics in gene therapy [71]. In order to determine population-based genetic risk variation for human illnesses and phenotypes, genome-wide association studies (GWAS) employ a statistical methodology that takes into account one single-nucleotide polymorphism (SNP) at a time across the whole genome [16]. The so-called high-dimension low-sample-size (HDLSS) problem [17], which is known to affect phenotypic prediction using genetic variation, makes it difficult to utilize deep learning for GWAS; hence, it has not been done yet. In order to tackle this issue, feature reduction techniques have been widely adopted [18]. However, feature reduction with high-dimensional genomic data is difficult owing to an NP-hard problem [19]. As a result, research is being done to address these drawbacks and construct a deep learning framework to find genetic variations using whole-genome data.

CNNs are frequently employed in AD detection utilizing image-based data such as MRI [72] or diffusion tensor imaging (DTI) [73]. This is similar to other image classification challenges. Either the CNN or the non-image data must be modified and tailored in order to employ the CNN with non-image data (such as gene expression). Using t-SNE [74], Sharma *et al.* (2019) [75] suggested a technique (dubbed "DeepInsight") to transform the non-image data into a 2D image, and a kernel principal component analysis (kPCA) then fed the modified data into the CNN. Authors used t-SNE or kPCA to bring related genes near to one another on a 2D picture plane because they believed that doing so would result in images that were suitable for CNN models. The discriminative qualities of genes are not taken into account by either t-SNE or kPCA, which are both unsupervised machine learning methods for visualizing high-dimensional data in a low-dimensional environment. Gene expressions are suitable for image-based classifiers like CNN thanks to a revolutionary image-formation approach that transforms a one-dimensional gene expression into a discriminative 2D picture. Fisher distance criteria, which maximize the distance between classes and minimize the variation within classes [76], was used in the proposed model to categorize the DEGs (Figure 14.5). Deep learning tactics that have frequently been used to propose a solution to predicting the risk of AD using multiple biomarkers or gene expression data are depicted in Table 14.1.

The image-based representation technique is carried out in two steps: first, the gene is categorized for discriminating power (that is, control vs. illness), and then, using their discriminating power, they are mapped into 2G pictures. The Convex Hull algorithm is used to

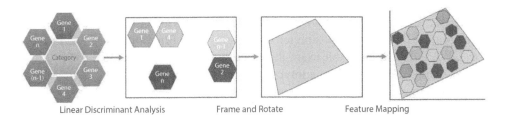

Linear Discriminant Analysis Frame and Rotate Feature Mapping

Figure 14.5 Use of linear discriminant analysis to locate the genes in the 2D image.

Table 14.1 Deep learning tactics for predicting Alzheimer's disease risk using gene expression.

Machine learning model	Dataset	Sample size for AD patients	Number of selected genes	Outcome (AUC)	Reference
CNN	GSE63060 + GSE63061 + GSE140829	1,262	482	0.875	[76]
DNN	GSE63060	145	353	0.874	[64]
	ADNI	63	922	0.657	[64]
SVM	GSE33000 + GSE44770	439	35	0.511	[77]
	GSE63061	139	188	0.804	[64]
	GSE5281	87	1,001	0.894	[78]
	GSE63060 + GSE63061	245	3,601	0.859	[79]
RF	GSE33000 + GSE44770	439	35	0.531	[77]
	GSE63061 + DCR	118	12	0.724	[80]

AD, Alzheimer's disease; AUC, area under curve; CNN, convolutional neural networks; DNN, deep neural network; SVM, support vector machine; RF, random forest.

create a minimal rectangle in order to reduce the sparse areas and produce a compact picture. In order for the minimal rectangle to fit within the 2D coordinate system, it is rotated. Each gene is positioned in the 2D picture at its correct location using the location system (Kalkan *et al.* [76], (2022)).

14.6   Deep Learning with Neuroimaging and Genomics in Alzheimer's Disease

The notion of combining neuroimaging and genomics has been around for at least two decades, and it was originally intended to leverage the concept of intermediate endophenotypes by combining the advantages of both types of research [81, 82]. This ensemble technique was formerly known as image genetics or imaging genomics, which are both interchangeable terms. These days, it is often referred to as "neuroimaging genomics," which is an example of how the two disciplines of "neuroimaging" and "genomics" overlap [83]. The Enhancing NeuroImaging Genetics through Meta-Analysis Consortium (ENIGMA) [84], which aims to comprehend how psychiatric disorders affect the brain by combining neuroimaging (such as MRI, diffusion tensor imaging, and functional MRI) and genomics (such as GWAS) data, is a notable example of neuroimaging genomics [84, 85].

The idea of intermediate endophenotypes in neuroimaging was thought to provide quantitative measurements for behavioral phenotypes, perhaps leading to a relationship between genes and behavioral phenotypes [86, 87]. The quantitative biomarkers of brain activity recorded by neuroimaging modalities are known as intermediate endophenotypes, and they may be used to assess neurobiological changes in brain processes impacted by conditions like AD [88]. According to certain theories [89, 90], AD-associated genetic variations may appear in the intermediate endophenotypes that may be evaluated using neuroimaging modalities and may be directly connected to AD. Additionally, it has been suggested that the problem of small effect sizes in genomics investigations can be resolved using the intermediate endophenotypes of neuroimaging [89, 90]. Contrarily, it is suggested that the results of neuroimaging genomics are only partially replicated, which may be due to small sample sizes, shaky study designs, and a dearth of multiple testing corrections [91, 92].

Such research on the combination exploration of neuroimaging and genomes or neuroimaging genomics are still uncommon in the present literature, particularly for AD prediction [93]. The design of integrating neuroimaging and genomics to predict AD risk is depicted in Figure 14.6.

14.7   Limitations and Challenges in Deep Learning-Based Neuroimaging Genomics Investigations in Alzheimer's Disease

Lack of cross-validation methods, conventional benchmark models, and large-scale, standardized benchmark datasets, hardware limitations, difficulty in understanding deep learning models, lack of open-source software platforms/packages, and instability and difficulties with mode collapse in the GAN model are just a few of the major problems

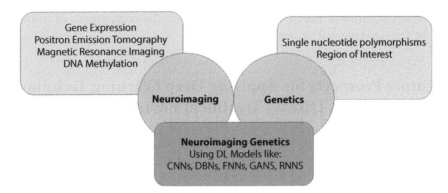

Figure 14.6 Integrating neuroimaging and genomics to predict AD risk. CNNs, convolutional neural networks; DBNs, deep belief networks; FNNs, fully connected neural networks; GANs, generative adversarial networks; RNNs, recurrent neural networks.

in the neuroimaging genomics studies pertaining to AD research [93]. Inferences of biomedical test processing with superior analytics [94, 95] and other domains like genomics classification [96] and the food industry [97] will suggest that technological advancements will improve healthcare services [98]. While effective in scoring AD categorization, prediction, and diagnosis, the current ML and DL models have major drawbacks like: (i) huge computing resources are required in order to train DL architecture on a big number of medical pictures, (ii) the difficulty in obtaining sufficient amounts of standard training datasets because they can be expensive and constrained by privacy concerns, and (iii) the requirement for more precise, focused, and monotonous regulation of various parameters throughout training.

In addition to the above-described restrictions, existing methods may have two drawbacks when it comes to DL-based AD diagnosis. They focus mostly on employing controlled learning systems for AD prediction or categorization. To educate the frameworks, they also need categorized data. However, these frameworks are pricey and difficult to use in actual executions to get enough AD data. Multi-view learning (learning with many perspectives), as a result, is seldom taken into account for MRI data, while learning from many perspectives might fully examine the functional characteristics and improve the accuracy of data calculation. Inspiring factors for multi-view data grouping include the fact that different views have different relevance and levels of early understanding. In order to develop unsupervised learning algorithms and create multi-view MRI data in order to achieve self-regulating AD diagnosis (Zhang *et al.* [99] (2021)). Despite numerous advancements, substantial obstacles still stand in the way of integrating DL approaches into the therapeutic environment. Although technical issues related to the generalizability and interpretability of frameworks are potential research areas, other issues like data privacy, accessibility, and ownership rights will require discussions in the healthcare system and society to come to a conclusion that they will be beneficial to all concerned collaborators. By using DL approaches, which have previously demonstrated their effectiveness in image processing and analysis, it may be possible to increase data quality specifically [97]. It will need interdisciplinary teams of doctors, engineers, computer scientists, ethicists, and legal professionals to incapacitate these flaws. It is one of the ways that people can genuinely comprehend the potential applications of DL in medicine to increase the competence of frontline staff and raise the standard of patient care [15].

14.8   Future Prospects for Applying Deep Learning Techniques in Alzheimer's Disease Treatment Environments

Notwithstanding that profound deep learning techniques have accomplished great outcomes, there are still a few pressing issues in AD recognition. In a few reviews and assortment of information, despite the fact that information upgrade and transfer learning strategies have abstained from over-fitting, the absence of adequate information might in any case cause speculation issues. To take care of this issue, data generation strategies [100] can be utilized to produce new images from existing pictures. The data set was expanded, but its efficacy is still unknown; research in this area will continue, and the image explanation is also another big task [101]. The labeling of medical pictures expects radiologists to comment on given picture information for explicit undertakings, which is a tedious task. Supervised learning has eased this issue and decreased the requirement for expert insight; however, further investigation is required. Albeit deep learning strategies have accomplished astounding outcomes, there are as yet numerous constraints and impediments in the field of AD detection. Tracking down the best blend of various biomarkers [102] requires a detailed clarification of the depth model, benchmarking stage, etc. Whether it can lessen clinical expenses and further develop clinical proficiency still cannot seem to be completely confirmed. Some fusion techniques may be helpful in AD studies, which are current areas of interest by several researchers [14].

Here two implications have been discussed; first, it offers insights into the aspects of using neuroimaging and deep learning on genetic data for predicting AD; and second, it demonstrates how, in utilizing these two forms of data, deep learning models might facilitate the diagnosis and prediction of AD. Numerous research have shown that deep learning models merging genomes and neuroimaging provide ground-breaking methods for the detection and prediction of AD [93]. Future research studies should concentrate on deep learning models to detect AD in the context of neuroimaging genomics as this could result in practical personalized medicine solutions in the fields of global health, public health, and population health, taking into account the crucial requirements of innovative methodologies [85]. Therefore, given the recent developments in disease diagnosis technologies and data-intensive healthcare science, we would anticipate that the fields of global health, public health, and population health could undoubtedly benefit from novel deep learning models with neuroimaging and genomics in the coming years [103, 104]. As a result, in the years to come, governments and the general public will both need to manage open issues and recently emerging concerns with considerable preferences [105–107]. The diagnosis and prediction of AD using deep learning models with neuroimaging and genomics would materialize for target-specific therapeutics in personalized medicine in the upcoming decade [108, 109]. This would depend on prospective large-scale investigations' ability to thoroughly evaluate the pertinent novel neuroimaging and genomics features.

14.9   Conclusion and Future Scope

The untreated loss in brain function characterizes AD, a neurodegenerative condition that is on the rise. Forecasting and diagnosing an illness call for effective, self-learning techniques since it is crucial to stop the condition's progression. Due to the nature of the multiple aspects of brain data, which are primarily extracted through neuroimaging using computer-aided algorithms, the idea of precise computer-aided diagnostic systems is made practical. Modern machine learning techniques fall short of deep learning, a cutting-edge machine learning approach, in their ability to recognize entangled patterns in multidimensional data that is difficult in nature. By identifying anatomical alterations in the brain, deep learning algorithms may be utilized to identify characteristics that carry information regarding AD. The prodromal phases of a disease might possibly be diagnosed early by using automated classification.

This chapter presents a thorough analysis of contemporary automated methods (neuroimaging genomics) to identify AD, which is based on a detailed reading of the relevant literature. The major focus was on neuroimaging genomics and supporting techniques, including deep learning-based detection of genetic variations (phenotype categorization and genome data fragmentation), as well as forecasting changed gene and mRNA levels in AD (genomics). Additionally highlighted are the research inference, challenges, and future study-related instructions. Important research hurdles with integrating neuroimaging genetics' deep learning capabilities into the therapeutic environment, and difficulties in starting to address the present difficulties are also mentioned. The practice of medicine may be profoundly changed by deep learning. Researchers have gathered information from a range of sources, including hospitals, labs, and online databases. In order to accurately predict AD, it is thought that MRI, PET, DNA methylation, and gene expression (neuroimaging) data, single-nucleotide polymorphisms, and genetic regions of interest (genetics) could be used. Fusion approaches have demonstrated appreciable accuracy for predicting AD in a small but accessible neuroimaging data set.

Deep learning techniques, which are a more complex kind of neural networks, are becoming more effective and seem to offer promise for the diagnosis of AD using neuroimaging genomics data. This is true because deep learning, which can be included into any kind of machine learning algorithms, tries to better grasp the data representations. Deep learning-based research on AD is still in its infancy; it is improving performance by integrating more data and enhancing transparency, which promote knowledge of certain disease-associated traits. In the near future, research on deep learning techniques in hybridizing nature-inspired systems will be taken into account in order to display neurological illnesses more accurately through prediction, classification, and diagnosis.

References

1. Rajput, M.S., Nirmal, N.P., Rathore, D., Dahima, R., Dimethyl fumarate exerts neuroprotection by modulating calcineurin/NFAT1 and NFκB dependent BACE1 activity in $A\beta_{1-42}$ treated neuroblastoma SH-SY5Y cells. *Brain Res. Bull.*, 165, 97–107, 2020.

2. Herrera-Espejo, S., Santos-Zorrozua, B.A., lvarez-González, P., Lopez-Lopez, E., Garcia-Orad, A., A systematic review of microRNA expression as biomarker of late-onset alzheimer's disease. *Mol. Neurobiol.*, 56, 12, 8376–8391, 2019.

3. Wingo, T.S., Lah, J.J., Levey, A.I., Cutler, D.J., Autosomal recessive causes likely in early-onset alzheimer disease. *Arch. Neurol.*, 69, 1, 59–64, 2012.

4. Cacace, R., Sleegers, K., Van Broeckhoven, C., Molecular genetics of early-onset alzheimer's disease revisited. *Alzheimers Dement.*, 12, 6, 733–748, 2016.

5. Harman, D., Alzheimer's disease pathogenesis: Role of aging. *Ann. New York Acad. Sci.*, 1067, 1, 454–460, 2006.

6. Chethana, H.P., Hemachandra, G., Sidhu, A., Biomarkers: Potential perspectives in detection, diagnosis, and prognosis of neurodegenerative disorders, in: *Functional Foods and Therapeutic Strategies for Neurodegenerative Disorders*, P. Elumalai and S. Lakshmi (Eds.), pp. 203–222, Springer, Singapore, 2022.

7. Koutsodendris, N., Nelson, M.R., Rao, A., Huang, Y., Apolipoprotein e and alzheimer's disease: Findings, hypotheses, and potential mechanisms. *Annu. Rev. Pathol.*, 17, 73–99, 2022.

8. Bhattacharyya, R., Teves, C.A.F., Long, A., Hofert, M., Tanzi, R.E., The neuronal-specific iso-form of BIN1 regulates β-secretase cleavage of APP and Aβ generation in a RIN_3-dependent manner. *Sci. Rep.*, 12, 1, 1–12, 2022.

9. Nayyar, A., Kumar, S., Agrawal, A., *Applications of computational science in artificial intelligence*, pp. 1–284, IGI Global, United States, 2022.

10. Venaik, A., Kumari, R., Venaik, U., Nayyar, A., The role of machine learning and artificial intelligence in clinical decisions and the herbal formulations against covid-19, in: *International Journal of Reliable and Quality E-Healthcare (IJRQEH)*, vol. 11, pp. 1–17, 2022.

11. Ilmudeen, A. and Nayyar, A., Novel designs of smart healthcare systems: Technologies, architecture, and applications, in: *Machine Learning for Critical Internet of Medical Things: Applications and Use Cases*, pp. 125–151, Cham: Springer International Publishing, Springer Nature, Germany, 2022.

12. Wellcome Trust Case Control Consortium, Genome-wide association study of 14,000 cases of seven common diseases and 3,000 shared controls. *Nature*, 447, 7145, 661–678, 2007.

13. Goldstein, B.A., Hubbard, A.E., Cutler, A., Barcellos, L.F., An application of random forests to a genome-wide association dataset: Methodological considerations & new findings. *BMC Genet.*, 11, 1, 49, 2010.

14. Gao, S. and Lima, D., A review of the application of deep learning in the detection of alzheimer's disease. *Int. J. Cog. Comp. Eng*, 3, 1–8, 2022.

15. Rajput, N.S., Rajput, M.S., Sarkar, P.D., Deep learning framework for prediction, classification and diagnosis of alzheimer's disease, in: *Machine Learning and Deep Learning in Medical Data Analytics and Healthcare Applications*, 1st ed, pp. 183–202, CRC Press, Taylor and Francis, FL, USA, Jan 2022.

16. Buniello, A., MacArthur, J.A.L., Cerezo, M. *et al.*, The NHGRI-EBI GWAS catalog of published genome-wide association studies, targeted arrays and summary statistics 2019. *Nucleic Acids Res.*, 47, D1005–12, 2019.

17. Auton, A., Brooks, L.D., Durbin, R.M., Garrison, E.P., Kang, H.M., Korbel, J.O., Marchini, J.L., McCarthy, S., McVean, G.A., Abecasis, G.R., A global reference for human genetic variation. *Nature*, 526, 7571, 68–74, 2015.

18. Yamada, M., Jitkrittum, W., Sigal, L. *et al.*, High-dimensional feature selection by feature-wise Kernelized lasso. *Neural Comput.*, 26, 185–207, 2014.

19. Guyon, I. and Elisseeff, A., An introduction to variable and feature selection. *J. Mach. Learn. Res.*, 3, 1157–82, 2003.

20. Rajput, M.S., Nirmal, N.P., Rathore, D., Dahima, R., Dimethyl fumarate mitigates tauopathy in Aβ-induced neuroblastoma SH-SY5Y cells. *Neurochem. Res.*, 45, 2641–2652, 2020.

21. Govaerts, L.J. and Bouhy, S.D., Pathogenesis of alzheimer's disease: Molecular and cellular mechanisms. *Rev. Med. Liege*, 62, 209–216, 2007.

22. Eckert, A., Keil, U., Marques, C.A. *et al.*, Mitochondrial dysfunction, apoptotic cell death, and alzheimer's disease. *Biochem. Pharmacol.*, 66, 1627–1634, 2003.

23. Rani, V., Verma, R., Kumar, K., Chawla, R., Role of pro-inflammatory cytokines in alzheimer's disease and neuroprotective effects of pegylated self-assembled nanoscaffolds. *Curr. Res. Pharmacol. Drug Discov.*, 4, 100149, 2022 Dec 20.

24. Zhang, M., An, C., Gao, Y., Leak, R.K., Chen, J., Zhang, F., Emerging roles of Nrf2 and phase II antioxidant enzymes in neuroprotection. *Prog. Neurobiol.*, 100, 30–47, 2013 Jan.

25. Habas, A., Hahn, J., Wang, X., Margeta, M., Neuronal activity regulates astrocytic Nrf2 signaling. *Proc. Natl. Acad. Sci. U.S.A.*, 110, 18291–18296, 2013.

26. Lee, V.M., Goedert, M., Trojanowski, J.Q., Neurodegenerative tauopathies. *Annu. Rev. Neurosci.*, 24, 1121–1159, 2001.

27. Spillantini, M.G., Murrell, J.R., Goedert, M., Farlow, M.R., Klug, A., Ghetti, B., Mutation in the tau gene in familial multiple system tauopathy with presenile dementia. *Proc. Natl. Acad. Sci. U.S.A.*, 95, 7737–7741, 1998.

28. Gotz, J., Chen, F., van Dorpe, J., Nitsch, R.M., Formation of neurofibrillary tangles in P301l tau transgenic mice induced by Abeta$_{42}$ fibrils. *Science*, 293, 1491–1495, 2001.

29. Wischik, C.M., Bentham, P., Wischik, D.J., Seng, K.M., Tau aggregation inhibitor (TAI) therapy with rember™ arrests disease progression in mild and moderate alzheimer's disease over 50 weeks. *Alzheimers Dement*, 4, T167, 2008.

30. Barber, R.C., The genetics of Alzheimer's disease. *Scientifica*, 2012, Article ID 246210, 14, 2012. https://doi.org/10.6064/2012/246210

31. Wilson, DM 3rd, Cookson, M.R., Van Den Bosch, L. *et al.*, Hallmarks of neurodegenerative diseases. *Cell*, 186, 4, 693–714, 2023.

32. Jindal, M., Gupta, J., Bharat, B., Machine learning methods for IoT and their future applications, in: *2019 International Conference on Computing, Communication and Intelligent Systems (ICCCIS)*, IEEE, pp. 430–34, 2019.

33. Samper-González, J., Ninon, B., Simona, B. *et al.*, Reproducible evaluation of classification methods in alzheimer's disease: Framework and application to MRI and PET data. *Neuroimage*, 183, 504–21, 2018.

34. LeCun, Y., Yoshua, B., Hinton, G., Deep learning. *Nature*, 521, 7553, 436–44, 2015.

35. Sharma, N., Kaushik, I., Bhushan, B., Gautam, S., Applicability of WSN and biometric models in the field of healthcare, in: *2020 Deep Learning Strategies for Security Enhancement in Wireless Sensor Networks*, pp. 304–29, IGI Global, United States, 2020.

36. Jo, T., Kwangsik, N., Saykin, A.J., Deep learning in alzheimer's disease: Diagnostic classification and prognostic prediction using neuroimaging data. *Front. Aging Neurosci.*, 11, 220, 2019.

37. Zhou, T., Thung, K.H., Zhu, X., Shen, D., Effective feature learning and fusion of multimodality data using stage-wise deep neural network for dementia diagnosis. *Hum. Brain Mapp*, 40, 3, 1001–1016, 2019.

38. Khani, M., Gibbons, E., Bras, J. *et al.*, Challenge accepted: Uncovering the role of rare genetic variants in alzheimer's disease. *Mol. Neurodegener.*, 17, 3, 2022.

39. Timpson, N.J., Greenwood, C.M.T., Soranzo, N., Lawson, D.J., Richards, J.B., Genetic architecture: The shape of the genetic contribution to human traits and disease. *Nat. Rev. Genet.*, 19, 110–24, 2018.

40. Frazer, K.A., Murray, S.S., Schork, N.J., Topol, E.J., Human genetic variation and its contribution to complex traits. *Nat. Rev. Genet.*, 10, 241–51, 2009.

41. Liu, C.-C., Liu, C.-C., Kanekiyo, T., Xu, H., Bu, G., Apolipoprotein E and alzheimer disease: Risk, mechanisms and therapy. *Nat. Rev. Neurol.*, 9, 106–18, 2013.

42. Jo, T., Nho, K., Bice, P., Saykin, A.J., Alzheimer's disease neuroimaging initiative. Deep learning-based identification of genetic variants: Application to alzheimer's disease classification. *Brief. Bioinform.*, 23, 2, bbac022, 2022.

43. Gunasekaran, J., Ramalakshmi, K., Arokiaraj, R.M., Kanmani, D., Venkatesan, C., Dhas, S.G., Analysis of DNA sequence classification using CNN and hybrid models. *Comput. Math Methods Med.*, 2021, 1835056, 2021.

44. Min, S., Lee, B., Yoon, S., Deep learning in bioinformatics. *Brief. Bioinform.*, 18, 5, 851–869, 2017.

45. Al-Ajlan, A. and El Allali, A., CNN-MGP: Convolutional neural networks for metagenomics gene prediction. *Interdiscip Sci.*, 11, 4, 628–635, 2019.

46. Collobert, R., Weston, J., Bottou, L., Karlen, M., Kavukcuoglu, K., Kuksa, P., Natural language processing (almost) from scratch. *J. Mach. Learn. Res.*, 12, 2493–2537, 2011.

47. Angermueller, C., Pärnamaa, T., Parts, L., Stegle, O., Deep learning for computational biology. *Mol. Syst. Biol.*, 12, 7, 878, 2016.

48. Alipanahi, B., Delong, A., Weirauch, M.T., Frey, B.J., Predicting the sequence specificities of DNA- and RNA-binding proteins by deep learning. *Nat. Biotechnol.*, 33, 8, 831–838, 2015.

49. Di Gangi, M.A., Gaglio, S., La Bua, C., Bosco, G.L., Rizzo, R., A deep learning network for exploiting positional information in nucleosome related sequences, in: *International Conference on Bioinformatics and Biomedical Engineering*, Springer, pp. 524–533, 2017.

50. Zhou, J. and Troyanskaya, O.G., Predicting effects of noncoding variants with deep learning-based sequence model. *Nat. Methods*, 12, 10, 931–934, 2015.

51. Quang, D. and Xie, X., Danq: A hybrid convolutional and recurrent deep neural network for quantifying the function of DNA sequences. *Nucleic Acids Res.*, 44, 11, e107–e107, 2016.

52. Kelley, D.R., Snoek, J., Rinn, J.L., Basset: Learning the regulatory code of the accessible genome with deep convolutional neural networks. *Genome Res.*, 26, 7, 990–999, 2016.

53. Umarov, R.K. and Solovyev, V.V., Recognition of prokaryotic and eukaryotic promoters using convolutional deep learning neural networks. *PloS One*, 12, 2, e0171410, 2017.

54. Hochreiter, S. and Schmidhuber, J., Long short-term memory. *Neural Comput.*, 9, 8, 1735–1780, 1997.

55. Koumakis, L., Deep learning models in genomics; are we there yet? *Comput. Struct. Biotechnol. J.*, 18, 1466–1473, 2020.

56. Montana, D.J. and Davis, L., Training feedforward neural networks using genetic algorithms. *Proc. 11th Int. Jt. Conf. Artif. Intell.*, pp. 762–767, 1989.

57. Williams, R.J. and Zipser, D., A learning algorithm for continually running fully recurrent neural networks. *Neural Comput.*, 1, 2, 270–280, 1989.

58. Shuang, Z., Fan, R., Liu, Y., Chen, S., Liu, Q., Zeng, W., Applications of transformer-based language models in bioinformatics: A survey. *Bioinf. Adv.*, 3, 1, vbad001, 2023.

59. Jim, C., Explainability in transformer models for functional genomics. *Briefings Bioinf.*, 22, 5, bbab060, 2021.

60. Orgogozo, V., Morizot, B., Martin, A., The differential view of genotype–phenotype relationships. *Front. Genet.*, 6, 179, 2015.

61. Fan, Y., Li, J., Song, S., Zhang, H., Wang, S., Zhai, G., Palmprint phenotype feature extraction and classification based on deep learning. *Phenomics*, 2, 4, 219–229, 2022.

62. Taghavi, N.S., Esmaeilzadeh, M., Najafi, M., Brown, T.B., Borevitz, J.O., Deep phenotyping: Deep learning for temporal phenotype/genotype classification. *Plant Methods*, 14, 66, 2018.

63. Muneeb, M., Feng, S., Henschel, A., Transfer learning for genotype-phenotype prediction using deep learning models. *BMC Bioinf.*, 23, 1, 511, 2022 Nov 29.

64. Lee, T. and Lee, H., Prediction of alzheimer's disease using blood gene expression data. *Sci. Rep.*, 10, 3485, 2020.

65. Mahendran, N., Vincent, P.M.D.R., Srinivasan, K., Chang, C.Y., Improving the classification of alzheimer's disease using hybrid gene selection pipeline and deep learning. *Front. Genet.*, 12, 784814, 2021.

66. Yamashita, R., Nishio, M., Do, R.K.G., Togashi, K., Convolutional neural networks: An overview and application in radiology. *Insights Imaging*, 9, 611–629, 2018.

67. Brigato, L. and Iocchi, L., A close look at deep learning with small data, in: *Proceedings of the 25th International Conference on Pattern Recognition*, Milan, Italy, 2020.

68. Tasaki, S., Gaiteri, C., Mostafavi, S. *et al.*, Deep learning decodes the principles of differential gene expression. *Nat. Mach. Intell.*, 2, 376–86, 2020.

69. Zheng, A., Lamkin, M., Zhao, H. *et al.*, Deep neural networks identify sequence context features predictive of transcription factor binding. *Nat. Mach. Intell.*, 3, 172–80, 2021.

70. Scherer, M., Schmidt, F., Lazareva, O. *et al.*, Machine learning for deciphering cell heterogeneity and gene regulation. *Nat. Comput. Sci.*, 1, 183–91, 2021.

71. Listgarten, J., Weinstein, M., Kleinstiver, B.P. *et al.*, Prediction of off-target activities for the end-to-end design of CRISPR guide RNAs. *Nat. BioMed. Eng.*, 2, 38–47, 2018.

72. Sarraf, S. and Tofighi, G., Classification of alzheimer's disease using fmri data and deep learning convolutional neural networks, 2016, 1603, arXiv 2016;arXiv:1603.08631.

73. Marzban, E.N., Eldeib, A.M., Yassine, I.A., Kadah, Y.M., Alzheimer's disease neurodegenerative initiative. Alzheimer's disease diagnosis from diffusion tensor images using convolutional neural networks. *PloS One*, 15, 3, e0230409, 2020.

74. van der Maaten, L. and Hinton, G., Visualizing high-dimensional data using t-SNE. *J. Mach. Learn. Res.*, 9, 86, 2579–2605, 2008.

75. Sharma, A., Vans, E., Shigemizu, D., Boroevich, K.A., Tsunoda, T., DeepInsight: A methodology to transform a non-image data to an image for convolution neural network architecture. *Sci. Rep.*, 9, 11399, 2019.

76. Kalkan, H., Akkaya, U.M., Inal-Gültekin, G., Sanchez-Perez, A.M., Prediction of alzheimer's disease by a novel image-based representation of gene expression. *Genes*, 13, 1406, 2022.

77. Park, C., Ha, J., Park, S., Prediction of alzheimer's disease based on deep neural network by integrating gene expression and DNA methylation dataset. *Expert Syst. Appl.*, 140, 112873, 2020.

78. Wang, L. and Liu, Z.P., Detecting diagnostic biomarkers of alzheimer's disease by integrating gene expression data in six brain regions. *Front. Genet.*, 10, 157, 2019.

79. Li, X., Wang, H., Long, J. *et al.*, Systematic analysis and biomarker study for alzheimer's disease. *Sci. Rep.*, 8, 17394, 2018.

80. Voyle, N., Keohane, A., Newhouse, S. *et al.*, A pathway based classification method for analyzing gene expression for alzheimer's disease diagnosis. *J. Alzheimer's Dis.*, 49, 659–669, 2016.

81. Hariri, A.R., Drabant, E.M., Weinberger, D.R., Imaging genetics: Perspectives from studies of genetically driven variation in serotonin function and corticolimbic affective processing. *Biol. Psychiatry*, 59, 88–897, 2006.

82. Rabl, U., Scharinger, C., Müller, M., Pezawas, L., Imaging genetics: Implications for research on variable antidepressant drug response. *Expert Rev. Clin. Pharmacol.*, 3, 471–489, 2010.

83. Mufford, M.S., Stein, D.J., Dalvie, S. *et al.*, Neuroimaging genomics in psychiatry—A translational approach. *Genome Med.*, 9, 1–12, 2017.

84. Thompson, P.M., Stein, J.L., Medland, S.E. *et al.*, The ENIGMA consortium: Large-scale collaborative analyses of neuroimaging and genetic data. *Brain Imaging Behav.*, 8, 153–182, 2014.

85. Lin, E. and Lane, H.Y., Machine learning and systems genomics approaches for multi-omics data. *Biomark. Res.*, 5, 2, 2017.

86. Gottesman, I.I. and Gould, T.D., The endophenotype concept in psychiatry: Etymology and strategic intentions. *Am. J. Psychiatry*, 160, 636–645, 2003.

87. Meyer-Lindenberg, A. and Weinberger, D.R., Intermediate phenotypes and genetic mechanisms of psychiatric disorders. *Nat. Rev. Neurosci.*, 7, 818–827, 2006.

88. Viviani, R., Lehmann, M.L., Stingl, J.C., Use of magnetic resonance imaging in pharmacogenomics. *Br. J. Clin. Pharmacol.*, 77, 684–694, 2014.

89. Braskie, M.N., Ringman, J.M., Thompson, P.M., Neuroimaging measures as endophenotypes in alzheimer's disease. *Int. J. Alzheimers Dis.*, 2011, 490140, 2011.

90. Chung, J., Wang, X., Maruyama, T. *et al.*, Genome-wide association study of alzheimer's disease endophenotypes at prediagnosis stages. *Alzheimers Dement.*, 14, 623–633, 2018.

91. Carter, C.S., Bearden, C.E., Bullmore, E.T. *et al.*, Enhancing the informativeness and replicability of imaging genomics studies. *Biol. Psychiatry*, 82, 157–164, 2017.

92. Pereira, L.P., Köhler, C.A., Stubbs, B., Imaging genetics paradigms in depression research: Systematic review and meta-analysis. *Prog. Neuro-Psychopharmacol. Biol. Psychiatry*, 86, 102–113, 2018.

93. Lin, E., Lin, C.H., Lane, H.Y., Deep learning with neuroimaging and genomics in alzheimer's disease. *Int. J. Mol. Sci.*, 22, 15, 7911, 2021.

94. Goyal, S., Sharma, N., Bhushan, B., Shankar, A., Sagayam, M., IoT enabled technology in secured healthcare: Applications, challenges and future directions, in: *Cognitive Internet of Medical Things for Smart Healthcare*. Studies in Systems, Decision and Control, vol. 311, pp. 25–48, 2021.

95. Panigrahi, N., Ishan, A., Jena, O.P., An expert system-based clinical decision support system for hepatitis-B prediction & diagnosis, in: *Machine Learning for Healthcare Applications*, vol. 4, pp. 57–75, 2021.

96. Patra, S.S., Jena, O.P., Kumar, G., Pramanik, S., Misra, C., Kamakhya, N.S., Random forest algorithm in imbalance genomics classification, in: *Data Analytics in Bioinformatics*, vol. 7, pp. 173–90, 2021.

97. Paramesha, K., Gururaj, H.L., Jena, O.P., Applications of machine learning in biomedical text processing and food industry, in: *Machine Learning for Healthcare Applications*, vol. 10, pp. 151–67, 2021.

98. Pattnayak, P. and Jena, O.P., Innovation on machine learning in healthcare services–an introduction, in: *Machine Learning for Healthcare Applications*, vol. 1, pp. 1–15, 2021.

99. Zhang, X., Yan, Y., Li, T. *et al.*, CMC: A consensus multi-view clustering model for predicting alzheimer's disease progression. *Comput. Methods Programs BioMed.*, 199, 105895, 2021.

100. Arbabyazd, L., Shen, K., Wang, Z. *et al.*, Virtual connectomic datasets in alzheimer's disease and aging using whole-brain network dynamics modelling. *eNeuro*, 8, 4, 1–33, 2021.

101. Choi, B.K., Madusanka, N., Choi, H.K. *et al.*, Convolutional neural network-based MR image analysis for alzheimer's disease classification. *Curr. Med. Imaging*, 16, 1, 27–35, 2020.

102. Jack Jr., C.R., Bennett, D.A., Blennow, K. *et al.*, NIA-AA research framework: Toward a biological definition of alzheimer's disease. *Alzheimers Dement.*, 14, 4, 535–562, 2018.

103. Lin, E., Lin, C.H., Lane, H.Y., Precision psychiatry applications with pharmacogenomics: Artificial intelligence and machine learning approaches. *Int. J. Mol. Sci.*, 21, 969, 2020.

104. Lin, E., Lin, C.H., Lai, Y.L. *et al.*, Combination of G72 genetic variation and G72 protein level to detect schizophrenia: Machine learning approaches. *Front. Psychiatry*, 9, 566, 2018.

105. Guney, G., Yigin, B.O., Guven, N. *et al.*, An Overview of deep learning algorithms and their applications in neuropsychiatry. *Clin. Psychopharmacol. Neurosci.*, 19, 206, 2021.

106. Lin, E., Kuo, P.H., Lin, W.Y. *et al.*, Prediction of probable major depressive disorder in the Taiwan biobank: An integrated machine learning and genome-wide analysis approach. *J. Pers. Med.*, 11, 597, 2021.

107. Lane, H.Y., Tu, C.H., Lin, W.C., Lin, C.H., Brain activity of benzoate, a D-amino acid oxidase inhibitor, in patients with mild cognitive impairment in a randomized, double-blind, placebo controlled clinical trial. *Int. J. Neuropsychopharmacol.*, 24, 392–399, 2021.

108. Lin, E., Lin, C.H., Lane, H.Y., Machine learning and deep learning for the pharmacogenomics of antidepressant treatments. *Clin. Psychopharmacol. Neurosci.*, 19, 4, 557–558, 2021.

109. Raza, M., Awais, M., Ellahi, W. *et al.*, Diagnosis and monitoring of alzheimer's patients using classical and deep learning techniques. *Expert Syst. Appl.*, 136, 353–364, 2019.

Artificial Intelligence Techniques in the Classification and Screening of Compounds in Computer-Aided Drug Design (CADD) Process

Raghunath Satpathy

School of Biotechnology, Gangadhar Meher University, Amruta Vihar, Sambalpur, Odisha, India

Abstract

The health problems created by pathogenic infections as well as genetic and metabolic disorders cause a public health challenge. Despite the success of developing medications to solve human health issues, some of these illnesses continue pushing high mortality rates. The traditional approach to the drug design process is complex, costly, and hence insufficient to address the issue. Therefore, computer-aided drug design (CADD) techniques perform a vital task in the discovery process of new drug molecules. Sophisticated computational tools are frequently used in major steps of the drug discovery pathways, starting from identification of target to lead molecule and metabolism study. However, artificial intelligence (AI) techniques are currently implemented to speed up the process. One of the crucial methods in drug design is screening the potential compounds from a more extensive compound database. However, AI algorithms can screen potential new drug compounds from a larger data set in a considerably faster and more accurate manner compared to the traditional methods. Due to automatization, the process reduces the time and money required for the procedure. The chapter provides the potential application of AI in the CADD process and highlights the methods and major algorithms, followed by the challenges in this emerging area.

Keywords: Artificial intelligence, CADD, machine learning algorithms, compound screening, molecular modeling, drug discovery process

15.1 Introduction

The development of new drug molecules is essential to address the global health problem. The drug discovery process is a multi-disciplinary subject in which screening, efficacy, pharmacokinetic property, and the safety aspects of the ligand molecule are evaluated with the specific target molecule. Computer-aided drug design (CADD) method is currently used worldwide to facilitate drug development. The drug development process starts from the identification and validation of the target molecule. The molecular targets for the therapeutic process are identified as essential proteins/enzymes of the pathogen that take part

Email: rnsatpathy@gmail.com

Abhirup Khanna, May El Barachi, Sapna Jain, Manoj Kumar and Anand Nayyar (eds.) *Artificial Intelligence and Machine Learning in Drug Design and Development*, (473–498) © 2024 Scrivener Publishing LLC

in prime roles in pathogenicity. The next crucial step is hit identification and validation, which involves recognizing the small molecule with the desired effect against the molecular targets. Hits can be identified by using several methods, such as high-throughput screening (HTS), knowledge-based methods, and virtual screening. The next step of the move is from the hit to a lead (probable drug molecule) validation and optimization. Optimization is necessary to improve deficiencies and maintain the desired structural properties. Furthermore, determining pharmacokinetic toxicity and other desired metabolic features can be considered. In this way, drug discovery brings different branches of science, such as computational chemistry, medical chemistry, drug metabolism, and other fields, into a single umbrella that allows us to provide unique insight into the process [1–3]. The property-based design of the novel small molecules has attracted significant attention among researchers in the drug discovery area. Recently, billions of small molecules have been synthesized and available in public and commercially available databases. However, one of the significant challenges in CADD is to find out the uniqueness of compounds from the compound database containing millions of compounds. Researchers had developed and adopted several computational methods that are adopted in the drug discovery pipeline. The primary objective of these methods aids the researchers to assist in the structure-based discovery and elucidation of bioactive compounds and to identify the molecular patterns for the target selectivity [4–7]. In this context, computational strategies, including artificial intelligence and machine learning algorithms, are frequently used in the modern discovery of small molecules as a drug. Artificial intelligence (AI) methods generally work by mimicking the human decision-making system to solve complex problems.

Furthermore, the performance of AI algorithms can be improved by continuously learning by doing specific tasks from the input data by the user. Recently, scientists also implemented an artificial neural network (ANN) to address the drug discovery issue to automate the drug design process quickly and accurately, ultimately speeding up the process [8, 9].

Organization of the Chapter

The rest of the chapter is organized as follows: Section 15.2 enlightens an overview of the drug design process. Section 15.3 highlights the computational tools and techniques in CADD, followed by Section 15.4 elaborating the concept of artificial intelligence (AI) and machine learning (ML) methods and followed by an explanation of major machine learning techniques and applications in molecular screening process in Section 15.5. Section 15.6 highlights challenges and opportunities. Finally, Section 15.7 concludes the chapter with future perspectives.

15.2   Overview of the Drug Design Process

The traditional methods of drug discovery are an expensive and time-consuming process. Millions of molecules are to be screened to obtain the desired drug molecules. After successful screening of the molecule, the safety aspects are measured by conducting *in vitro* and *in vivo* assays using animal models. However, animal studies most often fail to predict the clinical results due to differences in composition and biochemical pathways. Nearly about

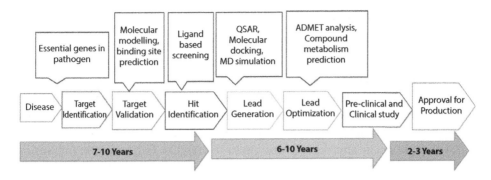

Figure 15.1 Overview of a computer-aided drug design process.

30% of screened molecules entering clinical trials fail because of safety aspects [10–13]. In this context, computer-aided drug design (CADD) plays a key role in the major steps of the drug development procedure, such as target molecule selection, lead compound, picking out optimized lead molecule, and assessing the metabolic performance of the drug. The computer application also reduces the time consumed in and the cost of the drug development process [14–16]. The method of computer-aided drug design is operated in an iterative manner and often makes progress through several paths before the establishment of a lead molecule to a functional drug molecule (Figure 15.1) [17–19]. The major steps of drug design is being described in the following sub-sections (15.2.1 to 15.2.5) [20–22].

15.2.1   Target Identification

Target identification in the drug discovery process is all about finding an agent with specific vital biological activity. The target can be any molecule to which the drug molecule can be targeted. In the case of infectious diseases, the target identification of the pathogen is one of the essential processes in the CADD process. The target can be any molecule to which the drug molecule can be targeted. Usually, the target should be chosen carefully in the principle that the biomolecule should be essential to the pathogen and non-essential to the host. Various techniques, such as genomics, metabolomics, and disease–protein networks, are applied to the target identification process to integrate the molecular information at different levels. The selection of the target protein to which the drug molecule will bind and inhibit the function is based on the metabolic pathway analysis. Several metabolic pathway databases are available; however, MetaCyc (http://metacyc.org) and KEGG (http://www.genome.ad.jp) are the commonly searched databases. These databases contain user-friendly platforms to retrieve and analyze specific organism-wise pathways using keyword searches. Once the target molecule is identified, the 3D structure prediction is essential to detect its drug binding site, geometry, stability, and so on. X-ray crystallography and 2D-NMR can be used to predict the experimental 3D structure. However, computational modeling, such as homology modeling methods, can also be used as an alternative when the experimental structure data is unavailable [23, 24].

15.2.2   Target Characterization

After the identification of the suitable target, the validation and characterization of the same is an essential step, and it requires several methods—for example, a commonly used way is to detect protein expression in pathogenic/clinical samples. Most often, *in vivo* studies are found to be a key factor to discuss the prediction of the target and involve protein inhibition studies. Several target features are analyzed to validate/verify the target molecule. One such approach is the identification of induced fit ligand binding mechanism (structural changes occur after ligand binding to the target). Furthermore, measuring the chemical kinetics is one of the crucial experimental methods that determine the order of the reaction exhibited by the ligand binding reaction. In the absence of experimental data, computational tools can be used to locate the protein active sites. Since most of the drugs function based on a competitive inhibition mechanism, the binding of ligands to the target is hence to be analyzed. Similarly, the allosteric nature of the compounds and their regulatory mechanism after binding to the target is also to be observed. Another important feature of the target characterization is analyzing the tissue-based location drug target in which it is expressed. This is essential to address the bioavailability issue—for example, if the target is only expressed in the tissue system such as the central nervous system (CNS), then the blood–brain barrier (BBB) permeability phenomena of the drug molecule must be adequately addressed. Another characterization approach is the identification of the *pharmacophore*. The pharmacophore is the three-dimensional portion of the target molecule responsible for the drug molecule's binding. The geometry of interactions, such as hydrogen bond donors (HBD), hydrogen bond acceptors (HBA), and hydrophobic interactions (HI) by the aromatic and hydrophobic groups, is analyzed. Target characterization is a tedious process that demonstrates the relevance of a molecule to a particular biological pathway, molecular process, or disease [25, 26].

15.2.3   Hit Identification

The term "hit" compound is obtained after a screening assay against the target. Various screening approaches exist to identify hit molecules, such as high-throughput, focused, and fragment-based screening (HTS). In the case of HTS-based methods, the total number of ligand (molecular) information is considered, and the binding activity is accessed on the target molecule for screening purposes. Two types of screening methods are used, one of which is known as *knowledge-based screening*, in which the selection of compounds from a library occurs based on the pre-existing information about the target (which may be obtained from the published literature). Similarly, the other i.e., *fragment screening* method uses the library of small-molecular-weight compounds, and screening occurs based on the small fragments that bind to the receptor module [27, 28].

15.2.4   Hit-to-Lead Phase and Lead Optimization

Progression from the hit to lead phase (lead generation) is a stage in early drug development. In this process, the ligand molecule hits from the screening process are analyzed keenly to identify propitious lead compounds. Furthermore, the confirmation of hit can be evaluated by analyzing its activity as tested over a range of concentrations (EC50/IC50), synthetic feasibility, different assays for stability, which is usually closer to the target physiological condition, and so on. Additionally, this phase of drug discovery aims to develop a compound(s) with enhanced properties that will correlate appropriately with the pharmacokinetics. For this, the chemical synthesis of compounds, along with different *in vivo* models, is studied. In this step, the continuous evaluation of structure–activity relationships is investigated for the selected hit compound. Finally, the final lead molecule (probable drug molecule) is discovered with optimal structural, metabolic, and pharmacokinetic properties [29–31].

15.2.5   Preclinical and Clinical Development

The optimized lead molecule is then tested in different animals to check their efficacy. After successful completion of the preclinical (animal-based) assay, it enters the next phase which is known as the clinical trial phase. The clinical trial stage comprises three main phases (phases I, II, and III), followed by a post-market survey stage. Phase I clinical trials are done by taking a small number of healthy volunteers. Phase II trials involve a group of diseased individuals to explore the drug molecule's therapeutic potential (safety and efficacy). Similarly, phase III trials are conducted on a much larger number of human subjects for a large-scale assessment of the efficacy and safety features of the drug. Furthermore, the post-market survey is the study to observe the drug's safety aspects that impact on larger populations [32, 33].

15.3   Computational Tools and Techniques in CADD

CADD is one of the key tools implemented to accelerate the design and development of new drug molecules. Based on the availability of the target, the CADD methods proceed in two different ways, such as structure-based drug design (SBDD), when the target structure is known, and the ligand-based drug design (LBDD). Both methods analyze the ligand–receptor interaction; however, the LBDD process starts with a set of ligand molecules that are considered and known to interact with the reference structures [34, 35].

Some of the essential computational methods that are frequently used in the CADD process are described below.

15.3.1   Homology Modeling

Homology modeling is a structure prediction method used whenever a protein target molecule's experimental structure is unavailable. The method works because *protein structures are more conserved than the sequences*. Hence, it uses the protein sequence and an experimental 3D structure (as template structure) to build the 3D structure of the query protein. Therefore, this is also known as the comparative modeling method [36, 37].

The modeling method works by using several steps such as:

1. Recognition of template structure and alignment
In this process, a suitable experimental structure that has sufficient homology with the query protein sequence is obtained. This is done by searching the structural database, such

as Protein Data Bank (PDB), with the user-given protein sequence by using BLAST (Basic Local Alignment Search Tool), available at https://blast.ncbi.nlm.nih.gov/Blast.cgi. An alignment percentage >80% is recommended, and the specific regions of alignment (query protein sequence template) are to be analyzed to understand the matching and mismatched regions.

2. Correction of the alignment region

This step is usually followed whenever there is a weak alignment between the query protein sequence and the template. Additionally, if the alignment contains any kind of violation, the rules of amino acid substitution rule, such as substitution of hydrophilic amino acid residues with the hydrophobic one in the protein core region and vice versa in the protein surface region. The correction/editing can be done manually after careful observation by using different software like Bioedit (https://bioedit.software.informer.com/).

3. Generation of backbone

After optimization of the target-template alignment, the backbone of the query protein is generated. This is performed by copying the atomic coordinates of the backbone of the template structure to the query protein as per the alignment.

4. Modeling of loop

Loops are the secondary structure of the protein. In several cases of modeling, every part of the query structure is not possible due to the lack of alignment of many protein regions. The prediction of the structure of these missing parts is performed in the loop region to complete the prediction of the final protein structure. Loop regions in protein structures often play important roles and are highly diverse in sequence and structure compared to other regions. This is done computationally by two approaches such as knowledge-based and energy-based. The knowledge-based approach is based on searching for loop conformation, those having similar sequences. The latter process adopts the model having the lowest energy conformation of the loop structure.

5. Modeling of side chain

Side chain modeling involves the prediction of the torsional angle (conformation) for each R group of amino acids attached to the protein's backbone. The side chains having lower energy conformations are known as *rotamers*. In this process, without considering all geometrically possible conformational space, a small number of rotamers can be used to describe the conformation of a side chain. Side chain modeling is usually knowledge-based. The rotamer libraries have been prepared from the PDB data, which is used for modeling purposes.

6. Optimization of the model

After the model is generated, the total energy minimization of the structure is necessary to reduce the total energy. This is done iteratively using different energy functions that compute the energy due to change in backbone and rotamer conformation until the stable state is achieved.

15.3.2   Molecular Docking

Once the target/receptor and ligand structure are known, the *docking* process is performed (Figure 15.2). Molecular docking is a computational method that involves the three-dimensional (3D) structure of two or more interacting molecules (ligand and receptor). Molecular docking aims to predict the binding affinity, conformation, and orientation of the ligand with the receptor by computing the binding energy. The molecular docking program uses specific sets of searching and scoring functions to calculate the binding energy of the ligand–receptor interaction. The prerequisite step of docking is to obtain the 3D structure of the ligand and target proteins (receptors). The 3D structure of the target protein is retrieved from the Protein Data Bank (PDB) and undergoes processing to remove the type of ligands, crystallographic water, missing atoms, etc. Then, the receptor molecule's active site is predicted using computational tools. Thereafter, the ligand molecules can be retrieved from numerous chemical databases and can be sketched by applying different chemical drawing software. Then, molecular docking process is performed, and the interaction of the docked ligand is analyzed (Figure 15.2). The docking program's accuracy and robustness depend on the choice of the *search* algorithm and *scoring* algorithm. Further evaluation of the analytical capability of a docking process may follow the solvation energy calculation and molecular dynamics simulation [38, 39].

15.3.3   Molecular Dynamics Simulation

Another important computational method that is frequently used in CADD is molecular dynamic (MD) simulation. Since it is difficult to obtain the dynamical molecular basis of interaction/atomic fluctuations and motions using an experimental basis, MD simulation is applied to understand the phenomena. The process consists of three basic steps—Step 1:

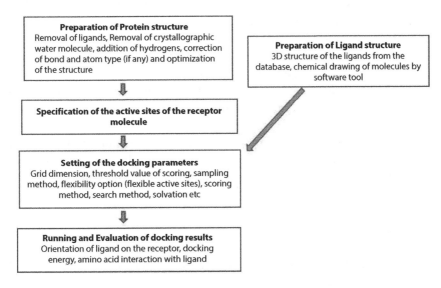

Figure 15.2 Process of molecular docking.

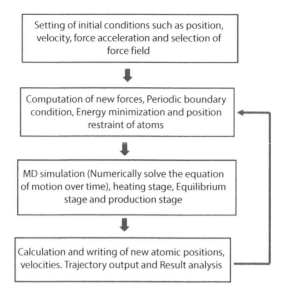

Figure 15.3 Methods to perform molecular dynamics simulation.

initialization, Step 2: heating, equilibration, and energy minimization; and Step 3: production run and analysis of the trajectory (Figure 15.3). Initially, the process starts with considering the given molecular structure, and initial position and velocities are allocated. Next, the equilibration step occurs by solving Newton's equations of motion for some defined steps. Then, the system is heated to calculate the rescaling of the velocities and its stability until the molecular system does not change with time and reaches a specific temperature. The system's energy can be computed using the *force field* (molecular parameters used for property calculations). The conformation of the system, whenever achieved to a lower energy conformation, is known as energy minimization. Energy minimization is done by choosing several minimization algorithms such as steepest descent, conjugate gradient, etc. In the third step, the model is then simulated under different conditions such as NVT (number of particles, volume, temperature) and NPT (number of particles, volume, temperature). In the final step, the running of the simulation is performed for a specific time period to obtain the trajectories as output. The trajectory files are written for the time steps chosen during the simulation and further analyzed to understand the desired properties of interest.

Several properties, such as free energy, kinetics, flexibility, conformational change in 2D and 3D structure, solvation energy contribution in receptor–ligand complexes, hydrogen bonding, salt bridge formation pattern during the simulation, etc., can be computed from the trajectory analysis [40–42].

15.3.4 QSAR Modeling

The quantitative structure–activity relationship (QSAR) modeling method aims to develop predictive models of biological activities and other physicochemical properties as a function of a compound's structural and molecular information. Typical quantitative molecular

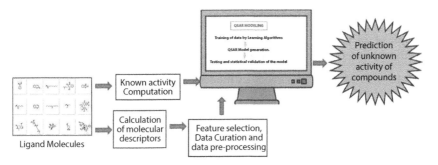

Figure 15.4 Steps followed in the QSAR modeling process.

parameters (descriptors) such as electronic properties, hydrophobicity, geometrical properties, and topology are determined by using sophisticated computational tools.

These features correlate with the ligand molecules' experimental binding affinity by using several statistical or machine learning techniques. There are basic steps followed in the QSAR modeling methods (Figure 15.4). The first step is the descriptor calculation of the compounds by using sophisticated tools. Molecular descriptors are the quantitative information (description) of the given molecule. Several categories of descriptors have been described based on the type of information. Some of the important types are constitutional (atomic constitution), geometric (values represent shape and size of molecule), physico-chemical (values of hydrophobicity, lipophilicity, solubility), quantum chemical (electronic structure of the molecule), and topological (bonding arrangement) descriptors. This step is followed by data processing and cleaning to avoid errors and inconsistencies (missing and incomplete) in the data, as these features hamper the accuracy of the model output. Furthermore, the variability in the distribution and range of each variable in the dataset is addressed by applying statistical and normalization techniques. The final selection of molecular descriptors is considered as the independent variable in building the QSAR model. The dependent variable is the biological activities of the compounds to be obtained from experimental results or the literature. Then, statistical and machine learning methods are implemented to get the relationship between the dependent and independent variables as a QSAR model. Then, the model's accuracy should be validated using testing and validation data computing several statistical parameters [43–45].

Furthermore, investigation of the properties like absorption, distribution, metabolism, excretion, and toxicity (ADMET) is essential to understand and predict the pharmacological properties. This is performed by rule-based calculation of different types of properties of the drug molecules by using computational methods. Above all, the drug-likeness rule is also used to screen the compound to be used as potential drug molecules. These rules consist of a set of guidelines focusing on the structure of compounds. In this context, Lipinski's rule of five is implemented to determine the drug-likeness of a chemical compound. The rule was first given by Christopher A. Lipinski in 1997. Lipinski's rule states that the compound should not have more than five hydrogen bond donors and 10 hydrogen bond acceptors, the molecular mass of the compounds should be less than 500 Da, and the octanol–water partition coefficient ($\log P$) should not exceed 5. After successful screening, if the compound is found suitable as a drug candidate, further preclinical trials (on animals)

Table 15.1 Major computational tools for drug designing (CADD) and applications.

S. no.	Name of the tools/ database/servers	Application domain	Availability
1	SWISS-MODEL	Homology modeling	https://swissmodel.expasy.org/
2	PyRx	Molecular docking	http://sourceforge.net/projects/pyrx/files
3	Gromacs 5.1.1	Molecular dynamics simulation	https://www.gromacs.org
4	PRODRG	Energy minimization	http://prodrg1.dyndns.org/submit.html
5	PROTOX 2	Toxicity prediction	https://tox-new.charite.de/protox_II
6	OSIRIS	Toxicity risk assessment	https://www.organic-chemistry.org/prog/peo/
7	PubChem	Chemical molecule database	http://pubchem.ncbi.nlm.nih.gov
8	Molegro data modeler version 1.0	QSAR modeling	https://molegro-data-modeller.software.informer.com/1.0
9	Ligand Scout	Pharmacophore modeling	https://mybiosoftware.com/
10.	Biovia Discovery Studio Visualizer	Binding site of ligand–receptor and molecular visualization	https://discover.3ds.com/discovery-studio-visualizer-download
11	*AutoDock Vina*	Molecular docking	https://vina.scripps.edu
12	PyMol	Molecular visualization	https://pymol.org
13	MOPAC 16	Quantum mechanical descriptor calculations	http://openmopac.net/MOPAC2016.html
14	Open Babel	Converting chemical file format	https://sourceforge.net/p/openbabel/news/2016/09/open-babel-240-released
15	Marvin Sketch	Chemical drawing and visualization	https://chemaxon.com/marvin
16	VMD	Molecular dynamics visualization	https://www.ks.uiuc.edu/Research/vmd
17	WEKA	Data mining and QSAR model validation	https://www.cs.waikato.ac.nz/ml/weka
18	CASTp	Binding site prediction	http://sts.bioe.uic.edu/castp/index.html?2011
19	MODELLER	Homology modeling	https://salilab.org/modeller/

and clinical trials are recommended on human subjects. Based on successful performance in the clinical trials, the necessary approvals from the approval committee for the drug are to be obtained so that it enters the market for its therapeutic use. Table 15.1 shows the computational resources that are widely used for drug design applications [46–50].

15.4 Concept of Artificial Intelligence (AI) and Machine Learning (ML) Methods

Artificial intelligence (AI) is defined as the science of making machines or intelligent computer programs using human intelligence. This method was developed in 1940 and is still used in the different application areas of science and engineering (Figure 15.5).

AI techniques take input data from the user and generate desirable output using computer algorithms (machine learning algorithms). Machine learning (ML) algorithms enable the process to deduce robust mathematical model-based input data (training data) to make predictions or classifications on new data sets. Recently, AI approaches have been successfully implemented in pharmaceuticals to discover novel antibiotics [51–53].

The implementation of AI techniques is applied in several steps in the drug discovery process and helps in understanding the process's mechanism and developing novel methods. AI techniques are nowadays getting popular due to their scientific and technical involvement in several domains, starting from robotics, speech translation, image analysis, drug discovery, and so on. Specifically, several developments have been made by the researchers to apply computers' intelligence in the core areas of medicinal chemistry, biology, pharmaceutical sciences, drug discovery, drug repurposing, drug metabolism prediction, drug toxicity analysis, and so on to resolve complex problems of the process [54–59]. The drug discovery pathway aimed at identifying and establishing new therapeutic molecules is labor-intensive, time-consuming, and a trial-and-error experimentation. In this context, AI-based methods provide a potential platform to speed up the process more efficiently and accurately [60, 61]. In the drug design strategy, *virtual screening* is an important *in silico* technique used in

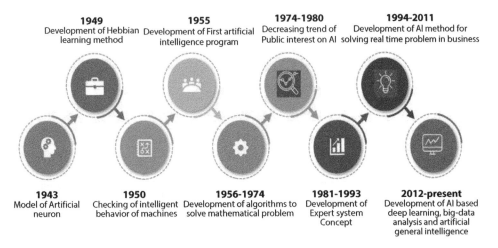

Figure 15.5 Major milestones of artificial intelligence development.

drug discovery. The virtual screening method comprises the technique in which the likely target-binding character of a set of chemicals (compounds) is evaluated by searching an extensive library of known chemical structures that bind to the specific target. Due to the less expensive and faster nature of virtual screening, it is more convenient in its use than the conventional and high-throughput screening methods [62–64].

15.4.1   Basic Steps Involved in the Implementation of AI Techniques in the Compound Screening Process

The AI method uses machine learning algorithms that enable the generation of statistical models by learning the specific pattern from large datasets. Then, the learning patterns are applied to predict the unknown data [65–67].

To perform molecular screening in the drug design process, the molecular data should be collected from the available databases and must be presented in a specific chemical format. Further machined learning algorithms can be implemented for effective classification and prediction purposes. The basic steps followed in this aspect are shown in Figure 15.6.

15.4.1.1   Searching Molecular Information from the Public Data Resources

Several public data resources that specifically provide the small molecules/ligands are available. In addition to the molecular structure, precise information such as molecular and physicochemical properties, target information, source of the compound, chemical formats, and synthesis details are available in these databases [68, 69]. Some of the popular small molecule databases available freely on the web are given in Table 15.2.

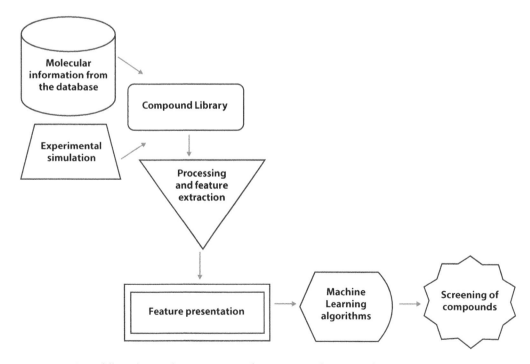

Figure 15.6 Steps followed in implementing AI in the screening of compounds.

Table 15.2 Small molecule database.

S. no.	Name of the database	Web availability	Remark
1	ChEMBL	https://www.ebi.ac.uk/chembl/	Compounds from the European Molecular Biology Laboratory (EMBL)
2	ChemDB	http://cdb.ics.uci.edu	Chemical database of small molecules
3	ChemIDplus	https://pubchem.ncbi.nlm.nih.gov/source/ChemIDplus	Identification of chemical substances cited in National Library of Medicine (NLM) databases
4	ChemSpider	http://www.chemspider.com/	A free chemical structure database providing fast text and structure search to over 100 million structures from hundreds of data sources
5	DrugBank	https://go.drugbank.com/	Online database containing information on drugs and drug targets.
6	DrugCentral	https://drugcentral.org/	Provides information on chemical entities, pharmaceutical products, drug mode of action, indications, and pharmacologic action
7	DTP/NCI	https://dtp.cancer.gov/	Specifically facilitates the discovery and development of new cancer therapeutic agents
8	eMolecules	https://www.emolecules.com/	Contains information of leading chemical compounds
9	PubChem	https://pubchem.ncbi.nlm.nih.gov/	The largest collection of freely accessible chemical information
10	ZINC	https://zinc.docking.org/	Free access to over 230 million purchasable compounds
11	SureChEMBL	https://www.surechembl.org/search/	Provides free access to chemical data extracted from the patent literature

(Continued)

Table 15.2 Small molecule database. (*Continued*)

S. no.	Name of the database	Web availability	Remark
12	SuperDRUG2	https://ngdc.cncb.ac.cn/ databasecommons/ database/id/5927	Containing information on approved/marketed drugs
13	COCONUT	https://coconut. naturalproducts.net/	Open source project for natural products storage, search, and analysis
14	DGIdb	http://www.dgidb.org	Provides information on drug–gene interactions and the druggable genome
15	DTC	http://drugtarget commons.fimm.fi/	Contains information on drug–target interactions
16	INPUT	http://cbcb.cdutcm.edu. cn/INPUT/	Automatically performing network pharmacology analysis
17	STITCH	http://stitch.embl.de/	Chemical protein–interaction network

15.4.1.2 Small Molecule Representation Format

Before the use of machine learning algorithms, the proper representation of the chemical molecule is essential. The traditional method of representing the molecules is as two-dimensional (2D) structure diagrams containing atomic bonds. Computers use several digitized quantitative information of the molecule for data processing for AI applications. It also influences the success rate of machine learning algorithms in model generation. Hence, it is essential to accurately represent the chemical structure to develop efficient AI models [70–72]. However, several formats are available for the computational processing of molecular information. Some of the major computational tools used to generate molecular properties are shown in Table 15.3. The three major types of presentations are as follows:

a) SMILE format

A simplified molecular input line entry system (SMILES) is a molecular representation method that uses (ASCII) characters to represent the molecular structure. SMILES strings can be given as the input to most molecular editors and can be converted to the corresponding two-dimensional (2D) or three-dimensional (3D) structures of the molecules. The length of the SMILE string varies with the molecular size—for example, drug molecules such as aspirin (2-acetyloxybenzoic acid (molecular formulae $CH_3COOC_6H_4COOH$) can be represented as CC(=O) OC1=CC=CC=C1C(=O) O.

b) Molecular fingerprint

The molecular fingerprint is represented by the *bit string* corresponding to the molecule's structural information. Two categories of molecular fingerprints are commonly used for the

Table 15.3 Some of the major tools involved in molecular property generation and analysis.

S. no.	Name of the tool	Web availability	Remark
1	Chemistry42	https://insilico.com/chemistry42	A software platform for *de novo* small molecule design and optimization by using artificial intelligence (AI) techniques
2	Molecule Net	https://moleculenet.org/	A platform for testing of machine learning methods based on molecular properties
3	ChemDoodle	https://www.chemdoodle.com/	Contains thousands of chemistry features of the compound
4	Hyperchem	http://www.hypercubeusa.com/	Computational property prediction uses methods such as molecular mechanics, molecular dynamics, semi-empirical and *ab initio* molecular orbital methods, and density functional theory (DFT)
5	Avogadro	https://avogadro.cc/	It is a molecule editor; visualizer also helps in molecular modeling and other bioinformatics analysis
6	ChemAxon	https://chemaxon.com/	Visualization and drawing of chemical compounds
7	BIOVIA Draw	https://www.3ds.com/products-services/biovia/products/scientific-informatics/biovia-draw/	Drawing and editing of complex molecules, chemical reactions, and biological sequences
8	ACD/ChemSketch	https://www.acdlabs.com/resources/free-chemistry-software-apps/chemsketch-freeware/	Drawing of chemical structures, including organics, organometallics, polymers, and calculation of molecular properties
9	DeepChem	https://deepchem.io/	Open-source tools that use deep-learning in drug discovery process
10	DeepCPI	https://github.com/FangpingWan/DeepCPI	Mainly applicable to generate features and make prediction
11	DeepDTA	https://github.com/hkmztrk/DeepDTA	Prediction of the binding affinity details drug–target complexes
12	Deep docking	https://github.com/vibudh2209/D2	Deep docking (DD) is a deep learning-based tool developed to accelerate docking-based virtual screening
13	GNINA 1.0	https://github.com/gnina/gnina	Molecular docking with deep learning
14	eToxPred	https://github.com/pulimeng/eToxPred	Estimation of the toxicity and synthetic accessibility of small organic compounds

representation of the molecules. One is key-based fingerprints which contain a pre-defined fragment library, and hash fingerprints, in which the exact fragment is converted to a fingerprint. One of the examples of key-based fingerprints can be generated by the Open Babel (https://openbabel.org/) software tool. The FP2-based fingerprint output of the molecule aspirin is given below:

04000000 00000808 20000108 00010200 00001000 00024000 02000000 00000800 00000100 00000840 00000000 40008020 02808002 00000000 01010001 0008200c 00020000 02008000 00000000 00420000 00000000 08020a20 10000000 00400004 00000000 80000000 00000800 00000001 00000300 00020000 c0004000 10000000

In this case, the structure of the compound is divided, and linear fragments of atomic length from 1–7 are generated by ignoring the atom fragments of carbon (C), nitrogen (N), and oxygen (O). When the atoms are involved in the ring formation, the fragment is said to be terminated. Furthermore, the fragment contains atoms, bonding details, and a complete ring structure and is considered as one fragment type of a molecule.

c) Graph-based methods
A graph is typically composed of nodes connected by edges. A molecule consists of atoms (nodes) and is connected by chemical bonds (edges) and also shows a similar pattern of graphical arrangement. Thus, molecules can be represented in graphical patterns to generate effective AI models for extensive use in classification and screening processes.

15.5 Major Machine Learning (ML) Techniques and Applications in Molecular Screening Process

In computer-aided drug discovery methods, several major machine learning algorithms, namely, decision trees, support vector machines, naive Bayesian, and random forest (RF), are frequently used.

15.5.1 Naive Bayes

In general, the Bayesian classification method assigns the most likely class of the given sample based on the variables presented in vector form. The algorithms work based on the Bayesian principle, which assumes that the variables are independent. This algorithm is simple, fast, and mainly implemented in classification problems. It has advantage such that the algorithm can learn from small data sets. However, in the instance in which the dimension of the data size is large, it may not work as an ideal algorithm [73, 74].

15.5.2 Support Vector Machines (SVM)

The support vector machines (SVM) method is one of the most widely used techniques due to its performance factor and the ability to work specifically in biological data having huge dimensions. The methods present a supervised learning model in which data analysis occurs for data classification and regression analysis purposes.

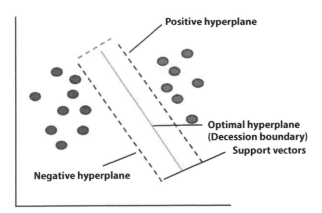

Figure 15.7 Support vector machine algorithms in the classification of compounds (shown in blue and green dots).

Support vector machine (SVM) is a tool that uses machine learning theory to maximize predictive accuracy while automatically avoiding over-fit to the data. They combine generalization control as a technique to control dimensionality. In general, the support vector machine takes all the (linear) data points from the variables and predicts the hyperplane (decision boundary) for the best separation between them (Figure 15.7). In a given data set with n dimension, the hyperplane divides the space into two parts corresponding to the entries of the two classes. The primary objective of the SVM is to predict the hyperplane that separates the objects from one class to another. However, in the case of complex datasets containing non-linearity and for the classification, a specific *kernel* function is used [75, 76].

15.5.3   Random Forest (RF)

A random forest (RF) algorithm is a supervised machine-learning approach commonly used for classification and regression purposes. It obeys the principle that the majority opinion is to be selected from the multiple opinions. The RF algorithm is a multiple decision tree classifier in which each decision tree is trained individually, and predictions are made from the average of the results. Large datasets and variables can be processed by this algorithm for more complex problems considering the combination of multiple classifiers [77, 78].

15.5.4   Artificial Neural Networks (ANN)

Artificial neural network (ANN) is analogous to biological neural working models and are considered massively parallel computing systems. These methods consist of a large number of processing elements interconnected with so-called nodes or neurons, which are configured in regular architecture.

Each neuron is used to be connected with another by a link, which is associated with particular weights containing information about the input signals. (Figure 15.8(a)). This kind of information is used by the neural network (nodes) to solve a particular problem. These weights are associated with each connection link, further computed by a mathematical function leading to the neurons' activation. The activation function applied to neurons

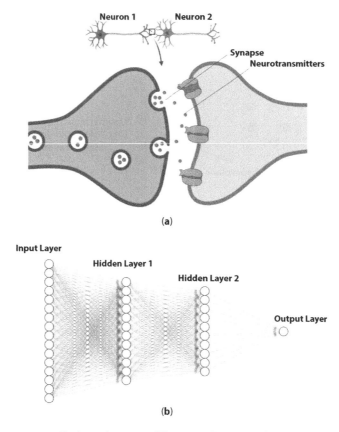

Figure 15.8 (a) Functioning of biological neurons. (b) Basic architecture of ANN.

in the network works by summating the inputs. Just like the learning process in biological systems, in this case, the adjustment connections occur as links and exist between the networks. The neural network comprises three main layers: an input layer, a hidden layer, and an output layer (Figure 15.8(b)). The input layer contains the inputs/information from the user for which the model will be learned. Input nodes send the data to the next hidden layer. The hidden layer is a group of neurons in which all types of *computation* occurs of the input data. There can be any number of hidden layers in a neural network. Furthermore, the output layer represents the output/prediction of the model resulting from all computations [79, 80]. A special case in the case of ANN is known as *deep learning*, which contains many interconnected neuron layers in which the information is processed hierarchically. In this case, each neuron layer tries to get more meaningful information—for example, the data's characteristics increase as it goes deeper into the network, and a complex relationship among the data is established [81, 82].

15.6 Challenges and Opportunities

Due to its wide application area, artificial intelligence (AI) is also regarded as a potential machine for the industrial revolution. In a drug development process, the time and cost are two key factors that can be reduced by the direct implementation of AI methods [83, 84]. Irrespective of the enormous potential benefits of the application of AI in the drug discovery process, several challenges and limitations are to be addressed [85–89].

A. Challenges
Some of these challenges are as follows:

a. Non-availability of recent, specific, and quality molecular data for analysis
Basically, big datasets are required for successful prediction by AI-based algorithms. Hence, considering a small amount of data may hamper the prediction process. Additionally, the data set should not contain incomplete or biased (inconsistent) type, which frequently happens due to data availability and accessibility issues. Using such data may lead to an inaccurate prediction of the result.

b. Lack of ability of different machine learning algorithms to work in a coordinated way
Several ML algorithms have the limitation of *algorithm bias*, in which the algorithm creator might have done biasing in which the information is processed in his way to generate predictions. The ML algorithms sometimes fail to establish links between different experimental variables, ultimately hampering the prediction accuracy of the model in forecasting future events.

c. The high dimensionality of the molecular data
Primarily, the molecular data used for AI-based processing are high dimensional in nature. Thus, machine learning algorithms may require huge computational resources (high-performance computing resources) for processing (training and prediction). Hence, the cost associated with this might be a significant barrier.

B. Limitations in interpretability by machine learning algorithms
One of the major drawbacks of ML algorithms is their less interpretability nature of the machine learning process. They need to reveal how a decision is made, making it challenging in the final prediction and explanation of the model. Furthermore, *overfitting* (poor performance of the model on new/unknown data) and *underfitting* (unable to recognize the pattern in the data) might be other drawbacks responsible for the weak performance of the algorithms.

Ethical Considerations
Machine learning models, especially in drug design aspects, can have significant unintended consequences as the prediction is associated with the life of the people. Hence, the ethical and fair use of AI for developing new therapeutic compounds must be adequately addressed, along with the data security and ownership criteria.

15.7 Conclusion and Future Perspectives

The discovery of a new drug molecule and assessing its therapeutic importance are multi-step, time-consuming, and high-cost processes. The primary risk factor associated with the process is the failure of the drug molecules, even at the end stage. Applying potential computational methods in several stages of the drug development process has significantly reduced the time frame. Artificial intelligence (AI) techniques have recently been integrated with the drug discovery process, resulting in promising opportunities in this emerging area. Several methods, such as Bayesian classifiers (naïve Bayes), support vector machines, random forests, and ANN, are prominent among the AI techniques used in several stages of the drug discovery process. Since the process is data-driven, the availability and selection of data quality are necessary for the successful application of AI in drug discovery. The latest developments in the learning method algorithms in AI make it possible to discover new drug molecules with therapeutic properties. However, in present situations, AI-based approaches cannot be a complete substitute for the (traditional) experimental methods and cannot replace human expertise and experience. As AI predictions are based on the available and preparation of data sets (user-defined data), human researchers must validate the prediction results. Hence, AI and traditional experimental methods can be combined to optimize the drug discovery process and accelerate the development of novel therapeutic compounds.

References

1. Paul, D., Sanap, G., Shenoy, S., Kalyane, D., Kalia, K., Tekade, R.K., Artificial intelligence in drug discovery and development. *Drug Discov. Today*, 26, 1, 80–93, 2021, https://doi. org/10.1016/j. drudis.2020.10.010.

2. Yang, X., Wang, Y., Byrne, R., Schneider, G., Yang, S., Concepts of artificial intelligence for computer-assisted drug discovery. *Chem. Rev.*, 119, 18, 10520–10594, 2019, https://doi. org/10.1021/acs.chemrev.8b00728.

3. Nelson, S.D., Walsh, C.G., Olsen, C.A., McLaughlin, A.J., LeGrand, J.R., Schutz, N., Lasko, T.A., Demystifying artificial intelligence in pharmacy. *Am. J. Health-Syst. Pharm.*, 77, 19, 1556–1570, 2020, https://doi.org/10.1093/ajhp/zxaa218.

4. Johnston, C.W., Skinnider, M.A., Wyatt, M.A., Li, X., Ranieri, M.R., Yang, L., Zechel, D.L., Ma, B., Magarvey, N.A., An automated Genomes-to-Natural Products platform (GNP) for the discovery of modular natural products. *Nat. Commun.*, 6, 1, 8421, 2015, https://doi.org/10.1038/ ncomms9421.

5. Nugroho, A.E. and Morita, H., Computationally-assisted discovery and structure elucidation of natural products. *J. Nat. Med.*, 73, 4, 687–695, 2019, https://doi.org/10.1007/ s11418-019-01321-8.

6. Giordanetto, F. and Kihlberg, J., Macrocyclic drugs and clinical candidates: What can medicinal chemists learn from their properties? *J. Med. Chem.*, 57, 2, 278–295, 2014, https://doi. org/10.1021/jm400887j.

7. Saldívar-González, F., II, Aldas-Bulos, V.D., Medina-Franco, J.L., Plisson, F., Natural product drug discovery in the artificial intelligence era. *Chem. Sci.*, 13, 6, 1526–1546, 2022, https://doi. org/10.1039/d1sc04471k.

8. Jiménez-Luna, J., Grisoni, F., Weskamp, N., Schneider, G., Artificial intelligence in drug discovery: Recent advances and future perspectives. *Expert Opin. Drug Discov.*, 16, 9, 949–959, 2021, https://doi.org/10.1080/17460441.2021.1909567.

9. Vamathevan, J., Clark, D., Czodrowski, P., Dunham, I., Ferran, E., Lee, G., Li, B., Madabhushi, A., Shah, P., Spitzer, M., Zhao, S., Applications of machine learning in drug discovery and development. *Nat. Rev. Drug Discov.*, 18, 6, 463–477, 2019, https://doi.org/10.1038/ s41573-019-0024-5.

10. Zhou, S.F. and Zhong, W.Z., Drug design and discovery: Principles and applications. *Molecules*, 22, 2, 279, 2017, https://doi.org/10.3390/molecules22020279.

11. Campbell, I.B., Macdonald, S.J.F., Procopiou, P.A., Medicinal chemistry in drug discovery in big pharma: Past, present and future. *Drug Discov. Today*, 23, 2, 219–234, 2018, https://doi.org/10.1016/j.drudis.2017.10.007.

12. Wouters, O.J., McKee, M., Luyten, J., Estimated research and development investment needed to bring a new medicine to market, 2009–2018. *J. Am. Med. Assoc.*, 323, 9, 844–853, 2020, https://doi.org/10.1001/jama.2020.1166.

13. Wouters, O.J., Berenbrok, L.A., He, M., Li, Y., Hernandez, I., Association of Research and Development investments with treatment costs for new drugs approved from 2009 to 2018. *JAMA Netw. Open*, 5, 9, e2218623, 2022, https://doi.org/10.1001/jamanetworkopen.2022.18623.

14. Prieto-Martínez, F.D., López-López, E., Juárez-Mercado, K.E., Medina-Franco, J.L., Computational drug design methods—Current and future perspectives, in: *In Silico Drug Design*, pp. 19–44, 2019.

15. Bassani, D. and Moro, S., Past, present, and future perspectives on computer-aided drug design methodologies. *Molecules*, 28, 9, 3906, 2023, https://doi.org/10.3390/molecules28093906.

16. Gurung, A.B., Ali, M.A., Lee, J., Farah, M.A., Al-Anazi, K.M., An updated review of computer-aided drug design and its application to COVID-19. *BioMed. Res. Int.*, 2021, 8853056, 2021, https://doi.org/10.1155/2021/8853056.

17. Anderson, A.C., The process of structure-based drug design. *Chem. Biol.*, 10, 9, 787–797, 2003, https://doi.org/10.1016/j.chembiol.2003.09.002.

18. Batool, M., Ahmad, B., Choi, S., A structure-based drug discovery paradigm. *Int. J. Mol. Sci.*, 20, 11, 2783, 2019, https://doi.org/10.3390/ijms20112783.

19. Wang, X., Song, K., Li, L., Chen, L., Structure-based drug design strategies and challenges. *Curr. Top. Med. Chem.*, 18, 12, 998–1006, 2018, https://doi.org/10.2174/1568026618666180813152921.

20. Kalyaanamoorthy, S. and Chen, Y.P.P., Structure-based drug design to augment hit discovery. *Drug Discov. Today*, 16, 17–18, 831–839, 2011, https://doi.org/10.1016/j.drudis.2011.07.006.

21. Tripathi, A. and Misra, K., Molecular docking: A structure-based drug designing approach. *JSM Chem.*, 5, 2, 1042–1047, 2017.

22. Singh, S., Malik, B.K., Sharma, D.K., Molecular drug targets and structure based drug design: A holistic approach. *Bioinformation*, 1, 8, 314–320, 2006, https://doi.org/10.6026/97320630001314.

23. Katsila, T., Spyroulias, G.A., Patrinos, G.P., Matsoukas, M.T., Computational approaches in target identification and drug discovery. *Comput. Struct. Biotechnol. J.*, 14, 177–184, 2016, https://doi.org/10.1016/j.csbj.2016.04.004.

24. Finan, C., Gaulton, A., Kruger, F.A., Lumbers, R.T., Shah, T., Engmann, J., Galver, L., Kelley, R., Karlsson, A., Santos, R., Overington, J.P., Hingorani, A.D., Casas, J.P., The druggable genome and support for target identification and validation in drug development. *Sci. Transl. Med.*, 9, 383, eaag1166, 2017, https://doi.org/10.1126/scitranslmed.aag1166.

25. Wyatt, P.G., Gilbert, I.H., Read, K.D., Fairlamb, A.H., Target validation: Linking tar- get and chemical properties to desired product profile. *Curr. Top. Med. Chem.*, 11, 10, 1275–1283, 2011, https://doi.org/10.2174/156802611795429185.

26. Siddharthan, N., Raja Prabu, M.R., Sivasankari, B., Bioinformatics in drug discovery a review. *Int. J. Res.Arts Sci.*, 2, 2, 11–13, 2016, https://doi. org/10.9756/IJRAS.8099.

27. Wang, T., Wu, M.B., Zhang, R.H., Chen, Z.J., Hua, C., Lin, J.P., Yang, L.R., Advances in computational structure-based drug design and application in drug discovery. *Curr. Top. Med. Chem.*, 16, 9, 901–916, 2016, https://doi.org/10.2174/1568026615666150825142002.

28. Yu, W. and MacKerell, A.D., Computer-aided drug design methods, in: *Antibiotics. Methods and Protocols*, pp. 85–106, 2017.

29. Guido, R.V., Oliva, G., Andricopulo, A.D., Modern drug discovery technologies: Opportunities and challenges in lead discovery. *Comb. Chem. High Throughput Screen.*, 14, 10, 830–839, 2011, https://doi.org/10.2174/138620711797537067.

30. Maruca, A., Ambrosio, F.A., Lupia, A., Romeo, I., Rocca, R., Moraca, F., Talarico, C., Bagetta, D., Catalano, R., Costa, G., Artese, A., Alcaro, S., Computer-based techniques for lead identification and optimization I: Basics. *Phys. Sci. Rev.*, 4, 6, 20180113, 2019, https://doi. org/10.1515/psr-2018-0113.

31. Xiang, M., Cao, Y., Fan, W., Chen, L., Mo, Y., Computer-aided drug design: Lead discovery and optimization. *Comb. Chem. High Throughput Screen.*, 15, 4, 328–337, 2012, https://doi.org/10.2174/138620712799361825.

32. Deore, A.B., Dhumane, J.R., Wagh, R., Sonawane, R., The stages of drug discovery and development process. *Asian J. Pharm. Res. Dev. Asian J. Pharm. Res. Dev.*, 7, 6, 62–67, 2019, https://doi.org/10.22270/ajprd.v7i6.616.

33. Zhou, S.F. and Zhong, W.Z., Drug design and discovery: Principles and applications. *Molecules*, 22, 2, 279, 2017, https://doi.org/10.3390/molecules22020279.

34. Wilson, G.L. and Lill, M.A., Integrating structure-based and ligand-based approaches for computational drug design. *Future Med. Chem.*, 3, 6, 735–750, 2011, https://doi.org/ 10.4155/fmc.11.18.

35. Sharma, V., Wakode, S., Kumar, H., Structure- and ligand-based drug design: Concepts, approaches, and challenges, in: *Chemoinformatics and Bioinformatics in the Pharmaceutical Sciences*, pp. 27–53, 2021.

36. Cavasotto, C.N. and Phatak, S.S., Homology modeling in drug discovery: Current trends and applications. *Drug Discov. Today*, 14, 13–14, 676–683, 2009, https://doi.org/10.1016/j.drudis.2009.04.006.

37. Nishant, T., Sathish Kumar, D., V. L., V., P. K., A., Computational methods for protein structure prediction and its application in drug design. *J. Proteom. Bioinform.*, 1, 2, 2011.

38. Satpathy, R., Application of molecular docking methods on endocrine disrupting chemicals: A review. *J. Appl. Biotechnol. Rep.*, 7, 2, 74–80, 2020.

39. Agarwal, S. and Mehrotra, R.J.J.C., An overview of molecular docking. *JSM Chem.*, 4, 2, 1024–1028, 2016.

40. Badar, M.S., Shamsi, S., Ahmed, J., Alam, M.A., Molecular dynamics simulations: Concept, methods, and applications, in: Transdisciplinarity, pp. 131–151, Springer International Publishing, USA, Germany, 2022, https://doi.org/10.1007/978-3-030-94651-7_7.

41. Salo-Ahen, O.M.H., Alanko, I., Bhadane, R., Bonvin, A.M.J.J., Honorato, R.V., Hossain, S., Juffer, A.H., Kabedev, A., Lahtela-Kakkonen, M., Larsen, A.S., Lescrinier, E., Marimuthu, P., Mirza, M.U., Mustafa, G., Nunes-Alves, A., Pantsar, T., Saadabadi, A., Singaravelu, K., Vanmeert, M., Molecular dynamics simulations in drug discovery and pharmaceutical development. *Processes*, 9, 1, 71, 2020, https://doi.org/10.3390/pr9010071.

42. Shukla, R. and Tripathi, T., Molecular dynamics simulation in drug discovery: Opportunities and challenges, in: *Innovations and Implementations of Computer Aided Drug Discovery Strategies in Rational Drug Design*, pp. 295–316, 2021.

43. Grover, A., Grover, M., Sharma, K., A practical overview of quantitative structure-activity relationship. *World J. Pharm. Pharm. Sci.*, 5, 427–437, 2016.

44. Satpathy, R., Quantitative structure–activity relationship methods for the prediction of the toxicity of pollutants. *Environ. Chem. Lett.*, 17, 1, 123–128, 2019, https://doi. org/10.1007/s10311-018-0780-1.

45. Abdel-Ilah, L., Veljović, E., Gurbeta, L., Badnjević, A., Applications of QSAR study in drug design. *Int. Res. J. Eng. Technol. (IJERT)*, 6, 06, 582–587 2017.

46. Kesharwani, R.K., Vishwakarma, V.K., Keservani, R.K., Singh, P., Katiyar, N., Tripathi, S., Role of ADMET tools in current scenario: Application and limitations. *Comput. Aided Drug Des.*, 71–87, 2020.

47. Davis, A.M. and Riley, R.J., Predictive ADMET studies, the challenges and the opportunities. *Curr. Opin. Chem. Biol.*, 8, 4, 378–386, 2004, https://doi.org/10.1016/j. cbpa.2004.06.005.

48. Jia, C.Y., Li, J.Y., Hao, G.F., Yang, G.F., A drug-likeness toolbox facilitates ADMET study in drug discovery. *Drug Discov. Today*, 25, 1, 248–258, 2020, https://doi.org/10.1016/j. drudis.2019.10.014.

49. Lipinski, C.A., Lead- and drug-like compounds: The rule-of-five revolution. *Drug Discov. Today Technol.*, 1, 4, 337–341, 2004, https://doi.org/10.1016/j.ddtec.2004.11.007.

50. Chen, J., Luo, X., Qiu, H., Mackey, V., Sun, L., Ouyang, X., Drug discovery and drug marketing with the critical roles of modern administration. *Am. J. Transl. Res.*, 10, 12, 4302–4312, 2018.

51. Solanki, A., Kumar, S., Nayyar, A. (Eds.), *Handbook of research on emerging trends and applications of machine learning*, IGI-Global, United States, 2019.

52. Nayyar, A., Gadhavi, L., Zaman, N., Machine learning in healthcare [Review], opportunities and challenges, in: *Machine learning and the Internet of medical things in healthcare*, pp. 23–45, 2021.

53. Zhong, F., Xing, J., Li, X., Liu, X., Fu, Z., Xiong, Z., Lu, D., Wu, X., Zhao, J., Tan, X., Li, F., Luo, X., Li, Z., Chen, K., Zheng, M., Jiang, H., Artificial intelligence in drug design. *Sci. China Life Sci.*, 61, 10, 1191–1204, 2018, https://doi.org/10.1007/s11427-018-9342-2.

54. Aliper, A., Plis, S., Artemov, A., Ulloa, A., Mamoshina, P., Zhavoronkov, A., Deep learning applications for predicting pharmacological properties of drugs and drug repurposing using transcriptomic data. *Mol. Pharmaceutics*, 13, 7, 2524–2530, 2016, https://doi.org/10.1021/acs. molpharmaceut.6b00248.

55. Li, Q. and Lai, L., Prediction of potential drug targets based on simple sequence properties. *BMC Bioinf.*, 8, 353, 2007, https://doi.org/10.1186/1471-2105-8-353.

56. Bharatam, P.V., Computer-aided drug design, in: Drug Discovery and Development, pp. 137–210, Springer, Singapore, Germany, 2021.

57. Venaik, A., Kumari, R., Venaik, U., Nayyar, A., The role of machine learning and artificial intelligence in clinical decisions and the herbal formulations against Covid-19, in: *International Journal of Reliable and Quality E-Healthcare*, vol. 11, pp. 1–17, 2022, https://doi.org/10.4018/ IJRQEH.2022010107.

58. Ilmudeen, A. and Nayyar, A., Novel designs of smart healthcare systems: Technologies, architecture, and applications, in: *Machine Learning for Critical Internet of Medical Things: Applications and Use Cases*, pp. 125–151, Springer International Publishing, Cham., Germany, 2022.

59. Lo, Y.C., Rensi, S.E., Torng, W., Altman, R.B., Machine learning in chemoinformatics and drug discovery. *Drug Discov. Today*, 23, 8, 1538–1546, 2018, https://doi.org/10.1016/j. drudis.2018.05.010.

60. Paul, D., Sanap, G., Shenoy, S., Kalyane, D., Kalia, K., Tekade, R.K., Artificial intelligence in drug discovery and development. *Drug Discov. Today*, 26, 1, 80–93, 2021, https://doi. org/10.1016/j. drudis.2020.10.010.

61. Griffen, E., Dossetter, A., Leach, A., Montague, S., Artificial intelligence in medicinal chemistry, in: *Burger's Medicinal Chemistry and Drug Discov.*, pp. 1–19, 2003.

62. Lyne, P.D., Structure-based virtual screening: An overview. *Drug Discov. Today*, 7, 20, 1047–1055, 2002, https://doi.org/10.1016/s1359-6446(02)02483-2.

63. Köppen, H., Virtual screening-what does it give us? *Curr. Opin. Drug Discov. Devel.*, 12, 3, 397–407, 2009.

64. Cerqueira, N.M., Sousa, S.F., Fernandes, P.A., Ramos, M.J., Virtual screening of compound libraries, in: *Ligand-Macromolecular Interactions in Drug Discov. Methods and Protocols*, pp. 57–70, 2010.

65. Vamathevan, J., Clark, D., Czodrowski, P., Dunham, I., Ferran, E., Lee, G., Li, B., Madabhushi, A., Shah, P., Spitzer, M., Zhao, S., Applications of machine learning in drug discovery and development. *Nat. Rev. Drug Discov.*, 18, 6, 463–477, 2019, https://doi.org/10.1038/ s41573-019-0024-5.

66. Tiwari, A.K., Introduction to machine learning, in: *Ubiquitous Machine Learning and Its Applications*, pp. 1–14, 2017, https://doi.org/10.4018/978-1-5225-2545-5.ch001.

67. Dubourg-Felonneau, G., Cannings, T., Cotter, F., Thompson, H., Patel, N., Cassidy, J.W. *et al.*, A framework for implementing machine learning on omics data. *Mach. Learn. Heal.*, 1, 1, 3–10, November 26, 2018.

68. Williams, A.J., Public chemical compound databases. *Curr. Opin. Drug Discov. Devel.*, 11, 3, 393–404, 2008.

69. Vazquez, M., Krallinger, M., Leitner, F., Valencia, A., Text mining for drugs and chemical compounds: Methods, tools and applications. *Mol. Inf.*, 30, 6–7, 506–519, 2011, https://doi.org/10.1002/minf.201100005.

70. Warr, W.A., Representation of chemical structures. *Wiley Interdiscip. Rev.: Comput. Mol. Sci.*, 1, 4, 557–579, 2011, https://doi.org/10.1002/wcms.36.

71. Hu, W., Liu, Y., Chen, X., Chai, W., Chen, H., Wang, H., Wang, G., Deep learning methods for small molecule drug discovery: A survey. *IEEE Trans. Artif. Intell.*, 5, 2, 459-479, 2024, https://doi.org/10.1109/TAI.2023.3251977

72. David, L., Thakkar, A., Mercado, R., Engkvist, O., Molecular representations in AI-driven drug discovery: A review and practical guide. *J. Cheminf.*, 12, 1, 56, 2020, https://doi.org/10.1186/ s13321-020-00460-5.

73. Zhang, H. and Li, D., Naïve Bayes text classifier, in: *IEEE International Conference on Granular Computing (GRC 2007)*, IEEE Publications, pp. 708–708, 2007, November.

74. Ren, J., Lee, S.D., Chen, X., Kao, B., Cheng, R., Cheung, D., Naive bayes classification of uncertain data, in: *Ninth IEEE international conference on data mining*, IEEE Publications, pp. 944–949, 2009, December, https://doi.org/10.1109/ICDM.2009.90.

75. Noble, W.S., What is a support vector machine? *Nat. Biotechnol.*, 24, 12, 1565–1567, 2006, https://doi.org/10.1038/nbt1206-1565.

76. Pisner, D.A. and Schnyer, D.M., Support vector machine, in: *Machine Learning*, pp. 101–121, Academic Press, London, United States, 2020.

77. Liu, Y., Wang, Y., Zhang, J., New machine learning algorithm: Random forest, in: *Information computing and applications. Proceedings of the 3: Third International Conference, ICICA 2012*, pp. 246–252, Chengde, China, Springer, September 14–16, 2012.

78. Schonlau, M. and Zou, R.Y., The random forest algorithm for statistical learning. *STATA J.: Promoting Commun. Stat. Stata*, 20, 1, 3–29, 2020, https://doi. org/10.1177/1536867X20909688.

79. Agatonovic-Kustrin, S. and Beresford, R., Basic concepts of artificial neural network (ANN) modeling and its application in pharmaceutical research. *J. Pharm. Biomed. Anal.*, 22, 5, 717–727, 2000, https://doi.org/10.1016/s0731-7085(99)00272-1.

80. Satpathy, R., Artificial neural network (ANN) techniques in solving the protein folding problem, in: *Advanced AI Techniques and Applications in Bioinformatics*, pp. 189–200, CRC Press, Boca Raton, United States, 2021.

81. Cao, C., Liu, F., Tan, H., Song, D., Shu, W., Li, W., Zhou, Y., Bo, X., Xie, Z., Deep learning and its applications in biomedicine. *Genom. Proteom. Bioinform.*, 16, 1, 17–32, 2018, https://doi.org/10.1016/j.gpb.2017.07.003.

82. Schmidhuber, J., Deep learning in neural networks: An overview. *Neural Networks, 61,* 85–117, 2015, https://doi.org/10.1016/j.neunet.2014.09.003.

83. Schneider, P., Walters, W.P., Plowright, A.T., Sieroka, N., Listgarten, J., Goodnow, Jr., R.A., Fisher, J., Jansen, J.M., Duca, J.S., Rush, T.S., Zentgraf, M., Hill, J.E., Krutoholow, E., Kohler, M., Blaney, J., Funatsu, K., Luebkemann, C., Schneider, G., Rethinking drug design in the artificial intelligence era. *Nat. Rev. Drug Discov., 19,* 5, 353–364, 2020, https://doi. org/10.1038/ s41573-019-0050-3.

84. Thomas, M., Boardman, A., Garcia-Ortegon, M., Yang, H., de Graaf, C., Bender, A., Applications of artificial intelligence in drug design: Opportunities and challenges. *Methods Mol. Biol. (Clifton, N.J.),* 1–59, 2022, https://doi.org/10.1007/978-1-0716-1787-8_1.

85. Linton-Reid, K., Introduction: An overview of AI in oncology drug discovery and development, in: *Artificial Intelligence in Oncology Drug Discovery and Development,* IntechOpen, 2020. http://dx.doi.org/10.5772/intechopen.92799

86. Ribeiro, M.T., Singh, S., Guestrin, C., 'Why should i trust you?' Explaining the predictions of any classifier, in: *Proceedings of the ACM SIGKDD International Conference on Knowledge Discov. and Data Mining,* vol. 13–17, August-2016, Association for Computing Machinery, pp. 1135–1144, August-2016, https://doi.org/10.1145/2939672.2939778.

87. Vamathevan, J., Clark, D., Czodrowski, P., Dunham, I., Ferran, E., Lee, G., Li, B., Madabhushi, A., Shah, P., Spitzer, M., Zhao, S., Applications of machine learning in drug discovery and development. *Nat. Rev. Drug Discov., 18,* 6, 463–477, 2019, https://doi.org/10.1038/ s41573-019-0024-5.

88. Minh, D., Wang, H.X., Li, Y.F., Nguyen, T.N., Explainable artificial intelligence: A comprehensive review. *Artif. Intell. Rev., 55,* 5, 3503–3568, 2022, https://doi.org/10.1007/ s10462-021-10088-y.

89. Karimian, G., Petelos, E., Evers, S.M.A.A., The ethical issues of the application of artificial intelligence in healthcare: A systematic scoping review. *AI Ethics, 2,* 4, 539–551, 2022, https://doi. org/10.1007/s43681-021-00131-7.

Empowering Clinical Decision Making: An In-Depth Systematic Review of AI-Driven Scoring Approaches for Liver Transplantation Prediction

Devi Rajeev[1], Remya S.[1] and Anand Nayyar[2*]

[1]*School of Computing, Amrita Vishwa Vidyapeetham, Amritapuri, Kerala, India*
[2]*School of Computer Science, Duy Tan University, Da Nang, Viet Nam*

Abstract

Effective clinical decision-making is critical in liver transplantation, as timely and precise assessments substantially influence patient outcomes. The chapter examine the possible benefits of artificial intelligence (AI) tools in improving clinical decision-making in liver transplantation. As part of this research, 44 relevant research papers are analyzed that satisfied the inclusion requirements. Various AI methodologies in liver transplantation, such as machine learning, deep learning, and predictive modeling are examined. This study aimed to assess whether AI-based scoring algorithms can improve the accuracy and efficiency of clinical judgments and predict outcomes such as graft failure, patient survival, and rejection. The findings suggest that AI-based models can improve clinical decision-making by providing accurate forecasts of critical outcomes and expediting evaluations, resulting in timely interventions. However, successfully integrating AI into clinical practice requires further research and validation. These insights benefit doctors, researchers, and policymakers interested in leveraging AI to enhance decision-making efficiency in liver transplantation.

Keywords: Liver transplantation, clinical decision-making, patient survival rate, healthcare decision support, predictive modeling, AI-driven scoring

16.1 Introduction

A liver transplant substitutes a healthy liver obtained from a deceased or living donor during a complex surgical operation known as a liver transplant. The importance of liver transplantation systems from their ability to prolong the lives of people suffering from severe liver impairment and enhance their quality of life. End-stage liver disease can develop from illnesses including cirrhosis, hepatitis, or hereditary abnormalities, and it can also cause organ failure and potentially fatal consequences [1]. AI approaches in liver transplantation can transform clinical judgment by assuring quick and accurate judgments that greatly influence significant survival and program effectiveness. The conclusions drawn from this

---

Corresponding author: anandnayyar@duytan.edu.vn

Abhirup Khanna, May El Barachi, Sapna Jain, Manoj Kumar and Anand Nayyar (eds.) Artificial Intelligence and Machine Learning in Drug Design and Development, (499–532) © 2024 Scrivener Publishing LLC

comprehensive study shed light on the potential of AI in liver transplantation and offer valuable recommendations for medical professionals, researchers, and policymakers interested in utilizing AI to enhance patient care and outcomes in this vital area of medicine. Patients on transplant waiting lists must wait an extended time since there is a much greater demand for live transplants. Additionally, delayed or ineffective decision-making during the examination, listing, and transplantation procedure might result in disease progression, complications, or even mortality for patients in desperate need of transplants. Researchers have investigated the use of AI algorithms to optimize decision-making in this crucial area of medicine in light of these difficulties.

A systematic investigation that included a thorough analysis of 44 pertinent research publications was carried out to look into the possible advantages of AI in liver transplantation. This research used various AI techniques, including machine learning, deep learning, and predictive modeling. They were chosen based on rigorous inclusion criteria. The chosen research covered a wide range of subjects, including how to enable quicker and more effective assessments and predict clinical outcomes, including graft failure, patient survival, and rejection.

This systematic study aimed to determine how well AI-based scoring algorithms may increase the precision of clinical decisions made in liver transplantation. Artificial intelligence (AI)-based models have the potential to provide precise forecasts of crucial clinical outcomes by utilizing machine learning algorithms and predictive modeling. The potential advantages go beyond simple accuracy, as new AI techniques also make assessments faster and more efficient, reducing the need for drawn-out decision-making procedures and enabling prompt intervention when required. Although the systematic study's results are encouraging, several issues must be resolved before AI may be effectively incorporated into clinical practice. Proper validation and additional research are crucial for AI-based models to be reliable and stable in actual medical contexts. Additionally, in order to protect patient privacy and keep the highest standards of medical ethics, the ethical issues surrounding the use of AI in healthcare must be carefully considered.

Identification and analysis of several AI algorithms utilized in liver transplantation research were among the technical elements of this work. The precision with which machine learning algorithms, deep learning networks, and predictive modeling techniques could forecast clinical outcomes was examined. These technical requirements were crucial in determining whether AI could increase the effectiveness of clinical decision-making and, ultimately, improve patient outcomes in liver transplantation. Although liver transplantation has achieved remarkable success, several difficulties are still involved. There is a massive need for donor organs and a considerable supply, which causes long waiting lists and high mortality rates for individuals awaiting transplants. Additionally, continuous risks are associated with post-transplant issues, including organ rejection, infection, and immunosuppressive medication side effects [2].

To overcome these difficulties, continuing research attempts to enhance several liver transplantation procedures, including organ preservation, surgical methods, donor selection, and post-transplant administration [3]. AI-based scoring techniques, among other developments in medical technology, have the potential to significantly improve the effectiveness and efficiency of clinical decision-making in liver transplantation. These developments aim to increase the efficiency of long-term graft and patient survival, forecast post-transplant results, reduce bouts of rejection, and optimize organ allocation [4].

16.1.1 Overview and Significance of Liver Transplantation

Effective clinical decision-making is essential because of liver transplantation's complexities and time constraints. Patients undergoing liver transplants continuously have advanced liver disease and urgently need medical attention. Effective clinical decision-making guarantees prompt organ evaluation, listing, and allocation to increase the likelihood of a successful transplant. Decision-making lags can affect patient outcomes negatively and raise mortality rates [5]. The quantity of accessible donor organs cannot keep up with the demand for liver transplants. Accurate evaluation and distribution of donor organs to the most qualified recipients are necessary for efficient clinical decision-making [6]. This necessitates considering variables, including the severity of the illness, blood type compatibility, body size compatibility, and organ availability. Reducing waiting periods and waiting list mortality and improving resource utilization are all benefits of optimizing organ allocation. Thorough assessment and risk classification of potential transplant recipients are necessary for effective clinical decision-making [7]. Examining elements, including the severity of the patient's liver illness, comorbidities, psychosocial characteristics, and anticipated post-transplant results, are all part of determining if a patient is a suitable applicant for transplantation. Appropriate patient selection improves graft and patient survival rates and ensures optimal resource utilization [8].

Intensive medical care, specialized medical teams, operating rooms, intensive care units, and immunosuppressive drugs are all necessary for liver transplantation. Effective clinical decision-making ensures that the individuals who most likely will gain advantages from transplantation give resources, which helps to maximize the utilization of these resources [9]. This increases the general effectiveness of healthcare systems and aids in addressing the rising transplant demand. Making clinical decisions in liver transplantation goes beyond the actual surgery. For the best possible patient outcomes, post-transplant care must be managed effectively, including immunosuppression, complication monitoring, and early intervention [10]. Well-informed post-transplant care decisions help lower the frequency and severity of problems, improve graft and patient survival rates, and enhance the long-term quality of life [11].

16.1.2 The Significance of Efficient Clinical Decision-Making in Liver Transplantation

Patients with chronic liver disease urgently need liver transplants since it is their last chance of survival. In order to maximize the patients' chances of survival, timely and effective clinical decision-making is essential for ensuring that patients are rapidly assessed, listed, and transplanted [12]. Patients needing transplants risk illness progression, complications, or even death if appropriate care is not provided. The difficulties patients face on transplant waiting lists are worsened by the vast disparity between the demand and supply of donor organs [13]. Effective decision-making, however, maximizes the use of available organs by matching patients with the most compatible organs, which increases the success rates of liver transplants and lowers mortality on the waiting list [14]. Additionally, the participation of diverse medical professionals from surgical teams, intensive care units, operating rooms, and post-transplant care facilities improves resource management, assuring the effective use of medical resources in liver transplantation programs [15]. Shorter waiting times raise the bar for care in these programs by improving patient and transplant survival rates and lowering the likelihood of post-transplant problems [16]. Effective decision-making is prioritized in liver transplantation programs, which has significant advantages for patients and the healthcare system.

Figure 16.1 elaborates on the procedures in clinical decision-making for liver transplantation. As these initiatives have positive results, they draw in additional organ donors, assisting in redressing the continued disparity between organ supply and demand. Additionally, good clinical decision-making provides fair organ allocation, enabling patients from various socioeconomic backgrounds to obtain life-saving transplants [17]. These programs increase the success rates of liver transplants by maximizing organ allocation and patient matching, giving patients a higher quality of life after the transplant [18]. Such programs' success and reputation also draw more interest and support, which results in additional funding and resources for liver transplantation initiatives.

For liver transplantation programs to be successful, which depend on efficient clinical decision-making, collaboration and coordination among medical specialists from diverse disciplines are essential. As a result, delays are reduced, and patient care is optimized [19]. Regular interdisciplinary meetings and discussions also improve communication and speed decision-making processes. Patients are given thorough and ongoing care during the transplant procedure thanks to the participation of surgical teams, intensive care units, operating rooms, and post-transplant care facilities. Effective decision-making also enables proactive patient care, allowing the early detection of high-risk patients and providing the required interventions and support [20]. Liver transplantation programs can efficiently

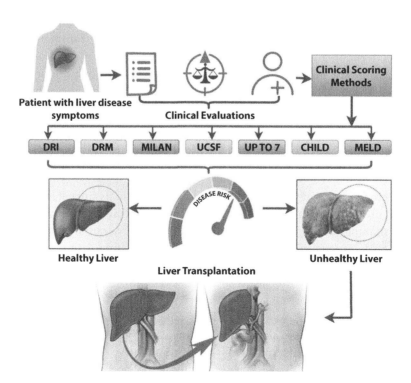

Figure 16.1 Efficient clinical decision-making in liver transplantation.

manage healthcare resources by drawing on the experience of many medical specialists, which will ultimately enhance patient outcomes and save healthcare costs [21]. Because of this, the success of these programs depends not only on the availability of organ donors but also on healthcare practitioners' commitment to putting evidence-based decision-making first and optimizing the use of their resources.

Effective clinical decision-making guarantees timely access to transplantation while minimizing liver disease progression and related symptoms. Prompt decision-making also eases the psychological strain on patients and their families, enabling them to make a more solid future. Cost-effectiveness in liver transplantation is influenced by effective decision-making. Healthcare expenditures related to evaluations, waiting periods, and post-transplant care can be reduced by precisely choosing acceptable candidates and optimizing resource allocation. Additionally, longer-term cost savings for healthcare systems are produced through reduced complications and better patient outcomes [22].

16.1.3   The Role of AI-Based Scoring Methods in Enhancing Efficiency in Liver Transplantation Decision-Making

AI-driven scoring techniques can help to maximize how donor organs are distributed among potential recipients. AI algorithms can produce allocation scores or rankings by considering various variables, including disease severity, patient characteristics, organ compatibility, and geographic location [23]. AI-driven scoring helps to find the best match between donors and recipients, increasing the likelihood that a transplant will succeed and lowering the waiting list mortality. This optimization improves efficiency by ensuring that organs are distributed to patients with the best chance of success [24].

AI-based scoring techniques can be helpful to clinical decision support tools for medical staff members working on liver transplants. These techniques can analyze patient-specific data and offer in-the-moment advice or risk [25]. AI-based scoring techniques can increase decision-making effectiveness, lower variability in clinical practice, and boost overall patient outcomes by supporting physicians in making evidence-based judgments. Large volumes of data are produced during liver transplantation, including patient information, test findings, imaging investigations, and clinical notes [26]. AI-based scoring techniques can automate data analysis, enabling a quick and thorough evaluation of medical data. These techniques streamline the data analysis process, saving time and allowing physicians to concentrate on crucial decision-making by extracting pertinent information, spotting patterns, and emphasizing essential insights [27].

This type of optimization increases overall efficiency in the transplantation process by enabling doctors to devote more time to direct patient care, multidisciplinary conversations, and strategic decision-making [28]. AI systems can continuously learn from new data and results and modify their behavior [29]. AI-based scoring techniques can improve prediction, recommendation accuracy, and efficiency over time as more data is gathered and analyzed. Through continuing clinical decision optimization made possible by this continuous learning, patient outcomes are enhanced, and efficiency is boosted [30].

Objectives of the Chapter

The objectives of the chapter are as follows:

- To explore various AI-based scoring methods employed in liver transplantation to enhance clinical decision-making efficiency;
- To assess the accuracy and predictive performance of these AI-based scoring methods in predicting post-transplant outcomes, encompassing graft failure, rejection, and patient survival;
- To examine the impact of AI-based scoring methods on clinical decision-making efficiency in liver transplantation, focusing on resource allocation, waiting times, workflow optimization, and overall transplant program outcomes;
- And, to analyze the characteristics that affect how well AI-based scoring techniques are implemented and integrated into routine clinical decision-making in liver transplantation.

Organization of the Chapter

The rest of the chapter is organized as follows: Section 16.2 offers the review methodology, which specifies the inclusion criteria and literature study for a comprehensive systematic review of AI-driven scoring methods in liver transplantation decision-making. At the same time, Section 16.3 includes a literature review of AI-driven scoring methods used to predict liver transplantation which delves into the information regarding various scoring methods employed to enhance clinical decision-making in liver transplantation. Section 16.4 presents the discussion and insights on the strengths and limitations of AI-based scoring methods and the implications of the findings for improving clinical decision-making in liver transplantation. Finally, Section 16.5 concludes the chapter with the future scope.

16.2 Review Methodology

A thorough literature search was done using predetermined search criteria in pertinent databases. Studies evaluating the performance and predicted accuracy of conventional and AI-based scoring techniques in liver transplantation were also included. A descriptive synthesis of the characteristics and conclusions was done after data extraction and quality assessment. A meta-analysis was completed if it was practical and appropriate. Survival rates, complications, and the effect on clinical decision-making were the key outcomes of interest. The inclusion criteria and the selection of research literature are elaborated in the upcoming sub-sections. It also includes the PRISMA flow diagram of this systematic review.

16.2.1 Inclusion Criteria

Randomized controlled trials (RCTs), observational studies, cohort studies, case–control studies, case series, systematic reviews, and meta-analyses are all types of research. Studies that only rely on editorials, commentaries, conference papers, or expert opinion should be disregarded. People receive a liver transplant for any reason, whether adults or children. Research involving transplants of organs other than the liver studies that assess artificial intelligence (AI)-based scoring techniques or predictive models explicitly created for clinical decision-making in liver transplantation is excluded from this study. Included research are those using support vector machines, artificial neural networks, machine learning, or other AI methods. Studies that do not use AI-based scoring techniques or concentrate on non-clinical liver transplantation features should be excluded.

It predicts post-transplant outcomes, including graft failure, rejection, patient survival, or disease recrudescence, with the accuracy and performance of AI-based grading techniques. Waiting periods, resource allocation, workflow optimization, transplant results, or the use of healthcare resources are all examples of efficiency metrics. Clinical results were linked to the application of AI-based scoring techniques, such as patient and graft survival rates, post-transplant problems, or long-term outcomes.

16.2.2   Selecting Research Literature for a Comprehensive Systematic Review on AI-Driven Scoring Methods in Liver Transplantation Decision-Making

The screening of the titles and abstracts found during the literature search serves as the first step in the research selection procedure. Studies that do not fit the inclusion criteria or are unrelated to the area of interest are rejected during this initial screening step. After the initial screening, the following process is to retrieve the full-text papers of the studies identified as possibly relevant. The articles' content was scrutinized at this step to determine how well it satisfies the predetermined inclusion and exclusion criteria. Then, to provide openness and accountability of the selection process, note the explanations for eliminating any research that does not match the criteria.

The included studies are meticulously documented, and pertinent information is retrieved for subsequent analysis, including study characteristics, study design, demographic characteristics, scoring systems, outcome measures, and significant findings. The research seeks to find and incorporate high-quality studies that satisfy the stated inclusion criteria by adhering to a stringent study selection process, ensuring the reliability and validity of the evidence synthesized in the review. A careful analysis of the literature review that was done to explore the importance of AI-driven scoring methods used for the prediction of liver transplantation is included in Section 16.3.

16.3   A Comprehensive Literature Review of AI-Driven Scoring Methods for Predicting Liver Transplantation Outcomes

This section comprehensively reviews AI-driven scoring methods used to predict liver transplantation. The studies obtained are classified into two main groups. Firstly, it focuses on AI-driven methods for predicting liver transplantation, including decision trees, random forests, support vector machines, neural networks, and deep learning. The second classification criteria focus on the integration of the clinical scoring method with the AI algorithms, which include the MELD score, CHILD score, Donor Risk Index score, donor–recipient matching score, MILAN score, UCSF score, and UP TO SEVEN score with AI algorithms. The analysis tries to identify these strategies' potential to enhance clinical decision-making by evaluating their accuracy. It also examines the effectiveness of clinical decision-making

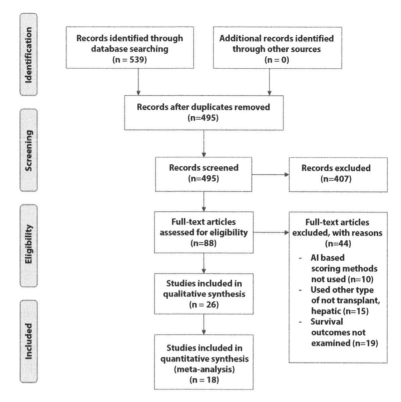

Figure 16.2 PRISMA flow diagram of systematic identification, screening, eligibility, and inclusion criteria for the systematic analysis.

in liver transplantation concerning AI-based scoring methodologies. This involves evaluating their capacity to optimize resource allocation, cut waiting times, streamline workflows, and improve transplant program outcomes. The analysis seeks to determine various strategies' practical advantages and disadvantages by assessing their efficacy [31]. A PRISMA flow diagram of systematic identification, screening, eligibility, and inclusion criteria for the routine analysis is shown in Figure 16.2.

Then, it will investigate the clinical effects of AI-based scoring techniques in liver transplantation. This process includes examining patient and transplant survival rates, post-transplant problems, and long-term results [32]. This entails evaluating the caliber of the included papers, pointing out any biases or confounding variables, and recommending areas that want additional study and examination. The goal is to offer suggestions for future research and clinical practice based on the comprehensive review results. This includes presenting recommendations for changes, emphasizing the demand for more validation studies, and discussing AI-based scoring techniques' potential application and integration into routine clinical decision-making in liver transplantation [33].

16.3.1   AI-Driven Methods Used for the Prediction of Liver Transplantation

AI-based scoring techniques can significantly improve productivity in several healthcare decision-making processes. To create prediction models, AI systems can analyze vast amounts of patient data, including clinical, genetic, and imaging data. The chance of post-transplant outcomes, such as graft failure, rejection, or survival, can be precisely predicted using these models [34]. AI-based scoring algorithms help doctors make more informed decisions about patient selection, organ allocation, and post-transplant treatment by giving fast and precise predictions. This facilitates decision-making processes and optimizes resource use [35].

Artificial intelligence in liver transplantation has enormous potential to alter patient care, optimize organ allocation, and improve clinical decision-making. AI-based techniques such as decision trees, random forests, neural networks, deep learning, and support vector machines are critical in predicting liver transplant outcomes.

Wingfield *et al.* [15] conducted a systematic analysis of research papers utilizing AI approaches to predict graft outcomes after deceased liver transplantation. They compared these to established predictive modeling and linear regression, such as the Donor Risk Index (DRI), the Model for End-Stage Liver Disease (MELD), and Survival Outcome Following Liver Transplantation (SOFT). In forecasting graft results, the results stated that AI approaches beat traditional models.

Zhuang *et al.* [36] discussed the fundamental applications of AI in transplantation, including organ allocation algorithms, determining whether to accept an organ for a specific recipient, developing a clinical prediction and decision support system to guide the physician, estimating mortality and morbidity on the waiting list, and post-transplant survival analysis. The authors emphasized the potential of artificial intelligence in improving clinical decision-making in transplantation.

16.3.1.1   Workflow of AI-Driven Methods in Liver Transplantation Prediction: Enhancing Clinical Decision-Making

The workflow of AI-driven methods used to predict liver transplantation is shown in Figure 16.3. The initial data collection phase includes gathering patient information, laboratory values, clinical history, and imaging data collected from electronic health records and appropriate databases. To ensure data quality and consistency, data preprocessing steps include data cleaning, addressing missing values, and normalization.

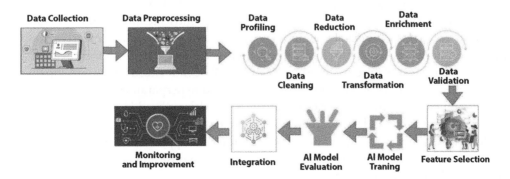

Figure 16.3 AI-driven workflow for liver transplantation prediction.

After that, feature selection techniques are used to discover the most significant variables for developing the AI model. After feature selection, preprocessed data is used to train AI models like decision trees, SVM, random forests, neural networks, and deep learning.

The models learn from prior patient data to forecast results and risk assessment in liver transplantation. Cross-validation or independent validation datasets assess the model's performance and generalization capabilities. Once the best-performing AI models are selected, they are integrated into the clinical workflow to help with liver transplant decision-making.

AI algorithms examine complicated patient data, such as clinical, genetic, and imaging, to give accurate risk assessments, personalized treatment plans, and efficient organ allocation. The following sub-section explains the ability of various AI algorithms to uncover hidden patterns and associations in data, allowing for real-time decision support, continuous monitoring of patient outcomes, and proactive management of potential complications. Ultimately, this will lead to improved patient care and overall results in liver transplantation.

16.3.1.2   Decision Trees

A decision tree is a sort of algorithm that examines patient data and generates predictions using a series of if-then expressions [37]. Decision trees can be used in liver transplantation to estimate a patient's chance of needing a transplant based on their medical history, test findings, and imaging investigations [38].

The quality and quantity of the dataset, the decision tree's complexity, and the unique traits of the patient group are only a few of the variables that might affect how accurately a decision tree predicts liver transplantation [39]. Depending on the application and dataset, the decision trees' accuracy can range from roughly 60% to over 80%. With the proper selection of characteristics and pruning methods, a well-built decision tree can frequently reach a respectable level of accuracy [40]. Remembering that accuracy cannot be the only criterion for measuring a prediction model's effectiveness is vital. The area under the receiver operating curve(AUC-ROC), precision, recall, F1 score, and other measures offer a more thorough assessment of the model's performance [41].

16.3.1.3   Random Forest

A machine learning technique called random forest makes better predictions by combining several decision trees. The random forest can be used in liver transplantation to analyze various patient data and produce more precise forecasts on the need for a transplant [42]. It is well known that random forest models can manage intricate interactions and identify non-linear patterns in the data. Combining the forecasts of many decision trees, it offers reliable and accurate liver transplantation predictions. It is crucial to remember, though, that the effectiveness of random forest models can still be influenced by the size and quality of the dataset as well as the selection of the features and hyperparameters [43].

Xu *et al.* [44] examined the various types of AI models utilized in clinical practice and concentrated on the boundaries of AI research in diagnosing, prognosis, and treating hepatocellular carcinoma (HCC). Authors concluded that AI supports in increasing equality in transplant recipient selection, prediction of treatment response and prognosis, and classification of ambiguous liver lesions.

16.3.1.4   Support Vector Machines (SVM)

The support vector machine (SVM) plays a vital role in liver transplantation by predicting patient outcomes and optimizing organ allocation. SVM is a supervised machine learning technique that uses certain features and variables to classify patients into distinct risk categories. In the context of liver transplantation, SVM may analyze diverse patient data, such as laboratory values, clinical indicators, and imaging findings, to assess disease severity, forecast short-term mortality, and identify patients who may gain the most from transplantation. Because SVM can handle both linear and nonlinear correlations in data, it helps capture complicated patterns in patient profiles.

SVM can identify high-risk patients by training on past data, allowing clinicians to prioritize those in greatest need of transplantation. This allows for more informed judgments concerning patient eligibility, transplantation timing, and post-transplant care. The classification capabilities of SVM considerably contribute to clinical decision-making in liver transplantation. Its ability to forecast patient outcomes, stratify risk, and optimize organ allocation improves patient care, resource management, and overall transplant success.

16.3.1.5   Neural Networks

Neural networks significantly impact liver transplantation because they improve risk assessment, patient management, organ allocation, and treatment options. By analyzing donor and recipient matching and post-transplant results, neural networks can predict graft survival following transplantation. This data can assist clinicians make informed decisions about donor–recipient matching and post-transplant treatment to improve graft survival in the long run. During critical scenarios such as organ availability and post-transplant problems, neural networks can provide real-time decision support to physicians. Neural networks can help with rapid and precise decision-making by analyzing data in real time, potentially increasing patient outcomes and lowering adverse occurrences. As AI and neural network technology advance, their impact on liver transplantation is projected to rise, resulting in more precise and successful transplants.

16.3.1.6   Deep Learning

A subtype of neural networks called "deep learning" can automatically analyze and learn from massive datasets. Deep learning can be used in liver transplantation to analyze patient data and generate more precise predictions about the need for a transplant. When working with particular data types, such as time series data or medical pictures, deep learning models, convolutional neural networks (CNNs), or recurrent neural networks (RNNs) can be used. These specialized systems can identify pertinent dependencies and patterns in the data for more precise predictions.

It is vital to remember that deep learning models may require more computing than conventional machine learning methods and frequently need significant volumes of data for practical training. Deep learning can also make it challenging to interpret models because of the complicated network topologies, which make it more difficult to comprehend how decisions are made. However, tools like feature importance analysis and visualization techniques might aid in understanding the model's behavior.

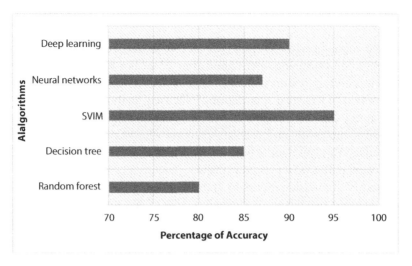

Figure 16.4 Accuracy assessment of AI-based scoring methods for liver transplantation prediction.

The influence of AI technologies on liver transplantation is predicted to be dramatic as they continue to evolve and be integrated into clinical practice, ushering in a new era of precision medicine and improved patient care. The accuracy shown by various AI algorithms for liver transplantation is shown in Figure 16.4. The literature study of AI-based scoring methods for the prediction of liver transplantation is elaborated in Table 16.1.

Table 16.1 Review of the state-of-the-art AI-based scoring methods for liver transplantation prediction.

Title	Study findings	Number of samples	AI algorithms	Outcomes measured
Artificial neural networks in prediction of patient survival after liver transplantation	Artificial neural network model for the survival rate of liver transplantation	Not specified	Artificial Neural Network (Multilayer Perceptron)	• 3-month mortality of patients after liver transplantation
Long-term survival prediction of liver transplantation using deep learning techniques	The FT-transformer model outperformed all other models	65535 donor recipient pairings	Random forest, artificial neural network, transformer, and k-nearest neighbor	• Survival following liver transplantation

(Continued)

Table 16.1 Review of the state-of-the-art AI-based scoring methods for liver transplantation prediction. (*Continued*)

Title	Study findings	Number of samples	AI algorithms	Outcomes measured
Artificial intelligence and liver transplant: Predicting survival of individual grafts	AI techniques can provide high accuracy in predicting graft survival based on donors and recipient variables	18,771	Supervised machine learning approaches	• Graft outcomes • Individual organ survival
Machine-learning algorithms predict graft failure after liver transplantation	A donor risk index predicts the outcome with an area under the receiver operating characteristic curve of 0.680 (95% confidence interval 0.669–0.690)	Not specified	Random forests, artificial neural networks, logistic regression	• Graft failure within 30 days
Predicting short-term survival after liver transplantation using machine learning	The proposed model achieves an area under the curve of 0.771 and a specificity of 0.815	13,629	Machine learning	• Postoperative survival within 30 Days
Machine learning for the prediction of red blood cell transfusion in patients during or after liver transplantation surgery	A model for predicting red blood cell transfusion during or after liver transplantation was successfully developed using a machine learning algorithm based on nine preoperative variables	1,193	Machine learning algorithm	• Red blood cell (RBC) transfusion during or after liver transplantation surgery
Application of AI techniques to predict survival in liver transplantation: A review	Artificial intelligence techniques are used to predict liver transplantation's endurance by detecting hidden patterns within large datasets	Not specified	ANN model	• Graft outcomes • Individual organ survival

16.3.1.7 Potential of AI in Enhancing Liver Transplantation Decision-Making

In my view, some observations based on these studies are that AI-driven methodologies have been employed to prognosticate liver transplantation procedures. These methodologies utilize artificial intelligence techniques, namely, artificial neural networks, decision tree classifiers, random forest, and naive Bayes classification models, to discern correlations between input variables and predict the potential outcomes of output variables. A novel investigation has developed an artificial intelligence approach that employs unceasing physiologic data streams to prognosticate the incidence of postoperative sepsis in hepatic transplantation recipients. Another study constructed a machine learning model to predict liver graft transplantation based on data collected during donor management, surpassing existing models. Furthermore, an artificial neural network has been utilized to predict acute kidney injury following liver transplantation. AI, machine learning, and deep learning techniques have also been implemented across various data formats in hepatology, including radiological imaging, electronic health records, liver pathology, wearable devices, and multi-omics measurements, to facilitate diagnosis, monitoring, and outcome prediction.

16.3.2 Integration of Clinical Tools with AI Algorithms for Enhanced Liver Transplantation Prediction: Comments and Observations

Clinical tools play a crucial role in liver transplantation, aiding clinicians in evaluating, making decisions, and managing patients. Integrating the clinical scoring methods with the AI algorithm improved the accuracy and efficiency of the prediction. By incorporating the clinical score with AI-based scoring methods, clinicians can benefit from improved risk assessment, enhanced outcome predictions, optimized treatment recommendations, refined transplant prioritization, and real-time assessment capabilities for adult and pediatric patients undergoing liver transplantation.

Clinical-based scoring techniques often used in liver transplantation include the Model for End-Stage Liver Disease (MELD), Child–Pugh Score, Donor Risk Index (DRI), Milan Criteria, University of California San Francisco (UCSF), donor–recipient matching, and UP TO SEVEN score. Based on patient and donor characteristics, these methods provide standardized metrics to assess illness severity, forecast outcomes, optimize organ allocation, and assure fair access to transplantation.

16.3.2.1 MELD Score with AI Algorithms

The Model for End-Stage Liver Disease (MELD) score, a popular grading system in liver transplantation, determines the severity of a liver disease based on the laboratory results. The three factors serum bilirubin, serum creatinine, and the international normalized ratio (INR) for prothrombin time are taken to calculate the MELD score. These factors were chosen because of their high correlation with the severity and mortality of liver disease. The MELD score objectively assesses liver dysfunction and forecasts the probability of short-term mortality by integrating these laboratory results.

The mathematical equation for calculating the MELD score is as follows:

$$\text{MELD score} = 3.78 \times \ln\left(\text{bilirubin}\left[\frac{\text{mg}}{\text{dL}}\right]\right) + 11.2 \times \ln(\text{INR}) + 9.57 \times$$

$$\ln\left(\text{creatinine}\left[\frac{\text{mg}}{\text{dL}}\right]\right) + 6.43 \tag{16.1}$$

The natural logarithm (ln) is used to normalize the distribution of the variables and ensure a linear relationship with mortality risk. The resulting MELD score ranges from 6 to 40, with higher scores indicating greater disease severity and higher mortality risk. Figure 16.5 demonstrates the 3-month mortality rate with various ranges of MELD score.

A MELD score of less than 9 indicates minimal liver impairment and a low risk of short-term mortality. A MELD score of 10–19 denotes moderate liver impairment and a moderate risk of short-term death. A MELD score of 20–29 indicates significant liver dysfunction and a high probability of short-term mortality. A MELD score of 30–39 indicates significant liver dysfunction and an exceeding probability of death in the immediate term. With a MELD score of 40 or higher, this stage denotes significant liver impairment with a high probability of short-term mortality. Patients in this stage may have advanced liver disease with multiple organ failures, decompensated cirrhosis, or abrupt liver failure.

The MELD score can be used as a feature in decision trees to produce a hierarchical decision-making procedure. Decision trees can create rules that help clinicians choose the best therapy or organ donation course based on a patient's MELD score and other pertinent parameters, analyzing extra patient data such as demographics, comorbidities, and laboratory results [45]. The MELD score can be used as one of the input features by SVM algorithms to categorize patients into various risk groups. By learning from prior patient data, SVM models can create a border that divides patients with multiple outcomes based

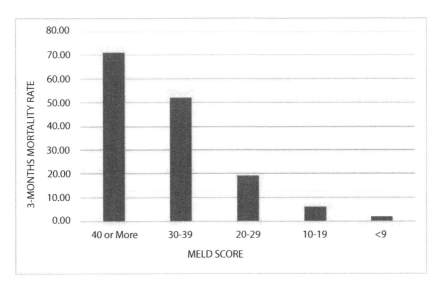

Figure 16.5 The 3-month mortality rate with various ranges of MELD score.

on their MELD score and other characteristics. Random forest models can provide a more thorough assessment of the risk connected with liver disease by taking the MELD score into account along with other patient-specific features [46].

16.3.2.2   CHILD Score with AI Algorithms

A system of scoring called the Child–Turcotte–Pugh (CTP) score is employed to evaluate the severity of liver disease and forecast prognosis in cirrhotic individuals [47]. The values of various parameters like serum bilirubin, serum albumin, prothrombin time, hepatic encephalopathy, and ascites are given in Table 16.2. The CTP score still has value in some clinical contexts [48]. It is a valuable tool in liver transplantation despite being mainly replaced by the Model for End-Stage Liver Disease (MELD) score for organ allocation. The CTP score classifies hepatic encephalopathy's severity as none (grade 1), mild (grade 2), or severe (grades 3 and 4).

By identifying patients who are at a high risk of death and who might benefit from liver transplantation, predicting the likelihood that the liver transplant will be successful, and matching donors and recipients to maximize graft survival, the CHILD score can be used in conjunction with AI algorithms to increase the effectiveness of clinical decision-making in liver transplantation [49]. Convolutional neural networks (CNN) and recurrent neural networks (RNN) are two deep learning techniques that can use the CHILD score as part of a monumental architecture that can process complex medical data [50].

A score of 1 to 3 is given to each criterion, with 1 denoting a less severe disease and 3 denoting a more severe disease. The results are then summed to get a final CTP score ranging from 5 to 15. The 2-year survival rate with a CTP score is presented in Figure 16.6.

The mathematical equation for calculating the CHILD score is as follows:

$$\text{CHILD} - \text{PUGH Score} = (1.7 \times \text{total bilirubin}) + (5.6 \times \text{INR}) + (3.8 \times \text{ascites}) +$$
$$(3.1 \times \text{hepatic encephalopathy}) + (4.0 \times \text{serum albumin}) \tag{16.2}$$

Deep learning models can look at the CHILD score combined with imaging data, genetic profiles, or other high-dimensional data to provide projections or risk evaluations. The CHILD score can be used as an input feature by neural networks [51].

Table 16.2 Parameters of CTP score and its values.

Points	Parameters				
	Serum bilirubin	Serum albumin	Prothrombin time	Hepatic encephalopathy	Ascites
1	2.0	>3.515	1–4	None	None
2	2 to 3	2.8–3.5	5 to 6	Minimal	Slight
3	>3.0	<2.8	>6	Advanced	Moderate

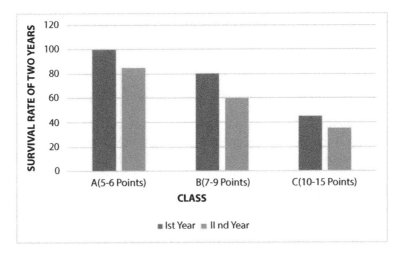

Figure 16.6 Two-year survival rate with CTP score.

16.3.2.3   *Donor Risk Index (DRI) Score with AI Algorithms*

The quality of deceased donor liver grafts used in liver transplants is evaluated using the Donor Risk Index (DRI), a rating system [52]. It was created to give an unbiased assessment of the caliber of donor organs and assist transplant facilities in making judgments about which organs to receive [53]. The DRI considers many aspects of the donor that may affect graft survival and post-transplant results.

The Donor Risk Index (DRI) score combined with AI algorithms like decision trees, SVM, random forest, neural networks, and deep learning can potentially improve personalized clinical decision-making in liver transplantation. Figure 16.7(a) illustrates donor factors such as donor serum sodium, donor age, cold ischemia time, and cause of donor death included in the Donor Risk Index. These algorithms can improve the decision-making process to select transplant candidates, enhance donor–recipient matching, forecast patient and graft survival, and pinpoint risk factors for problems, including disease recurrence [54].

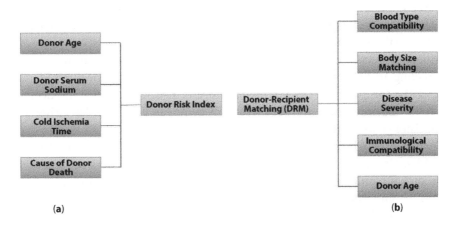

Figure 16.7 (a) Comprehensive overview of donor factors included in the Donor Risk Index (DRI) for liver transplantation. (b) Key features of donor–recipient matching for liver transplantation.

However, dataset imbalances, data privacy concerns, and a lack of research practices to test model performance in the actual world limit AI's clinical adoption in liver transplantation [55].

16.3.2.4   Donor–Recipient Matching (DRM) Score with AI Algorithms

Donor–recipient matching is essential for maximizing the success of liver transplants. A scoring method called the Donor–Recipient Matching (DRM) score is used to determine how well an organ donor and prospective recipient get along [56]. Choosing the best liver graft for transplantation considers several characteristics relating to both the donor and the recipient [57]. The DRM score gives each variable a numerical value DRM score, which determines an overall score or ranking. Features of donor–recipient matching, like blood type compatibility, body size matching, disease severity, donor–recipient immunological compatibility, and donor age, are shown in Figure 16.7(b). The decision-making process for choosing the best liver graft for a specific recipient is then guided by this score. The DRM score is only one component of the intricate decision-making process involved in liver transplantation. Other elements, including the urgency of transplantation, organ availability, and center-specific considerations, also play significant roles in organ allocation decisions.

Combining the Donor Recipient Matching (DRM) score with AI algorithms like decision trees, SVM, random forests, neural networks, and deep learning can enhance clinical decision-making in liver transplantation. These algorithms establish hierarchical decision-making procedures, categorize donor organs according to DRM scores, assess risk, forecast outcomes, and produce tailored recommendations for organ acceptance or allocation [58].

16.3.2.5   MILAN Score with AI Algorithms

Hepatocellular carcinoma (HCC) patients' eligibility for liver transplantation is determined using the Milan criteria, a grading system used in liver transplantation [59]. It was created to distinguish those HCC patients who are in the early stages and most likely to benefit from transplantation and have successful post-transplant outcomes [60]. The Milan criteria identify early-stage, locally advanced HCC patients who will most likely benefit from liver transplantation. Patients who meet these requirements have excellent long-term survival rates and minimal post-transplant tumor recurrence rates [61].

The Milan Criteria score can significantly increase the effectiveness of clinical decision-making in liver transplantation when paired with AI algorithms like decision trees, support vector machines (SVM), random forests, neural networks, and deep learning [62]. The following are some ways that these AI systems can use the Milan Criteria score to improve decision-making [63]. The Milan Criteria score can be used as a feature in decision trees to create a hierarchical decision-making process. SVM and random forests can combine the Milan Criteria score with other pertinent variables to assess the transplantation risk. To predict outcomes, neural network throughly works can learn intricate relationships between the Milan Criteria score and not to predict outcomes [64]. Deep learning techniques can use the Milan Criteria score with extensive patient data to generate personalized recommendations for patient eligibility and transplantation decisions. By integrating the Milan Criteria score with AI algorithms, clinical decision-making in liver transplantation can be optimized, resulting in improved efficiency and better patient outcomes [65].

16.3.2.6 UCSF Score with AI Algorithms

Hepatocellular carcinoma (HCC) patients' suitability for liver transplantation is determined using the University of California San Francisco (UCSF) criteria, a scoring system used in liver transplantation. Despite having a slightly more advanced disease, it helps identify patients who may benefit from transplantation by offering additional measures beyond the Milan criteria. Compared to the tight Milan criteria, the UCSF criteria allow for a larger spectrum of patients to be evaluated for transplantation and offer a more thorough review of patients with HCC. The UCSF criteria should be used in the context of a patient's full health, including liver function, general health, and responsiveness to other treatment methods, which is significant to mention [66].

The UCSF score can enhance clinical decision-making in liver transplantation using AI algorithms like decision trees, support vector machines (SVM), random forests, neural networks, and deep learning. By including the UCSF score as a feature in decision trees, they were categorizing patients into risk groups based on the score with SVM, combining the score with other variables in random forests, and learning complex relationships with neural networks and deep learning, AI algorithms using the UCSF score to improve decision-making processes. Clinicians can make better judgments and improve patient outcomes using AI algorithms with the UCSF score. However, data inconsistencies, privacy concerns, and a lack of benchmarking procedures restrict the use of AI in liver transplantation. Various parameters and ranges of MILAN and UCSF criteria are explained in Table 16.3.

Table 16.3 Various parametric values of MILAN and UCSF criteria.

	Scoring methods	
	MILAN criteria	**UCSF criteria**
Parametric values	One tumor ≤5 cm	One tumor ≤6. 5 cm
	Two or three tumors ≤3 cm	Two or three tumors ≤4.5 cm
	-	A sum of the longest diameter of each tumor ≤8 cm
	No imaging evidence of vascular invasion	No imaging evidence of vascular invasion
	No imaging evidence of extrahepatic Metastatic disease	No imaging evidence of extrahepatic Metastatic disease

16.3.2.7   *Up to Seven Score with AI Algorithms*

The "Up to Seven" criteria is a scoring system used in liver transplantation for hepatocellular carcinoma (HCC). It considers several tumor characteristics to assess patients' eligibility for liver transplantation. The criteria evaluate seven variables, and the sum of the scores determines the "Up to Seven" score. The "Up to Seven" score helps assess the risk of tumor recurrence after transplantation and guides the selection of patients for liver transplantation [67]. The parametric values of score 0, score 1, and score 2 in UP TO SEVEN score are elaborated in Table 16.4.

Steps to calculate the "Up to Seven" score:

- Assign a score to each of the seven variables based on the abovementioned criteria.
- Sum up the scores for all seven variables.
- The total score ranges from 0 to 14, with higher scores indicating more advanced tumor characteristics and potentially decreased eligibility for liver transplantation.

16.3.3   Assessing the Efficacy of AI-Based Scoring Techniques in Enhancing Clinical Decision-Making for Liver Transplantation

This systematic analysis aims to assess the efficiency of AI-based scoring techniques in enhancing the clinical decision-making process in liver transplantation. This study provided an in-depth overview of state-of-the-art Liver transplantation research. The state of the art of incorporating AI and clinical scoring methods to enhance the efficiency of clinical decision-making in liver transplantation is shown in Table 16.5. The systematic analysis

Table 16.4 Various parametric values of Up to Seven score.

Parameters	Score 0	Score 1	Score 2
Tumor size	≤2 cm	>2 cm and ≤5 cm	>5 cm
Tumor number	Single tumor	2 to 3 tumors	>3 tumors
Vascular invasion	No vascular invasion	Vascular invasion present	-
Extrahepatic spread	No extrahepatic spread	-	Extrahepatic spread present
Serum alpha-fetoprotein (AFP) level:	≤400 ng/mL	-	>400 ng/mL
Serum bilirubin level:	≤1 mg/dL	>1 mg/dL and ≤3 mg/dL	>3 mg/dL
Serum albumin level	≥3.5 g/dL	<3.5 g/dL	-

Table 16.5 A comprehensive review of AI and clinical scoring method integration to enhance clinical decision-making in liver transplantation.

Title of the study	Study findings	Number of samples	AI algorithm	Clinical scoring method used	Outcomes measured
Validation of artificial neural networks as a methodology for donor–recipient matching for liver transplantation	The application of artificial neural networks for donor–recipient matching in liver transplantation in various healthcare systems demonstrated good prediction skills, supporting the validation of these techniques	822	Artificial neural networks (ANNs)	MELD, CHILD, DRM	• Probability of graft survival (correct classification rate [Ccr]) • Nonsurvivable (minimum sensitivity [Ms])
Using artificial intelligence for predicting survival of individual grafts in liver transplantation: a systematic review	AI approaches can accurately predict graft survival based on donor and recipient factors	18,771	Artificial neural networks (ANNs)	DRI, MELD, SOFT	• Graft outcomes • Individual organ survival
Statistical methods *versus* machine learning techniques for donor–recipient matching in liver transplantation	Complex machine learning algorithms were unable to improve liver allocation performance	39,189	ANN, SVM	MELD, SOFT, and BAR	• 3-month end point • 1-year end point • 2-year end point • 5-year end point

(Continued)

Table 16.5 A comprehensive review of AI and clinical scoring method integration to enhance clinical decision-making in liver transplantation. (*Continued*)

Title of the study	Study findings	Number of samples	AI algorithm	Clinical scoring method used	Outcomes measured
Application of machine learning in liver transplantation: a review	Machine learning is being extensively researched in liver transplantation, with promising applications in both pre- and post-transplant settings	1379	Random forest, SVM, decision tree	UCSF, MILAN	• Patient survival • Graft rejection • Graft failure • Post-operative morbidity risk
Machine learning algorithms for predicting results in liver transplantation: the problem of donor–recipient matching	Artificial intelligence models can provide a considerable benefit by handling various factors, being objective, and assisting in circumstances of similar probabilities	Not specified	Artificial neural networks (ANNs), random forest classifiers, and SVM	MELD, MILAN, DRI	• Graft survival at 3 months • Outcome after transplantation
Clinical validation of a novel scoring system based on donor and recipient risk factors for predicting outcomes in liver transplantation	A unique prognostic-based grading system was designed and clinically verified utilizing donor and recipient characteristics	932	Decision tree, SVM	THE CLINICAL SCORING METHOD USED CHILD, DRM	• Patient survival • Risk of death • Retransplant • Fulminant hepatitis • Previous large abdominal/biliary tree surgery • Meld score • Serum creatinine before liver transplantation >1.5 mg/dL

(*Continued*)

Table 16.5 A comprehensive review of AI and clinical scoring method integration to enhance clinical decision-making in liver transplantation. (*Continued*)

Title of the study	Study findings	Number of samples	AI algorithm	Clinical scoring method used	Outcomes measured
Development and validation of an optimized prediction of mortality for candidates awaiting liver transplantation	Improved mortality prediction reliably and objectively prioritizes liver transplant candidates based on disease severity	Not specified	A state-of-the-art machine learning method, SVM	CLINICAL SCORING METHOD USED, MELD, CHILD, UP TO SEVEN	• 3-month waitlist mortality • Removal from waitlist

evaluates AI-based scoring techniques, precision, and prognostication capabilities in liver transplantation. This involves assessing how well they can foresee outcomes following transplantation, such as graft failure, rejection, and patient survival [68].

16.3.4   The Promise of AI Integration with Clinical Scoring Methods in Liver Transplantation Decision-Making

The potential for increasing efficiency and improving patient outcomes by combining artificial intelligence (AI) with clinical scoring methods in liver transplant decision-making is enormous. This remarkable development marks the beginning of a new era in liver transplant precision medicine, driven by ongoing research, collaboration, and inventiveness in the area.

However, careful attention must be paid to ethical issues and technical challenges to maximize AI's potential benefits fully. The investigation attempts to evaluate the accuracy and impact of AI-based scoring systems to improve clinical decision-making. In particular, it looks at how AI may improve how resources are distributed, shorten wait times, streamline workflows, and ultimately improve the results of transplant programs. The study also aims to pinpoint the advantages and disadvantages of these strategies in practical circumstances, helping to incorporate AI in liver transplantation responsibly. AI integration promises to transform liver transplantation decision-making and raise patient care and outcomes to new heights by embracing collaboration and upholding ethical standards.

16.4   Discussion and Insights

The systematic review aimed to determine how well AI-based grading techniques predicted liver transplantation results and how they affected clinician judgment. The number of studies found was: 539 potential studies after an extensive literature search across pertinent databases. The titles and abstracts of the remaining 495 studies were checked for relevance after duplicates were eliminated. After the initial screening procedure, four hundred seven studies were eliminated based on the predetermined inclusion and exclusion criteria.

The assessed studies included survival rates, post-transplant complications, graft failure, and length of hospital stay, among other end measures. The research shed light on traditional and AI-based scoring methodologies' predicted accuracy, sensitivity, specificity, and overall performance in the context of liver transplantation.

A strategy that holds promise for improving patient care and resource allocation is the incorporation of AI-based scoring algorithms in clinical decision-making for liver transplantation. The objective of this study was to conduct a thorough assessment of the literature on the use of AI algorithms in liver transplantation, including decision trees, SVM, random forests, neural networks, and deep learning, in conjunction with well-established scoring systems. The results showed that risk prediction, patient stratification, and treatment planning could all be enhanced by AI-based scoring approaches. MELD, CHILD, UCSF, DRI, DRM, and MILAN, UP TO SEVEN scores were combined with AI algorithms to show improved accuracy and individualized decision-making. These techniques provide the chance to enhance organ allocation, lower waitlist mortality, and enhance long-term results. However, issues including interpretability, biases, external validation, and ethical implications must be addressed. Future studies should concentrate on approving these procedures in various patient populations and addressing the moral and legal issues related to their proper application. Overall, AI-based scoring techniques can potentially transform clinical decision-making in liver transplantation, with implications for better patient outcomes and resource use.

16.4.1   Parameters in Clinical Scoring Methods

MELD, Child–Pugh, DRI, DRM, Milan Criteria, UP TO SEVEN, and UCSF score are clinical scoring techniques for liver transplantation that integrate numerous parameters that play an important role in assessing disease severity, forecasting patient outcomes, and prioritizing patients on the transplant waiting list. These parameters are significant because they help clinicians assess the urgency of transplantation, predict the likelihood of successful outcomes, and allocate organs to patients who need them the most. Clinical scoring methods for liver transplantation are essential tools used to assess the severity of liver disease, prioritize patients on the transplant waiting list, and predict post-transplant outcomes. These scoring methods often involve a combination of clinical and laboratory parameters to determine a patient's eligibility for transplantation and their prognosis. The key parameters and their influence on scoring methods are shown in Table 16.6.

16.4.2   Assessment of Clinical Scoring Accuracy Using Diverse AI Algorithms

When clinical scoring methods in liver transplantation are integrated with various AI algorithms, their accuracy can be greatly improved. Decision trees, random forests, neural networks, deep learning, and support vector machines are examples of AI algorithms that can handle huge and complicated datasets, find subtle patterns, and uncover hidden correlations between clinical characteristics. Clinical scoring methods in the context of liver transplantation are indispensable tools for evaluating the severity of liver disease, making critical decisions regarding organ allocation, and predicting post-transplant patient outcomes.

Table 16.6 Various parameters included in clinical scoring methods.

Parameters	Scoring methods						
	MELD	CHILD	DRI	DRM	MILAN	UCSF	UPTO SEVEN
Serum bilirubin	✓	✓					✓
Serum albumin							✓
Serum creatinine	✓	✓					
INR for prothrombin time	✓	✓					
Hepatic encephalopathy		✓					
Ascites		✓					
Ascites							
Donor age			✓	✓			
Cause of death			✓				
Donor serum sodium			✓				
Cold ischemia time			✓				
Blood type compatibility				✓			
Body size matching				✓			
DR immunological compatibility				✓			
Disease severity				✓			
Number of tumor					✓	✓	✓
Tumor size					✓	✓	✓
Tumor grade						✓	
Vascular invasion					✓	✓	✓
Extrahepatic spread						✓	✓
AFP level							✓

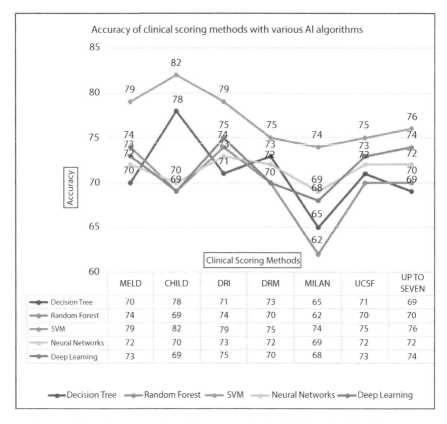

Figure 16.8 Accuracy shown by various clinical scoring methods in different AI algorithms.

The accuracy levels shown by various clinical scoring methods in different AI algorithms are shown in Figure 16.8. The integration of clinical scoring methodologies with AI algorithms offers significant promise for increasing risk prediction and clinical decision-making accuracy in liver transplantation.

16.4.3   Strengths and Limitations of AI-Based Scoring Methods

AI-based scoring techniques are advantageous in clinical decision-making due to a number of its advantages. First, these techniques improve accuracy by using cutting-edge algorithms to examine massive amounts of data. Compared to conventional scoring systems, AI models can offer more accurate forecasts and risk evaluations by seeing complex patterns and correlations within the data. Patients may benefit from better diagnosis, prognosis, and therapy planning [69]. Based on artificial intelligence scoring techniques can significantly increase productivity in medical settings. AI algorithms can help healthcare workers save time and money by automating jobs and optimizing operations. They enable clinicians to act swiftly by quickly analyzing patient data, producing insights, and offering recommendations. This effectiveness can result in more rapid and efficient patient treatment, particularly in life-or-death circumstances like organ transplants where seconds count [70].

It is crucial to understand the drawbacks of AI-based scoring techniques, however. The possibility of bias and discrimination is a significant drawback. The historical data AI algorithms use to train themselves may contain biases like racial or gender inequities. These biases can reinforce inequality in healthcare decision-making if they are not thoroughly observed and addressed. Identifying preferences and minimizing them during the development and validation phases is essential to ensure the equity and justice of AI systems. Another drawback is that some AI models are challenging to interpret. Deep learning algorithms, for instance, are frequently referred to as "black boxes" due to their intricate designs and challenging-to-understand decision-making processes. This lack of interpretability can bring concerns concerning trust, openness, and the capacity to understand and validate the results. To win the trust of medical professionals and patients, efforts are being undertaken to create explainable AI models that offer insights into the decision-making process.

Furthermore, the success of AI-based scoring techniques depends on their reliance on high-quality data. These methods for model training and model validation need extensive and varied datasets. However, getting hold of such databases can be difficult, mainly when working with rare diseases or particular patient populations. Incomplete or biased data might significantly impact the effectiveness and generalizability of AI models. Working with sensitive patient data also raises serious privacy and security risks, necessitating careful adherence to ethical and regulatory guidelines.

16.4.4   Implications of the Findings for Improving Clinical Decision-Making in Liver Transplantation

The findings on AI-based scoring algorithms are essential for enhancing clinical judgment in liver transplantation. First, AI algorithms with scoring systems like MELD, CHILD, DRI, UCSF, DRM, and MILAN and UP TO SEVEN scores can improve clinical decision-making's precision and effectiveness. These AI systems can analyze massive amounts of patient data, spot trends, and make predictions, giving clinicians helpful information to aid decision-making. Second, applying AI-based scoring techniques can result in more specialized and customized liver transplantation procedures. AI algorithms can offer patient-specific suggestions for eligibility screening, organ allocation, and post-transplant treatment by considering unique patient characteristics and risk factors. This individualized method can enhance the distribution of limited resources and optimize results.

Third, incorporating AI-based scoring techniques can help with resource management and patient outcomes. Clinicians may make well-informed decisions about transplant scheduling, patient prioritization, and post-transplant care thanks to accurate risk assessment and prediction models, which lower the risk of complications and increase long-term survival rates. Additionally, by improving resource allocation and utilization, AI algorithms' efficiency can maximize the benefits of liver transplant services. Overall, the results highlight the opportunity for AI-based scoring techniques to transform clinical judgment in liver transplantation. By utilizing these techniques, doctors can make more precise, fast, and tailored, thereby enhancing judgments of patient outcomes and maximizing resource allocation in liver transplantation. To enable the appropriate and successful integration of AI in clinical practice, it is essential to address the issues related to data quality, interpretability, bias, and ethical considerations.

16.5   Conclusion and Future Scope

The systematic study of AI-based scoring methods in liver transplantation shows that they can improve the effectiveness and efficiency of clinical decision-making. The precision and accuracy of clinical choices are greatly enhanced by merging well-established scoring systems with AI algorithms, such as decision trees, SVM, random forests, neural networks, and deep learning. These methods can potentially improve the long-term outcomes of liver transplant recipients, lower waitlist mortality, and maximize organ allocation through risk prediction, patient stratification, and personalized treatment planning. To ensure responsible and practical deployment in clinical practice, more study is needed in areas like external validation, interpretability of AI models, correcting biases, and ethical considerations.

One of the future priorities is conducting prospective studies to assess the efficacy and impact of AI-based scoring techniques in liver transplantation. Developing explainable AI models should also be prioritized to increase physician acceptability and comprehension. For the ethical use of AI algorithms in liver transplantation decision-making, it will be essential to address privacy, data security, and fairness issues. To thoroughly assess AI algorithms' efficacy and sustainability in clinical practice, the long-term effects of AI-based scoring methods should be investigated to assess quality-of-life indicators, post-transplant complications, graft survival rates, and long-term patient survival rates.

References

1. Schwartz, M., Dvorchik, I., Roayaie, S., Fiel, M.I., Finkelstein, S., Marsh, J.W., ... Llovet, J.M., Liver transplantation for hepatocellular carcinoma: Extension of indications based on molecular markers. *J. Hepatol.*, 49, 4, 581–588, 2008.
2. Mózes, F.E., Lee, J.A., Vali, Y., Alzoubi, O., Staufer, K., Trauner, M., ... Trautwein, C., Performance of non-invasive tests and histology for the prediction of clinical outcomes in patients with non-alcoholic fatty liver disease: An individual participant data meta-analysis. *Lancet Gastroenterol. Hepatol.*, 8, 8, 704–713, 2023.
3. Vagefi, P.A., Bertsimas, D., Hirose, R., Trichakis, N., The rise and fall of the model for endstage liver disease score and the need for an optimized machine learning approach for liver allocation. *Curr. Opin. Organ Transpl.*, 25, 2, 122–125, 2020.
4. Spann, A., Yasodhara, A., Kang, J., Watt, K., Wang, B., Goldenberg, A., Bhat, M., Applying Machine Learning in Liver Disease and Transplantation: A Comprehensive Review. *Hepatology*, 71, 3, 1093–1105, 2020, https://doi.org/10.1002/hep.31103.
5. Lin, J., Cui, C., Gao, Y., Zhou, L., W.X., Effect of perioperative clinical application of enhanced recovery after surgery on elderly recipients undergoing liver transplantation. *Organ Transplant.*, 6, 2023, Pesquisa.Bvsalud.Org. Retrieved June 10, 2023, from https://pesquisa.bvsalud.org/portal/resource/pt/wpr-965054.
6. Briceño, J., Ayllón, M.D., Ciria, R., Machine-learning algorithms for predicting results in liver transplantation: The problem donor–recipientient matching. *Curr. Opin. Organ Transpl.*, 25, 4, 406–411, 2020a, https://doi.org/10.1097/mot.0000000000000781.
7. Mitropoulou, P., Carroll, A., Fitzsimmons, S., Smith, L., 16 Screening for and monitoring Fontan-associated liver disease in a tertiary center, 2023, https://heart.bmj.com/content/109/Suppl_3/A19.abstract.

8. Shah, M., Mendoza, M., Bilhartz, J., Gupta, N., A Prospective Knowledge Assessment of Adolescent Liver Transplant Recipients after Tailored Education Intervention. *Int. J. Hepatol.,* 2023, 2023.

9. Kantidakis, G., Putter, H., Lancia, C., Boer, J., Braat, A.E., Fiocco, M., Survival prediction models since liver transplantation - comparisons between Cox models and machine learning techniques. *BMC Med. Res. Methodol.,* 20, 1, 1–14, 2020, https://doi.org/10.1186/s12874-020-01153-1.

10. Jarmulski, W., Wieczorkowska, A., Trzaska, M., Ciszek, M., Paczek, L., Machine-learning models for predicting patient survival after liver transplantation. *Comput. Sci.,* 19, 2, 223, 2018, https://doi.org/10.7494/csci.2018.19.2.2746.

11. Silberhumer, G.R., Györi, G., Brugger, J., Baumann, L., Zehetmayer, S., Soliman, T., Berlakovich, G., MELD-Na Alterations on the Liver Transplant Waiting List and Their Impact on Listing Outcome. *J. Clin. Med.,* 12, 11, 3763, 2023.

12. Silva, C.A.C., Fidelle, M., Birebent, R., Dalban, C., Zoppi, S., Reni, A., Rauber, C., Lahmar, I., de La Varende, M., A.-L., Rioux-Leclercq, N., Sautès-Fridman, C., Meylan, M., Vano, Y.-A., Beusenlick, B., Chouaib, S., Tantot, F., Escudier, B., Zitvogel, L., Derosa, L., Albiges, L., Serum soluble MAdCAM-1: A new biomarker for cancer immunotherapy. *J. Clin. Oncol.,* 41, 16_suppl, 4548–4548, 2023, https://doi.org/10.1200/JCO.2023.41.16_SUPPL.4548.

13. Mózes, F.E., Lee, J.A., Vali, Y., Alzoubi, O., Staufer, K., Trauner, M., ... Trautwein, C., Performance of non-invasive tests and histology for the prediction of clinical outcomes in patients with non-alcoholic fatty liver disease: An individual participant data meta-analysis. *Lancet Gastroenterol. Hepatol.,* 8, 8, 704–713, 2023.

14. Kalisvaart, M., Schlegel, A., Umbro, I., de Haan, J.E., Polak, W.G., IJzermans, J.N., Mirza, D.F., Perera, M.T.P.R., Isaac, J.R., Ferguson, J., Mitterhofer, A.P., de Jonge, J., Muiesan, P., The AKI Prediction Score: A new prediction model for acute kidney injury after liver transplantation. *HPB,* 21, 12, 1707–1717, 2019, https://doi.org/10.1016/j.hpb.2019.04.008.

15. Wingfield, L.R., Ceresa, C., Thorogood, S., Fleuriot, J., Knight, S., Using Artificial Intelligence for Predicting Survival of Individual Grafts in Liver Transplantation: A Systematic Review. *Liver Transpl.,* 26, 7, 922–934, 2020c, https://doi.org/10.1002/LT.25772.

16. Apostolov, R., Wong, D., Low, E., Vaz, K., Spurio, J., Worland, T., ... Sinclair, M., Testosterone is lower in men with non-alcoholic fatty liver disease and alcohol-related cirrhosis and is associated with adverse clinical outcomes. *Scand. J. Gastroenterol.,* 58, 11, 1328–1334, 2023.

17. Pramanik, P.K.D., Solanki, A., Debnath, A., Nayyar, A., El-Sappagh, S., Kwak, K.S., Advancing modern healthcare with nanotechnology, nanobiosensors, and internet of nano things: Taxonomies, applications, architecture, and challenges. *IEEE Access,* 8, 65230–65266, 2020.

18. Ganie, S.M., Pramanik, P.K.D., Malik, M.B., Nayyar, A., Kwak, K.S., An Improved Ensemble Learning Approach for Heart Disease Prediction Using Boosting Algorithms. *Comput. Syst. Sci. Eng.,* 46, 3, 3993–4006, 2023.

19. Abouhawwash, M., Tanwar, S., Nayyar, A., Naved, M. (Eds.), *Innovations in Healthcare Informatics: From Interoperability to Data Analysis,* IET, London, UK, 2023.

20. Ilmudeen, A. and Nayyar, A., Novel Designs of Smart Healthcare Systems: Technologies, Architecture, and Applications, in: *Machine Learning for Critical Internet of Medical Things: Applications and Use Cases,* pp. 125–151, Springer International Publishing, Cham, 2022.

21. Venaik, A., Kumari, R., Venaik, U., Nayyar, A., The role of machine learning and artificial intelligence in clinical decisions and the herbal formulations against covid-19. *Int. J. Reliab. Qual. E-Healthcar. (IJRQEH),* 11, 1–17, 2022.

22. CG, R. and Chandra, S.S.,.V., Artificial Neural Networks in Prediction of Patient Survival after Liver Transplantation. *J. Health Med. Inform.,* 07, 01, 1-7, 2016, https://doi.org/10.4172/2157-7420.1000215.

23. Tranchita, E., Cafiero, G., Giordano, U., Palermi, S., Gentili, F., Guzzo, I., ... Turchetta, A., Differences in Physical Activity Levels between Healthy and Transplanted Children: Who Needs More Tips? *Healthcare,* 11, 11, 1610, May 2023.

24. O'riordan, A., Johnston, O., Mcmorrow, T., Wynne, K., Maguire, P., Hegarty, J.E., Mccormick, A., Watson, A.J., Cagney, G., Gallagher, W.M., Ryan, M.P., Identification of Apolipoprotein AI as a serum biomarker of chronic kidney disease in liver transplant recipients, using proteomic techniques. *Proteomics Clin. Appl.,* 2, 9, 1338–1348, 2008.

25. Cruz-Ramirez, M., Hervas-Martinez, C., Fernandez, J.C., Briceno, J., De La Mata, M., Predicting patient survival after liver transplantation using evolutionary multi-objective artificial neural networks. *Artif. Intell. Med.,* 58, 1, 37–49, 2013.

26. Yang, L.S., Shan, L.L., Saxena, A., Morris, D.L., Liver transplantation: A systematic review of long-term quality of life. *Liver Int.,* 34, 9, 1298–1313, 2014.

27. Ma, E., Ai, J., Zhang, Y., Zheng, J., Gao, X., Xu, J., ... Wang, Z., Omicron infections profile and vaccination status among 1881 liver transplant recipients: A multi-centre retrospective cohort. *Emerging Microbes Infect.,* 11, 1, 2636–2644, 2022.

28. Meng, J., Liu, Z., Xu, X., Applications of neural networks in liver transplantation. *iLIVER,* 1, 2, 101–110, 2022.

29. Wang, M., Ge, J., Ha, N., Shui, A.M., Huang, C.Y., Cullaro, G., Lai, J.C., Clinical characteristics associated with posttransplant survival among adults 70 years old or older undergoing liver transplantation. *J. Clin. Gastroenterol.,* 10-1097, 2023.

30. Pomohaci, M.D., Grasu, M.C., Dumitru, R.L., Toma, M., Lupescu, I.G., Liver Transplant in Patients with Hepatocarcinoma: Imaging Guidelines and Future Perspectives Using Artificial Intelligence. *Diagnostics,* 13, 9, 1663, 2023.

31. Bertsimas, D., Kung, J., Trichakis, N., Wang, Y., Hirose, R., Vagefi, P.A., Development and validation of an optimized mortality prediction for candidates awaiting liver transplantation. *Am. J. Transplant.,* 19, 4, 1109–1118, 2019, https://doi.org/10.1111/ajt.15172.

32. Davari, H.R., Malek-Hosseini, S.A., Salahi, H., Bahador, A., Nikeghbalian, S., Nemati, M.H., ... Kazemi, K., Liver transplantation and aortic valve replacement. *Int. J. Organ Transplant. Med. (IJOTM),* 2, 1, 32, 2011.

33. Gillmore, J.D., Stangou, A.J., Tennent, G.A., Booth, D.R., O'Grady, J., Rela, M., ... Hawkins, P.N., Clinical and biochemical outcome of hepatorenal transplantation for hereditary systemic amyloidosis associated with apolipoprotein AI Gly26Arg1. *Transplantation,* 71, 7, 986–992, 2001.

34. Mohamed, Z.U., Keshavan, R., Muhammed, F., Santosh, D., Surendran, S., A focused survey of immediate postoperative practices in liver transplantation in India. *Indian J. Transplant.,* 11, 4, 181–183, 2017.

35. Remya, S. and Anjali, T., An Intelligent and Optimal Deep Learning Approach in Sensor Based Networks for Detecting Microbes. *IEEE Sensors J.,* 2023, 2023.

36. Zhuang, Q., Tu, B., Zhang, Y., Yao, J., Qiao, M., Chen, Y., 427.11: Assessment of Music Therapy on Psychological Stress And Immune Function in the Early Postoperative Period of Renal Allograft Recipients: A Prospective RCT. *Transplantation,* 106, 9S, S499–S499, 2022, https://doi.org/10.1097/01.tp.0000888124.66458.2c.

37. Kamaleswaran, R., Sataphaty, S.K., Mas, V.R., Maluf, D.G., Artificial intelligence may predict early sepsis after liver transplantation. *Front. Physiol.,* 12, 692667, 2021.

38. He, T., Fong, J.N., Moore, L.W., Ezeana, C.F., Victor, D., Divatia, M., ... Wong, S.T., An imageomics and multi-network based deep learning model for risk assessment of liver transplantation for hepatocellular cancer. *Comput. Med. Imaging Graphics,* 89, 101894, 2021.

39. Raju, J. and Sathyalakshmi, S., Application of AI Techniques to Predict Survival in Liver Transplantation : A Review. *2021 IEEE Pune Section International Conference (PuneCon),* 2021, December, https://doi.org/10.1109/punecon52575.2021.9686494.

40. Chen, S., Liu, L., Wang, Y., Zhou, X., Dong, H., Chen, Z., Wu, J., Gui, R., Zhao, Q., Advancing Prediction of Risk of Intraoperative Massive Blood Transfusion in Liver Transplantation With Machine Learning Models. A Multicenter Retrospective Study. *Front. Neuroinf.*, *16*, 2022, https://doi.org/10.3389/fninf.2022.893452.

41. Lee, H.-C., Yoon, S., Yang, S.-M., Kim, W., Ryu, H.-G., Jung, C.-W., Suh, K.-S., Lee, K., Prediction of Acute Kidney Injury after Liver Transplantation: Machine Learning Approaches vs. Logistic Regression Model. *J. Clin. Med.*, *7*, 11, 428, 2018, https://doi.org/10.3390/ jcm7110428.

42. Nair, B. and Nath, L.R., Inevitable role of TGF-β1 in progression of nonalcoholic fatty liver disease. *J. Recept. Signal Transduct.*, *40*, 3, 195–200, 2020.

43. Liu, C.-L., Soong, R.-S., Lee, W.-C., Jiang, G.-W., Lin, Y.-C., Predicting Short-term Survival after Liver Transplantation using Machine Learning. *Sci. Rep.*, *10*, 1, 5654, 2020, https:// doi.org/10.1038/s41598-020-62387-z.

44. Xu, X., Lu, D., Ling, Q., Wei, X., Wu, J., Zhou, L., Yan, S., Wu, L., Geng, L., Ke, Q., Gao, F., Tu, Z., Wang, W., Zhang, M., Shen, Y., Xie, H., Jiang, W., Wang, H., Zheng, S., Liver transplantation for hepatocellular carcinoma beyond the Milan criteria. *Gut*, *65*, 6, 1035–1041, 2015, https:// doi.org/10.1136/gutjnl-2014-308513.

45. Guerrini, G.P., Pinelli, D., Marini, E., Corno, V., Guizzetti, M., Zambelli, M., Aluffi, A., Lincini, L., Fagiuoli, S., Lucianetti, A., Colledan, M., Value of HCC-MELD Score in Patients With Hepatocellular Carcinoma Undergoing Liver Transplantation. *Prog. Transplant.*, *28*, 1, 63–69, 2017, https://doi.org/10.1177/1526924817746686.

46. Farr, M., Mitchell, J., Lippel, M., Kato, T.S., Jin, Z., Ippolito, P., Dove, L., Jorde, U.P., Takayama, H., Emond, J., Naka, Y., Mancini, D., Lefkowitch, J.H., Christian Schulze, P., Combination of liver biopsy with MELD-XI scores for post-transplant outcome prediction in patients with advanced heart failure and suspected liver dysfunction. *J. Heart Lung Transplant.*, *34*, 7, 873–882, 2015, https://doi.org/10.1016/j.healun.2014.12.009.

47. Ramos-Gonzalez, G., Elisofon, S., Dee, E.C., Staffa, S.J., Medford, S., Lillehei, C., Kim, H.B., Predictors of Need for Liver Transplantation in Children Undergoing Hepatoportoenterostomy for Biliary Atresia. *J. Pediatr. Surg.*, *54*, 6, 1127–1131, 2019, https://doi.org/10.1016/j. jpedsurg.2019.02.051.

48. Martínez, J.A., Pacheco, S., Bachler, J.P., Jarufe, N., Briceño, E., Guerra, J.F., Benítez, C., Wolff, R., Barrera, F., Arrese, M., Accuracy of the BAR score in the prediction of survival after liver transplantation. *Ann. Hepatol.*, *18*, 2, 386–392, 2019, https://doi.org/10.1016/j. aohep.2019.01.002.

49. Chang, C.-C.H., Bryce, C.L., Shneider, B.L., Yabes, J.G., Ren, Y., Zenarosa, G.L., Tomko, H., Donnell, D.M., Squires, R.H., Roberts, M.S., Accuracy of the Pediatric End-stage Liver Disease Score in Estimating Pretransplant Mortality Among Pediatric Liver Transplant Candidates. *JAMA Pediatr.*, *172*, 11, 1070, 2018, https://doi.org/10.1001/jamapediatrics.2018.2541.

50. Hsu, E., Schladt, D.P., Wey, A., Perito, E.R., Israni, A.K., Improving the predictive ability of the pediatric end-stage liver disease score for young children awaiting a liver transplant. *Am. J. Transplant.*, *21*, 1, 222–228, 2021, https://doi.org/10.1111/ajt.15925.

51. Alobaidi, R., Anton, N., Cave, D., Moez, E.K., Joffe, A.R., Predicting early outcomes of liver transplantation in young children: The EARLY study. *World J. Hepatol.*, *10*, 1, 62–72, 2018, https://doi.org/10.4254/wjh.v10.i1.62.

52. Silveira, F., Silveira, F.P., de Freitas, A.C.T., Coelho, J.C.U., Ramos, E.J.B., Macri, M.M., Tefilli, N., Bredt, L.C., Liver transplantation: Survival and indexes of donor-recipient matching. *Rev. Assoc. Med. Bras.*, *67*, 5, 690–695, 2021, https://doi. org/10.1590/1806-9282.20201088.

53. Lozanovski, V.J., Probst, P., Arefidoust, A., Ramouz, A., Aminizadeh, E., Nikdad, M., Khajeh, E., Ghamarnejad, O., Shafiei, S., AliHasanAlSaegh, S., Seide, S.E., Kalkum, E., Nickkholgh, A., Czigany, Z., Lurje, G., Mieth, M., Mehrabi, A., Prognostic role of the Donor Risk Index, the

Eurotransplant Donor Risk Index, and the Balance of Risk score on graft loss after liver transplantation. *Transplant. Int.*, 34, 5, 778–800, 2021, https://doi.org/10.1111/ tri.13861.

54. Jesudian, A., Desale, S., Julia, J., Landry, E., Maxwell, C., Kallakury, B., Laurin, J., Shetty, K., Donor Factors Including Donor Risk Index Predict Fibrosis Progression, Allograft Loss, and Patient Survival following Liver Transplantation for Hepatitis C Virus. *J. Clin. Exp. Hepatol.*, 6, 2, 109–114, 2016, https://doi.org/10.1016/j.jceh.2015.10.005.

55. Khalaileh, A., Khoury, T., Harkrosh, S., Nowotny, Y., Massarwa, M., Safadi, R., Mor, E., Nakache, R., Abu Gazala, S., Merhav, H., Multiplication product of Model for End- stage Liver Disease and Donor Risk Index as predictive models of survival after liver transplantation. *Eur. J. Gastroenterol. Hepatol.*, 31, 9, 1116–1120, 2019, https://doi. org/10.1097/ meg.0000000000001396.

56. Börner, N., Schoenberg, M.B., Pöschke, P., Heiliger, C., Jacob, S., Koch, D., Pöllmann, B., Drefs, M., Koliogiannis, D., Böhm, C., Karcz, K.W., Werner, J., Guba, M., A Novel Deep Learning Model as a Donor–Recipient Matching Tool to Predict Survival after Liver Transplantation. *J. Clin. Med.*, 11, 21, 6422, 2022, https://doi.org/10.3390/ jcm11216422.

57. Blok, J.J., Putter, H., Rogiers, X., van Hoek, B., Samuel, U., Ringers, J., Braat, A.E., The combined effect of donor and recipient risk on outcome after liver transplantation: Research of the Eurotransplant database. *Liver Transplant.*, 21, 12, 1486–1493, 2015, https://doi.org/10.1002/ lt.24308.

58. Nacif, L.S., Waisberg, D.R., Zanini, L.Y., Pinheiro, R.S., Rocha-Santos, V., Macedo, R.A., Ducatti, L., Haddad, L., Martino, R.B., Galvão, F., Andraus, W., Carneiro-DAlbuquerque, L., Clinical Validation of a Novel Scoring System Based on Donor and Recipient Risk Factors for Predicting Outcomes in Liver Transplantation. *Ann. Transplant.*, 27, 2022a, https://doi.org/10.12659/ aot.936271.

59. Xu, X., Lu, D., Ling, Q., Wei, X., Wu, J., Zhou, L., Yan, S., Wu, L., Geng, L., Ke, Q., Gao, F., Tu, Z., Wang, W., Zhang, M., Shen, Y., Xie, H., Jiang, W., Wang, H., Zheng, S., Liver transplantation for hepatocellular carcinoma beyond the Milan criteria. *Gut*, 65, 6, 1035–1041, 2015, https:// doi.org/10.1136/gutjnl-2014-308513.

60. Jang, H.Y., Choi, J.-I., Lee, Y.J., Park, M.Y., Yeo, D.M., Rha, S.E., Jung, E.S., You, Y.K., Kim, D.G., Byun, J.Y., Performance of Gadoxetic Acid–Enhanced Liver Magnetic Resonance Imaging for Predicting Patient Eligibility for Liver Transplantation Based on the Milan Criteria. *J. Comput. Assist. Tomogr.*, 41, 1, 25–31, 2017, https://doi. org/10.1097/rct.0000000000000476.

61. Jiang, N., Zeng, K.-N., Dou, K.-F., Lv, Y., Zhou, J., Li, H.-B., Tang, J.-X., Li, J.-J., Wang, G.-Y., Yi, S.-H., Yi, H.-M., Li, H., Chen, G.-H., Yang, Y., Preoperative Alfa-Fetoprotein and Fibrinogen Predict Hepatocellular Carcinoma Recurrence After Liver Transplantation Regardless of the Milan Criteria: Model Development with External Validation. *Cell. Physiol. Biochem.*, 48, 1, 317–327, 2018, https://doi.org/10.1159/000491731.

62. Zhang, H.-M., Jiang, W.-T., Pan, C., Deng, Y., Zheng, H., Shen, Z.-Y., Milan Criteria, University of California, San Francisco, Criteria, and Model for End-Stage Liver Disease Score as Predictors of Salvage Liver Transplantation. *Transplant. Proc.*, 47, 2, 438–444, 2015, https://doi. org/10.1016/j.transproceed.2014.10.046.

63. Qu, Z., Ling, Q., Gwiasda, J., Xu, X., Schrem, H., Beneke, J., Kaltenborn, A., Krauth, C., Mix, H., Klempnauer, J., Emmanouilidis, N., Hangzhou criteria are more accurate than Milan's in predicting long-term survival after liver transplantation for HCC in Germany. *Langenbeck's Arch. Surg.*, 403, 5, 643–654, 2018, https://doi.org/10.1007/s00423-018-1696-8.

64. Andreou, A., Gül, S., Pascher, A., Schöning, W., AlAbadi, H., Bahra, M., Klein, F., Denecke, T., Strücker, B., Puhl, G., Pratschke, J., Seehofer, D., Patient and tumor biology predict survival beyond the Milan criteria in liver transplantation for hepatocellular carcinoma. *HPB*, 17, 2, 168–175, 2015, https://doi.org/10.1111/hpb.12345.

65. Chaiteerakij, R., Zhang, X., Addissie, B.D., Mohamed, E.A., Harmsen, W.S., Theobald, P.J., Peters, B.E., Balsanek, J.G., Ward, M.M., Giama, N.H., Moser, C.D., Oseini, A.M., Umeda, N., Venkatesh, S., Harnois, D.M., Charlton, M.R., Yamada, H., Satomura, S., AlgecirasSchimnich, A., Roberts, L.R., Combinations of biomarkers and Milan criteria for predicting hepatocellular carcinoma recurrence after liver transplantation. *Liver Transplant.*, 21, 5, 599–606, 2015, https://doi.org/10.1002/lt.24117.

66. RM, J., Sethi, D.R., Hassan, I., Kundu, S., Bhattacharjee, B., Jayadeepa, R.M., Middha, S.K., Amrita School of Biotechnology, Amrita Vishwa Vidya Peetham, Kerala, India.

67. León Díaz, F.J., Pérez Daga, J.A., Sánchez Pérez, B., Fernández Aguilar, J.L., Montiel Casado, C., Aranda Narváez, J.M., Suárez Muñoz, M.A., Romacho López, L., Santoyo Villalba, J., Santoyo, J., Up-to-7 Criteria for Hepatocellular Carcinoma Liver Transplantation: A Retrospective Analysis of Experiences. *Transplant. Proc.*, 48, 9, 2969–2972, 2016, https:// doi.org/10.1016/j.transproceed.2016.08.035.

68. Ivanics, T., Patel, M.S., Erdman, L., Sapisochin, G., Artificial intelligence in transplantation (machine-learning classifiers and transplant oncology). *Curr. Opin. Organ Transplant.*, 25, 4, 426–434, 2020.

69. Lee, B.P., Roth, N., Rao, P., Im, G.Y., Vogel, A.S., Hasbun, J., ... Terrault, N.A., Artificial intelligence to identify harmful alcohol use after early liver transplant for alcohol-associated hepatitis. *Am. J. Transplant. (AJT)*, 22, 7, 1834–1841, 2022.

70. Khorsandi, S.E., Hardgrave, H.J., Osborn, T., Klutts, G., Nigh, J., Spencer-Cole, R.T., ... Giorgakis, E., Artificial intelligence in liver transplantation. *Transplant. Proc.*, 53, 10, 2939–2944, December 2021.

17

Pushing Boundaries: The Landscape of AI-Driven Drug Discovery and Development with Insights Into Regulatory Aspects

Dipak D. Gadade[1*], **Deepak A. Kulkarni**[2†], **Ravi Raj**[1], **Swapnil G. Patil**[3] **and Anuj Modi**[1]

[1]Department of Pharmacy, DSEU Dwarka Campus, Delhi Skill and Entrepreneurship University, Government of NCT of Delhi, New Delhi, India
[2]Department of Pharmaceutics, Srinath College of Pharmacy, Bajajnagar, Aurangabad (M.S.), India
[3]Drugs Control Department, Government of NCT of Delhi, Karkardooma, Delhi, India

Abstract

Artificial intelligence (AI) is revolutionizing the field of pharmaceutical and healthcare sector. The current understanding of drug development (DVPT) and discovery can be expanded with the aid of AI to benefit the health of the society. Current opportunities, where AI can be helpful include support in preclinical and clinical studies, target identification, hit identification, lead optimization, and clinical decision-making. The challenges that AI should overcome includes ethical aspects, intellectual issues, and regulatory aspects in drug DVPT and its clinical establishment. AI has various applications in drug discovery (DDS) and DVPT. The overall goal is to accentuate the importance of drug discovery and DVPT as well as the potential for AI to streamline the procedures and enhance better health outcomes. Furthermore, the recent updates of DVPTs in AI-related issues in regulatory affairs are highlighted in this chapter along with key moves that the pharmaceutical industry shall follow as it catches the benefits of AI-based applications.

Keywords: Artificial intelligence, drug discovery, preclinical, clinical, pharmaceutical, healthcare

17.1 Introduction

In recent years, artificial intelligence (AI) has made tremendous advancements in the fields of medicine and healthcare sector. It has completely changed how doctors identify, manage, and treat illnesses. Healthcare professionals can rapidly and reliably examine enormous volumes of patient data with AI, allowing better patient outcomes and more informed decision-making. AI has a wide range of possible applications in healthcare (Figure 17.1).

Clinical trials are conducted as part of the drug development (DVPT) process to evaluate effectiveness and safety in human subjects. This highly regulated process can take years

*Corresponding author: deepscpn@gmail.com
†Equal contribution as first author

Abhirup Khanna, May El Barachi, Sapna Jain, Manoj Kumar and Anand Nayyar (eds.) *Artificial Intelligence and Machine Learning in Drug Design and Development*, (533–562) © 2024 Scrivener Publishing LLC

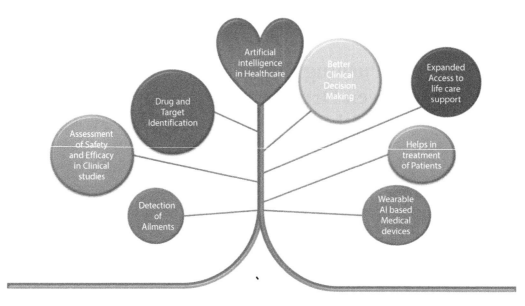

Figure 17.1 Potential applications of AI in healthcare.

to complete, including preclinical testing and post-marketing surveillance. In total, 13 to 15 years, at most, might pass during this period. Some drugs could require as high as 18 years of time from lab to bench side [1]. The ultimate objective is to obtain regulatory authorization to the medication for patients. The discovery and DVPT of new pharmaceuticals are essential to develop innovative and effective treatments for diseases and medical conditions. The first and most crucial phase in identifying potential new drugs and therapeutic targets is drug research and DVPT. As soon as a substance is identified as having therapeutic potential for the treatment of illnesses and disorders, the process of generating an active pharmaceutical ingredient (API) is initiated. It involves carrying out preclinical and clinical studies to determine the drug efficacy and safety in humans. It also includes acquiring approval from regulatory agencies in order to get marketing authorization [2].

AI has a latent role in the healthcare industry owing to its capacity to analyze tremendous amounts of data very quickly and accurately. Medical and healthcare practitioners may utilize AI to sift through patient data, including medical records, and genetic data, in order to uncover trends and risk factors that normal testing cannot detect. It helps clinicians make better educated diagnoses and clinical decisions, offer suitable treatments, and even anticipate future health challenges. Physicians may utilize AI to come up with personalized, tailor-made regimens for treatment that take the patient's needs into consideration. Treatment effectiveness can be optimized, as the risk of adverse drug reactions (ADR) or consequences can be reduced. It may assist biomedical researchers assess huge amounts of information and uncover novel concepts and patterns that would otherwise remain undiscovered in medical research. Furthermore, AI can assist to accelerate the discovery of novel therapies and treatments as well as increase our knowledge about complicated diseases. AI techniques enable the remote tracking of patients' health statuses. AI may gather information regarding the vitals of a person along with additional health variables *via* wearable smart devices and additional sensors, enabling healthcare practitioners to watch patients remotely and treat them as necessary. Hospital readmissions are lower, patient outcomes are better, and expenses for healthcare are lower. Medical pictures such as X-rays, computerized tomography (CT) scanning, and magnetic resonance bioimaging (MRI) may be analyzed by AI algorithms to detect anomalies and diagnose diseases. With the use of AI, ailments can be detected at an earlier stage. Despite all of the benefits stated, there are still challenges to be solved, such as data protection and regulatory compliance, but the prospective advantages of AI in healthcare are too large to ignore.

The need for expedited drugs research and DVPT is especially evident during the DVPT of COVID vaccines and therapies to combat a worldwide emergency [3]. It plays a vital role in the treatment of chronic illnesses like diabetes, tumors, and cardiovascular disease. DDS and DVPT in the pharmaceutical industry offer significant innovation and boost the economy [4]. The ability to advance research into novel medical treatments and drugs as well as to reinvent science and boost economic growth gains attention towards AI.

Objectives of the Chapter
The objectives of the chapter are:

- To give an overview of AI technologies, ethical considerations, IPR issues related to AI, and current regulatory developments related to AI;
- And, to illustrate the strategies to harness AI for better DDS and DPVT process.

17.1.1   AI for DDS and DVPT

"AI has been broadly defined as the science and engineering of making intelligent machines, especially intelligent computer programs. It can use different techniques, including models based on statistical analysis of data, expert systems that primarily rely on if-then statements, and machine learning" [5]. AI possesses the potential to revolutionize business sectors such as healthcare, banking, and transportation. However, there are particular ethical and cultural factors to consider, such as job displacement, discrimination, and privacy. DDS refers to the process of discovering and improving new pharmaceuticals for the prevention or treatment of ailments. This includes an array of steps, such as target validation and identification, preclinical testing, and clinical trials. This approach, which take many years, necessitates significant resources as well as collaboration among academics and other domains to expedite this process with the help of AI.

Organization of the Chapter
The rest of the chapter is organized as follows: Section 17.2 enlightens on the various classifications of AI in terms of narrow AI, general AI, and super AI. Section 17.3 gives an overview of AI technologies used in DDS. Section 17.4 focuses on the application of AI in DDS and drug DVPT. Section 17.5 highlights ethical considerations regarding the use of AI in DDS and DVPT. Section 17.6 illustrates IPR issues followed by Regulatory Approval and Market Access discussion in section 17.7. Section 17.8 elaborates AI in medicine's current DVPTs and strategy for pharmaceutical companies. Finally, section 17.9 concludes the chapter with future scope.

17.2 Classification of AI

AI is broadly classified as narrow AI, super AI, and general AI (Figure 17.2). It is discussed in the following subsections.

17.2.1 Narrow AI

Narrow AI is also referred to as weak AI. It can perform a single task way better than humans. Therefore, it may be utilized for process automation where a repetitive type of work is involved, such as X-ray or ultrasound imaging for the diagnosis of cancer. It is intended to carry out a certain activity or group of activities, such as image processing or language translation. Natural language processing (NLP) and artificial neural networks (ANN) could be used for information processing. These systems are trained to solve specific problems within a limited scope, and they do not possess human-like cognitive abilities [6]. However, it is not useful where problem solving in a broader perspective is required. The bias of such systems needs to be controlled during its training on the data [7].

Berg, an AI-based DDS and diagnostics company, has been acquired by a private equity investor group, BPGbio, for an undisclosed amount. The acquisition includes Berg's proprietary narrow AI software and Interrogative Biology platform that analyzes omics dataset to generate insights for clinical trials. BPGbio plans to explore partnerships for some of Berg's assets. The parenteral product BPM31510 containing ubidecarenone is under development for cancer treatment from BPGbio [8].

17.2.2 General AI

It is also known as artificial general intelligence (AGI). It has the ability to carry out cerebral tasks that humans can do. It would be able to think, reason, and learn in ways that are similar to human beings. AGI can perform unfamiliar tasks handled by humans. It is considered to be a representation of the brain and has the ability to perform at a similar capacity. AGI can perform given tasks creatively and with sensory perception. It could reflect a set of motor skills such as collecting a particular medicine from the shelves [9]. This type of AI is still a topic of research and DVPT and has not yet been fully realized. Some experts believe that neural networks can be a reliable method for developing the building blocks of general AI [10]. When achieved, it could revolutionize fields such as healthcare, transportation, and many more.

17.2.3 Super AI

Super AI is an innovative version of AI that has cognitive abilities that are equivalent or superior to those of a human being also called as artificial superintelligence. This type of AI can reason, learn, and solve problems in ways that are similar to human beings. Super AI has the potential to operate autonomously and make decisions without human intervention [11]. If it were to be developed, it could potentially revolutionize the field by being able to analyze vast amounts of data, design new drugs, and optimize clinical trial protocols.

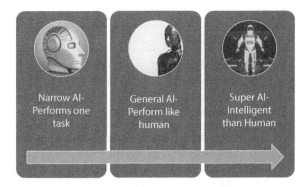

Figure 17.2 Classification of artificial intelligence.

17.3 Overview of AI Technologies Used in DDS

AI has the ability to evaluate huge amounts of complex datasets and spot those aspects that humans might overlook; AI has grown to be an increasingly vital tool in the DDS process. AI has the potential to speed up DDS, lower costs, and improve drug DVPT success rates. Different AI technologies utilized in the drug DVPT process are discussed below.

17.3.1 Machine Learning (ML)

"ML is an AI technique that can be used to design and train software algorithms to learn from and act on data. Software developers can use ML to create an algorithm that is 'locked' so that its function does not change or 'adaptive' so its behavior can change over time based on new data" [5]. ML involves teaching a computer algorithm to spot patterns in data and then utilizing that algorithm to predict outcomes for brand-new data. ML can be used in DDS to examine sizable molecular and biological data sets, identify promising drug targets, and forecast the effectiveness of potential drug candidates. Through diverse applications like qualitative structure–activity relationship (QSAR) analysis, hit discoveries, and *de novo* drug designs, ML methods improve decision-making in the drug industry to retrieve right outcomes. Complete working data shall be produced in clinical trials to address a variety of issues, including verifying ML methodologies, enhancing supervisory powers, raising awareness of ML approaches, and identifying risk failures in DDS [13]. The ML methods are classified in four categories as discussed in Table 17.1 [12].

ML-based devices has been recently helpful in the medication, screening, tracing, prediction, and estimating of COVID-19 cases. Such devices can track attributes related to a patient's family [14]. ML-based systems such as Gradient Boost, XGBoost, and AdaBoost have been reported for the prediction of heart diseases. These techniques can help medical practitioners in the diagnosis of cardiovascular diseases. About 92% of diagnostic accuracy was reported with these techniques [15]. Early diagnosis of metastatic breast cancer is possible with the examination of blood profiles by ML-based applications. It may reduce the healthcare expenditure by improving the diagnosis of cancer patients in the earlier stages [16].

Table 17.1 Types of ML [12].

Type of ML	Description
Supervised learning	The model/algorithm is trained on labeled data, with correct answers, and learns to make predictions based on this data. Commonly used for the predictive analysis of diseases, treatment methods, and patient care.
Unsupervised learning	The model is trained on data without any historical labels. The model must learn on the fly by itself, and the user can execute more complex tasks. Commonly used for clustering, anomaly detection, and neural networks. It may be used in DDS, patient health monitoring and medical diagnosis.
Semi-supervised learning	A type of ML that falls between supervised and unsupervised learning using labeled and nonlabeled dataset. The inputs are from the labeled dataset and apply to the nonlabeled dataset. It can make wonders by uncovering hidden patterns in DDS and for improving personalized treatment by early disease intervention.
Reinforcement learning	It uses a system of reward and penalty to train its algorithm. The model receives plunders for performing correctly and punishment for performing incorrect outputs and learns to maximize rewards and minimize penalties. Commonly used for personalized medicine, patient monitoring and care.

17.3.2   Deep Learning (DL)

Artificial neural networks are trained as part of DL to recognize patterns in data. DL is a type of ML. It involves ANN with multilayers, enabling the analysis of large and complex data sets. For tasks like predicting drug–target interactions and determining the likelihood that a compound will be toxic, DL has demonstrated promise in the field of DDS. DL has the ability to perform biological activity prediction, addressing issues in DDS and DVPT. DL-dependent tools, prediction models, and algorithms have been developed to aid the DDS and DVPT process, including tools for prediction drug receptor binding and its affinity, hit identification using virtual screening, pharmacokinetic property prediction, and drug activity prediction [17]. DL is helpful in improving the bioimaging quality by using convolution methods and kernel values [18].

BriefCase is an AI-based medical application developed by the Israeli company Aidoc Medical Ltd. It is intended to help radiologists in the diagnosis of biomedical imaging. Using DL algorithms, BriefCase analyzes medical images and flags potential abnormalities or areas of concern that require further attention from a radiologist. It can prioritize urgent cases and provide real-time notifications to radiologists, enabling them to quickly identify critical cases and make informed decisions. BriefCase has been trained on a vast dataset of medical images, allowing it to learn and adapt to new cases over time. This means that it can continue to improve its accuracy and effectiveness with continued use [19].

17.3.3   Natural Language Processing (NLP)

Another branch of AI called NLP involves training computers to explore and understand human language. Researchers can find new drug targets and potential drug candidates by using NLP to extract and analyze data from clinical trial data, patents, and scientific literature in the process of discovering new drugs. NLP has wide applications in model-informed drug DVPT and explores applications in clinical trials, pharmacovigilance, and regulatory submissions. Drug design, target identification, drug repurposing, liquid biopsy markers identification, and precision medicine are possible with the help of NLP [20].

17.3.4   Robotics

Robotics can be used to speed up and improve the effectiveness of DDS by automating laboratory procedures like large screening and drug synthesis. Robotics is used in the transport of food and hospital supply support, sanitation and cleaning in hospitals, surgical support, reduce the work of healthcare staff to accomplish administrative jobs, and telephonic assistance [21] PHArA-ON is AI-based technology which is aimed for the betterment of life quality, independence, and health of Europe's aging population through integrated and customizable ICT solutions [22].

17.3.5   Fuzzy Logic

To increase the prediction accuracy and lower the possibility of errors, fuzzy logic, a mathematical technique used to analyze complex systems with confusing or incomplete information, can be used in the DDS process. Differentiable fuzzy logics have the ability to integrate reasoning and learning by using logical mathematical formulae to express background knowledge [23]. Fuzzy logic in medicine has challenges in developing rules and membership functions, requires medical expertise and data, and lacks generalizability. However, it presents opportunities in neuroanatomy research, diagnosis and management of neurological diseases, and control of parameters in neurosurgical ICUs. Fuzzy logic-based controllers have been effective in maintaining stable intracranial pressure through varying the propofol infusion rates [24]. It can also be employed for drug repurposing in COVID-19, suggesting drugs like ribavirin, simeprevir, danoprevir, etc., which may be used for its treatment [25].

17.3.6   Swarm Intelligence

It is a type of AI that is based on the collective behavior of decentralized, self-organized systems. It is inspired by the behavior of social animals such as ants, bees, and birds, which are able to solve complex problems through cooperation and coordination. In swarm intelligence, a group of simple agents work together to accomplish a task or solve a problem. These agents communicate with each other and adapt their behavior based on feedback from the environment. Swarm intelligence can be used to resolve a variety of issues, such as optimization, routing, and scheduling [26]. It is considered as a combination of computer science, biology, and artificial intelligence. How biological systems solve complex problems is studied using swarm intelligence [27].

Swarm intelligence has the capacity to find optimal solutions in complex, dynamic environments. Since the agents work together to find solutions, the system is able to adapt to changing conditions and find solutions that would be difficult or impossible for a single agent to discover. Swarm intelligence has applications in fields such as robotics, transportation, and logistics.

17.3.7   Reactive Machines

Reactive machines are a type of AI systems that are designed to operate in the present moment based on the immediate sensory input it receives from the environment, without any explicit knowledge of the past or future. It typically uses a set of pre-programmed rules or algorithms to determine their actions in response to the current state of the environment. These rules or algorithms may be based on multiple variables, like the presence of particular objects or the occurrence of certain events [28]. Drone-based dynamic models can be used in contactless COVID-19 monitoring, sanitation, cleaning, and delivery of medicines to the patients [29].

AI has the capacity to transform the DDS process by giving researchers strong tools for digging deeper into complex data and producing more precise predictions. The requirement for high-quality data and the potential for biases in AI algorithms are two obstacles that must be overcome though.

17.4   Applications of AI in DDS and Drug DVPT

Designing tiny compounds, finding new pharmacological targets, and predicting medication efficacy and toxicity can all be aided by AI technologies. DL may be used to forecast the biological activity of drug candidates, while ML algorithms can be used to identify therapeutic targets. NLP may be used to retrieve data from scientific publications, while reinforcement learning (RL) can be used to improve medicine dosages [30].

By improving the effectiveness and precision of drug research and DVPT, AI has completely changed the DDS process. AI systems can examine enormous volumes of data and spot trends, which makes it simpler to forecast the efficacy of drug candidates and cut down on the time and expense involved in the generation of new medications [31].

To find and improve new drug candidates, AI has emerged as a crucial tool in the DDS process. Large-scale data analysis, pattern recognition, and prediction making are all made feasible by AI, which is something humans are not capable of doing on their own.

17.4.1   Preclinical Studies and Safety Testing

Before a new drug candidate is tested on humans, preclinical studies are carried out to determine its safety and effectiveness. By examining data from animal studies, pharmacological assays, and chemical structures, AI can assist researchers in identifying potential adverse effects and toxicological problems. By enabling researchers to recognize and discard drug candidates that will most possibly fail during trials and DVPT stages, this can help shorten the time and cost of drug DVPT [32].

Orion Pharma, a Finnish pharmaceutical company, is using AI to enhance preclinical toxicology studies aimed at evaluating the safety profiles of drug candidates. In one of their studies, the researchers had difficulty validating the results of a neurotoxicity study involving escalating doses of biomarkers excreted by astrocytes. The scientists were introduced to the Aiforia platform, which uses DLAI to evaluate histological changes. The tool allowed for the rapid deployment of AI models to develop algorithms to identify and visualize astrocytes and to produce quantitative data. The researchers noted the ease of use of the tool, its versatility, its ability to see subtle differences with greater accuracy, and its ability to remove subjectivity from histopathological analysis [33].

17.4.2 Target Identification and Validation

The first steps in DDS are the identification and validation of targets. The objective is to pinpoint a particular chemical or pathway that is implicated in the DVPT of the disease and may be addressed with medication [34]. To find possible targets, AI can evaluate massive databases including genetic information, protein interactions, and disease causes. The targets can also be validated using AI algorithms that identify potential negative effects and predict the likelihood that the targets will be effective [35].

In silico Medicine has announced that it has achieved a major breakthrough in AI-powered DDS by finding drug molecule and target for idiopathic pulmonary fibrosis. This is the first time that generative chemistry and biology have been linked together in this way to create a preclinical candidate based on preclinical and clinical study validation. It has made possible the target receptor identification and new drug molecule suggestion and validation in less than 2 years, costing around $1.8 million [36]. Amyotrophic lateral sclerosis (ALS) is a neurological disorder, and there is an urgent need for new therapeutic approaches. To address this issue, researchers used the PandaOmics AI-driven target discovery platform to analyze details related to the central nervous system (CNS). A total of 28 targets were identified, which were verified using the c9ALS *Drosophila* model [37].

17.4.3 Hit Identification and Lead Optimization

Finding chemicals that can control a target's activity comes after a target has been found and verified. To do this, compounds are screened for their capacity to bind to the target and alter its activity through hit discovery and lead optimization. AI can screen huge libraries of chemicals and forecast their future activity, cutting down on the time and expense of conventional screening techniques [38, 39].

Atomwise and Benevolent.AI are two companies that use AI for drug design. Atomwise uses a convolutional neural network called AtomNet for the prediction of the molecular binding affinity considering the structural information of the receptor. Miro1, a mitochondrial membrane enzyme target involved in Parkinson's disease, was identified by using a similar path. It was employed for the invention of 27 disease targets in association with academia and industry [39].

17.4.4 Prediction of Drug Efficacy and Toxicity

The effectiveness and toxicity of new therapeutic candidates can also be predicted using AI. This can be accomplished by examining clinical data from prior trials as well as data from preclinical research, including those involving animal models and *in vitro* experiments. In order to forecast how a medicine will perform in human trials, including its potential efficacy and adverse effects, AI systems can find patterns and links in the data [40].

The work of BenevolentAI, which used AI to find a viable cure for ALS, is one instance of how AI is being used to forecast the efficacy and toxicity of drugs. To find a new target for the treatment of ALS, the researchers employed AI to scan enormous datasets of gene expression data, protein interactions, and clinical trial data. A molecule that is now undergoing clinical trials for the treatment of ALS was found after using AI to predict the efficacy and safety of possible drug candidates. Benevolent.AI uses text mining to analyze patent database and bio-genomic information to establish relationships between molecular entities to identify intermolecular linkage [38].

17.4.5 Design of Clinical Trials

Clinical trial design with AI can be made more effective and efficient. AI algorithms can examine trial data from the past and spot trends that can be utilized to improve the trial design elements including patient selection standards, dose schedules, and endpoint assessments. AI can also be used to forecast a trial's likelihood of success, lowering the risk and expense of unsuccessful studies [40].

Pfizer used AI to expedite the DVPT and distribution of the COVID-19 vaccine. The company has been using AI in its research and DVPT activities for some time now, and this technology was useful during the COVID times. AI algorithms were used to identify signals from millions of data points in the vaccine trials, helping Pfizer to quickly analyze and interpret the data. Additionally, an ML tool called Smart Data Query was used to analyze and verify the data's quality, which significantly reduced the need for human intervention. As a result, Pfizer was able to expedite the vaccine DVPT process and distribute the vaccine quickly and efficiently. One way that Pfizer used AI was in the analysis of data from the vaccine trials. The company employed ML algorithms to help identify patterns and insights from the large amounts of data generated during the trials. This allowed Pfizer to analyze the data faster and make informed decisions about the vaccine's efficacy and safety. Another way that Pfizer used AI was in the optimization of the vaccine's production process. The company used AI to analyze data on the production process, identify areas for improvement, and optimize the process to increase efficiency and reduce waste. Therefore, the vaccine could be distributed to as many people as possible [41].

17.5 Ethical Considerations Regarding the Use of AI in DDS and DVPT

AI has revolutionized the fields of DDS and DVPT. It has potential to accelerate DDS by identifying novel drug targets and predicting the safety and efficacy of new compounds. However, the applications of AI in DDS always had a concern of ethical issues, including aspects related to data privacy, bias, and transparency. This section includes a discussion about the ethical considerations regarding the use of AI in DDS and DVPT and explores potential solutions to these challenges [42–44].

17.5.1   Data Privacy

Data privacy is an essential ethical consideration in the DVPT and application of AI in DDS. The pharmaceutical industry and research organizations collect vast amounts of personal health data to train AI algorithms for DDS. The personal health data creates the problem related to privacy and security of data. This section includes the discussion about data privacy in AI-driven DDS and DVPT and explore potential solutions to address these ethical considerations. Data privacy is an essential ethical consideration in AI-driven DDS and DVPT, and steps must be taken to protect the privacy of patients. Informed consent, anonymization, data security, transparency, and data governance are all critical components of ethical data management in DDS and DVPT [45, 46].

17.5.1.1   Informed Consent

The personal health data may be collected in DDS and DVPT based on informed consent. Patients must be made aware of the purpose behind the collection of data, how their data will be used, who will have access to their data, and how their privacy will be protected. Informed consent is particularly crucial in AI-driven DDS, as AI algorithms may identify patterns and correlations that were not initially anticipated. Therefore, it is essential to obtain consent that allows for the use of patient data for purposes beyond the specific research question [47].

17.5.1.2   Anonymization

Anonymization is the process of removing identifying information from personal health data to protect the privacy of patients. Anonymization can be challenging, particularly when dealing with longitudinal health data, where it may be possible to re-identify individuals based on their medical history. However, anonymization is a critical step in protecting the privacy of patients and should be considered wherever possible [48].

17.5.1.3   Data Security

The security of personal health data is critical in AI-driven DDS and DVPT. Health data is particularly valuable and vulnerable to cyberattacks, and data disclosure may result in various concerns for patients. It is important to have robust data security protocols for the protection of personal health data from unauthorized access, modification, or destruction [49].

17.5.1.4   Data Governance

Data governance refers to the process of managing and protecting data throughout its life cycle. Data governance includes policies, procedures, and controls for collecting, storing, using, and sharing data. Effective data governance can help ensure that personal health data is collected and used ethically and that the privacy of patients is protected throughout the DDS and DVPT process [50].

17.5.2 Bias

AI systems can analyze large datasets, generate insights, and predict outcomes, enabling scientists to identify potential drug candidates with greater speed and accuracy. However, the use of AI in DDS and DVPT also raises ethical issues, particularly regarding bias. Bias is an ethical consideration that needs to be addressed to ensure that AI systems do not reinforce or amplify existing biases in the pharmaceutical industry. Bias is the systematic deviation from an accurate estimate or judgment that is influenced by preconceived ideas or beliefs. Bias can arise due to several factors, such as personal beliefs, cultural background, and societal norms. Bias can be conscious or unconscious and can affect decision-making in various fields, including medicine and healthcare. In the context of DDS and DVPT, bias can occur in several ways. Bias can influence the selection of drug targets or the prioritization of certain disease areas over others. Bias can also affect the representation of patient populations in clinical trials, leading to a lack of diversity in the data used to train AI systems. This can result in AI systems that are biased towards specific patient groups, leading to ineffective or unsafe drugs for certain populations. Therefore, it is employed for training AI systems which can affect the accuracy and reliability of the predictions made by these systems. In the context of DDS and DVPT, bias can affect the entire drug DVPT process, from target identification to clinical trials [51, 52].

17.5.2.1 Target Identification

Bias can influence the selection of drug targets, leading to the prioritization of certain diseases over others. This can result in a lack of treatments for diseases that affect marginalized populations or for rare diseases. Bias can also influence the selection of molecular targets, leading to the exclusion of promising drug candidates that may be effective for specific patient populations [53, 54].

17.5.2.2 Compound Screening

Bias can also affect the selection of compounds for screening. Bias in the data used to train AI systems can result in the exclusion of potentially effective compounds that are not present in the training data. This can lead to the selection of compounds that are biased towards specific patient populations, leading to ineffective or unsafe drugs for certain populations [55].

17.5.2.3 Clinical Trials

Bias can affect the representation of patient populations in clinical trials. If the data used for training AI systems are biased towards certain patient groups, the AI system will be biased towards those groups as well. This can lead to the exclusion of patient populations that are not well represented in the training data, leading to ineffective or unsafe drugs for those populations [51, 56].

17.5.3 Transparency

Transparency refers to the openness and clarity in the process of deciding and the ability to trace the reasoning behind the decision. Transparency in AI-based DDS and DVPT is essential to ensure safety, accuracy, and accountability. Transparency in AI-based DDS and DVPT refers to the ability to explain and interpret the reasoning behind the decision-making process. In DDS and DVPT, transparency is critical for ensuring safety and accuracy. It is mainly important in the earlier phases of drug DVPT when the risks and benefits of a drug are uncertain. Transparency ensures that the decisions made by AI systems are consistent with ethical and regulatory standards and that they can be trusted by regulatory bodies, clinicians, and patients. Transparency in AI systems can be achieved through several mechanisms, including explainable AI (XAI) and open data sharing. XAI techniques include decision trees, rule-based systems, and model interpretation. Open data sharing refers to the practice of making data and algorithms available to the public, enabling researchers to replicate and validate AI-based DDS and DVPT processes [57].

17.5.3.1 Ethical Implications of Opaque AI Systems

The increasing use of AI in DDS and DVPT raises concerns about the ethical implications of opaque AI systems. Opaque AI systems are those that cannot provide explanations for their decisions, making it difficult to understand and interpret the reasoning behind their decisions. Opaque AI systems are particularly concerning in DDS and DVPT because they can lead to biases, inaccuracies, and safety risks. Opaque AI systems can be prone to biases due to the data they are trained on. The validation and replication of such systems are required to ensure accuracy and safety. In DDS and DVPT, accuracy and safety are critical because the consequences of inaccurate or unsafe drugs can be severe. Without transparency, it is difficult to identify errors or biases in the course of decision-making, and it is challenging to assure the safety and accuracy of AI-based DDS and DVPT processes [58, 59].

17.5.3.2 Importance of Transparency in AI-Based DDS and DVPT

Transparency is essential in AI-based DDS and DVPT for several reasons. First, transparency enables clinicians and regulatory bodies to understand and trust the decision-making process of AI systems. This is particularly important in drug DVPT, where the risks and benefits of a drug are uncertain. Transparent AI systems enable regulators to confirm that only safe and effective drugs are approved for use. Second, transparency enables the identification of biases and inaccuracies in the decision-making process. By providing explanations for their decisions, AI systems can be audited and validated, ensuring that they are accurate and unbiased. This is particularly important in drug DVPT, where errors or biases in the decision-making process can have severe consequences for patients. Third, transparency enables collaboration and innovation. Open data sharing enables researchers to replicate and validate AI-based DDS [60].

17.5.4 Accountability

AI is bringing unprecedented efficiency and accuracy to the DDS and DVPT process. However, this new technology has also brought a range of ethical considerations, including accountability. As AI is increasingly used in drug DVPT, it is essential to consider how accountability can be maintained and to ensure that the use of AI is ethically responsible. Accountability is an ethical consideration related to the use of AI in DDS and DVPT, including its definition, importance, challenges, and potential solutions. Accountability refers to the responsibility of individuals or organizations for their actions and the consequences that follow. In the context of AI in DDS and DVPT, accountability means ensuring that the use of AI is transparent, responsible, and ethically sound. The process involves fixing of accountability and responsibility during the process [61, 62].

17.5.4.1 Importance of Accountability

Accountability is crucial for the responsible use of AI in DDS and DVPT. Without accountability, the use of AI could result in negative consequences that are difficult to trace or remedy. If an AI system makes a mistake in the identification of potential drug candidates, it could result in significant financial losses for the drug DVPT company. In terms of decisions taken through the AI system about patient care, the consequences of incorrect decisions could be severe. Accountability is also important for building trust in the use of AI in DDS and DVPT. If people do not trust that AI is being used responsibly, they may be reluctant to participate in clinical trials or to use drugs that have been developed using AI. Ensuring accountability can help to build trust and confidence in the use of AI in drug DVPT [63, 64].

17.5.4.2 Challenges in Maintaining Accountability

Maintaining accountability in the use of AI in DDS and DVPT is not without its challenges. One of the biggest challenges in maintaining accountability is the lack of transparency in the use of AI. AI systems are often complex and difficult to understand, making it challenging to identify who is responsible for their actions. AI systems can be biased, which can result in unfair or discriminatory outcomes. This bias can be challenging to detect, making it difficult to ensure that the use of AI is ethically sound and accountable. The use of AI in DDS and DVPT is still relatively new, and there is a lack of regulation in this area. This lack of regulation can make it challenging to ensure that AI is being used ethically and responsibly. AI technology is rapidly evolving, making it challenging to keep up with new DVPTs and to ensure the ethical and responsible use of AI [65, 66]

17.5.5 Safety–Efficacy

AI is useful to identify new drug targets, the optimization of drug compounds, and the prediction of drug toxicity. However, as with any new technology, there are ethical considerations that must be taken into account when using AI in DDS and DVPT. One of these considerations is the balance between safety and efficacy of AI-generated drugs [67].

17.5.5.1 Safety–Efficacy Balance in AI-Based DDS and DVPT

DDS and DVPT processes are complex and expensive that involve the new drug target identification, the optimization of drug compounds, and the evaluation of drug efficacy and safety. AI algorithms can identify drug targets that were previously overlooked, leading to the DVPT of more effective drugs. However, these drugs may also be more potent and have a higher risk of side effects. AI can also be used to optimize drug compounds, leading to more effective drugs with fewer side effects. However, this optimization may also lead to the DVPT of drugs that are more potent and have a higher risk of side effects. The ethical implications of the safety–efficacy balance in DDS and DVPT are complex. Drugs that are more effective can lead to significant improvements in patient outcomes. Drugs that are not sufficiently tested for safety can lead to serious harm to patients. This balance must be carefully considered to ensure that drugs developed with the assistance of AI are safe and effective [68, 69].

17.5.5.2 Ethical Considerations Related to the Safety–Efficacy Balance in AI-Generated Drugs

Several ethical considerations must be taken into account when considering the safety–efficacy balance in AI-generated drugs. Patients should be made aware about the benefits and risk factors of AI-generated drugs before they agree to participate in clinical trials or use these drugs. This includes informing patients about the potential side effects of the drugs and the limitations of the AI algorithms used to generate them. The DVPT of AI-generated drugs must be transparent, and the algorithms used to generate these drugs must be made public. This will allow independent researchers to study the safety and efficacy of these drugs and identify potential risks and limitations. It includes testing in animal models and human clinical trials. These tests must be designed to identify potential side effects and to determine the optimal dosage and administration schedule for the drug. The DVPT and use of AI-generated drugs must be regulated by government agencies to ensure their safety and efficacy. This includes the establishment of guidelines for the DVPT and testing of these drugs and the monitoring of its safety and efficacy [70, 71].

17.6 IPR Issues

Intellectual property rights (IPR) are a crucial ethical consideration in the field of DDS and DVPT, especially in relation to the use of AI. AI accelerates DDS, reducing costs and improving the quality of medicines. However, the use of AI in DDS and DVPT raises complex ethical issues related to IPR, such as patentability, ownership, and licensing [72].

17.6.1 Patentability of AI-Generated Inventions

Patent protection is a crucial mechanism for incentivizing innovation and investment in drug DVPT. "In general, a patent is a legal document that gives the holder the exclusive right to make, use, and sell an invention for a certain period of time, usually 20 years." However, the patentability of AI-generated inventions is a complex issue that raises ethical questions.

Under the current patent laws, an invention must be novel, non-obvious, and useful to be eligible for patent protection. However, AI-generated inventions can raise questions about the identity of the inventor and the novelty and non-obviousness of the invention. In traditional DDS, the inventor is typically a human researcher who identifies a new drug target or molecule. However, in AI-driven DDS, the inventor may be an algorithm or a combination of algorithms that analyze large amounts of data to identify potential drug candidates. The issue of the inventorship of AI-generated inventions is a complex one that has yet to be fully resolved. However, it raises ethical questions about the fairness of patent protection for AI-generated inventions and the potential for bias in the patent system. If the law does not recognize AI as an inventor, it may disincentivize investment in AI-driven DDS and DVPT, which could slow down the pace of innovation in this area [73, 74].

17.6.2   Ownership and Licensing of AI-Generated Inventions

The ownership and licensing of AI-generated inventions also raise ethical questions related to IPR. Who should own the patent on an AI-generated drug and who should be licensed to use it? In traditional drug DVPT, the deciding inventorship and ownership of a drug patent is typically straightforward. The patent is owned by the company or researcher who developed the drug, and they can license the drug to other companies for a fee. However, in the case of AI-generated drugs, the ownership and licensing of the patent may be more complex. If the algorithm that generated the drug is owned by a third party, such as a technology company, they may claim ownership of the patent. This could lead to a situation where the company that developed the drug may not own the patent on the drug, and they may have to pay a licensing fee to use their own invention. The issue of ownership and licensing of AI-generated drugs is also complicated by the fact that AI algorithms may be trained on large amounts of data that are owned by third parties. An algorithm that analyzes patient data to identify potential drug targets may use data that is owned by hospitals or pharmaceutical companies. In this case, the ownership and licensing of the data may impact the ownership and licensing of the AI-generated drug [75–77].

17.7   Regulatory Approval and Market Access

Before a new drug can be marketed and sold to patients, regulatory approval is necessary. By analyzing clinical trial data and forecasting the likelihood of approval, AI can assist researchers in preparing regulatory submissions. This can increase the likelihood of success and cut down on the time and expense of the regulatory approval process.

The regulatory landscape for DDS and DVPT is complex and involves multiple regulatory bodies around the world. The 10 guiding principles for Good ML Practice (GMLP) were jointly identified by the health authorities of the USA (USFDA), Health Canada, and the UK. These guidelines are envisioned to apprise the DVPT of safe, effective, and high-quality medical devices that use AI and ML.

These guiding principles (Figure 17.3) are intended to provide a framework for the DVPT of safe, effective, and high-quality medical devices that use AI/ML. Developers and users of such devices should consider these principles in their design, DVPT, and use to promote patient safety and outcomes.

Principles	Summary
Patient Centricity	Medical devices that use AI/ML should be designed and developed with the needs and perspectives of patients in mind, with a focus on patient safety and outcomes.
Transparency	The AI/ML algorithms used in medical devices should be transparent and explainable to facilitate understanding and decision-making by users, patients, and regulators.
Bias Mitigation	Steps should be taken to identify and mitigate any biases in AI/ML algorithms that could result in unfair treatment or outcomes for certain patient groups.
Robustness and Security	Medical devices that use AI/ML should be designed and developed to be robust, reliable, and secure, with appropriate measures in place to protect patient data and privacy.
Performance	Medical devices that use AI/ML should be developed with appropriate performance metrics and validation studies to ensure they meet their intended use and performance expectations.
Clinical Responsibility	Developers and users of medical devices that use AI/ML should take clinical responsibility for their use, with appropriate training, oversight, and governance structures in place.
Regulatory Compliance	Developers and users of medical devices that use AI/ML should adhere to relevant regulatory requirements, including safety and effectiveness standards.
Evidence Generation	Medical devices that use AI/ML should be developed with a robust evidence base to support their safety, effectiveness, and clinical utility.
Data Quality	The data used to train and validate AI/ML algorithms should be of high quality, appropriately representative, and relevant to the intended use of the medical device.
Explainability	Developers and users of medical devices that use AI/ML should be able to explain and interpret the outputs of the algorithms used in the device to facilitate understanding and decision-making.

Figure 17.3 Ten guiding principles for good ML practices as developed by USFDA and MHRA.

In April of 2019, the USFDA published a "Proposed Regulatory Framework for Modifications to AI/ML-Based Software as a Medical Device (SaMD)—Discussion Paper and Request for Feedback." This framework was designed to help regulate medical device software and other digital health technologies that use AI/ML, and it included the following key points:

a. Risk-based approach: The framework proposed a risk-based approach under regulation, where the level of regulatory oversight would be proportionate with the level of risk posed by the device.

b. Predetermined change control plan: The framework also proposed the use of a determined change advance control plan to ensure that any deviations to the AI/ML algorithms used in medical devices were made in a controlled manner and with appropriate oversight.

c. Performance testing: The framework offered the use of performance testing to ensure that the AI/ML-based medical devices were safe and effective as well as met their intended use and performance expectations.

d. Transparency: The framework suggested that AI/ML algorithms used in medical devices should be transparent and explainable to facilitate understanding and decision-making by users, patients, and regulators.

e. Real-world performance monitoring: The framework proposed the use of real-world performance monitoring to ensure that AI/ML-based medical devices continued to perform as planned in practical settings.

f. Cybersecurity: The framework planned that AI/ML-based medical devices should be designed and developed with appropriate cybersecurity measures in place to protect the patients' data and privacy.

g. Evidence generation: The framework proposed that AI/ML-based medical devices should be developed with a robust evidence base to support their safety, effectiveness, and clinical utility.

The proposed regulatory context for AI/ML-based medical devices was intended to promote innovation while also ensuring patient safety and effectiveness. The USFDA sought feedback from stakeholders on this framework, which would inform the DVPT of future regulations and guidance related to AI/ML-based medical devices.

USFDA has issued a guidance document titled "Clinical Decision Support Software" to define the USFDA's regulatory approach. Here is a detailed explanation of the guidance:

a. Definition of clinical decision support (CDS): The guidance defines CDS as software that provides information and/or recommendations to a healthcare provider to assist in clinical decision-making. CDS software can be stand-alone or integrated into an electronic health record (EHR) or other clinical software.

b. USFDA's regulatory approach: The guidance explains that the USFDA will take a risk-based approach to regulating CDS software functions. The level of regulatory oversight will depend on the level of risk posed by the CDS function.

    c. Examples of low-risk CDS functions: The guidance provides examples of CDS functions that are considered low risk and generally will not be subject to USFDA oversight. These include software that provides information about a patient's condition, software that calculates a patient's body mass index (BMI), and software that provides drug–drug interaction alerts.

    d. Examples of higher-risk CDS functions: The guidance also provides examples of CDS functions that are considered to be of a higher risk and will be subject to USFDA oversight. These include software that diagnoses or treats a disease, software that provides treatment recommendations, and software that analyzes radiology images for the purpose of diagnosis.

    e. USFDA's approach to enforcement: The guidance explains that the USFDA will take a risk-based approach to the enforcement of CDS software functions. The USFDA will focus its resources on higher-risk functions and will exercise enforcement discretion for low-risk functions.

    f. Quality system requirements: The guidance also discusses the quality system requirements that apply to CDS software functions. These include requirements related to design controls, risk management, and software validation.

The USFDA's guidance on Clinical Decision Support Software provides clarity on the agency's regulatory approach to CDS software functions. By taking a risk-based approach to regulation and focusing its resources on higher-risk functions, the USFDA intends to encourage innovative ideas related to the DVPT of CDS software while also ensuring patient safety and effectiveness [78].

In addition to these bodies, there are also various international organizations that play a role in regulating pharmaceuticals, including WHO and ICH. Pharmaceutical companies must comply with the guidelines and regulations set forth by these bodies in order to bring their products to market. There are several medical devices that use AI/ML that have been approved by the various regulatory bodies; a few examples approved by the USFDA and their features are given in Table 17.2.

17.8 AI in Medicine Current DVPTs and Strategy for Pharmaceutical Companies

With the advent of AI, USFDA started evaluating the approval of AI-based medical devices. There are a total of 521 AI-based applications approved by the USFDA for medical use (Table 17.3) of which majority of the devices find application in radiology (75%), followed by cardiology (11%) [79]. The major players in the market of AI-based applications for use in the medical and healthcare sector are (a) GE Medical Systems SCS and their allied corporate divisions, (b) Canon Medical Systems Corporation, (c) Siemens Medical Solutions USA, Inc., (d) Philips Medical Systems and their divisions, (e) Quantib BV, (f) RaySearch Laboratories AB (Publ), (g) Aidoc Medical, Ltd., (h) Zebra Medical Vision Ltd., (i) HeartFlow, Inc., (j) Shanghai United Imaging Healthcare Co., Ltd., (k) Viz.ai, Inc., (l) Circle Cardiovascular Imaging Inc., (m) Clarius Mobile Health Corp., (n) CellaVision

Table 17.2 USFDA-approved AI-based applications.

Series no.	Name of AI-based medical device	Description	Features	Company
1	ABMD Software	Software for the analysis of hemodynamic parameters	Hemodynamic analysis	HeartLung Corporation
2	DLImage Reconstruction	Reconstruction of CT and MR images using deep learning	Image reconstruction using deep learning	GE Healthcare Japan Corporation
3	cvi42 Auto Imaging Software Application	Software for analyzing cardiovascular images	Analysis of cardiovascular images	Circle Cardiovascular Imaging Inc
4	Swoop Portable MR Imaging System	Portable MRI machine	Portable MRI imaging	Hyperfine, Inc.
5	DeepRhythmAI	AI system for detecting cardiac arrhythmias	Detection of cardiac arrhythmias	Medicalgorithmics S.A.
6	Viz SDH	AI system for detecting and analyzing strokes	Detection and analysis of strokes	Viz.ai, Inc.
7	AI4CMR v1.0	AI system for analyzing cardiovascular MRI images	Analysis of cardiovascular MRI images	AI4MedImaging Medical Solutions S.A.
8	Vivid E80, Vivid E90, Vivid E95	Ultrasound machines with AI capabilities	Ultrasound imaging with AI	GE Medical Systems Ultrasound and Primary Care Diagnostics (GEM)
9	EchoPAC Software Only, EchoPAC Plug-in	Software for analyzing echocardiogram images	Analysis of echocardiogram images	GEM

(Continued)

Table 17.2 USFDA-approved AI-based applications. (*Continued*)

Series no.	Name of AI-based medical device	Description	Features	Company
10	Libby Echo:Prio	AI system for analyzing echocardiogram images	Analysis of echocardiogram images	Dyad Medical, Inc.
11	Study Watch with Irregular Pulse Monitor	Wearable watch to monitor heart rate and rhythm	Heart rate and rhythm monitoring	Verily Life Sciences LLC
12	IDx-DR	Uses AI to analyze retinal images and detect signs of diabetic retinopathy	Detect greater than mild diabetic retinopathy (mtmDR) in new diabetic patients	Digital Diagnostics
13	Caption AI	Clinical decision support (CDS) software	Provide support to healthcare providers in the interpretation of chest X-ray images to help in the assessment of potential issues and to facilitate the triage and management of patients	Caption Health
14	Insilico Medicine	DDS platform	Uses AI to accelerate DDS and DVPT	Insilico Medicine, Inc.
15	OsteoDetect	Osteological diagnostic software	Analyze X-ray images and detect signs of wrist fractures	Imagen Technologies
16	Gauss Surgical Triton	Clinical decision support (CDS) software	Provide an objective estimate of blood loss during surgery	Gauss Surgical, Inc.

AB, (o) Arterys Inc., (p) DiA Imaging Analysis Ltd., (q) Hologic, Inc., (r) Hyperfine, Inc., (t) ImpediMed Limited, and (u) Caption Health, Inc.

There are several important steps that pharmaceutical companies can follow to take advantage of AI for DDS and clinical DVPT. Some key steps are discussed below [80]:

    a. Identification of areas where AI can be employed: Pharmaceutical companies should track areas such as DDS, clinical trials, and post-market surveillance of the use of AI. The relevant areas may include target identification and validation, drug design and optimization, clinical trial optimization, patient stratification, and real-world data analysis.

Table 17.3 Panel-wise USFDA-approved AI-based applications as medical devices [78].

Panel	No. of USFDA-approved AI-based applications as medical devices
Radiology	392
Cardiovascular	57
Hematology	15
Neurology	14
Ophthalmic	7
Gastroenterology–urology	6
Clinical chemistry	6
Microbiology	5
General and plastic Surgery	5
Pathology	4
Anesthesiology	4
General Hospital	3
Obstetrics and gynecology, Orthopedics, Dental	1 each

    b. Invest in AI talent and technology: Pharmaceutical companies should invest in AI talent and technology to build their capabilities in this area. This may involve hiring data scientists, AI experts, and software developers to build and implement AI solutions. Pharmaceutical companies need to build a team of AI experts who can develop and deploy AI solutions. This may require hiring data scientists, ML engineers, and other experts with AI skills. In addition, the companies need to invest in the infrastructure and computing resources needed to support AI initiatives.

    c. Build a robust AI infrastructure: AI requires large amounts of data to be effective, so pharmaceutical companies should build a robust data infrastructure to collect, store, and manage data. This infrastructure should be designed to support AI algorithms and ML models. Pharmaceutical companies should develop an AI strategy that aligns with their business goals and objectives. The strategy should identify the AI technologies and tools that will be used, the data sources that will be required, and the skills and resources needed to execute the strategy.

    d. Collaborate with AI startups: Pharmaceutical companies can collaborate with AI startups to gain access to cutting-edge technology and expertise. These startups may offer AI solutions that can accelerate DDS, streamline clinical trials, and improve patient outcomes. These partnerships can help pharmaceutical companies access cutting-edge AI technologies and expertise.

e. Develop partnerships with academic institutions: Pharmaceutical companies can also develop partnerships with academic institutions to gain access to research and expertise in AI. These partnerships can help pharmaceutical companies stay updated with the latest advances in AI and apply them to DDS and clinical DVPT.

f. Leverage existing data: Pharmaceutical companies should leverage the vast amounts of data that they have accumulated over the years, such as clinical trial data, electronic health records, and real-world data. This data may be useful to train AI models and develop predictive algorithms.

g. Train employees: Implementing AI in drug DVPT and medicine requires a workforce that is equipped with the necessary skills and knowledge. Therefore, pharmaceutical companies should invest in training programs to help employees understand AI and its potential applications in the industry.

h. Address ethical considerations: AI raises a number of ethical considerations, including issues related to data privacy, bias, and transparency. Pharmaceutical companies should ensure that they have policies and processes in place to address these concerns.

i. Ensure regulatory compliance: Pharmaceutical companies need to ensure that their AI initiatives comply with regulatory requirements. This may require working closely with regulatory agencies to ensure that the AI solutions are safe and effective, establishing quality management systems that follow the guidelines set by regulatory agencies to ensure that the AI systems are reliable, accurate, and meet safety standards, and ensuring data integrity by establishing data management systems that comply with regulatory guidelines. This includes having data security measures, data quality control, and traceability.

j. Foster a culture of innovation: Finally, pharmaceutical companies should foster a culture of innovation that encourages experimentation and risk-taking. By creating an environment that supports innovation, pharmaceutical companies can be more successful in implementing AI and other emerging technologies in drug DVPT and medicine.

17.9 Conclusion and Future Perspectives

In conclusion, the integration of AI into DDS and DVPT has the potential to revolutionize the entire process from preclinical studies to clinical trials. AI offers novel and innovative approaches to DDS and DVPT, which can greatly enhance the efficiency and success rate of the drug DVPT pipeline. The different applications of AI in DDS and DVPT, including preclinical studies, target identification and validation, hit identification and lead optimization, prediction of drug efficacy and toxicity, and design of clinical trials could pave the way for new drug DVPTs. Despite the significant potential of AI in DDS and DVPT, there are ethical and regulatory challenges that need to be addressed. The ethical considerations during the usage of AI under DDS and DVPT include concerns around data privacy and security, bias in data and algorithms, and transparency and accountability. Additionally, intellectual property rights (IPR) issues related to AI-generated discoveries and regulatory approval and market access also need to be addressed.

Looking ahead to the future, the integration of AI in DDS and DVPT is poised to see rapid growth, with significant investments being made in AI technologies by pharmaceutical companies based on the anticipation that it could bring more profits. The DVPT of strategic partnerships between pharmaceutical companies and AI technology providers is expected to accelerate the DVPT of new drugs, improve clinical trial design, and optimize patient selection for clinical trials. Furthermore, AI can help to identify new therapeutic targets and repurpose existing drugs for new indications, which can help to save the time making drug DVPT economic.

The strategic use of AI in DDS and DVPT can significantly improve the efficiency and success rate of the drug DVPT pipeline. AI algorithms can analyze molecular structures and predict drug interactions with specific targets. Applications such as drug designing, drug repurposing, drug screening, and targeting multiple proteins involved in diseases with AI are possible in the near future. Although the AI models are still not positioned adequately today for showcasing the real-world use, still it possesses the potential to alter the healthcare benefits. AI continues to evolve and improve in the near future; it will play a pivotal role in the revolution of the pharmaceutical industry. Therefore, it is essential for pharmaceutical companies and regulatory bodies to develop appropriate strategies and policies to harness the full potential of AI in DDS and DVPT. Continuous exploration could be undoubtedly helpful for safer and effective treatments for a wide range of diseases, benefiting patients and the society in whole.

References

1. Mohs, R.C. and Greig, N.H., Drug discovery and development: Role of basic biological research. *Alzheimer's Dement.: Transl. Res. Clin. Interv.*, 3, 4, 651–657, 2017, https://doi.org/10.1016/j.trci.2017.10.005.
2. Norris, S. M. P., Pankevich, D. E., Davis, M., Altevogt, B. M. (Eds.), *Improving and Accelerating Therapeutic Development for Nervous System Disorders*, National Academies Press, 1–24, 2014, https://doi.org/10.17226/18494.
3. Arora, G., Joshi, J., Mandal, R.S., Shrivastava, N., Virmani, R., Sethi, T., Artificial Intelligence in Surveillance, Diagnosis, Drug Discovery and Vaccine Development against COVID-19. *Pathogens*, 10, 8, 1048, 2021, https://doi.org/10.3390/pathogens10081048.
4. Paul, D., Sanap, G., Shenoy, S., Kalyane, D., Kalia, K., Tekade, R.K., Artificial intelligence in drug discovery and development. *Drug Discov. Today*, 26, 1, 80–93, 2021, https://doi. org/10.1016/j.drudis.2020.10.010.
5. USFDA, Artificial Intelligence and Machine Learning in Software as a Medical Device, 1–8, 2021, https://www.fda.gov/medical-devices/software-medical-device-samd/artificial-intelligence-and- machine-learning-software-medical-device.
6. Fleming, N., How artificial intelligence is changing drug discovery. *Nature*, 557, 7707, S55–S57, 2018, https://doi.org/10.1038/d41586-018-05267-x.
7. Labbe, M. and Wigmore, I., Narrow AI (weak AI), 2023, TechTarget, https://www.techtarget.com/searchenterpriseai/definition/narrow-AI-weak-AI.
8. Philippidis, A., Intelligence Mission: Berg Finds a Buyer. *Genet. Eng. Biotechnol. News*, 2023, February, https://www.genengnews.com/artificial-intelligence/intelligencemission-berg-finds-a-buyer/.

9. Hashemi-Pour, C., Artificial general intelligence (AGI), 2023, TechTarget, https://www.techtarget.com/searchenterpriseai/definition/artificial-general-intelligence-AGI?vgnextfmt=print. Accessed dated 09/03/2024.

10. Anirudh, V.K., What Are the Types of Artificial Intelligence: Narrow, General, and Super AI Explained, 2022, Spiceworks Inc, https://www.spiceworks.com/tech/artificial-intelligence/articles/types-of-ai/. Accessed dated 09/03/2024.

11. Kanade, V., Narrow AI vs. General AI vs. Super AI: Key Comparisons, 2022, https://www.spiceworks.com/tech/artificial-intelligence/articles/narrow-general-super-ai-difference/. Accessed dated 09/03/2024.

12. Manne, R. and Kantheti, S.C., Application of Artificial Intelligence in Healthcare: Chances and Challenges. *Curr. J. Appl. Sci. Technol.*, 40, 6, 78–89, 2021, https://doi. org/10.9734/cjast/2021/v40i631320.

13. Dara, S., Dhamercherla, S., Jadav, S.S., Babu, C.M., Ahsan, M.J., Machine Learning in Drug Discovery: A Review. *Artif. Intell. Rev.*, 55, 3, 1947–1999, 2022, https://doi. org/10.1007/s10462-021-10058-4.

14. Venaik, A., Kumari, R., Venaik, U., Nayyar, A., The Role of Machine Learning and Artificial Intelligence in Clinical Decisions and the Herbal Formulations Against COVID-19. *Int. J. Reliab. Qual. E-Healthc.*, 11, 1, 1–17, 2022, https://doi.org/10.4018/ IJRQEH.2022010107.

15. Mohammad Ganie, S., Kanti Dutta Pramanik, P., Bashir Malik, M., Nayyar, A., Sup Kwak, K., An Improved Ensemble Learning Approach for Heart Disease Prediction Using Boosting Algorithms. *Comput. Syst. Sci. Eng.*, 46, 3, 3993–4006, 2023, https://doi.org/10.32604/csse.2023.035244.

16. Botlagunta, M., Botlagunta, M.D., Myneni, M.B., Lakshmi, D., Nayyar, A., Gullapalli, J.S., Shah, M.A., Classification and diagnostic prediction of breast cancer metastasis on clinical data using machine learning algorithms. *Sci. Rep.*, 13, 1, 485, 2023, https://doi.org/10.1038/s41598-023-27548-w.

17. Nag, S., Baidya, A.T.K., Mandal, A., Mathew, A.T., Das, B., Devi, B., Kumar, R., Deep learning tools for advancing drug discovery and development. *3 Biotech.*, 12, 5, 110, 2022, https://doi. org/10.1007/s13205-022-03165-8.

18. Musa Jaber, M., Yussof, S., S. Elameer, A., Yeng Weng, L., Khalil Abd, S., Nayyar, A., Medical Image Analysis Using Deep Learning and Distribution Pattern Matching Algorithm. *Comput. Mater. Contin.*, 72, 2, 2175–2190, 2022, https://doi.org/10.32604/cmc.2022.023387.

19. Mills, T.T., 510(k) Summary Aidoc Medical, Ltd.'s BriefCas, 2022, USFDA, https://www. accessdata.fda.gov/cdrh_docs/pdf21/K213721.pdf.

20. Bhatnagar, R., Sardar, S., Beheshti, M., Podichetty, J.T., How can natural language processing help model informed drug development?: a review. *JAMIA Open*, 5, 2, 1–14, 2022, https://doi.org/10.1093/jamiaopen/ooac043.

21. Robotnik, Applications of robotics in medicine, 2022, https://robotnik.eu/applications-of-robotics-in-medicine/#pll_switcher. Accessed dated 09/03/2024.

22. PHArA-ON, Project Background, 2021, https://www.pharaon.eu/about/. Accessed dated 09/03/2024.

23. van Krieken, E., Acar, E., van Harmelen, F., Analyzing Differentiable Fuzzy Logic Operators. *Artif. Intell.*, 302, 103602, 2022, https://doi.org/10.1016/j.artint.2021.103602.

24. Uzun Ozsahin, D., Uzun, B., Ozsahin, I., Mustapha, M.T., Musa, M.S., Fuzzy logic in medicine, in: *Biomedical Signal Processing and Artificial Intelligence in Healthcare*, pp. 153–182, Elsevier, 2020, https://doi.org/10.1016/B978-0-12-818946-7.00006-8.

25. Masoudi-Sobhanzadeh, Y., Esmaeili, H., Masoudi-Nejad, A., A fuzzy logic-based computational method for the repurposing of drugs against COVID-19. *BioImpacts*, 12, 4, 315–324, 2022, https://doi.org/10.34172/bi.2021.40.

26. McClean, T., The Collective Power Of Swarm Intelligence In AI And Robotics, 2021, May 13, Forbes Media LLC, https://www.forbes.com/sites/forbestechcouncil/2021/05/13/the-collective-power-of-swarm-intelligence-in-ai-and-robotics/?sh=73392aab252f. Accessed dated 09/03/2024.

27. Nayyar, A. and Nguyen, N.G., Introduction to Swarm Intelligence, in: *Advances in Swarm Intelligence for Optimizing Problems in Computer Science*, Chapman and Hall/CRC, 53–75, 2019, https://doi.org/10.1201/9780429445927-3.

28. Mughal, F., Wahid, A., Khattak, M.A.K., Artificial Intelligence: Evolution, Benefits, and Challenges. *Internet of Things*, 59–69, 2022, https://doi.org/10.1007/978-3-030-92054-8_4.

29. Sharma, K., Singh, H., Sharma, D.K., Kumar, A., Nayyar, A., Krishnamurthi, R., Dynamic models and control techniques for drone delivery of medications and other healthcare items in COVID-19 hotspots, in: *Emerging Technologies for Battling Covid-19. Studies in Systems, Decision and Control*, Al-Turjman, F., Devi, A., Nayyar, A. (eds), vol. 324, pp. 1–34, 2021, https://doi.org/10.1007/978-3-030-60039-6_1.

30. Carracedo-Reboredo, P., Liñares-Blanco, J., Rodríguez-Fernández, N., Cedrón, F., Novoa, F.J., Carballal, A., Maojo, V., Pazos, A., Fernandez-Lozano, C., A review on machine learning approaches and trends in drug discovery. *Comput. Struct. Biotechnol. J.*, 19, 4538–4558, 2021, https://doi.org/10.1016/j.csbj.2021.08.011.

31. Vijayan, R.S.K., Kihlberg, J., Cross, J.B., Poongavanam, V., Enhancing preclinical drug discovery with artificial intelligence. *Drug Discov. Today*, 27, 4, 967–984, 2022, https://doi.org/10.1016/j.drudis.2021.11.023.

32. Sun, D., Gao, W., Hu, H., Zhou, S., Why 90% of clinical drug development fails and how to improve it? *Acta Pharm. Sin. B.*, 12, 7, 3049–3062, 2022, https://doi.org/10.1016/j.apsb.2022.02.002.

33. Aiforia, Orion pharma case study: accelerating preclinical neurotoxicity analysis with AI, 2020, https://www.aiforia.com/blog/preclinical-neurotox-case-study. Accessed dated 09/03/2024.

34. Deore, A.B., Dhumane, J.R., Wagh, R., Sonawane, R., The Stages of Drug Discovery and Development Process. *Asian J. Pharm. Res. Dev.*, 7, 6, 62–67, 2019, https://doi.org/10.22270/ajprd.v7i6.616.

35. Bagherian, M., Sabeti, E., Wang, K., Sartor, M.A., Nikolovska-Coleska, Z., Najarian, K., Machine learning approaches and databases for prediction of drug–target interaction: A survey paper. *Briefings Bioinf.*, 22, 1, 247–269, 2021, https://doi.org/10.1093/bib/bbz157.

36. Medicine, I., Insilico Medicine Achieves Industry First Nominating Preclinical Candidate Discovered by AI, 2021, February 24, CISION PR Newswire, https://www.prnewswire.com/in/news-releases/insilico-medicine-achieves-industry-first-nominating-preclinical-candidatedis-covered-by-ai-877449436.html.

37. Pun, F.W., Liu, B.H.M., Long, X., Leung, H.W., Leung, G.H.D., Mewborne, Q.T., Gao, J., Shneyderman, A., Ozerov, I.V., Wang, J., Ren, F., Aliper, A., Bischof, E., Izumchenko, E., Guan, X., Zhang, K., Lu, B., Rothstein, J.D., Cudkowicz, M.E., Zhavoronkov, A., Identification of Therapeutic Targets for Amyotrophic Lateral Sclerosis Using PandaOmics – An AI-Enabled Biological Target Discovery Platform. *Front. Aging Neurosci.*, 14, 914017, 1–16, 2022, https://doi.org/10.3389/fnagi.2022.914017.

38. Rashid, M.B.M.A., Artificial Intelligence Effecting a Paradigm Shift in Drug Development. *SLAS Technol.*, 26, 1, 3–15, 2021, https://doi.org/10.1177/2472630320956931.

39. Mak, K.-K. and Pichika, M.R., Artificial intelligence in drug development: present status and future prospects. *Drug Discov. Today*, 24, 3, 773–780, 2019, https://doi.org/10.1016/j.drudis.2018.11.014.

40. Seyhan, A.A., Lost in translation: the valley of death across preclinical and clinical divide – identification of problems and overcoming obstacles. *Transl. Med. Commun.*, 4, 1, 18, 2019, https://doi.org/10.1186/s41231-019-0050-7.

41. Sharma, A., Virmani, T., Pathak, V., Sharma, A., Pathak, K., Kumar, G., Pathak, D., Artificial Intelligence-Based Data-Driven Strategy to Accelerate Research, Development, and Clinical Trials of COVID Vaccine. *BioMed. Res. Int.*, 2022, 1–16, 2022, https://doi.org/10.1155/2022/7205241.

42. Naik, N., Hameed, B.M.Z., Shetty, D.K., Swain, D., Shah, M., Paul, R., Aggarwal, K., Brahim, S., Patil, V., Smriti, K., Shetty, S., Rai, B.P., Chlosta, P., Somani, B.K., Legal and Ethical Consideration in Artificial Intelligence in Healthcare: Who Takes Responsibility? *Front. Surg.*, 9, 862322, 1–6, 2022, https://doi.org/10.3389/fsurg.2022.862322.

43. Davenport, T. and Kalakota, R., The potential for artificial intelligence in healthcare. *Future Healthc. J.*, 6, 2, 94–98, 2019, https://doi.org/10.7861/futurehosp.6-2-94.

44. Karimian, G., Petelos, E., Evers, S.M.A.A., The ethical issues of the application of artificial intelligence in healthcare: A systematic scoping review. *AI Ethics*, 2, 4, 539–551, 2022, https://doi.org/10.1007/s43681-021-00131-7.

45. Bollier, D., *The Promise and Peril of Big Data*, The Aspen Institute, 1–61, 2010, https://www.aspeninstitute.org/publications/promise-peril-big-data/.

46. Patel, V. and Shah, M., Artificial intelligence and machine learning in drug discovery and development. *Intell. Med.*, 2, 3, 134–140, 2022, https://doi.org/10.1016/j.imed.2021.10.001.

47. Alharbi, E., Gadiya, Y., Henderson, D., Zaliani, A., Delfin-Rossaro, A., Cambon-Thomsen, A., Kohler, M., Witt, G., Welter, D., Juty, N., Jay, C., Engkvist, O., Goble, C., Reilly, D.S., Satagopam, V., Ioannidis, V., Gu, W., Gribbon, P., Selection of data sets for FAIRification in drug discovery and development: Which, why, and how? *Drug Discov. Today*, 27, 8, 2080–2085, 2022, https://doi.org/10.1016/j.drudis.2022.05.010.

48. Yoon, J., Drumright, L.N., van der Schaar, M., Anonymization Through Data Synthesis Using Generative Adversarial Networks (ADS-GAN). *IEEE J. Biomed. Health Inf.*, 24, 8, 2378–2388, 2020, https://doi.org/10.1109/JBHI.2020.2980262.

49. Blanco-Gonzalez, A., Cabezon, A., Seco-Gonzalez, A., Conde-Torres, D., Antelo-Riveiro, P., Pineiro, A., Garcia-Fandino, R., The Role of AI in Drug Discovery: Challenges, Opportunities, and Strategies, *Pharmaceuticals,* 16, 6, 891, 2023, http://arxiv.org/abs/2212.08104.

50. Winter, J.S., AI in healthcare: data governance challenges. *J. Hosp. Manage. Health Policy*, 5, 8–8, 2020, https://doi.org/10.21037/jhmhp-2020-ai-05.

51. Challen, R., Denny, J., Pitt, M., Gompels, L., Edwards, T., Tsaneva-Atanasova, K., Artificial intelligence, bias and clinical safety. *BMJ Qual Saf.*, 28, 3, 231–237, 2019, https://doi.org/10.1136/bmjqs-2018-008370.

52. Ntoutsi, E., Fafalios, P., Gadiraju, U., Iosifidis, V., Nejdl, W., Vidal, M., Ruggieri, S., Turini, F., Papadopoulos, S., Krasanakis, E., Kompatsiaris, I., Kinder-Kurlanda, K., Wagner, C., Karimi, F., Fernandez, M., Alani, H., Berendt, B., Kruegel, T., Heinze, C., Staab, S., … Bias in data-driven artificial intelligence systems—An introductory survey. *WIREs Data Min. Knowl. Discov.*, 10, 3, 1–14, 2020, https://doi.org/10.1002/widm.1356.

53. Shreve, J.T., Khanani, S.A., Haddad, T.C., Artificial Intelligence in Oncology: Current Capabilities, Future Opportunities, and Ethical Considerations. *Am. Soc Clin. Oncol. Educ. Book*, 42, 842–851, 2022, https://doi.org/10.1200/EDBK_350652.

54. Vamathevan, J., Clark, D., Czodrowski, P., Dunham, I., Ferran, E., Lee, G., Li, B., Madabhushi, A., Shah, P., Spitzer, M., Zhao, S., Applications of machine learning in drug discovery and development. *Nat. Rev. Drug Discov.*, 18, 6, 463–477, 2019, https://doi.org/10.1038/s41573-019-0024-5.

55. Yang, X., Wang, Y., Byrne, R., Schneider, G., Yang, S., Concepts of Artificial Intelligence for Computer-Assisted Drug Discovery. *Chem. Rev.*, 119, 18, 10520–10594, 2019, https://doi.org/10.1021/acs.chemrev.8b00728.

56. Delso, G., Cirillo, D., Kaggie, J.D., Valencia, A., Metser, U., Veit-Haibach, P., How to Design AI-Driven Clinical Trials in Nuclear Medicine. *Semin. Nucl. Med.*, *51*, 2, 112–119, 2021, https://doi.org/10.1053/j.semnuclmed.2020.09.003.

57. Vollmer, S., Mateen, B.A., Bohner, G., Király, F.J., Ghani, R., Jonsson, P., Cumbers, S., Jonas, A., McAllister, K.S.L., Myles, P., Grainger, D., Birse, M., Branson, R., Moons, K.G.M., Collins, G.S., Ioannidis, J.P.A., Holmes, C., Hemingway, H., Machine learning and artificial intelligence research for patient benefit: 20 critical questions on transparency, replicability, ethics, and effectiveness. *BMJ*, 368, l6927, 2020, https://doi.org/10.1136/bmj.l6927.

58. Collins, J.W., Marcus, H.J., Ghazi, A., Sridhar, A., Hashimoto, D., Hager, G., Arezzo, A., Jannin, P., Maier-Hein, L., Marz, K., Valdastri, P., Mori, K., Elson, D., Giannarou, S., Slack, M., Hares, L., Beaulieu, Y., Levy, J., Laplante, G., Stoyanov, D., … Ethical implications of AI in robotic surgical training: A Delphi consensus statement. *Eur. Urol. Focus*, *8*, 2, 613–622, 2022, https://doi.org/10.1016/j.euf.2021.04.006.

59. Héder, M., The epistemic opacity of autonomous systems and the ethical consequences. *AI Soc.*, 38, 1819–1827, 2023, https://doi.org/10.1007/s00146-020-01024-9.

60. Luo, Y., Peng, J., Ma, J., Next Decade's AI-Based Drug Development Features Tight Integration of Data and Computation. *Health Data Sci.*, *2022*, 1–3, 2022, https://doi.org/10.34133/2022/9816939.

61. Kerr, A., Barry, M., Kelleher, J.D., Expectations of artificial intelligence and the performativity of ethics: Implications for communication governance. *Big Data Soc.*, *7*, 1, 205395172091593, 2020, https://doi.org/10.1177/2053951720915939.

62. D'Antonoli, T.A., Ethical considerations for artificial intelligence: an overview of the current radiology landscape. *Diagn. Interv. Radiol.*, *26*, 5, 504–511, 2020, https://doi.org/10.5152/dir.2020.19279.

63. Doshi-Velez, F., Kortz, M., Budish, R., Bavitz, C., Gershman, S., O'Brien, D., Scott, K., Schieber, S., Waldo, J., Weinberger, D., Weller, A., Wood, A., Accountability of AI Under the Law: The Role of Explanation., Berkman Klein Center Working Group on Explanation and the Law, *Berkman Klein Center for Internet & Society Working Paper*, 2017, http://arxiv.org/abs/1711.01134.

64. Sharma, K. and Manchikanti, P., Regulation of Artificial Intelligence in Drug Discovery and Health Care. *Biotechnol. Law Rep.*, *39*, 5, 371–380, 2020, https://doi.org/10.1089/blr.2020.29183.ks.

65. Saboury, B., Bradshaw, T., Boellaard, R., Buvat, I., Dutta, J., Hatt, M., Jha, A.K., Li, Q., Liu, C., McMeekin, H., Morris, M.A., Scott, P.J.H., Siegel, E., Sunderland, J.J., Pandit-Taskar, N., Wahl, R.L., Zuehlsdorff, S., Rahmim, A., Artificial Intelligence in Nuclear Medicine: Opportunities, Challenges, and Responsibilities Toward a Trustworthy Ecosystem. *J. Nucl. Med.*, *64*, 2, 188–196, 2023, https://doi.org/10.2967/jnumed.121.263703.

66. Arrieta, A.B., Díaz-Rodríguez, N., Del Ser, J., Bennetot, A., Tabik, S., Barbado, A., Garcia, S., Gil-Lopez, S., Molina, D., Benjamins, R., Chatila, R., Herrera, F., Explainable Artificial Intelligence (XAI): Concepts, taxonomies, opportunities and challenges toward responsible AI. *Inf. Fusion*, *58*, 82–115, 2020, https://doi.org/10.1016/j.inffus.2019.12.012.

67. Smith, G.F., Artificial Intelligence in Drug Safety and Metabolism BT, in: *Artificial Intelligence in Drug Design*, A. Heifetz (Ed.), pp. 483–501, Springer, US, 2022, https://doi.org/10.1007/978-1-0716-1787-8_22.

68. Rani, I., Munjal, K., Singla, R.K., Gautam, R.K., Artificial Intelligence and Machine Learning-Based New Drug Discovery Process with Molecular Modelling, in: *Bioinformatics Tools for Pharmaceutical Drug Product Development*, pp. 19–35, Wiley, 2023, https://doi.org/10.1002/9781119865728.ch2.

69. Cova, T., Vitorino, C., Ferreira, M., Nunes, S., Rondon-Villarreal, P., Pais, A., Artificial Intelligence and Quantum computing (QC)as the Next Pharma Disruptors BT, in: *Artificial*

Intelligence in Drug Design, A. Heifetz (Ed.), pp. 321–347, Springer, US, 2022, https://doi.org/10.1007/978-1-0716-1787-8_14.

70. Bélisle-Pipon, J.-C., Couture, V., Roy, M.-C., Ganache, I., Goetghebeur, M., Cohen, I.G., What Makes Artificial Intelligence Exceptional in Health Technology Assessment? *Front. Artif. Intell.*, 4, 1–16, 2021, https://doi.org/10.3389/frai.2021.736697.

71. Jian, G., Artificial Intelligence in Healthcare and Medicine: Promises, Ethical Challenges, and Governance. *Chin. Med. J.*, *34*, 2, 99, 2019, https://doi.org/10.24920/003611.

72. Gerke, S., Minssen, T., Cohen, G., Ethical and legal challenges of artificial intelligence-driven healthcare. *Artif. Intell. Healthc.*, 295–336, 2020, Elsevier, https://doi.org/10.1016/B978-0-12-818438-7.00012-5.

73. Ramalho, A., Patentability of AI-Generated Inventions: Is a Reform of the Patent System Needed? *SSRN Electron. J.*, 1–32, 2018, https://doi.org/10.2139/ssrn.3168703.

74. Engel, A., Can a Patent Be Granted for an AI-Generated Invention? *GRUR Int.*, *69*, 11, 1123–1129, 2020, https://doi.org/10.1093/grurint/ikaa117.

75. Schwein, R.L., Patentability and Inventorship of AI-Generated Inventions. *Washburn Law J.*, *60*, Spring, 561–604, 2021.

76. Adde, L. and Smith, J., Patent pending: the law on AI inventorship. *J. Intellect. Prop. Law Pract.*, *16*, 2, 97–98, 2021, https://doi.org/10.1093/jiplp/jpab002.

77. George, A. and Walsh, T., Artificial intelligence is breaking patent law. *Nature*, *605*, 7911, 616–618, 2022. https://doi.org/10.1038/d41586-022-01391-x.

78. USFDA, Artificial Intelligence and Machine Learning (AI/ML)-Enabled Medical Devices, 2023, https://www.fda.gov/medical-devices/software-medical-device-samd/artificial-intelligence-and-machine-learning-aiml-enabled-medical-devices.

79. Joshi, G., Jain, A., Adhikari, S., Garg, H., Bhandari, M., FDA approved Artificial Intelligence and Machine Learning (AI/ML)-Enabled Medical Devices: An updated landscape. *Electronics*, 13, 3, 498, 2023, https://doi.org/10.1101/2022.12.07.22283216.

80. Ayers, M., Jayatunga, M., Goldader, J., Meier, C., Adopting AI in Drug Discovery, 2022, Boston Consulting Group, https://www.bcg.com/publications/2022/adopting-ai-inpharmaceutical-discovery.

18

Feasibility of AI and Robotics in Indian Healthcare: A Narrative Analysis

Rahul Joshi[1]* and Rhythma Badola[2]

[1]Department of Journalism and Mass Communication, School of Media Studies and Humanities, Manav Rachna International Institute of Research and Studies, Faridabad, Haryana, India
[2]Patanjali India Limited, Haridwar, Uttarakhand, India

Abstract

In contemporary times, the pivotal significance of robots, artificial intelligence (AI), and Internet of Things (IoT) technology has fundamentally transformed the healthcare sector. Healthcare businesses are progressively embracing artificial intelligence (AI) and its associated technologies in response to their growing prevalence in the corporate domain. The use of these technologies holds the promise of enhancing several aspects of patient care and administrative procedures within providers, beneficiaries, and pharmaceutical entities. There has been a growing potential for advanced robotics to significantly benefit the healthcare sector in recent years, owing to notable developments in several current technologies. A *robot* may be defined as a mechanized system that is programmed and actuated, with a certain level of autonomy. Medical robotics has seen significant advancements since the first development of prototypes based on industrial robots during the 1960s–1970s. Initial versions of these technologies have undergone significant development and have transformed into advanced and complex platforms that support doctors, patients, and attendants in modern healthcare environments. With time, robots have shown their utility and undergone advancements, enabling them to work inside restricted environments within the human anatomy, aid individuals in regaining the functionality of wounded limbs, and assist those with physical and cognitive impairments. Nevertheless, the use of robots in the healthcare sector may be controversial due to apprehensions about financial implications, accessibility of skilled workforce, and opposition towards embracing technological advancements. The dissemination of these technologies to the country's peripheral settlements and rural areas, which most people inhabit, poses the most significant challenge. This chapter presents a comprehensive review of the current state of robotics in the healthcare industry, highlighting the associated issues and obstacles.

Keywords: Artificial intelligence, robotics, surgical robots, assistive robots, clinical, India, challenges, healthcare

---

*Corresponding author: rahuljoshi.785@gmail.com

Abhirup Khanna, May El Barachi, Sapna Jain, Manoj Kumar and Anand Nayyar (eds.) Artificial Intelligence and Machine Learning in Drug Design and Development, (563–604) © 2024 Scrivener Publishing LLC

18.1   Introduction

18.1.1   Foundations of AI

Artificial intelligence is a computational system that can do activities often associated with human intellect, such as thinking, learning, adaptation, comprehension, and interaction. Currently, artificial intelligence is used in a multitude of domains. It executes certain functions or resolves predetermined issues using concepts and methodologies, including mathematics, logic, and biology. One notable characteristic of current computer-based intelligence advancements is their ability to effectively process diverse unstructured material, such as natural language text and images [1]. In recent times, the approaches of artificial intelligence and machine learning have gained prominence due to their efficacy in many applications. Machine learning enables a computational system to discover novel patterns and develop rules based on current data and situations.

There are many existing definitions of "artificial intelligence." Specific individuals directed their attention toward philosophical concerns, while others focused on mathematical difficulties or computer science. An example may be seen in the definition provided by the Academy of Medical Royal Colleges, which delineates artificial intelligence as the replication of human cognitive processes by technological means, namely, computer systems. The current scope of AI seems to be rather broad and lacking specificity. There needs to be more consensus over the meaning of this term, even within the healthcare domain. "AI" generally encompasses systems and technologies that exhibit characteristics like human intelligence, including reasoning, learning, adaptability, sensory comprehension, and interaction.

18.1.2   Objectives of AI

The following are the objectives of AI:

1) Logical and problem-solving skills: The field of logic and problem-solving has seen the development of algorithms that aim to replicate the cognitive processes involved in human puzzle-solving and logical deduction. During the late 1980s and 1990s, researchers in artificial intelligence made significant progress in addressing the challenges posed by uncertain or partial information. They achieved this by incorporating probability theory and economics principles into their methodologies. When faced with challenging issues, algorithms may need significant computing resources since they often encounter a phenomenon known as "combinatorial explosion." The trend pertains to the exponential growth in memory consumption or computational resources needed for issues of a particular scale, making them very challenging regarding computational requirements. The pursuit of more effective problem-solving algorithms is of paramount importance.

2) Data storytelling: The fields of data presentation and data design play a pivotal role in artificial intelligence investigation. A significant number of challenges that robots are anticipated to address will need a substantial amount of global knowledge. AI necessitates representing several elements, including objects, qualities, categories, and connections among objects. Additionally, it

requires the representation of circumstances, events, states, timeframes, and cause-and-effect linkages. Furthermore, AI systems must possess knowledge about meta-knowledge, specifically about what other individuals know about our knowledge. Lastly, several additional fields have received comparatively less academic attention.

3) Drafting: In the realm of drafting, intelligent agents need to possess the capability of establishing objectives and then attaining them. Individuals need the means to conceptualize forthcoming events, depict the global condition, and forecast the impact of their actions on this condition. Moreover, they should be able to make decisions that optimize the worth or usefulness of the alternatives. In the context of classical planning issues, it is customary for the agent to operate under the assumption that it is the only entity exerting influence within the given environment. This assumption gives the agent a level of certainty about the outcomes of its chosen actions.

4) Unsupervised learning: Machine learning, a core principle of artificial intelligence research since its birth, pertains to examining computer algorithms that can enhance their performance *via* experiential learning. Unsupervised learning is the capacity to identify and discern patterns within a continuous flow of incoming data. Supervised learning encompasses two fundamental tasks: classification and numerical regression. The categorization process involves assigning an object or concept to a specific category by examining several instances across various categories. Regression analysis aims to develop a mathematical model that characterizes the association between input variables and output variables, enabling the prediction of how the output variables are expected to vary in response to changes in the input variables.

5) Effective computing: It is also known as social intelligence and pertains to examining and advancing systems capable of seeing, comprehending, manipulating, and emulating human behavior. The area in question encompasses several disciplines, including computer science, psychology, and cognitive science. The field's inception may be attributed to early philosophical investigations into emotion, while its contemporary manifestation in computer science emerged from Rosalind Picard's seminal article on "effective computing" in 1995.

6) Cognitive ability: Numerous researchers believe their endeavors ultimately culminate in developing a machine with artificial general intelligence. Such a computer would integrate the talents mentioned earlier and surpass human capabilities in most, if not all, of these domains. There is a belief held by some individuals that the successful implementation of such a project may need the incorporation of human attributes, such as artificial consciousness or an artificial brain.

18.1.3 Healthcare and AI

Based on existing scientific research, AI exhibits promising prospects for use within the healthcare industry, primarily *via* four primary avenues. These include its application as a tool for supporting diagnoses, identifying personalized therapy plans, facilitating patient engagement, and modeling and enhancing the organizational infrastructures of medical institutions. A minimum of three modalities has the potential for AI to engage in interactions with not just healthcare professionals but also patients. However, there needs to be more knowledge about the potential effects of integrating artificial intelligence into medical practice on the patient–doctor relationship, a crucial element that significantly influences the efficacy of treatments. In the realm of medical practice, symptoms are often gathered, subjected to analysis, and afterward compared to existing scientific literature in order to identify disorders and choose appropriate treatment options. Following the principles of evidence-based medicine, doctors need to comprehensively understand the most up-to-date scientific literature to provide the most optimal solution [2].

Nevertheless, it is essential to acknowledge that theoretical and methodological investigations reveal notable deficiencies in current research:

a) It is worth noting that study samples often must accurately reflect the broader population.
b) Experimental settings often exhibit more artificiality than natural environments.
c) The cost associated with conducting experimental studies is sometimes prohibitively high.

While randomized studies are crucial for advancing scientific knowledge, medicine is now exploring using artificial intelligence as a novel approach to studying diseases and their corresponding treatments [3]. As previously mentioned, the field of artificial intelligence finds significant use in medicine and healthcare, particularly in diagnostics. Patients' clinical data from real-world evidence is analyzed using artificial intelligence equipment [4]. Consequently, the acquired data are juxtaposed with a substantial corpus of literature, including genetic testing, diagnostic imaging, electrodiagnostic results, records of physical examinations, clinical outcomes, and other relevant clinical information derived from various patient cohorts. Artificial intelligence (AI) serves as a diagnostic assistance tool in the medical field, aiding in identifying diseases and assisting clinicians in their daily tasks, including data manipulation and knowledge utilization [5].

Artificial neural networks can precisely identify and categorize patterns by effectively analyzing many biological, clinical, and pathological data. Furthermore, artificial intelligence can discern suitable treatment options that are customized to address the needs of individual patients, aligning with the principles of precision medicine. One instance illustrating this phenomenon is the use of artificial intelligence within the cancer domain, shown by the deployment of Watson for cancer [6]. There are two notable reasons why this topic has significant interest. Firstly, it offers the opportunity to determine the most effective remedy available. Secondly, it enables doctors to administer early therapies to delay the start of chronic pathological problems, which can potentially exacerbate over time [7].

Furthermore, artificial intelligence can potentially enhance patient participation throughout their healthcare journey. Digital gadgets, including eHealth, Digital Therapeutics, and Ambient Intelligence, are technological interventions designed to gather data, monitor individuals' health condition, and assist in managing patients' health by offering valuable advice to address daily health-related challenges [8]. This enables medical practitioners to provide healthcare services to patients outside the confines of traditional medical consultations, hence facilitating the provision of treatment inside the patients' homes. Individuals can get assistance to enhance their level of activity and assume more responsibility for their care [9]. Furthermore, artificial intelligence can potentially enhance the organizational architecture of medical facilities by offering valuable insights and recommendations. Healthcare systems are dynamic, undergoing constant growth and learning from experience. In the present environment, AI can provide recommendations for effectively managing challenges and augmenting organizational advancements in care coordination proficiency. This phenomenon illustrates the decrease in hospital visits resulting from the ability to self-administer various measurements.

This reduction can yield several benefits, namely:

a) A reduction in expenses associated with resource consumption, such as the use of emergency department services and the number of patients necessitating hospital stays.

b) The promotion of disease prevention by minimizing the need of in-person hospital visits for healthcare needs. To enhance preventative efforts, laboratories and clinics need to expedite the integration of artificial intelligence technologies to collect real-time data efficiently.

Additionally, institutions must ensure the continuity of their transition towards comprehensible procedures [10]. This measure will be beneficial in mitigating the incidence of infections and addressing other medical concerns about the healing process inside hospital settings. Undoubtedly, integrating artificial intelligence has great potential for enhancing healthcare systems, enabling them to become dynamic entities that continually evolve and improve. This is achieved by using AI's ability to learn from past experiences and actively pursue the implementation of ongoing process enhancements. When examining databases that exhibit a continuous data flow, consideration is given to the broader organizational structures and cycles involved in treating illnesses. This technique is consistent with the notion of illness management grounded in a multi-agent system (MAS), where many agents are situated within an interconnected environment and engage in interactions with each other [11].

The multi-agent system (MAS) method is designed to comprehensively model the intricate dynamics of individual patients, including their reactions to drugs and behavioral interactions, within the broader context of a society ecosystem. Implementing a global care coordination technology approach aims to efficiently establish, govern, and increase assistance for system enhancements, leading to enhanced medication responses and more efficacious treatments. Moreover, the expansion of scholarly inquiry into the field of "explainable artificial intelligence" (XAI) enhances the transparency and explanatory capabilities of AI systems, hence facilitating their integration into many professional domains [12]. In this manner, the dissemination of recent scientific discoveries might be facilitated by opensource platforms, enabling the aggregation and presentation of data for unrestricted access by medical professionals as readily available point-of-care information. This is made possible by the dataset's simplicity, readability, and clinical applicability [13].

In any case, the significance of doctors persists as a critical aspect, and now, it continues to be an area that lacks comprehensive research. The anticipated incorporation of AI inside healthcare environments is projected to influence the dynamics of doctor–patient interactions substantially. Artificial intelligence can fundamentally transform the provision of diagnosis, interventions, and therapies. However, it is imperative to acknowledge that AI should not replace the invaluable role played by human physicians in medical practice. Artificial intelligence in medicine presents a significant obstacle that aligns with the objectives of enhancing clinical decision-making processes and facilitating individualized treatment approaches. This contrasts the conventional notion of a "therapy for a disease" [14]. In contrast, medical treatments need to consider people's unique characteristics and requirements by actively including patients as decision-makers throughout their care journey. This is consistent with the adoption of a patient-centered approach, in which healthcare professionals and patients engage in a systematic collaboration to make informed decisions on treatments and interventions. This collaborative process is often referred to as shared decision-making [15]. From this perspective, online adaptive platforms can include people as active participants in their healthcare management by assisting patients in accepting their conditions within their everyday routines. Patients Like Me is one instance of a platform that facilitates patient communication and opinion exchange on their respective diseases. Additionally, this platform facilitates prompt access for doctors to get information on symptoms and physical issues patients report [16]. Maintaining communication with patients' perspectives and fostering the connection between people and the healthcare system would be advantageous. The significance of doctor–patient contacts in the treatment process necessitates healthcare providers to establish a customized setting that facilitates the exchange of information and empowers patients to take ownership of their illness management [17].

In summary, a diverse range of clinical data obtained from patients' medical records and wearable health sensors can offer suggestions regarding lifestyle adjustments and maintenance and augment understanding of developing healthcare strategies consistent with patients' habits and needs. There are ongoing challenges regarding accepting technologies and artificial intelligence among healthcare professionals. Based on the findings of several sources [18], critical determinants for assessing the inclination to use these technologies include perceived utility (the perception that technologies may effectively facilitate the attainment of goals), perceived simplicity of utilization, and the general acceptance of technological advances.

Longoni *et al.* [19] found that medical practitioners tend to place more trust in their medical perceptions as opposed to using models based on statistics. This phenomenon might be attributed to the assumption that individuals may be seen as having lower levels of competence and professionalism when they heavily depend on computerized decision aids. In a broad sense, there are two potential outcomes to consider. Firstly, physicians may be discouraged from using AI if they see themselves incapable of effectively managing it. Conversely, if professionals become too reliant on AI, there is a risk of diminishing the role of human competencies in the treatment process [20]. Physicians must navigate the interactions between AI and patients, enhancing their proficiency in handling data and effectively communicating with patients. In summary, most recent implementations of AI in medicine need more investigation, notably in the realm of human–machine interaction.

18.1.4   Latest Trends in Technology

The healthcare sector is undergoing rapid transformation due to prevailing universal trends in using artificial intelligence (AI). It is used in certain healthcare facilities to analyze complex medical situations, including cancer, and enhance the early detection of illnesses with heightened precision. An instance of a US firm, Enclitic, has successfully engineered medical imaging software that uses deep learning artificial intelligence to identify and locate cancers. The use of its design methodology enables the detection of human lung carcinoma *via* the examination of computed tomography (CT) scan data.

18.1.4.1   *Latest Trends in Health Industry*

The following points highlight the latest trends in health industry as follows:

1) Increasing popularity of telemedicine: Telemedicine enables the provision of medical consultations at a distance and offers several advantages, particularly for those living in underserved and remote areas. Using the metaverse allows patients to engage in remote consultations with physicians and specialists, obviating the need for physical travel and reducing healthcare costs. It provides many benefits to patients, including ease, efficacy, and cost-effectiveness. This alternative to traditional face-to-face consultations reduces the duration of waiting for appointments, streamlines the recuperation process, and offers a cost-effective solution. Furthermore, it facilitates care maintenance by enabling patients to get ongoing support and guidance from healthcare experts, leading to enhanced treatment results.

2) Proliferation of remote monitoring tools: Remote monitoring technologies are gaining popularity in India, driven by a growing number of individuals actively seeking avenues to enhance their overall health and well-being. Using these technologies, patients can actively engage in treatment and obtain prompt interventions as needed. Currently, a range of widely used remote monitoring equipment exists, including fitness trackers, blood pressure monitors, heart rate monitors, and glucometers. The gadgets may be worn by the patient or placed inside their house, facilitating frequent data transmission to the healthcare professional.

3) Transformational diagnostics: Transformational diagnostics play a crucial role in population health management by facilitating the identification of people who are susceptible to certain illnesses and disorders. Several transformative diagnostic methods have emerged as significant tools during the pandemic, including genomic sequencing, next-generation sequencing, whole-genome sequencing, and RNA-based testing. These tests have shown great promise in providing valuable diagnostic information. Furthermore, they are poised to revolutionize the healthcare business by offering enhanced precision and promptness in diagnosing and monitoring illnesses and medical conditions.

4) Emergence of healthcare software as a service: The use of healthcare software as a service (SaaS) has seen a notable surge in popularity among healthcare

institutions seeking to enhance their operational efficiency and the quality of treatment. Healthcare providers need practical solutions for storing electronic health records and population health management data. Software as a Service (SaaS) solutions are crucial in aiding healthcare professionals in managing patient medical data, appointments, and billing information.

5) Advancing healthcare *via* a digital twin: Research on digital twins has grown exponentially due to the quick development of communication technology, sensor technology, extensive data analysis, the Internet of Things, and simulation technology [21]. The definition of DT was changed to include digital representations of both living and non-living physical elements, which made it possible to use DT for people in areas like health and welfare. DT is a dynamic concept that virtually replicates human organs, tissues, cells, or micro-environments. It continuously adapts to changes in online data and may foretell the future of its corresponding counterpart. The DT is more than simply a virtual replica that may be linked to a physical twin *via* various cutting-edge technologies. Through the closed-loop optimization between DT and the surrounding environment, it is a living, intelligent, and developing model that can optimize the processes and continually forecast future states (such as flaws, damages, and failures). The technologies required for digital transformation may be classified into two distinct categories: mechanical models that integrate multi-scale knowledge and data and statistical models that are driven by data. The analytical model is utilized for structural analysis, whereas the numerical model is used to determine structural performance. The artificial intelligence model derives the real-time structural performance from real-time sensor data after being trained using samples and numerical data [22]. The digital twin is revolutionizing the healthcare industry and has been used by many significant businesses to boost productivity and identify issues.

6) Robotic surgery gain acceptance among surgeons: Like most emerging technologies, there was early opposition against robotic surgery. Furthermore, with the inherent challenges associated with adapting to change, several surgeons expressed a desire for further autonomy inside the surgical environment beyond the capabilities provided by robotic surgical procedures. At the outset, robotic technology in intricate surgical procedures seemed to possess more characteristics of a novelty rather than a paradigm shift in healthcare standards. Robotic surgery has gained significant popularity in medical operations, characterized by limited spatial constraints, challenging environments, and sometimes inaccessible regions. This spike in popularity may be attributed to incorporating advanced technological features such as a three-dimensional camera system and wristed tools inside the robotic surgical system. Robotic surgery has become more prevalent across several surgical disciplines, including general surgery, particularly treating abdominal wall hernias. This advanced technology facilitates the adoption of minimally invasive techniques, empowering surgeons to approach these procedures with enhanced precision and efficiency.

18.1.5 Limitations of AI in Healthcare

The following points highlight the limitations of AI in healthcare:

1) Complicated training: In order to achieve optimal performance, AI technology needs thorough training using carefully chosen datasets. Nevertheless, accessing some data required for comprehensive AI learning might pose challenges due to privacy issues [23].

2) Change is next to impossible: In some sectors, the process of implementing change might present significant difficulties. Given the criticality of the healthcare sector in providing optimal patient care, the medical community must ascertain the efficacy of artificial intelligence while formulating a comprehensive strategy to demonstrate its value to potential investors, justifying the associated expenses. All individuals collaborating with AI technology will be required to comprehensively understand this technology and its potential to facilitate their daily activities.

3) Still needs feedback from people: Artificial intelligence has made significant advancements in the healthcare sector. However, it is important to note that human involvement and oversight continue to play a crucial role in this domain. Human possess a unique ability to see and interpret behavioral patterns and demonstrate empathetic responses towards others in a manner that surpasses the capabilities of machines. Occasionally, these insights might play a crucial role in a medical diagnosis and serve to mitigate potential problems.

4) Increasing security risk: Artificial intelligence systems are susceptible to security vulnerabilities, presenting a significant challenge to the healthcare sector, where the utmost importance is placed on maintaining the confidentiality of patient data. The complexity and precision of cyber assaults are increasing, becoming them more challenging to anticipate and mitigate. Healthcare organizations must allocate substantial financial resources to safeguard against cybercriminal activities effectively [24].

5) Risk of increasing unemployment: Historically, there has been a prevalent notion that the rise of robots will result in the usurpation of human labor and the subsequent loss of employment opportunities. However, it is essential to acknowledge that the advent of artificial intelligence and automation presents a tangible and significant risk to several industries. The healthcare sector is not exempt from the potential impact of artificial intelligence since its implementation may lead to the obsolescence of several administrative positions.

Objective of the Chapter

There is a prevailing belief that the constraints on developing an effective human–machine cognitive processing engine extend beyond the limitations imposed by present technology. The involvement of emotions and cognitive skills is significant in comprehending diverse features *via* intelligent technology. This chapter thoroughly examines the current status of robotics in the healthcare sector, including an analysis of the various forms of robotics used in hospitals. Additionally, it sheds light on the challenges and barriers encountered in robotic surgery, specifically within the Indian healthcare system.

Organization of the Chapter

The rest of the chapter is organized as follows: Section 18.2 enlightens robotics and diverse types in healthcare. Section 18.3 stresses on pros of robotics in healthcare. Section 18.4 highlights the inclusion of robotics in India is increasingly gaining popularity. Section 18.5 elaborates limitations of robotics in healthcare. Section 18.6 discusses future applications of Robotics and AI. Finally, Section 18.7 concludes the chapter with future scope.

18.2   Robotics and Their Types in Healthcare

Integrating robots into the medical domain has significantly changed surgical procedures, supply management, disinfection processes, and healthcare provider–patient interactions. Intel provides a comprehensive range of technological solutions to support the advancement of medical robots, including various types such as surgical assistance robots, modular robots, and autonomous mobility robots.

The inception of robotics in the healthcare sector can be traced back to the 1960s, during which the development of medical robotic systems began. These systems were primarily influenced by industrial robots, leading to the creation of conceptual designs and prototypes [25]. The subject of surgical robotics saw significant advancements during the 1990s, during which several robotic systems were developed and implemented to address certain surgical domains [26]. Contemporary robotic systems can effectively grasp and operate several surgical tools with exceptional accuracy and dexterity. This advanced functionality enables surgeons to access anatomical regions that were previously deemed inaccessible for surgical interventions. Robotic surgery has been shown to enhance intervention results by reducing hospitalization duration, complications, and in-hospital mortality. This improvement may be attributed to surgical operations' heightened safety and precision [27]. Two significant limitations of this approach are the extended duration of the surgical procedure and the substantial financial expenses associated with it. The robotic surgery field is experiencing rapid expansion, with a compound annual growth rate ranging from 12% to 25% [28, 29].

In recent years, the integration of artificial intelligence technology with computer vision and data analytics has brought about significant advancements in medical robotics, expanding their functionalities across several domains within the healthcare sector. Robotic technology has expanded its use beyond the confines of the operating room, finding utility in clinical environments to bolster healthcare personnel and augment the quality of patient care. During the COVID-19 pandemic, hospitals and clinics increasingly use robots for a broader array of functions to mitigate the risk of disease transmission.

18.2.1   Types of Robotics

18.2.1.1   *Surgical Robotics*

These robots are used in procedures requiring high levels of accuracy and minimum invasiveness, such as chemical and radiofrequency ablation. The da Vinci Surgical System is

Figure 18.1 Surgical robot used in Max super Specialty Hospital, New Delhi, India.

a notable instance of a robotic system designed to aid in surgical procedures as shown in Figure 18.1. Prominent corporations are intensifying their research and development efforts in robotic surgical equipment. Intuitive Surgical has a significant share in the overall industry; however, the market dynamics are rapidly changing. The presence of prominent manufacturers like Johnson & Johnson and Medtronic in the MedTech surgical robotics industry bolsters its position. Every company has unique product portfolios focusing on specific therapeutic domains for minimally invasive robotic surgery. The da Vinci System is a versatile robot designed to perform several surgical procedures in urology, bariatrics, and gynecology. The MAKO System developed by Stryker is designed explicitly for orthopedic surgical procedures, focusing on partial and complete knee replacements. Surgeons prefer ergonomic workplaces that are situated away from hazardous radiological surroundings, as these workspaces have been shown to mitigate both physical and mental stress effectively [30]. Additionally, surgeons value the availability of a precise instrument with a high dexterity level, enabling it to execute specific tasks autonomously. Surgical simulations may also use medical robots [31].

18.2.1.1.1   Computer-Assisted Surgery

Robotic surgery is closely intertwined with computer-assisted surgery. The function of computer-aided systems (CAS) in medicine resembles computer-aided design/manufacturing/engineering (CAD/CAM/CAE) systems used in the manufacturing industry. The use of computer-assisted surgery (CAS) involves several applications such as surgical planning, patient–model matching, precise patient modeling, execution of pre-programmed surgical procedures, and the collection and analysis of patient-specific data throughout the pre-operative, intra-operative, and post-operative stages [32]. Within computer-assisted surgery (CAS), robots are seen as instrumental devices that enhance surgeons' skills, enabling them to carry out predetermined surgical treatments effectively. Figure 18.2 shows computer assisted surgery used in Apollo Hospital, New Delhi, India.

During the pre-operative phase, computer-assisted surgery generates a full computational model of a patient. In order to accomplish this objective, several data sets originating

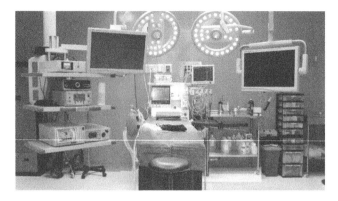

Figure 18.2 Computer-assisted surgery used in Apollo Hospital, New Delhi, India.

from sources such as medical imaging and laboratory tests are gathered and integrated with existing statistical data about human anatomy, physiology, and the specific ailment under investigation. Using the model facilitates anticipating the consequences of certain acts or the whole of an intervention, to optimize the intervention strategy for an individual patient. Within the confines of the operating room, the computer model is effectively aligned with the tangible representation of the patient. The usual procedure involves the identification of relevant landmarks or structures on both the preoperative model and the patient, which may be achieved by further imaging using a pointing device or the robot itself. During the operation, intra-operative imaging techniques and sensors are used to monitor changes in the patient's anatomical structure and revise the model. This enables the surgeon to assess the potential outcome of the surgery and make modifications if necessary. Following the completion of the operation, further data is gathered for patient follow-up. Patient-specific data might be saved in a subsequent phase. The data mentioned above has potential use in the context of surgical simulators, as it may serve as a valuable resource for training and evaluating surgeons. The data that has been evaluated may also be used to enhance statistical information for more effective pre-operative planning.

18.2.1.1.2   Mechanical Configuration for Robot-Assisted Surgery

The mechanical configuration of surgical robots is influenced by various factors, including safety considerations such as redundancy in both software and hardware, sterilization capabilities, and biocompatibility. Additionally, the choice of mounting location, whether on the floor, ceiling, surgical table or even on a patient, is an important parameter to consider. Furthermore, compatibility with other devices in the workspace, such as medical imaging devices, is also a crucial aspect to consider. This section focuses on examining a robot's end-effector, control methodologies, and their impact on the design of the robot. The control strategy plays a crucial role in determining the mechanical architecture of a surgical robot. There are three distinct methods by which a surgeon may exercise control over a surgical robot.

The first kind of robot is categorized as pre-programmed or active robots. This methodology has a resemblance to computer numerical control (CNC) machining. During the pre-operative phase, a surgeon formulates a control program for the robotic system by using medical data. During its operation, the robot effectively establishes a correspondence between the patient model and the actual patient *via* either medical imaging techniques or the implementation of fiducial pins that have been surgically inserted. Subsequently, the robot independently carries out predetermined instructions. To guarantee both safety and precision, the robot is under the surgeon's constant supervision and a range of sensors and medical imaging technologies. Pre-programmed control is only used in jobs characterized by a predictable environment, such as those involving fixed bone in orthopedic surgery. *Think Surgical's TSolution One* is an illustrative instance of an active robot [33].

The subsequent control methodology is referred to as teleoperation. According to Ghodoussi *et al.* [34] this strategy allows for a physical separation of several meters or even a transatlantic passage between a physician and a robot. The surgeon observes the surgical area using a camera affixed to the robot's end-effector and controls robotic instruments from a distant workstation. Simultaneously, the robot replicates these movements on the patient's side without delay. To enhance the overall effectiveness of the procedure, the robot employs a mechanism to effectively mitigate surgeon tremors and provide haptic feedback [35]. Active borders may also be a preventive measure to limit the robot's access to prohibited areas [36]. This methodology offers a surgeon an ergonomic workplace compared to traditional surgical methods. One significant constraint associated with teleoperation is the presence of time delay. The Da Vinci system, developed by Intuitive surgical Inc., is an illustrative example of such a system and finds applications across several disciplines [37]. Teleoperated control offers extensive flexibility for interactive surgical applications, including dexterous minimally invasive surgery or remote surgery [38].

The third methodology used is collaborative control. Collaborative robots, or cobots, are designed to facilitate direct contact between humans and robots in a shared environment. The surgeon adeptly seizes hold of the robot's end-effector and deftly maneuvers it like a conventional instrument, although with the exceptional accuracy characteristic of a robotic device. The force and torque sensors are integrated into each end-effector. These sensors detect the intended movement direction of the surgeon, and the robot is then commanded by the computer to execute the desired motion [39]. This methodology capitalizes on the inherent eye-hand coordination skills possessed by surgeons. In addition, using force sensors located at the end-effector enables the detection of invisible forces in human perception. The robot can amplify these forces to a level that allows the surgeon to experience resistance, proving advantageous in microsurgery. Like telerobots, collaborative surgical robots can mitigate hand tremors and implement active limits. One instance of such a robot is the Mako, developed by Stryker specifically for orthopedic surgical procedures [40]. The selection of the end-effector for a surgical robot's mechanical design is contingent upon the extent of the available workspace.

Generally, two primary categories of workspaces may be distinguished as expansive and restricted. A spacious work area provides enough room for accommodating an end-effector and its associated motions. Bone contouring or spinal surgery is often conducted inside clinical settings. In a broad operational environment, using a stiff end-effector equipped with high-precision actuators and sensors is common. High stiffness in a system contributes to precise operation by effectively minimizing repulsion that may occur during contact. Complex manipulations may be achieved by equipping stiff end-effectors with dexterous wrists in certain scenarios [41]. The second workspace contrasts with the first one since it is a restricted area with limited room for an end-effector and its corresponding movements. Restricted workspaces are often encountered in many surgical procedures, such as natural orifice transluminal endoscopic surgery, single-port access surgery, and intra-luminal surgery. These procedures include the deployment of end-effectors inside the human body, surrounded by delicate soft tissues. The end-effector must possess sufficiently compact dimensions to accommodate insertion into the human body while still possessing the capability to maneuver inside the body without causing harm. One effective approach to simultaneously fulfill both criteria is using a continuum robot equipped with a flexible body like a snake [42]. These robots exhibit various architectures and actuators, with dimensions reaching 2 mm [43, 44]. Continuum robots can flex at any given location within their structure, facilitating secure traversal inside the human anatomy.

Unconventional robotic systems, such as robotic capsules and microrobots, are employed in specific locations for the objectives of diagnosis and intervention. Robotic capsules are specialized automated equipment specifically created to examine the gastrointestinal tract. Several movement methods include mechanical systems such as worm-type, legged, wheeled, crawling approaches, and magnetic means. The anatomical structure in question is commonly referred to as the stomach. The robots demonstrate motion in coordination with the physiological phenomenon referred to as peristalsis within the lower gastrointestinal tract. The utilization of microrobots has been proposed as a prospective strategy for conducting minimally invasive interventions within the circulatory system. The systems that may be considered encompass the urinary tract, the ocular system, and the neurological system. A range of therapeutic interventions are accessible for individuals in such circumstances. Robotic systems exhibit diverse applications, including but not limited to targeted brachytherapy, drug delivery, material removal, and telemetry. The introduction of regulated structures has been implemented. A variety of mechanisms can achieve locomotion. The flagella demonstrate helical motion and are pushed through using magnetic forces, while piezoelectric mechanisms drive the traveling-wave flagella. Motors, also called external magnets, find applications in several fields. Microrobots collect electrical energy *via* passive or active mechanisms. An external source facilitates the transmission of mechanical or thermal energy.

18.2.1.1.3 Applications for Robot-Assisted Surgery

The following points highlight the diverse applications of robot-assisted surgery:

1) Cardiac surgery: Endoscopic coronary artery bypass (TECAB) surgery and mitral valve replacement have been undertaken. Closed chest, endoscopic mitral valve procedures are currently being conducted using the robot.
2) Gastrointestinal surgery: Various treatments have been conducted using the Zeus or da Vinci robotic systems, including bariatric surgery.
3) Gynecology: The area of robotic surgery in gynecology is seeing rapid growth and development. The use of the da Vinci surgical system in benign gynecology and gynecologic oncology is included within this context. Robotic surgery has shown efficacy in treating several gynecological conditions, including fibroids, atypical periods, endometriosis, ovarian tumors, pelvic prolapse, and female malignancies. Automated technology enables gynecologists to do surgical procedures such as hysterectomies, myomectomies, and lymph node biopsies. The need for extensive abdominal incisions is effectively eliminated.

Additionally, it has potential use in tubal re-anastomosis, hysterectomies, and ovary resection procedures.

4) Neurosurgery: There are now many stereotactic intervention systems available in the market. The Neuro-Arm, developed by MD Robotics, is recognized as the pioneering surgical robot compatible with magnetic resonance imaging (MRI) technology. Surgical robots have been used in several surgical techniques, including complement-image-guided and radiosurgery.

5) Orthopedics: The ROBODOC system was introduced to the market in 1992 by Integrated Surgical Systems, Inc. Surgical robots have found use in several orthopedic surgical procedures, including complete hip arthroplasty operations such as femur preparation and acetabular cup replacement, knee surgery, and spine surgery.

6) Pediatrics: Surgical robots have been used in a variety of operations, such as tracheoesophageal fistula repair, cholecystectomy, Nissen fundoplication, Morgagni hernia repair, Kasai portoenterostomy, congenital diaphragmatic hernia repair, among others. The first sophisticated computer-assisted robot-enhanced surgical operation in the United States was conducted on January 17, 2002 by doctors at the Children's Hospital of Michigan in Detroit.

7) Radiosurgery: The Cyber-Knife Robotic Radiosurgery System employs image guidance and computer-controlled robotics to treat tumors in various body regions, irrespective of their orientation.

8) Urology: Urology encompasses surgical procedures, such as prostate gland removal for cancer, kidney obstruction repair, bladder abnormality correction, and sick kidney removal, often performed by the da Vinci robot.

18.2.1.2 Rehabilitation Robotics

Rehabilitation refers to the systematic approach to address problems after a stroke. Impaired limbs are well recognized as prevalent consequences of stroke, necessitating the intervention of a qualified therapist to facilitate the rehabilitation process and achieve complete or partial restoration of limb functionality. As a result of the scarcity of therapists and other factors to be considered, scholars have been engaged in creating robots capable of executing the rehabilitation procedure. Over the last two decades, many robots have been developed to assist rehabilitation operations. The domain of rehabilitation robotics is often classified into two distinct areas: therapy robots and aid robots. Furthermore, the field of rehabilitation robotics encompasses several components, such as the advancement of artificial limbs (prosthetics), the implementation of functional neurostimulation (FNS), and the use of technology to diagnose and monitor individuals during activities of daily living (ADLs). Typically, therapeutic robots are used by two primary stakeholders concurrently: individuals with disabilities undergoing treatment and therapists responsible for configuring and overseeing the robot's engagement. Various therapeutic interventions have seen notable advancements *via* the integration of robotic assistance. These include upper- and lower-extremity movement therapy, facilitating communication for children diagnosed with autism, and promoting educational inquiry for children affected by cerebral palsy (CP) or other developmental disorders. A robot has the potential to serve as a viable substitute for a physical or occupational therapist in terms of providing hands-on intervention.

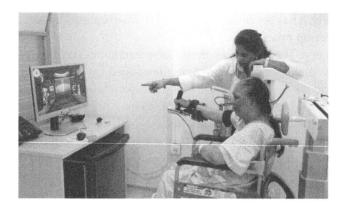

Figure 18.3 Rehabilitation robotics process in Kokilaben Hospital, Mumbai, India.

Figure 18.3 demonstrates the use of rehabilitation robotics process. There are several factors that support this such as:

a) Once appropriately configured, an automated exercise machine can consistently administer therapy for extended durations without experiencing fatigue.

b) The robot's sensors can assess the patient's exertion and objectively quantify any improvements in functionality that may have transpired, potentially surpassing the limitations of current clinical measurement scales. This measurement aspect can serve as a significant motivation for individuals to persist with their therapy.

c) The robot may be able to involve the patient in therapeutic exercises beyond the scope of a human therapist, such as amplifying movement errors to elicit adaptive responses.

18.2.1.2.1   Structural Approach in Rehabilitation Robots

Rehabilitation robots may be categorized as end-effectors and exoskeleton robots [45]. End-effectors refer to uncomplicated robotic devices with a moveable handle at the distal end. Patients can affix their hands to this handle and track a predetermined trajectory [46]. This kind of robot is distinguished by its capacity to adjust to various sizes and motions, as necessitated by the rehabilitation process [47]. One limitation of end-effector robots is their inability to perform rotational movements, rendering them unsuitable for pronation and supination motions. In recent times, there has been a development of end-effectors that provide bilateral rehabilitation training. This training approach involves the affected limb mirroring the movements of the unimpaired limb in a synchronous manner. Several studies have shown that bilateral rehabilitation stimulates the affected hemisphere *via* the synchronization of movements on both the left and right sides of the body.

Exoskeleton robots are distinguished using a splint or bionic framework to encase the limb [48]. Exoskeleton robots use torque calculations for individual joints to regulate and govern limb motions [49]. Exoskeletons need a reduced operational space when contrasted with end-effector robots. It includes limb joint axes for precise and targeted movements. Moreover, using exoskeleton robots for bilateral rehabilitation has challenges since the exoskeleton designed for the right leg cannot be effectively employed for the left limb.

Furthermore, the cost of developing separate exoskeleton robots for both the right and left limbs to facilitate bilateral rehabilitation training is a significant factor to consider.

18.2.1.2.2 Examples of Rehabilitation Robots

The following are some of the prominent examples of rehabilitation robots:

1) MIT-MANUS: The Massachusetts Institute of Technology has created a robotic workstation, MIT-MANUS, designed to rehabilitate upper limbs in individuals who have experienced a stroke [50]. It is an interactive workstation that requires patients to interact visually with a personal computer game to execute specified movements [51]. It offers five degrees of freedom, namely two degrees of freedom for translation in the elbow and forearm. These degrees of freedom are represented by flexion/extension for the elbow and pronation/supination for the forearm. Furthermore, the wrist possesses three degrees of mobility: flexion/extension, pronation/supination, and abduction/adduction. Utilizing a magnet safety lock facilitates the secure attachment of the patient's hand to the device, offering a straightforward method for releasing the patient from the device. In addition, it should be noted that the MANUS workstation offers low torques. In order to ensure the safety of the patient, therapy sessions must be supervised by a qualified therapist.

2) MIME: The Mirror Image Movement Enabler (MIME) is a robotic system based on the CPM (continuous passive motion) technique. It comprises a wheelchair and a table that can be adjusted in height. The patient is seated in the wheelchair and places their damaged limb on the table [52]. The limb that has been impacted is secured into a forearm splint, which limits the range of motion of both the wrist and hand. MIME encompasses three distinct treatment modes, namely passive, active-assistive/active-resistive, and bilateral modes. Furthermore, the utilization of MIME is prevalent in both the passive and active-resistive modes. The robot moves the limb towards the target in a precise trajectory in the passive mode. The active-resistive mode is characterized by restricting limb motions along a specified trajectory by applying a viscous resistance. MIME is employed to enhance muscular strength and the range of motion in the limbs.

3) L-EXOS: The L-EXOS system is designed with a primary emphasis on delivering repetitive movements and offering a concurrent assessment of therapeutic advancement [53]. The L-EXOS system integrates the use of augmented reality to guide patients in order to achieve a predetermined trajectory [54]. Regarding safety considerations, the L-EXOS system offers a rotational velocity of 10 revolutions per minute (rpm), with a maximum torque limit of 120 Newton meters (Nm). Furthermore, it offers five degrees of freedom, with each movement equipped with a corresponding sensor.

4) T-Wrex: The T-Wrex or the therapeutic Wilmington exoskeleton is a robotic active upper limb rehabilitation device. It possesses five degrees of freedom [55]. This program is designed to cater to persons who experience pronounced arm weakness, offering a comprehensive intensive exercise regimen. The T-Wrex incorporates gravity correction, sometimes known as antigravity, to

enable the entire arm to feel a sensation of weightlessness in a spatial environment. Furthermore, the T-Wrex offers a substantial three-dimensional range of motion, thereby simulating the natural movements of the upper limbs. It is comprised of two links that are affixed to the forearm and upper arm. The robot incorporates position sensors and unique grip sensors to enhance safety. These sensors facilitate the monitoring of upper limb movement.

5) ARMin: The ARMin robot is designed for upper limb rehabilitation and offers seven degrees of freedom (DOF). These include three-dimensional shoulder rotations, elbow flexion/extension, forearm supination/pronation, wrist flexion/extension, and the ability to assist with hand closing and opening [56]. The ARMin system comprises a chair and a robotic arm. In this setup, the patient, while seated, connects his hand to the robotic arm and changes its length to achieve the optimal position. The ARMin device incorporates a three-tier safety system consisting of multiple sensors that collectively identify and address potential malfunctions. Additionally, it should be noted that the ARMin device is designed without any sharp edges, ensuring the safety of its users. Furthermore, the device's joints are specifically engineered to operate within a human limb's natural range of motion.

18.2.1.3   Socially Assistive Robotics

The field of socially assistive robotics involves the development of robotic systems that demonstrate social attributes that closely resemble those observed in humans. Furthermore, the discipline has placed significant focus on utilizing the robot's physical form to develop communication and contact with people in a socially immersive manner, in addition to its core functions of autonomous movement and action. One of the essential aspects of this field involves the study of socially assistive robotics, which prioritizes assisting human users through social interaction rather than physical means [57]. The domain of human–robot interaction under the framework of socially assistive robotics applications spans a range of scholarly disciplines, including robotics, healthcare, the social and psychological sciences, and neuroscience.

In contrast to interactive robotics, which primarily serves entertainment purposes and facilitates fundamental interactions with human users, assistive robots are designed to aid those with specific requirements in their daily activities. Assistive robots, encompassing socially assistive robotics as well, hold the capacity to augment the overall well-being of various user demographics. The demographic cohorts being examined include elderly individuals, individuals with physical impairments, those undergoing rehabilitation therapy, and individuals with intellectual disabilities and behavioral and social challenges. However, these systems pose a new challenge in effectively meeting the demands of the entire population while simultaneously accommodating the distinct requirements of everyone within the designated recipient group. Figure 18.4 displays the socially assistive robotics designed by NAO Robots.

18.2.1.3.1   Key Determinants of Socially Assistive Robotics
The following points highlight the key determinants of socially assistive robotics:

1) Social conduct: Social conduct is crucial in assisting individuals, including those with special needs. The physical manifestation of the robot, including

Figure 18.4 Socially assistive robotics made by NAO robots.

its presence, look, and shared context with the user, plays a crucial role in establishing a sustained and captivating interaction with the user. It is postulated that implementing an adaptive, dependable, and user-friendly hands-off robot can establish a sophisticated and comprehensive human–robot relationship. This robot would be capable of delivering a personalized therapeutic protocol that engages and motivates participants in many settings, including schools, clinics, and, eventually, homes. In order to achieve this objective, such robots must possess interaction skills and capabilities geared toward human beings. Additionally, they should demonstrate proper social conduct that is contextually relevant to the user. Furthermore, these robots should prioritize the user's needs and goals by directing their attention and communication toward accomplishing specified objectives.

2) Embodiment: The physical manifestation of the robot is a crucial factor in determining its efficacy in assisting. The concept of embodiment encompasses not only the tangible aspects of physical existence but also individuals' active engagement and involvement. The concept of embodiment holds significant importance within Maurice Merleau-Ponty's phenomenology of perception [58].

The work identifies three distinct interpretations of embodiment, which are as follows:

a) The term "embodiment" pertains to the tangible representation of an individual human entity.

b) The concept of human movement involves the acquisition of body capacities and contextual responses.

c) Cultural competence refers to the comprehensive cultural skills, talents, and knowledge that individuals gain *via* immersion in a certain ethnic setting.

3) Personality: It serves as a significant factor in shaping human social connections. Numerous studies have demonstrated a clear correlation between personality traits and behavioral patterns [59]. According to personality psychologists, the behaviors that hold the utmost significance exhibit the following characteristics:

a) They are very prevalent in an individual's lifestyle, demonstrating a certain level of consistency across various settings.
b) They remain relatively constant in an individual's lifestyle over time.
c) They serve as indicators of the person's distinctiveness or uniqueness.

Therefore, personality is crucial in human–robot interaction (HRI) [60]. The motivation in building the personality of robots is driven by the desire to create companions and assistants for people, modeled after our understanding of ourselves. There has been a contention that the personality of a robot should align with that of its human user. Although a universally accepted definition of personality does not exist, one definition, derived from scholarly sources, characterizes personality as the composite arrangement of an individual's character, conduct, temperament, emotions, and mental attributes that exhibit stability across many contexts and endure through time.

4) Empathy: The construct of empathy is a thought-provoking concept that elicits discussions regarding its measurement within various contexts, as well as its possible implications in the field of robotics. The field of socially assistive robots holds excellent importance in patient-focused therapy due to its ability to facilitate understanding an individual's internal experiences and promote a mutual understanding of sentiments. Empathy's significance in therapeutic enhancement is evident, as it serves as a mediator for pro-social conduct. According to Rogers [61], it was demonstrated that their therapist provided patients with empathy, authenticity, and unconditional positive regard and had a more rapid recovery. Hence, it is postulated that the presence of empathy may positively impact patient satisfaction and motivation to recover, as well as improve adherence to therapy programs within the patient-therapist dynamic. Empathy is not a capacity that machines possess. Nevertheless, it is feasible to develop robots exhibiting explicit empathy manifestations. To effectively simulate empathy, a robotic system must possess the ability to identify the user's emotional state, engage in communication with individuals, exhibit emotional responses, and demonstrate the capacity for adopting different perspectives. The ideal manifestation involves the ability to comprehend and replicate the emotional states of individuals and exhibit responsive behavior that suggests susceptibility to the influence of these emotions. Individuals undergo emotional experiences and subsequently convey these emotions through interpersonal communication.

5) Engagement: Engagement is crucial in socially assistive robotics since it establishes and maintains a shared connection between an individual and the robotic entity. For a robot to engage in social interactions, it must understand the presence of humans and recognize when individuals express a willingness to engage in interaction. This assumption is based on human-human interactions serving as a fundamental framework. In order to facilitate a seamless engagement, the

robot must possess the capability to capture attention proactively. These objectives can be accomplished through sustained eye contact or directing one's gaze toward the individual while maintaining an appropriate physical distance that promotes effective social engagement. The utilization of nonverbal as well as verbal exchanges is crucial in developing a meaningful and captivating interaction. The robot should be able to communicate with the user through both spoken and nonverbal modalities—for instance, during the user's speech, the robot should exhibit signs of active involvement or disinterest in the dialogue and appropriately convey agreement or disagreement through nodding or displaying displeasure. Research studies had been conducted on the utilization of essential agents and robots in order to enhance engagement [62, 63].

6) Adaptation: The acquisition of communication abilities and the capacity to adapt our behavior based on received information has been a crucial factor in human evolution. Designing machines that possess sophisticated abilities on par with those exhibited in people has proven exceptionally difficult. In socially assistive robotics, the learning process must effectively address immediate differences arising from individual variances and enduring adaptations that facilitate engaging interactions over extended periods, ranging from months to even years. The automated device should be able to obtain information from the user and adapt its operations based on the user's traits, feelings, and preferences, enabling customized interaction. There is a need for further scholarly investigation that examines explicitly the educational dimensions of extended social engagement. A multitude of learning techniques for interaction between people and robots have been proposed in academic literature. However, these methodologies must consider the user's profile, preferences, and personality. Considering the interaction of socially assistive robots with susceptible humans, the robot must exhibit the capacity to engage in discerning contemplation about the distinct needs and constraints of the user.

7) Transfer: One of the key goals in the domain of socially helpful robotics is to provide a significant and captivating interaction for the user during their engagement with the robot and to facilitate enduring modifications in behavior—for example, it is advantageous for a child who has been diagnosed with autism to participate in social activities with a robot in order to develop and improve their social skills, as well as to see the transfer of these skills to their relationships with colleagues and families. In a similar vein, the goal is for robots utilized in the context of physical therapy for individuals recovering from stroke to not only enhance and oversee the therapy process but also to exert a lasting impact on the patient's inclination and motivation to engage in physical therapy, independent of the robot's reminders. Moreover, the objective is for senior adults who participate in social narrative sessions with a robot to have a heightened inclination to interact with their friends and family members. While research is now available regarding optimizing the transfer of abilities and changing behavior through human-human interactions, the most optimal method for organizing interactions between robots and humans to enhance skill transfer has yet to be established. Measuring success for various forms of socially assistive technology often hinges upon

transferring skills and behaviors in numerous aspects. To effectively illustrate this transfer, it is necessary to conduct longitudinal research, including persons regularly in contact with robotic systems. Conducting long-term user investigations involving research prototype devices entails encountering substantial as well as intricate technical challenges.

18.2.1.4   *Non-Medical Robots*

In contrast to the robots discussed earlier in preceding sections, other than medical robots find application inside the medical industry. However, they do not directly participate in patient treatment. Healthcare organizations employ robotic systems for routine functions, such as logistics management, cleaning operations, patient counseling, and vital signs measurement [64]. Certain occupations, such as cleaning, exhibit the capacity to be executed by domestic robots, service robots, or adapted iterations of mobile assistive robots [65]. Robots with specific designs are required for various additional tasks, such as decontamination [66], intra-hospital patient transportation [67], transferring patients between a bed and a wheelchair [68], medication dispensing, and assisting with medical interventions. This project constitutes an integral part of the continuous process of digitizing hospital operations.

The importance of healthcare robots has been heightened during the corona-virus pandemic due to the urgent necessity to minimize face-to-face encounters, especially inside hospital environments where the danger of infection is elevated. The rapid spread of the pandemic and the limited availability of medical professionals have accelerated the adoption of automation inside hospital settings. This is due to the ability of robots to perform duties that have historically been performed by human healthcare workers, while unaffected by the risk of infection and fatigue. Implementing robotic systems in healthcare facilities was initiated during the pandemic's initial stages to mitigate the coronavirus's transmission. The rise in demand has resulted in the emergence of novel airborne and terrestrial robots designed to clean buildings and streets. Furthermore, a notable advancement has emerged in non-contact temperature sensing devices and robotic systems, which furnish persons with crucial information about COVID-19 and preventive procedures, alongside several other innovative solutions.

18.3   Pros of Robotics in Healthcare

The following highlights various pros of robotics in healthcare:

1) Exclusive patient care: Socially assistive robots (SARs) have emerged as a product of the advancement in artificial intelligence and the integration of physically supported technologies. Socially assistive robots (SARs) possess emotional intelligence, enabling them to provide personalized and exceptional patient care. These machines are equipped to engage in emotional communication with patients, fostering a deeper connection and understanding. Various reaction categories can be identified, namely interaction, communication, friendship, and emotional attachment [69]. The prudent utilization of robotics within the healthcare system guarantees optimal patient care, flawless procedures in medical environments, and a safe environment for patients

and healthcare practitioners. The utilization of autonomous robots in healthcare significantly reduces the likelihood of human error and carelessness. The health and social care sector have seen significant transformation due to the emergence and ongoing advancement of SARs.

2) Protecting working conditions: Robots have the potential to effectively fulfill the responsibilities traditionally carried out by nurses, ward boys, receptionists, and other healthcare staff. Various categories of robots, such as receptionist robots, medical servers, and nurse robots, have demonstrated remarkable efficiency in executing the abovementioned responsibilities [70]. Automated mobile robots (AMRs) find extensive application in healthcare settings, where they perform various tasks, including distributing medical supplies and linen, collecting patient data, and providing food and water to hospitalized individuals. These robots play a crucial role in safeguarding the well-being of medical professionals by minimizing their exposure to pathogens, thereby effectively mitigating the risk of infection transmission. Hence, these robotic systems were extensively employed throughout the current COVID-19 epidemic. During the COVID-19 pandemic, commendable efforts were made in pandemic preparedness, screening, contact tracing, disinfection, and the enforcement of quarantine and social distancing measures. The Arogya Setu application, designed by the National Informatics Centre and the Ministry of Information Technology, has emerged as a valuable tool in effectively handling the COVID-19 crisis. Social robots perform physically demanding tasks such as lifting heavy beds or transporting patients, mitigating the physical burden on healthcare personnel.

3) Organized operational task: Automated mobile robots (AMRs) facilitate the standardization of routine tasks, alleviate the physical strain on healthcare professionals, and ensure the implementation of more accurate protocols. These robotic systems have the potential to mitigate the issue of human shortages, maintain a comprehensive record of activities, and ensure timely placement of orders. They assure the availability of medicines and other

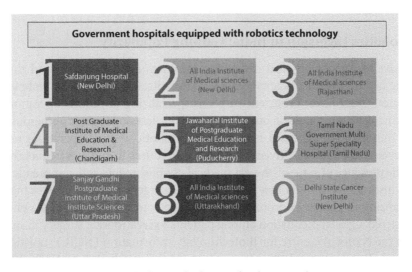

Figure 18.5 List of government hospitals that used robotic technology in India.

equipment on time. Automated robots facilitate the expeditious cleaning and sanitization of rooms, ensuring their prompt readiness for arriving patients. This enables healthcare workers to allocate their time towards other crucial patient-related tasks. Artificial intelligence can be effectively employed in utilizing robots to diagnose various ailments. Radiologist robots, possessing computational imaging skills, diagnose medical conditions using artificial intelligence through deep learning techniques. Robots are utilized in the medical field to perform diagnostic procedures such as MRIs and X-rays, providing significant benefits to healthcare professionals by safeguarding them against the hazardous radiations employed in these processes.

18.4   Insights Into Robotic Surgeries in India

The emergence of automated surgery inside India's medical system has yielded many noteworthy breakthroughs. The increasing prevalence of robotic surgery in India has garnered considerable attention from international patients. As of January 2023, India has witnessed the establishment of over 70 robotic installations across various governmental and private institutions, accompanied by a cohort of over 500 surgeons who have received specialized training in this domain. At present, there are a total of nine large-scale government-operated hospitals that are utilized for various medical purposes, as listed in Figure 18.5.

In addition to government-funded universities and medical colleges, India is home to many private training institutes that offer training courses, fellowships, and observer-ships in robotic surgery. In addition to structured training sessions, junior professors and resident's doctors may receive informal training in robotic-assisted procedures. In the current setting, it is seen that consultants engage in specialized training through robotic surgery fellowships, enabling them to transfer from conducting open surgical procedures to those that are supported by robotic technology. As the transition from open surgery to robotics occurs, junior professors, fellows, and residents' doctor concurrently acquire skills, techniques, and valuable experience. This phenomenon exemplifies the widespread endorsement of robotic-assisted surgery from the general populace and governmental and private entities.

18.4.1   Robotics Inclusion in India: Gaining Popularity

The imperative to uphold physical distancing measures amidst and beyond the COVID-19 pandemic has prompted Indian surgeons and medical institutions to embrace robotic-assisted surgical procedures. Proficient surgeons specializing in robotic operations in India have gained increasing recognition outside national borders due to their numerous successful treatments. Although the expenses associated with robotic-assisted operations remain considerably elevated, the cost-effectiveness of such procedures in India is frequently noteworthy due to the presence of state-of-the-art medical establishments and commendable success rates. Many institutions in India that provide robotic surgery typically possess highly skilled teams specializing in clinical coordination and patient care. The convergence of these variables has fostered a global inclination among patients to seek robotic surgery in India.

Based on the National Centre for Biotechnology Information (NCBI) statistics, the success rate of robotic surgery in India ranges from approximately 94% to 100%. Robotic surgery exhibits a significantly reduced incidence of complications compared to conventional

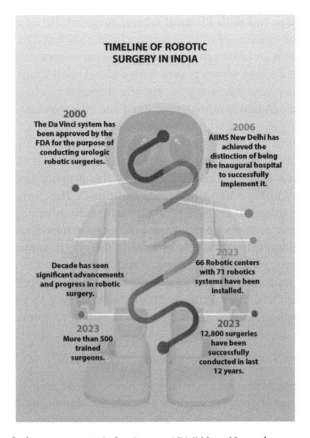

Figure 18.6 Timeline of robotic surgery in India. Source: APAC News Network.

surgical methods. Additionally, there has been a decrease in the duration of the surgery. Robotic surgery additionally guarantees a notable reduction in blood loss, contributing to increased surgical success rates. According to the standards set forth by the Insurance Regulatory and Development Authority of India (IRDAI), wellness policies in India must provide coverage for robotic surgery operations. Health insurance companies typically cover various aspects of robotic surgery, encompassing expenses related to hospitalization, surgical procedures, physician fees, nursing care, intensive care unit charges, pre-hospitalization, and post-hospitalization costs, and occasionally even ambulance services.

Robotic surgery has yielded significant advantages in the practical and accurate execution of intricate medical procedures. Numerous diseases exhibit intricate pathophysiological mechanisms, hence necessitating the utilization of robotic surgery to enhance surgical precision, dexterity, and maneuverability for the operating surgeon. Therefore, in contemporary times, many surgeons in India are increasingly using robotic-assisted surgical procedures to get optimal outcomes. The efficacy of a surgical intervention relies on various elements, such as the number of situations, the standardization of operations, and recurrent exposure to an identical illness. These elements contribute to the reinforcement of rigorous management protocols and the optimization of resource utilization cost-efficiently. The exponential growth of India's population has emerged as a significant societal issue, leading to a single surgeon being responsible for treating an exceedingly large number of patients. This phenomenon might be seen as a fortuitous occurrence since it facilitates the acquisition of knowledge and skills for most robotic surgeons, hence affording them many learning prospects. The timeline of robotic surgery in India is listed in Figure 18.6.

Several establishments in India offer training programs in robotic procedures, with the support and expertise of experts from government-funded institutions and private medical centers. The "Vattikuti 1-year fellowship" in robotic surgeries has been designed to incorporate a training approach that is more streamlined and effective, hence offering improved opportunities for young surgeons who aspire to specialize in this field. Furthermore, the da Vinci Basic Surgical Skills Training Centre in India has been initiated to offer supplementary training prospects. Advancements in robotic technology have extended the age at which surgeons may effectively utilize surgical capabilities. This is mainly attributed to improvements in ergonomics, motion scaling, and tremor filtration. The demand for surgeons in a country like India is consistently rising, making it particularly advantageous. Surgeons with exceptional laparoscopic abilities frequently exhibit a comparative advantage and experience a reduced learning period when transitioning to robotic surgery. Laparoscopy has gained significant prominence and widespread adoption within the medical community in India. Hence, the transition from a laparoscopic surgeon to a robotic surgeon is distinguished by a smooth and uninterrupted progression, leading to a decrease in the time required to acquire proficiency and an acceleration in skill development.

18.4.1.1 Conditions Treated by Robotic Surgeries in India

The incorporation of machine learning in surgery has been determined to benefit the skilled and precise performance of complex medical procedures. Numerous diseases exhibit intricate processes. In instances of this nature, the utilization of robotic surgery proves to be quite advantageous for surgeons, as it enables them to maintain a high degree of flexibility and control. Therefore, in contemporary times, a significant number of medical practitioners in India are increasingly adopting robotic-assisted surgical procedures in order to get optimal outcomes. The conditions treated by robotic surgeries in India are listed in Figure 18.7.

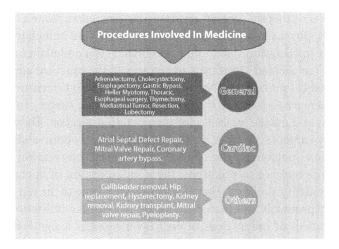

Figure 18.7 Procedures involved in robotic surgeries.

18.4.2 Strengths of Robotic Surgeries in India

The following points highlight the diverse strengths of robotic surgeries in India:

1) Patient volumes: The efficacy of a surgical program relies on several critical factors, including a significant number of cases, the uniformity of surgical techniques, and recurrent exposure to the same condition. These elements contribute to establishing rigorous management protocols and ensure the efficient utilization of resources in a fiscally responsible manner. The increasing population of India is a noteworthy social concern as it results in a considerable burden on individual surgeons due to the higher number of patients requiring medical attention. The lucky occurrence leads to accelerated skills development for most robotic surgeons, presenting several learning opportunities.

2) Expanding GDP: India is currently ranked as the fifth largest economy globally regarding nominal GDP and holds the third position in purchasing power parity (PPP). The healthcare sector in India has had significant growth, emerging as one of the leading industries in the country. It is projected that the healthcare market will witness a threefold increase by the year 2023. The observed expansion might be ascribed to the escalating incidence of lifestyle-related ailments and the growing demand for cost-effective medical treatment mechanisms. The current economic growth trajectory and the healthcare industry's rapid expansion have led to a decentralization of institutions. This decentralization is anticipated to facilitate the establishment of additional hospitals that offer robotic procedures, thus reducing treatment costs.

3) Highly skilled laparoscopic surgeons: The necessity of possessing laparoscopic experience prior to engaging in robotic surgery is a subject of ongoing debate. Nevertheless, it is indisputable that surgeons possessing exceptional laparoscopic abilities would have a distinct advantage and a reduced learning period. Laparoscopy has gained significant prominence and widespread adoption within the medical community in India. Hence, a smooth and uninterrupted process distinguishes the shift from a laparoscopic surgeon to a robotic surgeon, leading to a decreased learning curve and accelerated acquisition of skills.

4) Instruction and supervision: In India, several institutes presently offer training programs in robotic surgery. These programs are conducted by knowledgeable consultants from government institutions and privately owned hospitals. The implementation of the "Vattikuti 1-year fellowship" in robotic surgery has introduced a training strategy that is more efficient, hence offering improved opportunities for young surgeons who aspire to specialize in this field. Moreover, the development of the da Vinci Basic Surgical Skills Training Centre in India seeks to provide additional training opportunities.

5) Increased insurance: The National Health Protection Scheme, known as "Ayushman Bharat," was introduced in the General Budget 2018–2019. Its primary objective is to extend health coverage to over 100 million economically disadvantaged and vulnerable households. The introduction of this insurance policy will enhance accessibility to robotic surgery for a broader range of patients, particularly those belonging to lower-income demographics, hence facilitating their receipt of associated advantages.

18.4.3   Opportunities for Robotic Surgeries in India

The following points enlighten the various opportunities for robotic surgeries in India:

1) Expansional scope: There is potential for further development in robotic surgery in India as other medical specialties gradually recognize its value. The multidisciplinary application of this technology offers the possibility of reducing related maintenance expenses, enhancing its cost-effectiveness.

2) Medical tourism: India has become a highly desirable destination for patients worldwide due to highly skilled physicians and surgeons offering health-care services comparable to those in Western nations. This, combined with renowned Indian hospitality, cost-effectiveness, and minimal waiting periods, contributes to the country's appeal. Now, India's medical tourism sector has reached a valuation of 2 billion USD. The presence of robotic surgery capabilities has the potential to appeal to a more significant number of international patients who may necessitate not only robotic operations but also other surgical interventions that do not include robotics.

3) Newer robotic systems: There are ongoing developments in the field of robotic systems that are specifically designed for therapeutic purposes. These systems facilitate the emergence of a competitive market for intuitive surgery, perhaps reducing initial investment and maintenance costs. Consequently, this could enhance these systems' affordability and widespread adoption among the Indian populace.

18.4.4   Real-Time Success Stories of Robotics Utilization in Indian Hospitals

The following are various examples of success stories of real-time usage of robotics in Indian hospitals:

1) Total knee replacement using the CUVIS Joint Robotic System at Artemis Hospital: This system enables surgeons to customize 3D CT imaging for operation planning which Artemis Hospital recently bought in Gurugram. The technology is easy to use and gives surgeons freedom with various cutting possibilities. The techniques used demonstrate high precision, little invasiveness, and a strong emphasis on patient safety. It enables surgeons to insert implants precisely, resulting in a more natural sensation following surgery. Patients benefit from the reduced risk of injury to adjacent tissues and the less probability of complications after surgery performed using robotics. As a result of the use of smaller incisions, patients experience lower blood loss and a notable decrease in pain. Since the implants last longer, patients' knees perform better over the long run and have a higher quality of life.

2) Introduction of Versius Robotic Surgical System in AIMS Hospital: The Asian Institute of Medical Sciences (AIMS) in Faridabad has just incorporated the Versius Robotic Surgical System, therefore introducing the first 3D Advanced Minimal Access Surgical Robot in the vicinity. The stated sophisticated surgical robot has the capacity to significantly transform the domains of cancer and urology, with a specific emphasis on kidney nephrectomy. Moreover, this technology

exhibits significant promise in augmenting thoracic surgery and many general surgical operations, including, but not limited to, the extraction of gall bladder stones and the careful healing of complex hernias, alongside numerous other intricate surgical interventions. Integrating 3D visualization, artificial intelligence, and machine learning has led to the emergence of a highly advanced and efficient robotic solution. This solution aims to augment surgeons' proficiency by offering increased degrees of accuracy, precision, and safety. Furthermore, it offers enhanced surgical treatments, particularly in anatomical areas that are often difficult to access. According to Dr. N. K. Pandey, the Chairman and Managing Director of Asian Hospital, the utilization of advanced robotic surgery in the upcoming generation offers numerous benefits. These advantages include heightened precision leading to decreased tissue trauma, minimal blood loss, reduced risk of infection and complications, improved mobility, enhanced early functional recovery, and shorter post-surgical hospital stays for patients.

3) Installation of a robotic system for spine surgery at BLK Max Super Specialty Hospital: The BLK-Max Super Specialty Hospital has recently included an advanced integrated robotic system tailored explicitly for spine surgery. Artificial intelligence is used to graphically depict the anatomical structure of the spine inside the complicated framework of surgical operations. Robotic surgical treatments benefit from data integration, making them beneficial for spine surgeries. This allows medical practitioners to customize the surgical approach to accommodate each patient's unique requirements. The integrated spinal robot has undergone training to navigate and execute surgical operations inside the spinal area proficiently. Moreover, incorporating surgical navigation and guidance inside this robotic system offers significant advantages for spine surgeons. The technology has been purposefully developed to optimize procedural efficiency. The use of robotic surgery augments the objectivity of the approach *via* its increased dependence on predetermined plans. Dr. Puneet Girdhar, Senior Director, and Head of Orthopedic Spine Surgery at BLK Max Super Specialty Hospital, asserts that robotic spinal procedures have become the preferred method in modern medical practice for treatments requiring high levels of precision and accuracy. In addition to offering guarantees of positive outcomes, these entities strive to minimize complications throughout the surgical process.

4) Intuitive deployed its 100th surgical system at the UN Mehta Institute of Cardiology: Intuitive, a corporation in Sunnyvale, California, has just completed the deployment of its 100th robotic-assisted surgical system inside the borders of India. As mentioned earlier, the achievement was accomplished at the UN Mehta Institute of Cardiology located in Ahmedabad. Intuitive's robotic projects are primarily deployed inside notable private and government hospitals, medical education institutes, and state government medical schools nationwide. Before attaining this recent milestone, Intuitive achieved notable advancements in augmenting minimally invasive healthcare in India *via* advanced robotic technology. A dynamic and ever-evolving ecosystem, including many educational opportunities, services, and solutions, has enabled advancement. The progress of Intuitive's da Vinci technology

may be due to the active involvement of over 800 trained surgeons in its use. Mandeep Kumar, the Vice President and General Manager of Intuitive India, thanked the team for improving patient care outcomes, optimizing patient and care teams' experience, and decreasing the total treatment costs.

5) Arterial bypass surgery in Northern India conducted by Apollo Delhi: The first instance of a fully automated arterial bypass surgery for triple vessel coronary artery disease was occurred at Indraprastha Apollo Hospitals in New Delhi. This groundbreaking achievement represents a noteworthy advancement since it is the foremost technique to be executed in northern India. The surgical procedure was performed under the guidance of a team of highly qualified medical professionals, including Dr. MM Yusuf, a specialist consultant in robotics. According to Dr. MM Yusuf, the person responsible for overseeing the robot-assisted surgery, robotic-assisted coronary artery bypass grafting (CABG) is considered the least intrusive cardiac operation. The collaboration between advanced technology and surgical proficiency constitutes a symbiotic relationship. The use of minimally invasive techniques in medical procedures provides significant short- and long-term advantages. These benefits include reduced incisions, less blood loss, diminished discomfort, accelerated recuperation, and expedited resumption of daily activities. In contrast, open chest surgery has challenges in achieving these outcomes. Total artery bypass surgery is known to have superior long-term outcomes and a reduced probability of requiring further intervention in the future.

6) First gynecology procedure in CARE Hospitals, Hyderabad: The first implementation of the Hugo Robotic-Assisted Surgery (RAS) system for gynecological procedures, including hysterectomy, occurred in Asia-Pacific. This significant milestone was achieved *via* a partnership between the CARE Hospitals Group, based in Hyderabad, and India Medtronic Private Limited (MPL). The milestone therapy was administered by the skilled clinical team of CARE Hospitals, under the supervision of Dr. Manjula Anagani, at their primary hospital in Banjara Hills. The patient, a 46-year-old female, presented with a protracted case of adenomyosis, a medical disorder characterized by the thickening and enlargement of the uterus. The patient had a surgical intervention known as a robotic-assisted complete hysterectomy, during which the uterus afflicted by the condition was extracted using the Hugo Robotic-Assisted Surgery (RAS) system. CARE has achieved the distinction of being the first hospital in the regions of Telangana and Andhra Pradesh to use the novel robotic-assisted surgical system developed by MPL. In reference to the surgical procedure, Dr. Manjula Anagani said: "Utilizing the new RAS system from Medtronic for hysterectomy, which was APAC's first gynecological procedure, is a testimony to our dedication to providing high-end clinical care. It is a proud moment for all our teams, and we look forward to using this innovative robotic system to expand access to the powerful benefits of minimally invasive surgery to more patients."

7) SSI MANTRA launched by Rajiv Gandhi Cancer Institute, Hyderabad: The SSI Mantra (Multi-Arm Novel Tele Robotic Assistance) surgical robotic system, developed by SS Innovations, has been introduced as India's first medical

robotics surgical system. The Rajiv Gandhi Cancer Institute completed its first pilot study on human patients, during which the surgical team successfully performed 18 complex surgeries in urology, gynecology, and general surgery in less than 1 month. The advent of robotic-driven surgery in India can be traced back to its first occurrence in 2001, with further implementations at AIIMS in 2006 and RGCI in 2011. However, it is noteworthy that the current development is the first instance of a fully indigenous robotic surgical system being created in India. According to Dr. Sudhir P. Srivastava, 85 letters of intent have been submitted for the MANTRA project, including submissions from government hospitals. Currently, a total of 72 systems exist, with an additional two systems anticipated to be accessible shortly. Moreover, there are around 500 surgeons who have received the necessary training to conduct surgical procedures using the system mentioned above proficiently.

18.5 Limitations of Robotics in Healthcare

While robotic surgery is considered a significant advancement in modern technology, it has drawbacks. Let us examine the drawbacks associated with this sophisticated surgical technique:

1) Malfunctioning of robots: The various aspects of a robotic surgery procedure are meticulously examined and scrutinized. Properly inspecting all surgical components, including the instruments and the robotic system employed in robotic surgery, is essential. However, it should be noted that machines are artificial entities and, as a result, are susceptible to experiencing malfunctions. Therefore, mechanical malfunction represents a prominent drawback associated with this surgical procedure [71]. In addition, the presence of malfunctioning devices has the potential to induce nerve palsies, tissue damage, and various other complications. These difficulties serve as an impediment to the effective execution of surgical procedures [72].

2) Incorrect data entry: Including a robotic system does not imply the complete substitution of a surgeon in the context of surgical procedures. The system functions as a supportive tool for a surgeon during the execution of a surgical procedure. In order to execute the surgical procedure, medical practitioners must accurately enter the relevant data into the robotic apparatus. If the provided information is inaccurate, it may lead to unforeseen problems. There is a possibility that the robotic system may encounter difficulties in accessing the intended surgical location, perhaps resulting in inadvertent harm to the surrounding anatomical regions. Moreover, it has been shown to result in mortality in a few instances. Therefore, a physician needs to exhibit certainty in such circumstances.

3) Less available centers: While several hospitals are nearby, it is essential to note that just a few may provide comprehensive amenities. Therefore, those in need may encounter challenges like the lack of access to robotic surgery. Hospitals may lack the necessary equipment to conduct technologically sophisticated robotic surgeries effectively.

4) Expense: Robotic technology in surgical procedures, which enables enhanced maneuverability and visualization of intricate anatomical regions, incurs

additional costs and expenditures. Therefore, the financial feasibility of robotic surgery is limited to specific patients' financial capacities. Moreover, using sophisticated machinery and complex methods, including cutting-edge technology, increases costs. Consequently, many individuals are compelled to reconsider their actions due to the increased financial implications of the abovementioned process.

5) Latency during the procedure: The processing and execution of scheduled tasks by a computer need a certain amount of time. Therefore, it is necessary to provide a certain amount of time for a computer to transmit the acquired information to the robotic arms involved in the surgical procedure. The matter or element in question may not have substantial importance or relevance in the context of regular surgical procedures. However, the requirement for expeditious medical interventions, such as heart operations, might elicit considerable concern. Hence, a medical practitioner must exercise caution and adequately anticipate the repercussions of the machine's delay in such circumstances.

18.6   Future Applications of Robotics and AI

The healthcare sector is widely acknowledged as one of the largest and most dynamic sectors on a worldwide scale. This initiative aims to enhance the pace of growth by implementing modernization strategies and innovative ways. In the past, this industry heavily relied on manual procedures that necessitated more time and were susceptible to human mistakes. Recent advancements in machine learning have sparked a significant transformation within the healthcare industry, with a primary objective of developing intelligent computers capable of emulating human-like behaviors and responses. Despite being in its early stages, the use of artificial intelligence and robots in the healthcare industry has promising potential in terms of acceptance and feasibility.

The domains that exhibit a high degree of susceptibility to the rapid integration of artificial intelligence and robots within the healthcare sector include the following:

1) Providing care for the elderly population: According to expectations, the global adult population will see a twofold increase by 2050. The increasing desire for social assistance may be addressed *via* the emergence of socially assistive robot technology. Several vital variables contribute to increased loneliness among older individuals who live alone, including homeownership, marital status, poor health, and a lack of social support networks. According to research done by Wada *et al.* [73], social robots play a significant role in providing healthcare services to older individuals. While many survey participants expressed reluctance in acknowledging the importance of robots assuming their caregiving responsibilities, it became apparent that they harbored similar reservations about human carers. The participants reached a consensus, acknowledging that humanoid robots are equipped with beneficial human attributes, rendering them more dependable than their human counterparts. The utilization of robots in the care of elderly individuals can be regarded as a significant development in the current context, characterized by a growing elderly population

in India due to enhanced healthcare services. This development is particularly noteworthy due to the evident disparity between the demand for trained healthcare professionals in hospitals and the available supply, necessitating alternative solutions. The development of mental commitment robots is underway to treat elderly individuals in hospital settings. These robots can exert psychological, physiological, and social influences on individuals *via* direct physical interaction. The study findings indicated that the emotional state of older individuals saw a positive change as a result of the intervention [74]. Numerous ongoing investigations are being conducted to investigate the potential for enhancing social robots' communicative capacities to provide improved interaction with humans [75]. The acceptance of a robot among older individuals is significantly influenced by its physical appearance. Companion animal robots have shown favorable outcomes in elderly persons who have dementia. Previous studies have shown that companion animal robots with appropriate proportions, weight, and shape have the potential to provide cognitive stimulation to individuals in the elderly population who are impacted by dementia. The use of animal-like robots such as PARO, created by the National Institute of Advanced Industrial Science and Technology (AIST) in Japan, has shown notable benefits in enhancing the cognitive capabilities and sleep patterns of elderly individuals [76].

2) Drug development: The use of artificial intelligence has significant potential in the field of drug development, being a crucial area where its application may prove advantageous. On average, using conventional methodologies, bringing a new pharmaceutical to the market requires 14 years and an expenditure of around 2.6 billion dollars. Artificial intelligence enables the expeditious execution of identical tasks. In 2015, the containment of the Ebola virus outbreak in West Africa and certain European countries was facilitated by using artificial intelligence. This technological advancement played a crucial role in expediting the identification of an appropriate pharmaceutical intervention, effectively preventing the worldwide dissemination of the illness. Moreover, research has shown that using artificial intelligence may expedite the completion of clinical trials for newly discovered drugs. Artificial intelligence may differentiate between cardiotoxic and non-cardiotoxic anticancer drugs. Moreover, it can identify prospective antibiotics from a vast pool of molecules, facilitating the discovery of new antibiotics. Furthermore, these algorithms are now being used to identify compounds that can mitigate the development of antibiotic resistance resulting from microbial resistance [77]. Presently, research is being conducted to investigate the potential contribution of artificial intelligence in addressing the escalating issue of antibiotic resistance [78].

3) AI in diagnosis: According to available sources, an estimated annual mortality rate of approximately 80,000 persons may be attributed to erroneous medical diagnosis. Historically, several instances characterized by insufficient information have led to significant blunders. Artificial intelligence can expedite the sickness prediction and diagnosis process due to its immunity to these limitations. Artificial intelligence is widespread in the field of cancer diagnostics, particularly in cases when the timely identification and forecasting of

the disease are of utmost importance. Many organizations are using artificial intelligence technology to diagnose and detect different cancer forms [79].

4) Rise in clinical trials: Historically, clinical research was characterized by a sluggish pace and limited success rates. Before 2000, only 13.8% of individuals who applied successfully navigated the clinical trial process, including all three stages. AI has significantly reduced the duration of production cycles, leading to notable enhancements in manufacturing expenses and outcomes. The artificial intelligence system assists in managing, storing, and maintaining the ongoing stream of data generated during clinical trials. The analysis of computerized patient data provides an opportunity to extract valuable insights that may be used in future research endeavors, resulting in significant time and cost savings. Consistent monitoring of patients and exchanging data across several computer systems is practical. Additionally, it has high efficacy in regularly monitoring patients and facilitating data sharing across several computer systems. The potential of artificial intelligence to learn autonomously enhances the digital consultation mode [80]. The primary objective of digital consultation is to decrease the need for hospital visits in cases with uncomplicated diseases that may be adequately managed at home with the oversight of a medical professional. In the next era, the most pragmatic and efficacious approach to addressing prevalent maladies would include digital consultation facilitated by artificial intelligence. Integrating artificial intelligence with online healthcare facilities might potentially enhance the accessibility of reliable healthcare practitioners near patients' residences.

5) Remote tracking of patients: The concept of remote patient monitoring has seen rapid advancement *via* AI sensors and advanced predictive analytic techniques. Advanced technologies are being developed, including intelligent implants and smart prostheses, used in post-operative rehabilitation to mitigate potential challenges that may arise after surgical procedures. In addition to personal health monitoring devices such as glucometers and blood pressure monitors, these systems are used. Novel implantable devices monitor patients' physical activities, muscle endurance, and other essential physiological parameters critical to their recuperation rate. Sensors implanted into the muscles or nerves have the potential to provide reliable data on the ongoing healing process of patients. Recently, novel forms of patient monitoring, such as digital pills, nanorobots, and intelligent fabrics, have emerged [81]. Monitoring technology aims to ensure consistent medication delivery, wound care, and treatment of cardiac diseases by monitoring patients' emotional, physiological, and mental states [82]. According to a projection, almost half of the population in developed countries will use wearable devices and other artificial intelligence-driven monitoring systems by 2025. Mobile devices with Wi-Fi or Bluetooth functionalities collect preliminary data and precise details at discharge. Furthermore, the data is securely stored in a cloud-based system and subject to continuous monitoring to mitigate challenges and reduce hospital readmissions. The patient is provided with online assessment and recommendations.

6) AI in nanotechnology: Recently, the field of medicine has benefited from nanotechnology research. Integrating AI technologies with nanotechnology

has shown to be effective in comprehending the many phenomena occurring inside nano systems. Developing nano systems may contribute to the design and development of medications. The topic of nanomedicine has had significant growth and ongoing advancements [83]. Various effective ways have been explored to deliver therapeutic agents in precise and predefined quantities. The development above has significantly contributed to attaining effective outcomes in combination treatment.

7) Prediction of an epidemic outbreak: One notable capability of artificial intelligence in the field of healthcare is its ability to predict the occurrence of an epidemic outbreak. While it cannot exert control on or limit the epidemic, it can provide warnings, enabling timely measures to be made. The system collects, evaluates, and analyses the incoming data using machine learning algorithms or social networking platforms to identify the endemic's central point [84, 85]. The calculating process involves the development of an algorithm that gathers data from several sources, including news bulletins in multiple languages, airline booking information, and reports about plant and animal illnesses. On December 30, 2019, the Blue Dot AI engine identified clusters of a typical pneumonia case emerging in Wuhan, China's wet and dry markets. It promptly notified relevant governmental authorities and other involved parties. The warning signal marked the first indication of the unique COVID-19 pandemic.

18.7   Conclusion and Future Scope

The nascent use of robotics in the healthcare sector has several prospects for medical practitioners, particularly within metropolitan environments. The undeniable importance of artificial intelligence is evident in several domains, including medication development, illness diagnosis, digital medical consultations, robotic surgery, remote patient monitoring, and epidemic breakout prediction. The increasing use of robots in providing care for older individuals has garnered recognition and is progressively gaining acceptance within Indian culture. In the current context, deploying and monitoring health services would be impractical without using artificial intelligence and robots. There are several emerging strategies being developed for the use of robots in the healthcare industry, which have the potential to become more economically advantageous in the following years. However, it is essential to ensure the quality of robotic processes by implementing a rigorous and ongoing monitoring system [86].

The use of artificial intelligence and robots in the healthcare industry in India has the potential to enhance the current state of healthcare services significantly. This approach has effectively addressed the issue of insufficiently trained healthcare workers and the significant shortage of physicians, nurses, and paramedical personnel. The primary obstacle is accessing the nation's geographically isolated areas that need more infrastructure and a dearth of new technology. The significant financial implications associated with using artificial intelligence and robots within the healthcare industry provide a substantial obstacle in providing equitable access to these advancements for marginalized communities. In addition to this, mistakes and mechanical breakdowns can occur due to inadequate maintenance plans, which might lead to severe repercussions. The Indian government must assist organizations in investing in artificial intelligence and promote public–private partnerships

(PPPs) within the AI and health sectors. Policymakers must address the ethical concerns surrounding using artificial intelligence and robots within the healthcare industry to promote their effective implementation. Upon careful examination of the available information and considering the feasibility, it can be argued that there is a need to gradually increase the use of robots in India, starting with well-established and well-equipped hospitals. The viability of this approach is contingent upon its sensible use with the implementation of a standardized reporting and monitoring system.

Future Scope

The healthcare system in India is a very dynamic and complex industry inside the country. There are numerous obstacles in the healthcare sector, including issues related to pricing and accessibility. However, one particularly pressing concern is the need for more medical professionals, such as doctors, and the paucity of skilled nurses, technicians, and enough infrastructure. In India, the availability of quality healthcare services is predominantly concentrated in proximity to tier 1 and tier 2 cities, resulting in an uneven distribution of healthcare accessibility throughout the country regarding physical reach. In addition, the advancement of artificial intelligence will lead to a decrease in the overall cost of healthcare due to enhanced efficiency. The integration of an AI-enabled system has been found to positively impact the reduction of medical errors and the enhancement of productivity. Artificial intelligence has the potential to address the obstacles to accessibility and effectively tackle the challenge by utilizing early detection techniques and afterward making appropriate diagnostic judgments. Moreover, case studies from India in robotic surgeries could be discussed, experiences of Indian doctors and medical practitioners could be compared with the experiences of foreign doctors. The security of patients' data can be investigated while also focusing on social robots, their need for meaningful activities, and a holistic approach. The relationship between robots and emotions may also be discussed. Technical regulations of AI in India and technical and clinical trials of software as a medical device created with the application of AI can be explored.

References

1. Raheem, F. and Iqbal, N., Artificial Intelligence and Machine Learning for the Industrial Internet of Things (IIoT), in: *Industrial Internet of Things*, pp. 1–20, CRC Press, United States, Oxon, London, 2022.
2. Knottnerus, J.A. and Tugwell, P., Evidence-based medicine: Achievements and prospects. *J. Clin. Epidemiol.*, 84, 1–2, 2017.
3. Castaneda, C., Nalley, K., Mannion, C., Bhattacharyya, P., Blake, P., Pecora, A., Goy, A., Suh, K.S., Clinical decision support systems for improving diagnostic accuracy and achieving precision medicine. *J. Clin. Bioinf.*, 5, 4, 2015, https://doi.org/10.1186/s13336-015-0019-3.
4. Pravettoni, G. and Triberti, S., *Il medico 4.0: Come cambia la relazione medico-paziente nell'era delle nuove tecnologie*, Edra, Florida, United States, 2019, September.
5. Sarwar, S., Dent, A., Faust, K., Richer, M., Djuric, U., Van Ommeren, R., Diamandis, P., Physician perspectives on integration of artificial intelligence into diagnostic pathology. *NPJ Digital Med.*, 2, 1, 28, 2019.

6. Liu, C., Liu, X., Wu, F., Xie, M., Feng, Y., Hu, C., Using artificial intelligence (Watson for Oncology) for treatment recommendations amongst Chinese patients with lung cancer: Feasibility study. *J. Med. Internet Res.*, 20, 9, e11087, 2018.

7. Triberti, S., Durosini, I., Pravettoni, G., A "third wheel" effect in health decision making involving artificial entities: A psychological perspective. *Front. Public Health*, 8, 117, 2020.

8. Cirillo, D., Catuara-Solarz, S., Morey, C., Guney, E., Subirats, L., Mellino, S., Mavridis, N., Sex and gender differences and biases in artificial intelligence for biomedicine and healthcare. *NPJ Digital Med.*, 3, 1, 81, 2020.

9. Zhuo, R. and Sun, X., Design of personalized service system for home-based elderly care based on data fusion, in: *Big Data Analytics for Cyber-Physical System in Smart City: BDCPS 2019, 28-29 December 2019, Shenyang, China*, pp. 412–419, Springer, Singapore, 2020.

10. Danso, S.O., Muniz-Terrera, G., Luz, S., Ritchie, C., Application of big data and artificial intelligence technologies to dementia prevention research: An opportunity for low-and-middle-income countries. *J. Glob. Health*, 9, 2, 1–4, 2019.

11. Grzonka, D., Jakóbik, A., Kołodziej, J., Pllana, S., Using a multi-agent system and artificial intelligence for monitoring and improving the cloud performance and security. *Future Gener. Comput. Syst.*, 86, 1106–1117, 2018.

12. Gunning, D. and Aha, D., DARPA's explainable artificial intelligence (XAI) program. *AI Magazine*, 40, 2, 44–58, 2019.

13. Tjoa, E. and Guan, C., A survey on explainable artificial intelligence (xai): Toward medical xai. *IEEE Trans. Neural Networks Learn. Syst.*, 32, 11, 4793–4813, 2020.

14. Pravettoni, G. and Triberti, S., *P5 eHealth: An agenda for the health technologies of the future*, p. 189, Cham, Switzerland, Springer Nature, United States, 2020.

15. Renzi, C., Riva, S., Masiero, M., Pravettoni, G., The choice dilemma in chronic hematological conditions: why choosing is not only a medical issue? A psycho-cognitive perspective. *Crit. Rev. Oncol./Hematol.*, 99, 134–140, 2016.

16. Hendler, J., Mulvehill, A.M., Hendler, J., Mulvehill, A.M., Who Will Be Your Next Doctor?, in: *Social Machines: The Coming Collision of Artificial Intelligence, Social Networking, and Humanity*, pp. 14–28, 2016.

17. Gorini, A., Mazzocco, K., Triberti, S., Sebri, V., Savioni, L., Pravettoni, G., A P5 Approach to m-Health: Design suggestions for advanced mobile health technology. *Front. Psychol.*, 9, 2066, 2018.

18. Davis, F.D., Perceived usefulness, perceived ease of use, and user acceptance of information technology. *MIS Q.*, 13, 3, 319–340, 1989.

19. Longoni, C., Bonezzi, A., Morewedge, C.K., Resistance to medical artificial intelligence. *J. Consum. Res.*, 46, 4, 629–650, 2019.

20. Lewis, D.R., The perils of overconfidence: Why many consumers fail to seek advice when they really should. *J. Financ. Serv. Mark.*, 23, 3, 104–111, 2018.

21. Li, L., Lei, B., Mao, C., Digital twin in smart manufacturing. *J. Ind. Inf. Integr.*, 26, 100289, 2022.

22. Tao, F., Xiao, B., Qi, Q., Cheng, J., Ji, P., Digital twin modeling. *J. Manuf. Syst.*, 64, 372–389, 2022.

23. Mahapatra, B., Krishnamurthi, R., Nayyar, A., Healthcare models and algorithms for privacy and security in healthcare records, in: *Security and privacy of electronic healthcare records: Concepts, paradigms and solutions*, p. 183, 2019.

24. Abouhawwash, M., Tanwar, S., Nayyar, A., Naved, M. (Eds.), *Innovations in Healthcare Informatics: From Interoperability to Data Analysis*, Institution of Engineering and Technology (IET), USA, 2023.

25. Messier, C.F.E., History and future of rehabilitation robotics. *Worcester Polytechnic Institute, An Interactive Qualifying Project Report*, pp. 1–58, Project No. AHH-0901, 2010.

26. Takács, A., Nagy, D. Á., Rudas, I., Haidegger, T., Origins of surgical robotics: From space to the operating room. *Acta Polytech. Hung.*, *13*, 1, 13–30, 2016.

27. Sheng, S., Zhao, T., Wang, X., Comparison of robot-assisted surgery, laparoscopic-assisted surgery, and open surgery for the treatment of colorectal cancer: A network meta-analysis. *Medicine*, *97*, 34, 1–9, 2018.

28. By Product, S. R. M., Service (Instruments and Accessories, Systems, Service), Application (Urological Surgery, Gynecological Surgery, Orthopedic Surgery), End User (Hospitals, Ambulatory Surgery Centers)—Global Forecasts to 2025, 2020. https://www.marketsandmarkets.com/Market-Reports/ambulatory-surgical-center-market-182183086.html

29. Kolpashchikov, D., Gerget, O., Meshcheryakov, R., Robotics in healthcare, in: *Handbook of Artificial Intelligence in Healthcare: Vol 2: Practicalities and Prospects*, pp. 281–306, 2022.

30. Wee, I.J.Y., Kuo, L.J., Ngu, J.C.Y., A systematic review of the true benefit of robotic surgery: Ergonomics. *Int. J. Med. Robot. Comput. Assist. Surg.*, *16*, 4, e2113, 2020.

31. Liss, M.A. and McDougall, E.M., Robotic surgical simulation. *Cancer J.*, *19*, 2, 124–129, 2013.

32. Taylor, R.H., Menciassi, A., Fichtinger, G., Fiorini, P., Dario, P., Medical robotics and computer-integrated surgery, in: *Springer Handbook of Robotics*, pp. 1657–1684, 2016.

33. Emara, A.K., Zhou, G., Klika, A.K., Koroukian, S.M., Schiltz, N.K., Krebs, V.E., Piuzzi, N.S., Robotic-arm–assisted knee arthroplasty associated with favorable in-hospital metrics and exponentially rising adoption compared with manual knee arthroplasty. *JAAOS- J. Am. Acad. Orthop. Surg.*, *29*, 24, e1328–e1342, 2021.

34. Ghodoussi, M., Butner, S.E., Wang, Y., Robotic surgery-the transatlantic case, in: *Proceedings 2002 IEEE International Conference on Robotics and Automation (Cat. No. 02CH37292)*, vol. 2, pp. 1882–1888, IEEE, 2002, May.

35. Freschi, C., Ferrari, V., Melfi, F., Ferrari, M., Mosca, F., Cuschieri, A., Technical review of the da Vinci surgical telemanipulator. *Int. J. Med. Robot. Comput. Assist. Surg.*, *9*, 4, 396–406, 2013.

36. Marayong, P., Li, M., Okamura, A.M., Hager, G.D., Spatial motion constraints: Theory and demonstrations for robot guidance using virtual fixtures, in: *2003 IEEE International Conference on Robotics and Automation (Cat. No. 03CH37422)*, vol. 2, pp. 1954–1959, IEEE, 2003, September.

37. Koukourikis, P. and Rha, K.H., Robotic surgical systems in urology: What is currently available? *Invest. Clin. Urol.*, *62*, 1, 14, 2021.

38. Morelli, L., Guadagni, S., Di Franco, G., Palmeri, M., Di Candio, G., Mosca, F., Da Vinci single site® surgical platform in clinical practice: A systematic review. *Int. J. Med. Robot. Comput. Assist. Surg.*, *12*, 4, 724–734, 2016.

39. Haidegger, T., Benyó, B., Kovács, L., Benyó, Z., Force sensing and force control for surgical robots. *IFAC Proc. Vol.*, *42*, 12, 401–406, 2009.

40. Kalavrytinos, D., Koutserimpas, C., Kalavrytinos, I., Dretakis, K., Expanding robotic arm-assisted knee surgery: The first attempt to use the system for knee revision arthroplasty. *Case Rep. Orthop.*, *2020*, 1–5, 2020.

41. Palep, J.H., Robotic assisted minimally invasive surgery. *J. Minimal Access Surg.*, *5*, 1, 1, 2009.

42. Burgner-Kahrs, J., Rucker, D.C., Choset, H., Continuum robots for medical applications: A survey. *IEEE Trans. Rob.*, *31*, 6, 1261–1280, 2015.

43. Le, H.M., Do, T.N., Phee, S.J., A survey on actuators-driven surgical robots. *Sens. Actuators, A*, *247*, 323–354, 2016.

44. Runciman, M., Darzi, A., Mylonas, G.P., Soft robotics in minimally invasive surgery. *Soft Rob.*, *6*, 4, 423–443, 2019.

45. Nef, T., Quinter, G., Müller, R., Riener, R., Effects of arm training with the robotic device ARMin I in chronic stroke: three single cases. *Neurodegener. Dis.*, *6*, 5–6, 240–251, 2010.

46. Islam, M.R., Spiewak, C., Rahman, M.H., Fareh, R., A brief review on robotic exo-skeletons for upper extremity rehabilitation to find the gap between research porotype and commercial type. *Adv. Robot. Autom*, 6, 2, 10–4172, 2017.

47. Bertani, R., Melegari, C., De Cola, M.C., Bramanti, A., Bramanti, P., Calabrò, R.S., Effects of robot-assisted upper limb rehabilitation in stroke patients: A systematic review with meta-analysis. *Neurol. Sci.*, 38, 1561–1569, 2017.

48. Cesqui, B., Tropea, P., Micera, S., Krebs, H., II, EMG-based pattern recognition approach in post stroke robot-aided rehabilitation: A feasibility study. *J. NeuroEng. Rehabil.*, 10, 1–15, 2013.

49. Głowiński, S. and Błażejewski, A., An exoskeleton arm optimal configuration determination using inverse kinematics and genetic algorithm. *Acta Bioeng. Biomech.*, 21, 1, 45–53, 2019.

50. Hogan, N., Krebs, H., II, Charnnarong, J., Srikrishna, P., Sharon, A., MIT-MANUS: A workstation for manual therapy and training, in: *[1992] Proceedings IEEE International Workshop on Robot and Human Communication*, IEEE, pp. 161–165, 1992.

51. Hesse, S., Schmidt, H., Werner, C., Bardeleben, A., Upper and lower extremity robotic devices for rehabilitation and for studying motor control. *Curr. Opin. Neurol.*, 16, 6, 705–710, 2003.

52. Lum, P.S., Burgar, C.G., Shor, P.C., Majmundar, M., Van der Loos, M., Robot-assisted movement training compared with conventional therapy techniques for the rehabilitation of upper-limb motor function after stroke. *Arch. Phys. Med. Rehabil.*, 83, 7, 952–959, 2002.

53. Dehem, S., Montedoro, V., Edwards, M.G., Detrembleur, C., Stoquart, G., Renders, A., Lejeune, T., Development of a robotic upper limb assessment to configure a serious game. *NeuroRehabilitation*, 44, 2, 263–274, 2019.

54. Frisoli, A., Bergamasco, M., Carboncini, M.C., Rossi, B., Robotic assisted rehabilitation in virtual reality with the L-EXOS, in: *Advanced Technologies in Rehabilitation*, pp. 40–54, IOS Press, Amsterdam, Netherlands, 2009.

55. Rehmat, N., Zuo, J., Meng, W., Liu, Q., Xie, S.Q., Liang, H., Upper limb rehabilitation using robotic exoskeleton systems: A systematic review. *Int. J. Intell. Robot. Appl.*, 2, 5–6, 283–295, 2018.

56. Mihelj, M., Nef, T., Riener, R., ARMin II-7 DoF rehabilitation robot: Mechanics and kinematics, in: *Proceedings 2007 IEEE International Conference on Robotics and Automation*, pp. 4120–4125 IEEE, 2007, April.

57. Feil-Seifer, D. and Matarić, M.J., Socially assistive robotics. *IEEE Rob. Autom. Mag.*, 18, 1, 24–31, 2011.

58. Merleau-Ponty, M., *Phenomenology of perception (C. Smith, trans.)*, Routledge, CRC Press, London, UK, 1962.

59. Christensen, H., II and Pacchierotti, E., Embodied social interaction for robots. *AISB-05*, pp. 40–45, 2005.

60. Nakajima, H., Yamada, R., Brave, S., Morishima, Y., Nass, C., Kawaji, S., The functionality of human-machine collaboration systems-mind model and social behavior, in: *SMC'03 Conference Proceedings. 2003 IEEE International Conference on Systems, Man and Cybernetics. Conference Theme-System Security and Assurance (Cat. No. 03CH37483)*, vol. 3, pp. 2381–2387, IEEE, 2003, October.

61. Rogers, C.R., Empathic: An unappreciated way of being. *J. Couns. Psychol.*, 5, 2, 2–10, 1975.

62. Sidner, C.L. and Dzikovska, M., A first experiment in engagement for human-robot interaction in hosting activities, in: *Advances in Natural Multimodal Dialogue Systems*, pp. 55–76, 2005.

63. Michalowski, M.P., Sabanovic, S., Simmons, R., A spatial model of engagement for a social robot, in: *9th IEEE International Workshop on Advanced Motion Control, 2006*, pp. 762–767 IEEE, 2006, March.

64. Khan, Z.H., Siddique, A., Lee, C.W., Robotics utilization for healthcare digitization in global COVID-19 management. *Int. J. Environ. Res. Public Health*, 17, 11, 3819, 2020.

65. Gupta, A., Singh, A., Bharadwaj, D., Mondal, A.K., Humans and robots: A mutually inclusive relationship in a contagious world. *Int. J. Autom. Comput.*, *18*, 185–203, 2021.

66. Begić, A., Application of service robots for disinfection in medical institutions, in: *Advanced Technologies, Systems, and Applications II: Proceedings of the International Symposium on Innovative and Interdisciplinary Applications of Advanced Technologies (IAT)*, pp. 1056–1065, Springer International Publishing, Germany, Cham, Switzerland, 2018.

67. Wang, C., Savkin, A.V., Clout, R., Nguyen, H.T., An intelligent robotic hospital bed for safe transportation of critical neurosurgery patients along crowded hospital corridors. *IEEE Trans. Neural Syst. Rehabil. Eng.*, *23*, 5, 744–754, 2014.

68. Mukai, T., Hirano, S., Nakashima, H., Kato, Y., Sakaida, Y., Guo, S., Hosoe, S., Development of a nursing-care assistant robot RIBA that can lift a human in its arms, in: *2010 IEEE/RSJ International Conference on Intelligent Robots and Systems*, IEEE, pp. 5996–6001, 2010, October.

69. Bora, G.S., Narain, T.A., Sharma, A.P., Mavuduru, R.S., Devana, S.K., Singh, S.K., Mandal, A.K., Robot-assisted surgery in India: A SWOT analysis. *Indian J. Urol.: IJU: J. Urological Soc. India*, *36*, 1, 1, 2020.

70. Raje, S., Reddy, N., Jerbi, H., Randhawa, P., Tsaramirsis, G., Shrivas, N.V., Piromalis, D., Applications of healthcare robots in combating the COVID-19 pandemic. *Appl. Bionics Biomech.*, *2021*, 1–9, 2021.

71. Abdi, J., Al-Hindawi, A., Ng, T., Vizcaychipi, M.P., Scoping review on the use of socially assistive robot technology in elderly care. *BMJ Open*, 8, 2, e018815, 2018.

72. Ilmudeen, A. and Nayyar, A., Novel Designs of Smart Healthcare Systems: Technologies, Architecture, and Applications, in: *Machine Learning for Critical Internet of Medical Things: Applications and Use Cases*, pp. 125–151, Cham: Springer International Publishing, Germany, Cham, Switzerland, 2022.

73. Wada, K., Shibata, T., Saito, T., Tanie, K., Effects of robot assisted activity to elderly people who stay at a health service facility for the aged, in: *Proceedings 2003 IEEE/RSJ International Conference on Intelligent Robots and Systems (IROS 2003) (Cat. No. 03CH37453)*, vol. 3, pp. 2847–2852, IEEE, 2003, October.

74. Moyle, W., Jones, C., Sung, B., Bramble, M., O'Dwyer, S., Blumenstein, M., Estivill-Castro, V., What effect does an animal robot called CuDDler have on the engagement and emotional response of older people with dementia? A pilot feasibility study. *Int. J. Soc. Rob.*, 8, 145–156, 2016.

75. Al-Turjman, F. and Nayyar, A., *Machine Learning for Critical Internet of Medical Things*, Springer International Publishing, Germany, Cham, Switzerland, 2022.

76. Thodberg, K., Sørensen, L.U., Christensen, J.W., Poulsen, P.H., Houbak, B., Damgaard, V., Videbech, P.B., Therapeutic effects of dog visits in nursing homes for the elderly. *Psychogeriatrics*, 16, 5, 289–297, 2016.

77. Bohr, A. and Memarzadeh, K. The rise of artificial intelligence in healthcare applications. Artificial Intelligence in Healthcare, pp. 25–60, Academic Press, 2020. https://doi.org/10.1016/B978-0-12-818438-7.00002-2. https://doi.org/10.1016/B978-0-12-818438-7.00002-2.

78. Kumar, A., Krishnamurthi, R., Nayyar, A., Sharma, K., Grover, V., Hossain, E., A novel smart healthcare design, simulation, and implementation using healthcare 4.0 processes. *IEEE Access*, 8, 118433–118471, 2020.

79. Martin, L., Hutchens, M., Hawkins, C., Trial watch: Clinical trial cycle times continue to increase despite industry efforts. *Nat. Rev. Drug Discovery*, 16, 3, 157–158, 2017.

80. Nayyar, A., *Computer Methods in Medicine and Health Care: Proceedings of the CMMHC 2022 Workshop*, vol. 26, IOS Press, Amsterdam, Netherlands, 2022.

81. Batth, R.S., Nayyar, A., Nagpal, A., Internet of robotic things: Driving intelligent robotics of future-concept, architecture, applications and technologies, in: *2018 4th International Conference on Computing Sciences (ICCS)*, pp. 151–160, IEEE, 2018, August.

82. Becker, K., Thull, B., Käsmacher-Leidinger, H., Stemmer, J., Rau, G., Kalff, G., Zimmermann, H.J., Design and validation of an intelligent patient monitoring and alarm system based on a fuzzy logic process model. *Artif. Intell. Med., 11,* 1, 33–53, 1997.

83. Nayyar, A., Gadhavi, L., Zaman, N., Machine learning in healthcare: Review, opportunities and challenges, in: *Machine Learning and the Internet of Medical Things in Healthcare*, pp. 23–45, 2021.

84. Venaik, A., Kumari, R., Venaik, U., Nayyar, A., The role of machine learning and artificial intelligence in clinical decisions and the herbal formulations against covid-19. *Int. J. Reliab. Qual. E-Healthc. (IJRQEH), 11,* 1, 1–17, 2022.

85. Pramanik, P.K.D., Solanki, A., Debnath, A., Nayyar, A., El-Sappagh, S., Kwak, K.S., Advancing modern healthcare with nanotechnology, nanobiosensors, and internet of nano things: Taxonomies, applications, architecture, and challenges. *IEEE Access, 8,* 65230–65266, 2020.

86. Lim, C.P., Chen, Y.W., Vaidya, A., Mahorkar, C., Jain, L.C. (Eds.), *Handbook of Artificial Intelligence in Healthcare: Vol 2: Practicalities and Prospects*, vol. 212, Springer Nature, Cham, Switzerland, 2021.

19

The Future of Healthcare: AIoMT—Redefining Healthcare with Advanced Artificial Intelligence and Machine Learning Techniques

Wasswa Shafik[1,2]

¹School of Digital Science, Universiti Brunei Darussalam, Gadong, Brunei Darussalam
²Dig Connectivity Research Laboratory (DCRLab), Kampala, Uganda

Abstract

The Internet of Medical Things (IoMT) has transformed healthcare by enabling medical devices to connect and exchange information through the Internet. The convergence of artificial intelligence (AI), machine learning (ML), and IoMT has resulted in the artificial intelligence of the Internet of Medical Things (AIoMT) paradigm, which has immense potential in healthcare delivery. This chapter provides an overview of how AIoMT is transforming the healthcare industry and unlocking the full potential of IoMT. It also reviews the cybersecurity aspects of this rapid technological advancement, including different cyber-attacks and threats, suggested countermeasures, and future directions. AIoMT has revolutionized healthcare by integrating AI and ML with IoMT, providing better diagnosis, treatment, and patient care. Through advanced data analytics and automation, AIoMT has the potential to enhance the diagnosis, treatment, and prevention of diseases as well as improve patient outcomes and reduce costs. For AIoMT to reach its full potential, it is crucial to collaborate and coordinate between healthcare providers, data scientists, and technology experts. AIoMT is not just a catchphrase but a game-changer in the healthcare industry. Lastly, to ensure the safety and security of patients' data, it is necessary to address the cyber-related challenges associated with AIoMT.

Keywords: Artificial intelligence, machine learning, Internet of Medical Things, good health and well-being, healthcare cybersecurity, drug development

19.1 Introduction

With the technological advancement in the 21st century, the world has witnessed numerous technological breakthroughs, and the Internet of Things (IoT) can be considered one such breakthrough that advances the faith of humanity by offering various services to ease our lives [1]. The IoT aims to connect every digital object to the Internet, allowing machine-to-machine (M2M) communication between these devices and yielding immense benefits for

Email: wasswashafik@ieee.org

Abhirup Khanna, May El Barachi, Sapna Jain, Manoj Kumar and Anand Nayyar (eds.) Artificial Intelligence and Machine Learning in Drug Design and Development, (605–634) © 2024 Scrivener Publishing LLC

shaping humans in a variety of domains such as surveillance, agriculture, military, manufacturing, energy generation, and healthcare, among others [2].

In this regard, healthcare is one primary domain this IoT serves. Hence, IoT in healthcare is also known as the Internet of Medical Things or IoMT [3]. Most of the IoMT applications and services in healthcare possess the capabilities for providing quality and comprehensive patient care within less time and can be applied in various clinical contexts such as hospitals, nursing homes, communities, and homes, among others [4]. AIoMT combines the power of AI and ML with IoMT to provide better diagnosis, treatment, and patient care [5]. It has facilitated the analysis of large datasets to generate insights that improve medical decision-making, disease diagnosis, and treatment. Personalized healthcare solutions are also possible with AIoMT [6]. Nevertheless, the evolving nature of AIoMT and its ability to process large volumes of patient data make it vulnerable to cyber-attacks that may result in data leaks, loss of life, and tarnished reputations of medical service providers [7].

Within smart healthcare, a significant component of smart cities, artificial intelligence (AI) is highly used in line with IoMT for inferring the meaning of the gathered pathological data and making timely and precise decisions on the underlying pathological conditions [8]. This collection is called AI of the Internet of Medical Things or AIoMT [9]. Currently, the IoMT and AI play a momentous role in enhancing the health and well-being of billions of people worldwide. In various aspects of healthcare, especially in disease diagnosis, patient condition monitoring, clinical environment monitoring, surgical procedures, and pandemic situation management and surveillance, these AIoMT technologies are highly used owing to their ubiquitous nature and yield benefits such as making timely and precise decisions [10]. This has also given rise to many healthcare applications, such as those for elderly care, remote health monitoring, chronic disease management, and fitness programs, to mention a few [11].

In recent years, this AIoMT has attracted so much attention from academia, industry, and researchers due to its potential to alleviate the massive burden in healthcare caused by

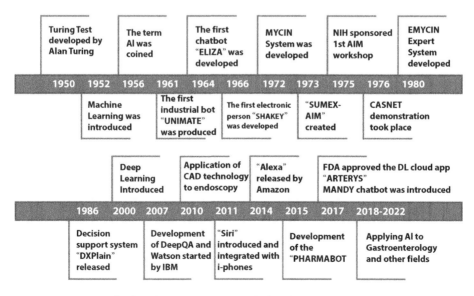

Figure 19.1 1950–2022 artificial intelligence evolution in the healthcare industry [13].

a shortage of medical staff and the rise of global pandemics [12]—for example, severe acute respiratory syndrome coronavirus, the recent COVID-19 deadly pandemic, the rise of an aging population, and the rise of chronic diseases are demonstrated in Figure 19.1 [13]. Moreover, the AIoMT ecosystem is often involved in dealing with sensitive patient data; owing to the ever-changing attack vectors in the modern threat landscape, this AIoMT is becoming a critical and frequent target that various cyber attackers are paying greater attention to [14].

19.1.1   Artificial Intelligence and Machine Learning Overview

AI is a field of study that involves the development of computer systems that can perform tasks that typically require human intelligence, such as speech recognition, decision-making, and natural language processing [15]. AI is considered a significant driver of technological progress, with potential applications in various industries, including healthcare, finance, and transportation [16] and [17]. The concept of AI can be traced back to the 1950s when researchers began developing algorithms to simulate human reasoning and decision-making [18]. Nevertheless, progress in the field was slow until the 1980s and 1990s, when computer hardware and software advancements made it possible to process and analyze large amounts of data [19].

There has been a significant increase in the use of AI for various applications, including image and speech recognition, natural language processing, and autonomous systems [20]. Some key trends in AI include the development of deep learning algorithms, which use artificial neural networks to learn from data, and the increased use of cloud computing and big data technologies to support AI applications [21]. However, the biggest challenge facing AI is the bias in algorithms, which can result in discriminatory outcomes [22]. There is also a shortage of skilled AI professionals, which has led to increased competition for talent and higher salaries. In addition, the complexity of AI algorithms and the need for large amounts of data can make it challenging to implement and deploy AI systems in real-world settings [23].

Efforts are underway to address some AI challenges, such as developing more transparent and explainable algorithms and using data augmentation and transfer learning to mitigate bias [24]. There is also a growing emphasis on AI's ethical and social implications, with organizations working to establish standards and guidelines for the responsible development and deployment of AI systems [25]. In addition, there is ongoing research into new AI algorithms and architectures and the use of reinforcement learning and other approaches to enable machines to learn and make decisions autonomously [26].

ML is a field of study involving algorithms and statistical models to enable computer systems to improve their performance on a task through experience. ML has become increasingly important in recent years due to its ability to analyze and make predictions from large and complex datasets [27]. Also, ML can be traced back to the 1950s and 1960s, when researchers began developing algorithms to teach computers how to recognize patterns in data [28]. However, progress in the field was slow until the 1990s, when computer hardware and software advancements made it possible to process and analyze large amounts of data [29].

ML has significantly increased in recent years for various applications, including image and speech recognition, natural language processing, predictive analytics, and autonomous systems [30]. Some key trends in ML include the development of deep learning algorithms that use artificial neural networks to learn from data and the increased use of cloud computing and big data technologies to support ML applications. However, one of the biggest challenges facing ML is the bias in algorithms, which can result in discriminatory outcomes [15]. There is also a shortage of skilled ML professionals, which has led to increased competition for talent and higher salaries. In addition, the complexity of ML algorithms and the need for large amounts of data can make it challenging to implement and deploy ML systems in real-world settings [19].

Efforts are underway to address some ML challenges, such as developing more transparent and explainable algorithms and using data augmentation and transfer learning to mitigate bias [26]. There is also a growing emphasis on ML's ethical and social implications, with organizations working to establish standards and guidelines for the responsible development and deployment of ML systems. In addition, there is ongoing research into new ML algorithms and architectures and the use of reinforcement learning and other approaches to enable machines to learn and make decisions autonomously [31].

19.1.2   Artificial Intelligence and Machine Learning from a Medical Perspective

AI and ML can revolutionize medicine by enabling more accurate and personalized diagnosis and treatment options. In recent years, there has been a significant increase in the use of AI and ML in medicine, with applications including medical imaging analysis, drug discovery, and personalized medicine [32]. The field faces several challenges, including the need for high-quality and diverse data, increased transparency and explainability of AI and ML models, and concerns about bias in these models [9] and [33].

Efforts are underway to address these challenges, including developing standardized datasets and algorithms, using techniques like federated learning to improve data privacy and security, and establishing guidelines and frameworks for the responsible use of AI and ML in medicine [34]. Moreover, ongoing research is focused on developing new AI and ML algorithms and architectures and exploring new applications for these technologies in healthcare [35]. With continued progress and innovation, AI and ML have the potential to improve healthcare outcomes and patient experiences significantly [36], like those presented in Figure 19.2.

One area where AI and ML significantly impact is medical image analysis. AI algorithms can analyze medical images with greater accuracy and speed than human radiologists, helping to detect abnormalities and improving diagnostic accuracy [37]. This could reduce the need for invasive procedures and improve patient outcomes. Another area of promise is drug discovery, where AI and ML can help identify promising drug candidates more quickly and accurately than traditional methods [4]. By analyzing large amounts of data on drug targets, molecular structures, and chemical properties, AI algorithms can identify drug candidates with a higher likelihood of success, potentially reducing the time and cost of drug development [26].

If the intruders can penetrate such AIoMT devices, they can access personal and medical information stored on the devices and gain control over them, eventually leading to significant health issues and the potential loss of life. Nevertheless, they could also have had access

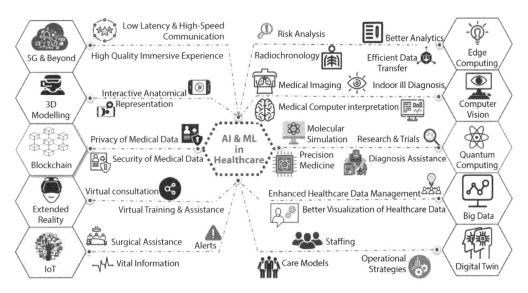

Figure 19.2 Artificial intelligence and machine learning applications in healthcare.

to the underlying, susceptible patient information and could have sold this information for higher prices in the black market, especially on the dark web, which eventually tarnishes the reputation of medical organizations [38]. As for that, greater attention must be paid to the security of the entire AIoMT ecosystem; otherwise, that will endanger patients' lives and tarnish the reputation of medical organizations [39].

Objectives of the Chapter

The objectives of the chapter are as follows:

- To provide a comprehensive overview of artificial intelligence and machine learning techniques in the health industry;
- To explore how these technologies are used in drug design and development, accelerating drug discovery, reducing risks and costs, and personalized treatments;
- To propose a secure AIoMT framework for smart healthcare, including primary care services, payers (PHCS), secondary care services (SCS) and life science care (LSC), MeDP on the body sensors (BS) for heat rate, temperature, proximity pressure among others, sensor-based health devices; these devices handle basic and emergency medical operations, health payer system (HPS), sensor-based care devices (SBCD), sensor life science devices (SLCD), bio_fog systems (BFS), healthcare fog system (HFS), payer_fog systems (PFS) and life science fog systems (LFS), patients' cloud cluster (PCC), primary healthcare cloud cluster (PHCC), secondary healthcare cloud cluster (SHCC), and life science cloud cluster (LSCC);
- To examine different AIoMT cybersecurity aspects in terms of threats, attacks, and countermeasures;

- And, to elaborate top healthcare case studies like: early detection of diabetic retinopathy, chatbots for mental health, and predictive analytics for patient outcomes.

Organization of the Chapter

The remainder of this chapter is organized into seven sections: Section 19.2 describes the different applications of AI in smart healthcare. Section 19.3 proposes a secure AIoMT framework for smart healthcare in smart cities based on edge technologies; Section 19.4 highlights the cybersecurity aspect of AIoMT in a smart city; and the threats and cyber-attacks targeting the IoMT, as well as the proposed countermeasures, are discussed in Section 19.5. Section 19.6 presents some healthcare case studies using AI. Finally, Section 19.7 concludes the chapter with future scope.

19.2   Application of AI and ML in Drug Design and Development

The drug discovery and development process is long and complex, involving identifying potential drug candidates, preclinical testing, clinical trials, and regulatory approval. AI and ML have the potential to revolutionize this process by enabling faster and more accurate identification of promising drug candidates, reducing the time and cost of drug development, and improving patient outcomes. The following are some of the critical applications of AI (first subsection) and ML (second subsection) in drug design and development:

19.2.1   AI in Drug Design and Development

This section demonstrates how AI is revolutionizing drug design and development by enabling faster and more efficient identification of drug candidates, predicting their efficacy and toxicity, and optimizing their properties for clinical use.

19.2.1.1   Predictive Modeling

Predictive modeling in drug design and development involves using machine learning algorithms to predict the efficacy and safety of drug candidates [40]. By analyzing large datasets, these algorithms can identify patterns and relationships to predict a drug's potential interactions with biological targets, side effects, and pharmacokinetics [30]. In conventional drug development, the identification of drug candidates often relies on time-consuming and expensive trial-and-error experimentation. The failure of numerous drug candidates during clinical trials due to safety concerns or lack of efficacy further prolongs and elevates the cost of drug development.

Nevertheless, with the emergence of AI in drug design and development, predictive modeling can be utilized to assess the safety and efficacy of potential drug candidates more accurately. As a result, researchers can allocate resources to the most promising candidates, thereby reducing the time and cost associated with drug development [28]. AI also allows for analyzing vast amounts of data from diverse sources such as genomics, proteomics, and clinical trials. This data-driven approach provides researchers with a better understanding of the underlying mechanisms of diseases, aiding the identification of novel therapeutic targets and potential drug candidates [41].

19.2.1.2 Drug Repurposing

Drug repurposing is an innovative drug development approach that utilizes machine learning algorithms to analyze vast biological and clinical information datasets to identify new therapeutic uses for existing drugs [28]. The algorithms identify similarities between diseases or biological pathways, allowing researchers to repurpose existing drugs for new indications or patient populations. This approach reduces the time and cost of drug development as existing drugs' safety and pharmacokinetic properties are already established.

Drug repurposing can potentially improve patient outcomes, extend the lifespan of existing drugs, and create new revenue streams for pharmaceutical companies. As a result, the need for extensive preclinical and clinical trials is minimized by repurposing existing drugs, and the process of bringing drugs to market can be accelerated [38]. Drug repurposing can lead to identifying new therapeutic uses for drugs already approved for other indications, providing new treatment options for patients with unmet medical needs. Therefore, drug repurposing has emerged as a promising strategy in drug development, and the integration of machine learning algorithms has further facilitated the identification of potential new therapeutic uses for existing drugs.

19.2.1.3 Clinical Trial Optimization

Clinical trial optimization is an application of machine learning in drug design and development that involves using algorithms to optimize the design and execution of clinical trials [42]. ML algorithms can analyze large amounts of data from clinical trials, including patient characteristics, treatment protocols, and outcomes, to identify factors most likely to lead to successful clinical trials [43]. Using ML to optimize clinical trials, researchers can improve the efficiency and accuracy of the drug development process. These algorithms can help identify the most promising patient populations, dosage levels, and treatment protocols while minimizing the risk of adverse events [44]. Clinical trial optimization can also help reduce the cost and time required for drug development. Using ML to optimize clinical trials, researchers can increase the likelihood of success, reducing the need for expensive and time-consuming trials.

19.2.1.4 Personalized Medicine

Personalized medicine is an application of AI in drug design and development that involves tailoring medical treatments to individual patient characteristics, such as genetics, lifestyle, and environment [43]. AI algorithms can analyze large datasets of patient information to identify patterns and relationships between patient characteristics and treatment outcomes, allowing healthcare providers to develop personalized treatment plans [44]. Algorithms can also analyze large amounts of genomic data to identify genetic variations associated with disease risk or drug response [45]. This information can identify patients more likely to respond to a particular treatment, reducing the need for trial-and-error approaches to treatment selection [46]. Personalized medicine can improve patient outcomes by identifying the most effective treatments for individual patients, reducing the risk of adverse effects, and improving overall treatment efficacy [44]. It can also help reduce healthcare costs by avoiding unnecessary treatments and reducing hospital readmissions.

19.2.1.5   Drug Safety and Toxicity Prediction

Drug safety and AI toxicity prediction are vital in drug design and development. It involves using machine learning algorithms to predict the potential adverse effects of drug candidates on human health. These algorithms analyze large chemical and biological information datasets to identify patterns and relationships between drugs and toxicities, allowing researchers to predict potential toxicities before drugs are tested in vivo. By anticipating potential toxicities early in the drug development procedure, researchers can eliminate unsafe drug candidates before investing time and resources in expensive clinical trials [47]. AI algorithms can also help identify safer dosages and drug administration routes, reducing the risk of adverse patient effects. Drug safety and toxicity prediction using AI have the potential to significantly reduce the time and cost of drug development while improving patient safety [34]. By identifying potential toxicities early in development, researchers can focus their resources on the most promising drug candidates, increasing the chances of successful drug development.

19.2.1.6   Virtual Screening

Virtual screening is an application of AI in drug design and development that involves using machine learning algorithms to analyze large databases of chemical compounds and identify those most likely to be effective drug candidates [43]. These algorithms can predict chemical compounds' activity, selectivity, and toxicity based on their chemical properties, allowing researchers to identify potential drug candidates quickly and efficiently. Virtual screening using AI can reduce the time and cost of drug development by eliminating ineffective drug candidates early in the development process. It can also help researchers identify compounds with a high probability of success, increasing the chances of successful drug development [42]. AI algorithms can also optimize the selection of chemical compounds for screening, reducing the need for expensive and time-consuming experimental screening. This can significantly accelerate drug discovery and reduce the time to market for new drugs.

19.2.1.7   De Novo Drug Design

De novo drug design, enabled by AI, is an emerging strategy in drug development that leverages machine learning algorithms to create novel molecules with desired properties for drug development. These algorithms can design molecules from scratch or modify existing ones to improve their properties, such as affinity and selectivity for a particular target [38]. AI in de novo drug design can accelerate drug discovery by reducing the reliance on trial-and-error approaches to molecule design, thereby minimizing the time and cost associated with traditional drug development.

AI can facilitate the design of molecules with specific properties not found in nature, such as improved efficacy, reduced toxicity, or increased bioavailability. With the advent of

AI in drug design and development, researchers can now access and analyze vast amounts of chemical data and generate molecules with optimized properties, which was not feasible before [19]. *De novo* drug design is an exciting application of AI in drug development that holds great promise for creating new and effective drugs to treat various diseases. It can also help researchers design molecules with specific properties not found in nature, such as improved efficacy, reduced toxicity, or increased bioavailability [16].

19.2.1.8   *Biomarker Discovery*

Biomarker discovery is a promising application of AI in drug design and development that aims to identify biological markers, or biomarkers, using machine learning algorithms. Biomarkers are indicators of a biological state or condition, such as the presence or absence of a disease, and can be used to predict disease progression, drug efficacy, and toxicity. AI can analyze vast amounts of data from various sources, such as genomics, proteomics, and clinical trials, to identify potential biomarkers to inform drug design and development [48]. Biomarker discovery using AI can also improve the efficiency and accuracy of clinical trials by identifying patients more likely to respond to a particular treatment or experience adverse effects, reducing the time and cost of drug development while improving patient outcomes. In addition, biomarker discovery can lead to the development of companion diagnostics, diagnostic tests used to identify patients most likely to benefit from a particular treatment [19]. Finally, biomarker discovery using AI can also improve the efficiency and accuracy of clinical trials by identifying patients more likely to respond to a particular treatment or experience adverse effects [26]. This can help reduce the time and cost of drug development while improving patient outcomes.

19.2.1.9   *Protein Structure Prediction*

Protein structure prediction is an application of AI in drug design and development that involves using machine learning algorithms to predict the three-dimensional structure of proteins [24]. This is important for understanding the molecular basis of diseases and designing new drugs that interact with specific protein regions. AI can analyze vast amounts of data from various sources, such as genomics, proteomics, and structural biology, to predict the structure of proteins with high accuracy [49]. Protein structure prediction using AI can accelerate drug development by providing insights into the molecular mechanisms of diseases and drug targets.

It can also help identify new drug targets and design more effective drugs interacting with specific protein regions, improving drug efficacy and reducing toxicity [50]. AI can optimize the properties of existing drugs by predicting their binding affinity and specificity to protein targets, reducing the time and cost of drug development [51]. AI-enabled protein structure prediction is promising in drug design and development, providing researchers with the tools to design more effective and targeted drugs for various diseases [52]. Protein structure prediction using AI can accelerate drug development by providing insights into the molecular mechanisms of diseases and drug targets [26]. It can also help identify new drug targets and design more effective drugs interacting with specific protein regions.

19.2.1.10   Pharmacokinetic Modeling

Pharmacokinetic modelling is an application of AI in drug design and development that involves using machine learning algorithms to predict how drugs are absorbed, distributed, metabolized, and eliminated by the body, known as absorption, distribution, metabolism, and excretion (ADME) properties. These algorithms can analyze large chemical and biological datasets to learn the relationships between molecular structure, drug formulation, and pharmacokinetic properties [32]. This information can be used to design drugs with improved pharmacokinetic properties, such as increased bioavailability and reduced toxicity, and to optimize dosing regimens to improve drug efficacy and safety [11].

19.2.1.11   Adverse Event Prediction

Adverse event prediction is an application of AI in drug design and development that involves using machine learning algorithms to predict the potential adverse effects of drugs before they are tested in clinical trials [37]. These algorithms can analyze large biological and clinical data sets to identify patterns and associations between drugs and adverse events. This information can predict the likelihood of adverse events and identify patients at higher risk of experiencing them [53]. As a result, pessimistic event prediction using AI can improve patient safety and reduce the cost and time of drug development by allowing researchers to identify potential safety issues earlier in the drug development process.

19.2.1.12   Natural Product Discovery

Natural product discovery is an application of AI in drug design and development that involves using machine learning algorithms to identify and analyze natural compounds with potential therapeutic properties [43]. These algorithms can analyze large chemical and biological datasets to learn the relationships between the chemical structure of natural compounds and their biological activity. This information can be used to identify natural compounds that have the potential to be developed into new drugs or to optimize existing drugs based on natural product structures [15]. Natural product discovery using AI can accelerate drug development by providing a large pool of potential drug candidates to explore, with the potential for improved efficacy and reduced toxicity.

19.2.1.13   Drug Formulation Optimization

Drug formulation optimization is an application of AI in drug design and development that involves using machine learning algorithms to optimize the formulation of drugs for improved efficacy, safety, and stability [42]. These algorithms can analyze large physicochemical and biological datasets to identify relationships between drug formulation, drug properties, and pharmacological activity. This information can be used to optimize the formulation of drugs, including selecting the most appropriate excipients, optimizing the dosage form, and designing targeted drug delivery systems [15]. As a result, drug formulation optimization using AI can improve drug performance, reduce toxicity, and increase patient compliance while reducing the time and cost of drug development [54].

19.2.1.14   Quality Control

Quality control is an application of AI in drug design and development that involves using machine learning algorithms to monitor and maintain the quality of drugs during manufacturing [28]. These algorithms can analyze large manufacturing and quality control datasets to identify patterns and anomalies that may indicate deviations from established quality control standards [44]. This information can be used to optimize manufacturing processes, detect potential quality issues, and ensure compliance with regulatory requirements. As a result, quality control using AI can improve the efficiency and accuracy of quality control processes, reduce the risk of defects and recalls, and ultimately improve patient safety [34].

19.2.1.15   Regulatory Compliance

Regulatory compliance is an application of AI in drug design and development that involves using machine learning algorithms to assist with regulatory compliance activities, such as identifying safety issues and adverse events and ensuring compliance with regulatory requirements [55]. These algorithms can analyze large datasets of clinical trial data, adverse event reports, and regulatory guidance to identify potential safety issues and ensure that the drug development process complies with regulatory requirements. This information can be used to optimize drug development strategies, identify risk areas, and ensure that regulatory requirements are met throughout the drug development process [40]. As a result, regulatory compliance using AI can improve the efficiency and accuracy of regulatory compliance activities, reduce the risk of compliance issues and penalties, and ultimately improve patient safety [56].

19.2.2   Application of ML in Drug Design and Development

This sub-section presents different ML applications concerning drug design and development.

19.2.2.1   Virtual Drug Screening

Virtual drug screening is an application of machine learning in drug design and development that involves using computational methods to predict the potential effectiveness of large numbers of drug candidates [26]. ML algorithms can analyze large chemical and biological datasets to identify the relationships between chemical structure and pharmacological activity [40]. These algorithms can then be used to virtually screen large libraries of drug candidates and identify those with the most significant potential for success. As a result, virtual drug screening using machine learning can significantly reduce the time and cost of drug development by identifying promising drug candidates early in the drug discovery process [44]. It also enables drug researchers to explore more drug candidates than is possible with traditional laboratory-based screening methods.

19.2.2.2   De Novo Drug Design and Development

De novo drug design is an application of machine learning in drug design and development that involves using computational methods to design utterly new drug molecules from scratch [38]. These algorithms can then be used to predict the properties of new drug molecules based on their chemical structure, such as their affinity for specific targets or their likelihood of causing adverse side effects [42]. *De novo* drug design using machine learning can significantly accelerate drug development by enabling researchers to rapidly explore large chemical spaces and identify promising drug candidates with a high likelihood of success [2]. It also has the potential to generate entirely new classes of drugs that may have been impossible to discover using traditional drug discovery methods.

19.2.2.3   Biomarker Detection

Biomarker detection is an application of machine learning in drug design and development that involves using computational methods to identify molecular or cellular markers indicative of disease or drug response [26]. ML algorithms can analyze large datasets of genomic, proteomic, and clinical data to identify patterns and relationships between these markers and the presence or progression of the disease. By identifying specific biomarkers associated with drug response, researchers can develop personalized drug treatments tailored to the individual patient's genetic makeup and disease characteristics [19]. Biomarker detection using ML can accelerate drug development by enabling researchers to identify promising drug candidates more quickly and accurately.

19.2.2.4   Scientific Trial Optimization

Clinical trial optimization is an application of machine learning in drug design and development that involves using computational methods to optimize the design and execution of clinical trials—for example, machine learning algorithms can analyze large datasets of patient data to identify patient subpopulations that are most likely to respond to a particular drug and predict the likelihood of adverse events or other negative outcomes [43]. This information can be used to design more efficient and effective clinical trials that maximize the chances of success and minimize risk to patients [37]. By optimizing clinical trials using ML, researchers can accelerate the drug development process and bring new treatments to market more quickly and with greater confidence in their safety and efficacy.

19.2.2.5   Patient Mobile Medicine

Patient mobile medicine is an application of machine learning in drug design and development that involves using mobile devices to collect and analyze patient health data in real time. ML algorithms can analyze large datasets of patient-generated health data, such as sensor data from wearables or health-related activity logs, to identify patterns and relationships between patient behavior and health outcomes [41]. By collecting this data in real time, researchers can gain insights into how patients respond to drug treatments and other interventions and can use this information to refine treatment protocols and develop personalized treatments tailored to the individual patient's needs [73]. Patient mobile medicine using ML has the potential to significantly improve patient outcomes by providing clinicians with real-time insights into patient health and enabling them to provide more personalized and effective treatments [44].

19.2.2.6   Toxicity Prediction

ML algorithms can analyze large chemical and biological information datasets to identify patterns and relationships between chemical structure and toxicity [38]. By analyzing these patterns, machine learning algorithms can predict the likelihood of toxicity for new drug candidates, enabling researchers to identify and eliminate potentially toxic compounds early in the drug development process. This can help reduce the risk of adverse drug reactions and improve patient safety [28]. By using ML to predict drug toxicity, medical researchers can accelerate drug development by eliminating potentially toxic compounds early in the process and focusing resources on the most promising drug candidates.

19.2.2.7   Protein Structure Prediction

Protein structure prediction is an application of ML in drug design and development that involves using computational methods to predict the three-dimensional structure of a protein. By predicting the structure of a protein, researchers can gain insights into its function and potential drug targets, which can aid in developing new drugs [39]. Using ML to predict protein structure, researchers can accelerate drug discovery and development by identifying potential drug targets and designing drugs that can interact with these targets more effectively.

19.2.2.8   Drug Repurposing

Drug repurposing, also known as drug repositioning, is an application of ML in drug design and development that involves identifying new therapeutic uses for existing drugs. Such algorithms can analyze large molecular and clinical datasets to identify potential new uses for drugs that have already been approved or are developing [19]. Researchers can accelerate the drug development by repurposing existing drugs, reducing the time and cost required for preclinical and clinical studies. Machine learning algorithms can also help identify potential drug targets and predict the efficacy of drug candidates for new indications, which can aid in designing clinical trials and developing personalized treatments [50].

19.2.2.9   Quality Controller

Quality control is critical to drug design and development, ensuring the final product is safe and effective. ML algorithms can aid in the quality control process by analyzing large datasets of manufacturing data and identifying potential quality issues early in the development process [39]. Therefore, scientists can minimize the risk of costly delays or recalls by detecting and addressing potential quality issues early on. ML algorithms can also help optimize manufacturing by identifying areas where efficiency can be improved and reducing waste [44].

The use of AI and ML in drug design and development can significantly improve the efficiency and success of the drug development process. As these technologies advance, we expect more personalized and effective treatments for various diseases and conditions. A summary of the AI algorithms applied in healthcare, including logistic regression, random

Table 19.1 Summary of AI algorithms and their applications in AI-enabled healthcare.

AI algorithms	Applications in healthcare	References
Support vector machine	Psychiatric disorders	[62]
	Cancer diagnosis	[75]
	Predicting surgical site infection	[76]
	Surgery	[77]
Neural network	Covid-19 prediction	[36]
	Cancer diagnosis	[78]
	Image-based cardiac monitoring	[79]
	Diabetes prediction	[80]
Naïve Bayes	Disease prediction	[65]
	Medical diagnosis	[81, 88]
K-nearest neighbor	Disease prediction	[82]
	Computer-aided diagnosis	[83]
	Healthcare monitoring	[9]
	Heart disease prediction	[84]
Decision tree	Glucose monitoring for diabetes	[85]
	Medical diagnosis	[54]
	Surgery	[84]

forest, decision tree, naive Bayes, support vector machines, neural networks, and k-nearest neighbor, is depicted in Table 19.1.

19.3   Secure AIoMT Framework for Smart Healthcare

The framework in this section is deployable for the personal area and home area-oriented remote medical surveillance based on edge technologies. The framework captures, transmits, analyzes, and stores health data from multiple sources (Figure 19.3)—for example, a data source could be sensors, smart watches, wristbands, smartphones, or other medical data acquisition systems [89]. Despite the numerous potentials envisioned by the framework, the immediate challenge to be addressed is accessing the information without compromising privacy.

The privacy concern concerns who accesses what information and the authentication and authorization of different actors like doctors, patients, guardians, nurses, and hospital

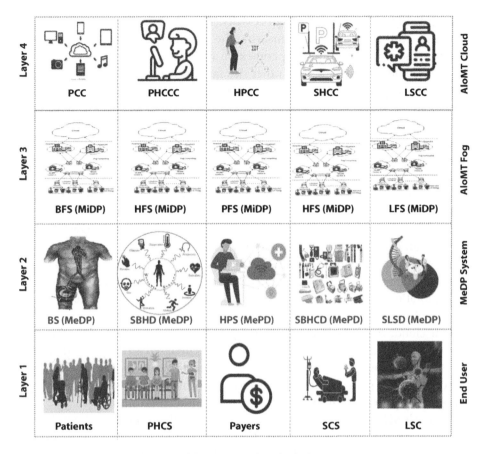

Figure 19.3 Secure artificial intelligence of the Internet of Medical Things ecosystem.

administration [90]. All data captured from the patient is sent from the medical endpoint device (MePD) to the medical midpoint device (MiPD) (fog, mist, edge) for processing using AI systems. In some situations, the data could be complex, requiring more advanced AI methods that may not fit the processing power of MiPD. In such a case, the data is transmitted to be processed in the cloud system for medical applications. At each level, AI-enabled processing derives the meaning and relationships underlying the data collected in real time from MePD [90].

This framework is modeled with security components at each level to secure data security and related insights by detecting suspicious activities to breach the system [91]. The services provided by this framework enable doctors, nurses, and other hospital staff to gain controlled access to the information to be used in clinical situations to diagnose, treat, and predict future ailment trends of the patient. The framework in Figure 19.3 is proposed to deter MePD's challenges, including limited system resources (memory, energy, processing power, and interoperability). Also, the diverse and heterogeneous nature of MePD limits the scalability and performance of the whole AIoMT system [91].

In this framework, processing large data is forwarded by MiPD, whereas big processes are pushed to the cloud via AIoMT. The MiPD runs AI algorithms because they have better resources and provide real-time processing of unstructured, structured, and complex data that is ever-growing and produced at high velocity, let alone being very diverse [61]. Earlier studies have noted the importance of ensuring the safekeeping of medical and healthcare information in the security and privacy context in which the cloud and fog applications in IoMT introduced non-compliance and other risk factors in a medical environment [59].

MePD devices capture data about the patients and the environment through sensors, actuators, smart wristbands, and other medical data acquisition systems, which provide continuous monitoring that generates massive medical data (big medical data), upon which health workers can make rational decisions about medical events [89]. The information processing can be used for medical transactions that happen daily, weekly, monthly, and quarterly. Further processes support decisions at the hierarchies of the health system, starting from the transactional level to the executive level, which requires the knowledge and experiences of doctors and consultants [87]. This knowledge extraction and analysis follows a complex process that must be secured to ensure that no third parties have access to the data and that authorized access is limited to the needed data.

Due to the resource limitations of MePD, the generated data is sent to MiPD (the Edge/Fog device) through a secure gateway, which ensures the security of the data and performs analysis, exploration, and filtering of the collected information [81]. While in the fog, AI models are applied to the data to classify private and non-private data to be securely transmitted to the cloud, where health professional personnel can securely access the information to provide quality diagnosis, decisions, and treatment based on the cleaned information [91]. The AI models significantly reduce the workload of health personnel and costs and eliminate other health hazards, such as radiation exposure in traditional imaging systems, while recognizing patterns that the human eye would otherwise miss [83].

The secure AIoMT ecosystem is rapidly expanding, with an increasing number of connected medical devices and sensors generating vast amounts of data. As a result, there is a growing need for secure AI algorithms that can analyze and extract meaningful insights from the data while protecting patient privacy and maintaining data security. The proposed secure AI of the IoMT ecosystem aims to address these challenges by developing secure and efficient AI algorithms for analyzing medical data [62]. The system employs a combination of encryption, multi-party computation, and differential privacy techniques to ensure patient data remains secure and private. One of the technical highlights of this system is its use of federated learning, which enables AI models to be trained on decentralized data without data sharing [92].

This ensures that patient data remains in its original location, minimizing the risk of data breaches or privacy violations. Another technical highlight is homomorphic encryption, which enables data to be encrypted while still allowing computations to be performed, maintaining data security and privacy [26]. The secure AI of the IoMT ecosystem also employs robust data governance frameworks to ensure that data is collected, stored, and used transparently and ethically. This includes obtaining patient consent, ensuring data anonymity and confidentiality, and adhering to regulatory requirements. Moreover, the proposed secure AIoMT ecosystem aims to incorporate various security measures such as encryption, authentication, and access control to prevent unauthorized access and ensure the confidentiality and integrity of patient data [36]. The system will also use anomaly detection techniques to identify and prevent potential cyber-attacks.

Regarding technical highlights, the secure AIoMT ecosystem will utilize advanced machine learning algorithms such as deep learning, reinforcement learning, and transfer

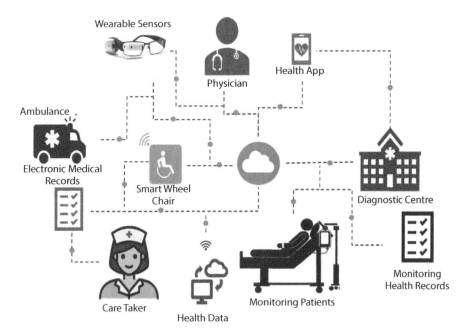

Figure 19.4 Real-time artificial intelligence of the Internet of Medical Things ecosystem implantation.

learning to analyze large datasets of patient data, including medical records, physiological signals, and medical images. The system will also leverage edge and cloud computing to enable real-time data processing and provide scalable and flexible computing resources [28]. In addition, the secure AI of the IoMT ecosystem will adhere to industry standards to ensure interoperability and compatibility with existing healthcare systems. The system will also be designed with modularity and flexibility, allowing for easy integration with other healthcare systems and devices.

The proposed secure AIoMT ecosystem that can be implemented as shown in Figure 19.4 has the potential to transform healthcare by providing personalized and efficient medical care while ensuring the security and privacy of patient data. However, it is essential to address ethical and regulatory concerns and ensure that the benefits of AI in healthcare are balanced with appropriate safeguards and ethical considerations. The proposed secure AI of the IoMT ecosystem aims to provide a secure and efficient platform for analyzing medical data, enabling the development of new insights and improving patient outcomes while maintaining data privacy and security.

19.4 AIoMT Cybersecurity Aspects

Securing MePD, which generates vast amounts of data from connected devices, is challenging for most IoMT systems. This is because devices in such networks capture sensitive data about patients, compatibility, and complex issues that are often private. Security and privacy issues in the MePD are difficult to resource due to their heterogeneous nature among IoMT systems. This is because devices in such networks capture sensitive data about patients, compatibility, and complex issues that are often private. Security and privacy issues in the MePD are difficult to resource due to their heterogeneous nature. Most security vulnerabilities and breaches occur during medical emergencies when medical personnel rush to use IoMT solutions without considering security [93]. Security and confidentiality, integrity, and availability (CIA) issues are ignored during this period. The security concerns raised included controlling, monitoring, and operating the MePD.

The confidentiality component deals with data protection from unauthorized users; therefore, the authorization of MePD and individuals on the network raises questions like maintaining confidentiality at the MePD and user levels while ensuring proper data management [85]. Integrity ensures the authenticity of the data being transmitted and stored on the system so that no creation or modification of data occurs without proper authorization. Availability guarantees that authorized personnel can access data on the system whenever needed. Authentication ensures that all MePDs confirm one another's identities, ensuring that only authorized personnel and devices can access the information and that it is only limited to the information for which they have access permissions [67].

Additionally, the IoMT system enforces privacy regulations in the IoMT environment and provides access to various users' private information. These rules are designed to prevent unauthorized disclosure of patient data and should adhere to legal and ethical laws of privacy, for example, the General Data Protection Regulation (GDPR) and the Health Insurance Portability and Accountability Act (HIPAA) [94]. The non-repudiation aspect ensures that the communicating parties within an IoMT environment cannot deny participation in exchanging information [95].

19.5   AIoMT Threats, Attacks, and Countermeasures

With many IoT devices being connected in smart healthcare, they face countless threats and attacks that can lead to patient data leaks, which may result in patients being publicly harassed and traumatized, tarnishing the reputation of medical organizations. Inappropriately, a search in scholarly repositories shows no one-size-fits-all security solution for IoMT systems to safeguard against security and privacy breaches [96]. In this section, we discuss the attacks and threats against the IoMT together with their proposed countermeasures.

Multi-vector attacks on IoMT devices in smart cities, such as distributed denial of service (DDoS) attacks, have the potential to disrupt the end-user experience in the IoMT environment by denying legitimate users (patients and medical personnel) access to MePD or systems [62]. Such an attack affects the system and medical device availability and ultimately prevents access to medical records by medical personnel, and the patients will be denied access to their prescribed medication and care [38].

Malware attacks are other forms of attacks to which IoT environments are prone. This malware includes spyware, worms, trojans, viruses, ransomware, and many more that can exploit security and loopholes and spread quickly across the network, thereby threatening the integrity and confidentiality of the IoMT network and devices [97]. Their ability to have unauthorized access to medical records can lead to the modification, loss, and leakage of patient records. Therefore, combating malware attacks on medical systems becomes crucial to mitigate the fallout from loss and unauthorized access to patient and medical-related data within the IoMT environment.

Attacks such as eavesdropping have been reported, which have the means to listen and collect information from medical sensors [98]. Identification of the man-in-the-middle (MITM) attack as a typical attack on IoMT systems and proposed countermeasures [46]. Such an attack can identify healthcare emergencies in patients being monitored and replay the unchanged physiological data to prevent the healthcare system from raising the alarm [84]. Therefore, a system that prohibits a MitM from disrupting performance and preventing alarms by the remote healthcare monitoring system was proposed.

IoMT devices are susceptible to botnets or zombie attacks, which can potentially cause physical harm to human patients [62]. As described in their modus operandi, these botnets can logically exploit a drug dose that can kill or result in life-threatening complications when prescribed to a patient. Additionally, IoMT devices can be remotely hijacked and used for targeted assassinations by terrorists [29]. Other reported attacks in the IoMT environment include brute force, jamming attacks, packet analysis attacks, flooding attacks, resource depletion attacks (such as buffer overflow, sleep deprivation, and battery drain), false data injection, hardware Trojans, and social engineering [69].

A hybrid deep learning-driven intelligent software-defined network (SDN)-enabled malware detection framework for timely and efficient detection of sophisticated malware attacks in the IoMT environment was proposed [92]. This framework can leverage the underlying resource-constrained IoMT devices without exhausting them. Also, an intelligent and dynamic system that mitigates the spread of ransomware in integrated health environments was proposed [69]. This system leverages machine learning techniques to detect and classify the spreading phases of ransomware in integrated health environments.

Threats can be attributed not only to the technical skills of the hackers when targeting IoMT systems but to the unskilled end-users as well. Authors indicated that issues such as stakeholders' unfamiliarity with security and privacy solutions and overlooking the inbuilt features of medical devices could create attack opportunities [43]. Such threats can lead to severe breaches in the IoMT environment by unsuspecting individuals, resulting in patient data loss. As a countermeasure, the authors proposed an ontology-based security recommendation framework consisting of context-aware IoMT protocols that empower stakeholders to make well-informed decisions [6]. The overall mechanism of this framework ensures the classification of security threats in the IoMT environment and provides automatic recommendations for the required security controls to be applied for each threat.

Also identified is the low battery power limitation of MePDs as posing risks to the overall cybersecurity of the IoMT environment in terms of integrity, confidentiality, and availability [6]. To negate such risks, he proposed transferring software details to the cloud-based platforms of service providers and deploying lightweight cryptographic keys to safeguard patient data. Proposed attributes to the cybersecurity solutions in the IoMT environment, such as lightweight MePDs with low power consumption rates, policies that regulate and ensure data on the IoMT network is protected at all levels from the collection, transmission, and storage, as well as lightweight fundamental management mechanisms since MePDs' must communicate securely amongst themselves [67]. Other studies proposed a system for secure data sharing that guarantees information protection, allowing access to mutual information and preventing the transmission of incorrect computations from customers through integrity verification test [86].

The heterogeneity and ubiquitous nature of IoMT devices further create a problem of ensuring secure holistic communication among them due to the uniqueness of the security measures inherent in them from their manufacturers. Such differences allow hackers to exploit weak and obscure security measures, which may compromise the entire network's security. Therefore, a multiparty trust negotiation system was deployed to countermeasure using the Soter framework that secures communication among MePDs and healthcare personnel [59]. This was achievable by gradually exchanging established digital credentials based purely on personalized access control policies.

Data encryption has been used to protect data confidentiality in resource-restricted IoMT devices and ensure the integrity of the transmitted data in the IoMT edge network environment. Furthermore, the authors devised a cloud-based security and privacy solution for IoMT that used the asymmetric encryption standard (AES), where keys were generated using the attribute-based encryption (ABE) protocol [59]. Such cryptographic methods maintain the security and privacy of IoMT-generated patient data.

A four-component blockchain-based framework for IoMT (BIoMT) security and privacy preservation for smart healthcare. These components included the cloud server, network cluster, medical facility, and intelligent medical devices, which provided a non-significant overhead capable of meeting most of the security and privacy requirements of the IoMT environment [66]. Also, others proposed the MedRec prototype, another blockchain-based secure e-health records storage management system [54]. This prototype addressed patient privacy issues, improved the secure presence of medical research data, and prevented modification of patient records using cryptographic-based hashes. Demonstrating how a deep recurrent neural network (DRNN) and machine learning models such as random forest, k-nearest neighbor, decision tree, and ridge classifiers can be deployed to classify and forecast sophisticated cyber threats was done [73]. Their proposed model outperformed the existing models by optimizing the features with the help of a bio-inspired particle swarm algorithm.

This system has the potential to save lives, as medical personnel are becoming constantly reliant on MePDs to make health-related decisions [72]. The security and privacy-preserving mechanism of the architecture lies in its ability to allow authenticated and trusted MePDs in the IoMT environment to serve patients through an encryption-based communication protocol [69]. This architecture's security services are accessible on demand with the aid of an application.

19.6   Selected Case Studies

As AI and ML get enhanced, different specific case studies can be explored and examined to properly under the application, support, and limitations, including early detection of diabetic retinopathy, predictive analytics for patient outcomes, personalized treatment recommendations, chatbots for mental health, and early detection of Alzheimer's disease are some of the selected cases.

19.6.1   Early Detection of Diabetic Retinopathy

Diabetic retinopathy is a common complication of diabetes that can cause damage to the blood vessels in the retina, leading to vision loss and blindness if left untreated.

Early detection and treatment of diabetic retinopathy are essential to prevent vision loss and improve patient outcomes [70]. Though traditional screening methods for diabetic retinopathy are time-consuming and costly, leading to delays in diagnosis and treatment. To address this issue, Google's DeepMind collaborated with the UK's National Health Service to develop an AI-based system that can detect diabetic retinopathy at an early stage [68].

Hybrid adaptive deep learning classifier for early detection of diabetic retinopathy using optimal feature extraction and classification. The system uses a deep learning algorithm that analyzes high-resolution images of the eye, detecting abnormalities and identifying areas that require further examination [71]. The system was trained using a dataset of 128,000 retinal images, allowing it to achieve an accuracy rate of 94%, which is on par with human ophthalmologists. This technology has the potential to significantly improve early detection rates and reduce the risk of blindness for patients with diabetes.

The AI-based system can analyze large volumes of retinal images quickly and accurately, allowing for early intervention and treatment. It also has the potential to reduce the burden on ophthalmologists and improve the efficiency of the screening process. Furthermore, the collaboration between Google's DeepMind and the UK's National Health Service highlights the potential for public-private partnerships to improve healthcare outcomes using AI and machine learning technologies [68]. This partnership shows that AI-based systems can be developed and implemented successfully in real-world healthcare settings, leading to better patient outcomes and more efficient healthcare delivery [74].

19.6.2   Predictive Analytics for Patient Outcomes

Predictive analytics for patient outcomes involve using AI and machine learning algorithms to analyze patient data and predict the likelihood of adverse health outcomes. These algorithms can identify patients at risk of developing complications or adverse events by analyzing patient data such as vital signs, laboratory values, and medication orders. This early identification allows healthcare providers to intervene earlier, preventing or mitigating the risk of adverse outcomes and improving patient outcomes [67]. Predictive analytics in healthcare can revolutionize delivering healthcare by providing personalized and proactive patient care. By identifying patients who are at high risk for adverse outcomes, healthcare providers can allocate resources more effectively and provide targeted interventions to those who need them the most [66].

Also, predictive analytics can help reduce healthcare costs by preventing complications and reducing hospital readmissions. Predictive analytics is becoming increasingly widespread in healthcare, with applications in various areas such as sepsis detection, readmission prevention, and chronic disease management. However, implementing these technologies requires careful consideration of ethical and privacy issues and ensuring that the algorithms are reliable and accurate [65]. Nevertheless, with proper implementation and oversight, predictive analytics can transform healthcare delivery, improving patient outcomes and reducing healthcare costs.

19.6.3   Personalized Treatment Recommendations

Personalized treatment recommendations involve using AI and machine learning algorithms to analyze patient data and provide customized treatment plans based on individual patient characteristics. One example of a successful application of personalized treatment recommendations is IBM's Watson for Oncology [62]. This AI system analyzes patient data such as medical history, laboratory values, and imaging results to provide treatment recommendations tailored to the individual patient. In addition, the system considers various factors, such as the patient's age, sex, comorbidities, and the latest medical research and guidelines [38].

By providing personalized treatment recommendations, Watson for Oncology has the potential to improve patient outcomes and reduce healthcare costs by ensuring that patients receive the most effective and appropriate treatments. The system has been used successfully in various healthcare settings, including hospitals and cancer centres, and has demonstrated promising results in improving patient outcomes [37]. However, implementing personalized treatment recommendations requires careful consideration of ethical and privacy issues and ensuring that the algorithms are reliable and accurate. Additionally, there is a need for further research and validation to ensure that personalized treatment recommendations are practical across a range of healthcare settings and patient populations [28]. Despite these challenges, personalized treatment recommendations can revolutionize healthcare delivery, providing more effective and efficient patient care.

19.6.4   Chatbots for Mental Health

Chatbots for mental health are AI-powered conversational agents that can provide support, guidance, and counselling to individuals experiencing mental health issues. These chatbots use natural language processing and machine learning algorithms to simulate human-like conversations, providing a personalized and accessible resource for individuals seeking mental health support [11]. One example of the successful implementation of chatbots for mental health is Woebot, a chatbot developed by Stanford University researchers. Woebot uses cognitive–behavioral therapy techniques to provide support and guidance to individuals experiencing symptoms of depression and anxiety. The chatbot engages users in conversation and provides personalized resources and exercises to help them manage their symptoms [14].

Woebot is an effective tool for improving mental health outcomes, with users reporting reduced symptoms of depression and anxiety after using the chatbot. Using chatbots for mental health can revolutionize how mental health services are delivered, providing accessible and personalized support to needy individuals [44]. However, implementing these technologies requires careful consideration of ethical and privacy issues and ensuring that the algorithms are reliable and accurate. Additionally, the effectiveness of chatbots for mental health may vary across different populations and cultures, highlighting the need for further research and validation [64].

Despite these challenges, using chatbots for mental health can address the mental health crisis and support individuals who may not have access to traditional mental health services—for instance, in 2018, the National Institute of Mental Health launched a pilot study to test the effectiveness of a chatbot called "Woebot" in treating depression and anxiety [63]. The chatbot uses natural language processing and cognitive–behavioral therapy techniques to provide personalized mental health support to users [62]. The study found that users reported a significant reduction in symptoms after just 2 weeks of using the chatbot.

19.6.5   Early Detection of Alzheimer's Disease

Researchers at the University of Bari in Italy developed an AI-based system to detect early signs of Alzheimer's disease by analyzing patterns in brain scans. The system achieved an accuracy rate of 86%, which was significantly higher than the accuracy rate of traditional diagnostic methods [14]. This technology can potentially improve early detection rates and enable earlier interventions, which could improve patient outcomes. Early detection of Alzheimer's disease is a critical area of research and development, and AI and ML algorithms play an increasingly important role in this field.

The algorithm uses machine learning to analyze brain scans and identify subtle changes that indicate the onset of Alzheimer's disease [62]. The system was trained using a dataset of over 800 individuals and achieved an accuracy rate of 84% in identifying individuals who went on to develop Alzheimer's disease. This technology can revolutionize how Alzheimer's disease is diagnosed and treated, allowing for early interventions that may delay or prevent the onset of symptoms [58]. Early detection can also help in developing new treatments for Alzheimer's disease by identifying patients who are at high risk of developing the disease and including them in clinical trials. However, implementing these technologies requires careful consideration of ethical and privacy issues and ensuring that the algorithms are reliable and accurate [59]. Nevertheless, with proper implementation and oversight, AI and ML algorithms can transform how Alzheimer's disease is diagnosed and treated, improving patient outcomes and reducing the burden of this devastating disease [38].

19.7   Conclusion and Future Scope

Around the world, healthcare systems are under much pressure because of an increase in population and the number of disaster incidences because of global climatic changes, let alone the appearance of new strains of diseases that do not have treatment available. In addition, our lifestyle over the years has made communicable illnesses rampant. The world's overall population is expected to hit close to 9 billion by 2050, and yet the number of health professionals is likely to be 5.73 per 1,000 persons; this makes healthcare expensive and exclusive, thereby requiring the adoption of healthcare technology. Adopting health technologies helps care providers increase their capacity to engage more patients and achieve better outcomes, putting them one step ahead of their counterparts.

AIoMT is expected to improve the precision of wearable devices in collecting data about patients' conditions. This will enable doctors to engage with their patients using telemedicine to gain better healthcare services. The new ways of getting healthcare services will considerably lower the cost of healthcare for all groups of patients. Secondly, as a base technology beneath virtual and augmented reality [61], AIoMT will provide a tool for doctors to acquire data and experience of the patients in real time, allowing for the precise prescription of medicine and other related healthcare procedures.

Furthermore, AIoMT forms the foundation of chatbot technologies (voice assistants) that provide transparent information about clinical processes and measurements of patients' activities and healthcare support, especially during health emergencies or pandemics. Voice assistants such as Apple Siri, Google Assistant, and Amazon Alexa have been instrumental, along with WhatsApp text-based chatbots, which could respond to COVID-19-related general questions [60]. These trends are seen to transform healthcare systems in the future as they become fully embraced.

Adopting intelligent things and medical big data analytics as applied in AIoMT technologies will trend healthcare toward digitized healthcare, cutting across digital health records that may be useful in remote diagnosis, medical communication, and body and biohacking [35]. This could involve numerous trends in gene editing and advancements in prosthetics in addition to increasing the body's ability to live healthily and longer [59]. Another visible trend is seen in robots and nanobots finding their way into a healthcare setting as effective devices that can perform surgery and AI-based exoskeletons for disabled people that enable them, for example, to walk [58]. Generally, the trends cited here form a very lucrative place for the AIoMT, estimated to be worth more than $158 billion soon [57].

Finally, this chapter discussed how AI influences the health sector in light of the rise in IoT devices in smart cities and the convergence of AI and IoMT in intelligent healthcare. In it, we have provided the ecosystem of AIoMT based on edge technologies, discussing the cybersecurity aspect of smart healthcare, threats, countermeasures, and future directions. The major strength of this review lies in its ability to guide readers on the different ways AI is revolutionizing the health sector, together with the threats that many Internet-facing medical devices in the IoMT environment face and their solutions. The future trends and aspects discussed are yet to be fully utilized, as the adoption of smart healthcare is still slow. In summary, as different cities adopt the many opportunities brought by the increased application of AI in smart healthcare, they should not forget the many cyber threats and attacks capable of leaking patient data, tarnishing the reputation of medical service providers, and potentially leading to loss of life. Therefore, MePD manufacturers, software developers, and security architects should put security measures in place to mitigate the fallout from any cyberattack on the IoMT environment.

References

1. Kaur, P., Kumar, R., Kumar, M., A healthcare monitoring system using random forest and internet of things (IoT). *Multimed. Tools Appl.*, 78, 14, 19905–19916, 2019, https://doi. org/10.1007/s11042-019-7327-8.

2. Jun, Y., Craig, A., Shafik, W., Sharif, L., Artificial intelligence application in cybersecurity and cyberdefense. *Wirel. Commun. Mob. Comput.*, 2021, 1–10, 2021, https://doi. org/10.1155/2021/3329581.

3. Ahmed, S.M. and Rajput, A., Threats to patients' privacy in smart healthcare environment, in: *Innovation in Health Informatics*, vol. 1, pp. 375–393, Elsevier, Amsterdam, The Netherlands, 2020, https://doi.org/10.1016/ B978-0-12-819043-2.00016-2.

4. Meng, H., Shafik, W., Matinkhah, S.M., Ahmad, Z., A 5g beam selection machine learning algorithm for unmanned aerial vehicle applications. *Wirel. Commun. Mob. Comput.*, 2020, 1–16, 2020, https://doi.org/10.1155/2020/1428968.

5. Joyia, G.J., Liaqat, R.M., Farooq, A., Rehman, S., Internet of medical things (IoMT): Applications, benefits and future challenges in healthcare domain. *J. Commun.*, 12, 4, 240–247, 2017, https://doi.org/10.12720/jcm.12.4.240-247.

6. Mohan, N. and Kangasharju, J., Edge-Fog cloud: A distributed cloud for internet of things computations, in: *2016 Cloudification of the Internet of Things (CIoT)*, Paris, France, pp. 1–6, IEEE, 2016, https://doi.org/10.1109/CIOT.2016.7872914.

7. Shafik, W., Wearable medical electronics in artificial intelligence of medical things, in: *Handbook of Security and Privacy of AI-Enabled Healthcare Systems and Internet of Medical Things*, pp. 21–40, IGI Global, Hershey, Pennsylvania, 2024, https://doi.org/10.1201/9781003370321-2.

8. Shafik, W., IoT-based energy harvesting and future research trends in wireless sensor networks, in: *Handbook of Research on Network-Enabled IoT Applications for Smart City Services*, pp. 282–306, IGI Global, Hershey, Pennsylvania, United States, 2023, https://doi.org/10.4018/979-8-3693-0744-1.ch016.

9. Kaur, H., Atif, M., Chauhan, R., An internet of healthcare things (IoHT)-based healthcare monitoring system, in: *Advances in Intelligent Computing and Communication: Proceedings of ICAC 2019* (pp. 475-482). Springer Singapore, 2020.

10. Verma, H., Chauhan, N., Awasthi, L.K., A comprehensive review of 'Internet of Healthcare Things': Networking aspects, technologies, services, applications, challenges, and security concerns. *Comput. Sci. Rev.*, 50, 100591, 2023, https://doi.org/10.1016/j.cosrev.2023.100591.

11. Alshehri, F. and Muhammad, G., A comprehensive survey of the internet of things (IoT) and AI-based smart healthcare. *IEEE Access*, 9, 3660–3678, 2021, https://doi.org/10.1109/ACCESS.2020.3047960.

12. Kalinaki, K., Fahadi, M., Alli, A.A., Shafik, W., Yasin, M., Mutwalibi., N., Artificial intelligence of internet of medical things (AIoMT) in smart cities: A review of cybersecurity for smart healthcare, in: *Handbook of Security and Privacy of AI-Enabled Healthcare Systems and Internet of Medical Things*, pp. 271–92, IGI Global, Hershey, Pennsylvania, United States, 2024, https://doi.org/10.1201/9781003370321-11.

13. Pandya, S., Thakur, A., Saxena, S., Jassal, N., Patel, C., Modi, K., ... Kadam, P., A study of the recent trends of immunology: Key challenges, domains, applications, datasets, and future directions. *Sensors*, 21, 23, 7786, 2021.

14. Bragazzi, N.L., Dai, H., Damiani, G., Behzadifar, M., Martini, M., Wu, J., How big data and artificial intelligence can help better manage the COVID-19 pandemic. *Int. J. Environ. Res. Public Health*, 17, 9, 3176, 2020, https://doi.org/10.3390/ijerph17093176.

15. Habibzadeh, H., Nussbaum, B.H., Anjomshoa, F., Kantarci, B., Soyata, T., A survey on cybersecurity, data privacy, and policy issues in cyber-physical system deployments in smart cities. *Sustain. Cities Soc.*, 50, 101660, 2019, https://doi.org/10.1016/j.scs.2019.101660.

16. Shafik, W., A comprehensive cybersecurity framework for present and future global information technology organizations, in: *Effective Cybersecurity Operations for Enterprise-Wide Systems*, pp. 56–79, IGI Global, Hershey, Pennsylvania, United States, 2023, https//doi.org/10.4018/978-1-6684-9018-1.ch002.

17. Shafik, W., Matinkhah, S.M., Asadi, M., Ahmadi, Z., Hadiyan, Z., A study on Internet of things performance evaluation. *J. Commun. Technol. Electron. Comput. Sci.*, 28, 1–19, 2020, http://dx.doi.org/10.22385/jctecs.v30i0.312.

18. Shafik, W., Matinkhah, S.M., Sanda, M.N., Afolabi, S.S., A 3-dimensional fast machine learning algorithm for mobile unmanned aerial vehicle base stations. *Int. J. Adv. Appl. Sci.*, 10, 1, 28–38, 2020, https://doi.org/10.11591/ijaas.v10.i1.pp28-38.

19. Syed, L., Jabeen, M.S., Alsaeedi, A., Smart healthcare framework for ambient assisted living using IoMT and big data analytics techniques. *Future Gener. Comput. Syst.*, 101, 136–151, 2019. https://doi.org/10.1016/j.future.2019.06.004.

20. Shafik, W., Matinkhah, M., Etemadinejad, P., Sanda, M.N., Reinforcement learning rebirth, techniques, challenges, and resolutions. *JOIV: Int. J. Inform. Visualization*, 4, 3, 127–135, 2020, http://dx.doi.org/10.30630/joiv.4.3.376.

21. Panesar, A., Machine learning algorithms, in: *Machine Learning and AI for Healthcare*, pp. 85–144, Apress, Berkeley, CA, 2021, https://doi.org/10.1007/978-1-4842-6537-6_4.

22. Shafik, W., Cyber security perspectives in public spaces: drone case study, in: *Handbook of Research on Cybersecurity Risk in Contemporary Business Systems*, pp. 79–97, IGI Global, Hershey, Pennsylvania, United States, 2023, https://doi.org/10.4018/978-1-6684-7207-1.ch004.

23. Andreu-Perez, J., Poon, C.C.Y., Merrifield, R.D., Wong, S.T.C., Yang, G.Z., Big Data for Health. *IEEE J. Biomed. Health Inf.*, 19, 4, 1193–1208, 2015, https://doi. org/10.1109/JBHI.2015.2450362.

24. Kappassov, Z., Corrales, J.A., Perdereau, V., Tactile sensing in dexterous robot hands-Review. *Rob. Auton. Syst.*, 74, 195–220, 2015, https://doi.org/10.1016/j. robot.2015.07.015.

25. Fleck, E., Staley, S., Ryszka, K., Potkay, J.A., BIO16: Toward a blood-compatible, 3D printing resin for microfluidic artificial organs. *ASAIO J.*, 68, 2, 18–18, 2022, https://doi. org/10.1097/01. mat.0000840800.55807.ab.

26. Kruse, T., Pandey, A.K., Alami, R., Kirsch, A., Human-aware robot navigation: A survey. *Rob. Auton. Syst.*, 61, 12, 1726–1743, 2013, https://doi.org/10.1016/j. robot.2013.05.007.

27. Alaziz, S.N., Albayati, B., El-Bagoury, A.A., Shafik, W., Clustering of COVID-19 multi-time series-based K-means and PCA with forecasting. *Int. J. Data Warehous. Min.*, 19, 3, 1–25, 2023, https://doi.org/10.4018/IJDWM.317374.

28. MacDonald, S., Steven, K., Trzaskowski, M., Interpretable AI in healthcare: Enhancing fairness, safety, and trust, in: *Artif. Intell. Med.*, Singapore, pp. 241–258, Springer Nature, Singapore, 2022, https://doi.org/10.1007/978-981-19-1223-8_11.

29. Shafik, W., Matinkhah, M., Sanda, M.N., Network resource management drives machine learning: a survey and future research direction. *J. Commun. Technol. Electron. Comput. Sci.*, 2020, 1–15, 2020, http://dx.doi.org/10.22385/jctecs.v30i0.312.

30. Patel, T.A., Puppala, M., Ogunti, R.O., Ensor, J.E., He, T., Shewale, J.B., Chang, J.C., Correlating mammographic and pathologic findings in clinical decision support using natural language processing and data mining methods. *Cancer*, 123, 1, 114–121, 2017, https://doi. org/10.1002/cncr.30245.

31. McKinney, S.M., Sieniek, M., Godbole, V., Godwin, J., Antropova, N., Ashrafian, H., Shetty, S., International evaluation of an AI system for breast cancer screening. *Nature*, 577, 7788, 89–94, 2020, https://doi.org/10.1038/s41586-019-1799-6.

32. De Fauw, J., Ledsam, J.R., Romera-Paredes, B., Nikolov, S., Tomasev, N., Blackwell, S., Ronneberger, O., Clinically applicable deep learning for diagnosis and referral in retinal disease. *Nat. Med.*, 24, 9, 1342–1350, 2018, https://doi.org/10.1038/s41591-018-0107-6.

33. Shafik, W., Making cities smarter: IoT and SDN applications, challenges, and future trends, in: *Opportunities and Challenges of Industrial IoT in 5G and 6G Networks*, pp. 73–94, IGI Global, Hershey, Pennsylvania, United States, 2023, https://doi.org/10.4018/978-1-7998-9266-3.ch004.

34. Liu, X., Faes, L., Kale, A.U., Wagner, S.K., Fu, D.J., Bruynseels, A., Denniston, A.K., A comparison of deep learning performance against healthcare professionals in detecting diseases from medical imaging: A systematic review and meta-analysis. *Lancet Digit. Health*, 1, 6, 71–297, 2019, https://doi.org/10.1016/S2589-7500(19)30123-2.

35. Shafik, W. and Tufail, A., Energy optimization analysis on internet of things, in: *Advanced Technology for Smart Environment and Energy. Environmental Science and Engineering*, J. Mabrouki, A. Mourade, A. Irshad, S. Chaudhry (Eds.), vol. 1, pp. 1–16, Springer, Cham, Dordrecht, Netherlands, https://doi.org/10.1007/978-3-031-25662-2_1.

36. Iskanderani, A., II, Mehedi, I.M., Aljohani, A.J., Shorfuzzaman, M., Akther, F., Palaniswamy, T., Alam, A., Artificial intelligence and medical internet of things framework for diagnosis of coronavirus suspected cases. *J. Healthcare Eng.*, 2021, 1–7, 2021, https://doi.org/10.1155/2021/3277988.

37. Liu, A., Seal, S., Yang, H., Bender, A., Using chemical and biological data to predict drug toxicity. *SLAS Discovery*, 28, 53–64, 2023, https://doi.org/10.1016/j.slasd.2022.12.003.

38. Erikainen, S. and Chan, S., Contested futures: envisioning 'Personalized,' 'Stratified,' and 'Precision' medicine. *New Genet. Soc.*, 38, 3, 308–330, 2019, https://doi.org/10.1080/14636778. 2019.1637720.

39. Shokoor, F., Shafik, W., Matinkhah, S.M., Overview of 5G & Beyond Security. *EAI Endorsed Trans. Internet Things*, 8, 30, e2, 2022, http://dx.doi.org/10.4108/eetiot.v8i30.1624.

40. Cai, C., Lin, H., Wang, H., Xu, Y., Ouyang, Q., Lai, L., Pei, J., miDruglikeness: Subdivisional drug-likeness prediction models using active ensemble learning strategies. *Biomolecules*, 13, 1, 29, 2023, https://doi.org/10.3390/biom13010029.

41. Schiff, G.D., Volk, L.A., Volodarskaya, M., Williams, D.H., Walsh, L., Myers, S.G., Rozenblum, R., Screening for medication errors using an outlier detection system. *J. Am. Med. Inf. Assoc.*, 24, 2, 281–287, 2017, https://doi.org/10.1093/jamia/ocw171.

42. Talat, A. and Khan, A.U., Artificial intelligence as a smart approach to develop antimicrobial drug molecules: a paradigm to combat drug-resistant infections. *Drug Discov. Today*, 28, 103491, 2023, https://doi.org/10.1016/j.drudis.2023.103491.

43. Sarkar, C., Das, B., Rawat, V.S., Wahlang, J.B., Nongpiur, A., Tiewsoh, I., Sony, H.T., Artificial intelligence and machine learning technology driven modern drug discovery and development. *Int. J. Mol. Sci.*, 24, 3, 2026, 2023, https://doi.org/10.3390/ ijms24032026.

44. Kavidopoulou, A., Syrigos, K.N., Makrogkikas, S., Dlamini, Z., Hull, R., Marima, R., Lolas, G., AI and big data for drug discovery, in: *Trends of artificial intelligence and big data for e-health*, pp. 121–138, Cham: Springer International Publishing, Germany, 2023, https://doi. org/ 10.1007/978-3-031-11199-0_7.

45. Shafik, W., Matinkhah, S.M., Ghasemazade, M., Fog-mobile edge performance evaluation and analysis on internet of things. *J. Adv. Res. Mobile Comp.*, 1, 3, 1–17, 2019, http://doi.org/10.5281/ zenodo.3591228.

46. Yang, Z., Jianjun, L., Faqiri, H., Shafik, W., Talal Abdulrahman, A., Yusuf, M., Sharawy, A.M., Green Internet of things and big data application in smart cities development. *Complexity*, 1–15, 2021, https://doi.org/10.1155/2021/4922697.

47. Yamada, H., Computational toxicology in drug safety research. *Nihon Yakurigaku zasshi. Folia Pharmacologica Japonica*, 158, 1, 82–88, 2023, https://doi.org/10.1254/fpj.22098.

48. Santana, M.M., Gaspar, L.S., Pinto, M.M., Silva, P., Adão, D., Pereira, D., de Almeida, L.P., A standardized protocol for blood and cerebrospinal fluid collection and processing for biomarker research in ataxia. *Neuropathol. Appl. Neurobiol.*, 49, 2, e12892, 2023, https://doi.org/10.1111/ nan.12892.

49. Ali, S., Hafeez, Y., Jhanjhi, N.Z., Humayun, M., Imran, M., Nayyar, A., Ra, I.H., Towards pattern-based change verification framework for cloud-enabled healthcare component-based. *IEEE Access*, 8, 148007–148020, 2020, https://doi.org/10.1109/ACCESS.2020.3014671.

50. Pramanik, P.K.D., Pareek, G., Nayyar, A., Security and privacy in remote healthcare: issues, solutions, and standards, in: *Telemedicine technologies*, pp. 201–225, Academic Press, Cambridge, Massachusetts, USA, 2019, https:// doi.org/10.1016/B978-0-12-816948-3.00014-3.

51. Mahapatra, B., Krishnamurthi, R., Nayyar, A., Healthcare models and algorithms for privacy and security in healthcare records, in: *Security and privacy of electronic healthcare records: Concepts, paradigms and solutions*, p. 183, 2019, https://doi.org/10.1049/PBHE020E_ch8.

52. Nayyar, A., Gadhavi, L., Zaman, N., Machine learning in healthcare: review, opportunities and challenges, in: *Machine Learning and the Internet of Medical Things in Healthcare*, pp. 23–45, 2021, https://doi.org/10.1016/B978-0-12-821229-5.00011-2.

53. Shafik, W., Matinkhah, S.M., Shokoor, F., Sanda, M.N., Internet of thing-based energy efficiency optimization model in fog smart cities. *Int. J. Inform. Visualization*, 5, 2, 105–112, 2021, http://dx.doi.org/10.30630/joiv.5.2.373.

54. Ilmudeen, A. and Nayyar, A., Novel designs of smart healthcare systems: technologies, architecture, and applications, in: *Machine Learning for Critical Internet of Medical Things: Applications and Use Cases*, pp. 125–151, Cham: Springer International Publishing, New York City, United States, 2022, https://doi.org/10.1007/978-3-030-80928-7_6.

55. Shafik, W., Matinkhah, S.M., Ghasemzadeh, M., Theoretical understanding of deep learning in uav biomedical engineering technologies analysis. *SN Comput. Sci.*, 1, 6, 1–13, 2020, https://doi.org/10.1007/s42979-020-00323-8.

56. Azaria, A., Ekblaw, A., Vieira, T., Lippman, A., MedRec: Using blockchain for medical data access and permission management, in: *2nd International Conference on Open and Big Data (OBD)*, Vienna, Austria, pp. 25–30, 2016, https://doi.org/10.1109/OBD.2016.11.

57. Shah, V. and Khang, A., Internet of Medical Things (IoMT) Driving the Digital Transformation of the Healthcare Sector, in: *Data-Centric AI Solutions and Emerging Technologies in the Healthcare Ecosystem*, pp. 15–26, CRC Press, Boca Raton, Florida, United States, 2023, https://doi.org/10.1201/9781003356189-2.

58. Simoens, P., Dragone, M., Saffiotti, A., The internet of robotic things. *Int. J. Adv. Rob. Syst.*, 15, 1, 1729881418759424, 2018, https://doi.org/10.1177/1729881418759424.

59. Manickam, P., Mariappan, S.A., Murugesan, S.M., Hansda, S., Kaushik, A., Shinde, R., Thipperudraswamy, S.P., Artificial intelligence (AI) and internet of medical things (IoMT) assisted biomedical systems for intelligent healthcare. *Biosensors*, 12, 8, 562, 2022, https://doi.org/10.3390/bios12080562.

60. Sezgin, E., Huang, Y., Ramtekkar, U., Lin, S., Readiness for voice assistants to support healthcare delivery during a health crisis and pandemic. *NPJ Digital Med.*, 3, 1, 122, 2020, https://doi.org/10.1038/s41746-020-00332-0.

61. Dwivedi, R., Mehrotra, D., Chandra, S., Potential of internet of medical things (IoMT) applications in building a smart healthcare system: A systematic review. *J. Oral. Biol. Craniofac Res.*, 12, 2, 302–318, 2022, https://doi.org/10.1016/j.jobcr.2021.11.010.

62. Zhao, L., Zhu, D., Shafik, W., Matinkhah, S.M., Ahmad, Z., Sharif, L., Craig, A., Artificial intelligence analysis in cyber domain: A review. *Int. J. Distrib. Sens. Netw.*, 18, 4, 15501329221084882, 2022, https://doi.org/10.1177/15501329221084882.

63. Yaacoub, J.P.A., Noura, M., Noura, H.N., Salman, O., Yaacoub, E., Couturier, R., Chehab, A., Securing internet of medical things systems: Limitations, issues and recommendations. *Future Gener. Comput. Syst.*, 105, 581–606, 2020, https://doi.org/10.1016/ j.future.2019.12.028.

64. Orrù, G., Pettersson-Yeo, W., Marquand, A.F., Sartori, G., Mechelli, A., Using support vector machine to identify imaging biomarkers of neurological and psychiatric disease: A critical review. *Neurosci. Biobehav. Rev.*, 36, 4, 1140–1152, 2012, https://doi.org/10.1016/ j.neubiorev.2012.01.004.

65. Langarizadeh, M. and Moghbeli, F., Applying naive bayesian networks to disease prediction: A systematic review. *Acta Inform. Med.*, 24, 5, 364–369, 2016, https://doi.org/10.5455/ aim.2016.24.364-369.

66. Seliem, M. and Elgazzar, K., BIoMT: Blockchain for the internet of medical things, in: *IEEE International Black Sea Conference on Communications and Networking*, Sofia, Bulgaria, pp. 1–4, 2019, https://doi.org/10.1109/BlackSeaCom.2019.8812784.

67. Varshney, T., Sharma, N., Kaushik, I., Bhushan, B., Architectural model of security threats and their countermeasures in IoT. *International Conference on Computing, Communication, and Intelligent Systems*, Greater Noida, India, pp. 424–429, 2019, https://doi.org/10.1109/ ICCCIS48478.2019.8974544.

68. Hemanth, S.V. and Alagarsamy, S., Hybrid adaptive deep learning classifier for early detection of diabetic retinopathy using optimal feature extraction and classification. *J. Diabetes Metab. Disord.*, 22, 1–15, 2023, https://doi.org/10.1007/s40200-023-01220-6.

69. Shafik, S.M., Matinkhah, S.M., Ghasemzadeh, M., Internet of things-based energy management, challenges, and solutions in smart cities. *J. Commun. Technol. Electron. Comput. Sci.*, 27, 1–11, 2020, http://dx.doi.org/10.22385/jctecs.v27i0.302.

70. Jiang, H., Hou, Y., Miao, H., Ye, H., Gao, M., Li, X., Liu, J., Eye tracking based deep learning analysis for the early detection of diabetic retinopathy: A pilot study. *Biomed. Signal Process. Control*, 84, 104830, 2023, https://doi.org/10.1016/j.bspc.2023.104830.

71. Silva-Viguera, M.C., García-Romera, M.C., López-Izquierdo, I., De-Hita-Cantalejo, C., Sánchez-González, M.C., Bautista-Llamas, M.J., Contrast sensitivity assessment in early diagnosis of diabetic retinopathy: A systematic review. *Semin.Ophthalmol.*, 38, 4, 319– 332, 2023, https://doi.org/10.1080/08820538.2022.2116289.

72. Ben Amor, L., Lahyani, I., Jmaiel, M., AUDIT: Anomalous us data detection and isolation approach for mobile healthcare systems. *Expert Syst.*, 37, 1, e12390, 2020, https://doi.org/10.1111/ exsy.12390.

73. Saheed, Y.K. and Arowolo, M.O., Efficient cyber attack detection on the internet of medical things: A smart environment based on deep recurrent neural network and machine learning algorithms. *IEEE Access*, 9, 161546–161554, 2021, https://doi.org/10.1109/ACCESS.2021.3128837.

74. Shafik, W., Matinkhah, S.M., Ghasemzadeh, M., A fast machine learning for 5G beam selection for unmanned aerial vehicle applications. *Inf. Syst. Telecommun.*, 7, 28, 262–278, 2019, https:// doi.org/10.7508/jist.2019.04.003.

75. Sweilam, N.H., Tharwat, A.A., Abdel Moniem, N.K., Support vector machine for the diagnosis of cancer disease: A comparative study. *Egypt. Inf. J.*, 11, 2, 81–92, 2010. https://doi.org/10.1016/j.eij.2010.10.005.

76. Chang, M., Canseco, J.A., Nicholson, K.J., Patel, N., Vaccaro, A.R., The role of machine learning in spine surgery: The future is now. *Front. Surg.*, 7, 54, 2020, https://doi.org/10.3389/fsurg.2020.00054.

77. Soguero-Ruiz, C., Fei, W.M., Jenssen, R., Augestad, K.M., Álvarez, J.L.R., Jiménez, I.M., Skrøvseth, S.O., Data-driven temporal prediction of surgical site infection, in: *AMIA Annual Symposium Proceedings,* vol. 2015, p. 1164, American Medical Informatics Association, 2015, https://pubmed.ncbi.nlm. nih.gov/26958256.

78. Svoboda, E., Artificial intelligence is improving the detection of lung cancer. *Nature*, 587, 7834, S20, 2020, https://doi.org/10.1038/d41586-020-03157-9.

79. Shafik, W., Matinkhah, S.M., Shokoor, F., Sharif, L., A reawakening of machine learning application in unmanned aerial vehicle: Future research motivation. *EAI Endorsed Trans. Internet Things.*, 8, 29, e3, 2022, http://dx.doi.org/10.4108/eetiot.v8i29.987.

80. Kwon, Y.T., Kim, H., Mahmood, M., Kim, Y.S., Demolder, C., Yeo, W.H., Printed, wireless, soft bioelectronics and deep learning algorithm for smart human–machine interfaces. *ACS Appl. Mater. Interfaces*, 12, 44, 49398–49406, 2020, https://doi.org/10.1021/ acsami.0c14193.

81. Shen, Y., Li, Y., Zheng, H.-T., Tang, B., Yang, M., Enhancing ontology-driven diagnostic reasoning with a symptom-dependency-aware Naïve Bayes classifier. *BMC Bioinf.*, 20, 1, 1–14, 2019, https://doi.org/10.1186/s12859-019-2924-0.

82. Uddin, S., Haque, I., Lu, H., Moni, M.A., Gide, E., Comparative performance analysis of K-nearest neighbour (KNN) algorithm and its different variants for disease prediction. *Sci. Rep.*, 12, 1, 6256, 2022, https://doi.org/10.1038/s41598-022-10358-x.

83. Li, C., Zhang, S., Zhang, H., Pang, L., Lam, K., Hui, C., Zhang, S., Using the K-nearest neighbor algorithm for the classification of lymph node metastasis in gastric cancer. *Comput. Math. Methods Med.*, 876545, 2012, https://doi.org/10.1155/2012/876545.

84. Galbusera, F., Casaroli, G., Bassani, T., Artificial intelligence and machine learning in spine research. *JOR Spine*, 2, 1, e1044, 2019, https://doi.org/10.1002/jsp2.1044.

85. Shokrekhodaei, M., Cistola, D.P., Roberts, R.C., Quinones, S., Non-invasive glucose monitoring using optical sensor and machine learning techniques for diabetes applications. *IEEE Access*, 9, 73029–73045, 2021, https://doi.org/10.1109/ACCESS.2021.3079182.

86. Yaqoob, I., Ahmed, E., Hashem, I.A.T., Ahmed, A., II, Gani, A., Imran, M., Guizani, M., Internet of things architecture: Recent advances, taxonomy, requirements, and open challenges. *Wireless Commun.*, 24, 3, 10–16, 2017, https://doi.org/10.1109/ MWC.2017.1600421.

87. Martin-Isla, C., Campello, V.M., Izquierdo, C., Raisi-Estabragh, Z., Baeßler, B., Petersen, S.E., Lekadir, K., Image-based cardiac diagnosis with machine learning: A review. *Front. Cardiovasc. Med.*, 7, 1, 2020, https://doi.org/10.3389/fcvm.2020.00001.

88. Goswami, M. and Sebastian, N.J., Performance analysis of logistic regression, KNN, SVM, naïve bayes classifier for healthcare application during COVID-19, in: *Innovative Data Communication Technologies and Application*, pp. 645–658, 2022, https://doi.org/10.1007/978-981-16-7167-8_47.

89. Oniani, S., Marques, G., Barnovi, S., Pires, I.M., Bhoi, A.K., Artificial intelligence for internet of things and enhanced medical systems, in: *Bio-inspired Neurocomputing*, pp. 43–59, 2021, https:// doi.org/10.1007/978-981-15-5495-7_3.

90. Podder, P., Mondal, M.R.H., Bharati, S., Paul, P.K., Review on the security threats of internet of things. *Int. J. Comput. Appl.*, 176, 41, 37–45, 2020, https://doi. org/10.5120/ijca2020920548.

91. Shafik, W., Toward a more ethical future of artificial-intelligence and data science, in: *The Ethical Frontier of AI and Data Analysis*, vol. 1, pp. 362–388. IGI Global, Hershey, Pennsylvania, United States, 2024. https://doi.org/10.4018/979-8-3693-2964-1.ch022

92. Singh, P. and Singh, R., Energy-efficient delay-aware task offloading in fog-cloud computing system for IoT sensor applications. *J. Netw. Syst. Manage.*, 30, 1–25, 2022, https://doi.org/10.1007/s10922-021-09622-8.

93. Si-Ahmed, A., Al-Garadi, M.A., Boustia, N., Survey of machine learning based intrusion detection methods for internet of medical things. *Appl. Soft Comput.*, 22, 110227, 2023, https://doi.org/10.1016/j.asoc.2023.110227.

94. Shafik, W., Navigating emerging challenges in robotics and artificial intelligence in Africa, in: *Examining the Rapid Advance of Digital Technology in Africa*, pp. 124–144. IGI Global, Hershey, Pennsylvania, United States, 2024. https//doi.org/10.4018/978-1-6684-9962-7.ch007.

95. Newaz, A., II, Sikder, A.K., Rahman, M.A., Uluagac, A.S., A survey on security and privacy issues in modern healthcare systems: Attacks and defenses. *ACM Trans. Comput. Healthc.*, 2, 3, 1–44, 2021, https://doi.org/10.1145/3453176.

96. Mosenia, A. and Jha, N.K., A comprehensive study of security of internet-of-things. *IEEE Trans. Emerging Top. Comput.*, 5, 4, 586–602, 2017, https://doi.org/10.1109/ TETC.2016.2606384.

97. Hasan, M.K., Ghazal, T.M., Saeed, R.A., Pandey, B., Gohel, H., Eshmawi, A.A., Alkhassawneh, H.M., A review on security threats, vulnerabilities, and counter measures of 5G enabled Internet-of-Medical-Things. *IET Commun.*, 16, 5, 421–432, 2022. https://doi.org/10.1049/cmu.2.12301.

98. Aslan, Ö., Aktuğ, S.S., Ozkan-Okay, M., Yilmaz, A.A., Akin, E., A comprehensive review of cyber security vulnerabilities, threats, attacks, and solutions. *Electronics*, 12, 6, 1333, 2023, https://doi.org/10.3390/electronics12061333.

Index

Printed and bound by CPI Group (UK) Ltd, Croydon, CR0 4YY

27/10/2024

14580181-0004